# When It's Time To Say Good-Bye

## Marti Tote

Marti Tote
RENO, NEVADA

Printed in the United States


ISBN: 978-1-4196-9670-1

Marti Tote
Reno, Nevada
www.AngelicSensations.com

I dedicate this book to all of us who never give up—
in loving memory of my dad, Eddie Littlefield.

# Acknowledgements and Special Thanks

T HERE ARE MANY friends and family members whom I must acknowledge for their belief in me, as without them, I probably would have never gotten this book into print.

A special and most heartfelt thanks must first go out to my big sister Jodie who has always believed in me and who has spent countless hours over the past fifteen years listening to me and reading this book over and over and over again.

To Mr. Roy Rogers Jr., a most heartfelt thank you for allowing me the honor of using his mother's lyrics for my story. Happy Trails to You My Friend!

To Kwikset Lock and Key for employing my father for twenty-six years and for accommodating his desperate desire to feel needed toward the end.

To my psychologist and conscience Diane, without whom I'm quite positive I would have been writing this story with a crayon in an establishment somewhere high upon a hill surrounded by fences topped with barbed wire.

To my husband Bob for understanding all of the weekends lost as I sat writing while he kept the home fires burning.

To my Uncle Calvin who always listens, never judges, and wrote the check to get this story into print.

To my friend and attorney Bruce who has gotten me out of more than just a few binds and who took the time to read this story and give his much appreciated opinion and ideas.

To my best friend Jane who tends to our precious horses, who wishes that time would stand completely still, and who loves story time on Saturday mornings.

To my once so very close friend Gina, with whom I spent countless hours on the living room floor, laughing, crying and reading this book from cover to cover when we should have been working. Pass the peas!

My deepest and most genuine appreciation to my editor, Gail Chadwick, who truly earned her bread and butter by taking on this project, as I am certainly *not* a punctuation person by any means! She also gave me the faith I so desperately needed to believe in myself as a writer. I sincerely thank you Gail, with all of my heart!

To my four youngest sisters—Margaret Jayne, Melodie June, Melissa Jan, and Lianne Larae—for all playing an unknown part in this beautiful story. I know you all love me and for that I am so very thankful. I love each and every one of you as well.

To my mom in loving memory—Mary Martha Beuchat—from whom I am sure I inherited my writing capabilities. Thanks for taking the heat throughout this entire story. I hope you have now found true peace and happiness, Mom. I really and truly did love you!

And last but certainly not least—to my precious children and grandchildren, whom I love with all I have in me and who will all, someday, carry on my legacy in some way once I, myself, am gone from this most wonderful place—Jason, Michael, Jack, Jessica, Bryce, Donovan, Lindy, Sheena, Kim, Taylor, Dylan, Kaycee, Cody, and Shelbie, wherever you are.

# Prologue

WHEN I BEGAN to write this story, it was 1992. I simply meant to save some precious memories when I came home from my dad's house after spending the last three weeks of his life with him and then laying him to rest. It was never meant to become a memoir. I actually began this story on a little Macintosh computer. So as I continued to write for about six months, the story ended up on two floppy discs. Then it sat in a desk drawer for about six years until I bought my first real computer and asked my big sister to transfer my discs to my new computer. When she did, she found this manuscript and began to read. Then—she called me one day and said, "Dad's story, your memories, make a beautiful memoir. It needs to be told." I thought she was nuts. She begged me to separate it into chapters, which I did in my spare time, which took about four more years.

Then, in the late '90s, I sent this manuscript to a publishing house in West Virginia. In response, I not only received a letter from the editor but also a phone call. They offered to publish my book! I was elated! I should have just let them have it but a lawyer friend of mine told me not to. He felt I should query other publishing houses, which I really never did, so it sat for a few more years—on my computer—until another friend of mine, also an attorney, offered to read it. He loved it and told me he felt it needed some rewrites, which took me another three years. He is also the one who suggested I self-publish it and see if a larger publishing house just might pick it up. And so here we are.

My desire to finally share this story was mostly because I wish I'd had a book like this to read before my dad had been diagnosed with cancer. Perhaps our journey may have gone a little smoother in the end. But— who's to say?

Throughout this story I make many comparisons to the classic *The Wizard of Oz*. Most of us have seen the movie and, if you haven't, please do so. To some of us, it is just an old film that captured our hearts as children, a magnificent fairy tale. To others, perhaps it should have been labeled a horror story, with its trees that slap people and its flying monkeys and Munchkins and, of course, the witches—some good, some bad—and the powerful wizard himself. But to me, it is a brilliant masterpiece that explains the path of life. Yes, the very path that each and every one of us will travel whether we like it or not. That legendary yellow brick road! Follow the yellow brick road! Why not? For crying out loud, it was the only road *to* follow! It was the only stinking road out of town! Life.

I truly believe that most of us can certainly relate to Dorothy. She's content and yet—she just knows there's more that life must have to offer and she just can't see what she has because she's too damned busy chasing an unknown dream (or rainbow) of how she thinks things should be. I don't know about all of you, but I think she had it pretty darned good. But isn't that just the way we are? It is so easy for each of us to make decisions for someone else. We can always see clearly what our neighbor or friend *should* be doing. Human nature, I suppose. And doesn't she make the most obvious mistakes throughout this whole movie? Sure she does! She runs from her troubles, only to find out that they weren't so bad in the first place and mostly because, each and every time she comes up against another one, something worse happens to override the earlier problem. Yup, sure sounds like life to me.

In a nutshell, this movie has everything that life has to offer. Good friends, crappy neighbors, folks we meet who are clearly different in appearance than ourselves. Different places other than home, some good and some not so good. It has good witches and bad witches. I know I've met a few of both in my lifetime. And let us not overlook the decisions she had to make throughout the whole darned ordeal. Such as, which way to go on that notorious, yellow brick road. It is one of her very first dilemmas, a crossroad, if you will. And let's not forget she meets a wonderful friend at each and every one of those crossroads, as well as a few enemies. But each and every true friend she meets along the way is always there for her at the most critical times in her journey and they help her make those most important decisions. And the whole darned movie is centered around believing in someone she has never even seen. She knows only that he has the solution to all of her problems. It is her belief in someone she has never even seen. Did you catch that? I, myself, just happen to pray each and every day to someone I have never seen. Hum?

I also find it quite a coincidence that he resides in a place called the Emerald City. You know, streets paved with, well, not gold, but a yellow brick road. Huh. Anyway—and what about those stinking ruby slippers, huh? We find out that those blasted red sparkly little possessions hold the very key to getting her what she's been wanting all along. If only she had known. Ah, but had that been the case, she would have missed the journey. Not to mention, the movie would have been over long before it even began. Those slippers create a whole lot of problems for her. Something she is given that someone else desperately wants that she doesn't particularly care about in the first place. A possession she obviously takes for granted. Sounds familiar now, doesn't it?

And when it's time for her to leave—to say good-bye to all of her friends—it's final. There is no talk of exchanging letters or visiting each other again, because they all know she isn't coming back. They all know it is the end. And they all thank her for everything she has taught them and all the memories they have of her which they will now hold so very close to their hearts. Sounds like the final exit to me and, in the end, she ends up right back where she started. Odd? Perhaps. But, oh, so comparable to life, wouldn't you agree?

Sometimes, we don't really pay attention to the rainbows we are running through as we are trying to get to the rainbows in the distance. I hate that, but whether I hate it or not, it is true. Can't really grasp the idea that I, myself, have no control over such things. Huh, something to ponder later on I suppose and I will. Someday—much later.

For right now, I'd like to invite you to simply sit back, relax and enjoy this most heartfelt story about life, love, sacrifice, and the sorrow of *When it's time to say good-bye.*

Welcome aboard, my friends!

# Chapter One

## *Memories*

*It is strange how the memory of a man may float to posterity on what*
*he would have himself regarded as the most trifling of his works.*
Sir William Osler 1849-1919 In Aphorisms from
his Bedside Teachings (1961) p. 112

I N THE BEGINNING, when my dad was diagnosed with cancer, I truly thought that someone had made a terrible mistake. Or so I prayed. I mean, guys like my dad didn't get cancer. Guys like my dad didn't die at the tender age of seventy-two either. No, because, you see, guys like my dad went peacefully in their sleep. When—and only when—they turned old and gray: *really* old and *really* gray. Sadly, I was wrong.

Subsequently, once I had to face the realization that no mistake had in fact been made, I then decided that we would be an exception to the rule. I prayed again. I truly thought that we would be one of the few who would beat this horrible disease and the beast we all know as death. Again, I was wrong. But I want you all to know that it was certainly not because I didn't try. No, siree! I tried harder to fight this monster than I had ever tried to do anything else in my entire life. But as you will soon find out, it really wasn't my battle to begin with. It was my dad's—and he had decided, long before I ever came into the picture, *whatever will be will be.*

Nonetheless, I still continued to secretly hope, throughout this whole experience, that somehow, sometime, some way, there would be a reprieve. You know? Sort of a second chance, or perhaps a miracle, if you will. What I didn't see at the time was that I was right smack-dab in the middle of my second chance as well as a full-blown miracle all along. I just didn't realize it until it was all over. Guess that's just the way life is sometimes—or it most certainly seems to be anyway. And I'll be the first one to admit—I don't really care for it much.

1

I guess the best place for me to begin would be at the beginning. Usually works out best that way when someone is telling a story such as mine. However, when I think about it, I don't really know where the beginning is. It seems like it was so very long ago. Almost like a distant dream clouded by my own inability to face the fact that someone I once loved with everything I had in me, is now gone. And along with all the emptiness, comes all of the grief that I sometimes think will never go away. But I guess it does eventually. Well—sort of. Time may heal some wounds, but certainly not deep lacerations of the heart. And you can quote me on that.

Trouble is, is that every time I try to think back to where all of this began, I seem to get a little distracted; I mean, can somebody please tell me why in the name of God, someone like my dad had to go when there are plenty of more-deserving human beings out there who might just as well have been able to go first? Like, why not take some unlikable person instead? Someone miserable and mean. You know, someone who is much more deserving of death.

Sounds pitiful doesn't it? Yes, indeed, I realize that it most certainly does. But isn't this just the way we feel when someone we love has been taken from us? I believe it is. I also believe that somewhere, way down deep inside the very chambers of all of our hearts, lies a very selfish and horrible pit where we keep hidden all of our most intimate feelings. And I'm not real sure, but I think it has something to do with good old fashioned honesty. It may not be very socially acceptable—honesty—but it's there. And I don't care much for that either.

Perhaps it will be for the best, if I introduce to you the man my father really was. Yes, that does seem appropriate for starters. And it shouldn't be too difficult in that I think we have all met a person such as my father at one time or another in our lives—the sort of person who, once he walks away, leaves us all wondering just how in the heck he managed to do what he just did. Always happy, always smiling, and always so stinking positive. Geeze, it's all you can do not to reach out and slap the happiness right out of folks like him. Well, he was my dad, and as you will come to find out during the course of this story, we were the closest any two people could possibly be, and I still can't tell you how he did it. Nope, I can't for the life of me even figure out *why* for that matter. Why and how he was always so darned happy just may always be a mystery to me. And perhaps it doesn't really even matter now that he's gone. But I can tell you this. I am so very thankful every day of my life that he was the person he was—and I can only hope that he has left me even a tiny portion of the magic that he was able to bestow on anyone who ever knew him.

Standing short at about five feet eight inches tall, perhaps the secret of his happiness lay in the fact that my dad never really grew up. As a matter of fact, I believe we just might be on to something there. Now listen, we are talking about a guy who told his children that cows stood on the hillsides to eat because they had been born with two legs shorter than the other two. Incidentally, while we're on that subject, I think I was about twelve years old or so before I realized that this little myth just might not be true. So, sometime on—or around—or close to my twelfth birthday, I made the stupid mistake of asking my dad why he had told me such a tale. I don't have the slightest clue what came over me that day. Guess it had something to do with entering puberty, for the answer I got went to the tune of, "Because it was true!" And unless I ever hung around long enough to wait for those lopsided cows to walk back up to level ground, then I had no proof that it wasn't true. And you know, sometimes to this day, deep inside that wonderful part of my own heart that never grew up, I do still find myself wondering.

Characteristically, my short little myth-believing dad was a dead ringer for George Burns—although I think his ears were a little bigger than George's—but just the same, he was equally as charming as George. OK, a lot more wrinkled but equally as charming. You get the picture, I'm sure. He very rarely went to any trouble at all to be—well—simply himself. He seldom wore anything other than a pair of jean overalls, a white T-shirt, and tennis shoes. And if he did, it was a pair of sweatpants, a white T-shirt—and tennis shoes. He was a plain and simple man as he lived and, as you will come to find out, he was a plain and simple man right up until the very day he died. Yes, indeedy, I saw to that little chore all by myself.

Now, I'm not real sure, but I think my dad just may have been the very first Toys"R"Us kid. And although there is no documentation to substantiate this claim, I myself, believe it to be true. A big kid at heart as well as in body, mind, and spirit. Plain and simple and although eventually his childlike personality would come to be my mother's sole reason for their divorce; ironically, it was also the very same reason why I myself, loved him so very much.

My dad had certain characteristics that made him—well—unique. I guess we all do—but for the most part his were, shall we say, very differently unique. Some may even call them weird. I quite frankly wouldn't allow it, but just the same, others just might think so, and that is really OK with me.

My dad wasn't really a dead ringer for George Burns as much as—well—he sort of—looked like—a chimpanzee. His eyes; he had the deepest wrinkles around his beautiful brown eyes, like rock-tossed rings in a puddle. Sometimes I wonder if God had simply placed them there to catch all of the tears he would certainly cry later on in life. Now that I think about it—that is a very nice thought indeed. As far back as I can recall my dad always had wrinkles. I mean the kind that cut really deep into the skin all the way down to the bottom of his neck. He was much too young a man to have had those wrinkles so many years ago. He always told me they had come from the war, from being out in the sun day in and day out with no shelter for four years. I have my own ideas about that story. Yes, a war perhaps, but certainly not the kind he was talking about. He had huge ears that stuck out from the side of his head, which, unfortunately, is a genetic trait, and thank God I didn't get them! His nose was wide but proportioned well for his face and then—there was that smile. The smile that lit up a room accompanied by a certain twinkle in his eye and when he became extremely excited or happy or—God forbid—sad, really sad—he would stretch those wrinkles for all it was worth and he would not just feel but actually throw his emotions for anyone who was lucky enough or unlucky enough to catch them. He had a loud and booming voice when he was happy, and he whispered when he was sad. He would have never greeted someone with a simple hello. No, because you see, a simple hello would have been, well, too simple and not so unique. My dad bellowed a hearty "Hi, there!" when he greeted someone and just as hearty a "Bye now!" when he parted. And whether it was a "Hi, there!" or a "Bye now!" he always held both of his arms up in the air and waved both hands as though he were, well, drunk! But he wasn't. He was just—happy. That was my dad.

He was also very blatantly honest and that sometimes became a problem, as you will come to find out as we get a little deeper into this story. However, his unrefined honesty was something I came to depend on as the years went forward. Although, toward the very end I found myself wishing he would have lied, just once in his life for *my* own pitiful sake!

His language was just as unique as the man himself. Oh, my gosh— no, my father very seldom swore, I surely didn't mean it that way. It was his words themselves that were unique—as well as his phrases. So unique, in fact, that sometimes I wondered if he just might have been from another planet. I think he actually made most of them up, quite frankly. Goofy and silly things came out of his mouth and they were his, well, his trademark, his very own language. Nowadays, some may have thought he was a little, uh, strange as dum-dum, nitwit, pea brain, knucklehead, or my favorite, sh-t bird, which was always pronounced "chit bird," may have been blurted out as a result of something we had done wrong. Sometimes we needed to "use our heads for something besides a hat rack," or if we needed to comb our hair or wash our faces, we may have resembled "the east end of a horse going west!" Always said with a half chuckle or a smile—and always with love. If we asked permission to go somewhere or do something, he blurted out a hearty "Why sure!" or "Why not!" as if there should never have even been a question asked in the stinking first place. And he could drag a one syllable word into a several-syllable word. "W-h-y n-o-t!" Silly as it sounds, that was my dad. Things were going to happen, "come hell or high water," that is, "if the good lord was willing and the creek didn't rise," which, come to think about it now, makes me wonder how I ever obtained the courage to learn how to swim! Mere survival, I suppose.

He had to have been the most excitable grown-up I had ever known in my entire life, which incidentally came with a warning label: "Don't get your bowels in an uproar!" When we shared something exhilarating with him, he would exclaim, "Oh, goody!" or, my favorite, "Well, I'll be go to hell John!" And if we shared something not so exhilarating, he still exclaimed some harebrained phrase that would eventually become a permanent part of *our very own* everyday vocabularies as well. Bullpucky! And if something just didn't seem quite right to my dad, he would loudly exclaim that it didn't make one damned bit of sense to him what–so–ever–at–all!

The five of us girls—yes, he had five—were never known as his daughters. We were his "five beautiful brown-eyed baby doll girls." I was second to the oldest. And there were no more than three years between each of us. As a matter of fact, the two youngest of my sisters were only eighteen months apart. That part of the tale will come a little later down the story road. If he addressed us one at a time it was very seldom by name. It was always dear or baby doll or skeezics or calf eyes or brown eyes—or nitwit—anything at all but our first names. I know he knew our names though because on the rare occasion that he did call us by our birth names he always said our first and middle names together. He was from Oklahoma—he had two names—he was proud of it! He also had a nickname. For hell's sake, shouldn't everyone? Well, quite frankly and honestly—if you lived in my dad's world, then the answer to that question would certainly be yes. He sang us songs when we were up and sang us songs when we were down. Quite frankly, he sang songs any old time he felt like it, which was just about all the time—and he didn't hum or murmur the words either, he *belted* them—not caring where he was or who was listening either. That was my dad.

We grew up to the tunes of "You Are My Sunshine," "Beautiful, Beautiful Brown Eyes," and "The Old Gray Mare, She Ain't What She Used to Be," which became a classic in our family the year my mother divorced him. It also just happened to be our favorite tune to sing while driving in the car. And driving in the car just happened to be my dad's favorite thing to do. And God forbid if someone ever sped by us in a rush, because, "They were just in a hurry to get nowhere!" As we would invariably, almost each and every time, catch up with them at the next light or stop sign. My dad loved his cars and took impeccable care of them throughout the years, as you will soon find out. And again, in his very own language (I suppose most men's language) he always referred to each one as a "she." There was no such thing as *the* car or *he* cars, only *she* cars. Perhaps he had always been partial to girls and perhaps it was just as well, as God had blessed him with five of them. He never had a son and swore up until the very day he died that he never wanted one. That was my dad. I don't suppose some snakes-and-snails-and-puppy-dog-tails little boy would have responded well to "You Are My Sunshine," anyway.

He not only loved to sing but he loved to dance! That was my dad—and any old tune at all would do, as he would begin feeling the beat with a bounce in his step, which would then get him to raise his arms about midway in the air, and his hands seemed to be able to scout out anyone who was fortunate enough—or unfortunate enough—to be standing in the room with him, as they instantaneously became his dance partner. When we were very young, we were bestowed with the honor of dancing on top of his feet, which in comparison was like flying! As we got a little older our dance steps simply came naturally, as we had been standing upon Fred Astaire's feet for so long that we knew each and every footstep by heart. Oh, how my father could dance! And after each and every honor he would end it with a gracious bow and a big fat smooch—followed by a loud and boisterous, "I–love–you–baby– doll! Let's go back to your place!" That was my dad. Then he'd make up some silly-ass word or phrase for being a great dancer, like "bug legs" or "skeezics" (whatever in the hell that meant), and that became our name for the day. It was an honor—plain and simple. He could put emphasis upon any word in the dictionary and give it a stronger meaning. Whether it was adding syllables or making up a whole new phrase, somewhere along the way, my dad's vocabulary became the all new edition of Mr. Webster's redefined dictionary.

Something couldn't just be "fast," for instance; it had to be "like a bat out of hell!" And if someone were less than intelligent, they were always and forever "dumber than Thompson's colt!" Thompson, incidentally, was a farmer who had a colt that would cross the river just to get a drink of water. I'm not really sure if he ever existed or not. My dad swore he did, but that basically meant that maybe he did, or maybe he didn't. And now, I'll probably never know for absolute sure anyway.

When my mom would start in on him, "harping" about something that just wasn't worth harping about because, "life was just too damned short to be wasted on bickering," and she would not stop for hours once she got started—he would abruptly end the one-sided argument by finally waving his arms in the air and exiting the room, telling her to "go piss on a flat rock!" I didn't quite understand the whole meaning of that phrase until I was much older. And at the time, I didn't much care because I was too preoccupied with the cussword my dad had just blurted out at my mother. "Piss" was a cuss word in *our* house and I always followed my dad out of the room, admiring him for being able to cuss and get away with it—and at my mom, no less! He was cool! He was also dumber than Thompson's colt! Because no one crossed my mother! No one! Not and lived to tell about it anyway. No one except my dad, that is—if you dare to call his life after the divorce living.

A fairy tale, that's exactly what my childhood was up until the age of eight, consisted of: a land of make-believe. Full of stories and fantasy, courtesy of none other than the most wonderful man who ever created a dream. (Well, besides those guys who write for Mr. Disney and Martin Luther King.) I would bet a dime to a doughnut hole that there wasn't a minute in my father's day that he wasn't busy thinking up some wildly concocted harebrained story, for one silly reason or another. And I really can't say why. Come to think of it, that's one question I never did ask him. (I guess the lopsided cow thing had been enough for me.) Maybe it was so that I could tell this story once he was gone. I may never know. But if I had to guess, I would have to say that he told these stories because somewhere deep down inside that wonderful part of him that never grew up, he himself believed them to be true with all of his heart.

I'm thinking by now, you all have a pretty good idea of who my dad was. And if you are still holding on to this book after all I have shared then I should also let you in on how very much my father loved children. A lot—no, actually more than anything else in the whole entire world. For you see, he believed that children held some sort of key that unlocked the secret magic to true happiness through make-believe and that they lost the ability to use that key once they became adults. He believed that it was a very special person indeed, who could make it safely into adulthood and not lose the ability to imagine and dream. And you know, now that I think about it, maybe he had something there. Yes, if I do say so myself, I truly believe he did.

Oh, now don't get me wrong. My dad had all the normal, dull, humdrum, adult responsibilities, the same as everyone else. I think he just chose to deal with them differently than most.

He had a wife, who was, coincidently, also my mother. He had five beautiful little girls, four of whom were my sisters and one of whom was me; a large five-bedroom two-story house with a mortgage to match; three cars, a dog, and a load of bicycles, skates, and wagons in the garage. He worked two full-time jobs to pay for it all and he slept only in between all the shenanigans that five busy little girls could muster up. Sounds pretty grown-up to me. And it also sounds like I may have just answered my own question. Maybe it's not that he *didn't* grow up as much as it was that he didn't *want* to grow up. And now that I really think about it, I can't truthfully say that I blamed him. As a matter of fact, now I can't believe he lived as long as he actually did—but for that, I am truly thankful.

Again, my dad was probably one of those guys who people just might wonder about nowadays and mostly because he was the kind of guy who spent a lot of time with his girls. Actually, and in all honesty, it was because he just naturally fit in. He enjoyed playing with us and he actually enjoyed listening to us as we would prepare all day long to put on our silly puppet shows, using paper lunch sacks with faces drawn on them just for the sheer pleasure of knowing that in the end, he would whoop and holler and clap as though he had just seen a Broadway play. To put it simply, it tickled him pink to participate in our world. You see, my dad believed in the wisdom of the child. He believed that if more grown-ups listened to the children, they would learn so much more. He believed if world peace were left up to the children—well, there just might not be any need for war. Oh, maybe a few names would have been called and then someone might have chanted, "Sticks and stones may break my bones," but then with all of the forgiveness that only a child can embrace, all would have been forgotten. Perhaps he was truly on to something there. Perhaps. If nothing else, it sure gives us all something to think about.

So you see, mostly my dad was a very unique grown-up because he treated us with respect. And simply because he believed that in order to receive respect, you had to first give it. Which, in turn, meant you had to earn it. Huh, what a concept. He didn't believe that adults had the right to call all the shots just because they were bigger or older. Bigger and older didn't make them wiser! As a matter of fact, my dad used to say that bigger and older made some adults a whole heck of a lot dumber than Thompson's colt. And as I have already shared with you, that's pretty damned dumb!

My dad was a very serious thinker when it came to real-life proceedings, as you will come to learn throughout the course of this story. Yes, a very serious thinker indeed. He'd squint his wrinkled chimpanzee eyes and gaze into midair, rubbing his chin and pondering when asked a question that was too complex for an adult to answer for a child. And we would hold our breath just waiting for the secret answer. Oh sure, he could have given the same old reply that most adults gave at times such as those. He could have said, "I'll tell you when you're older." But there again, my dad's beliefs compelled him to answer the darned question and get it out of the way! Put it to rest once and for all! Because surely we wouldn't give up asking until we got an answer that satisfied us anyway. Perseverance was a true child attribute.

I can't ever remember a time when I asked my dad a question and was told that he would give me the answer when I was older. No matter what the question was or what it was about, I got an answer right then and there. Now I will tell you, if he couldn't figure out an answer to a question that one of us would ask—why then, he'd simply just make one up. That's what all that squinting and pondering was about, I suppose. And this quite frankly, is also where the fun began. I believed he was the smartest man in the world. Well—if not the smartest, then certainly and to say the least, the cleverest. That's how the cow story got started in the first place. I was just stupid enough to have asked him one day, how those cows stood lopsided for so long on the hillside— and the rest became history!

My dad was a truly remarkable adult in that he knew beyond a shadow of a doubt that the things children dreamed up in their pretty little heads were absolutely true. He knew stuff that was top-secret kid info only. He was truly amazing! The only grown-up I ever encountered who not only knew about the boogeyman and monsters—but he believed in them too! If I do say so myself (and I do), acknowledgement can do wonders for a child's curiosity.

He understood the things that most parents couldn't understand, really important things. Things that kids are gonna believe no matter how many times they are told not to. Perhaps the real secret to his wondrous knowledge was that he simply and beyond a shadow of a doubt knew how very important it was to believe in *us*. Yes, again, I think we just may be on to something there. My gosh, we sure are uncovering a whole lot of mysteries, aren't we?

One of my fondest memories of the greatest storyteller who ever lived, is how he always managed to keep my imagination alive. Heck, if it wasn't for him, I might have turned out—well, let's just say for the sake of argument, I owe him a lot. I mean we are talking about a grown man who would physically throw himself on the mercy of the monsters who lived in my closet, solely to satisfy some crazy notion I conjured up in my silly little head. And I think you know the very notion I'm talking about. The one that used to keep us all up at night watching endlessly in the dark for some horrible slobbering vision of ugly to jump out and gruesomely murder us just as we were going to sleep. Uh huh, that's the one. Well, there was no need to worry about such things when you resided in the very same dwelling with the greatest monster fighter who ever lived.

Now listen, fact is fact, and no kid can be expected to go to sleep safely until there has been a thorough investigation of monsters lurking, now, can they? Well can they? No, of course they can't. And my dad knew it. So he would proceed to wildly beat the pee-waddlings out of the underside of my bed as well as the inside of my closet before I went to sleep at night. Hey, someone had to do it. So it might as well have been the greatest monster fighter who ever lived. My knight in shining— uh—overalls! My dad. And you know, there had never been a doubt in my mind as to who would win. Never. Because anyone who was ever someone knew that if you believed in God with all your heart, that you could surely beat any monster you might ever have to come face to face with. A solemn promise from the very man who knew it all—and then some.

You see, he was aware of secrets about stuff that no other grown-up knew, and certainly not because they hadn't been told, but because they simply chose not to believe. Such as—the man in the moon. Now, let's discuss this character, shall we? Because in our home he was very real and existed for the sole purpose of following you at night just to keep an eye on you. It was his God-given job. Just watch the moon sometime at night while driving if you don't believe me. He always follows you. We were very thankful to have him and, as a matter of fact, each and every night before we went to bed, we called him up on the phone just to tell him good night and to thank him for watching over us when we couldn't see God because he was probably busy with some other little kid who needed him more than we did, simply because maybe they didn't have parents or a grandma or grandpa or some other reason that was just devastating enough to convince us not to ask why. And—we didn't. We were simply satisfied and honored at the fact that *my dad* and *only my dad* had his phone number. And each and every night up until the day my daddy left home, he dialed that number and we said our prayers and good night to the man in the moon before we turned in. It was a family ritual, plain and simple. And I suppose the man in the moon must have gone with my dad when he left, because after that horrible day—we never called him up again. My mom was an adult and obviously, therefore, didn't know the number.

Now, if you'll allow me after that tale to share another, I'll let you in on another little tidbit of info that few kids even know. Ready? OK, here it is. The boogeyman is real. Yes, siree, Ida, just as real as you and me. Problem was that he had simply been pinned with a bum rap, a terrible miscarriage of justice on the old guy's part, if I do say so myself (and I do). You see, the boogeyman wasn't a bad monster at all. Heavens, no. In all actuality, he was just some little kid's stuffed animal that had been left out in the rain. And that little ditty just happened to explain why he was so ugly. If you were covered with fur, and someone left you out in the rain, why then, you'd be ugly too. So you see, when he showed up in some unsuspecting child's closet or at the window, he was only looking for the child who left him behind. He was lost and lonely and wanted to find a safe and warm bed to sleep in, nothing at all to be afraid of really, plain and simple.

Now I'm going to explain something to all of you that has been a mystery to all children (and maybe even some grown-ups) since time began, maybe even longer. Those so-called house-settling noises.

I don't know about you, but I remember laying in my bed at night with the house perfectly quiet, minding my own business, when all of a sudden, I'd hear a crack so loud it would stand my hair on end. And I have to be honest with you; the house-settling thing just didn't cut it for me. I mean, let's try to reason here a minute. If the house really needed to do something like, settle—which I seriously doubted, then how come we never heard those noises during the day? Uh huh, I didn't think I was the only one who didn't buy it. Well, I'm about to share with all of you, one of the best-kept secrets in little kid history. Those noises weren't the house settling at all. Nope. They were in all actuality, my stuffed animals creeping up to the side of my bed at night checking to see if I was asleep yet, for when and only when I finally fell asleep at night, all of my stuffed animals came alive to play with one another! And I have to say that they must have been quick little varmints, because each and every time I tried to catch them in the act—well—you know.

In turn, this little well -known fact explained why I couldn't find a certain something when I knew exactly where I had left it. See, I told you he had an answer for everything. I would frantically search for a certain something I had lost until I had no alternative other than to have to ask my dad for his help, which would in turn prompt one…of… those…looks. You know, the dreaded parent look? The one where only one eyebrow goes up and then the head sort of turns half cocked to one side?

Yes, indeedy—that would be the one! The look that clearly stated without a word being said that, *it was them*—my stuffed animals—and, quite frankly, at that point, to tell you the truth, I simply stopped looking. *It* would probably turn up when—and only when—*they* were done playing with whatever it was I had been looking for in the first place. I would suddenly realize that I didn't really need it that badly after all. You know, badly enough to have to go up to my room and look under the bed or in the closet before a thorough monster check had been done—because monster checks lasted only until dawn the next day. Heck, any kid who was ever someone knew that. Sheesh!

Now, I grew up believing most of the stories I have already shared with you and more. Much more. And I always felt confident in knowing that I could ask my dad any question to which I would always get an answer, so I had no problem boasting about such things to all of my friends. Which I'm sure, at some point in time, caused some problems for my parents; I just never really wanted to know so I didn't ask. Anyway, let's see—ah yes, I was just about to explain how I had become the neighborhood Ann Landers.

You see, my little friends found out about the answer guru, whom I called my dad, from someone who boasted about it quite often and they would send me to find out all the secrets of the universe from the man who knew it all. When they sent me for information, my friends knew beyond a shadow of a doubt, that I would always come back with an explanation. I was very reliable, you know.

Now, of course I asked the questions that most of us do when we are children. I mean, just because my dad was a loon, doesn't mean I, myself, wasn't perfectly normal. So, I was sent out on missions to ask the universal questions such as, where do people go when they die and where do babies come from, and so on and so on and so on.

I think most of us can relate to the first question, huh? I mean we still don't really know for absolute sure where people go when they die, now, do we? Not for absolute sure we don't. Not yet anyway. Well, not to worry, because I'm about to put that question to rest for all of us once and for all. OK, my friends, here it is. The truth.

When people die—they go to live with Santa Claus at the North Pole. If they die when they are children, they become elves so they will always have lots of toys to play with and always have forever to play. Because everyone who's anyone knows that when someone dies, it sadly is forever. If they are adults, they are sent to watch over the children. Plain and simple. Well—if nothing else, it's certainly a comforting thought, now isn't it? Well, it might be until we get to the end of this story anyway. And let's not forget the baby question. Land sake's alive, I almost forgot to tell you one of the most important answers to one of the most frequently asked questions in little kid history. Where do babies come from? Well, I'm about to tell you just that. Ready? OK, here it is! Babies come from Santa Claus! Duh! And this is how it works: Every Christmas, Santa hides a seed inside the cookies of certain houses of people who want to have a baby that year. Then, at some time or another, the mother eats that certain cookie and the seed is planted in her tummy. So sometime during the next year when the mom and dad decide they want a baby the seed begins to grow. And voila! It takes about nine months for the baby to form and then the mother goes to the hospital where Santa meets her and he takes the baby out with Christmas magic. You know, the very same Christmas magic he uses to come down the chimney when it's too small for him to fit? Yes indeed, *that* Christmas Magic! Make sense? Why sure it does, especially if you're a little kid trying to find some answers in a grown-up world. Best of all, the key word here is "answer." And that's more than any of my other friends ever got, a lot more. Well, unless they asked me of course.

Now, it's quite clear that all of these wonderful traits are probably what sent my mother screaming over the edge in the end. I'm sure it had a whole lot to do with it. Actually, I know it did. And I'm not real sure, but I think where she made her first mistake was when *she* decided to grow up. I could be wrong. Highly doubtful, but I could be. She just didn't seem to appreciate the simple things in life anymore and anyone who ever knew my dad knew that the simplest things in life were what made him the absolute happiest.

A beautiful day for instance, or finding a baseball game on television as he was flipping through the channels on a weekend afternoon, a good home-cooked Sunday dinner, a peaceful little nap in the middle of the day, a beautiful sunset—oh, and gadgets. Yes, unfortunately, you read it correctly. Gadgets. If it ticked or sang or chirped or buzzed or did anything at all out of the ordinary, it classified as a gadget— and my dad had to have one or give one to somebody!

He gave *me* a gadget, as a matter of fact, for Christmas about a year before he died. It was a movie rewinder for my VCR. Sounds harmless enough, I realize, but you see, it looked like a car and when you put the movie in to rewind it, the headlights came on. Geeze, the way he carried on when that silly thing lit up, you would have thought he had invented it himself. Laughing hysterically, waving his hands in the air, proclaiming that it was "something else again." These little acts were exactly the reasons why my mom couldn't handle life with the smartest man in the world anymore. And they also, just so happened to be, the very memories I cherish the most. Funny how some things turn out, isn't it? Well, not really funny. That's simply just a figure of speech.

Most of my memories of my dad are good ones, like the ones I have already shared with you, but there are some sad ones that push their way through from time to time as well. Sad memories that don't make me sad really, as much as they make me—well—proud; memories that define the man my father really was. Not as if the memories I have already shared weren't enough to do just that. I mean they do pretty much sum my dad up in a nutshell, or—as a nutshell. But, believe it or not, he had a serious side to him too, a very serious side that didn't take an adult to see. As a matter of fact, I have sometimes wondered if it was only the heart of a child who could find it.

One of those memories is of a time when I was just a small girl. Actually, all of them are, until we get to the very end, but this is the first I have chosen to share with you. I truly don't know how old I was, but I was young. That will just have to do for now.

My dad and I were sitting in our living room in the very early morning hours of the day, he reading his paper and me watching my cartoons. when all of a sudden, I realized he was oh...my...God...crying! Well, I couldn't hardly move as fast as I wanted to, not really knowing if it was due to paralyzation of my heart or the slick bottoms of my feet pajamas—but I did manage to get my tiny self moving and up next to him on that couch—and fast!

Then—carefully scooting right up next to him, wiping his face with a tiny corner of my pajama sleeve—I leaned my cheek directly against his, and quietly, oh so very quietly, whispered, "What's the matter, Daddy?"

And with the compassion that only my dad could portray, he welcomed my comfort by taking hold of my trembling little hand, just exactly like he would do twenty-some odd years later while he lay dying, and he slowly began to explain by telling me of a story he had just read, a story of a man who had been arrested for abusing his child!

Can you imagine? Well, I, for one, can tell you my dad sure as heck couldn't. It was absolutely inconceivable to him! Always had been and always would be up until the very day he died. Then, looking at me through tear-filled eyes, he asked me a question that I would never forget. A question that to his dying day, not even my dad could answer. "Who," he asked, "who could ever do such a thing to a child?" And you know, my friends, I didn't know *who* actually could do something like that to a child. Not at that time in my life anyway. I couldn't have ever imagined anything like that in my worst nightmares. For you see, my dad had never raised his voice or his hands to me in anger in my entire little life, for he believed that if a child ever needed comfort, how could the child ever find it in the very arms that would sometimes administer pain? Didn't make a damned bit of sense to him. And, thank God, it didn't make a damned bit of sense to me either. And I'm here to tell you, it truly never has.

My dad had always been an easy crier. He was a very emotional man. He had soft feelings and a soft heart. And he was never embarrassed to cry in front of us

13

girls either. No siree, he cried whenever he darned well felt the need. As a matter of fact, that's another memory in itself. I can remember each and every time I saw my daddy cry. Maybe it's because it was so devastating. I mean things have to be really bad for a dad to cry. Dads aren't supposed to cry. Dads are supposed to be stronger. I, myself, never saw an episode one where Ward Cleaver ever lost it, did you? No, of course you didn't, because that would've meant that he just might have had to depend on good old June to be the strong one for a change. And that wasn't about to happen, now, was it? So perhaps that explains the feeling of worry that would come over me each and every time my dad would turn on the waterworks. A feeling of complete loss of control like my whole entire world was coming apart. Dads were the very foundation of all that was tough for God's sake, and we weren't taught any differently in those days. I didn't realize until I was much older, just how very fortunate I was, to have had my emotional, tear-dropping, compassionate little dad. And isn't that just the way it is sometimes? We just don't see how very fortunate we are until we've lost whatever it is we realize we were fortunate enough to have had in the first place. Such are the complications of life, I suppose. We don't have to like it, but that's just the way things are.

Now that little episode wasn't the first time I had ever seen my dad cry. To be truthful with you, it's hard for me to differentiate the first from the last. But I do remember certain times better than others and another one of them, perhaps a day most of us who were alive at the time can recall, was the day the whole entire world stood completely still.

November 22, 1963. President John F. Kennedy had just been shot!

Yes, my friends, my dad cried on that day alrighty, just about as long and as hard as he could. And to be perfectly honest with all of you, what I remember most about that day wasn't *how* my father cried, as much as I can remember *why* my father cried. I mean, he didn't cry because he would miss the president. He didn't even know him. So it wasn't a saddened cry, as much as it was a scared cry. Scared because some lunatic had shot and killed the leader of our great country and no one had stopped him because no one ever thought anything that horrible could ever happen. He cried because in his day, there wasn't a family to be found who didn't proudly fly the American flag from their porch on Memorial Day or Veteran's Day or any old darned day for that matter, let alone shoot the very president of the United States of America for Pete's sake. Things they were a changing, and that fact frightened my father more than anything.

On the other hand, having the choice to fly the American flag or not to fly the American flag was exactly what made America, America, home of the free and land of the brave, apple pie, and the strength of the American family. And that was just exactly the kind of man my father was which leads me to another memory of my father's tears. It was four years later; 1967 to be exact. I was nine years old and about to learn the true facts of life, the hard way. This was the year my mom decided that after thirteen years of marriage and five beautiful little girls, that she just didn't want to be married anymore to a man who never grew up. She decided it would be best for all of us if my dad moved out.

Well, if nothing else, I learned two very important lessons that summer, ladies and gents. The first was that the world did not, in fact, end in 1967, although I'm still not totally convinced. The second was to never let someone else make my decisions for me.

In the doorway of that very same two-story house which had harbored all of the skates and bikes and wagons and love, there stood my dad, holding his suitcase under one arm and his portable TV under the other with the pain of realization streaming down his cheeks, assuring me that everything was going to be all right. I knew he was lying, but I chose to believe that lie over the painful truth that the smartest man in the world, not to mention the greatest monster fighter who ever lived, was walking out of my life and there wasn't a darned thing anyone could do to stop him. So there I sat—on the stairway, long after the door had closed behind him, watching—waiting for him to return. But he never did. At least not for a long, long time.

You see the pain of losing his family was the worst he had ever experienced. I didn't know it then—but years later, three weeks before he died, to be exact, he would share these feelings with me, along with all the other things I ever wanted to know about life but had been too preoccupied to ask—until then. And not to worry, because I will be sharing them with you as well.

Yes, growing up around a man like my dad was a constant adventure. And, if nothing else, it certainly made for some wonderful memories. Which, in the end, is all we really have, isn't it? Sad but true. Perhaps if he had been a drab or boring person then his loss might have been a little easier to accept. Maybe. Highly doubtful—but maybe.

No, he certainly wasn't a drab or boring person in any sense of those words. He was a silly, compassionate, live-and-let-live, happy, dancing, singing, simple-minded, life-loving, quirky little man. He was my dad. And for the life of me I just couldn't seem to let go. No matter how much time I had been given to prepare for the worst.

Letting go. Let's talk about that for a moment, shall we? Just exactly what in the hell does that mean anyway? What a stupid term. Letting go. Like we have a choice when the time comes, huh? Well we don't— and I know because I'll be the first one to tell you that if not letting go of someone meant they could stay as long as we could hold on, then I'd have had my dad surgically attached to my very soul!

Which brings me to share something else with all of you. Something so crazy that I can't believe I thought of it. An idea so shameful—well, you know.

Sometime during the tormenting months after my dad was diagnosed with the horrible disease that would eventually take his very last breath, I was desperately trying to figure out ways to preserve his memory, seeing that he had already made it perfectly clear that there wasn't a snowball's chance in hell to preserve anything else. And I am ashamed to admit that I had some extremely drastic thoughts during all of my panic. Humiliating thoughts. Thoughts so embarrassing that I can't believe I'm about to share them with a bunch of perfect strangers. Although, we really aren't strangers anymore now, are we? No, I guess we really aren't. Very well then, on with the truth.

Let's see, where were we—oh yes. I believe I was just about to hang my head in shame. For what I am about to share with you is the extreme example of the end of one's rope.

I was so desperate to hold onto my father, no matter what the cost, that one evening—one cold and lonely miserable evening about two days after he died, I went so far as to ask my oldest sister, who, coincidently, is also my dad's oldest daughter, if she thought that maybe someone could make a wax replica of him. Now, that is pitiful. Yes, to say the least, it is. Look, I already told you I was ashamed. And I will also share with you that just as soon as it came out of my mouth, I felt like I was listening to one of those silly early-morning radio shows, where the DJ says something really stupid and all of a sudden you hear a prerecorded crowd of people booing, hissing, and heckling. But once I said it, I knew it was too late to take it back, just as sure as I knew my own name. I guess it was the look on my sister's face, as I could almost see her flipping through the yellow pages of her mind trying to decide which mental facility would be the best and cheapest one for me. Hey, now look, I know it was absurd, but I was a woman who was under a considerable amount of stress, as you will soon find out. And I'll tell you something else on behalf of me and my wild imagination. I don't think for one minute that I'm the first person to ever think of such an act. Maybe I'm the first to be brave enough to admit it, but certainly not the first to think about it by far. Hell, Roy Rogers stuffed Trigger, for crying out loud! And let's not forget, there is that wax museum where all of the stars have been preserved, so to speak. I was desperate! And desperation can make us do some of the damnedest things, as you will soon find out. Of course, my older sister had absolutely no problem in reaching out and grabbing me by both shoulders and shaking me until the absurd thought left my mind; nonetheless, I did think about it. And why did I think about it? Well, because—I didn't want to let go.

Sound familiar? Yes, sadly I thought, it might, especially to those of us who have had to suffer the loss of someone very special. Well look, no sense in all of us going to the nuthouse. You don't have to reveal your deepest, darkest, most harebrained ideas now. Simply allow me to make an absolute fool out of myself on your behalf, and that my friends, is exactly why I shared it with you, to make a point.

I'm not weird, really. I just simply didn't want to let go of someone I loved more than anything. Not so hard to understand, is it? Well, is it?

Now on the less stranger side of things, you'll all be glad to hear that I did, in fact, realize a more decent way to preserve my father's memory. One that would be a little more acceptable to people like my oldest sister (the stick-in-the-mud that she is). Yes, my friends, at the time, I owned a handy dandy little gadget that came to be one of my most soothing comforts on those long sleepless nights right after the death of my father, a piece of equipment that can preserve more than just a memory—my tape recorder. And I used it. Not only did I use it, but I also told my dad why I was using it. Sound a little scary? Well, it should. I mean anyone who's someone knows that no one in his or her right mind likes to talk about—well, you know—the inevitable. Especially to the person it's happening to. And I'm not real sure, but I think it has something to do with the fact that if we talk about it, then it makes it real. I hate that. But, I had to do it. I would have preferred videotaping; however, my dad did not want to be seen nor remembered that way. Therefore, sadly, someone (me) had to think of something else. And you have to admit, it was a hell of a lot better of an idea than the first one I'd had. Yes, I didn't think you'd have a problem agreeing with that.

Preserving a memory. Sounds impossible, but it can be done. And what made me do it were the memories I already had. The memories I never forgot, the memories that make all of us who we are for one silly reason or another.

Memories, the bloody little creepers, those misty water colored—well, you know. I don't know why we need them except for the fact that we might not ever find our way home again. Think about it; if it weren't for all the memories, none of us would be sad at all after someone died. Then the pain wouldn't be there. And the tears and the misery and the— well, enough said. I think you get the picture.

All of the stories I have shared with you thus far are memories. Memories of a man who was more than special to me for reasons I have already shared with you and for some that I am about to. Reasons that, perhaps, I just might owe my very sanity to.

You see, not only do I remember all of the wonderful stories my dad told me when I was young, but I remember other things as well. Things that shaped me to be the person I am today. And, as you will soon discover, the odds of my becoming a normal functioning human being after my daddy left home, were virtually nil. But I did it. It was a miracle, but I truly did it. And I believe with all my heart that I owe it all to the memory of a man who absolutely stood for everything great there could be.

As I shared with you earlier, my parents obtained a divorce when I was only nine years old. In the first place, probably like most small children who are dragged through the heart-wrenching ordeal of every child's worst nightmare, I couldn't understand for the life of me just what in the Sam hell a divorce really was, not to mention how it could happen to *my* family. I had only heard other children talk about it at school and had seen it on TV, but I just knew beyond a shadow of anyone who was ever someone's doubt that my parents would never get one. Never. Just as well as I knew that—my daddy would never die.

You see, if my daddy left home, that would've meant that all we had left was our mother—and she was definitely an adult. Very scary fact to the mind of a child who had been best friends all of her tiny life with not only the smartest man in the world but the only living adult left on the face of the earth who knew about monsters and the real secret behind the boogeyman. And the very worst part was that there were no warning signs. None. No arguments. No yelling matches at two in the morning. No sirens or flashing lights. Not even a black and white fuzzy bull's-eye, blaring a test and only a test of the Emergency Broadcast System, that in the actual event of an emergency would have instructed me of just exactly what in the hell I was supposed to do as my tiny little life was falling apart before my very heart. Nothing. I simply woke up one morning to find that my daddy was gone. And my life as I had come to know it, was to never again be the same. The only other time in my life that I can remember feeling that empty was twenty-six years later—on the night he died.

We sometimes do things in our lives that we can no more understand than if we were strangers to ourselves. And in a sense, that's exactly what I did, without even realizing it.

I had preserved another memory. Or maybe I had found a way to take back some of the control that I had lost so long ago. Heck, now that I think about it, maybe I did both.

You see, about four months before he died, my dad gave away his youngest daughter, who, coincidently, also just happens to be my baby sister, at her one and only wedding. And we fortunately have a ton of videotape starring our still seemingly healthy, funny, and sentimental dad sporting not a pair of overalls and white T-shirt and tennis shoes, but a handsome tuxedo and top hat with a pair of shiny black dress shoes. And you know, being as short as he was, with all due respect, he really did resemble a penguin.

Well, on the night he died, I put that tape into the VCR, which just happened to be setting directly next to that silly-ass car rewinder that had at one time brought so much joy to someone who was now just a memory—and I sat there hitting play and rewind, play and rewind, over and over again. I guess in my mind, it kept him alive as I sat there staring at the man I would never again be able to touch. It seemed that four months earlier had been forever ago. Forever—only when someone dies.

I realized while watching that video that I had been the only one at the time who knew my dad was dying. That's the way he wanted it. He didn't want anyone feeling sorry for him. And then a scene I had viewed many times before came dancing onto my TV set, yet on this night, it held a completely different meaning. The prayer.

Before the ceremony, my dad and sister knelt before the altar for prayer. But you see, my sister had to say the prayer simply because my dad was crying so hard he couldn't even speak. (Shouldn't come as a shock to any of us). He knelt on bended knee shaking his bowed head from side to side with tears screaming the years of pain down his cheeks, so choked up I thought he just might succumb to a heart attack right then and there. For you see, *this* sister was only eighteen months old when my dad left home and, as you will soon find out, a lot of tears and arguments had come between them throughout the years and what I was witnessing on that video was healing. And there was something else! Yes, something else indeed. It was then, at that moment, that something suddenly dawned on me. His life had now been completed. He had not only found all of us again, but he had lived to see all of his five little girls of yesterday, become women of today. End of chapter. Now all that was left for him to do was to prepare himself to have to leave them once again, but this time for the last and final exit. And that, my friends, is why I believe my dad was crying so uncontrollably that day. And not just because it gives my aching heart such soothing comfort on those endless, sleepless, nights—but because he told me this himself, just a week before he died.

Well, I suppose by this time, you all must have a pretty good idea of just who my father was. He was just my dad, that's all. The only one I will ever have. And now he's gone. It's just as simple as that.

His ideals and beliefs were created by him and him alone. Live and let live, no matter what the circumstance. No matter what race, creed, or color one's skin may be, don't judge anyone until you have walked a mile in his or her sneakers—and even then—we were not put on this earth to judge other human beings but to simply get along with one another until we pass away and go to wherever it is we really do go when we end our journey here. And although it may seem that he was a little nutty at times, he was a man of his word and his word was as good as the man who gave it.

I would imagine that a few of you might even think that some of the stories he told were—uh—unnecessary. Perhaps.

For instance, why make the monsters or the boogeyman real? Why hadn't he just told me that they weren't real; that there was nothing there that could hurt me; that those creatures were simply all a figment of my cute little overactive imagination?

*Marti Tote*

Well, I think you all just might have the answer to that question already. But for the sake of any misunderstanding, I'll set the record straight.

In the first place, that sort of response would have made my dad just like every other adult in the world, and I think that just may have bothered him more than the pain he suffered in the end. Secondly, I don't know about you, but I knew that no matter what any grown-up said, the things I imagined were very real and no amount of anything told to me would have convinced me otherwise. Well, my dad knew that too. He knew not to tell me how or what to believe. And just as he did throughout my entire life, no matter what, he knew he had to always believe in me.

I've said it a least a million times before and I'll say it another million if that's what it takes. I owe all of my ability to cope with life to the wonderful memories I have from my short-lived childhood. And those memories were created and shared unselfishly by a man who cared enough to take the time to enhance the imagination of a tiny little girl so very long ago. Who would have ever thought that, based on those memories alone, I would make a decision twenty-six years later, that would give back to my father everything he had ever given to me and more? I can tell you, certainly not him—and sure as heck not me.

❧

# Chapter Two

## Relationships

*Almost all of our relationships begin and most of them continue
as forms of mutual exploitation, a mental or physical barter,
to be terminated when one or both parties run out of goods.*

W.H. Auden 1907–1973 Dyer's Hand (1963) "Hic et llle"

IN THE YEARS following my parents' divorce, my safe and secure life, as I had
come to know it, would become a shattered menagerie of broken dreams. If
I had known what was in store for me the day my daddy left home I would
have grabbed onto his legs as he was on his way out that door, hoping to become a
permanent part of his body's anatomy forever—never having to return again.

You see, it's not that my mom made a decision only for herself on that grave day
back in 1967. She also made some devastating choices that would affect my sisters
and me for the rest of our lives, the most major of those decisions being the presence
of a stepfather.

In the years to follow we would be tragically subjected to a life that could only
be described as your worst nightmare. We were thrown from our world of magic and
make-believe into a world of horrible and harsh realities full of the most vicious abuse
ever imagined. My next book will fill in the years that I am now about to gracefully
dismiss. Twenty long years would go by before I came to really know my father again.

After the divorce we left our big two-story home in Orange County, and moved
to a smaller home much farther away. Over the next seven years we would move eight
times. It was a far cry from the stable surroundings that we as children had come to
know and trust. Not that we didn't move a lot before then, because we did; yes, we
most certainly and sadly did. You see, my mom had itchy feet and my dad followed

happily along, scratching them each and every inch of the way. But at least we moved and scratched together.

The division of our family started out right along the path of a normal divorce, I suppose, if there is such a thing. My dad came and picked us up on Sundays and then we'd go get an ice cream and play at the park or we would go to my grandmother's house, which had also become my father's home as well. It certainly didn't take me long to understand the meaning of divorce. No siree. It meant my heart felt like it was breaking.

Our only time spent together with our dad was shared in the ways I have just described to you, so I probably don't have to tell you that going to get that ice cream every Sunday became a very priceless and cherished excursion for me. And I didn't know it at the time, but it would also become one of those memories that many years later would prove to be an absolute lifeline.

We would begin our visits together almost always by heading downtown to the local Dairy Queen or to the corner drugstore to get the biggest ice cream we could possibly carry in our fat little hands. Then we would go over to a park or my favorite, just sit on the curb in the parking lot of the shopping center and eat it. Oh, how I loved those afternoons. Oh, how I sometimes wish we could really go back. Although in a sense I guess that's exactly what I'm doing right now, isn't it? Yes, I guess it is.

Now I'll share another one of my juicy little secrets with you. Oh, it's nothing as intense as the others I have shared but I think you'll enjoy it just the same.

You see, it wasn't that I was starving or anything like that, although we weren't permitted such treats as ice cream any longer in our new surroundings, but I would always get the biggest ice-cream cone that was ever made available to a little girl in little kid history. And why, you might ask. Well, I'm about to tell you just that. It wasn't because I was a kid with eyes bigger than my belly; it was so we could sit there as long as possible. That's why. See, I had figured out that once the ice cream was gone it was time to go home, so the bigger the ice cream, the longer the visit. Not bad figuring for a little kid, huh? Nope, if I do say so myself (and I do), not bad figuring at all. I guess that's what tearing a family apart can do for a child. Makes 'em think better, to say the least. I found just as much pleasure in savoring every moment as I did in savoring every bite. Nope, didn't take me long at all to get the hang of a divorce—quick learner that I was—not too long at all.

Thinking back now, I realize those ice-cream excursions must have been quite a challenge for my dad. I never really had the heart to ask him but I'm sure it's true. I mean, having to take five giggly little girls for ice cream all at the same time? Kinda makes you wonder if he really wasn't just a tad bit crazy after all, huh? Can you imagine, all five of us chatting away with ice cream dripping down our chins and my dad making like an octopus with his arms full of napkins? OK, maybe he was just a little crazy. But he was happy, by golly. Yup, he sure as heck was. When he was with us, he was always happy. And that's all I have to say about that!

Now being that I was such a little girl at the time, I don't recall what our conversations during those outings *did* consist of, as much as I can very clearly recall what they *didn't* consist of. And what they absolutely didn't consist of—was talk about our home life.

You see, the eyes of the man who had once held so much love and life had grown sadly dim. His soul had painfully died and he was just going through the motions. And because of the absence of his sparkle, I can remember wondering if he knew about the man who had moved into our home. Naw, he didn't know. Cause if he had known, wouldn't he have put up his dukes like he had done time and time before—to battle yet one more, but this time, very real monster? Sure he would have. And then he would've brushed himself off and come home again and we would've been done with the whole damned nightmare that had consumed my life and dreams once and for all! This time though, for the first time in my life, I must share with all of you, that there was definitely a doubt in my mind as to who would win. For my dad wasn't mean enough—or ugly enough—or hateful enough—to battle this monster. Nope, I truly don't think that even Godzilla teamed up with King Kong and a whole closetful of beasts could have done the trick. And I began to learn very quickly that some of the stories I had always believed in—just might not be true. Because no matter how much I believed in God and no matter how much I prayed, this monster continued to win. And I really came to know that anyone who was ever someone couldn't even have figured it out. But you know it really didn't matter anyway, because I wasn't allowed to tell. So not only had I lost all the life and luster that my dad had worked so hard to create, but I was then taught to lie and to deceive the only person in my life whom I could trust. What a horrendous amount of guilt to be placed upon such a small child. Yes, if I do say so myself (and I do), it most certainly and disgustingly was.

In all the moves that would follow, we would be taken farther and farther away from the man who held the very key to my heart. Therefore, it became more difficult for this tired, beaten, gentle, little man to see his girls. He had no more fight left in him with each and every month that went by. And with each and every month that went by, my mom took with her all he had ever dreamed of. And like his dreams, we became a fond and distant cloud of shattered hopes that he would never have within his reach again. Not until much later in his life anyway.

Well, I have always believed that all things happen for a reason. And I'm not really sure, but I think I now have some proof.

The year was 1987 and somehow by the grace of God, my grown sisters and I all ended up in the same state and even in the same town. You see (and I'm sure this won't come as a shock to anyone who was ever someone), we all left home before we turned sixteen, scattering ourselves wherever we could, hoping to leave behind the treacherous past we had so bravely survived.

During the twenty years since the divorce, I saw my dad only on occasion and just long enough to visit with him for an hour or two. And although I love you's would be exchanged as we parted, they no longer held the power that they once had, between a little girl and her knight in shining overalls, so many years ago.

I made sure to call him on Father's Day and on his birthday throughout the years, desperately trying to recapture what I had lost, but it wasn't until the summer of 1987 that I not only began to recapture what I had lost, but I re-entered into a relationship with my dad that would prove to be far more powerful than anything we had ever hoped for or could have ever imagined.

First of all, let's go over the past a bit. A little history lesson, if you will.

During my growing-up years, especially after my dad left home, my opinion of him was that he was ignorant. Now I realize that ignorant is such a harsh word. I too think it very well is. Nonetheless, this is what I was told. I presume I was told this myth so that I would stop thinking about the smartest man in the world. This happens sometimes when a divorce has taken place. Or perhaps my mom had decided to follow in my dad's footsteps and take up storytelling as a second hobby of her own. I have never really figured it out. But if I had to guess, my guess would be that I was told this absurd piece of information so that I would, in fact, stop thinking about the greatest monster fighter who ever lived. Huh, like any story in the whole United States of America could've done that anyway!

I was told my dad was stupid and that he didn't have a brain in his head at all, because he only had an eighth-grade education, which, incidentally, was also supposed to explain why he had been *only* a janitor all of his life. Well, when you're a little kid, you somehow tend to believe certain things that have been told to you because they appear to be fact, especially when told to you by an adult, and extra especially when that adult is your own mom. Well, low and behold, anyone who was ever someone learned much later in her life, that that little tidbit of info was a mere figment of my mom's wild imagination. Huh, guess she really did have it in her after all. To put it in much simpler terms, this was a whole lot of horse malarkey! A stinking lie!

First of all, just to set the record straight, my dad had obtained a *tenth*-grade education, which, for someone who was born in 1920, was quite an accomplishment to begin with, and second of all, my dad truly enjoyed janitorial work! So much, in fact, that he held the very same job with the very same company for twenty-six years, right up until about two months before he died! And let's not forget to mention the fact that janitorial work is a fine profession! A hard-working profession that not just anyone can do either! Oh, and also, just for the record, my dad did, in fact, quit high school in the tenth grade, so that he could join the United States Army at the tender age of seventeen, to help support his mother! Before that, he did odd jobs around town and at the age of twelve, he opened up a little bicycle repair shop in his garage, to help make ends meet. Now, I don't know about all of you, but that doesn't sound very ignorant to me!

Let's see now, where was I? Oh yes, I was just about to explain the significance of my opinion of my father's intelligence or—lack there of.

Because of what I had been told regarding my father's intellect and because of growing up the way I did—never to be rescued from the hellhole we now called home—I just assumed that he did, in fact, know about the abuse and that he simply chose not to do anything about it due to his ignorance. Well, in the first place, you know what they say about those who assume, and in the second place, as you are about to find out it was another horrendous, colossal, and stupendous crock full of bull, horse, cow, and pig malarkey!

My dad began his visits to my home during the summer of 1987 just like no time had ever passed. He simply called me up one day right out of the blue, told me he was coming, and just as quickly as he had vanished from my life, he reappeared. He still lived in Southern California and I lived in northern Nevada. Wasn't like it was a hop, skip and a jump but *that*, my friends, was just the kind of guy he was. No need to explain. Just the fact that he showed up should have said it all. And I'm here to tell you that it surely did.

Being with him again was like stepping through a looking glass into my childhood fantasies. I mean to tell you, he hadn't changed a bit. Oh, he was a little older, but he had aged so very gracefully. (Let's hope that's a genetic trait.) And let's face it; a herd of wild elephants couldn't have dragged the child out of my dad. Nope, he was still the very same man who took me tenderly by the hand so long ago and led me into a land where make believe dreams come true.

I had always felt in my heart that a part of my dad's life stood completely still after the divorce. And I was absolutely right. He couldn't tell you what he did yesterday, but he could sure as heck recall details regarding those tender years of my childhood. And so many of our conversations in the beginning of our visits were centered mostly around just that, what happened and why. And although neither one of us could ever come up with anything substantial to explain the divorce we both did agree on one thing—that my mother went off the deep end back in 1967, and succeeded in becoming a Joan Crawford clone.

We spent many teary-eyed conversations during his summer visits. Reminiscing about the past of which we were so rudely robbed. Yes, now that I think about it, it seems to me that most of our initial conversations each and every time he arrived led into talk of the good—as well as—the bad old days. And he would share with me during those intense and lengthy conversations that he just knew beyond a shadow of a doubt that had he and my mother stayed together, all of us girls would have stayed at home, and gone on to college to successfully become doctors and lawyers and homeowners! The old two-story house would have been paid for by now and we would have handed down to his grandchildren all of the skates, bicycles, and wagons! Imagine that—after all those years he could still get me caught up in a good fairy tale and just like all the others—I know he believed them with all his heart to be true. I guess some things really don't ever change. Thank God.

During the next five years, my dad's visits would gradually advance to two a year. Every July for his week vacation and every November for four days at Thanksgiving and a lot of phone calls in between, consisting of discussions centered around those lost years belonging to him and me, but the one discussion that would reacquaint me with the true personality behind the man who was once my most cherished childhood friend, was the one that will remain in my memory until those lopsided cows walk back up the hillside.

It was his first summer visit and he arrived with all the excitement of a small child. He fell in love with my home right away being that it was a big two-story house complete with dogs, cats, husband, and kids. I don't think I need to explain why he loved coming here. By now I think we all understand completely.

I woke up the morning of his first arrival at the ungodly hour of 4:00 a.m. when I heard him stirring around downstairs, getting his coffee and taking a smoke on his pipe. My dad never just smoked his pipe, he took a smoke, just like he took a drink of coffee, took a little nap, well—you get the picture. I laid in my bed listening to his morning noises that first visit and my mind began to wander back to a time when those noises were my cue to wake up and spend special moments with my dad. Moments full of whispers and kisses in the dark before he would have to begin his day and all of a sudden—I felt a complete rush of excitement, just as I had so many years ago, as a child waking up and ever so quietly sneaking downstairs with the bottoms of my little feet pajamas scraping across the hardwood floors every inch of the way, just to spend those couple of minutes alone with the greatest story teller who ever lived.

We would have a little chat and he would take a little smoke of his pipe in those wee, dark, quiet hours of the morning and then, with lunch pail in hand, he would kiss me good-bye as he tucked me back into bed. Oh, how I loved those precious moments of my past and, oh, how I longed for them so badly once again. And before I knew what was happening, by golly, I felt an opportunity to take back some of the things that were mine. So I got up, put my slippers on and tiptoed down the stairs as quietly as could be (this time minus the feet pajamas), and as I rounded the corner there he stood—in the kitchen—with his coffee cup in one hand and his pipe in the other. All that was missing was his lunch pail. And for what had to be the longest moment in history to the child inside, I stood there, leaning against the doorjamb, simply gazing upon the man who never grew up, as he meandered about the kitchen enjoying every moment of his new day.

Once he caught sight of me, he greeted me the same way he always had and always would until the very day he left me forever. With his eyes holding the element of surprise while both of his arms were outstretched toward me, he whispered, "Hi, Baby Doll," which was always followed by a tender smooch and gentle hug. Geeze, it was all I could do not to ask him to wipe my nose and tuck me back into bed. This was ecstasy, my friends. This was like reliving a dream. This was my dad. And he was home again!

We piddled around, getting coffee and exchanging whispers between us before we strolled into the living room where there was a big picture window directly in front of the couch, allowing us to watch the sun come up. We sat on the couch drinking our coffee and eating our doughnuts, which just so happened to be my dad's favorite breakfast, me with my bare feet tucked up underneath my bottom, leaning next to him, and him, well just sitting next to me close and snug. I remember that morning felt like no other. It was as if I had been given a secret peek into heaven. And perhaps I had. Because that morning something happened to my daddy and me that I can only explain as—well—true and complete understanding. I turned my gaze to him from the window and told him how very much that moment meant to me. And as I desperately looked into those eyes that had lost their sparkle so very long ago, I started to see somewhat of a rekindling. Yes, as a matter of fact, I knew I did! He was very peaceful and satisfied and those big brown chimpanzee eyes held a twinkle once again, as he gazed out upon the beginning of a new day. It was one of the many treasured moments I will always cherish. And even though that monster of my past had tainted my trust by tricking me into believing that moments shared together meant having to do the unthinkable, I felt completely safe and comfortable laying my head on the shoulder of the man who had taught me to believe in myself. And as we sat with our hearts entwined—one with the other—my dad broke the silence of our peaceful serenity with what must have been a lifetime of wonder as he then turned his gaze to me and asked for me to honestly tell him what happened after he'd left home.

Well, I couldn't believe what my heart was hearing, as I sat there staring into the eyes of the most ignorant janitor who ever lived. Totally shocked beyond disbelief I looked at him with careful consideration wondering if he really didn't know. And once I witnessed the sincerity in his tired old storytelling eyes that *no*, he really *didn't* know, then I wondered if I should take the risk of breaking his spirit once again.

"All of it?" I asked.

"Yes," he replied, with the most terrified look I had ever seen come across his face. "All of it."

And so I began. And I don't mind telling you, that our morning conversation proved to me that my once-thought-to-be ignorant father was, in reality, an extremely intelligent man.

You see, my dad did not, in fact, realize the horror that took place in my life after the divorce. He had an idea something wasn't right, but a man like my father couldn't have ever dreamed of the nightmares that were indeed taking place. And I did not, in fact, realize the horror that had taken place in his life either, until that very morning.

He shared with me a story that was his account of his own nightmare that began after that grave day back in 1967. A nightmare that described a very desperate man who went to court and to private detectives time and time again depleting his, as well as his parents' savings, to try and reclaim what was rightfully his. A story of a janitor, *just* a janitor, who thought that *maybe*, just *maybe* there was a man living in his home with his daughters who might be harming them. I guess I obviously hadn't been the only one who had noticed the absence of a sparkle in someone's eyes. And because he was *just* a janitor, and hadn't the funds nor the credibility to prove such a horrible accusation, there wasn't a lawyer or a private detective or a judge, for that matter, who would listen to him, let alone who even cared. Looking back, 1968 was not the year of the single father. He made barely enough money to pay the $150 dollars in child support each month, let alone raise five little girls on his own. What would he have done had he been able to prove it? He couldn't afford to raise us; therefore, perhaps the welfare department would not only take his little girls from their mother but they might just also rip them from the very existence of their father too (again), only to be placed in a home with foster parents! Surely our mother wouldn't allow another man, a stranger, to harm her children. I mean, she hadn't ever been even close to being the monster fighter he had been back in his day, but she had to love us girls as much as he did. Didn't she? Not to mention the fact that he didn't have the money to prove otherwise. So, he prayed, just like anyone who was ever someone would have done back in 1968. He was beaten and he knew it.

He was so tired of running into dead ends. So tired of not being able to see his daughters due to some lame excuse that was given more often than not—by the woman who at one time had held so much love for him. So tired of having to drive farther and farther every year just to make the attempt to see his little girls—so tired of living with the fact that he knew there was another man in our lives, just as well as he knew there wasn't a damned thing he could do about it. But he thought maybe if he could just prove it, then wouldn't the law have made that man move out? Well, or so he thought—or so he wished.

Yes, he was tired of it all. So tired, in fact, that one day back in 1969, he tucked a .22-caliber Ruger into the small of his back and started out the door of my grandmother's house to put a stop to all of his pain once and for all!

Well, thank God I also had a grandfather, because he's the one who stopped my dad from making what would have been the worst mistake of his life. Although, I am ashamed to admit that sometimes I still wonder. Yes, sadly, sometimes I do wonder.

My dad was heading for the front door of his parents' house that morning on a mission like no other when from the dark confines of the living room, his pop's voice very calmly came from somewhere in the dark, asking where he was going. Turning his head slightly to the right without completely turning around, my dad whispered to my grandfather that he had something to do. My grandfather asked if it was so important that he couldn't wait just a few minutes to sit a spell and talk. My dad, hand on the door knob, released his grip and that was the end of that.

You know, I love that story. I asked my dad to tell it to me time and time again. You see? It made me see a man in my father that I had no idea existed. It's a heroic part of him that I still love to secretly fantasize about to this very day. Who's to say that all wouldn't have worked out better had he made it out the door that morning? Really nothing wrong with thoughts like that, now, is there? Naw, they're just thoughts, for Pete's sake. No one else really knows about them besides you anyway. No harm done. But it sure is funny how one person's decision can alter so many futures, isn't it? Yes, it sure as hell is. The kicker is, some of us never even know about it. Matter of fact and on second thought, I take that back. It's really not funny at all.

So there we have it. A heroic story and the rekindling of a once thought- to-be lost relationship. What more could we ask for—I mean, besides a happy ending, which we already know isn't gonna happen as far as this story goes. Well, at least not the traditional happy ending that we are all accustomed to anyway. Although, I have learned throughout this whole inspirational experience that like beauty, happy endings are in the eyes of the beholder. And I want you to hold on to that thought, my friends, for you're soon going to need it. Yes, you most certainly and sadly will.

From the first summer visit with my dad, I would continue to take chances on trust. I would come to learn for the second time in my life what a parent really was. And together he and I would learn to build a relationship so close that in the end, it would prove to be our only pillar of strength. Each other. What a beautiful gift. But then again, most true relationships are, now, aren't they?

Those summer visits gave back to us most of the quality time we had lost. All of which was possible to reclaim that is. Together, we took walks to the market. We watched old movies. We spent several warm summer evenings talking on the patio in my backyard. Several mornings on that very same patio, drinking coffee and having adult conversations that had once belonged to a sleepy eyed, tiny little girl and her daddy. And another most wonderful happening began to take place as well. For you see, my children also came to know some of the magic and charm that only my dad could convey. What a heartwarming experience it was, to watch my dad interact with my children. Them just being kids and him just being—well—my dad.

I can't begin to describe the feeling that came over me, the first time I watched my daughter lay in my father's lap, with her thumb tucked securely in her mouth, watching TV, mumbling away about whatever she had on her mind, and my dad sitting there totally engrossed in a program, all the while answering her about every two minutes with, "Uh huh," "Why not!" and "Why sure!"

I stood there completely mesmerized as my thoughts went back to a time when those little chats were so tenderly taken for granted. I remembered how safe I felt laying in my daddy's lap. How truly comforting it was to trust someone with my very being and soul. So I silently thanked God at that very precious moment in time, for giving my daughter the chance to experience the wonderful love my dad had to offer, that only a child could receive. And I also thanked him for allowing me to relive a moment that I had believed to have been gone from my heart and my memories forever.

It was a wonderful new beginning. A beginning full of anticipation and hope, a new beginning between two very special people who had once been cheated out of trying. And I didn't know it then, but it was also the new beginning of a very priceless and fragile relationship that had to be prepared with just the right amount of love, so that years later it would be strong enough to endure a most difficult and tragic ending. And you know, it truly did become that strong and more. Much, much, more.

Only God could've known at the time why it was so important that my dad and I try to reclaim all that we could of our relationship. I can tell you, I sure as heck didn't know. I'm embarrassed to say that just as sure as I know my own name, I knew I'd have my dad around forever. I mean—all you had to do was look at him, for Pete's sake. He was spry and healthy and full of life! Wonderful sweet life! Why should I have thought that anything was ever going to happen to him? I mean, what in the heck kind of world would this be, if we all sat around contemplating all of the tragedies that could happen? Exactly my point, ladies and gents. We don't, do we? Well, of course not. But sometimes, things do happen, don't they? Yes, they most certainly and tragically do. I guess sometimes we tend to take even the most precious gifts for granted, don't we? Ah, if only hindsight really *were* twenty-twenty.

My dad and I came to be extremely close over the next five years, learning to share thoughts and feelings that we believed to be very intense and emotional at the time. And they were, don't get me wrong. But I'll be the first one to admit, that we had absolutely no clue what intense and emotional could really be and we wouldn't discover its meaning until the year he died.

It was actually the summer of 1989 when I realized that my first rainbow had come to an abrupt end. Well, for a short time anyway, until the next storm, I suppose. You see, that was the summer that my dad had become just a little too preoccupied with someone other than me. Yes, you read it correctly. No need to adjust your eyes, although it probably would have done me some good to have adjusted my heart for this one. My dad, as we already know, was everybody's friend. If they were male they were his buddies and if they were female they were always his girlfriends. That's just the way it was. And I have to say that I never heard a complaint from either side. My dad's buddies were fellas he worked with and his girlfriends were females he worked with—plain and simple. He didn't really have a life outside of work. He did when he and my mother were together. Oh yes, they most certainly did. They bowled together and went out dancing together and had friends over to play cards on certain nights of any given week and they had even been known to enter cross-country car races together and—they won!!! But that was a long time ago. Long before the winds of change became a full blown tornado.

Let's see, where was I? Ah yes, I was just about to introduce to you one of the greatest upsets in my life since the divorce! Well, besides the day I realized that the horse wouldn't come out of my National Velvet paper doll set. That was a horrible upset. I tore that folder to smithereens trying to get that damned horse to come out only to find out that, well, I had torn my paper doll folder to smithereens for nothing. Anyway, where was I? Ah yes, I was just about to explain the second most greatest upset in my life since the divorce. A girlfriend. No let me rephrase that. A GIRL— FRIEND!!!!! A real one! The kind that didn't just work with my dad but the real kind! The kind that saw him every day and NOT just at work. The kind that kisses and stuff. OH, MY HELL! This had to be the most ridiculous stunt my father had ever pulled. A girlfriend? No way! There was no one for my father except my mother! And God knows she had destroyed him long ago never to love again so—uh—he—didn't need anyone else—ever—again. He had me. Oh my crap—that is so, well, so selfish. Yup, that's me! Little Miss I'm-the-most-important-thing-in-the universe!

I began hearing of this girlfriend as she would filter into our telephone conversations. No big deal at the time. My dad had a lot of girlfriends. SO WHAT! Everyone loved my dad so how in the hell could he tell one girlfriend from the other??? How sick is this dialog, folks? Anyway, I began hearing more and more about one girlfriend in particular and by the summer of 1989 it became apparent that this gal wasn't going anywhere. She was hanging on like a bad leach and—it got even worse! She had kids, for hell's sake! They were nearly grown but, nonetheless, they existed just the same. And so the story goes.

It was that dreaded summer that my dad decided to bring her along on his visit to my home. Don't ask me. I just went along with it for kicks and giggles. He didn't tell me she was coming either. She just showed up with him and he was like—well—OK, happy. He was proud of her and it was weird because he acted as though he loved her. This was absurd! And she was, well, I suppose, she acted as though she loved him as well. Oh, this was not meant to be, folks. I had never planned on my dad finding someone else. I mean, why would he have needed to do such a thing after all those years of being alone? Why not just bite the bullet and go for it all the way until he died? Alone. Never having felt the touch of another. I mean, for Pete's sake, he was nearly sixty-nine years old. He had been alone for all of those years. OK, this dialog is really getting sicker by the minute and heading absolutely nowhere.

Well, the fact is, is that my dad had indeed found someone and had fallen in love. And what made it worse was that she was nothing like my mother. I need some serious therapy.

She was quiet and polite and she moved ever so gracefully. She was part Indian, which gave her the appearance of an ageless beautiful woman. Her hair flowed freely, long and straight, and ended well below her behind. She was, well, as sick as it sounds, beautiful in a plain sort of way and—she appeared to be deeply devoted to my father. She didn't say much at all unless you spoke to her. Ah, but when my father laughed, she laughed. And when he made an ass of himself like he loved to do, she would blush. And when my father kissed her she didn't pull away. She touched his cheek ever so gently and smiled. Nothing like my mother! How could he possibly love this gentle butterfly? Yup, I'm heading straight for therapy directly after this very paragraph.

All kidding aside, I fell in love with her the very moment I met her. And for no other reason than because my father loved her so—and this was as obvious as the stuck-up nose on my pathetic face. She was perfect for him and he for her. He had done what he felt my mother should have done. He had patiently waited. He knew the good lord would bring him someone someday. He also knew, he was never stepfather material. So he had chosen someone who had older children. He had waited for twenty-two long years to finally have a companion. And she—well—completed him. She was submissive and accommodating. She was flawless. Uh huh. Yup. Flawless. She was also twenty years younger than my father and harbored more mysteries and hidden secrets than the book of Revelation. AH HA! Nonetheless, I wouldn't come to know this until the very end. And I am thankful my father never knew. Or so I thought at the time anyway.

My father's girlfriend would continue to accompany him on his visits to my home from that summer forward. And they moved in together shortly after that first visit. My father was happy and she was—well— uh—oh yeah, happy too. Yes, she was very happy. Piss on a flat rock!!!!!

Just for argument's sake, let's call her the bad witch. Yes, I think I like that. It is fitting and quite appropriate for where we are heading. She was so nice until she realized that I wasn't giving up those ruby red slippers willingly. Hell, I had no clue she even wanted the damned things until the very end. Curses!

My most trusting nature began early on in their relationship. I knew something had to be amiss. Something always is, it seems. First of all, everyone has a story. I don't care who we are, there is a story trailing behind us. For some of us, it could be a fairy tale and for most of us it's a mystery but then there are some who have a full-blown nightmarish Stephen King absolute horror story lurking within them. Yup, that about explains it.

It became very complex just calling my dad's house because, luckily, I would get her on the phone before him. It was difficult for me to accept the fact that I was now calling him a lot more than he was calling me. Sometimes I would call and she would inform me that dad was sleeping and that she would have him call me back—but he didn't. Sometimes, I would try to have a conversation with her but I couldn't. I could never get her to talk. And this may come as a shock to some of you, but I came to never really like her at all. I thought it was jealousy at first. But I knew me better than that. No, it was something more sinister. Something I have come to learn is a gift I have. It was something more powerful. My own flipping opinion!!!

So, time marched on, as it usually does for some stupid reason, and I took a backseat to the girlfriend. I really didn't mind though, because each and every time I spoke to my dad he was—happy. He was—content. He was whole. And as difficult as that was for me to swallow, I had to accept that little ditty of a fact—for his sake. After all, how many times had he done it for me?

Now, as if this particular summer hadn't thrown me enough of a curveball to keep me swinging wildly in the old batter's box for quite some time, there was even more to come. Yes, indeedy, this had been only the first inning, folks. Hell, this had been only my first time up at bat for that matter. Gosh, I hate sports. The summer of 1991 was just around the corner and just before that visit in July my dad called me and informed me that he and his wonderful, whimsical new love had decided to tie the noose—I mean knot. What a crock of hullabaloo!

"Fantastic," I proclaimed! "How wonderful for you," I exalted!

"When?" I asked with loathing exhilaration.

"This summer," he said. "At your house. I want to be married in your backyard, dear."

"Great," I said with my stomach churning up all I had eaten over the past year. "I can't wait," I screamed! "What can I do to help?" Perhaps put my order in for nothing but rain for the entire month of July? Oh wait, I know, I can finally have that swimming pool that I've always wanted put in. You know, completely tear up the backyard and with the rain I'm ordering it should be nothing but a muddy flipping pile of mush when you get here. Yes, that will work out just fine.

"Well," he interrupted as my devious plan was just about to take off to places unknown, "Could you find a preacher?"

Sure—why not? I was thinking more along the lines of a mortician, however, a preacher will do, I suppose. And that, my friends, was that! I was asked by my father to begin preparing for his wedding, in my very own backyard. July? Stupid month for a wedding anyway, wouldn't you agree? Track with me here, people.

So, as the story goes, he and his, uh, blushing (gushing) bride (witch) showed up in July and I had the wedding planned. I called all of my sisters and we decorated the backyard with a beautiful arch and chairs and flowers. We bought a wedding cake and set up a beautiful table with wine goblets for the bride and groom and a cake server set with their names engraved on them, which explains why I didn't take that very serving knife and kill her with it. My name was on the bill. We found a local preacher at a nearby church who was more than happy to come over on a Saturday to marry an older couple. And they arrived on a Friday to obtain the license, which in my state takes only a matter of seconds and viola! We had created the setting for a beautiful ceremony. My dad was elated and I was, well, not. Now, I'm not sure how the other girls felt about my father's new love, but I know how I felt and, quite frankly, it's my story so my opinion is all that counts. Well, right now anyway. Actually, and in all honesty, I think the younger girls liked her. Now, doesn't that just figure? Dumb-Asses. They also liked my mother.

So, that fateful day finally arrived and I want you all to know that I tried to bond with my father's new bride that day. I tried to get her to speak or nod or something else besides just stand there and purse her lips but to no avail. Nope, ladies and gents, I had come to the sad conclusion that I would never be able to see or understand whatever in the hell it was my father saw in this woman. And as this writer continues throughout this story, you will come to find out I damned well never did. But what I did come to find out was far worse than I could have possibly imagined anyway. My mind doesn't allow me to think such things. Thank God!

OK, so where is the end of this damned rainbow and who in the hell moved my yellow brick road? Never mind that; had I known all I needed at the time was a pail of water to dump on her, I would have done so and saved us all a whole lot of heartache. But I didn't know at the time. Hell, I should have caught on when she wore a black hat to get married in! A huge wide brimmed black hat to be exact. Too busy chasing other rainbows, I suppose.

So, married they became. And I was glad when it was all over. My dad was so happy. As a matter of fact, I don't think I had seen him that happy in a very long time. Which, in turn, made me, well, I guess happy too. Well, sort of.

We spent the rest of that week's visit, well, visiting. I tried to get to know the new bride but to no avail. About the only thing she would talk about were her kids but never in front of my dad. And I, myself, found this to be odd indeed. She had a daughter who I realized my dad really had no opinion of what–so–ever–at–all, which I found out through certain conversations. And—she had a son. He was older than I—and— my father would not—and I mean absolutely would not—talk about him. And she wouldn't talk about him in front of my dad. So, I did what any other red-blooded American daughter would have done in just such a situation. I tried to get the scoop on the dirt. I mean this was absurd! Ah ha! There was her story! And it was a good one! I just couldn't figure out what in the hell it was on my own. And as much as I hate to admit it, I didn't figure it out until the very end. And for that—I am damned thankful. Of that you can be sure.

First of all, I had never known my father to be tight-lipped about anything. So I had to get to the bottom of this. You know, dig out the dirt. Therefore, one evening after the wife (witch) had gone to bed, I got myself a cup of coffee and meandered on downstairs to the family room where my dad was sitting, watching the news. "Coffee?" I asked.

"No thank you, dear," he said. "I'm getting ready to go up to bed as soon as the news is over."

I had to make my move fast. I sat down next to him on the sofa and I scooted over close to him and laid my head on his shoulder, coffee cup in hand. He reached his hand over and rested it on my knee. After a few moments of listening to the evening news, I prompted, "Happy?" "Uh huh," he replied.

"Good," I said, and meant it. A few more moments went by before I dropped the bomb. "Dad?" I said.

"Uh huh," he mumbled, acknowledging me.

"I was wondering something."

"Uh huh," he said again.

"What is the deal with the kids?" I waited. And I truly expected my dad to answer me with it was none of my damned business.

But he didn't. He simply took a long pause, a deep breath, and then very matter-of-factly exhaled his answer. "She mothers them too much."

*OK,* I thought, *I'm a mother. I can relate.* But wait. I didn't want to relate. Not to her anyway. "What do you mean," I prompted?

Again, he inhaled and then slowly exhaled, reached for his pipe, and put it to his lips before he said, "The girl is OK, I suppose. At least she can wipe her own nose."

Great! That told me a whole lot! Ah Ha! We have a daughter who can wipe her own nose. Comforting news for the tissue companies but not me! I trudged forward.

"Do you like her?" I asked.

Silence—and then he simply mumbled, "I suppose." Then he followed that with, "She's OK."

Oh, for crying out loud! Great! I got it! The daughter was O flipping K! Can we please have a conversation here?

"Do they live with you?" I asked.

Pause. And then, "Nope, they used to though."

WHAT???? How long had this romance been going on? They used to? Used to when? Like how old was I and why oh why had no one thought to tell me? Me, of all people? I mean after all, I was the special one!

"How old is she, Dad?" I asked but quickly followed it up with they.

"How old are they?"

Again, my dad gripped his fat little hand around the bowl of his pipe, put the darned thing to his lips, sucked in its smooth and soothing tobacco flavor, and said, "Oh, I suppose the girl is a little younger than you and the boy is a little older than you."

Holy crap! I was thirty-four years old! Had this romance been going on for more than—Oh, my holy heck—fifteen years? Uh, do you think there was something you should have maybe told me about—a flipping decade ago?

"How long have you two been seeing each other?" I prompted, afraid that at any moment my dad would get up, slam his pipe down on the table, and politely tell me that he was done with this conversation. But he didn't. Nope. He sure as hell didn't, although I wish he had. Instead, he began to tell me a story.

Yup, they had been dating for more than a decade and both the son and daughter had lived with them for a short time in her apartment. Although, my dad never really gave his place up. Commitment City, Folks. Anyway, he proceeded to ruin my night with a story of how "those kids," as he put it, lived off their mother and how the son was on drugs and never worked and how the witch—and I don't mean Glinda the Good Witch—would give them money and buy what they needed while she and my dad would work for *their* money. Of course, the very honor my father stood for. And then he did it. He screwed everything up from the word Go—or Screw, whichever you prefer. He told me a story that I couldn't believe and that I would never forget; it would proceed to haunt me throughout this whole stinking ordeal. He told me that he and the son had it out one night and that this Damien son had taken a swing at my father. Hold on, back up here. W H A T? Taken a swing? At my dad? Who in his right mind could have ever taken a swing at my dad? Oh, my hell, this guy had to be inhuman! Never mind that, I was headed upstairs to wake my husband up and demand that he go immediately to Southern California and beat the living whatever out of this guy! Go right now, I would have screamed! And don't stop until you find this Damien person and then you make him go away! And while you are out Damien hunting, I'm gonna go get a pail of water and put a stop to this charade once and for all!

Of course, I didn't do anything of the sort. I know it's hard to believe but I didn't. Instead, I scooted closer to my dad and I listened. And as I listened I watched his expressions so intently that I forgot where we were. I was mesmerized. I was shocked. And I wondered why, oh, why did my dad—how, oh, how *could* my dad—love this woman? Well, we all know the answer to that dumb-ass question already now, don't we? Of course we do. Because he was, well, my dad. And I knew at that moment, that very stinking horrible, awful, nasty, ghastly, hideous, horrific moment that will be forever etched into my pea-size memory, that my dad would never know the meaning of true love. Hell, maybe most of us never do anyway. But my dad deserved to know what it felt like to be loved back. The way he knew how to give love. However—that wasn't going to happen here, folks. Not in his lifetime anyway. And that little ditty of a fact made me very angry. More like furious. Or maybe just sick, I'm not real sure. But what could I do? He had chosen to marry this woman and if I said anything against her, well, let's just say for argument's sake that it probably wouldn't have been a very good idea to do so. So, there I sat. On the couch, staring into the eyes of my father as he told me his tales of woe and I did nothing. I said nothing. I simply listened. But in my mind, I knew that this had been a terrible mistake and that it would all come out in the wash some day. Ah, yes. My dad himself had a saying. He'd say, "Shit always floats to the top." And, as far as I can tell thus far, he was absolutely correct. And it was certainly no different in this situation. But I could have never dreamed that I'd be the one left to clean up the mess. Not to mention, the horrible calm before the mess. I reckon I was just meant to be a cleanup person. Perhaps I inherited that fantastic little trait from my father himself. Although the messes I would be cleaning up were far worse to deal with, in my opinion. They are the kinds that keep coming back. Like shoveling mud uphill—with the rain still pouring down—in the middle of a hurricane—naked—I'll stop there.

After sitting and listening for what seemed like an eternity, I shifted my rear a little closer to my dad. Put my hand on his arm and gave him a gentle tug. He wouldn't look at me. So I tugged again and his gaze wandered my way as he took in long and seemingly enjoyable puffs of his pipe but his eyes never made it to mine. He was afraid to look at me. This was a new feeling and I didn't much care for it. And I might share with all of you that this was only the beginning. There would be so very many more of these non-communicating moments to come. Finally, I very softly whispered, "Dad?"

"Huh?" was his only reply.

"Why did you marry her?" I asked with my heart pounding so loudly I couldn't hear myself think! Now I'd gone and done it. What business was that of mine anyway? Well, probably none of my damned business at all but I had to ask. I mean for crying out loud, he had just married this witch person and here we sat talking about all the wonderful memories he had thus far and my heart was just a tad bit confused. And I'm not really sure but I could've sworn there was a silhouette forming on the wall in the shape of Alfred Hitchcock!

He cleared his throat and finally turned his head and then shifted his entire body toward mine, placed his stubby little hands on my knees, and he looked me right in the eye and said, "Because she needs security if something were to happen to me."

OK, hold it the hell on here! Security is purchasing a gun or a big-ass Doberman dog with bad breath. Security for what???? Oh, perhaps for that Damien person. Uh huh, OK—she'd need a much bigger dog than a Doberman. And perhaps a few hand grenades rather than a gun.

"Security for what?" I asked, puzzled as all get out. "Like, for money if you die?" I asked, as though he might reach out and slap me at any given moment.

"Well, yes," he continued, as though I were dumber than Thompson's colt, "That and health insurance. She has nothing," he blurted out as though I couldn't have heard him had he spoken in a normal tone of voice.

I jumped and he was immediately sorry. What in the hell had just happened here? My dad was raising his voice at me and I was jumping at the tone. This was so out of the ordinary that I was almost positive that that silhouette on the wall had now become one of those monsters that used to live in my closet.

"So," I pushed, "you married her to—take care of her?"

"Well, yes," he stammered! Like duh!

Oh crap, this was going nowhere and damned fast. I mean at warp speed! Let's recap, shall we? Oh to hell with recapping. Did he even love this woman or had he chosen her simply because she was needy? Oh, for hell's sake. This was just awful. And I could tell he was getting cranky by the minute. Cranky? My dad? OK, I had definitely wandered into the twilight zone this time. Why was he getting so—well— cranky? Unless— he—Oh, my hell! That was it! He was sorry! He was damned sorry he married her! He wanted out! He was desperate—that had to be it! No need to worry. I could fix that. Why, we'd just hop our happy little asses right on down to the county courthouse and get ourselves an annulment Yes, indeedy—that is exactly what we would do. And then we send that witch person home to her Damien son and her "not so bad" daughter—and we'd be done with her once and for all. Yup, had it all figured out. Sure as hell did. Damn, he was so lucky to have me.

"So," I continued, "you do love her though, right?" Please say no, please say no, please say no.

"Well, for crying out loud, yeah, I love her!" he shot back at me.

Dang, he didn't have to be so damned curt! Geeze. All I asked was did he love the woman he just married on that very same godforsaken day! Idiot! What a dumb-ass!

"I thought so," I said. "I mean, I knew so," I covered.

"Well, what kind of a question was that," he quipped.

Oh, the kind that makes you kind of wish you were invisible. You know—the kind of question that only dumb-ass half-witted daughters ask when they are trying to destroy a relationship with their father. Uh huh, that kind of a question. How in the hell did I know what I was asking? I was deranged and half nuts by then.

"Well, use your head for something besides a hat rack," he quipped.

OK, I will, just as soon as I get it unstuck from where I sit down.

"Sorry, Dad," I said and meant it. It's just that, well, you know, all I have to compare this to is Mom and—uh huh, and what—Baby Doll? Are you now going to tell him that you don't think he ever really loved your mother? Oh, that's just great. Who needs terrorists when they have me?

He was talking to me. "And?" he urged.

Think fast, cutie pie.

"And, I don't want you to ever be that unhappy again." Oh, that was great! Encore! Encore!

By this time I was nearly crying. And not that I hadn't meant what I had just said, I did. But it's not what I wanted to say. However, what I wanted to say would have made him love that "Damien" and that "She's OK, I guess—not so bad" daughter a hell of a lot more than me. Oh, hell yes.

"Well," he said, "and I don't ever want to be that unhappy again either."

No kidding? Because I could swear you are heading straight down that very same road, my friend. Oh, yes! I mean what in the hell is it about you and women? Why do you always pick the ones that will for sure, beyond a shadow of a doubt hurt you—you dumb-ass, dear old dad of mine?

"Good," I said. "Then that is that." And there we both sat, together, knowing damned well that nothing had gotten accomplished. I know he was unhappy. I know he was sitting there reflecting on just what in the hell he had done. I knew it just as well as I knew my own name, it was "Dumb-Ass!" Moral to this part of the story? Don't ever ask someone if they are happy on their wedding day. Or—if you are born with a big mouth, have your tongue removed at a very young age. Or—try to remember moments when you feel guilty because somewhere down the road I can just about assure you that you will not feel guilty at all. As a matter of fact you will probably have a moment when you say to yourself—Ah ha! I knew it!

They left at the end of that week in July and I felt, well, lonely. No, more like I had just lost my best friend. Oh and let's not forget that my best friend had just gone home with his new Frankenstein bride.

Something was amiss and I was going to get to the bottom of it come hell or high water! I just didn't know when. Oh—and I didn't know how either. But I knew I would and when I did, that witch person had better put her pointy hat where the sun didn't shine and kiss her rump good-bye, because once I exposed her for what she really was—why—she wouldn't be able to crawl low enough. Just had to figure out what I thought she really was. Ok, of that I wasn't sure but I just knew it was bad. She was bad and I was going to prove it so my dad could see, uh, so my dad would realize, uh, that he—had blown it again? Oh, crap. This was a bad idea. So, I really did nothing. I just had to come to grips with the fact that my father had just married the woman of his dreams and I quite frankly didn't care much for her. That was all. No big deal. He was just the only parent I had, (that I could relate to anyway). And I had just rekindled a long-lost relationship with him but, hey, long-lost relationship rekindlings are overrated anyway.

I'm glad I didn't know at the time what was in store for my father and me. It may have just sent me over the edge earlier than I had already anticipated. And so the story goes on once again.

As I have already shared with you, it was 1992 when my dad's youngest daughter decided it was time to tie the knot. But sadly, she never really knew my dad. You see, she was just a baby when he left home. Eighteen months old to be exact. And the years that followed, sure as heck didn't give her one iota of a hint as to who the person behind the man, really was. Every-other-weekend visits, simply just doesn't cut the mayonnaise when it comes to a sincere and fulfilling relationship, now, does it? No, unfortunately, it sure as heck doesn't. And I find that to be a very sad fact of life. Especially when we consider how many children in the world are still growing up, exactly the same way.

Well, it just so happened that as my dad's youngest daughter began preparing for the most important day in her entire life, she felt a compulsive need to get to know the species of humankind that other children throughout her existence had strangely called Dad. Oh now, of course I had told her many stories, just like the ones I have shared with you, but she had to find out for herself, you see? And she had tried in vain on several other occasions to do just that, but something always seemed to get in the way of her ability to recapture something she never really had to begin with. And as pitiful and sad as this sounds it was true. I was old enough when my dad left home, to have wonderful memories to remind me of who he was. She had nothing.

This fact was, indeed, also very disturbing to my dad. He wanted to give her what she so unfairly missed out on but he truly didn't know how. How in the hell do you go back? Well, for those of us who live in the real world, we all sadly know that you just can't, now, can you? You can try but it's never really the same. Therefore, he did not know her—and she did not know him. But something happened in 1987. Something that can be described only as the meddlings of someone a whole lot more powerful than ourselves—and He must have really had his work cut out for Him knowing only what He, Himself could have known at the time—because, let me tell you, He had very little time to soften some hearts and get this little event into motion.

I guess the best way to begin to tell you what happened next is to first give you a little background. Seems only proper given the circumstances at hand.

You see, my dad's three youngest daughters felt just like any other persons might feel given their position. After all, as far as they were concerned, our dad is the one who left *us*. I had never shared the things I knew about the divorce simply because it was something my dad had shared exclusively with me. Not to mention the fact that they just didn't seem to have the ability to comprehend anything when it was in reference to my dad. And why would they? They didn't even know him. They only knew who and what he represented, compliments of none other than my mother. Therefore I would imagine they probably thought that he was simply just a dumb-ass, good for nothing janitor guy who had walked out on us. I truly felt that when they were ready to open their hearts to listen, only then—would they be able to hear. That's just the way life is sometimes. We don't have to like it. But it truly and sadly and quite simply is—a fact of life. One that very matter-of-factly sucks rope, if I do say so myself. (And I do).

41

What a mess! The way I see it is that it was easier to dislike a man they never knew than it was to have to come to grips with the fact that the only parent they'd ever had, may have perhaps deceived them. You know the old adage, what you don't know won't—or some things are better left—well, you get the picture.

It's unfortunate, but life can sometimes deal a harsh hand. And although it should be up to us to play it right, sometimes some of us aren't able to play with a full deck to begin with. It's sad but true. Well, it seemed to me that throughout my life, knowing when to hold 'em or when to fold 'em simply wasn't enough. You see, after the divorce my sisters and I weren't dealt a very legal hand, to say the least. So we never really had an option to play our cards right. We had no options at all, nor did we have any rights or choices. Yes, ladies and gents, I believe whoever the nut was who said that "time heals all wounds," had obviously *never* been abused.

Well, there did finally come a time in my life when it became obvious that it was going to take a lot more than just time to heal all my wounds. After three failed marriages and several years of trying to live the life of the Cleavers with an Addams family background, I decided that something just might be wrong with me. I know it was a long shot, but nonetheless, I decided to seek what we call therapy. Now, this was not an easy decision for me. I mean, who in their right mind would ever want to face the fact that they just might need a little help—just to get by and live day to day? Well, sure as heck not me, I can tell you that! But I can also tell you this; it was either therapy or some form of ending it all—and quite frankly, I thought I'd try therapy first. (It's a little less strenuous on the system.) So, off I went into the world of mind invaders, to try to put together the pieces of my past so that I might be able to function properly or, well—socially—in my present as well as my future. And I must say, all kidding aside, it was the smartest move I ever made.

Now you would think that because my dad was from the old school, so to speak, that he just might think this therapy thing was for the birds. I wasn't really from the old school and I can tell you, I sure as heck did. But remember now, we're talking about my dad here. And you may have already guessed; his feelings on the subject were quite the contrary. Yes, he actually thought the therapy thing was "just peachy," even though in his day, people went to shrinks only when they'd already jumped off the deep end. You know, like closing the barn door after the geese had already escaped. However, as we already know, my dad was a man of change and he felt that if I thought it would help me to overcome the terrible past from whence I came and it made me feel better about myself, then "whhhhy not!" Not to mention the fact that his daughter had finally seemed to get her droppings together as a result of that peachy therapy. And so the story goes.

I began therapy in March of 1986 and, believe it or not, it actually began to shed some light on the heavily wooded area of my past. Yes, my friends, I actually began to like myself again and I learned how to trust myself and my own instincts for the very second time in my whole life. I also learned to communicate openly and honestly once again. What a concept, huh? No lies, no deceit, just good old-fashioned down-home honesty. Imagine that.

In the meantime, my dad's wheels began to turn inside that simple little mind of his. And as a result of all that wheel turning, he decided that it was high time someone took on some responsibility for all that had happened to me in my past. So at the age of seventy, once again displaying his ability to give something of himself, he obligingly volunteered to go along with me to a couple of my therapy sessions. Now, how's that for a twist? No—he really didn't have a whole hell of a lot to do with the choices that had been made for me after he'd left home. Not really. And I do want to point out that I realize that perhaps I am taking him off the hook a little more so than he deserves. But to be perfectly honest with you, he gave more back to me than any other adult ever had in my whole entire life. Perhaps it doesn't excuse his neglect of the situation as much as it at least gave me something and more importantly *someone* to hold on to for the first time in my life since the divorce. And let me tell you, to an abuse survivor, validation of any sort is priceless!

My dad felt that as my parent he owed me some answers—and a future—and that *somebody* should try and give back to me some of what I had lost. There really was no end to the gifts he was willing to give and I can tell you that there are no words to describe what it was like to sit in that office and watch my dad tearfully reflect his feelings on the loss of my childhood. Finally, someone had taken some responsibility. And what's more, someone was willing to release all of the guilt. What a relief!

He went through an awful lot of *should haves* and *could haves* before we finally decided that if hindsight could be bottled and sold—it would truly be worth millions. Of course, how do you put a price on replacing someone's childhood? Huh, I suppose you really can't, now, can you? But at least my dad was willing to try. And that's more than I can say for the rest.

Perhaps now it will be a little easier for you to understand the distance between my dad and his three younger daughters. My younger sisters never had the opportunity to experience the emotion that only my dad could deliver. Well, not yet anyway. Ah, but they would. Yes, indeedy, and sooner than they thought!

As I was saying earlier, my dad's youngest daughter decided in her heart that it was time to take a risk. Having a traditional wedding meant more to her than anything else in the world, and you can't very well have a traditional wedding without the traditional father. Well, I guess you can, but she just simply didn't want to. So when she finally decided that it was time to tell the old man how she felt, she got the surprise of her life—and then some.

After careful consideration, she called him on the phone one daring afternoon and tried one more time to make a connection. She finally decided it was time to tell my dad that she felt like he had abandoned her and that those Sunday visits just hadn't been enough! "Why in the hell didn't you do something more?" is what I believe her exact words were. Sounds logical when you think about it—now, doesn't it?

Now, being that she had been raised right alongside the rest of us, she expected a lot of excuses along with a lot of *becauses* and *whys* and *what else did you expect me to do*? Ah, but she had never experienced a confrontation with the likes of the most ignorant janitor in the universe. Nope, she sure as heck had not. And what she received, perhaps for the first time in her life (or that she could remember anyway), was full and complete honestly and compassion from none other than the most courageous monster fighter who ever lived. Her father.

He began their conversation by tearfully telling her that she was absolutely right. That there was no excuse in the world that could be given for the decisions he made or didn't make so very long ago, just as there could be no forgiveness. He then proceeded to share with her his account of what had truly happened back in 1967, all the while making sure not to exclude himself from blame. And I wasn't there, but I understand that at the end of that conversation, there were some *I love you's* exchanged, but this time, they were sincere and heartfelt *I love you's* and my little sister started to feel some earth-moving changes within her soul that could be identified only as actual father–daughter bonding.

The conversation ended about two hours later and with no real concrete commitments as far as the wedding was concerned, in that my dad told her he just didn't know if he could get the time off to make it in August, being that he would still have to take his scheduled vacation in July as always. Doesn't sound like he was very committed now, does it? Nope, of course not. But this was a tactic my dad used to prepare for a surprise attack. Oh, how he truly loved to give the gift of a good surprise. And a good surprise is exactly what his youngest daughter received.

Yes, ladies and gents, it was all in the game plan. For two weeks later he showed up at my door totally unannounced to accept my sister's invitation in person. That was simply his style. He felt that this was much too important an issue to the daughter he never really knew to handle over the phone. So once again, my dad, displaying his ability to give of himself, resulted in the introduction of his youngest daughter to her true father.

Well, he wanted to surprise her and, believe me, he did. And he surprised me as well—showing up, totally unannounced, at my front door very early on a Saturday morning, which meant he had driven all night. I couldn't imagine who in the world could've been knocking at my door at seven o'clock on a Saturday morning, and I sure as heck would have never guessed it was my dad, that's for darned sure. But there he stood, in the flesh, with his arms extended and his lips ready for a smooch! Yes, indeedy, there he surely stood. And I don't mind telling you, that I'm really glad he chose to surprise his youngest daughter, for it was a very wonderful and pleasant surprise for me as well. What better comfort was there to wake up to, than a hug and a kiss from the very man who had rescued me time and time again? My knight in shining overalls! My dad! And I will never forget the anticipation and excitement he exhibited that morning.

He bounced through my front door beaming with all the energy of a small child on Christmas morning. He never even stopped to rest! He was like a tornado of emotion! He was on a mission and he wanted to complete it promptly and gracefully. But most importantly (especially to a guy like my dad), he wanted to complete his mission traditionally.

He proudly answered my look of bewilderment that morning, with the fact that he had come in person to tell his youngest daughter that he would be proud to escort her on what was very obvious to him to be the most important day of her life. But you know, ironically, the most important day of her life would now, in fact, change because of his decision. Yes, indeedy, my dad was about to change the course of history!

After he dropped off his little overnight bag at my house, he went on his way to complete his heartfelt rescue mission—to accept what he felt was a true and inspiring honor. So with his chest out and his head high— and a hearty "High ho, Silver and away!"—he was gone.

Again, I wasn't there (seems like I miss all the good stuff), but from what I understand, it was a very touching, very overwhelming moment for both of them. Now, don't you just love these kinds of stories? Boy, I know I sure do.

My dad came home from my sister's looking better than I had seen him look in quite some time, which just goes to show you how love does wonders for the soul, doesn't it? He shared with me that they both had a wonderful talk and that in less than two months, he would proudly escort his youngest daughter down the aisle of holy matrimonial bliss. Boy, was he proud of her, and of himself, for that matter. As he very well should have been, don't you think? Plain and simply done. And with that little step out of the way, he got up the next morning and left for home.

That was June of 1992. The next month, my dad would still make his scheduled visit for a week. But this time, he and his youngest daughter would be reunited and they would be able to start to get to know one another. It was another wonderful new beginning we had to look forward to. I was truly starting to feel like someone had just given me a gold mine. Today my dad's youngest daughter, tomorrow—who knew? Yes, my friends, there was no limit to the happenings that could take place now. Things were coming together really nicely, wouldn't you agree? As it isn't every day that we are given a second chance to try and right a wrong, now, is it? Nope, it sure as heck isn't. And I, for one, am not the sort of person to look a gift horse in the mouth, or the eyes or ears or—well, you know what I mean. To put it simply, I felt as though nothing could ever go wrong again.

*Somewhere, over the rainbow, Way up high, There's a land that I heard of Once in a lullaby.*

*Somewhere, over the rainbow, Skies are blue, And the dreams that you dare to dream Really do come true.**

What a crock of crap!!!! * (Lyrics by E.Y. Harburg).

# Chapter Three

## Life

*Life is a gamble at terrible odds— if it
was a bet, you wouldn't take it.*
Tom Stoppard 1937- Rosencrantz and
Guildenstern Are Dead (1967) act 3

WELL, LADIES AND gents, as we well know by now, life seems to deal out the bitter along with the sweet more than we care to acknowledge. For it was during my father's next visit that I discovered totally by accident that he was dying.

Not only was I surprised to see my dad at the front door—simply because he arrived one day earlier than expected (love those surprises)— but I was also surprised and fear stricken because of his appearance. For the first time in my life and his, for that matter, I noticed how old he looked. And not only had he aged tremendously in just one month but his skin actually had a yellow tint to it. Did he have more wrinkles? How could I have missed that before?

Now because of my background, I'll be the first one to admit that I do tend to think the very worst of a situation in the beginning. However, I have learned to try to then tell myself that there's no reason to worry until I have all the facts. You know, sort of a calm-down talk between me, myself, and I. Therefore, I simply assumed that there just had to be a logical explanation for his appearance. I was sure of it. Maybe he was tired. I mean he was in his seventies, for heaven's sake and he was still working full time. Yes, of course, that was it. So, I decided that I would simply tell him that I thought it was time for him to slow down a bit. Yes, I believe I felt better already. As for the yellow skin, well, I knew from everything I had ever read on the subject of cancer that yellowing of the skin comes right along with the package. So rather than lose my sanity and my bowels both at the very same moment, I simply decided that my dad was eating just too many darned yellow vegetables. Yes, indeedy— happened all the time. He had probably become a vegetarian in his old age—that was all. I'd simply have to tell him it was time to slow down on those vegetables too. As a matter of fact, that was probably why he had also dropped about twenty pounds in just one month. The man needed to eat some meat and potatoes or something. Or maybe that witch was slowly poisoning him! Oh, my heck—I just knew she was horrible and this would prove it! See, there was no reason to panic. I had already figured it out on my own. I'd simply have to tell him to start eating more meat and dairy products and get rid of that wife of his—that's what. Come to think of it, old people don't really eat enough dairy products, do they? Nope, they sure as heck don't. That's why their bones get so very brittle. I read that somewhere. Yup, I'd simply have to have a talk with that man about his nutritional intake as well as his personal life—again? Oh boy. Yes, indeedy, my friends, that's exactly what I was gonna have to do. Geeze, are a daughter's worries ever put to rest?

You know, as I'm sure I don't have to point out to you by now, it's truly amazing how the human mind actually has the ability to fool itself—isn't it? Yes, indeed, truly amazing! Especially when it's panic stricken and has lost all control of a situation. I have to tell you, it absolutely fascinates the crap right out of me—as I'm sure it will all of you—as we continue on.

After we shared our hellos and he had settled in a bit, my dad went upstairs to take a little nap. At that point, I decided that I would pick up around the house so that I could spend some nice visiting time with him once he awoke. So, I found myself going through his little ice chest, putting things away, and talking with the witch person while he was napping, minding my own bleedy little business, when I came across a box of what very clearly seemed to be medicine. OK, now I was getting somewhere. This would clear up everything. No need to worry any longer. He was probably on medication for—well—I didn't know what. But I was sure it was something that old people have to take because they're, uh, old or because they aren't getting enough meat and dairy products in their diets. Or an anti-serum to reverse the effects of poison! OK, truthfully, I had no clue what it was but I was about to find out.

I turned to the bad witch and asked, "What's this?"

She stared at me for a moment and shrugged her shoulders.

"You don't know?" I asked. What in the hell kind of a wife are you anyway???? It's the poison, isn't it? Isn't it?? Answer me, you wicked old witch person you!!! I calmly walked toward the table and showed the box to her as though she had never seen it before and asked again, "What is this?"

She was silent. OK, this is not a good time for her to play coy with me. For I could actually reach out and slap those little monkeys right out from under her skirt!

When suddenly out of nowhere, she spoke. Very quietly and almost in a whisper she said, "You'll have to ask your father."

Oh really? Will I? Have to ask my father, huh? Well, what if I don't want to ask my father? What if I'd rather just slap the crap right out of you until I get an answer? Huh? How's that sound, you dumb half-witted witch person, you!

"Why?" I asked. "Why can't you tell me?" I urged. She was silent again. Geeze–La–Weeze! Had she ever learned to communicate normally? I mean, have a heart here, lady! I was getting just a little bit frightened (I'm frightened, Auntie Em) and I couldn't feel my legs!

"I don't want to ask my father," I blurted! "I'm asking you! Is he sick?"

Silence again. She was now looking down at the floor.

What? Do I have roaches? Or might the answer to the question I am asking you be written in the tile of my stinking kitchen floor? I walked closer to the table and begged, "Please tell me why my dad is taking medicine?"

"I can't," she said. "It isn't my place to tell you."

OK, I liked her again. Not really, but she seemed to be genuine in that she really didn't feel right about telling me. I knew something was seriously wrong though. Because otherwise she could have told me, right? Well, duh!

Now, don't judge me too quickly here yet. Cause there's more to come. Yes, ladies and gents, there's lots more fun ahead. You see, it just wasn't enough that I had to find the box that contained medication, but then I just had to go and do something really intelligent. Since I couldn't get a straight answer out of St. Mary, I decided to open the damned box and look inside. Boy howdy, did I. And to my horror, it wasn't a medicine box at all. It was Pandora's box! For it not only contained a bottle of medication but a syringe to boot! Oh, dear, things were definitely getting worse by the second. OK, there had to be a logical explanation for all of this. Well, didn't there? Uh huh, like hell there was.

I frantically looked all over the box for the word insulin. Nope, it wasn't there! Not anywhere! As a matter of fact, I couldn't understand a word that had been typed upon that box. Might as well have been written in some other language. All righty then, a diabetic he wasn't. Therefore, I would just have to stay calm and, when my dad woke up, he would simply tell me that what I had found in his little ice chest was a miraculous medical breakthrough cure for the common cold! Common colds can be very harmful to the elderly, you know? Well, and if you didn't know before, you can consider yourselves informed as of now! Hell, I hear tell that some old folks can even die from a common cold! Goes right straight to their lungs and turns into pneumonia! However, had it simply been just a common cold, I think "Little Miss Tight Lips" would have told me, huh? Yeah, seems logical. But she wasn't talking—which meant I could probably just about bet the farm on the fact that it wasn't a cure for the common cold.

I don't guess I have to tell all of you how very frightened I was. No, I'm sure you all get the picture. I was more frightened than I had ever been, perhaps in my whole life (and after all I have shared with you already, you have to know that I was pretty damned frightened, to say the least) not to mention the fact that his nap must've been the longest taken since Rip Van Winkle's! How in the hell could he sleep so damned long in the daytime anyway?

While he continued to nap and I continued to spend time with his new bride, who had all of a sudden developed a severe case of mute, I piddled around the kitchen and tried to create a dialogue over and over again in my mind. What would I say? What could I say? *Dad, I was going through your ice chest and I came across a box that has very matter-of-factly scared the living hoopala right outa me—and now, I would like for you to tell me one of your spiced-up fairy tales, and this one better be the granddaddy of 'em all—so this whole stinking episode can have a happy damned ending!* There you see? No need to worry. No need to worry at all, nope—none, what–so–ever–at–all. Damn it!

Well, I have to admit that when he finally did come downstairs, sleepy eyed and full of charm, I felt an incredible urge to just forget the whole damned thing. I mean, for crying out loud, I should've been thankful that my dad had been chosen to participate in a medical breakthrough experimental cure for the common cold. I would just throw the box of medicine away and slap the sickness right out of him and get that man some vitamins or some good dairy products. Hell, I'd buy him a whole damned cow if I had to. Maybe even the whole damned dairy! See, I told you it was going to get better.

He got himself a cup of coffee, greeted his bride as she politely excused herself and went upstairs, which was a really good place for her at that particular moment—and then he sat down at the table to take a smoke of his pipe, all the while me sitting there, watching his every move, staring at him like he had just revealed the fact that he was a goat. I couldn't take my eyes off him! Like, what was I expecting him to do? Maybe start hacking and coughing, break out in a rash, grab his chest and die right there on the spot? Well, to be perfectly honest with you— perhaps.

Quite frankly, I was just about to get up and run like hell all the way to wherever it is people run to when they're so scared that they consider buying whole dairy farms for their sick fathers, when something came out of my mouth that I hadn't said for at least twenty-five years.

It was a game I used to play with my dad when I was a little girl. Whenever I had a problem or when my dad had to get the truth out of me, we would say to each other, "We love each other and we are always honest with each other, aren't we?" Then we would proceed to say whatever it was that had been on our minds. It kind of set the stage to prepare each other for a serious talk. So, without even thinking about it, my primeval instincts took over and it was out of my mouth before I even knew what was happening.

Looking at me with a startled but inquisitive look, he replied to follow suit. "Yes," he said, "We *do* love each other and we *are* always honest with each other."

Okeydokey, I thought, so far so good. So I proceeded on as I exhaled my words.

"Well, Dad, I was putting some stuff in your ice chest away, you know just cleaning up a bit—and I found some—uh—medicine." I sure as hell didn't want to admit that I opened it up and found syringes. Good Lord, like if maybe I didn't tell him, they would disappear. What a daughter! What a heroine! What courage she has! What a blooming doodoo head! Spit it out, girl. Open your mouth and get it over with, for someone's sake, before you lose what nerve you have left! I pushed on, being ever so careful not to look at him until I finally asked, "Dad, are you sick?"

There—it was out. No turning back now, "Little Miss Baby Doll, Nosey Body." Nope. Whatever was going on inside of that box, which was residing in my refrigerator, was about to hit the fan at that very moment.

He looked down at his hands and kind of fidgeted a little, and then he looked at me—and then down at his hands again, before he calmly looked at me again, but this time right square in the eye and very matterof- factly said, "I have the cancer."

Well, howdeeflippendoo! I, very matter-of-factly, wanted to slap the living crap right out of him. Oh, by the way, did I fail to mention the fact that I have cancer, pass the carrots. I have cancer, get the door. I have cancer. Call an ambulance for the heart attack my lunatic daughter is about to have!

Everything went dim! My life was flashing before my very eyes and I wasn't even the one who was dying! This just absolutely could not be happening! Gosh darn it, old man, ha, ha—you really had me going this time! Boy, what a kidder! I tell you, this guy missed his calling. He could've been a comedian! What a storyteller! A regular—uh—a regular—oh, to hell with it. I knew damned well he wasn't kidding. No one in their right mind would ever kid about something like that. Not even my dad. But when I heard those words, this was one time in my life that I wished with everything I had in me, that he *was* kidding. That this was just another little story he had concocted just to get a laugh out of me. But I wasn't laughing at all. And he—wasn't either.

Well, how in the hell do you like that, ladies and gents? Now he'd gone and done it. He'd gone and told me the truth. This was just great! This was just fantastic! This was a stinking nightmare!

There must have been a terrible mistake! Yup, that was it. They must have read the tests wrong, if there were any tests. Were there tests? Of course there must have been. How else would he have known that he had cancer? Sure, that was it. Happened all the time. Whew, what a close one.

Oh sure—now, don't get me wrong. I knew that people got cancer. I watched "Dateline" and "Oprah" and read *People Magazine*, for God's sake! But surely not people like my dad. He's such a cute little man (like cancer only preys on the mean and ugly or perhaps someone should have asked my permission first, huh?). Of course if, in fact, cancer did prey only on the mean and ugly; I, for one, knew just a man who would fit that bill. Yes, I most certainly and sure as hell did. So just wait right there, God—I'll run and go get him for you!

But I didn't go anywhere. To be perfectly honest, I couldn't have moved had someone dumped fire ants down my britches. Nope, as a matter of fact, I just sat there, trying to work up enough courage to say something—anything at all to break the silence.

"What kind?" I asked. Oh beautiful sweet cakes. That was good. Like it really mattered! Cancer is cancer really, isn't it? But don't some people fight it and win? Sure they do, don't they? Well don't they, gosh darn it? Sure— some do. But at his age? Chances were probably slim. About as slim as the chance of that wife of his finding her voice again—oh, and speaking of that wife person, just wait until I got my hands on her! But not just yet—for just as I was about to contemplate shaking her until she herself wished she had cancer, my dad stopped me dead in my tracks. For it was then, at that very moment, that he slowly reached one comforting hand across the table and gently took mine and then with the other hand, he reached down and took hold of the bottom of his trademark T-shirt and lifted it to reveal his right breast where there was a horrible black lump protruding from it. And then, with all the compassion that only my dad could portray, he proceeded to tell me the horrible truth. And on that very morning, within the confines of my own kitchen, I truly believe that a part of me died.

All that my cute little truth-seeking dad knew was that his cancer was terminal and that it was throughout his whole body. It was from the tips of his fingers to the tips of his toes and, at the risk of sounding like a troubled promiscuous teenager, I asked, "How could this have happened?"

Well, my friends, my simple-minded, gadget-loving, storytelling little dad didn't even know what kind of cancer he had, let alone how it had happened. He thought that terminal was a good enough explanation for him. After all, terminal means the end—*hasta la vista*—*happy trails to you*—*good night, Irene*! And things were worse! Oh yeah, a whole lot worse. They had given him six months to live six months ago! Well, howdeedo!

Talk about feeling the earth moving under your feet. And just to make matters a little bit more bizarre, to tell you the truth, I really don't think he would have thought this subject important enough to tell me anytime soon either. I mean, after all, it was *his* problem. Why bother with worrying anyone else over something that absolutely nothing could be done about? I mean everyone who was ever someone should know that once your number is up—well, there isn't a damned thing that anyone on the face of this earth can do about it. Now then, that's the end of that.

The conversation that followed that day would become the first of many containing all kinds of things that people never have to talk about unless one of them is dying. And you know, to be quite truthful, it made me feel kind of—well—sick. Yes, I do believe that's the word I'm looking for. Sick as well as sad. Sad at the fact that we don't say the things we should say, when we should say them, unless something like this happens. Do you follow me? I mean to tell you that if you get anything out of this story at all, please get this! We don't call the shots when it comes to fate. Get it? So the next time you feel like saying something to someone you love and you find yourself doing like most of us do, thinking that you can just say it later—when the timing might be better or whatever excuse we can conveniently come up with—stop! And for the sake of love, say it now! For you may not ever get another chance.

It became more than obvious to me, and probably after the last paragraph, to you as well, that the first thing I had to do, was get a hold of myself as well as my emotions. However, my efforts proved to be about "as worthless as tits on a boar hog." No matter how hard I tried, the ugly truth hung over my heart like a dark cloud. No, more like a thundercloud. No, more like a full-blown tornado! My dad was dying! And, it was right then and there, that I realized, that we absolutely have no idea what the future holds for us. Not a whole damned lot gets by me now, does it?

I asked a lot of questions that morning. And I said a lot of things that I would have never said before then. Things that could've waited—until I found out what I had just indeed found out, and I want you to know I did it with the intention of not dropping one tear. Good old faithful and brave daughter that I was. I knew that my dad had confided in me for a reason and I wasn't about to let him down. Now, isn't that cute? Like he really expected me to handle all of this without showing any emotion. Well, to be honest with all of you, I only lasted about an hour, before I just couldn't hold those bulging floodgates any longer. Yes, siree, I cried all right and once I started—so did he.

I realize now, that I was trying to avoid the very emotion that was much-needed for relief. I guess I just didn't want to start crying because then my dad would've started, and I hated to see my dad cry. It's a very uncomfortable feeling to cry with someone who is hurting when you can't make it better. It sucks! As a matter of fact, it kind of makes you feel, well, worthless. Yes, I do believe that's the word I'm looking for. Well, and that's OK. Because the truth is that as a problem solver I was indeed worthless in this situation. But as a support system I was priceless.

Once I cried, I realized that it then gave him permission to cry. And he shared that very secret with me. He hadn't cried yet. Can you imagine? Where in the hell had his partner been? Surely she damned well knew. And, well, yup—she did. But they never talked about it. My father chose not to. And I hate to admit it, but I almost felt sorry for her at that very moment. "Why talk about it? Nothing in this world could be done for it." Those were his seventy-two-year-old words, coming from his seventytwo- year-old way of thinking. Wow.

He shared with me that he had been in a state of denial and disbelief for the last six months. And that made me cry even more. What a lonely feeling that must have been. What a true relief it must have been for him to finally say it out loud to someone who would receive it with the empathy he had hoped for. And most of all, what a treasure we had both received, feeling comfortable enough with each other to be able to speak our hearts and our minds, without the fear of disappointment. Well, oh goody for us! If this was what life was all about, I didn't want any part of it. I was, quite frankly ready to go with him, selfish but true. And just wait a minute here. Wait just a gosh damned cotton-picking minute. Maybe he could be cured! What in the heck had I been thinking? Just maybe there was some kind of treatment we could do. You know, some sort of miraculous cure that no one else on the face of this earth even knew about. Yes—why the hell not? They made movies about this sort of situation all the time. It could happen, you know! I had to get on this. And I had to get on it fast!

*Was* there something we could do? Could there be a chance? These were some of the questions that I had to pursue for myself as well as for my dad. But most importantly and desperately of all, I had to pursue them for the mere sake of hope.

I was so panic stricken that I could conjure up all kinds of things in my busy little mind. I felt desperate and scared to death! As a matter of fact, at one point during his visit, we were sitting on my sofa, chatting away about things that people chat away about when they are scared gutless, when I did something that to this day, I am ashamed of. Out of nowhere, with no warning what–so–ever–at–all, I abruptly reached out to him, grabbed his little white T-shirt and begged him not to leave me! Like he was just preparing to go to Hawaii or something—not to mention the fact that he had just come face to face with another disaster in his life, that he couldn't do a damned thing about. Well, that little act of selfcenteredness was only the beginning of some of the selfish little treasures that I would find hidden within my behavior throughout this whole ordeal. Yup, I had lost control all right. Seems like there was nowhere to turn, nothing anyone could do! Geeze, don't you hate that? I felt like a dog chasing his tail. No stinking wonder they just give up and lay down.

Yes, I was truly in a panic situation all right. There just had to be something I could do! But what? What could I do? What could I possibly do to stop this horrible happening from taking place?

Well, ladies and gents, that's when it hit me. Sometimes, not always— but sometimes—there's not a damned thing we *can* do. However, it seems that for some stupid unknown reason throughout our lives, we all have this inner voice that keeps chanting, "Never give up. Never say die." I have no doubt that it's the same voice of that very same idiot who says that "time heals all wounds." I'd really like to know who in the hell that person is. I'd also like to know why we all feel like we can be the exception to the rule when a tragedy strikes. I suppose it could be because there are those of us who have actually been through a tragedy and beat it, that's why. Well, whoever you are, good for you. And God bless you. I, for one, will be the first person to stand by your side yelling, "In your face, tragedy!" I will also be the first person to tell you how very blessed and courageous you truly are.

I too couldn't give up. Nope, no matter how hopeless the situation seemed, I just couldn't give up. Problem was, my dad had. Well, or so he thought at the time anyway.

You see, he simply figured that this was the way God had intended for him to leave this old world and "why question the good Lord?"

I was willing to do whatever it took to find something to prolong his life, while all along he had simply accepted things just the way they were. Now, I ask you, just exactly what is wrong with this picture?

He shared with me that he had lived a good life. He said, "We all gotta go sometime and who are we to question when or how?" He also had a saying that he then repeated to me for the umpteenth time in my life. "We are all born dying, dear." And you know, the scary thing is, is that when you think about it—that statement almost makes sense, doesn't it?

Well, I don't know about you, but I know that I, myself, would like to live to be—well—old. But most of all, I would like to die in my sleep. Sounds very pleasant, doesn't it; however, the frightening fact of the matter is that we don't really know what the game plan is, now, do we? Nope, we sure as heck don't. I mean, think about this: People who die unexpectedly, such as in a car accident on the way home from work, probably didn't wake up on that very morning saying to themselves, "I think I just might die today, so I'd better get all of my errands run, as not to burden those whom I will so sadly leave behind." Nope, not hardly. Which proves my theory. We have absolutely no control over what might happen. I told you, not a lot gets by me. Nope, you'd have to get up pretty–darned–early–in–the–morning, if you want to get one by me, alrighty—that's for darned sure!

So there I sat. Saddled with a decision. I wasn't sure if I should try real hard to prolong his life or if I should just let it be. Perhaps this was my dad's fate. Perhaps he was meant to leave this world by way of cancer. Huh, could be. Or perhaps, just maybe, these things weren't really *Little Miss Baby Doll's* decisions to make! Huh, now, that was one to ponder. But oh, how I wanted to. Oh how I so pitifully and desperately wanted to.

Then, right smack-dab in the middle of all this panic, I got this crazy notion. Surprising, isn't it? All of a sudden, I felt the need to do all kinds of things all at once! I wanted to go back and relive my childhood so that it would be fresh in my mind forever. I wanted to find a cure for cancer. I wanted to make time stand completely still. But most of all, I wanted to find a way to stop fate. All in a day's work. All in a day's work, indeed. Of course, all of these things were sadly impossible, weren't they? What I wanted and what was real were two completely different issues. And I think we will find they usually are.

But not to worry, I simply decided for the mere sake of my own sanity, to get down off my "Lone Ranger" dream cloud that I had so happily been riding on and take each day at a time. Yes, believe it or not, not even *I* could change the situation at hand. No kidding. I found it hard to believe myself. But it was painfully true.

So, unwillingly I decided to let go of all of the things that I had absolutely no control over and just enjoy my dad while he was with me. I didn't like it, but sometimes, that's just the way the bell rings, ladies and gents.

Now, not like I was fooling anyone who was ever someone. Letting go of all of the things I had no control over would indeed take time. After all, Rome wasn't built in a day and neither was the creation of change. And I'm here to tell you, that I can wholeheartedly vouch for that!

So, I'll tell you exactly what I decided to do, I sorted out in my mind the things that I desperately wanted and placed them into two categories, realistic thinking and wishful thinking. After I completed this little step, I then decided to meet the wishful thinking list halfway with realistic solutions. Wasn't perfect, but it was a start.

OK, so I couldn't make my dad's cancer disappear, *well, not right now, anyway;* that was more than obvious. And I couldn't relive my childhood either, now, could I? Which meant that the treasures in my memories were just gonna have to do. However, I could relive some of those precious moments today. Yes, by golly, I sure as heck could, by a process known as reenactment. That was very realistic and very possible. And I knew it was, because I'd seen them do it on all of the soap operas. And we have all heard at least a dozen times throughout our lives, how some dumb-ass person was acting like a child. Going through a second childhood, someone would say, acting like a real jack—well you get it. And it was then, at that very moment, when I decided to join the lifestyles of the dumb and childish.

With that little thought in tow, the very next afternoon, I asked my dad if he would care to go up to the corner drugstore with me to get an ice cream. Yes, of course I was up to something. I had a specific plan in mind. I was on a mission, a mission that my dad was completely unaware of at the time. Geeze, don't you just love a good mystery? Then again, it's probably not such a mystery after all; as I'm sure you have already figured it out by now. Yes, indeedy, I just wanted to sit and have an ice cream with my dad just one more time. And come hell or high water, I was going to do just that. *If the good Lord was willing and the creek didn't rise.*

Now, we also all know by now, that I had never been able to experience this delightful form of entertainment without the feeling of anxiety. And it just so happens that I was in the mood for a good, stiff recreated memory. By golly, all I wanted to do was sit on the curb (it didn't matter what curb, any old curb would do) with my dad and talk about everything and anything that came to mind with no secrets, no sadness, and no shame. Imagine that! Yes, indeedy, it was another first in the making.

After going to great lengths to try to keep this futuristic episode a secret, my excitement gave way to my inability to keep my big mouth shut, and so I ended up sharing this little ditty of information with my dad after all. Guess I never really was any good at keeping secrets from him anyway. Nope, those days were over for good. Well, until the end of this story anyway. Well, sure as heck, and much to my delight, my simple-minded, memory-seeking, little dad was wholeheartedly all for it. How could we have ever had a doubt?

So with that little decision out of the way, we headed out that next afternoon for Thrifty Drug Store. It wasn't on the corner anymore and it was a lot larger than the one I had remembered so many years ago, but it would just have to do—and it did—and very nicely, I might add. Oh, and for the record, I did invite the wife;

however, she had no hankering for an ice-cream cone and she sure as hell about fainted when I mentioned sitting on a curb. I'd have to work on her. Yup, if she was gonna hang around for this adventure, she was gonna have to get with the program. Funny, that is exactly how my mom would have reacted. Huh, I'll have to get back to that thought later.

When we arrived at the drugstore, I once again found myself wishing, hoping to hear the soft whining cries of the violins. This was a tender moment, gosh darn it. Shouldn't CNN have been there covering this story or something? Uh huh, *or something* was right. For goodness sake, you would think that someone would've given a damn. Or you might just think that maybe, just maybe, we were the only ones whom it *really* mattered to. Perhaps, but I just couldn't seem to get it through my thick noggin that there we were, getting ready to relive a special moment, and not *one* other person on the face of this earth seemed to care. Now, that's sad, isn't it? Well, sure it is, but isn't that just the way things are sometimes? Yes, it surely and sadly seems to be. And again I'll say we sure as hell don't have to like it. I'll also remind all of us that one person's worry or sorrow is another person's—well, on second thought, never mind.

Getting out of the car was a lot less stressful than I had remembered. Huh, my sisters weren't with us, so it was much easier, not to mention the fact that I could now wipe my own chin, so I'm quite sure my dad was looking more forward to our little adventure as well—or so it seemed. Oh, and I was driving; perhaps that's why he was so damned anxious to get out of the car. Huh. So anyway, off we went, strolling into the drugstore, acting like a couple of kids, the adventure-seeking duo that we were. My dad shaking his head from side to side, laughing that unmistakable hearty laugh of his—that I miss so very much—now— today.

As we entered the cool confines of the drugstore, I was taken not only by the rush of cold air, but I was also completely consumed by a rush of deja vu, as my mind was hurled back to a time when it was *so* very wonderful to feel the chilled floor beneath my tiny bare feet as they shuffled to keep up with my dad. Although this time, sadly, it was he who was shuffling to keep up with me.

The aproned women at the counter had no idea who we were or what she was about to take part in as she smiled, asking if she could help us? Could she help us? Well that was certainly an understatement, as I proceeded to order the biggest bubble gum ice-cream cone ever made in little kid history.

My simple-minded sherbet-loving little dad, on the other hand, ordered just that, in the color of orange and size small.

We walked out to the parking lot with my dad still shaking his head from side to side in disbelief, as I was trying to steady that hunk of blue ice cream at the same time I was attempting to sit on the curb. Everything seems to become a little harder as we become a little older. Ever notice that?

My dad was following right behind me, trying to keep up, licking and slurping every step of the way when all of a sudden he paused, looking across the street. Then he looked back at me—then back across the street again, raising his eyebrows and tossing his head toward that same direction. What the—oh, alrighty. It wasn't going to take a cow to kick me in the head to make me realize what he was trying to say. I got it. Yes, siree! I got it just fine, as a matter of fact. Much to my delight, he was into this more than I had ever expected him to be. So stopping my rear, already in progress on its way to the curb, I stood up.

"You want to walk over to the park?" I asked. Stupid question. What the hell did I think? He was just standing there making that motion to hear the rocks in his head rattle? Sheesh. Of course that's what he meant. Well, actually, no he didn't, at least, not exactly.

Seeing that we were both a little older now, not to mention the fact that my dad tired so easily, walking seemed to be out of the question. Not a problem. Not a problem at all. We just hopped into his little minivan and drove across the street to the lawn-roving haven that awaited our arrival. Then, we found a good curb in the shade of a great tree and, by golly, we sat down to eat our ice creams! What a wonderful experience! And with it, came a sad but tender sign of the precious cycle of life. For this time, I was the one who was making like an octopus, wiping my dad's chin, all the while with him chatting away about whatever was on his mind. And you know this would be only the beginning of many role reversals yet to come. And it would also be the beginning of many new memories that would be tenderly created.

I wished for more time when I was young and I found myself wishing for it then as well, maybe even more so. I wished our trip to the park could have lasted forever. I guess some things never really do change, do they?

When we or I should say, he, finally decided that it was time to go home I felt saddened and, well, panicked. But I also felt fulfilled. For I realized that I had received the treasure I had hoped for: to have ice cream with my dad just one more time and to feel the sensation of actually wanting to go home. And I can tell you, it felt pretty darned good! So this is how it must have been for a happy child, eh? Not bad, not bad at all.

During our serene ride home we were both contently satisfied with the silence. Looking back now, I'm sure we looked like a couple of canary-seeking cats that had just gotten lucky. And once again, I sadly found myself experiencing one of life's role reversals, as it was me in the driver's seat turning the steering wheel toward home, while my dad was nodding off to sleep, strapped safely into his seatbelt with his belly full of ice cream. And for a split second, I felt a complete sense of control and I wondered if I might be able to keep him there—right there in that very seat, sleeping peacefully for the rest of our lives. Yes, it was an extremely powerful feeling, if I do say so myself. But gee whiz, after what we had just re-experienced, how much gas did I think it might take to just keep driving all the way to—well, I don't know where. But there just had to be a place where daughters take their dying fathers so that they can undergo some sort of lifesaving transplant, only to wipe their brows afterward, proclaiming how that was a close one. Well wasn't there? Another fairy tale, I suppose. Yes, another wonderful fairy tale indeed.

No sooner did we pull in to the driveway and he was groggily awake and opening the van door. He then sadly took just a few seconds to catch his breath before he began heading steadfastly for the front door of the house. Then, once at the front door, he paused again for a few more seconds before he bolted through the door and up the stairs to my daughters' bedroom to take a little nap—with me right on his heels.

He lay down at one end of the bed on his back with his hands tucked tightly up behind his head and I laid at the opposite end of the bed in the same position so that we were facing each other. And we laid there in that very position, just like we had so many years before, only this time, he didn't have to keep chanting, "Close your eyes, go to sleep!"

Now I never really meant to have a conversation with him at that time. Nope, I solemnly swear I didn't. My only intention was to take a little nap with a nice breeze blowing through the window on a beautiful, warm afternoon, listening to summer sounds of lawn mowers blazing away in the distance, with an occasional outburst of children's laughter faintly coming from somewhere in the neighborhood—with my belly full of bubble gum ice cream and my dad by my side. This was without a doubt, true ecstasy! And I want you all to know that I was doing just that. Minding my own business, staring off into some distant daydream, enjoying my moment, when I suddenly realized that he wasn't sleeping! Nope—he was looking right at me! And it wasn't just any look either. It was *that* look, the same exact look that had been on his face that summer morning on my couch when he had asked to become a part of my past. The same look that not many months later would become my cue to brace myself for a tear-filled conversation with my dad.

As the terror I was feeling was completely paralyzing my heart, I then wondered if he was going to cry. I didn't like that look. I didn't like that look at all. As a matter of fact, I hated that look. Now, what was he gonna tell me? Now, what was he going to say that would absolutely convince me of the fact that my heart was breaking. Panic rushed over me so rapidly that it was actually making me dizzy. Then, I had this overwhelming urge to run like hell again to anywhere else in the world other than where I was right then. Yes, my friends, I was scared all right. Boy howdy, was I. Scared of what he might be about to say. Scared of how I would have to answer, and scared mostly of having to allow the tears that were welling up in my heart to flow freely.

To be perfectly honest with you, by this time in my life I had gotten fairly used to the feeling of wanting to run like a jackrabbit each and every time I felt afraid. Yes, indeedy, because of my past, I believe it had become a permanent part of my personality. And to be just as honest with you, who in the heck could blame me? But for some stupid reason it was time to stop running. I don't know who decided that or why, or even when for that matter, but I think it was me and I think it was because I was tired of feeling afraid. So, instead of running, I did the unthinkable.

I very bravely, very secretly, and very carefully, fastened my imaginary safety harness securely around my heart and prepared myself for another heart-wrenching, tear-jerking collision with my dad's thoughts. And I'm not going to lie to you. I hated it. I felt squeamish, uncomfortable, trapped and wishing at that very moment that I could somehow disappear. But I couldn't. I didn't like it but there truly does come a time in one's life when they just have to plain and simply go for the gusto. And then I got to thinking, for crying out loud, what was the worst thing that could happen? Just exactly what in the world so terrible could actually happen? Well, let's see, for starters he could say something that would make me cry. Or maybe he was about to say something that would absolutely convince me of the fact that my heart was breaking. Or maybe—just maybe, he simply had something on his mind and needed to share it with me. Uh huh, nice try, for after all that worry, I wish I could say that it had been needless—but I can't because just as I had feared, *that* look, the very same look that would later become my cue to drop many a heartfelt tear during his final days with me, was indeed followed by another sad little thought running around in my dad's busy little mind.

So, what did I do? Well, in the first place, what in the heck was I supposed to do? What should I have done? Abruptly excuse myself from his presence screaming all the way out the front door, running to wherever it is daughters run to when they don't want to face the fact that their fathers are dying? Well, to be perfectly honest with you, perhaps— simply because I had come to expect this of myself. But I didn't. Nope, believe it or not, I didn't run at all. Instead, I simply looked into those big brown, tired and comforting old chimpanzee eyes and very tenderly, very carefully, very bravely said, "A penny for your thoughts." And to this very day I have no clue what gave me the courage to say that—and sometimes, I wish I hadn't.

He laid there for just a little longer, kind of squinting, all the while his eyes never leaving mine and with the seriousness that only my dad could portray, he whispered his thoughts to me. And if I live to be very old myself, I will never forget that afternoon's conversation, with the greatest monster fighter who ever lived, as he quite frankly and quite seriously, looked me in the eye and began to make his request.

"I don't want to live so long that I become a burden, dear. Do you understand?" he said. "I pray that when I get to the point that I can't get up by myself or go to the bathroom by myself or I just can't do the little things in life that I like to do, like watch my shows or take a little walk, that God will see it in his heart to come and get me. I don't want to live like that."

Well, I quite frankly didn't want him to have to live like that either. But did we have to talk about it, for Pete's sake? Did we have to lie there on a beautiful summer's day and talk about this crap? Did we have to interrupt our private serenity with all of this hullabaloo? Well, quite honestly, yes, we most certainly did. And why, you might ask. Well, I suppose it's because he damned well felt the need to do so, that's why. And I'm here to tell you—I surely didn't care for *that* very much either. As a matter of fact, I hated every minute of it.

Just exactly how much more did he expect me to take? That's what I wanted to know. I just simply and quite frankly wanted all of the heartbreak to stop! That was all. I had already had just about all I could take! Whatever in the hell it was that I had done to deserve all of what was happening to me—I would've taken it back, just to stop my heart from breaking! Uh huh, my heart from breaking, my pain, my suffering, my anguish—my ass! Oh my heck, did I sound like a whining selfish dope or what? Yeah, or what—is a great question. So what do you think I said? Well, after knowing how I truly felt you might be just as surprised as I was. For the voice of the woman who would have done anything in the world to keep her father alive—agreed with him.

"I don't blame you," I said. "I wouldn't want to live that way either," I whispered, ashamed of myself for agreeing with him. And as I lay there I realized I couldn't look at him. I could feel his eyes boring a hole through me but I just couldn't return his gaze. Just for a few minutes. For I just knew he was crying. When I finally allowed myself to glance his way, his eyes were indeed moist with tears. And that glance was all it took for me to drop a few myself. I propped myself up on my elbow and braced my hand up underneath my head and I continued to gaze into the eyes of my father. He gazed back at me and I suddenly made a face at him, as if to say, *Crap, what do we do now?* He returned my look with one much the same. Our cheeks scantly revealed our sorrow as we reflected on the short conversation we'd just had. And it was at that very moment that a thought came to mind that had never occupied space there before. Geeze, why would it have? I wondered about folks in the past who had participated in assisted suicide. Hadn't really ever given it serious thought before that moment on that very afternoon but it was there now and so I thought I'd share my question with my dad. I broke the silence with a rasp in my voice, cleared my throat and then I said, "Dad?"

"Uh huh?"

"What do you think about people who take their own lives when things do get so bad that they just don't have any quality of life left?"

He never even hesitated before he answered. "I don't know," he said.

"I don't like to judge what other people do but I don't think I could do it. I know that there is a doctor out there running amok that does that sort of thing but I think I should wait it out and trust that the good Lord will come and get me when he's good and ready and not until then."

*Thank God,* I thought. I wouldn't have known how to get a hold of that fella anyway.

"Do you believe that people should have the right to take their own lives," I pressed?

"I believe to each his own," he said.

"Yeah, me too," I agreed. "But," I continued, "If you wanted to I would help you, Dad."

He stared at me for a long moment and with the dew of his sadness still puddling under his eyes, he said, "I know you would, dear."

"But I'm glad we won't have to," I added.

"Uh huh, me too," he answered.

I *was* my father's daughter—and at that very moment I had come face to face with the true meaning of what is clearly known as unconditional love. All of a sudden, all that really mattered to me was *his* comfort and happiness and nothing else. Imagine that. I was beginning to see the whole picture, although I didn't consciously realize it until much later.

We lay there for just a little while longer that afternoon sharing with one another what we felt the future held until my dad finally drifted off to sleep. But before he did, he gave me something to ponder. In a groggy voice with his eyes closed he mumbled, "No need to worry, dear. It will never go that far anyway. I'll be long gone before I get to that stage."

Sleep? Easy for him! I was left to lay there with his lingering words stabbing at my bleeding heart. What exactly was that statement supposed to have meant anyway? Maybe with a little luck he would die quickly? What in the hell had just taken place here? Let's go over it, shall we, just in case there's a pop quiz at the end of this decade. He was waiting for the good Lord to come and get him! Waiting to die? He had already given up, for Pete's sake! And now, as I look back, as much as I hate to admit it, I think I too was beginning to let go. Or for the time being anyway—oh hell—who did I think I was kidding? No I wasn't, but I sure as heck wanted to believe I was.

I lay there for what seemed like forever watching him sleep, going over and over again in my mind the conversation we had just had. I mean, Geeze–La–Weeze; no one ever has to go over such things in real life do they? These things only happen in the movies. You know, then the movie is over and we feel sad for just a couple of minutes until we are able to say to ourselves, *Oh heck, it was only a movie, someone else's pain.* And then we go about our own menial, merry stinking lives! We don't ever think these things will actually happen to us! They only happen to other people whom we do feel sorry for, but hey, that's a tough break—and their problem.

As I lay there with these most selfish thoughts on my mind, I then found myself wondering and fearing what my life would be like without him for the second time in my life and that sent me crawling up to lay right next to him on the bed.

I found myself touching his face and stroking his arms while listening to the whisper of his steady breathing, when my mind began to wander back once again, to a time when I was Daddy's little girl living in a big two-story house with my family intact and all of life's fulfilling hopes and dreams at my feet.

It was very early in the wee hours of the morning and I had just woken up with a most horrible nightmare. The most ghastly of all horrific nightmares to be exact; I dreamed my daddy had died, and even though I was terribly afraid of the dark, I knew I had to go see if he was OK. So I wandered down the long dark hallway that led to my parents' bedroom, shivering with absolute, unmistakable, nightmare fear as I shuffled my little feet into their room and right over to my dad's side of the bed and then—just stood there, with my chubby little arms folded across my heaving chest, watching and waiting to see if he was breathing. My nose was cold and my cheeks were wet with nightmare tears as I stood there with my little kid legs quaking underneath me. I couldn't tell if he was breathing or not, but I just knew beyond a shadow of a doubt, that if I leaned over at that very moment and kissed him, he wouldn't be dead. I knew that *my* kiss would save my dad from the reality of my horrible nightmare, because I was a kid and kids had such secret powers. So I very carefully, very quietly, and very gently leaned over and tenderly kissed my dad just like the prince had kissed Snow White, so that he could live for a very long time and happily ever after, probably never to discover that it was indeed *me*, his daughter in shining feet pajamas who had saved his very life on that night so long ago.

So as I laid there now, with my nose cold and my cheeks wet—but this time with *very real* nightmare tears—I kissed him again, and in my grown-up heart with a little girl's memory, I truly believed that for at least a little while longer, I had saved my dad again. And as I quietly then crawled up and over him to leave him sleeping peacefully, I paused briefly at the bedroom door, before closing it and a faint smile came across my face as I then remembered how I had slept in the hallway right outside of his bedroom for the rest of that dark morning long ago, guarding and protecting my most precious possession—my most secret treasure—my bestest friend in the whole wide United States of America—my dad. And I didn't know it then, but that was another memory I would soon be reliving.

We spent the rest of his visit trying to share as much time as we possibly could with each other. But you know, I felt a great deal of disappointment because it just didn't feel like how it was portrayed in the movies. I guess I was waiting to hear the big boom of a symphony orchestra every time we touched or the sound of whining violins each and every time we cried. But neither one of those things happened at all. Not a single one. And it didn't take me long to figure out that it was, in fact, *only* in the movies that those things really do happen, simply because I couldn't remember ever feeling as sad as I did, for as long as I did, after a movie had ended.

When my dad's visit had finally come to an end, I felt terribly lonely and out of control. Makes sense really, when you stop to think about it. Life itself had become out of control—literally!

I stood at the front door saying my good-byes wondering if it would be the last time I would ever see him alive. And as deja vu once again began to push its way into my memory, I realized that for the second time in my life, I was tearfully standing in the doorway of a big two-story house watching my dad walk out of my life and there wasn't a damn thing I could do about it. But this time I was older and this time I was wiser so this time—shouldn't I have been able to stop him? Shouldn't I have been able to do something? I couldn't just stand there and let him go, could I? Then what? Just–what–exactly should I have been able to do besides stand there and let him leave?

Pitiful wasn't it? Yes, it most sadly and certainly was. It took every ounce of strength I had in me not to reach out and grab him, holding him close to me while I proceeded to yell at God, that he just absolutely could not take my dad away from me! And this little feeling of urgency wasn't new either. Oh, heck no, it wasn't new! In all honesty, it had actually been brewing inside me for quite some time; however, I quite simply hadn't cared to identify it. This feeling was more overwhelming than fear itself. More overpowering than any amount of heartbreak I had ever suffered. More frightening than all the loss of control I had experienced throughout this whole ordeal thus far. Yes, my friends, little Miss Control Freak had clearly come face to face with the feeling of desperation.

I was helpless and I was beaten and perhaps for the first time in my life I had to come to grips with the fact that maybe, just maybe, there wasn't anything I could do. Absolutely nothing. And if you don't mind me saying so, gosh darn, that's a cruddy feeling, the feeling of defeat. I mean, for crying out loud, I had already survived so many tragedies throughout my life, you would think I could have come up with a way to stop death, now, wouldn't you? Well wouldn't you? Uh huh— okey doke. Not very likely, I suppose. Not even *I* could come up with a way to stop death. Imagine that. Which is exactly my point. Sometimes we just have to give up. And it's not defeat, it is just—well, reality. Some things just aren't possible. And once again I'll remind us all that we don't have to like it. But sometimes, that's just the way the old wind blows.

I followed my dad out to his car that day for more good-byes, more smooches— more torture. I don't know what in the heck I expected. I guess I thought that by following him every inch of the way that I could somehow stop fate—perhaps chase the cancer right out of him and watch it run screaming down the street—or maybe that orchestra would finally get their stinking act together just for my sake.

But not one of those things took place. Nope, not a silly stinking one. He simply kissed me good-bye, told me he loved me, put his wife in the car and began his long journey home. And that was the end of that. Like he had the right to do that. What about me? What about my broken heart? Oh sure, go ahead and go home like nothing's ever happened. I'm the one who's hurting! I'm the one who has to stay behind and learn to live without *you*! I mean, after all, you are only the one who's dying! *Only* the one who is *dying*?

Pathetic wasn't it? Yup, in just one short week I had become an out-of- control, unrealistic, desperate, pathetic little mess. Isn't life grand?

Well, thank goodness that along with all of these charming little characteristics that had become a part of my equally charming personality, also came my ability to create an understanding and forgiveness of myself. As much as I didn't care to, I had to learn for the sake of my sanity, once again, to take my time and feel whatever it was I wanted or needed to feel and after all of the undesirable traits that I had so unwillingly acquired had run their course, lovable, huggable, cute little me would return. Sadly though, I didn't know this at the time. I simply thought that I was doomed to live the life of a very unhappy, miserable, possessed person never to want to experience happiness again. Which just goes to show you that you don't have to give up hope. Because anyone who was ever someone knows that the horrible trouble-making little demon that comes to reside inside of our bodies during a tragedy can be exorcized with the power to love and forgive yourself for simply being human. I know it's difficult to believe, but the proof is in the Jell-O, my friends. Yes, indeedy, I too was once a guilty, miserable little mess. And just look at me now. Uh huh, just sit and take a good, hard, long look at me now. On second thought—well—maybe you'd better not. Some things *really are* just better left unlooked-at.

# Chapter Four

## Fear

*Fear is the main source of superstition, and one of the main sources of cruelty. To conquer fear is the beginning of wisdom, in the pursuit of truth as in the endeavor after a worthy manner of life.*
Bertrand Russell 1872–1970 Unpopular Essays
(1950) "An Outline of Intellectual Rubbish"

D URING THE WEEKS to follow, after my father's visit, I found that I had yet, another cross to bear. Hard to believe, isn't it?

Being that my dad had been somewhat of a private man all of his life, he asked me to do him just a slight, teensy, weensy, little favor. He asked me to keep his illness a secret. Just for a little while. Oh sure, like why in the hell would I need to tell anyone? I could handle it just fine all by myself. I mean, after all, I *had* already become quite the little queen of denial. If anything was going to get any tougher, why, I'd just simply and quite frankly pretend that it wasn't really happening at all! Yes, siree, it was as simple as that. Anyway, if the witch could do it, then so could I. I mean let's get serious here for just a minute, folks, shall we? Just exactly how long had *she* known that my father was dying? Interesting. Could she have known before the wedding, hum? Perhaps. Maybe before she moved in with him? Oh, for crying out loud! How in the hell long had my father had this horrible disease? And—just exactly how long had she known about it? Never mind that question for the moment. We'll come back to that one. For right now I had enough to deal with and on my own because my dad just absolutely did not want me to tell anyone. Not one single solitary stinking soul.

Now, his reasons for this request were genuinely justifiable, I suppose, if there is such a thing—but I didn't have to like it. And I sure as hell didn't, thank you very much.

First of all, he didn't want his misfortune to interfere with my sister's wedding. He didn't feel it would be fair to take her hopes and dreams away because of some unfortunate and harsh realities. Leave it to my dad to put things into perspective.

Second of all, and perhaps the most crucial, he didn't want the girls to feel like they were obligated to make amends. As he put it, he didn't want any pity or guilt love. He felt that if they wanted to get to know him, it shouldn't be because he was dying. He felt that it would be like one big major guilt trip. He felt that God would stir things up before he finally had to go, if it was meant to be. Well, howdy do! He sure as hell felt an awful lot. I felt like I needed about thirty more years to get used to the whole damned idea. Now, not only did I feel dumped and lonely, I also couldn't share my misery with anyone else! For hell's sake, how much more was I expected to endure? I didn't want to be the only one hurting. I wanted everyone else to feel as miserable as I did! That seemed fair enough to me. As a matter of fact, it made a whole hell of a lot more sense to me than anything else had thus far.

I was now entering into the wonderful world of self-pity, blame, anger, and revenge. Take a number, wait in line, no pushing, no shoving—let's all learn to play nicely and get along well with others. Oh, suck rope! What thoughtful little feelings we harbor inside of ourselves at times. Oh heck—and that was nothing. I discovered feelings inside of me that I never knew I was even capable of displaying! Ah, what a broken heart can do to a person.

The self-pity was easy. Of course I was the only person in the world who had ever been close to her father and now I was losing him. Yup, I had to be the only person on the face of this earth who had ever lost a loved one. I had totally and completely mastered self-pity, not to mention the fact that I had also totally and completely lost my ever-loving mind. Halleflippinluyah! Oh, and after I had mastered this feeling, another sensation suddenly came over me that I'll be happy to share with you. Why not place blame? Yes, indeedy, I believed that would make me feel much better seeing that I liked myself way too much to have carried all of this guilt around on my own. Now, that too makes a whole hell of a lot of sense, doesn't it? Uh huh, my point exactly.

Now, I sure as heck couldn't blame God—plain and simply because I felt like he might get really mad at me and take someone else away, not to mention the fact that he wasn't visually available and what I wanted was to actually witness pain being suffered by another human being. Therefore, I came to the sad realization that I couldn't blame the witch either, for I don't think she knew how to display pain. Hell, maybe she didn't feel at all. Another point we will get to the bottom of later on. So I started out on a quest to find someone I could blame for all of the misery I was carrying around with me. Now, don't you just hate it when something like this happens? Boy, I know I sure did. And do you know why? Well, I'm about to tell you. Because we just know that someday we're gonna have to take responsibility for feeling this way. That's why. Yes, siree, just as sure as shingles, someday we will have to admit to someone, somewhere, someplace at sometime—that we actually had these selfish, vindictive little thoughts. And even if that someone is *only* and *just* ourselves, I, for one, can sure as heck tell you that it's still extremely embarrassing.

Now, where was I? Ah yes, I believe I was just about ready to expose a part of my charming personality that I swore I'd never expose.

You see, as I was searching my mind for someone who was worthy to accept all of this hatred which had come to exist inside of me, a horrible thought came to me. As a matter of fact, it was so hideous that I could hardly believe that I was the one who thought of it. Now, brace yourselves my friends, for what I am about to share with you is another miserable little thought I found running around in my pretty little head.

My stepfather! He was alive and well and worst of all, he *wasn't* dying! Now, what kind of justice was this? How in the world was I supposed to accept this? How could a wonderful little man like my dad be stricken with cancer when a monster like that was still alive and breathing? Go figure. This, quite frankly, didn't make a damned bit of sense to me and to put it nicely, it matter-of-factly pissed me off! Yes, to say the least, I'd had it! This was a totally unacceptable situation as far as I was concerned! Actually, it should have been a totally unacceptable situation as far as anyone in their right mind was concerned, don't you think? I mean to tell you, I was damned angry, to say the least, and that's when I decided that I wanted revenge! And as ashamed as I am to admit it, that's also when a whole lot of hateful, ugly little thoughts started to fester inside my broken little heart—and, by golly, someone was going to pay for this! And that's when I got to really thinking, so hold on to your hats, because here it comes.

I figured that since I considered God to be one of my closest friends, I would ask him to do me a real unheard of favor. I wanted him to help me place my anger. After all, what are friends for, right? So, I wanted him to take my stepfather instead!

Oh now, before you all go off half-cocked hanging your heads in shame once again, just hold on a minute. Yes, of course I know it was an awful request and again I will share with you how very ashamed of myself I truly am for even allowing myself to go that far. And I challenge anyone who was ever someone to have the guts to stand up and say that they've never had the same thoughts themselves—any takers? Uh huh, well, if there are, I sure as heck have a great deal of respect for you and I wish to thank you at this time for your input. But most of all, I thank God himself for having the capability to forgive me, for having such a vengeful and vindictive thought. They say that he is a forgiving God and I hope to shout he'd darned well better be for my own pathetic sake, if you know what I mean. But you know, all dramatics aside, I truthfully just couldn't seem to justify in my mind why that horrible excuse for a man got to live and my dad had to be taken away. It just, quite frankly, didn't seem fair! And to tell you the truth, it still doesn't—and it probably never will. But these are some of the things in this world that we just have to deal with, I guess, and again I'll remind us all that we sure as hell don't have to like them but, then again, situations like this happen every day, don't they? Yes, and sadly whether we like them or not.

Now, because of the stories my dad had shared with me, I knew why little children had to die, but never did my dad *ever* tell me a story as to the whys of a situation such as this. And sadly, my friends, I believe that this is a question that can be answered only by God himself and I have to have faith in that belief, as not to lose every bit of sanity I've ever had. And I'm quite sure that I'm not the only one who sees things this way either. A lot of situations that come our way in life don't seem quite fair, do they? Nope, they sure as heck don't—and I've decided that I don't much care for this either!

The anger I felt was overwhelming, to say the least. So overwhelming, in fact, that it actually started to become unhealthy. And that's when I finally decided that I just might have to come to grips with the fact that there are always going to be situations in our lives that we just can't justify. It's painful and, no, it sure as hell isn't fair, but again reality had reared its ugly head. And sometimes, that's just the way the feather falls. I'll be the first to admit that it sucks rope—but that's just life—plain and simple.

Now I'll share another little secret with you. After I had taken the time to cool off and examine the situation thoroughly, I knew in my heart that I was, in fact, just looking to place blame where there was nowhere to really place it at all. I was scared gutless and, quite frankly, fear can do the darnedest things to otherwise really nice people. We all should know this to be true. But you see, there was a problem and the problem was that unless my stepfather had a little toy voodoo doll, sporting a pair of overalls, that he had dipped into a vat of cancer cells, I couldn't blame him at all. Don't you just hate it when realizations like that happen? Now, I could hate the situation and I could even hate my stepfather. Lord knows that no one deserved my anger more than he did. But to be true to myself in this particular situation, there really was no *one* person to blame. And just for the record, I've never been any good at hating anyone in my entire life. Not my stepfather, not my mother, not the witch. No one. I'm too stinking forgiving. And I hate that too.

Geeze, what an ugly realization, and just when I was getting used to feeling like a real lowlife.

Well, you'll all be happy to know that I did eventually begin to get a grip on all of this. And as soon as I got my crap together, incidentally, another phrase that makes no sense what–so–ever–at–all, I decided that what I needed to do was to put all of this negative energy into positive actions. What a concept. It was also easier said than done. However, this too was so very necessary. But best of all, it was possible. And at that point, at least something was.

I realized that my emotions had gotten way out of hand due to the fact that I was so afraid. Do ya think? Scared crapless, to put it honestly. And quite frankly, fear, as we have already discussed, can make us do the darndest things, now, can't it? For instance, like imagining that someone could actually be dipping an "Over-All Sporting Replica" of someone's father into a vat of cancer cells. Sure is amazing, what the mind of a scared and angry person can conjure up, isn't it? Yes, if I do say so myself, it most certainly and embarrassingly is.

Well, to be honest, I discovered a lot of amazing little things about myself throughout this situation. Not only did I obviously have quite an imagination, but I also had quite an extraordinary ability to deal with tragedy. And quite frankly, I think we all do. It's just another one of those things that isn't asked of us every day, so again, we don't get a lot of practice. And let's thank God (or whomever you choose) for that.

So, I began putting first things first, which led me to understand that perhaps my dad's feelings, *not* mine, should have been of the utmost importance. Another wonderful concept! Hallelujah!

I began to put myself in my dad's place, so that I would know how to be there for him. And—well—quite honestly, this just about scared the pee-waddlings right out of me.

How do you deal with death? I mean, once you're gone it's over, isn't it? Well, here on earth anyway. Right?

Funny thing about death—well, not really funny; that's simply just an expression. Death is something that we all know is inevitable. We hear about it all the time. We watch it on TV. We read about it in the newspapers and most of us feel sad about it, or we will say things like "Gosh, that's too bad" or "What a shame." Some of us, probably most of us, fear it all of our lives. Which reminds me of something a very close friend of mine once said to me.

"We are the only species who are born with the knowledge that we will die." Uh huh, now, let that sink in a minute. Now that I've probably just about scared the pee-waddlings out of you too, relax. I just had to make a point.

Until we are faced with the inevitable, we as human beings are truly remarkable in that we can push certain things, uncomfortable things, to the back of our minds, or if you're anything like me, you can actually put them away in a locked closet in your mind, hoping never to have to find the bloody key. You see, even when it's right under our busy little noses and we see and hear about it every day, we simply choose not to deal with it or think about it. I just have to say it again. We human beings *really* are truly remarkable. Yes, indeedy, I believe we most certainly are.

So you see, my dad didn't really think that his dreaded disease known as cancer should get the best of him. As a matter of fact, I'm sure he was probably just like any other human being who is told they are dying. He thought that just maybe he would be the *one* exception to the rule. Sound familiar? Yes, I thought it might. I believe this is where the story began.

Now, also just like any other human being, he wasn't really thrilled with the fact that he was no longer in control of his own body, not to mention his own life and emotions. But he sure as hell tried to take control where control could be taken. Therefore, he made a few decisions that just might not make a whole hell of a lot of sense to some of us. And that's OK. They were *his* decisions and *his* decisions alone to make.

You know, all hell breaks loose when your body becomes terminally ill. It's like your mind goes out for revenge. For instance, as in the case of my father, one might find oneself thinking that, by God, they might not be able to physically do the things they want to do, but they can sure as heck still make decisions concerning what's left of their own life, now, can't they? And I'll share with all of you, that sometimes, because of some horrifying realizations that we have absolutely no control over, we may tend to make some pretty hasty decisions. And in my dad's situation, hasty was all he had left.

Therefore, he did make a few decisions as a way to regain some control. And I didn't particularly care for some of them either. But, hey, who in the hell was I? And there was one decision in particular that he made that I still wonder about to this day, and I probably always will. He decided to go off the shots and stop the chemotherapy.

Now, it's not like this was an easy decision. As a matter of fact, I know it wasn't. I was there. But, come to think of it, life itself would never be easy again. Not as if it had already been like a trip to Disneyland. But I could settle for a comparison of more like a trip to Knott's Berry Farm. All right then, in all honesty, more like a trip to the sanitation department, which would explain why sometimes life really stinks! During his last visit to my home, my dad shared with me that for six months he had been taking those shots and they made him very sick. He said they also screwed with his taste buds causing his food to taste like metal so he had stopped eating as much, simply because it just wasn't as enjoyable anymore and he *was* dropping weight very quickly so he truly needed to eat. And let's face it, if you can't taste your food, why would you want to eat it? So, with that little thought in mind, he simply decided that he'd rather die happy on a full stomach and somewhat in control of his own life than to die miserably, hungry, and out of control. Boy, that's showing 'em, now, isn't it? Yes, siree, that's really showing 'em good!

Now, as sure as I was at the time, that we had made the right decision, I'll admit to you that, after he died, I spent many sleepless nights wondering about that decision. Wondering if maybe I should have talked him out of it. Maybe he could have lived a little longer had he stayed on those shots. Or maybe, just maybe, I really had no say in the matter at all. For once again, as much as I hate to admit it, it just simply wasn't *my* decision to make. But again, I sure as hell wanted to. Oh, how I so desperately wanted to. And once that little decision was out of the way, I figured my heart was safe. But I was wrong. Because there was still yet another decision that my dad had made without me. Imagine that! And this one was probably tougher than the last, if you can believe that.

You see, he had simply decided that he wanted to die at home. No hospitals, no chemo, no life support, no IVs—no nothing. Yes, a simple man he was while he lived and a simple man he would be as he died. End of conversation! Now, how in the heck do you like them apples?

Putting myself in his place was one thing, but being *me* and having to allow him to make these decisions for himself, while I could do nothing about it, was another. The real kicker was that all of his decisions were just that. All–of–his decisions! Do you think I would ever get that? Well, rest assured, I did. But I fought it—just about right up until the day he died. Oh, come, come now, didn't I know what was best for him? Or perhaps the actual truth was, is that I knew what was "best for him" is what made *me* more comfortable. Yup, to be quite honest, I believe that just about summed it all up in a pea shell.

Putting myself in my dad's place taught me a very valuable lesson. I think it goes something like "Do unto others." Well, either that or "Oh, crap!" It was finally time to learn or to admit that I had to give him the respect he so much deserved. I had to stop doing what was *best for me* and start understanding what he felt was *best for him*. Yuk, this was becoming more and more difficult as time went on. And it actually and very matter-of-factly put me in my place. Don't you just hate that? Well if you don't, then you're a much better person than I! Much, much better—OK, a trillion times better but who's keeping track?

Well, the month of September was upon us and the wedding had come and gone. I was wrong in July when I watched my father walk out my door. It wasn't the last time he would be at my home. For as we already know, he did make it for the wedding and when he left in August that would, in fact, be his last visit. And I knew it would be, just as well as I saw him standing there twenty pounds lighter than he'd been from July to August. And just like the leaves were slowly beginning their descent from the trees, so was my dad's life beginning its descent from existence.

Well, whether I liked it or not (and I didn't, thank you ever so much), one of the first things I realized I had to do after my dad's departure, not really counting the nervous breakdown, was to start dealing with the situation at hand. And oh, boy, was I in for the very ride of my life!

You see, just as sure as I knew my own name, I knew I had to face my fears in order to conquer them. Oh goody! This was going to be a ripsnorter. I knew I could count on that!

Now, this was another step that sure as heck wouldn't come easy and like anything else worthwhile, it would take a lot of hard work. And some of us even have to pay a price to get there. Learning to face my fears was a little trick I had learned long ago and it sure as hell wasn't by choice either. However, later on in life, on or around, or about the time I began therapy, I realized it was a very healthy thing to do. Wonderful! I truly felt better already.

Geeze, could things become any more complicated? Well, to be perfectly honest with all of you—yes, my friends, things could and sure as heck would sadly get much more complicated. But I sure didn't know it then. However, what I did know was that facing my fears and replacing them with knowledge was an imperative step that I had to take, compliments of none other than that charming little woman who has called herself my therapist for the last too many years. Also being someone I love with everything I have in me, but sometimes—well, just like any step to a healthy outlook—it sucked big bananas because I finally had to face the dreaded reality that my dad just quite possibly could be dying.

So with that little thought in mind, I did the unthinkable once again. As a matter of fact, doing and saying the unthinkable had become a permanent part of my everyday lifestyle. Yes it most certainly had. And I realized this well-hidden little fact as I reached for the phone and quite confidently dialed my dad's doctor's office in Orange County with the intention of getting some answers. And here's another little lesson to be learned, ladies and gents. Be oh, so careful what you ask for, because answers are exactly what I got.

Now, the nurse who came on the line knew my father very well, just as anyone who had ever been fortunate enough to come in contact with him did. Quaint, wasn't it?

I then, very courageously explained to her who I was and that because my father wasn't really sure of his condition, that I, myself, would politely like to know, just exactly what in the Sam hell was going on!

Well, that charming little nurse person saw absolutely no harm in talking to me about my father's condition, seeing that my dad had already told them that I would probably be calling. Wonder how he knew that? So she asked me to hold the line while she promptly fetched his chart.

Now I was getting somewhere, probably nothing at all. My dad had probably gotten his facts mixed up or his wires crossed and the nurse would come back on the line joyfully exclaiming that he actually had six years to live instead of six months, six months ago, silly little dad of mine. And I honestly thought that facing my fears was gonna be difficult. Ha! I was amazing!

I sat tapping my pen patiently on the table as I listened to Barry Manilow thanking Mandy for coming and giving without taking while I waited for the good news of my dad's biggest mistake in janitor history. Geeze, you would think they could find more upbeat music for those damned hold lines, for crying out loud! And where in the hell did she have to go to get that chart anyway? Cleveland? Well, I'd tell her what. If she didn't hurry up, I'd just hang up the bloody phone and that would show her! Then I would never have to deal with reality and that would teach someone a lesson and it sure as hell wouldn't have been me! Uh huh—and that's all I have to say about that!

She did finally come back on the line and just in the nick of time for her sake, I might add. And with her cheery little professional nurse voice she proceeded to tell me that my father was a charming little man. One of a kind, as a matter of fact, and that he was dying from melanoma. Better known to some as skin cancer. The fastest spreading form of cancer there is. Pass the stinking carrots just one more slaphappy time, please!

Geeze, was I the only one here who wasn't getting this, first the old man and now, this joyful little Joan of Arc impersonator. Didn't anyone understand how stinking devastating the term cancer really was? I felt like I had just walked into one of Rod Serling's best, for God's sake! Well, this information was simply not acceptable to me. No stinking way! He wasn't marked up with spots all over his body at all! Nope, you must be sadly mistaken, missy. As a matter of fact, she was wrong. Dead wrong! And she'd better pray to whomever it was she prayed to and real quick like, I might add, because she was just about ready to get hurt real bad. But she didn't. Nope she sure as hell didn't. She didn't pray nor did she even come close to acting like she was afraid. She simply continued on to explain to me that my father had had an MRI done six months ago and that his cancer was throughout his entire body. He had metastasized tumors on his spine, on his head and on his right breast. As a matter of fact, that is where they believed the cancer had begun its journey. IN HIS BREAST!? His lungs were infested as well as his liver and most of his internal organs. As a matter of fact, she could hardly believe he had held on this long, to be perfectly honest with me. Well, Geeze–La–Weeze! For crying out loud, don't let me stop you! On second thought, all right already! Enough! You can shut up any time now! I didn't want to hear any more. Never, ever again for that matter! The least she could have done was break the phone call up into about sixteen sessions so that I could've had time to digest all of this a little bit at a time, don't you think? Well, it shouldn't matter that I asked for it. I didn't want to hear it! Any of it! As a matter of fact, all I really wanted to do at that time was cease to exist myself.

She then proceeded to explain to me that my dad was definitely on borrowed time. He had been living with cancer in his liver for six months, which is almost unheard of. Three months was usually the norm. Like we were talking about the life expectancy of a car battery! "He is definitely a tough little guy," she said. I could hear her turning pages on the other end of the line. "The best and only thing left for us to do now, was to make him as comfortable as possible."

Well how about them apples! Perhaps there is a speeding bus somewhere with your name on it, you dumber–than–Thompson's–colt nurse, you. You need to use your head for something besides a hat rack, lady! For crying out loud, maybe he should be inducted into the hall of fricking fame for the longevity of life award! I couldn't believe what I was hearing! It was far worse than I had expected. Skin cancer? Breast cancer? Spreading throughout his internal organs? Make him as comfortable as possible? Oh, someone was in big trouble now! I want to talk to your boss and right now, lady, because it has become completely obvious to me that you are a total lunatic! My dad can't possibly have skin cancer, you delirious, dumb, professional nurse person, you! He doesn't even like the sun! So he has a few moles! So what! That's certainly nothing to get excited about, not to mention getting bent out of shape over, is it?

Yup, that was me and those were my thoughts alrighty. No question about it. And then I thought of something really stupid. But this time I actually said it out loud. I never even took a minute to think about it, so I can't really even say it was a decision, but before I knew which end was up, it came out of my mouth just as easy as you please. I told her that I was on my way to Southern California to stay with my dad until he died. What in the hell had I just said? Never mind that. Just where in the hell do you think that came from? Oh, and it got even better. I then proceeded to tell her that he brought me into this world and that I felt I wanted to be there to help him leave. Well, how stinking noble of me, don't you think? What I really wanted to know was, who in the hell was this person who had taken over my body?

Well, folks, it was me, the real me. She was back and she was determined! But she was also so scared completely out of her wits that it's a wonder she didn't go with a coronary before her father went with cancer.

The nurse then shared with me that she too, felt that my dad would soon need someone to take care of him. *Oh, God, that's exactly what he didn't want to happen!* Did he know this? Oh, geeze, this just couldn't possibly be happening, could it? Well, to be perfectly honest, yes, it most certainly could—and it was indeed happening. And right before my very heart.

It was real, my friends. The situation was very real. It had to be, didn't it? Because nurses don't lie to concerned, scared–half–out–of–their–wits daughters, now, do they? Well, for the mere sake of argument, let's assume they don't.

I then asked her, in her opinion, how long did he have? Now, why did I have to go and ask a stupid question like that? When you ask a question, don't you usually get a damned answer, you no–brain, had–to– be–concerned daughter, you!

She then told me we were looking at weeks. Weeks? That wasn't good enough. I had to proceed. How many weeks? "Well," she said, "Three, maybe four. But if he does hold on for four weeks, it will only be because you are there. More realistically, your father probably has only about two more weeks to live." *Here we go again, pass the stinking carrots!*

You know, I was fine until I made that phone call. Yup, finer than frog hair. I should have hung up when I had the chance. Right after Mandy sent Barry packing. As a matter of fact, I was a heck of a lot more comfortable not knowing the truth than I was at that particular moment. So I'll tell you what, you just go about your merry little nursing day, lady, and save some lives and I will hang up this phone and we will just simply pretend this stinking conversation never existed. Sounded good to me. No, let me rephrase that, it sounded great to me!

Sad, pitiful and maybe even a tad bit embarrassing, however, that was me. I can look back now and, while I don't think I will ever be able to do so and laugh about it, I do know I have at least learned from it. OK, not really. But for the sake of this story, it sure sounds good, doesn't it?

How was I going to prepare myself to say good-bye to my dad in just two to four short weeks? For crying out loud, it sounded like a weight loss commercial. How was I supposed to call and tell him that I was on my way to help him die? Did I say help him? Never mind that. How in the heck was I going to tell my husband and four children that for the first time in their lives I was leaving them for an unknown amount of time, when I didn't even know it myself until about two minutes before that?

Oh, boy, I had never bargained for this mess. This was all getting quite out of hand. Where in the world did I get the idea that it was my responsibility to stay with my dad? Where did I learn that kind of nobility? From whom could I have learned that kind of loyalty? Well, I think if we all just take a minute here, we can probably figure that one out now, can't we? Yes, indeedy, I think we already know the answer to that question. And none of us has to be a brain surgeon to do so either.

I thanked her for her frankness and honesty and the sick thing about it was I really meant it. Then I told her I would contact their office when I arrived at my father's.

"Oh, there's just one more thing" she said, as I proceeded to hang up the phone. She felt it was important for me to know that my dad had been on pain medication since last April. "The pain he'd been experiencing was starting to get more severe and he would need some stronger medication soon to accommodate the pain that was yet to come."

Well, howdy do! What in the heck was she talking about now? Listen, lady, in my book you have just about worn out your welcome! First, you politely tell me that the world's last living real monster fighter is on his way out and sooner than we all think. Then, in your charming little nurse way, you proceed to explain to me things about him that I should have already known to begin with, but I didn't because he didn't choose to share them with me. And now you tell me that he'll need more pain medication soon because the pain he's already been experiencing is going to get a little worse, when I knew nothing about any stinking pain in the first place! God, I hate to be the last one to know everything!

So what did I do? Well, I'll tell you. I then politely and very intelligently asked what kind of pain medication. Geeze, I never cease to amaze myself.

She told me that as soon as I got to my dad's house, she would send a nurse over to start my dad on morphine patches. Morphine? Oh, my God! He could become addicted, couldn't he? Uh huh, and he could just take that addiction right on up to heaven with him, you moron! Addiction was the least of a dying man's worries. And let's not all get sidetracked here and forget what the nice, little, nurse person just said. Morphine! Now, I don't know about any of you, but where I come from, that's some pretty serious pain medication.

She then continued on to explain how he would need help after he was put on these morphine patches. Patches? What in the heck is a morphine patch? She went on and on about how these patches were the greatest thing anyone ever invented because you wear them and the medication goes right through the skin and into the bloodstream and they hold their peak for three days at a time and it would make it a lot easier on my dad cause he was having a problem swallowing the pain pills at this point. As a matter of fact, he was having trouble swallowing period.

Oh, was he? Well, whoop-de-do! My dad had not shared any of these things with me. So therefore, you must be lying, you pants–on–fire– dumb–old nurse, you!

I then asked how long had my dad been in pain. There it was again. Why can't I just leave things well enough alone?

She said for quite some time now. His internal organs were on a rampage to try to fight the horrible disease that had invaded his body. She also informed me that they would put him on oxygen as soon as I arrived just to help him breathe a little easier.

Oxygen? Oxygen! Why? His breathing had been just fine while he had been at my house, hadn't it? Hadn't he always been a heavy breather? No, you doo-doo head, that's just a small oversight on your part. Think back to the last time you saw him or to the last time you talked to him on the phone. He wasn't just breathing hard cause he ran to get the phone on the first ring, you knucklehead! As a matter of fact, didn't it always ring several times before he even picked it up?

I tuned back in and told her I would call her as soon as I got there and thanked her once again for her time. Oh, and I'd also like to thank you for making my life a living nightmare once again and if I can ever return the favor, PLEASE feel free to give me a call, you witch–in– nurse's–clothing, you. And there I sat, with the hum of the dial tone signaling to me that I had just been cut off from a part of the world that harbored a living hell for my dad and me.

My God, I hadn't known he was in pain. I called him every day and he said he was doing fine. He said he had his good days and he had his bad days but for the most part he felt great. Great compared to what, is what I wanted to know. What I *needed* to know.

If I had listened to myself long enough for all of this to have made sense, I would have realized that my dad had always felt great! He just simply wasn't a person who ever complained. He wasn't the type of man to collect sympathy. Hell, we should all know that by now! What was the matter with me? How had I become so engrossed in the situation that I didn't even notice how sick he had really become? I believe it must have had something to do with not being able to see the ostrich in the forest, or sticking my head in the trees. Or—oh, crap, you know what I mean.

Well, out of all of this mess one thing was for sure. I felt like I had been dreaming and a pinch wouldn't have done it for me. I needed something more like the Jaws of Life to wake me up from this one. I didn't know who was going to take care of my family while I was away. I didn't know who was going to pay for my plane fare. I didn't know how I was going to allow my dad to die. Worst of all, I didn't know who in the hell cared besides me. But what I did know was that I *was* leaving. And it had to be soon. For we were already way over our limit on borrowed time as it was.

And there was just one more thing. One more tiny, little, teensy-weensy thing. Where in the hell had the witch been through all of this? That nurse person had not even mentioned that my father had a wife. No, remember? She had said that my dad told them *I'd* be calling. Me. The nurse and my father both had expected *me* to call—and. And what? Why hadn't she said, *I'm sure he'll be fine, after all, he has his wife.* But she didn't. No, I'm sure she didn't even know my father was married. Why? Never mind why but how? How in the hell does a man venture into the journey of hell, the valley of the shadow of death, without his wife right by his side? I was baffled. Why was I going there? What was she doing that was so almighty important that she couldn't put it aside for the last few weeks of her beloved husband's life? Oh, and how about a phone call? How about, *I thought I'd better call to tell you that your father is in pain.* Huh? How about that for starters? How about, *he's getting worse and he can't swallow anymore.* Does anyone besides me think that that little ditty is an important fact? What exactly was that woman thinking? What was she doing, just waiting for him to die? Waiting for the burden to be gone? Was she stupid? Or, was she—very, very wise?

No, this just wasn't possible. Perhaps I was mistaken. Of course, I had to be. I was simply reading something in that wasn't even there. I have been known to love a good book. I've also been known to put things where they don't belong. Yup, that's me. Silly–ass, make–believing, storytelling, imaginative little me.

Intelligent, intuitive, right–on–the–money me.

# Chapter Five

## Leaving

*All conservatism is based upon the idea that if you leave
things alone you leave them as they are. But you do not. If
you leave a thing alone you leave it to a torrent of change.*

G.K. Chesterton 1874–1936 Orthodoxy (1908) ch. 7

WELL, MY FRIENDS, I've said it before and I'll say it a million times more
if that's what it takes. All things definitely do happen for a reason. And
I had reason to believe that statement more than ever. Simply because
solutions just began falling into place and, as they did, the fear began to subside.
Well, at least for a little while anyway.

You see, there was one really great occurrence that came out of all the years we
lived with the monster. Another sister. A half sister if you will—however, I have never
thought of her that way until this very moment. Although, I do suppose it will make it
a little easier to identify her throughout my story. So, half sister it is, for now anyway.

I was thirteen years old when she was born and although I hated her father,
I loved her with everything I had in me. She and I had developed a special bond
throughout her childhood that can be explained only by my overwhelming feeling
of compassion for her because of the man who fathered her—and although she came
into this world having to grow up with some very obvious hurdles, she had become
quite a fine young lady. And it just so happened that at the time of my father's illness
she was living and going to college in another state and had just decided that she was
ready for a break. Hard to believe, isn't it?

When I called to talk to her about my dilemma I was quite simply and harmlessly
looking for a shoulder to cry on. She was safe. No one had told me I couldn't tell *her*.
So I decided to take advantage of this little newly discovered treasure. Of course,

this certainly hadn't been the first time I had taken advantage of her understanding heart. But it sure would prove to be the most memorable. Or so I thought at the time. Another book, another story.

During our tear-filled conversation, as I was sobbing and trying at the same time to explain what had been happening, she obligingly and compassionately decided that she would come to my rescue and play the part of a live-in nanny until I could return home. She felt like it would give her the much-needed break she was looking for and at the same time, it would give her the opportunity to do something in a situation that no one could do anything about. A role we would all come to be looking for before this whole damned mess was over.

So, it looked like fate had intended for me to go to my father's all along. Coincidence—or a little help from up above? Well, I know what I think; however, what I think usually turns into a novel. So I won't go into it just now.

With that little step out of the way, all there was left to do was tell my family. Shouldn't be so hard. I'd just tell them the truth. Usually works out best in all situations. And the truth was that I was so scared and confused that I didn't know what the next step should really be.

You see, I have a real problem with trust. I know it's hard to believe but it's a fact and I sure as heck wasn't in the habit of gallivanting off and leaving my children with one of my sisters to fulfill my own desires. On the other hand, this certainly wasn't a pleasure cruise we were talking about now, was it? And to say the least, this was not a desire by a long shot. Nonetheless, I was torn between my feelings of responsibility to my children and my feeling of responsibility to my father. And both harbored a love so strong that Sampson himself would have been jealous.

Now, the ideal situation would have obviously been to bring my dad home to my house. Uh huh, ideal for *me* but not for *him*; remember, he wanted to die at home. Decisions were so very much easier when I was selfish.

The next step was to tell my family all about the preparations I had made for *them*, without consulting *them* and to inform *them* ever so gently if there was such a way, of my father's condition. All in the same evening? This was moving along about as smoothly as the voyage of the Titanic. And perhaps that would explain the sick, sinking feeling I'd had in my gut since this whole damned pleasure cruise began.

My first move was a classic. I decided to tell the kids and my husband of my great heroic plans for the future during dinner that evening, taking a big chance on one or all of them choking to death before my very eyes.

Throughout the preparation of dinner, I tried hard to be calm, cool, and collected and, quite frankly, wishing that I had prepared a seventeen trillion-course meal.

As I was setting the table I felt like I was just minutes away from bolting like hell out the front door, leaving everyone standing around shaking their heads, wondering just what in the Sam hell had gotten into me this time. She'll come back they'd say as they gathered around the table trying to pick through the remains of what I hadn't dumped on the floor during my whirlwind exit. Relax, I didn't. But I wanted to.

Oh, sure, they knew that Grandpa had cancer, and they knew he was going to die, and they knew not to tell my sisters, and my husband had been cradling my tears for quite some time by then, however, none of them were aware of the fact that the time we all had been dreading had finally come. Hell, I had just found out myself!

As I put the last bowl on the table and summoned for everyone to come and eat, I knew it wasn't going to be easy. I sat looking at all of them while they chatted away about their day's events, passing food to one another, oblivious to the volcano that was just about to erupt from within my soul.

It wasn't *just* me anymore. I had to tell *them*. I had to bear the news that their grandpa was, in fact, dying and that they would probably never see him again. And for the icing on the bloody camel's back, I had to go away to be with him. So not only were they going to have to deal with losing their Grandpa, they also had to do it without their mother there to console them. No problem, not a problem at all.

Should I be dramatic and slow? Or matter-of-fact and fast? Well, to tell you the truth, blurting out "Grandpa's dying, please pass the peas" just wasn't my way of doing things contrary to everyone else's obvious and previous beliefs. Not to mention the fact that there weren't even any peas on the table. I'm telling you, things just couldn't get any better than this.

So, I started out slowly beginning with "I spoke with my dad's doctor's office today." They all paused long enough to show attention, so far so good. Like what did I expect? I hadn't really said anything of great significance yet.

They all continued their much-enjoyed meal with a few glances my way with some raised eyebrows to show that they were listening when I finally dropped the bomb.

"Things aren't real good." Oh great! Like that was a big secret to begin with. Slowly I said, "They seem to think that Grandpa has only a couple of weeks to live."

I would have killed for a bowl of peas at that point. Actually, I would have killed for anything at all to look at other than the faces that were staring back at me right then and there. And I truly believe that it was the only time ever in my house that you could have heard a pin drop.

I don't know what I was thinking when I made the stupid decision to tell everyone during dinner. I guess I chose that particular time because it's the one time every day that we were all together. What I didn't stop to think about was the fact that dinnertime was a time to share positive information, not devastating, gut–wrenching, make–you–want–to–hurl news, for Pete's sake!

Needless to say, no one finished his or her dinner. And there were a lot of questions as to the whys and whats of these goings on before I finally told them that I had decided to go to Grandpa's house and take care of him until he passed away. Again, the silence was overwhelming. And then, just like most things we spend our time worrying about, it had been proven needless.

They were very supportive, understanding, and sad all at the same time. Each of them had personal sorrow to deal with, so sending me to go and be with my dad was their way of being able to do something in this mess that no one could do anything about. It gave them a sense of control. And it gave me the permission to go without guilt or regrets. Yes, my friends, looked like the road was now clear and I had everyone's blessings. So all that was left for me to do was to get the heck out of there.

You know, I'm ashamed to admit it, but in my heart I think I was secretly hoping for a roadblock. This was going to be tough and I knew it. It wasn't like I was just going for a visit to spend some time with my dad and we would enjoy each other's company and then I would kiss him good-bye and come home looking forward to the next visit. Uh, uh, not this time—this was it. The end. After this visit—there would be no more. Damn, that was haunting!

Well, if that wasn't the most depressing outlook on a situation that I had ever been up against, I don't know what was. I just had to keep myself from thinking about it that way. So, I secretly told my heart to hang on and we would get through this somehow. We always had before. Yes, I think I was still fooling myself into believing that my dad would somehow pull through this tragedy unscathed. To be truthful, this was the only way I could keep from losing my sanity.

Speaking of losing my sanity, hadn't someone better tell my dad that he was about to have a houseguest? Might be a good idea except for the fact that I was too afraid to call him. And why, might you ask? Yes, I thought you might. Well, once I tell you, you're not going to believe it anyway. Then again, you pretty much know me by now so you just might, so here goes: I was afraid that if I told him I was coming, then he just might have found out that he was truly dying—that's why. Uh huh, go ahead and snicker.

Like he didn't know. Like he hadn't been trying to tell me this for weeks now. Uh huh, well, let me tell you something else. I knew it too. I still just didn't quite want to believe it. I figured that by not talking about it, it might just somehow go away. But no matter how much I tried to ignore this particular situation, it seemed to just get worse. See, nothing ever happens in real life the way it does in the movies.

I just really hate that! I guess it goes without saying that besides the fact that I quite obviously and really was losing what little mind I had left, this would indeed be a very difficult phone call to make.

I had been calling him daily since he left my house in August, so simply calling wasn't the problem at all. Sometimes the phone would ring and ring and ring and I would get so panicked that I thought my heart would stop beating right then and there. Then he would finally answer very obviously perturbed because I woke him up. Or the witch would answer and quite curtly tell me that my dad was sleeping and she would tell him I called. Then I would try to engage her in some sort of conversation about—oh—I don't know, maybe how things were going at the castle or how her flying monkeys were doing, but to no avail. Yup, these conversations I was used to. It was the topic of this particular conversation I was trying to avoid.

But honestly, haven't we all had to experience this sort of thing before? Well, excluding asking about someone's flying monkeys. I mean having to talk to someone without really addressing the issues at hand? Sucks, doesn't it?

Well, before I knew it, the phone was ringing and I was actually the one who had dialed. Maybe I'd just tell him I was coming for a nice little visit. Uh huh, like I could ever successfully lie to my dad. Five rings so far, the witch must have been out on her broom somewhere.

On about the seventh ring his tired, gruff old voice said, "Hello?" Did I say gruff? When did that start? He was impatiently again saying, "Hello?"

Would have been nice if I could have spoken, but I had this tremendous lump in my throat. Finally, I began with "Hi, Dad, it's me."

"Well, hello, me!"

"Were you sleeping?" I asked.

"No, dear, I was just watching one of my shows is all. What cha know, Baby Doll? Is everything all right?"

No, everything is not all right! You're dying and I, the stinking pathetic brown-eyed baby doll girl, have made the stupid decision to come and stay with you until you complete your miserable journey.

I continued, "Oh, yes, everything's fine, Dad. Just wanted to call and see how you are."

Oh, well, he was just as fine as he had been the day before, just as fine as he had always been, you nitwit. He answered the bloody phone. That was a plus!

I told him that I had been thinking about it and I felt like I'd like to come and stay with him for a while. There was an incredibly long pause of silence and I realized that silence is not very damned golden at all.

"Dad?" I prompted. *You idiot! You've killed him!*

"That's great!" he finally blurted out, scaring the living hoopla right out of me.

"That's wonderful! When will you be here, dear?"

*Great? Wonderful? When will you be here, dear?* What in the hell was going on here? This was not supposed to be. This was not the way I had planned it at all. Wasn't I expecting him to say no, it wasn't necessary? Wasn't I hoping? Wasn't I praying? What in the heck ever happened to *"Don't bother, dear, I'm fine"*? That's exactly what I had been hoping for. How about a good old-fashioned *"No, no dear, don't trouble yourself."* Yes, indeedy. Now, that would have been great for starters. Followed up with the classic *"Oh no, you can't possibly leave your family for that length of time."* Then finally ending with the all-time favorite, *"I'll be fine, don't you give it a second thought."* Uh huh, and then perhaps Dick Clark could stop by and host the rest of the top forty that we have left unsaid.

Again, as I tuned back into the conversation, he was asking when I would be there.

Well, by now we all know that there is just something about my dad that has always been able to drag the honesty right out of me so before I knew what I was saying it was out of my mouth. I told him that I had spoken with the nurse at his doctor's office and that they seem to have the silly idea that he didn't have a whole lot of time left, so I would be leaving within the week. And once again, I was taken totally by surprise when my dad responded with *"I don't think it will be long either."*

What in the hell did he just say? Stop the music! Stop the flipping music right here and now and go get Dick! Just exactly what in the heck was he trying to tell me? Don't be shy, just stand right up here, close to the mic and spit it out, for cripe's sake!

Well, you see, he decided to share with me at that very moment that he had given in—or up—whichever you prefer. He had decided to share with me all the facts that had been left unsaid. The fact was that he felt a little weaker every day and he had been having a hard time keeping food down. He had been having trouble breathing and he just, quite frankly, had had enough of it all. The most heartbreaking confession that he shared with me was the fact that he was starting to get just a little bit frightened and he would be delighted to have me come stay with him. And I can sure as hell tell you after he said that, I would have gotten there if I'd had to *walk* every step of the way! I believe I would have crawled across the desert on my bare and bleeding knees. Yup, I know I would have. And then he asked the question I had been dreading. I actually had been hoping he wouldn't ask, but he did. "How long will you be staying, dear?"

Hadn't I already said until he had to go? Perhaps not; small oversight on my part I suppose. This was it! I had to tell my dad that I believed he was dying. Actually, no, I had to first tell myself.

After a long pause I bravely and tenderly replied, "Until you leave me, Dad." And it was done. I had said it. Just like that it came rambling out of my mouth just as easy as you please.

Right away, I thought, geeze I shouldn't have said that. Why did I say that? It sounds so—final. But then, it was final, wasn't it? I mean, death is, after all, the grand finality of life! And as always, he answered with a simple reply that made everything seem so natural.

He said, "I would like that, dear, very much. No one should be alone when they die. It will be nice to have you here with me."

You know, all I can remember thinking at that very moment was that no one *should* be alone when they die. No one should *ever* have to experience the pain of losing someone they love either. But we do, don't we? I truly and sadly don't know why or how, but we do.

He then, all of a sudden, decided that he'd been on the phone too long and it was time to hang up as he left me with his notorious, "I love you, dear, I'll see you when you get here, bye-now!" And there I sat. With the phone in my hands listening to a distant voice chanting, "If you'd like to make a call, please hang up and dial again." I was vaguely aware of the fact that I had just solidified my plans. It really didn't hit me for a couple of heart-screaming seconds. Not until after I had hung up the phone and started to pack did I realize what in the hell I was actually doing and even then, I didn't really know—as we will soon find out. I can tell you one thing for sure though; my dad had said that he wanted me there with him. I couldn't back out now, even if I wanted to. I had to go whether I could make up excuses or not and deep down inside, I really wanted to go. I really did! I wanted to go and have a nice visit and come home. I wanted things to be the way they used to be. I wanted everything to be OK again. I wanted my dad back, the way *he* used to be. I wanted him to live—forever.

It became very clear to me that my wants were easily identified. It's what I *didn't* want that was scaring the hell out of me. And what I *didn't* want was to have to say good-bye to my dad, forever. Plain and simple. (Forever—only when someone dies.) The problem was that I really didn't have to go if I didn't want to. I could have called my dad and made up some lame excuse and he would have understood. He would have had no problem with that what–so–ever–at–all, because that's just the kind of person he was.

The truth is that it was me. And that's just the kind of person I was—and still am, and I hope to always be. That is exactly why I had to go. Oh, he did a terrific job of fathering me, now, didn't he? Out of all of the precious gifts that I had received from his charming personality, it was more than clear to me that I had chosen compassion above them all. And you know, when you really think about it, that's not so bad, now, is it? Nope, I don't believe it is at all. But it sure would've made my life a heck of a lot easier had I inherited something less troublesome, like maybe his nose.

With all of my hurdles out of the way, I then felt this incredible, overwhelming urge to hurry. All of a sudden, there was now this overpowering sense of urgency running around inside of me. As a matter of fact, I found myself feeling so anxious that it just about put me into the worst panic attack in therapeutic history. What if he didn't wait for me? What if he died before I got there? What if he fell down and he couldn't get up? (I truly hate that commercial.) Oh, my God, what if? What if—well, I didn't know, but if I gave myself time enough to think about it, I'm sure I could've created some horrible circumstance in my mind that I could do absolutely nothing about.

Sad, isn't it? Those what ifs will get you every time. I am totally convinced that the *what ifs* are related to the *I should haves* and are probably distant cousins of the *Why didn't I's,* and all of them are easy ways for us to accept blame and guilt for a situation that we can do nothing about, which in turn explains why they also have a way of making us feel really helpless and miserable. It totally fascinates the poo right out of me to think that we actually get through these things.

For the rest of the week until I actually left for my dad's house, I felt all of these lovely little wonders of the blame and guilt family. So I continued to call my dad every day, searching for a way to release some of these unwelcome intruding feelings. But the sad truth of the matter was that only *I* could let them go. It wasn't up to my dad to do it for me. Nope, it most certainly wasn't. However, I continued to feel like there must be *something* I could do. I should have made him stay on the shots. Why hadn't I told him he had to take those shots? What if he dies and I feel like it's all my fault just because I wasn't more demanding? Don't suppose it had dawned on me yet that perhaps these little ditties were all out of my control. Nope, by the looks of things thus far, I would have to say that not a whole lot of anything really dawned on me at all. And it wouldn't for quite some time yet.

As I made my daily phone calls to my dad I became more aware of his deteriorating condition. He sounded so very tired all the time. His voice had become very raspy and his breathing was extremely heavy. But there was something else. Something that I just couldn't put my finger on. Something that had touched my heart in a much different way than ever before. Something about his personality. Yes—I believe that was it. His personality was becoming almost childlike. He was becoming very dependent on me. That was it! That is what had been breeding the urgency. He sounded like a child, a very frightened child!

He wanted to know when I would be there. *"Today?" "Tomorrow?"* How was I going to get there? Was I going to fly? Oh, how he loved to fly! How long would it take me to get there? You know, those airplanes were remarkable, weren't they? Oh—yeah, Dad, those airplanes were flipping remarkable alrighty, about as remarkable as an Eskimo sitting in an igloo drinking hot chocolate! What in the hell was going on? This was all just about enough to make me sick. Really sick, like actual wrenching, vomiting sick! But I managed to refrain from doing so. All I could do was keep telling him I'd be there soon. And deep in my heart I knew it wouldn't be long before all of this too would become just another precious memory. And then another thought occurred to me. A thought I had never had before. A thought that had, quite frankly, never dared cross my mind. Hard to believe, I know.

What if his mind was going too? My God, I could have handled anything else but I truly didn't think I could have handled that. How would the daughter of the greatest storyteller who ever lived deal with the fact that he might not ever be capable of telling another story again? He didn't want to live so long that he couldn't use his mind anymore. And I didn't want him to. And as I sat there with that thought lying heavy within my soul, I became absolutely heartsick over the many people who have to endure the agony of watching a loved one succumb to a mind robbing disease. We have no guarantees in this life and I was frightened as hell to think about what could possibly lay ahead for my dad and me.

Needless to say, just as soon as my sibling in nanny's clothing arrived, I'd be making a beeline for the airport. There was, however, just one more little minor detail that I had overlooked. My sisters! Hadn't someone better tell them what's going on—and soon? Oh, I supposed—and guess who that ever so lucky someone was?

After discussing (arguing) this matter with my dad over the telephone one afternoon, we both agreed (finally) that it was indeed time for my sisters to be told. And it's a darned good thing too, because I truly don't know what I would've done had he not agreed with me. I explained to him that I felt there was a good reason for the type of illness that he had been stricken with, as cancer doesn't kill you overnight. And sometimes I believe we are given a warning or a second chance that we *had* so fortunately been given for a reason, even if it did have to be pushed upon some of us (me). So, I decided the best place to start was at the top, with my oldest sister.

Now we all have to understand that my oldest sister had always been—well—the oldest, and this role I had been playing was usually hers. Therefore, I hadn't had much practice being the teller. I had always been the receiver. And I don't mind sharing with all of you that I was just a tad bit nervous about the whole darned idea. I was actually and more honestly worried that she might be upset with me for knowing first—which, of course, I had no control over but nonetheless, she just might have felt—well—left out. I sure as hell found myself wishing that someone had kindly left me out.

We were on our way to the library the Saturday before I was due to leave (nothing like waiting till the very last minute) when I decided that it was as good a time as any to somehow try to gently tell her that our dad's days were numbered. Of course, if we stop and think about it, all of our days are numbered—nonetheless—his number had, in fact, come up and there, quite frankly, is no easy way to tell someone something like that—now, is there? Well, if there is, I sure as hell wish someone had told me how because no matter how many times I practiced, the words seemed so—well—unnatural, which in itself is sort of ironic, don't you think, in that death, just like birth is—very natural.

We had just pulled into the parking lot of the library when I carefully began by asking her what she had thought of our dad's appearance at the wedding. Subtle enough, I thought. She turned her head and looked at me as if I had actually transformed myself *into* Thompson's colt. A look I was getting pretty used to by that time. "What do you mean?" she asked. *What do you mean, what do I mean,* I thought. What part of the question do you not understand? Didn't you kind of notice that he was a little thin, for crying out loud, not to mention the fact that he was as yellow as the ribbon around Tony Orlando's old oak tree! Geeze, why can't these things ever be easy?

I continued. "Do you think he looked well?"

She thought a minute, then answered me with, "Well I don't know, I guess."

"Well," I said, "the truth is that Dad is very sick."

She looked at me and with a most distrusting tone in her voice she asked, "How sick?"

Oh, I don't know, how sick would he have to be for you to stop answering my questions with questions, you moment-robbing dumb-ass sister of mine?

"Well," I said, "there really is no easy way to say this so bear with me here a minute. And after a long pause, I blurted out, "He has cancer and it's terminal and he is dying." Pass the freaking peas for the last and final time!!!!

Now, my big sister has always been a calm, matter-of-fact, let's– get–all–the– details–first–before–we–do–a–Manson–rain–dance–on– somebody's–face kind of person, so she looked me square in the eye and very calmly asked, "How long does he have?"

How long does he have? How long does he have? Was I the only idiot who wanted to know all of the dirty little details? What in the hell was wrong with me?

I looked her back, square in the eye, and finally told her the harrowing secret that I had been living with for quite some time and my heart went out to her as I gazed upon her bewildered expression.

We sat in the car that day for what turned out to be the better part of an hour, as I shared the whole nightmare with her down to the very last detail and together, she and I both decided that she, herself, would be the one to tell the rest of the girls, while I was in Southern California, so that I would have no more obstacles to prevent me from starting on my way.

Great—just what I wanted. I realized that there were no more obstacles to keep me from my journey—and we never did make it to the library.

Unfortunately, I realized something else as well. I realized that sharing this secret with my big sister was just like old times. For once again, she had been told a secret that she could do absolutely nothing about. And once again she felt like she should be able to take the pain away from her little sister's heart, because she was the oldest and shouldn't it be her responsibility to do something? Anything? Well, not hardly. Because just exactly like old times, there wasn't a damned thing she could do in this world to make the situation better. She was helpless and she knew it, once again.

Preparing to leave proved to be very difficult for me. I found myself once again feeling like I wanted the best of both worlds. It would have been so much easier just to have brought my dad to *my* house. I think it goes something like—wanting to have your cake and eat it too. And, incidentally, I never really did understand that little ditty anyway. If you have a piece of cake, what in the heck else are you supposed to do with it?

My children, the ones who had always been so dependent upon me, were beginning to show a change—or maybe I had just never taken the time to notice how independent they really were. How long had they been able to get themselves ready in the morning? How long had they been able to actually think for themselves? How long had I been defeating their capabilities just so that I would feel needed? Yes, I believe that was the real question here. For they had obviously been humoring me for quite sometime. So along with the dreaded task of leaving my children, also came the realization that I had done my job as a mother and done it well. Halleflippenluyah!

My husband had always been a team player, pitching in with the laundry, cooking, cleaning, and the kids as well as working a ten-to twelve-hour day outside of the home. Geeze, I felt like my job had already been deleted, but in all honesty, I needed every one of these signs to be able to get on *that* plane and go.

Perhaps they all knew this and they just put on one hell of a show, or perhaps they had all become exactly what I had prayed so hard for all of my life: A real family—a family that pulled together during a crisis, giving each other the strength and compassion to endure any situation. Well, whether we meant to or not, that's exactly what we had proudly accomplished. Well, I'll be go to hell John!

So, with nothing left to hold me back, it was finally time to go as I went frantically searching throughout the house trying to remember if I had forgotten anything. How in the heck is a person supposed to be able to remember if they have forgotten anything anyway? Huh, I suppose it's just another one of those phrases that don't make a damned bit of sense, what–so–ever–at–all!

This was it! I was ready. And as I went racing out the door to catch my plane on time, I realized there *was* a slight obstacle. My kids! I had to kiss and say good-bye to my children.

Good-bye. Damn, I was getting tired of that. I was already sick of it all and I hadn't even left yet. Well, ladies and gents, to be perfectly honest with you, I had absolutely no idea what the phrase *sick of it all* really meant because had I known at the time what my future held, I would've unpacked that little suitcase of mine, put on my feet pajamas, crawled into my bed with my blankey and my ba ba and pulled the covers up over my head until it was all over. You can bet your sweet pajama bottoms on that!

Finally, I realized that it *really was* time to go, as I summoned each one of the kids, scattered throughout different areas of the house and outside with my half sister on my heels every step of the way.

Upon each location as I made my journey toward the car, I stopped and tenderly kissed each one of my children, taking into my memory their smells and touches, knowing that the next time I saw them, my dad would only be but a memory of the same senses.

We put my bags in the car and I took one last glace as I kissed my sister and climbed in and closed the door. Sure is strange how the slamming of a car door can lock in silence. Strange indeed.

As we rounded that very same corner that I had taken so carefully with my dad by my side just weeks before that—which now seemed like hundreds of years ago—I looked back just one more time, knowing in my heart that I would become homesick long before my children would become mother-sick. I watched them resume their normal activities once the last wave had been given. What a horrible and unsettling feeling. Where in the hell were the banners? Where was that stupendous brass band? How about some news coverage or something? For crying out loud! I was leaving home for the very first time ever! And all I got was a kiss and a look that said, see you, Mom, have a great trip, go bury Grandpa and we'll catch you on the flip side. Well—or so it seemed anyway.

My husband and oldest sister accompanied me to the airport and I somehow felt that I couldn't have been in better hands if All State themselves had been at the wheel, with the both of them trying to convince me of the fact that my plane absolutely and beyond a shadow of a doubt, would not go down over the desert somewhere, never to be found again.

You see I'm not really crazy about flying. Never have been. I had flown only a couple of times before that and I was feeling, once again, like I wanted to call this whole thing off. Just kidding, everyone! Grandpa's not really dying. I was just checking to see if we could actually pull this whole silly episode off and—we—did! Boy howdy, did we! Ha Ha, what a funny joke. Aren't I just the absolute most! A real comedian! Well—or so I would liked to have thought anyway. But it quite sadly didn't happen that way. Sure would have been nice though.

As I stood in the passenger area of the airport, waiting for the boarding call, I watched in amazement as all the people were rushing around, hurrying to their appointed destinations and I wondered how many of them were on their way to complete a task as difficult as mine. Probably none of them—because weren't most of them smiling, or just simply talking away without a care in the world?

But wait a minute, hadn't I been the one who had smiled at the flight attendant after she checked my ticket and gave me permission to board? Yup, I think that was me.

It sure is strange, isn't it? We never really know what might be going on in the minds of others, do we? Kind of made me want to hop up on the counter, right smack-dab in the middle of the airport and yell, "Haaaay, if there's anyone here who is on their way to say good-bye to a loved one forever, please report to me at once! I'm feeling pretty lonely and scared right about now, which means that you quite probably might be too. So maybe we could get together and feel very stinking sorry for each other because no one else in the whole wide world could possibly know how awful we feel besides us!"

Relax, I didn't.

As my sister and I stood waiting for my husband to catch up with us, after stopping for a cup of coffee, I noticed her gazing at me like she was some sort of lovesick fool. And that's not all I noticed. Had she always looked so beautiful? No, radiant was the word. Yes, I believe she was almost beaming.

And just before I had time to find somewhere else to be, she reached out her hand and very gently placed it on my arm as she said, "I love you. I always thought that I would be the one to go. I really always thought it would be me. But it's not. It's you. You decided to do this on your own and in your heart of hearts you took full responsibility to love our dad like the rest of us never could. I don't think I can ever remember a time when I've been more proud of you than I am right now." And as I stood completely still, staring into her tear-filled eyes, she said something else to me. Something I'll never forget as long as I live. She said, "Here we are, once again faced with another trauma that we can do nothing about. But we've done it before and we will do it again, and I know that—because we are survivors. That is also exactly how I know you will make it through this. You have to be the strongest you have ever been now, because the situation that you are about to face is the most painful you will ever experience. Do you understand? But I know you can do it. Because you have always been the strong one."

Oh, for crying out loud! Why did she have to go and say a thing like that? It wasn't enough that I had to leave my children and my husband, was it? It wasn't enough that I was just about to board the biggest piece of scrap metal in tin can history, not to mention the fact that in my simple mind all I kept asking myself was, "How in the hell do you think those trillion-pound pieces of shark-shaped tin actually catch air?" But now she had to go and open the floodgates to my emotions. Oh, go piss on a flat rock!

As my husband approached us, I'm sure he had thoughts that while he had been gone just around the miserable corner, to get a stinking cup of coffee, we had received "THE" phone call and it was all over, as we stood teary-eyed and wiping our noses laughing at the look on his face and crying at the same time.

There was my boarding call. I truly felt like I was gonna throw up. How do you say good-bye at a time like this? There aren't enough lingering moments in all the world.

Before I knew it—there I was. Me. Standing in line with everyone else, lost in the crowd of nameless people—all heading for somewhere that I was sure held happier moments than my own destination. Of that I was positive. And as I started down the long hallway, I glanced back over my shoulder and caught one last glimpse of my sister and my husband and I knew in my heart at that very moment, that the next time they saw me, I would be a completely different person. I knew beyond a shadow of a doubt that I would never again be the same.

# Chapter Six

## *Realization*

*The only limit to our realization of tomorrow will be our doubts of today. Let us move forward with strong and active faith.*
Undelivered address for Jefferson Day, Apr. 1945 (the day after
Roosevelt died) In Public Papers (1950) vol. 13, p. 615

WELL, I GUESS it's pretty obvious that my plane didn't go down over some sand-filled dessert never to be recovered because otherwise—well, you know.

My experience flying in over Ontario was extremely dissatisfying in that I was absolutely heartsick over the color of the clouds. The smog was thick with a brown blanket of filth that hovered over the city, leaving me to wonder just what in the name of God have we done to this planet? And I believe, if I'm not mistaken, that it was at that very moment that I decided I really needed to start recycling.

A few months before all of this mess had begun; I had located and reunited with one of my most cherished, childhood friends. As a matter of fact, she was the *only* childhood friend I'd ever really had. I guess that would explain why I cherished her. Well, that and the fact that she was the only one I ever told. You know—about The Monster. She had remained in the Southern California area and we had arranged for her to be the one who would meet me and take me to my dad's. So, as I stepped off the plane, it was a bittersweet reunion, considering the circumstances. However and nonetheless, it was beautifully obvious that the past years had been very good to her. She was lovely. And she harbored many of my most intimate secrets from my childhood and she kept her promise. She never told a soul. Damn it. Damn it all to hell!!!

After we embraced and hugged and cried and talked and hugged and cried some more, a little healthy reminiscing, if you will, we began our intended journey to my father's house. I hadn't been back to Southern California since we left The Monster with our very lives almost twenty years before and I became truly fascinated at how fast paced it was. The vast energy and hustle was consuming. Perhaps it had always been that way and I had just been too young and preoccupied to notice. Geeze, getting onto the freeway took an act of Congress alone. I must compliment the brave people of Southern California, for I realized just then that I was truly a wimp.

As I watched speeding cars darting and dashing on and off the freeway, I also had to commend my father. He deserved a medal for not succumbing to a heart attack, before the cancer. Of course, I learned later on that he never drove the freeways. There was just no end to his intelligence.

My mind wandered during the drive as we sped through the city of Diamond Bar. *Diamond Bar.* My God, it had been years since I had thought of that place as almost instantly, my memories took me back to a time of sadness, as I could very clearly recall the look on my dad's face as he entered our home to take his girls for a much-needed reprieve from hell.

He would walk through the door with the biggest smile on his face and at the same time, with the worst pain in his eyes that I had ever seen. Heck, that look had become all too familiar to me, come to think about it. We all harbored that same exact look, each and every time he arrived. Except for the fact that one of our eyes had to always be focused on The Monster.

I couldn't stand the thought of how very painful that must have been for my father. Having to beg for permission to take his own little girls from the very same man who had moved into his home just one week after he had moved out. This wasn't treatment fit for a pig and yet my dad went through this ritual each and every time he came to get us. Boy, I sure do love those memories. About as much as I loved facing the task I had before me. They sure do come at the damnedest times, don't they? Made me wonder if I would have ever recalled that one particular episode had I not seen the name of the city on the freeway sign. I then decided probably not. Why would I have wanted to?

Before I knew it, we were approaching my dad's trailer park and just in the nick of time, for if you don't mind me saying so, I don't think my heart could've taken another precious childhood memory.

As we rounded the last corner into the tiny little community that my dad had for so long called home, I was so taken by the neatly groomed modest lots with their tidy lawns and their nicely swept porches. What a nice little place for my dad to live. What a thought. For then I realized that it would now also, become—a nice little place for him to die as well.

Well, here we were. As my personal taxi came to a halt and I slowly emerged from the car, I paused to glance at the outside of my dad's tiny little home with its mailbox standing proudly at attention and its neatly groomed flower beds ready for inspection. The front porch was blanketed with an immaculate deep green indoor-outdoor carpeting that also covered three little steps that led to the driveway where we stood. Awnings that wore their stripes proudly—discretely shaded the windows. Yup, this was the place. This was my father's barracks with all its treasures ready for his departure. And just up those steps and beyond that door was my dad, waiting anxiously for me to arrive. Now, I really *did* want to throw up. Either that or run screaming all the way back home just as fast as my cowardly little legs would carry me. But I didn't. Nope I surely did not. Instead, I said my good-byes to my friend, making promises to call soon, took a deep breath as I jerked my trillion-pound suitcase from the truck—and headed on up the steps. What in the hell had I put in there anyway? God only knew, which leads us into another valuable lesson to be learned from these experiences. Don't ever pack your suitcase while in shock. You are liable to end up with all shoes and no underwear.

As my friend drove away, I paused on the first step, taking a moment to cast a final wave, before I turned once again and faced the terror before me. I then took another deep breath and up the second step I went to his little front porch. I took it real well too. Seeing that there was only one more step before I would be standing directly at his front door, I truly couldn't understand why my legs were so wobbly.

What in hell's tarnation had I been thinking anyway? That maybe this would be easy? No, of course not. I knew this journey would be far from easy.

All right then, what? Perhaps I thought I would open the door to find him sprawled out on the floor never to awaken again? For crying out loud, can you believe that? Well, of course you can. This is me we're talking about. Nonetheless, I just couldn't open that door.

What if he had lost more weight? What if he was really sick? Oh, that's good. Like he wasn't really sick. OK then, what if he looks so bad that I gasp when I see him, scaring the holy living hoopla right out of the both of us? Not to worry. I would simply have to keep my composure. Yup, it was more than clear to me that the dreaded what ifs were back again and in full force. So I got to thinking. What if there was one of those great big whopping California earthquakes right at that very moment that would have, in fact, knocked me right off that front porch, cracking my head open on the pavement leaving me dead—never having to face the reality of walking through that door? What a mouse! What– A–Mouse! And with that little thought in tow, I simply reached forward to open the door when I stopped dead in my tracks. Holy crap! A most horrendous thought smacked me back down the step from whence I had just come and left me breathless. Had he even told his wife I was coming, because I sure as hell hadn't. Oh–my–heck! The wicked witch probably had no clue I was coming to stay. Huh, that would teach her not to engage in conversation with me when I called, which we would never have to worry about again, once this little episode was over with anyway. However, I surely didn't know that little ditty at the time. Yup, I'd betcha a dime to a doughnut hole that my dad never even bothered to tell her I was coming. And that little thought, my friends, gave me both the courage and strength to walk back up those steps and open that sliding glass door with a most Cheshire cat smile on my cute little unwhiskered face.

As I slid the door to my left, I had to push the curtains out of my way to walk through the opening and as I did, the sheer panels brushed against my face, welcoming the smell of my father's home to my senses. *Pipe tobacco. Borkum Riff.*

I slowly entered the dwelling that would come to be my home for the next three weeks and as I did the first sight to my tired and wandering eyes was the man who just had to be the world's oldest and most tired Captain Kangaroo fan of all times.

There he sat, Indian style in his big recliner, wrapped in a blanket, smoking his pipe, with headphones wrapped around his ears, watching TV.

There was smoke coming out of the pipe. That was a good sign. At least he was breathing. His eyes lit up like sparklers the minute he saw me as he tried to stand up and fumbled around so as not to get his feet caught up in the blanket—took a couple of steps forward—with his arms extended and with that big, happy, wonderful smile that only my dad could portray, he very softly said, "Hi, Baaaby Doll," which was followed by one of the tightest hugs I think he had ever given me.

My luggage fell to the floor, as I wrapped my arms around his frail little body closing my eyes, which were stinging from the moisture of my broken heart. What was happening here? He was so very thin. His beautiful head of thick black hair had gray patches sneaking around in various places. But at that moment, these things just didn't seem to matter. This was my warm, darling and charming little dad and his arms were wrapped so very tightly around my body that if the world had ended at that very moment, rest assured my every want and need in my whole entire life would have just been fulfilled.

"You look good," I muffled into his neck. Oh geeze, what in the heck did I say that for?

"Oh, I feel fine," he said.

Well that's just great! I'll be going now, nice seeing ya. Thanks for the hug. Hate to smooch and run but I have got much better things to do than stand here looking at a shell of the man who used to be my father.

The conversation began slowly as he told me I could put my things anywhere I felt comfortable putting them. Problem was, I felt comfortable putting them back at home, safe under my bed where I, myself, would like to be and stay for the next decade. On the other hand, just as I bent over to pick up my suitcase, I caught a glimpse of *her* out of the corner of my eye. She was sitting on the couch just to the right of the doorway. No, I decided. I wanted to stay after all. At this point, she had become a bigger mystery than my father's illness. She didn't stand up right away, however, she did greet me and announced that she had only learned I was coming that very morning. Perfect!

"Well, geeze," I said, "I talk to you on the phone just about every day. I assumed you knew." Perhaps if you could do more than just breathe into the phone we may have gotten to this subject. No—let me rephrase that; perhaps if you gave a damn— oh, never mind.

She then, as if forced out of common consideration, stood up and we insecurely embraced—well, sort of, and as I stood there with my arms loosely around her and hers the same around me, I watched my dad as he shook his head from side to side and walked back toward the bedroom. What in the hell was that, I wondered? Come to think of it, I had a question for her anyway. Seeing that my dad had so conveniently left the room, I took the opportunity to ask the burning question that had been eating at me since my phone conversation with that dumb nurse person. I took a step back from her and focused my gaze upon hers, under that notorious wide-brimmed pointy black hat. OK, she wasn't really wearing a hat but it sure seemed so as I stood before her. What in the hell kind of wife was she anyway? Why hadn't she, herself, arranged for someone to come in and take care of my dad? Yup, that's exactly what I wanted to know. However, all in due time, my little pretty, all–in–due–time.

After we exchanged our hellos, and I moved my suitcase from one spot to the next in my father's tiny living room about six times, finally leaving it sitting exactly where I had dropped it in the first place, my simple-minded get–to–the–point little dad, wanted to do just that! Get to the point, as he came back from the bedroom with his blanket in tow. He was cold, he announced. Cold? For crying out loud it was only October and this was Southern California!

I hadn't been there twenty minutes before he wanted to start discussing funeral arrangements and his will! Leave it to my dad. How about a cup of coffee first? Never mind the coffee. How about a good stiff shot of gasoline or maybe something a little stronger, like cyanide. I felt pushed, hurried, and, quite frankly, like I wanted to scream. It's like, when you're standing over the edge of a swimming pool on a hot summer day with your toes just barely touching the water, contemplating jumping in. You know you'll jump sooner or later but you just want to wait for the right time until you're ready. So you stand there, minding your own business, enjoying the moment, perhaps even humming a little tune—when out of nowhere—some idiot comes along and pushes you! Well, that was exactly how I felt. And—I believe, if I'm not mistaken—I just called my dad an idiot.

I wasn't ready to jump! Yes, I came there to dive in but I would have liked to have had the time to at least think about it first. You know, get used to the water a little. Dip my toe in, swish it back and forth.

Not my dad. He obviously felt an urgency to get these matters discussed and now!

Well, cow crud, not me! I was still waiting for that shot of cyanide! But seeing that I had already been pushed, I felt like I might as well at least begin treading water. I really didn't have much of a choice. I didn't like it, but I would do it.

Again, there I was, wanting to do things my own way, on my own terms within my own time frame. Gosh I hate it when I do that! As I sat there looking at my dad, I had to get it through my head once and for all, that what I wanted was not important anymore and it probably never would be again. And it's not that what I wanted wasn't important to my dad—it was. But the simple fact was that the things on his mind at that moment were *more* important to him. Thus began a whole new meaning to the word unselfish.

He had me cornered. No kids, no phones, no distractions at all. He had obviously come to the time in his situation to admit to himself that it was over. And it was equally important for him to say it out loud to someone who could and would receive it properly. And that ever so lucky someone was me. Remember? I had qualified myself for that lovely position while he had been at my house. And I guess I had now proven, that by being there at *his* house, I was truly worthy of this responsibility. Yup, things were already becoming extremely complicated and I hadn't even been there thirty minutes!

How in the cat doo had I gotten myself into this mess? Perhaps by being there for him when he needed me the most? *Well, I'll be go to hell John!* And let's face it; if the time to talk about these things had been left up to me, I would still be sitting there to this very day—wondering just how in the heck I was going to begin the conversation. It's sad but it's true, folks. So very painfully and embarrassingly true. So, I got myself a cup of coffee, as there was no gasoline or cyanide available—that I could see anyway—and I sat down on the floor of my father's living room across from him in front of his coffee table and I prepared myself for a long and enjoyable conversation.

Now, we didn't talk for very long that evening, but we did break the ice just a little. And what glaziers were left would certainly not have time to melt before I was caught up in another world that my father would once more create for me in the way that only he could.

The subjects we did cover that evening, however, were more than just important to my dad, simply because they weren't just subjects to him, they were his "secret desires." Secret desires that he obviously felt were vitally important and had to be discussed at that very moment in time. Funny how a simple task like dying can shake up the secret desires in the best of us now, isn't it? Well—not really—oh, forget it!

He began with his most intimate wishes. Wishes such as, how he wanted to be buried. Now, this might come as a shock to all of you, which I can completely understand, so brace yourselves once again, my friends, for another silly idea that had been running around inside my dad's little storytelling head.

My simple-minded, clothing-hating little dad wanted to be buried in the nude. Now, he had been saying that as far back as I could remember. But I will share with you that I wasn't exactly sure if he'd been serious until that very moment. And let me tell you, he was serious. And why, we might be asking ourselves at that very moment, did he feel the need to tell me that he wanted to be buried in the nude? Well, two reasons that I could figure. One, of course, being for the simple reason that he felt that he came into this world nude so he figured (in his own words) that it was "a compliment to God himself to leave this old world the very same way he had entered it." And the other was, I guess he thought he'd better tell me right then and there, just in case he died in the middle of the night. Otherwise, I have no damned clue as to why.

I feel it's important to share with all of you that this was only the beginning of several conversations that created the memories that are so special to me now. So I'm glad he shared them with me the way he did, *when* he did—well, now anyway. However then, at the time, I still couldn't believe we had to talk about it. He was such a silly little man.

Now, not only did he share his wishes with me that first night but he also made some requests. Special requests that would prove to be very important to my sisters after this whole damned mess was over with. More coffee!

You see, he had been a longtime fan of old country-western music, and he had specific albums that he wanted to go to each daughter. His Hank Williams collection was his most treasured and it was imperative that it went to the daughter who he felt would appreciate it the most and so on and so on. And, yes, he just had to tell me these things right then and there. So he did. We discussed who would get what albums for the reasons that only my dad could justify. And while he spoke, I became engrossed in his every word as my mind began to wander. I was hearing the sound of his voice but the words were not clear to me as my thoughts and my heart were focused on the face of the man who had always been my daddy. I found myself wondering once again, just what in the hell was happening here? How could this be real? And those eyes, those tender, caring, understanding, eyes that had once cried for the abuse suffered by someone else's child. Yes, I thought, those eyes could still hold a sparkle, even as he spoke of things that were too painful to bear. I wanted to reach out and kiss his soft wrinkled little face and ask him to stop. But this was so very important to him. He was displaying such bravery. He was saying to me, "See, I have accepted this and I want you to accept this too."

Well, my friends, I couldn't! And I wouldn't! And that was that! He could just go right on ahead and keep talking about whatever tickled his little fancy but I absolutely refused to accept that fact that I was losing my dad! I just knew I'd come up with something before he died—some incredible, miraculous way to save him. But for now, I'd just let him go right on along sharing all he had to share. I needed to be aware of it all anyway for when the time came that he really was dying. Like when he was a lot older and grayer and not just seventy-two.

He was growing tired now. I noticed that it had become a real task for him to speak for a long period of time. His speech was becoming thick and slurred and his eyes were growing heavy. I was so very saddened, as I sat there with the realization of my father's illness bearing down so heavily on my very soul.

I suggested that it might be time for him to go to bed now. We could talk more about these things tomorrow or the next day or never would have suited me just fine.

Yes, he was tired and as he started to get up and out of his recliner, I truly do believe that my heart may have actually stopped momentarily, as the blanket fell from around his shoulders revealing his bony naked neck and chest and immediately I noticed a peculiar marking on his right breast!

I then thought that I just might actually throw up as I focused in on the lump that was protruding from beneath his chest. It was black. It looked just like a bruise. I had seen it before, however, I didn't remember it being that large. And what in the hell was that lump protruding from his neck? My God, it had to be the size of a tangerine!

As he headed for the sink to get one last drink of water before bedtime, my eyes followed him with extreme compassion and sorrow as it took about all the strength he had, just to get to the kitchen and by the time he got there he was completely winded. My heart was breaking. This was it! My dad was deteriorating before my very eyes and there wasn't a damned thing in this world that I could do about it. But little did I know, the worst was yet to come, and not a thing in this world could have prepared me for what was about to happen.

As he stood over the sink drinking his water he then began to choke! No, it was more like a cough. No, it was more like a gag. Nothing came up, mind you, however he continued to display this horrible occurrence for about five minutes.

Well, you can just about imagine what I was doing by that time, now, can't you? Or then again, maybe you can't because I simply did nothing— absolutely nothing—and mostly because my feet couldn't move. They were frozen. So were my hands. And so was my shattered heart.

He was hunched over the kitchen sink holding his stomach with one hand and with the other he was signaling for me to stay put. No need to worry there. I wasn't going anywhere.

I glanced over at the witch for an explanation. My eyes were wide with a question. But she didn't return my gaze. She simply sat on that couch in the same exact spot where she had been perched all evening and stared at the floor.

Finally it seemed to subside for the most part and he straightened up a bit, looked at me with a bewildered kind of smirk, shaking his head slowly from side to side as if to say, *Isn't this just the darndest thing you have ever witnessed?*

Well, as a matter of fact it most certainly and most painfully was. And afterward, he never even thought to give me any sort of an explanation as to what in the hell I *had* just witnessed! He simply began his shuffled journey back to his bedroom, with me right behind him every step of the way.

I pulled his bed down for him and asked him if he needed anything, anything at all, like maybe a pistol or a razor blade of sorts? No, he was just fine. He just wanted to go to bed.

As I stood there staring at him, watching him get settled in, I was totally mesmerized and I realized I had to ask a question that would keep me up all night if I didn't ask it right then and there. So as he was stooped over, fluffing his little pillows, I asked, "Dad, how long have you been gagging like that?" He finished his little bedtime ritual and then turned and sat down on the edge of the bed with his hands interlocked together and his head down. He then looked up at me as though he were ashamed and through squinty eyes he said, "Oh—I guess for about a week now."

Alrighty, I thought, now we're getting somewhere. I had no clue where—but somewhere. I then, taking my time, speaking slowly and clearly, asked another puzzling question that would surely have made me a suicidal maniac by morning if I didn't get an answer right then and there. I began really gently with, "Dad, how long has it been since you have eaten?"

He was sitting in the same position so he raised his head again with the same look in his eyes and said, "Oh, about a week I guess, something like that."

A week?! A WEEK?! Geezus criminy!!! People don't just go a whole week without eating! And they sure as hell don't take it so stinking lightly! Do they? Well, do they? Well, guess again, little missy! They sure as hell do if they have terminal cancer. Yesiree, they most certainly do! And what's more, they really don't give a fat rat's patoot about it either! Because food is the very last stinking thing on their minds!

He was still sitting there in the same position as I continued our harrowing conversation. I wondered why he was sitting there like that but I didn't pursue that wonder. I had more important things on my mind, like how I was gonna get home!

I continued on. "Dad, are you hungry?"

He looked up at me again and very matter-of-factly said, "No, not really." What in the hell did he mean by that? What kind of answer was no, not really? You're either hungry or you're not! Aren't you? Oh, this was not good. Not good at all.

He then asked me not to worry. Oh, no stinking problem. I'll just go to bed with visions of cute little sugar plumbs dancing in my already nutty head, and you just go right on ahead and continue to starve yourself to stinking death before my very eyes, you dumb old simpleminded dad, you! Ninny! Ninny! Ninny!

So what did I say? Well, by golly, I let him have it! Immediately I came back with the only thing I could think of. "Dad, I have to worry, I love you. You're the only dad I have." Boy that was showing him! Thompson's colt! Thompson's colt!

He just sat there, looking up at me. And then he smiled a most wonderful smile before he replied with, "Well, I love you too, Baby Doll, but worrying about the situation isn't going to change anything at all. It is—what it is."

Hey, why hadn't I thought of that? And hadn't I heard that somewhere before? Yes, I believe I had. And what's more, he was exactly right. I didn't like it much but he was as right as rain. And I did worry. And my worrying did not, in fact, change a darned thing. But you see, I had to do something and as it turned out, the worrying would not stop until the day my father died. And when I think of all the time I spent just simply worrying about a situation that I could do absolutely nothing about, I wish I had a nickel—well, you know how it goes.

As I helped him lay down, pulling the covers up over his skinny little legs, I replied with, "Well, maybe worrying about the situation won't change anything but just the same, I do worry." Oh, that's good, great comeback, you idiot! How poetic of me!

He answered me just one more time, before he drifted off to sleep with, "Uh huh, I know, dear."

That's it? Uh, huh, I know, dear. Great! Now, what in the hell was that supposed to mean? And there I stood. Staring at him in disbelief while he was peacefully drifting off into slumberland. I continued to stand there for quite some time, watching and listening to him sleep.

Had he always been able to fall asleep so fast? Never mind that, what about that heavy breathing? My God, it hurt just to watch him. He was taking such deep breaths and that wasn't even the worst part of this whole damned scenario either! There were twelve-to fifteen-second intervals in between each of those breaths. Yes, my friends, I had just been introduced to the silent killer. I couldn't see it, but I could sure as hell see what it was doing and I don't mind telling you that it matter-of-factly made me sick.

I realized over a period of about ten minutes, that standing there watching him sleep wasn't getting me anywhere at all really, however, without my even knowing it, I was slowly being educated, and I can tell you, that there's no learning that can compare to the hands-on training that I was about to receive, and this was only night number one!

I turned to tiptoe out of the room to leave him to his much needed rest, when I stopped short for just a moment, as I noticed something on the wall next to the door that I hadn't seen in years. It was a painting. A most wonderful painting that had always hung in my parents bedroom, and I supposed it had now always hung in my dad's bedroom throughout the years as well.

The painting was of a cowboy sleeping on a bed of clouds with his head rested up against his saddle with his hat pulled down over his eyes. Above him was a beautiful clouded woman riding a running horse, with her hair flowing freely behind her as though he were dreaming of her. The painting was in its original frame which was braided with rope from a lariat. I simply stood and stared at it for quite some time as I could recall its presence in all of our homes of happiness from long ago. Since it was hung on the wall directly in front of the foot of his bed, I assumed it was the first thing he saw each and every morning when he awoke and probably the last thing he saw each and every night as he turned in to go to sleep. *That is, until his nit wit daughter had arrived.* I loved that painting and only because my dad had always loved it so. Now keep this little thought in tow my friends, because just like everything else we are about to discover, *that* painting will hold quite an element of surprise for me down this old story road. Yes it most mysteriously and undeniably will!

Gently closing the door behind me, I had thousands of questions running throughout my mind. But it didn't take long for me to toss them aside for the time being. I'd had too much sorrow to deal with for one night already.

Just a couple of steps from the bedroom door and I was standing in the living room. I walked over and plopped myself down on the couch, next to the witch, and said nothing, finally taking the time to realize how very exhausted I had become—and as I sat there in the silence of my warm and comforting surroundings, my eyes began to explore my newly found home.

Over in the left corner of my dad's neat and tidy living room, sat a hug, big screen TV. I then remembered when he had bought it and what a big deal it had been for him to actually own something like that. He had called me up and told me all about it with the excitement of a small child on an early Christmas morning. Geeze, he got excited over the darndest things. And I don't mind telling you that the memory in itself didn't touch my heart even half as much as the sight that sat on top of that TV. Nope, not even half as much.

I sat staring in total bewilderment at the treasures on top of his big screen as I recognized them to be trinkets from our childhood displayed proudly as if they had been placed there to deliberately spark a memory. What in the hell was going on here?

There was a plastic replica of Donald Duck that had been on my youngest sister's seventh birthday cake. My word, it had been years since I'd seen that. I then wondered how he had obtained it, and a comical visual came into view as I imagined my dad walking into our home and sliding that silly thing down his pants. Must have held some kind of a special memory for him. The divorce had been final almost six years by then. I began to think about how much this would mean to my youngest sister when I suddenly remembered a phone call I had received from my dad in July, the minute he had returned home from accepting her wedding invitation in person.

He was crying hysterically and I was very afraid that something had happened on his long drive home. He kept attempting to speak through sporadic sobs and I kept saying, "What is it, Dad, what's wrong?"

When he had finally gained enough control to speak clearly, I was able to understand that the reason behind his tears was his concern regarding my sister's disappointment in the event that something might happen to him before the wedding. He was saying, "This means the world to her and if something goes wrong before she walks down that aisle, she will never be able to get over it."

I tried to reassure him as much as I could in between my own sobs, that nothing would happen that wasn't meant to be, and now I had the precious memory of that wedding to accompany the memory of my dad's deep and genuine concern for his youngest daughter's happiness.

You know, that memory made me painfully aware of how very quickly yesterday becomes a part of our past. Sad, isn't it.

As my eyes began to focus back in on the present, I noticed to the right of Donald Duck sat a plastic bust of Mickey Mouse that had belonged to my second-to-the-youngest sister. I recalled a picture in my memory of her chewing on its nose, realizing that it wasn't good enough as I got up off the couch and walked over to it. Yup, there they were. Tooth marks where she had scratched the paint right off its nose. Oh, how I wished at that moment that my sisters and I were all young again. Yes, I knew it was impossible, but that surely didn't stop the want inside me. No, it surely and sadly did not.

As I gently ran my finger across the tip of Mickey's nose I noticed that directly in front of him was a wedding picture of my oldest sister and her husband. And although they had been married for only a couple of years at that time, the picture seemed ancient to my eyes.

To the right of the TV set was a stereo cabinet, which contained my dad's record player, and his much cherished albums, and on top of it were more treasures.

A small Polaroid picture of a man in a nice suit shaking my dad's hand and handing him a miniature grandfather clock. My dad was wearing a pair of blue jeans, a white T-shirt and suspenders. Surprise, surprise. It wasn't hard to tell that the picture had been taken the year before. My dad still had a belly and some meat on his bones.

Beside that picture was another picture of a cake, which portrayed a man in a pair of overalls holding a broom. Across the top of the cake it read, "Congratulations, Eddie on Twenty-Five Years of Keeping it Kleen!" Behind the pictures, stood three bowling trophies, all from various bowling leagues of long ago and all with his name neatly engraved on a tiny flat plate of gold.

To the right of the bowling trophies sat a baseball. A most wonderful home run baseball from the Babe Ruth League of 1991 with my second oldest son's signature scribbled across the center. Oh, how my dad loved those late-night summer games. He would hoop and holler with the best of them. By God, that was his grandson!

As I stood there reminiscing, my eyes then wandered across the living room, to the wall leading into the kitchen. There, directly above the light switch, hung a small bulletin board with a calendar and several business cards strewn about fastened securely with tiny different colored pins and up in the right-hand corner of this neatly kept message center, from one of those pins, hung a small brown rubber monkey.

This monkey had belonged to my middle sister when she too was very small. She had bitten off the tip of the monkey's tail one afternoon while riding home in my father's car after an ice-cream outing, and as I walked over to check out my memory it was coarsely confirmed, which led me to wonder why in the hell my sisters chewed so damned much!

Not wanting to admit it to myself, I realized that I was indeed searching everywhere I could possibly think of for something that reminded my dad of me. But there was nothing. Not one single solitary thing! I couldn't find one single bit of evidence that could point to me as this man's daughter.

My heart was destroyed and breaking as I sadly walked back over to the couch, stepping on my lip every inch of the way wondering why. Why didn't my dad want a remembrance of me anywhere? Geeze, I was the one he talked to all the time. I was the one who never forgot Father's Day or his birthday or any other old day for that matter. I was the one–who–was–there! I–was–the–one. I'm the one he had chosen to spend his final days with. He didn't need a remembrance of me anywhere because he damned well knew that in the end, I, as always, would be there.

Well he must have thought that he was pretty darned smart. He knew all along that I couldn't have left him to die alone. As a matter of fact, he probably knew it before I did. And I'll share with you that by the time he finally died, he did share that little secret with me and then some.

Well I'll be that monkey's uncle. What a nice way to end my first evening at my dad's house, I thought, as I smugly sat there giving all of my newly discovered treasures one last glance before bedtime. As I lay there trying to steady the beat of my heart, a most sad and discomforting thought came to mind.

So, this was how it all ended. With your name on a couple of ancient bowling trophies and a picture of some guy, who no doubt makes three times the amount of money that you do, handing you a miniature grandfather clock for twenty-five years of keeping it kleen. Well, howdeedoo!

Gosh that's sad, isn't it? Well now, yes it would be if that really was the way it ends. But it isn't. Nope, not at all, because, you see, I believe that every person on this earth has touched someone else in a special certain way and because of that touch, we who remain behind, will in some way be just a little bit different. Now, that's a very pleasant thought, isn't it? Well, it certainly was a very pleasant thought for me as I sat there in my father's living room that evening. As a matter of fact, that thought gave me a lot of comfort so I decided to tuck it away safely into my bag of survival techniques so that I could retrieve it when the need arose. And believe me, my friends, that need would definitely arise and sooner than I could ever have dreamed.

The witch was still sitting on the sofa with broomstick in hand, right where I had left her before my walk down epiphany lane, although she was looking at me more intently now than she had been earlier. I wandered over and sat down next to her on the sofa. And—there I sat without one word being spoken between the two of us. Crap, did she ever initiate a conversation?

I finally cleared my throat and asked how she was. I didn't really care but the environment had produced some extremely uncomfortable silence so I asked anyway.

Oh, she was fine, she said. More silence until I finally asked, "How long has he been gagging like that?"

She sat there for a few seconds before she answered me with, "Oh, probably about two weeks."

"Two weeks." I asked her, "Why?" She didn't know.

"Well, what does the doctor say?" I asked. She didn't know.

"Has anyone told the doctor?" I asked. She didn't know that either.

OK, just exactly what *did* she know? I mean after all, did she not live with him? And maybe my dad would be more inclined to share things with her if she would take that hideous hat off and put her broomstick down!

"Your father does not inform me of what goes on during his visits with the doctor," she finally said.

A little animosity, I thought? Perhaps.

I pursued the subject anyway.

"Why not," I asked.

She pursed her lips and answered me with, "I don't know, I guess he doesn't feel it's any of my business. He tells you more than he tells me."

OK, now I was really uncomfortable.

Do you ask, I said? "Because I have to ask him. He won't just volunteer information. He doesn't want to worry anyone," I defended.

She was silent and I was uncomfortable again.

"Are you guys OK?" I asked. She squirmed before she answered.

"Well, I guess. Your father just doesn't share a lot," she said.

Hum, where had I heard that before? I, myself, had no problem communicating with him. Yes, I had to pry and poke and prod to get some things out of him, but perseverance always prevailed with my father. I didn't know where to take the conversation from there. I could feel her anger but I didn't know what to do with it or even if I wanted to do anything with it at all. I had just arrived and the last thing I wanted to do was get into it with my dad's beloved wife. After all, I just knew beyond a shadow of a doubt that she had a dungeon somewhere in that house stuffed with flying monkeys and a big huge-ass hour glass just waiting for me.

She interrupted my thought with a statement.

"You seem to be the only one he cares to share anything with at all," she said. "He's mad at me because of my son. He doesn't like the fact that I help him out."

Damien! I knew that son of a gun would come up again. Wow, this was none of my business. I didn't want to know any of this crap. Especially concerning this son of hers who was the very one who took a swing at my dad years ago.

OK, so how do I get out of this conversation? I wasn't about to give her any sympathy concerning Damien. Now it was I who was squirming.

"My dad doesn't have any respect for those who don't help themselves, that's all. He is from the old school and he believes that your son is old enough to be on his own without his mother's help." I had probably already said way too much. I could tell by the way she was calling for those monkeys to come and scoop me up. Get her! Get her and bring her to me now!!!!

"No," she said. "He has always hated my son. It wouldn't matter what he did."

"Do you really believe that?" I asked.

"Yes," she quipped with the insinuation that I was some kind of an idiot.

"I don't think my dad knows how to hate anyone," I quipped back.

"Well then, you don't know your father like I do," she said smugly.

OK, this had gone far enough. I wasn't about to sit there and argue with her over my father's feelings or lack there of. Where was the Tin Man? Where was Toto? Never mind that. Where in the hell was that proverbial pail of water? I'd put an end to this crud once and for all.

However, I didn't. Nope, instead, I just sat there in silence. I truly didn't want to speak to her at that moment nor any moment in the near or far future for that matter. Perhaps I didn't know my dad like she did. Perhaps she was right. And—perhaps that was because I had never put myself in a situation such as that with my dad. And, God willing, I never would.

Finally, after sitting there and allowing her to feel smug about getting the last word, I ended the silence with a statement.

"Well," I began, "I may not know my dad like you do, And for that I am thankful. I have never known my dad to hate anyone. Disrespect— yes, but hate— never. And if he disrespects your son, I am sorry for him."

I could have taken it further but I didn't. I just couldn't. My father was dying for heck's sake and I really didn't give a rat's hat if he did or did not hate her son. I, myself, didn't particularly care for him and I had never even met him! I was tired. I had had a long day and I didn't want to talk to her anymore. She would just have to go scare some Munchkins or something. I was obviously no match for her. Not on this night anyway.

I finally broke the silence by sharing with her that I was tired and I needed some sleep.

She said nothing.

I really was feeling a little sleepy after all of the bonding we had just gone through. So I decided it was time to find a place of comfortableness for myself in this new haven that had temporarily become my home. And I do mean home! It seems my dad had replaced my mom quite conveniently. I would have to commend him for a job well done when I saw him the next day. Great job, Dad! You found someone just exactly like Mom!!!!

And as I looked around for space to call my own, I spied a most remarkable object.

Across from the couch where I had been sitting, there was a gadget of a sort. A futon.

Now a futon is certainly not your run-of-the-mill kind of gadget, mind you. For those of you who have never seen one, I'll explain: A futon is a small couch by day and a sleeper by night. Simple enough, I suppose.

My dad thought it to be one of the coolest things he had ever gotten his hands on, and that, my friends, as we already know, is what classified it as a gadget.

I decided that cool or not, it was definitely time to get some sleep, if I was going to make my dad's early morning wake-up call, so I scooted on over to this eighth wonder of the world and began tugging on the heavy mattress that had been in disguise by day.

Good Lord, that thing was heavy! It took all of the strength I had just to pull it off its wooden base. Kind of a cute idea, I thought, but it could stand some perfecting in the opinion of a scrawny woman.

OK, now all I had to do was find an overnight home for the stuffed bear and the monkey that I had just so gently uprooted. Huh, funny how I didn't even think twice about the stuffed animals that resided in my father's living room. I suppose that's because they were just part of the family. Always had been as a matter of fact. You see, my dad not only loved stuffed animals, but he spoke to them too. I mean, after all, just because they came alive only at night, didn't mean they couldn't understand what was going on during the day. Duh! And just as all of these silly little things were going through my just as silly little mind, I wondered when my dad had removed that two-foot teddy bear from the passenger side of his pickup truck. Yes, indeedy, folks, my dad drove around town with that teddy bear strapped in a seat belt just as though he were his companion and that's because, well, I suppose he was! And why, you might be asking yourselves. Well, I'll tell you why. Because there was always a chance that while they were out, putzing around town, they just might happen upon a car with a kid in the back seat. And this would prompt my dad to reach his right arm over and behind that bear to lift its arm to the window to wave at whatever kid would be lucky enough to see it. That's why. Oh, how my dad got a kick out of that little prank. He always proudly proclaimed how *all* kids *always* waved back. Because *they believed*—and I think this is where we came in—and so the story goes.

Needless to say, I couldn't just toss them off the futon. That was their home!

So, standing there holding both the monkey and the bear in my arms, searching the room for a place to put them—I decided to—well, she was still sitting down or I just might have found a real good place for the both of them.

However, I simply decided that they could sleep with me! Who would ever know? I mean besides all of you? Oh, and that wretched witch person. However, she had suddenly gotten up and headed toward the bedroom anyway. Funny, she didn't even kiss me good night.

Yup, this was going to be one hell of a ride—that was for darned sure. I hadn't even been there a day yet and already I had made myself an enemy but I didn't really care about her anyway. I wasn't there for her. I was there for my dad. And I would have to stay focused on that. Boy howdy, would I.

After I had nestled myself and my bed partners in, one to sleep on each side of me, I then had to find a blanket of some kind. I gazed over in the direction of the recliner and voila! There laid my dad's snuggle blanket. That would do just fine. Now for a pillow. Let's see, if I were my dad where would I keep a spare pillow? Ah ha! Right beside the recliner on the opposite side, next to the wall. That wasn't so hard, which simply meant that Thompson's colt would just have to remain the dumbest one after all—for the time being anyway.

OK, now all I had to do was lower my adrenalin so I could get some sleep. I lay down beside my furry buddies, covered all of us up and proceeded to do just that—get some shut-eye.

I had been laying there for about fifteen minutes before I started to drift off to dreamland when suddenly I felt something. What in the heck was that? Well, quite frankly I had no clue. Something startled me awake and that something could only be described as weight on my back!

I sat straight up on top of my futon mattress and proceeded to frantically look around the room for a cat that my dad would never own!

Now, I was not the type of person to jump to conclusions without a logical explanation and seeing that I was definitely alone it must have been something that fell from the ceiling fan that was hanging directly over my head. (Comforting thought in itself.) So I calmly (actually calmly is putting it rather lightly) began beating my bedding half to death, searching for a foreign object of some kind, any kind, that could explain the sensation that I knew I had just experienced.

Nothing. Alrighty—must have been my imagination. Lord knows I have an active one. I looked at my furry little friends and wondered. *No, that's kid stuff you doo-doo brain.*

As I made a second attempt to lie down and get some sleep, a horrible thought crossed my busy little mind. It could have been a spider!

All right, that's just fine and jim-dandy. Let's just forget for one tiny heart-stopping little moment that I am deathly afraid of those eightlegged hairy little beasts, not to mention the fact that had it, in fact, been a spider, it would had to have been wearing five-pound cleats and headgear, you pea brain!

OK, I'd simply just chalk this one up as being overly tired and exhausted and having one hell of a wild imagination. Oh, that would work. Uh huh, that would work just fine.

As I lay back down to try to attempt just one more time to get my much-needed rest, I tried to identify the feeling I had just experienced. Well, my friends, I couldn't. All I knew for sure, was it had felt like something heavy on my back. Not very comforting, however, that was the only honest explanation I could come up with.

It wasn't long before I had drifted off to sleep again, when once more I felt the same sensation as before but this time, I knew exactly what it was. I could clearly and unmistakably identify it as being a hand on my back!

I mean to tell you, I shot up off that futon like a rocket! Which left me standing in the middle of the living room frantically looking around like I had just lost a thousand-dollar bill. It would have been some good footage for someone's home videos, I'm sure.

Nothing! Positively—absolutely nothing!

Now look, I thought—I *know*—that what I felt was a hand. There was no one else in the room with me, but I know that is exactly what I felt. So, searching for an answer, I tiptoed back to my dad's room to make sure he was asleep.

I very quietly opened the door and peeked in. Yup, he was asleep alrighty and what did I actually think *that* was going to prove? At seventytwo years old and riddled with cancer there is no way he could've come in and touched me and gotten back into bed without my seeing him. Not as fast as I had shot up off that mattress! Hell, at sixteen with a track medal he couldn't have done it, you bubble brain. The witch was asleep as well. Sure, like she came in to the living room with a change of heart and tried to wake me by rubbing my back and then had a change of her darkened heart and flew back into the bedroom on her broomstick before I could see her. You know, I really needed a life.

Slowly, I walked back into the living room and the first thing I did was turn on a light. Always good to be able to see where you're going, you know, not to mention the fact that monsters don't come out in the light.

In a haze of bewilderment and disbelief, I sat down on the couch. Just exactly what in the Sam hell was going on here? I began to try and reason with myself. OK, I know what I felt was a hand on my back. I also know that I am the only one here. Uh huh, well then, that should explain everything, now, shouldn't it?

I was, to say the least, scared half out of my mind, which didn't leave me much to work with. I didn't know what was going on. I didn't know how to make sense of all of this. However, in the midst of all of this *not* knowing, I *did* know one thing. I sure as hell wasn't getting back on that mattress to go to sleep! I would just simply pick up my pillow, blanket, and my furry little friends—and sleep on the couch. That's exactly what I was gonna do! Just as soon as I could muster up enough courage to get up off the sofa.

One thing I knew for sure though, was I had to get some sleep. Morning at my dad's house came very early and I was exhausted, long before I had gotten there, as it was.

So—I very leisurely got up off the sofa and, looking around every step of the way, I slowly and cautiously walked over to the mattress and, with a case of chills that would have given a goose a good run for its money, I leaned over, picked up the blanket, pillow, and friends with one fell swoop and with one incredible but cowardly leap, I was back on the couch and feeling like I was about to succumb to a heart attack. And I sat on that couch, knees up to my chin with the pillow by my side and the blanket tucked tightly in my fists, which were knuckled up around my face, and I continued to sit there until I finally fell asleep. My reprieve from the unexplained didn't last but a couple of hours before I was awakened by my dad's quiet morning sounds.

I had somehow managed to lie down during my sleep, so as I heard him stirring around in the dark of the living room, I first realized that he had turned off the light that I had so bravely left on. Dumb-ass! He would definitely have a word with me about that come daylight. Power bills aren't cheap, you know. Then I wondered if I should get up with him, or just continue sleeping. I focused my eyes on the clock that I recognized as the one he had been given for twenty-five years of "keeping it kleen" and I needed a double take. It was only two o'clock in the flipping morning for crying out loud! What in the heck was he doing up that early?

I'm sure he was unaware that I was watching him as he gently packed his pipe full of that wonderful-smelling tobacco and proceeded to step over the mattress from hell so that he could sit down on the floor and—now what was he doing? Squinting, I watched as my quiet little moment-seeking dad opened the door to his stereo cabinet, plugged in his headphones and placed them on his head. He then leaned over to reach the glass doors, which harbored his treasured melodies and took out an album, gently set it on the turntable and then he flipped the slender lever to turn it on.

I continued to watch him with amazement as he sat Indian style on the floor in front of his stereo in the dark, taking short peaceful puffs off his pipe, enjoying his music, in the quiet of the morning.

Gosh, I thought, what simple pleasures my dad enjoyed and I so badly wanted to get up with him—but for the first time ever—it wasn't a good idea. This was how he had chosen to enjoy his final days. This was perhaps the only form of entertainment left for my simple-minded little dad. Well, except for maybe his shows or perhaps the late-night antics of his second-oldest daughter. Oh, how I wish to this day that I could witness his pleasures again. Oh, how I do so wish.

Well, I didn't fall back to sleep that morning after all. Instead—I chose to enjoy my dad from afar, so to speak, with the faint sounds of country-western music crackling from his headphones.

When the album had run through both sides, he quietly got up, took his headphones off, clicked his much-enjoyed gadget to the off position and wandered back toward his bedroom. As I continued to lay there very quietly and very still, as not to give myself away, I could hear him stirring around and I could hear him talking rather faintly. *What in the world was he saying?* This was very disturbing to me. I had never known my dad to talk to himself. But wait a minute; he wasn't just talking to himself, was he? No, he wasn't. He was having a conversation! I could hear the tone of his voice rising and falling. But he was whispering loudly and I didn't hear the witch.

What in the hell was going on now, for crying out loud? I swung my feet over my blanket, causing it to fall to the floor and I stood up, trying to lean toward the bedroom so that I could maybe hear just a little bit better.

Cow dung! Here he came! He was shuffling his way back into the living room!

I quietly but ever so swiftly jumped back onto the couch searching frantically for my blanket but it was too late. Before I knew it, he was standing directly in front of the coffee table, which was directly in front of the couch.

As I lay there with my eyes closed, trying to breathe real steady, he walked around the coffee table and was now standing directly over me! He stooped down and picked up my blanket and gently placed it over me. I stirred a little to make it look good, as he tucked it securely under my chin and around my shoulders, then my midsection, and finally my feet. He then leaned down and kissed my forehead before he turned and walked toward the kitchen.

I opened my eyes again, trying to secretly follow him with my gaze, which was now quickly puddling with tears. I had forgotten what it had been like to have my dad tuck me in. I had never expected to receive such a precious gift. I expected my visit to his home to be horrible. I expected my visit to be unbearable. I never could have imagined just exactly how valuable all of this would be until that very moment. I had been so worried about the pain my heart would suffer that I completely overlooked the treasures I would receive. And remember this, my friends, for someday your heart just might need a little advice.

I continued to listen to him as he filled his water glass and I heard him talking again and this time I could hear *exactly* what he was saying! It seemed to me that time stood completely still, as I clearly heard him whispering, "Yah, I know, OK, all right, yah, yah, OK."

I just absolutely could not believe what I was hearing and I didn't have enough time to even worry about it before he began to go through his sporadic ritual of gagging once again. Geeze, did this happen every single time he drank water? Should I get up and offer to help? No, you ninny, because don't you remember the last time? He wanted you to stay put.

So, I did nothing. Absolutely nothing. I just lay there listening to the heartbreaking sound of my father's body giving way to this dignityrobbing disease and as I lay there, in the dark, helpless to do anything at all, I began to get angry all over again.

This just wasn't fair! What could my quiet-time, loving, little dad have ever done in his life to deserve such torture? Gosh damn it! I just couldn't grasp what in the hell was going on here!

Problem was that I was trying to find reasons for a situation that had none.

Who's to say why certain things happen? I mean, I know we have doctors to explain *how* they happen, but *why* is a completely different issue, isn't it? Yes, it most certainly and sadly is. Which brings me to the brink of one of my opinions, once again.

I believe that we, as human beings all share a common illness. Yes, indeed, I sure do. It's known as the "it will never happen to me" syndrome. Now, most of you know about the syndrome I'm talking about, don't you? Oh, sure you do. It's the one where we continue to do dangerous things to our bodies, thinking the whole time that it will never happen to us. Well, I'm here to tell you that it most certainly *can* happen to us. However, I'm also here to tell you that it took me a lot longer than my first night with my dad to believe it.

You see, all of my life I had been a sun baby. Yes, I know what they say about sun tanning and the dangers but skin cancer only got the dumb people who didn't use protection, and besides I would have quit if I had ever noticed a mole out of place anyway. Because didn't people with skin cancer have terrible patches of rash-looking spots all over them? Geeze, you would think that once someone noticed something like *that* they would have it taken care of right away, wouldn't you? Well, wouldn't you?

Well, my friends, what we don't know about skin cancer, was an alarming fact I learned while watching my father succumb to this horrendous disease. Perhaps I shouldn't say we in this instance. For there are those of you out there who may have learned a whole lot sooner than myself.

You see, once a mole starts changing, it is sometimes, already too late. Now, if that doesn't wake you up real quick like, maybe this will. We don't just get a little rash that can be a warning sign. Sometimes, there is no warning, get it? Once a mole has cancerous little cells living inside of it, it is very discreet about moving into our bloodstream. Yes, it could take some time, maybe even years, but the harsh facts are that once those lovely little cancerous cells work their seething little way into the underside of your skin, beneath that mole, they then hit the bloodstream, and once they hit the bloodstream, it's party time for those ruthless little killers.

These are the facts that we don't care to acknowledge in all the magazine articles that we so swiftly flip by because don't we already know what all that tanning does to us? Haven't we all heard that the ozone layer is a mess? Yah, so what.

That is exactly how I used to feel each and every time I would hear or read about the dangers of skin cancer. However, what I so nonchalantly failed to acknowledge while reading those magazine articles or what I so conveniently ignored, is that once your bloodstream becomes invaded by those tiny microscopic demons, it's chemo time, ladies and gents, as well as a dramatic and desperate fight for your very life!

My dad had a mole on his right breast that had been there since God himself was a child. It wasn't black or ugly, it was just your run of the mill mole but it was starting to grow. So he went to the doctor with the intentions of having it removed. Well, the doctor removed it all righty, right along with half of his nipple and then sent it in for a biopsy. Simply standard procedure; however, while that tiny little mole was going through standard procedure, an extremely hard mass of a lump became a houseguest where that mole had previously been residing. By the time the doc received the biopsy back from the lab, which was about a week, that little lump began to breed and multiply underneath my father's skin.

It seems to be a fact that has become very obvious to me in that cancer cells get kinda lonely. They seem to breed very happily amongst themselves. They don't give a damn who lives there either. They just find a place to reside and move in! They aren't prejudiced in the least! As a matter of fact, they seem to be extremely sociable. They like all races, all sexes, and all ages. Once they move in, all that partying they do beats the hell out of the landlord and, providing the landlord is able to find the strength to rebuild, then he might have a fighting chance. Yes, sometimes we can rebuild from the damage they have done. Sometimes, we can even beat it. But for the price and the toll our bodies have to pay just to get to that point, it is definitely not worth the risk.

No, there are no guarantees in this life, I realize. Some of us will get cancer no matter how well we follow the rules. No matter how well we take care of our bodies. That is the very reason why this disease is such a damned mystery. But keep in mind that we do have some reasons for the cause and those reasons are really important for us to listen to. Also keep in mind that I am not a professional. These thoughts were simply shared with you from the breaking heart of a very distraught daughter who watched her father fight for his very life, and in the end she then witnessed his horrifying defeat.

No, you sure as hell don't have to be professional to feel the heartbreaking pain of defeat now, do you? Unfortunately, just like cancer, it also has no prejudice.

So the next time you feel a bout of "it will never happen to me" coming on, remember the information this friend passed along to you. Hopefully, it will slap the ignorance right out of your pretty little heads. I pray it does anyway, I truly do pray that it most certainly does.

After my dad's heart-wrenching ritual ended, he wandered back over to his chair, which was located about a foot from the couch. He then packed his pipe full of tobacco once again, put the headphones to his big screen atop his little head and turned on the morning news.

Geeze, I thought, no wonder he sleeps all day. I left him to himself for quite some time before I began to stir, giving the warning of my awakening.

The darkness was beginning to give way to much-welcomed morning light, when I sat up and tried to look as though I had been sleeping, rubbing my eyes and acting like I was trying to focus.

He immediately took his headphones off his head and greeted me with a wonderful, "Good morning, Baby Doll, did you sleep well?"

No, as a matter of fact, Baby Doll didn't sleep worth a doo-doo. She was too busy listening to you dying before her very heart and talking to someone who wasn't there, you cute little water-gagging, mysterious conversationalistic dad of mine.

Looking him square in the eye, I lied. Yes, I told him, I had slept just fine. I then asked, "Did you?" He then looked me square in the eye and in return answered me with a lie. Oh, yes, he had slept fine too.

OK, now that it is completely obvious that we can both lie to one another, what in the hell does this prove? Uh huh, my point exactly, that we are both a couple of real serious liars, that's what.

He then ordered me to get myself some coffee or anything I wanted at all for that matter. Coffee? Yes, that would do just fine right about now, seeing that I had slept for only two stinking hours before I was so rudely awakened by the force of God only knew what, because I sure as hell still hadn't figured it out!

I hadn't taken but a sip of my hot and soothing eye-opener before I noticed that he was looking at me with one of those funny faces that only my dad could portray. Then, all of a sudden, he stuck his tongue out at me and started to laugh. This was my dad's way of showing me that he was in a good mood. I would then return his gesture with my tongue protruding from my mouth and then I would say something like, "Man, you are sooo ugly." Which would in turn prompt his response of "No I am not! My mommy always told me I was beautiful, so *you* are lying, because my mommy wouldn't lie to me!" Then, I would surely mumble something under my breath regarding his mother and the conversation would be over.

These little quips of conversation would always end with me waving my hands at him with a—get away from me—kind of motion and then we would go about our business. So you see, life does continue on even in the midst of tragedy, doesn't it? And I, for one, am so very thankful that it does. Aren't you? I mean, what would life be like if all we did was sit around and pay attention to the obvious? Yup, exactly.

119

Life wouldn't be very fulfilling at all, now, would it? No it most certainly and most sadly would not. There were, in fact, a lot of little instances throughout our ordeal that were humorous. At first, I truly thought I was either extremely morbid or that I simply had missed the train when it came to getting some compassion. But just wait, ladies and gets. You are about to be a witness to one of the most compassionate stories ever told. And through it all, there were indeed times of happiness as well as sadness. It's a part of life, my friends, a truly miraculous and wonderful part of life.

# Chapter Seven

## *Miracles*

*A miracle, my friend, is an event which creates faith.*
*That is the purpose and nature of miracles...Frauds*
*Deceive. An event, which creates faith, does not deceive:*
*Therefore it is not a fraud, but a miracle.*

George Bernard Shaw 1856–1950 Saint Joan (1942) sc.2

W E SAT THERE that first morning, enjoying each other's very presence for just a little while, before I realized that it was Monday and the hospice people would be there soon. Now, I had no clue who these hospice people were, except that I had been told by my father's nurse that they were an organization of doctors and nurses who made house calls to monitor the condition of terminally ill patients. Uh huh, monitor their condition for what purpose is what I wanted to know. If you're terminally ill, then you are terminally ill, if you know what I mean. Well, aren't you? What the hell good does it do to monitor someone's decline, for crying out loud?

Well, little Miss Smarty Pants, better known to some of us as Baby Doll, had a good lesson in life coming right up. Yes, siree, and boy howdy! She sure as heck did.

In the meantime the witch had gotten up and walked into the bathroom and I heard the shower running. She was getting ready for work. Good, that was a great place for her to hang out all day. Actually any old place except there with us would have suited me just fine. Her castle on the hill was waiting and I'm sure her monkeys needed to be fed. Maybe needed their wings waxed—or whatever.

After finishing my coffee, I then decided it was time to jump into the shower myself so that I could be ready for these hospice people who would be monitoring my dad's decline, but before that I thought it best to remind my dad that they were coming.

He kind of looked at me with a—I don't give a doo—look and continued to watch his show. OK, I thought, my sentiments exactly. And with that, I headed for the bathroom.

What a cute little place my dad had made for himself to cleanse his body and brush his teeth, everything neatly in its proper place. There were freshly laundered towels hanging from the small sliding doors that harbored his sparkling clean little bathtub.

Over the toilet, there were steps of shelves, which were supported by two chrome polls, proudly standing at attention to display my dad's little collection of toiletries. Yup, and just as I had suspected, there was the bottle of baby powder and a small peach-colored powder puff balancing itself atop it. There wasn't a day in my dad's adult life that he didn't apply baby powder to himself after a shower or bath. And why, we might ask. Well, simply because he said it made him feel good all under, that's why. However, I personally think there were other reasons. And as this story progresses, perhaps you will share in my opinion.

There was an electric razor and several other items neatly placed on each shelf. I was pleasantly enjoying my sightseeing tour as I undressed, preparing to take my shower, when I noticed a tall, fat, brown bottle with prescription writing on a small white sticker, which was slapped onto the front of it. Kind of looked like one of those old-fashioned medicine bottles from long ago. I leaned a little closer, as I was careful at the same time not to touch it. Let's see, what did it say?

Oh, is that all. It was just a bottle of liquid morphine. LIQUID MORPHINE!!!! What in the hell was my dad doing with liquid morphine? Take two teaspoons full every four hours as needed for pain. Pain? What pain? What in the hell was going on here now?

It was all I could do, not to run out into the living room at that very moment, like a stark-raving mad and naked lunatic, shaking this heavy old fashioned brown bottle at my dad, demanding an explanation and right now! But I didn't. Nope, I sure as hell didn't. Instead I simply sat down on the seat below his toiletry shelf—put the towel over my face— and cried.

After my shower of both cleanliness as well as tears, I came out of the chamber of horrors that had been neatly disguised as the bathroom and I rounded the corner to find that my dad had fallen asleep sitting straight up in his recliner with his headphones intact. Huh, lucky for him, I thought, because I wanted some answers and I wanted them now! Uh huh, like I was really going to confront him with what had obviously not been hidden from me. Confront him for what exact purpose, Little Miss Panic Attack? So that perhaps he would have to say out loud that he was in so much pain that he had to resort to drinking liquid morphine? Just what in the hell would that prove? Uh huh, exactly. That he was in so much pain that he had resorted to drinking liquid morphine, that's what.

I made a quick swoop of the house and it seemed as though the witch had already flown. And once again, she didn't kiss me!!! Gone for the day. Whatever would we do without her?

I found myself standing in front of my dad's recliner surveying the living room. All was clear and as I stood gazing at him sleeping. I then got a good look at the tumor on the side of his neck that had seemed to have grown by leaps and bounds since I last saw him at my house. It was awful. It was, in fact, the size of a tangerine and as I stood there looking at it, I became very angry all over again!

How dare that ugly intruder take up residency inside my father's neck! I wanted it out of my dad, and I wanted it out of him right then and there! As I stood frozen in the moment, quietly trying to get hold of myself, I realized that my tears had already spoken out loud.

I didn't know it then but in the weeks to come, my anger would rapidly grow at the same rate as that horrible and vicious trespasser. However, in the end, all of my anger would be in vain, for the trespasser would finally and truly be the successor in this brutal battle.

I began picking up a little around the house, mostly just to keep myself busy and my mind occupied until the hospice nurse arrived and, come to think of it, when she did get there, she'd better darned well have some answers!

I had no sooner turned around from opening the sliding glass door to allow the screen to push some fresh air through the living room, when I heard footsteps approaching the front door.

I turned back around to face the door and there stood a woman, sporting a white doctor's smock, with a stethoscope draped around her neck, and a smile on her face, which was a most warm and welcoming one. Ah hah! She has "nurse" written all over her, I thought, as I walked over to the door to let her in.

She introduced herself as the hospice nurse and then guessed that I must be the patient's daughter. Brilliant deduction, Florence!

We exchanged hellos and as we did I felt all of the doubt about this organization starting to diminish as she touched my arm and told me what a wonderful daughter I was for simply being there. She then walked directly over to where my dad was still sleeping and sat down across from him on the "futon from hell," lifting her briefcase up and over her tiny little slender legs, setting it squarely on top of her lap. She then clicked open its flaps to reveal the contents inside.

As she asked me in a soft whisper how my dad had been feeling, he woke up, startled at first, but then realizing who she must be as she kindly then said to him, "Hi, Eddie, I'm from hospice, how are you feeling?" And you know, it wasn't what she said, as much as it was *how* she said it, which just seemed to create a feeling of warmth in the room. She was so sincere and concerned and we hardly had just met her. Not to mention the fact that just her very touch had made me feel more trust for her than I had felt for most people I had known my entire life. Yes indeed, there was a certain aura about this woman that simply could not be overlooked. With her long hair flowing in a ponytail that easily touched the back of her knees; she was almost angelic as she began a soothing and heartfelt conversation with my dad.

She began with questions concerning his food intake. Could he still eat solid food? Could he drink water? Had he begun throwing up after drinking or taking his medication? Was he having trouble sleeping at night? Did he drift off to sleep without even realizing it during the day? Did he get winded from just short little walks around the house?

What the hell? Had she been hiding somewhere in the walls? How did she know all of this? How did she know my dad so well after just meeting him? And most importantly of all, how in the name of God was she able to be so feeling and understanding and caring when she had just met us not even ten minutes ago?

Well my friends, I don't know the answers to these questions either. But I have just introduced to you, the wonderful caring and special organization that is known as hospice.

I swear to you that these people must be secret angels sent to earth by the Lord himself. They are trained professionals on the subject of death and the dying. You see, it is their love in life to escort the terminally ill into the glorious land of no return. It is their passion to support the family members left behind, and it is their heartfelt duty to teach both the patient and the family how to accept the unacceptable with pride and dignity. Boy, am I thankful there is such an organization, for if it weren't for them, well—you'll see.

I listened to my dad answer her questions with my heart breaking once again as he blatantly told her that all he wanted to do was eat again and shake this God-awful feeling inside of him. He wanted to feel good again. He wanted to stop throwing up air. As I listened to my father plead with a woman for something she couldn't possibly give to him, I was so taken by her extraordinary ability to comprehend every one of his pleas, making no promises yet at the same time, giving him all of the understanding in the universe.

We then, both my dad and I at the same time, asked why he was throwing up absolutely nothing after he drank water. We shared with her that we were both very concerned about this. I then asked if there might be something that could be done to stop it. You know? Like maybe she might have something in her little briefcase there that just might stop and kill his cancer. Sure, that would be just great for starters.

With the concern and warmth that I was soon to learn only she could display, she explained to us that these terrible gagging bouts, in her opinion, were the body's way of trying to reject the cancer. She gently explained how my father's body was shutting down. She shared with us that it could possibly be a tumor that had taken up residence in my dad's esophagus. She then said it could be any number of things, *all* of which we could do nothing about. God, what a helpless feeling.

She then removed the stethoscope from her briefcase and very gently listened to my dad's heart and joked with him, saying that there must be something going on in there because after all, his ticker was still going, and then she told him he had a strong heartbeat.

Yes, I thought to myself, if there is one good healthy organ left inside my wonderful little dad, it would have to be none other than his caring and loving heart.

With all of the talking going on, my dad had grown tired and he asked if she was through with him, which she answered him politely with "Certainly." So, with that, he got up from his chair, shuffled his way to the bathroom for a short pit stop and then on to the bedroom for his restful little nap, waving good-bye in a backward motion over his head.

The nurse waited, listening for him to get settled before she began her private conversation with me, which she began by saying that my dad was a charming little man.

I sat down in my dad's recliner, moving his headphones aside, and then focusing my eyes on this woman who had, no more than forty-five minutes ago, successfully taken hold of my heart. She was just finishing up her notes when she looked up from the folder, closed it, and handed it to me.

She whispered that she would record my father's daily progress in this folder each time she visited so that we would be aware of any changes for the better as well as the worse. I looked down at the folder, which was now resting on my lap, and my heart was touched as I read the words that were inscribed across the center. "Hospice, When There Is No Cure— Comfort Always." Gosh, I thought, what a pleasant way to describe this truly remarkable organization.

She then leaned forward and placed her hand on my leg and sincerely whispered, "Are you OK? I'm sure you have plenty of questions and fears of your own." She then told me that's what she was there for, so she didn't want me to be afraid to ask her whatever might be on my mind.

Uh huh, sure I would. Just as soon as I could swallow, I sure as hell would. I realized at that moment that I just couldn't believe that it was *me* sitting there! There I was, caught up in a situation that was totally inconceivable to me. I was overwhelmed with all of the feelings inside of me at that particular moment so she would just have to please excuse me while I fell apart.

My eyes welled up with tears and I couldn't speak for a moment or two and then, through short quiet little sobs I asked, "How long do you think he has?"

She very compassionately told me there was really no way of telling. This was an answer that only God could give. She could tell by the look on my face that this wasn't good enough so she proceeded on.

She said, "By the look of things maybe a couple of weeks."

I asked, "If he's lucky, do you think he can last a month?"

She looked down at her already folded hands and said, "Maybe."

She explained to me how she had been doing this for quite some time now and she had seen people whom she thought would last for another year go the very next day and vice versa, so she really could not honestly say.

Well, of course she couldn't. What in the hell did I think she was anyway, a guru? How could I have expected her to give me answers like that? Well, I don't know but I did. I wanted her to give me a time and a place and a day. I wanted her to have all the answers because God knew I needed some right about then, but she couldn't, now, could she? No, of course she couldn't. But oh how I desperately and shamefully wanted her to.

I was helpless and beaten for the second round and I didn't feel like I had it in me to go for the third. I was ready to give up and I hadn't even been there twenty-four hours. *What a mouse! WHAT–A–MOUSE!*

In the midst of all my self-pity, she interrupted with a question, a question that took me by surprise, to say the least. She asked if all of my dad's affairs were in order, his will, his wishes, etc.

Now, I want you all to know that I sat there for a minute trying to regain some composure before I told her no. I didn't mean just no either, I meant *hell* no! *Hell no*, I hadn't put my dad's affairs in order yet. I didn't even have my own crap together yet! Heck, at that point in the game, I hadn't even come to grips with the fact that anything was *really* wrong! I mean, for Pete's sake, my dad looked just fine! So what if he couldn't eat. Lots of people don't eat. Hell's bells, he would get hungry sooner or later. Wouldn't he? Well, wouldn't he?

I explained to her that it was part of the reason I had to come. I then asked why she had asked. Yah, just exactly what was it to her anyway?

She told me that some terminally ill people hold on for just the littlest things and that once everything is in order it's like giving them permission to go. As a matter of fact, she told me, that once everything was in order it might be a good idea for me to tell my dad that I felt it was all right for him to leave.

Well, how dee doo! Do you hear what she had just said? Was she nuts? Oh sure, like I was gonna give my dad permission to leave me—just like that. Uh huh, when elephants fly, my friends. When elephants damn well fly!

Well great then. I suddenly got this incredible idea. I would never get any of it done. Not the will, not his wishes, and I sure as hell would not give my dad permission to go anywhere—ever! Period. So that was that. My dad wouldn't be dying after all. What a concept! This hospice thing was getting better by the minute, wouldn't you say? Yes, I could get the hang of this real quick like.

When I tuned back in to the conversation that was taking place without my bubble-brained attention, the nurse was saying that it is very important, especially to the elderly, to have their affairs in order toward the end. There was that word again. How many times did I have to tell people that my dad was not elderly! Gosh, didn't anyone ever listen anymore? OK then, Baby Doll, at seventy-two, just exactly what was he then? Well, he was old, that's what. He was just plain and simply old–er. Why, he had another ten to twenty years before he became elderly, didn't he? Well, didn't he?

Uh huh, I know, it's obvious that I was losing the battle within myself too. I was being forced to accept the fact that all of this was going to run its course with or without my approval. I don't know about all of you but I truly do hate to be forced to do anything. However, considering the circumstances, something had to happen within me and pretty damned soon too.

She continued on with the conversation, sharing what she felt I needed to know to get through this. Get through this? She was meaning to tell me that people actually got through this crap? Yah, right. *How* is what I wanted to know. As a matter of fact, *how* was what I desperately wanted and *needed* to know!

Well, folks, this was the very conversation that would clue me in to the secrets of open and honest communication. And how to deal with all of this was right at the top of the list. This woman was an absolute goddess, as she sat there giving me permission to be angry and to feel sorry for myself. Giving me permission to place blame or to try and find reasons. Giving me permission to fall apart if that's what it took because in the end it wouldn't matter, the results would be the same. My dad had a terminal illness and he was absolutely, beyond a shadow of a doubt, dying. So she shared with me that I might as well put all of my self-pity aside until after the funeral and share all of my most secret and intimate feelings with my dad now, while there was still time, while I still had him there with me to share those things with. There would be plenty of time for all of my mixed feelings later. But now, now was the time to say everything that had to be said. To do everything that needed to be done. To share my true feelings about my dad, with my dad, while he could still hear it. After all, what did I have to lose, besides my best friend in the whole world? Might as well have him leave with some of the wonderful treasures he had given me throughout the years. Made perfect sense to me. I still didn't like it—but it made perfect sense.

The hospice nurse stayed for the better part of about forty-five more minutes, making sure she answered all of my questions. That is, all of the questions she could possibly give me an answer to. It was during this that she explained to me about my dad's medication and she also explained the miracle of morphine patches.

This was the beginning stages of the age of the patch, my friends. They seemed to have one for just about everything imaginable. The liquid morphine was playing hell with the lining of my dad's tummy so these patches would serve him a lot better. She explained how to put them on and that they needed changed only once every three days. Unlike a pill or liquid medicine that keeps its peak for only about an hour, then slowly begins its decline, the morphine patches actually hold their peak for the full seventy-two hours, not to mention the fact that the patient doesn't have to keep track of time every four to six hours. Now, doesn't that make it nice for the elderly? Yes, I believe it was me who just said elderly.

She then took the time to explain to me how to use the oxygen tank equipment that had been dropped off the day before I arrived. This was extremely difficult to listen to as she gently explained how my dad might need a little help breathing toward the end, just to make him a little more comfortable. She made it very clear to me that it wouldn't save his life but it would, in fact, ease his breathing so that he didn't have to work so hard just to simply inhale God's precious gift of life.

When it came time for her to leave, I felt as if I were saying good-bye to an old and dear friend. And as I said those good-byes, she promised to be back every other day. When it looked like my dad was nearing the end of his seventy-two-year journey, she then would visit daily.

As I watched her step down the front porch steps, I felt like screaming "Please don't leave me here alone! You guys are used to this crap! I don't know what to do. Even if I did know what to do, I don't want to do it! So won't you please come back here and stay with me until it's all over? Please!"

Sad, isn't it? Well the truth is that it is sad. Very sad, because no one really knows what to do when it's time to say good-bye now, do they? I mean, isn't there some sort of ritual that should be followed? Shouldn't we be doing something to stop this? It sure as hell isn't natural to have to sit and wait for someone to pass away, is it? No, it sure as hell shouldn't be. But it did, in fact, become very natural in the weeks to follow. As a matter of fact, I probably wore a permanent path in the carpet from the living room to my dad's bedroom checking on him in his sleep. Wondering each and every time if that would be the time I might find he had left me. Oh, if only hindsight really could be bottled and sold—well—I would have at least been able to save the carpet.

I felt extremely empty during the first hour after her departure. I wanted to wake my dad up and ask him to hold me. Yes, of course, that would have been an act of pure selfishness and I knew it, although I will share with you that during the next three weeks, I did wake him up more than just a couple of times for the mere reason of self-satisfaction, and each and every time, acting as if it had been an accident. Just another one of those shameful little secrets.

At 10:00 a.m. my dad came wandering out of the bedroom heading straight for his chair. *The Price Is Right* was on, for crying out loud! Get the heck out of his way! I would soon come to learn that this was an everyday routine.

He went to bed at around eight thirty in the morning for a little nap, which was actually his afternoon simply because he got up so darned early. He would then automatically wake up at exactly five minutes to ten, go to the bathroom and then make a beeline for his chair to watch *The Price Is Right*.

At 11:00 a.m., after his show was over, he would then fool around with trying to eat something (usually to no avail), and then he would go back to bed and sleep till around five minutes to two in the afternoon.

At that time he would wander into the bathroom once again and afterward, once again, make a beeline for his chair to watch *Matlock*. Oh, how he loved his shows. And you know, it didn't take me long at all to make the obvious connection between those two most treasured shows and my dad himself. I mean after all, what better way to spend his day than with Bob Barker and Andy Griffith? He'd been watching them both for years, each on various shows throughout those years. I think they were all about the same age too. So you see, it was like three old friends sitting down every day to enjoy each other's company. What a pleasant feeling that had been for my dad.

How nice it was of him to share those thoughts with me in his final days. And you know something else? The sad part of it is that neither Mr. Barker nor Mr. Griffith suffered the loss of their old friend when he died. But I bet if they had known him they would have, for my dad was a very loyal friend to the both of them. After all, they grew old together and I find that to be a very comforting thought. And I'll tell you something else too; it touches my heart to think of all of the other elderly people out there who tune in every day for the very same reasons. My dad said that Bob and Andy were all that was left of the original TV era. The way TV was meant to be. No foul language, no nudity, just honest-to-goodness darned good entertainment. And I'll clue you in on another one of my little secrets; each and every time I hear "Come on Down," or the theme song to *Matlock,* I wonder if my dad just might be nestled comfortably in some old cloud formation somewhere enjoying still—his two oldest and dearest friends. I truly do hope so, yes, simply for my heart's sake, I truly do hope so.

During the first week of my visit, I really did think that my dad was gonna be around for at least another five years. He seemed to be fine. He seemed to be strong. He seemed to be trying to at least eat something every day. But as you and I both know, things most sadly are not always what they *seem* to be, are they? No, they surely and truly are not.

What I so conveniently overlooked, or what I didn't care to acknowledge, was that *everything* he tried to eat eventually came back up. But somehow I managed to fool myself into believing that only a portion of what he ate was coming up, simply by telling myself that something had to be staying down. Well, didn't it?

As for his strength, well, I guess it really doesn't take a whole lot of anything at all to walk from the bedroom to the bathroom and then to the living room but then again, if I had been truthful with myself, I would have realized that it did, in fact, take all the strength he could muster to do just that. Makes you just hate the truth, now doesn't it?

For the first week, my dad and I simply sat in the silence of each other's company most of the time that we were together. We hadn't yet learned how to make better use of our quiet time yet. Ah, but we would.

He was sleeping about five hours out of every eight-hour period. And once again, thinking that it couldn't possibly get any worse, nor could he sleep any longer, simply making allowances once again, for my own inability to cope with the facts which were, quite frankly, staring me directly in the heart.

As I think back, another precious role reversal was indeed taking place. For we come into this world much the same way, don't we? Tired and sleeping most of the time, and after my little three-week vacation in hell, I came to realize that we go out of this world the very same way. Now, there's just got to be something to all of this, don't you think? Yes, there certainly must be, or let's pray so anyway.

I spent most of my days trying to get used to his schedule and most of my nights trying to sleep in between his waking-up periods. Up and down, up and down during the night. I'd like to have thought I was caring for an infant most of the time, or maybe I secretly wished I were, because at least they have a future.

Each and every time I checked on him during his sleep, I felt the same anxiety that I had experienced so many years before each and every time I checked on my own precious sleeping babies. Because just like every other loving mother, I knew there was always that chance that I could lose one of them to SIDS and that thought was always in the back of my mind each and every time I checked on one of them. It's one of those fears that no one really likes to talk about. But it's there and those of us who are mothers know it's there, don't we? Now, there was always that chance each and every time I checked on my dad that I just might find that he had already left me. It is truly a wonder that I didn't succumb to a heart attack with all of this worry, now, isn't it? Uh huh, just wait.

It very quickly became routine to hear him up at all hours of the night. I'd tearfully listen to him gagging and then he would wander throughout the house, doing all of the little things that were important to him, like lighting his pipe and enjoying his music. I eventually learned to half sleep during his 2:00 a.m. adventures. But part of me always kept a very watchful eye and ear out for some sort of trouble. The part of me who knew damned well that trouble, sadly, was the name of the game.

Later on in the afternoon of that first day, another woman from hospice arrived introducing herself as my father's case manager. She too, was an extremely warm and caring person and, like the nurse, she was just as cute as a button. (Must have been one of the qualifications for the job.)

It was her duty to make sure that everything was being done properly and it was also her duty to answer questions and console both the patient and the family, to tend to the emotional needs. Boy, these people covered every base, didn't they? As well as the outfield, the stands, and the bathrooms—well, you get the picture.

The case manager, like the nurse, spent time with my dad as well, explaining why he couldn't eat and why he felt so damned awful at times and it was during one of her initial conversations with him, that I realized how much my dad enjoyed talking about his illness.

Yes, I know that sounds ridiculous, but it's true. You see, even as nightmarish as it was, it was *his* illness and *his* alone and he felt he was battling it just fine, if he did say so himself. It was *his* experience and *his* pain. I think he was more than proud of the fact that he was actually coping with it. And you know, if he wasn't he should have been. Yes, he sure as hell should have been. As should anyone who has ever had to experience such an illness, don't you think? For in my eyes, these people are true warriors. Battling every day of their lives for the very something that most of us take so casually for granted. Life itself. When you think of it that way, it's not hard to understand why it is called such a precious gift, now, is it?

Both of the hospice women took special care of my dad's wants and needs. They also took my dad's complaints as well as his pleasures very seriously. Making arrangements to come before or after his shows and naps. Now, you have to know that my dad surely wasn't their only patient. No, of course not, but you would have never known that by all the attention he was given. It was courteous and it was, to say the least, deserved. I mean, after all, the elderly have been here longer than anyone. So if anyone deserves to be treated with dignity and respect it's truly the elderly. Why, they are like survivors of a great battle. And I think if we will all just take a minute to realize in which direction this world is heading, I'm sure we will all agree.

When it came time for the case manager to leave, I became very sad again, as I had when our nurse left. Let's face it, folks, I just didn't like being left alone.

We exchanged hugs and she too promised to return in a couple of days, making me promise to call if we had any questions or fears of any kind. She made it clear that that's exactly what they were there for. And you know, at that very moment, I felt like pitching a tent in my dad's living room and begging her to stay with us until it was all over.

After she left, I walked back into the house from the front porch to find my dad sitting in his recliner, looking at me with that inquisitive look once again. You know the look? Yup, the very same one that made me feel like I just might absolutely go insane!

Oh, cow dung, now what in the heck was he gonna say this time that would make me feel completely helpless?

Trying to ignore him, I walked over and sat down on the couch, bracing myself for yet another heartfelt conversation with my dad, not really wanting to, but knowing that he damn well *would* be spilling his guts soon anyway.

He sat there squinting for just a minute before he spoke. When he did, my heart felt like it was once again being torn completely apart.

He said, "This is it, dear, isn't it? I'm on my way out, aren't I?" And before I even had a chance to reply, he continued.

"I never thought it would be this way, and I sure as hell didn't want it to be, I can tell you that!"

I swallowed hard, trying to choke back the pain and, after a moment or two, I looked at him and tried to speak. It didn't work. Then clearing my throat and viciously swiping at my tears at the same time I accomplished a sentence. "What way, Dad?"

He then took a minute to clear his own throat but not bothering to wipe the tears away from his own eyes, as he said, "This way. You know, being sick and weak. Hell, just look at me! I can't keep anything down at all. I can barely even put my pipe in my mouth anymore. It gags me. And if I can't even smoke my pipe anymore, then what in the hell is there left for me to enjoy?"

And you know, I couldn't have come up with an answer for him if a bolt of lightening had struck me in the caboose at that very given moment! Nope, and I wouldn't have spoken if I had miraculously found an answer for him anyway because something happened to me at that very instant and I really can't explain it. All I can tell you is—it was powerful!

It was like a blanket of acceptance had fallen from the sky and gently wrapped itself around me as I simply looked him directly in the eye and said, "Well, I guess there really isn't anything left for me to say—is there, Dad?" Wow. I was at a loss for words. Or—was I?

With a deep breath, I continued; "Perhaps not. Perhaps you can't enjoy the simple things anymore. Not all of the time anyway but sometimes is certainly better than no times, isn't it Dad?" No answer—I continued.

"You know what? For the time being we *do* have each other—*and*— we have what little time there is left to share together."

Another deep breath as if it just may have stopped the tears from falling, "OK, so you can't eat anymore—as long as you're not hungry, then no harm done, because the fact of the matter is that you *are* going to die and from what everyone else says—it will be soon!"

And as much as I tried not to allow them to fall, the tears began to well up in my eyes and proceeded to overflow as they splashed their unwelcome dew upon my cheeks. "So," I continued angrily, swiping at the soggy intruders that had taken up residency upon my face, "I just want you to be comfortable. I want you to be thankful for the time we have been given, OK?"

Waiting for a reply, gazing into his eyes that had also become a well of tears, I noticed the old canals that God had created down my father's cheeks to channel the overflow and, although he had always been wrinkled, for the very first time I realized that those wrinkles served a darned good purpose.

"OK," he finally choked. "OK."

I then suggested that he not to try to smoke his pipe so often. "You're slowing down, Dad, and therefore, so are your pleasures—so just enjoy what you can, when you can. Let's try that for a while, OK?"

Uh huh, now, just who in the hell was this and what had she done with my father's daughter? Never mind that, where in the heck did all of that sincerity crap come from? Never mind that, how had I learned to be so convincing? Well, I'll tell you—on second thought, I can't—because I have absolutely no clue what I'm talking about.

I guess the sincerity came straight from my bleeding little heart, and as for the convincing part, I still to this day don't know, and I don't mind telling you that after I had said all of what I had indeed just said, I wondered just how in the hell long this new attitude of mine would be staying.

We both sat there very quietly for the next couple of minutes before either one of us spoke again, both of us staring at the floor as our rivers slowly ran dry.

He then broke the silence as he cleared his throat once again and prepared to speak. "You know? I suppose you're right," he began. "Let's not spend time worrying about things we just can't change."

"Right," I said. "Let's just enjoy each day to its fullest and when there are no more—then I guess it will be *me* alone left to enjoy my life to its fullest. And let me tell you, Dad, I have learned to do just that! It isn't going to take a brick from heaven to fall on my knotty little head to convince me either," I blurted out!

He chuckled—and then I chuckled—and then we both looked away from one another, our gazes falling to the floor, once again to ponder.

Life was definitely precious—and I was going to enjoy it to its fullest as soon as this whole damned mess was over, I had decided. I may not have known how I was going to fulfill that little notion, but I was damned well going to do it somehow.

He then shared with me one of his little tidbits of info that I had warned you were coming earlier in the story. Oh, I know, I've already shared a few of them with you, but I promised that I would, in fact, tell you everything! Uh huh! E-v-e-r-y-t-h-i-n-g!

Trying to keep his composure, he very quietly began to speak his words of wisdom—and I sat studiously and attentively as I listened to my wise little info bestowing Dad as he told me to tell my husband to cash in his retirement when he turned thirty-five or forty, so that he could enjoy his hard-earned money while he still has his health—and youth—to do so.

He said, "Don't wait to retire till you're so old you can't live anymore. Don't leave your money behind for the family to fight over, for God's sake, because they will and you can't take it with you! Tuck a little away for emergencies and spend the rest on something that will make you feel worthwhile. Something that will bring joy to the both of you now."

Now, how's that for sound advice? Uh huh, I know. Sort of kicks you right smack-dab in the keister, now, doesn't it? But if you think about it, he really had something there. Yes, he really did!

You see, just like most of the elderly, my dad had waited just a little longer to retire so that he could have a little more money saved to live on for the rest of his life. Well, the problem obviously was that the rest of his life, all of a sudden—consisted of mere days. The rest of his life—was over. He was so sick that he couldn't even walk out into his tiny yard to enjoy the fresh air without feeling like he had just run a marathon, so just exactly what good was all of his hard-earned money doing for him now? Again, I will remind us all that we just can't tell the future and we sure as hell don't call the shots. It's unfortunate, and it matter-of-factly sucks— nonetheless, it's true.

Now, I certainly don't expect all of us to run right out and drain our savings accounts, either. But I sure do see things a whole hell of a lot differently, more so now, than I ever did before. I feel that there just might have been a slight hint of hindsight to my dad's point of view. Uh huh, I know. I didn't race home after his funeral and tackle my husband to the ground, pulling his arm back until he cashed in his retirement either. However, I did understand what my dad was trying to say that day, and I think you do too. I know that I, for one, have learned to rearrange my priorities and appreciate the simple things in life, more so now than I ever did before. As a matter of fact, I now have a phrase that I have become quite fond of: "It's only money,"—and as my dad used to say, "You sure as hell can't take it with you!" My children have become accustomed to that saying now. Perhaps someday, when I'm gone, they will tell a story similar to this one, and I think I like the idea of leaving that legacy behind. As a matter of fact, I believe there has just simply got to be something to all of this! Yes there most certainly must be. I just have to figure out what.

Perhaps this is why some of us are left behind. So that maybe we will take heed and be able to correct someone else's mistakes to benefit our own lives. Huh, what a concept! But it's just a thought. It's not set in stone or anything. It's just another simple little thought that I found trickling throughout my beady little brain—and not to worry—because there's more where that came from. Oh, heck yes—a hell of a lot more!

I do wish my dad had been able to spend some of his retirement money. Oh—he wouldn't have traveled to faraway places—or bought a fancy new car—nor would he have plunked it into a mansion. But I bet you a dime to a doughnut hole that he would have bought another new and BIGGER TV. I'll bet he may have put a new paint job on the old Chevy. Had he found another unusual piece of furniture to add to his already weird collection, he may have bought it too. Who's to say because now he's gone and I will never know. Or will I????

# Chapter Eight

## *Family*

*There is no such thing as society. There are Individual men and women, and there are families.*

Margaret Thatcher 1925 Women's Own 31 Oct. 1987

D URING THE DAYTIME, while my dad was napping, I spent most of my time desperately trying to find things to do to keep myself from going crazy.

Writing letters to my husband and children as well as calling them three times a day was one way of doing just that. As much as I didn't want to admit it, I could feel the loneliness for my family beginning to escalate inside my heart.

Yes indeed, the loneliness had already become quite a burden. So much, in fact, that I found myself wondering if maybe I shouldn't have invested in some stock from the phone and local postal companies before I had left home. However, I did also find that I had become very resourceful in times of great despair. Not exactly the training required for landing a good job nor could I actually put it on my resume—but it will come in handy if I ever need to get through another hardship.

I had to search for ways to keep myself busy and occupy my time. The hospice visits were one deterrent. They sort of broke up the monotony of things and the hospice nurse as well as the case manager had become my friends—in a business sort of way.

My weekends were spent mostly watching old movies and reading anything I could get my hands on. The Sunday paper for Orange County can take all the way to Wednesday to finish, for God's sake. However, there comes a time when reading just doesn't do it for you. Neither does a phone call or cleaning or writing or making faces in the mirror at yourself or dodging witches. Don't you just hate that feeling of restlessness? You know the feeling I'm talking about? When there is absolutely nothing to do. Well, there is, but you don't want to do that particular thing at that particular time. I was extremely lonely and I would have given just about anything at times—just to have someone to talk to. Someone who could have made sense out of all of this turmoil. Someone who had a clue as to why this was all happening. Now, before you all go off half-cocked, pacing and wringing your hands and moaning for me in my time of loneliness—don't. And I'll tell you why. Because there is no need.

You see, my friends, I have a relative whom I had become very close with just about the time I had rekindled my relationship with my dad and this relative was a most unusual one in that he was my dad's younger brother. Now, that's not so unusual, is it? Well, of course it isn't, but that's not the point. We're getting to the point.

Now, how much younger he was than my dad, no one really knows for sure, because each and every time he is asked just how old he is he replies with the same answer of, "I have lived three lifetimes." He refers to God as the "Great Spirit" and he wears his hair in a braid that reaches well below his knees. Yes, ladies and gents, here comes the unusual part: my uncle is a full-blooded Native American.

Now, how can I explain this strange skeleton from my dad's side of the family closet? Well, I myself wondered that very same thing just about all of my childhood years.

First of all, I grew up thinking that I must be an Indian too seeing that when I was a tiny little girl I spent a whole lot of time over at my grandmother's house and there were Indians everywhere. Now, to a child this can be very confusing, especially when I was told that these brownskinned human beings were my aunt, uncles, and cousins. My grandma's skin was as white as a sheet, as was my father's. So in my little kid mind, I just figured that God had given my grandma some Indian babies because only *she* could love them like they should be loved. Sounded logical to me at the time, and it, quite frankly, wasn't really far from the truth.

I also thought that there was a real good chance that maybe their parents had been killed by the cowboys and they needed a really nice lady to take care of them, and God knows my Grandma fit that bill to a tee—and so the story goes.

It wasn't until I was about eight years old that I got the true and correct story straight from the Indian's mouth. Oh, I knew, as I grew older that they must have been adopted; however, there is a heartwarming story that tells it all and it goes like this:

My grandmother, a wonderful, gentle, and loving woman, gave birth to my father in the bed at home with the help of a midwife. Well, it wasn't a good delivery and she was told not to have any more children. Now, that was like telling Willie Wonka that he couldn't have any more chocolate, in that my grandmother loved and adored children more than anything else on the face of this earth. It certainly isn't a mystery as to the hows and whys of my dad's personality, now, is it?

Let's see now, where was I? Ah yes, back to my gammy.

My gammy divorced my grandfather when my dad was just a little guy, because she felt that he didn't have the patience it took to raise a young boy. As a matter of fact, she left my father's father because when my dad was just a little tyke, he got a pair of cowboy boots for his birthday and he somehow left them out on the porch in the rain and they got wet and he got a spanking and my grandfather got served divorce papers. "There was no need to spank that boy."

So, from that time on, for many years to follow, my dad and my gammy were alone during an era when that sort of situation was unheard of, unless of course the husband had been killed in the war. However, between the two of them, they made it just fine. When it came time for my dad to lie about his age and enlist in the Army—well—his mother was more than proud of him and gave him her blessing. But this created a new dilemma you see, for she had just finished raising her only child and she became lonely.

Well, my dad became a soldier and began hanging out in certain taverns where one might meet other soldiers and all from different branches of the service and, in frequenting these fine establishments, my dad took up a great friendship with a Native American Marine. An officer, to be exact, who was not married and so my dad introduced this Indian Marine to his mother and the rest was history.

Now, you're probably thinking that you have this whole Indian mystery figured out by now, don't you? Of course, the Indian kids came after she married my grandpa, but that isn't at all how the story ends. Remember? She wasn't able to bear any more children.

Well, she did, in fact, end up marring this big Indian Marine officer and he went overseas quite a bit. But that didn't bother my gammy because during the years of raising my father alone, she had gone to school and had become a nurse, an OB nurse. During World War II, while my dad was fighting a war, and my grandpa was giving orders to do so in another part of the world, my gammy was busy delivering babies in a hospital close to an Indian reservation, and as I have already explained that was like leaving a kid in charge of a candy store. She once told me that each and every time my "Paw Paw" went off on a tour of duty he came home to another little papoose. She had a big heart and she figured, who better to give your love to than an unwanted child.

So there you have it. That is how my uncle the Indian, came to be my uncle the Indian.

Now wasn't that a nice story? It got right to the plot and the ending real quick, just so we could all understand what I am about to share with you a little better. Whew, writing a book is a lot of work!

Now, this uncle of mine wasn't my only uncle, but he was my favorite. He had always been closest to my dad, which is hard to figure out simply because my dad had already left home by the time all these baby Indians started taking up residency at my gammy's reservation and to make the odds of their close relationship a little bit higher, my favorite uncle, who incidentally was also my dad's closest brother, was the youngest and the last one to arrive, the last of the Mohicans, if you will.

Nonetheless, that's the way it was and, you know, I think that some of my gammy's magic touched that last little Indian baby just as delicately as it had touched my dad, because in the end, my uncle would be the one to stay behind and care for both of my grandparents during their final days here on this earth. He gave ten unselfish years of his life, caring for Paw Paw, who was dying of cancer, and Gammy, who was dying simply from old age. Giving back to the two people who gave him a life to begin with. Again the role reversals we perform in this life, truly are priceless.

So, probably needless to say but I will anyway, my uncle came to be my leaning post as I spent those final weeks at my dad's house, for he understood all too well the emotional turmoil that had come to reside inside my broken heart.

My uncle had accompanied my dad on most of his summer visits to my home and it had been during the time of all of those visits that I had decided that although he was a little older than I remembered him to be, he was still my very same uncle "the Indian." He had been the closest thing I had ever had to a brother and the years had certainly not interfered with that bond between us.

Don't you just love these stories? I know I do. Sometimes I even forget it's my family we're talking about.

So, let's see, where was I? Ah yes, back to the story.

A couple of nights a week my uncle would stop by my dad's house, always bearing gifts of playing cards or take-out dinner or magazines or whatever he felt might bang my shutters at the time. I enjoyed our close relationship so very much and it sure felt comforting to have someone to lean on. This was actually turning into quite a domino kind of situation wasn't it? Yes, it sure as heck and most certainly seemed to be. My uncle was a sight for sore eyes on those restless nights when my dad wouldn't, couldn't wake up. He was always there with a word of comfort or wisdom. And when all words of comfort and wisdom were expired he also had one heck of a sense of humor. I'll tell you what I enjoyed even more—watching him and my dad interacting with one another. Yes, I have to say that there was just something about seeing the two of them together that took my breath away.

Perhaps it was the fact that my uncle paid very special attention to his older brother. Yes—that truly could have been it, I suppose. He had great respect for my dad and he loved him with everything he had in that old, tired, worn-out heart of his. But I believe that the idea of losing his big brother just two short years after the loss of their mother had become an overwhelming heartache for that old Indian. I also believe, that after the loss of my dad, that tired old Indian was never the same.

My uncle would usually show up late in the evening after working all day, just to sit and chitty chat with my dad about anything and everything and sometimes about nothing really at all. No matter how tired he was, no matter how long his day had been, if his older brother wanted to talk, then by golly they would talk. Sometimes during their conversations, he would reach over with a caring hand and gently touch my dad's shoulder when he spoke, or sometimes he would laugh at the silly little things my dad would say, or sometimes (most of the time), he would harbor a look of sorrow as my dad would share his feelings on the subject of dying with his youngest and closest brother. And sometimes, I would simply and quite easily, just break down and cry. I, myself, will die knowing that I was witness to one of the most heart-touching situations I have ever been blessed enough to see, which was watching that old Indian slowly letting go of his big brother.

I got a lot of solace out of listening to their conversations. My father thanking his little brother for taking care of their mom and pop, and asking him to look after me when it came time for him to go. Kind of makes a person want to—well—to be quite honest with you, kind of makes me want to throw up.

My dad had developed a new worry during his last and final days here, not like dying wasn't a big enough worry to begin with but he had also become terribly worried about what would happen to me after he died. That in itself is a heartbreak to beat all heartbreaks. But I find that to be so very fitting of my father's personality. There he was withering away to almost nothing with each and every day that went by, and yet he was worried about me. Yup, that is definitely one of those traits that made it so difficult for me to let him go. But that, my friends, was also just the way my dad was. And I thank God for that precious little detail, each and every single day of my own existing life.

One evening, a very heartfelt conversation took place between my uncle and my dad, one that would sadly also become one of the last conversations I would witness between the two of them.

My dad had been experiencing horrendous pain in his kidneys. It began out of nowhere and stayed until the very end. He was sitting on the edge of the bed with his hands folded and his head down and my uncle was sitting right next to him. It had become a rough night for my dad. The vomiting had gotten worse as well as his frame of mind. The time I had been dreading was growing near and I knew it just as well as I knew my own name, although, I'm ashamed to admit that at the time, you'd have played hell trying to convince me of that fact.

My uncle sat rubbing his brother's skinny little back trying to ease the pain, when my dad suddenly looked up, turned his head toward his brother, and out of the blue, said, "I don't want to go like Pop did. I don't want that chemotherapy. No way, do I want that to happen! I tried that stuff and I didn't like the way it made me feel. Sick all the time."

He then, just as easy as you please, resumed his position as my uncle continued to rub, promising him that we wouldn't allow anything like that to happen. Of course, he didn't have to really even entertain the idea of chemo at that point; however, my dad didn't know that. My uncle never missed a beat and gave my dad his word that he would never allow that to happen. And to my dad, there was nothing stronger than the word of an Indian. Well, at least that particular Indian for sure. And to tell you the truth, my friends, after my uncle had gone through chemotherapy treatments with my grandfather, I don't think my dad had a thing to worry about. A hundred Appaloosas couldn't have dragged him to sit through something like that again. No problem, but instead of sharing those horrible details with my dad, he just simply told his buddy not to worry.

*His Buddy.* My uncle had always referred to my dad as Buddy, instead of Eddie. Lots of folks did, simply because it fit him well. My uncle had shared with me that it had been my dad's nickname as far back as he could remember. He had never been Eddie as much as he had been Buddy, and, you know, it truly touches my heart to think that somewhere along the path of my dad's life, someone had seen fit to give him a nickname that portrayed his wonderful personality. Yes indeed, Buddy fit him just fine.

In turn, my dad had a nickname for my uncle as well. He simply called him "The Indian."

Oh, once in a while, he might call him something like "knot head" or "dumdum" but not very often. Most of the time he referred to him as just the Indian. And that was just plain and simply my dad's way.

Now, after all I have shared with you so far, it would be very dishonest of me if I didn't give credit where credit is justly due, although I'd truly like to say I, myself, did it. But in all fairness I must admit that with very little time left, it was, in fact, my uncle who decided to take responsibility for getting my dad's will done. Quite frankly, after burying both of my grandparents without one, he knew all too well the importance of having this little task completed before it was too late. Not to mention the fact that if it had been left up to me, we'd still be sitting here wondering which day would be best to begin.

Now, he didn't feel any more comfortable than I did having to ask my dad the questions that needed to be asked in order to get those things completed; however, I don't know of anyone who does enjoy such tasks. Well, not personally anyway. But you know, I will say that I think it helped having the two of us to do it together. We were great support for one another. Kind of like the buddy system—no pun intended. And just like everything else we sit around worrying about, it was needless. But then again, that's another valuable lesson we will all learn before the end of this story, I can promise you that.

Now, my dad was very matter-of-fact about everything he ever did in his life and making his last will and testament was no different, as he proudly announced his wishes. It didn't seem to bother him half as much as it bothered us. And you know, isn't that the way it usually is?

Hospice had provided a living will for him already, stating that no lifesaving procedures were to be performed when it came time for him to go. So that was taken care of. Halleflippenluyah! Gee whiz, at least we didn't have to worry about that little ditty, huh? Sure as hell took a load off my happy little preoccupied shoulders! Of course, in all seriousness, I will share with you that this procedure is mostly for the family members of a terminally ill patient, so that they don't do something stupid like dial 911 if the patient goes into cardiac arrest—simply because those guys and gals who answer those calls are trained and prepared to save a life, living will or not, which is a comfort to most of us, but certainly not to a terminally ill patient. I, for one, was more than happy to hear that. Overjoyed! On the other hand, one of the first things that the hospice nurses taught me was to call them first, no matter what. And of course going back to the basics, these had been my father's wishes from the very beginning. Remember? He absolutely, beyond a shadow of a doubt, did not want anyone bringing him back if he started to go. Talk about abnormal! I mean, aren't we taught all of our lives to sustain life? Well, heck yes, we are! Of course we are! There aren't many of us out there who wouldn't go that extra mile in an emergency to lend a hand to our fellow man if he was in trouble or hurt, now, is there? It's a natural response, for God's sake. So needless to say, this was absolutely abnormal! My heart was telling me that I had to let him go. That's the way he wanted it. Those were his wishes. Gosh, and I think if I had to hear that just one more time—well, I'm sure I would have thought about doing something really crazy. Let's just leave it at that.

My dad had already shared with my uncle and myself all of his wishes. Yup, he knew just exactly what he wanted done with all of his belongings and his valuables. Kind of made me wonder just how long he had really been preparing. Of course, maybe I'm over reacting again. I mean, most of us have probably had those thoughts from time to time, I suppose. Thoughts like, who might want what of ours when we—well, you know. It just seemed a bit—well, overwhelming, having to hear it coming from my dad, himself. Now, truthfully, isn't it easier when we hear those sorts of things coming from someone else's loved one? Yup, as we all hang our heads in complete shame—if I do say so myself, it most certainly is.

So, now that we all agree with the fact that these conversations we have in our final days matter-of-factly suck rope, I'll share another memory with you. And this memory just so happens to be one of the most heart-touching decisions my dad made in his final days here on this blessed earth.

He had made the decision to leave his most cherished possession, his 1982 Chevy Step-Side Pickup, to his youngest daughter's son.

Now, it didn't matter to my dad that his grandson was only thirteen years old at the time. Being the old sentimental guy that he was, the only thing that mattered to him was the fact that his baby daughter, had given her son my father's last name at birth, simply because it had been her last name at the time. And I can promise you that she had absolutely no idea of how important that decision would prove to be until years later, which was now, as my father lay dying and he realized that with five daughters, there was no one left to carry on the family name, until my sister's son was born. Yes, indeedy, folks, her son was my father's *only* namesake.

Now you all have to know by now, that this meant as much to my father as my sister's wedding had meant to her. In my dad's opinion, a man's name was everything. And that 1982 Chevy Step-Side Pickup couldn't even make a dent in the amount of thanks my father was willing to offer. That Chevy Step-Side Pickup was his most treasured possession, and therefore, it should be handed down to someone who would own it forever, someone who was truly worthy of receiving such a fine heirloom. What a special exchange of precious gifts, wouldn't you say? A heart for a heart, a gift for a gift, thought for a tear, that's poetry in motion, my friends, plain and simple.

I had originally planned to tape my dad's will, as well as having it in writing, however, when we sat down to do so, he kept getting confused, so we had to write it down so that he could go back and reread it to make sure he had covered everything and everyone. Leaving someone out was totally unacceptable to a man like my dad. It took a good week to complete the rough draft. But I can tell you it was a week I will never forget.

A week full of laughs as well as tears, as I would sit and recite what my dad had just said, only for him to say, "No, wait a minute now, that's not right—do it over." How will "So" and "So" feel if I leave that for "So" and "So." Quite frankly the man was lucky he was already dying, if I may be so honest, but then again, no matter how frustrating, any amount of time spent with my dad was cherished.

Remembering what the hospice nurse had said to me regarding all affairs to be in order, I have to admit I was a little scared the night my uncle bounced through the front door waving the will in his hands, proclaiming its completion. I knew in my heart that once my dad signed that waving piece of proverbial heritage that he wouldn't have anything left to stop him from going. All would be done and he would have nothing more left to do.

Well, ladies and gents, let's see, how can I put this—how about plain and simple. Boy, was I wrong.

You see, as the days continued to pass, my dad's health continued to deteriorate. The hospice nurses continued to make their scheduled visits and I continued preparing myself for the worst. So just how in the heck does one prepare for the worst exactly? Beats the duke right out of me, my friends, but I was trying. I was truly and desperately trying, and let me tell you, if I may be so bold, nothing I had ever learned in my entire life could have prepared me for what I was about to endure. There is no way that you can ever prepare to lose someone. OK, maybe you can prepare but you will never be ready. Especially family.

Family is something that goes on and on. Dead or alive the tree just keeps branching out. And someday, we all become a branch on that tree that is forgotten. Sixty years from now, my great-grandchildren will only see my father's name on that tree. They will never know the pain I endured of letting him go. They will never know his humor or kindness. They will not ever be aware of his illness. But they will carry his traits. His blood will run through their veins. And somewhere, sometime, someday, both my dad and I will be family again.

⌒⌒⌒⌒

# Chapter Nine

## Challenge

*The ultimate measure of a man is not where he stands in moments of comfort and convenience, but where he stands at times of challenge and controversy.*

Martin Luther King 1929–1968 Strength to Love (1963) ch. 3

A T THE END of the first week, a doctor from hospice called upon my dad. A very tall, distinguished-looking gentleman, with graying hair, who appeared to be in his late forties or early fifties, showed up one day, unannounced, little black bag and all. He had come to check my dad over and see if there was anything he could do for him! I myself wasn't aware that doctors still made house calls.

Now, I have no clue what made me do it, but when this gentleman walked through the door, I reached over and turned on the tape recorder. Guess it must have been fate.

By the end of the first week, both my dad and I had accepted his condition as well as we possibly could have at the time anyway, and we spoke of the unspeakable daily. He woke up in the mornings and shared with me how he was feeling and I would open my little medical book I had brought from home and assessed where we stood. Of course, I really had no possible way of actually knowing such facts, but I thought I did as I would read to him his decline and he would listen intently and then we would both diagnose where he was in his decline. Sounds sick, I realize; however, it was a coping technique and we were comfortable with it.

Well, sadly Little Miss Daughter of the Year and her trusty steed of a father were not medical personnel nor were we fortune tellers. We were simply and finally winding down. We had both stopped trying to figure a way out of this mess. We had ceased trying to force food down his throat as well. It simply wasn't working. He couldn't even drink a glass of water without it coming back up. We both, somehow without uttering a word of acceptance out loud, had come to know that we were fighting a losing battle. And if you don't mind me saying so, this situation that we had come to accept very matter-of-factly and quite frankly—made me sick.

So, by the time the doctor showed up, we had both finally quit trying to find ways to prolong my father's life (or so we thought at the time anyway). I guess you could say the doc was a day late and a lifetime too short.

So, when this gentleman walked through the door, addressing my dad as "sir," asking him if there was anything he could do for him, well, my dad sort of grinned at me and then turned to look that doctor square in the eye with a serious, pleading look on his face and he said, "Yah, as a matter of fact there is. Could you kindly make me want to eat something?"

The doctor sorrowfully told my dad, "No, sir," there wasn't anything he could do to make my dad want to eat again. My dad answered him with a trailing reply of, "Uh huh. I didn't think so."

After that, each and every time the doctor asked my dad a question, my dad answered him with "OK, all right" and "Will do." The doctor was very kind to my dad and I don't think my dad meant to be rude at all. He just knew that there was nothing that could be done, so why talk about it?

As the doctor got ready to leave, he told my dad to try to drink a milkshake or eat some ice cream. My dad answered him with "OK, will do, thank you" and his notorious "Bye now." And with that, folks, my father dismissed the doctor. He then, turned his heart away from the being that we all seem to rely on in our lives for a miracle or two. But this time, there were no miracles to be found in his little black bag of cures. My dad had sadly come to the end of cures in his life. They were all used up, and isn't that really all that happens when we die? Why sure it is. We just simply and sadly use up all of our cures.

After the doctor had walked down the steps and vanished, my dad sat down on the futon and looked over at me shaking his head with tears in his eyes.

"There's not a damned thing they can do, dear. Nothing! No matter how hard anyone tries, it's over."

I sat there for a couple of minutes, looking at him with that same ache in my heart that had come to be a permanent feeling for me, before I was finally able to clear the lump from my throat and said, "I know, Dad. He was just trying to help."

After a long pause, as he too was probably trying to clear the lump in his throat, he said, "I know they are." So there we sat, two lumpy throated, helpless pieces of dog doo.

He then broke the silence, as he always well did, with a request, and it never ceases to amaze me how I jumped at his every command.

He asked me to get him a milkshake out of the freezer. He wanted to give it a try.

"Are you sure?" I asked with hope in my voice.

"No, I'm not sure," he answered sounding a tad bit perturbed, "but I'd like to try."

Well, I just about made it to the kitchen in one leap. Flinging open the freezer door and with the grace of a drunken ballerina, I reached into the tiny frozen food section of my dad's kitchen and grabbed a chilled milkshake, popped off the top, and grabbed a spoon out of the drawer. Good heavens, you would have thought I was blind the way I was trashing the place.

"Do you want me to soften it up a little?" I asked.

"No, I want it just like that," he answered.

"Do you want a spoon?" I asked.

"Well, of course, what do you want me to do, lick it with my tongue?

Well, hell's bells, how was I to know what he was going to do with it? I was so pumped up with adrenaline and hope that I had no stinking idea as to what I was even doing for crap's sake.

I leaped back over the coffee table and like a king's faithful servant, I extended my arm to him with his tasty freeze at attention.

He thanked me and at the same time, gave me a get–the–heck–away– from–me sort of look and proceeded to eat his dessert.

Well, folks, within the first three bites, before I even had time to sit down, he was gagging, and all the hope that I had harbored for just those couple of minutes vanished as I jumped up to help him get to the bathroom just in time for him to throw up those three little stinking bites of tainted frozen memories.

I stood next to him in the bathroom rubbing his bony little back, whispering to him that I was so sorry, as he held one hand up as if to say he was all right. However, he turned briefly and our eyes met for just seconds, but seconds was all it would take for me to see the tears of realization streaming down his cheeks.

I left him there for just a couple of minutes, walking out to the living room with my hands cupped over my quivering lips, quietly trying to control my sobs, and as I regained control of my emotions, I gently reached over and turned off the tape recorder.

You know, I have listened to that conversation many times since my father's death and each and every time I laugh a little and at the same time I cry a little too, remembering how I desperately continued to hold on to the hope throughout those last days. And although that may seem a little strange, I, for one, am so very thankful that—*we*—no matter how bleak a situation becomes, can and will always continue to hold on to the hope.

With each and every day that passed my dad became a little weaker, and each day he lost a little more weight. By the end of the first week, we had not only come to the realization that there was nothing more we could do, but we had also become painfully aware of the fact that no matter how difficult it was, it had come time for us to say what was on our minds, for we understood all too well, that if we waited, we just might not get another chance. And now that I think about it, isn't that the way it should be all of the time anyway? Yes, it most certainly should be, but sadly it is not. Ah, but by the end of this story, I guarantee that each and every one of you will walk away from this book with an incredible urge to seek out someone you love and tell them just that. And if you don't mind me saying so, it shouldn't have taken this story for all of us to realize that common little error that hides so cowardly inside of us all. Then again, it took me losing my dad to get it, so feel lucky, my friends. Better me than—well, on second thought, never mind.

Now, most of these "say what was on our minds" conversations began harmless enough in the beginning. I would reach over and touch his tired old cheek from time to time and tell him how very much I would miss him once he left me, or I would catch him looking at me, and with just a cock of my head or a raise of an eyebrow, I would prompt a similar statement from him. However, I must warn you that just like anything else in this life that we practice, we practice and practice until we begin to get so good at it that we tend to want more. We want to get better and better. And with that little thought in tow, our conversations began to take a turn for the—well—they began to take a turn for the honesty. Real honesty. And those conversations are sometimes very hard to bear. So, on second thought, I guess our conversations, like my father's health, began to take a turn for the worse.

The questions from my dad were the most difficult. Of course, that's terribly easy for me to say now. Seeing that he's not here to defend his own opinion. However, I must say that I see them as the most difficult for that very reason, because he isn't here anymore to defend himself. My book, my opinion!

I believe his questions were so harsh and painful to my ears due to the simple fact that he was so damned honest. Questions such as, did I think he could slip into a coma due to starvation before he died, or he would ask me if I could actually stand by and watch, while he had a heart attack and not call for help?

How in the hell do you answer questions like that? Well, in all truthfulness, beats the hell out of me—but for the most part, you answer with all the honesty you can muster up inside your already confused little heart, that's how. Because quite frankly, I truly didn't know, so I would tell him that I could only promise to do my best to carry out his wishes. As for the starvation question, I told him that I hadn't really thought about it, but that I would rather him slip into a coma, before I had to stand by and watch him succumb to a heart attack. Great choices, huh?

We spent many conversations over the next three weeks, wondering just exactly how he might go, and I don't mind telling you, I didn't like it at all! Not one damned bit! However, now, as I look back, I'm so very proud of all we accomplished during our last days together. We were like two soldiers in a foxhole waiting to run, knowing damned straight well that he would be the one to take the bullet. That is bravery, my friends, plain and simple.

I'll tell you what else I didn't like. I didn't like watching my father's body going through its decline. Before then, I had never even thought of the process the body goes through when it is declining. Of course not, why would I have? Why would anyone in his or her right mind, think of those things, for heck's sake?

Each day it seemed that one at a time each organ would take its place in line. Slowly and ever so slightly, something would stop working the way it always had. So until I was right smack-dab in the middle of a new situation, I had no clue what to expect, and *that,* in my opinion, had to be the worst.

Oh, the hospice nurses would give me hints as to what I could expect, however, I couldn't even have possibly imagined, until some of those things were upon me. For instance, the first time I had to help my dad go to the bathroom.

First of all, I had never in my entire life seen my dad naked. As we all know, my dad was a very proud and proper man and there are just some things that are not meant for a daughter's eyes. And knowing about my past only made him more modest and determined.

Now, I don't know why I hadn't expected for this to happen, seeing that I was there to do just those sorts of things. I mean, hadn't I known that he might need help toward the end? Well, of course I did, but I never could have guessed that one of those things meant my having to help him go to the bathroom! After all—he had a wife! She was never really there— but I swear to you, I really thought she would dig deep when we needed her most. And—once again, that's what I get for thinking. And let me tell you, the very first time I had to help my dad in the bathroom—was indeed the most difficult as well as the most heart wrenching task I had encountered thus far.

He had been sitting with me that morning, watching one of his shows and he and fallen asleep in his chair. He hadn't even been able to stay awake long enough to finish watching his program, when he groggily awoke, looking at me with his eyes barely open and softly said, "I have to go to the bathroom, dear—and I don't think I can make it on my own." *Oh, Lord!*

"OK," I said, with not a bit of hesitation. "Let's try to stand you up." He tried to steady himself but it was too difficult and this day was about to become the first of many when I noticed an apparent—as well as horrifying decline.

I stood him up and tried to hold him by wrapping his arm up around my neck. The wounded soldier stance, how fitting; however, I realized that if he went to fall, I wouldn't have been strong enough to catch him, so I quickly invented the way that became our ritual to help him get around.

I stood in front of his frail, little body, with my back to him, placing his hands on my shoulders, and we walked slowly together, like we were imitating a choo choo train. This way, if he went to fall, I could have easily bent forward to catch his full weight on my back. And, sadly, his full weight had become less than my own, so I was sure I could handle him.

So off we went, scooting across the floor like two kids from a "Romper Room" rerun. It wasn't until we reached the bathroom door, and I turned around to face him, that I realized that someone had to help him go!

Oh, geeze, what was I gonna do? And he realized it too. So there we stood, both of us looking at each other with an understanding that could have only been exchanged between those two hearts.

As I stood facing him, trying bravely not to hesitate, he touched my face and said, "I'm so sorry, dear."

Sorry? Why, he had absolutely no reason in the world to be sorry! He hadn't done a gosh darned thing to be sorry for! This situation, as uncomfortable as it had already become, had gotten way out of hand! It was clearly time for me to buck up and smell the—well—reality! My past was then—and this was now, for cripe's sake! Look what had happened. My dad was standing there apologizing to me for needing help! And this, my friends—was totally unacceptable!

So, I took his hand from my face, making sure to keep it tightly tucked in mine and I didn't have to say a word. We exchanged an understanding glance with one another, as I simply looked over his shoulder, reached down and helped him with his sweatpants.

As he sat down, I simply turned my back to give him some dignity. And when he was through, I helped him up the very same way, thanking God that I made it through this ordeal without fainting from embarrassment for the both of us. We then got in to our train formation and headed for the bedroom. And I truly do believe, that for the second time in my life, I all too well understood what it meant to be robbed of one's dignity.

This was to become the first of many episodes to follow. Even when the witch was home, he called upon me to help him. I don't think she could have gotten through the bathroom door with that hat on anyway.

From that day forward, my dad would need my help just about every time he went to the bathroom. And, yes, it was an extremely difficult task for the both of us, mentally. But you know, after a while (practice, practice, practice), it simply became a part of a normal day. And I'll tell you something else. If given the choice, I would have gladly continued to do it for the next fifty years.

At one point, shortly after that first experience, he shared with me that if my past hadn't been my past, he thought it might not have bothered him so much. I shared with him that his acknowledgement of those things was the very reason I could perform those tasks. So, as always, we had come to an understanding of one another's feelings within one another's hearts. But I will also tell you this. With each day that went by, I was becoming angrier and angrier at the witch. Where in the hell was she in his times of need? His wife should have been the one there helping him through his dignity-robbing moments! Perhaps it would have made it a little easier on everyone concerned. But as I have already shared, she was rarely ever there and when she was, she simply sat and watched as we choo chood to the bathroom. And, yes, for those of you who might be wondering, when she was present, I did ask her if she'd like to accompany him. She politely declined. Keep that tucked away for now.

I have come to realize that the challenges we face in this life, seem to very seldom be decided by us. We simply wake up one day—and find that we are faced with one or several. Some are little and some are major, but all are important. And equally important are the ways by which we choose to face our challenges, and sometimes, it seems that the way we choose, isn't our choice to begin with either. But all in all, we deal with them, don't we? Well, maybe so, but I'll be the first one to stand up and admit that I don't like them. Not one stinking, solitary, damned bit! However, have you ever noticed how good it feels, once we've accomplished one of those challenges?

Uh huh, well, I'm here to tell you that this was one of the—no—it was THE toughest challenge I had ever had to face. And I did accomplish what I set out to do in the end. Well, sort of. And I must say, that for being in the midst of the toughest challenge in my entire life, thus far, once completed, I felt worse than I had before it all began. So, how's that for screwing up the natural balance of things? Uh huh, just what I thought. Challenges, like beauty, are simply in the eyes of the—oh, just forget it. Besides, as you are about to find out, these hadn't been challenges at all. Nope. They were simply figments of my perception of a challenge. Yup, Little Miss Baby Doll, as smug as she had become, was still in for the very ride of her life!

# Chapter Ten

## Wishful Thinking

*Time, you old gypsy man, will you not stay?*
*Put up your caravan just for one day?*

Ralph Hodgson 1871–1962 Poems (1917) "Time, You Old Gypsy Man"

D URING THE BEGINNING of the second week of my stay, my dad decided that it was high time to start taping his life story. I'm sure his reasoning was that we might as well while he still had the strength to do so. OK, if not his reasoning then it certainly and sure as heck was mine. I mean, after all, that was one of the biggest reasons for my stay. To be able to preserve memories, remember?

So, one afternoon, right after *Matlock* was over, he asked me to get my tape recorder and accompany him into the bedroom. Obligingly, I unplugged it from the living room socket and with gadget in hand and dread in my heart we choo chooed back to the bedroom.

As my dad sat on the bed trying to prop his pillows, I searched for an outlet to accommodate my gadget's plug. I quickly found one, on the wall, opposite the foot of the bed. I then plugged the tape recorder in and carefully placed it on the middle of the bed and proceeded to get myself comfortable.

My dad was sitting propped up on pillows, watching and waiting for me to get ready, when he suddenly began to laugh at me. I kind of stared at him for a minute and I asked him what in the hell was so funny?

He said, "You are. You're a funny little dum-dum."

Well, I can tell you that I do believe my heart must of actually skipped a beat right then and there. He hadn't said that to me in years. As a matter of fact, it touched my feelings to the point that I all of a sudden got this incredible urge to take back some more of what was mine. Prepare yourselves, ladies and gents. Here it comes.

I decided for some unknown, silly-ass reason or another, that at that very moment, I wanted to jump on the bed just for the sole reason of irritating him. Sadistic? Well, perhaps. But for those of you who feel you really know me, then it really wasn't as sadistic as it was touching.

So, I slowly got up on my knees and trying to balance, an act that I had long forgotten, I began to steadily stand on the bed.

With an inquisitive look he sort of cocked his head and asked, "Now what in the heck do you think you're doing, girl?"

I continued to rise until I was in a standing position. Well, he began laughing so hard, that I wondered if it wasn't good for him, yet at the same time he kept threatening to hurt me if I didn't stop it.

He was saying, "Now you're gonna get hurt here in a minute, cause I'm gonna get up from here and hurt you myself."

Well, with all due respect, he still hadn't learned how to put the fear of God into me, so I then proceeded to jump. Not hard, mind you; as a matter of fact I don't think that my feet ever really left the mattress. It was just enough to make the bed shake a little.

Oh, how I wanted him to be better. Oh, how wonderful it was to hear him laugh out loud again. But most importantly was—oh, how great it felt to see tears of joy streaming down that tired old face at a time when it was difficult to find any joy at all. And with that, my own tears began to fall along with my laughter. However, I will share with all of you, that my tears were not from joy. For as I continued to jump, I realized that he had begun to cough uncontrollably from laughing and all of a sudden the horrible reality of the present had pushed its way into our moment. The cancer had spread to his lungs and it was becoming difficult for him to breathe.

I don't know *why* I did *what* I did that day. I guess I saw an opportunity to relive another memory. Or perhaps I simply wanted to be happy at a time when happiness had just about become obsolete. Whatever the reason was, I can tell each and every one of you that I am certainly glad I did it. For sometimes, I can close my eyes and still remember how happy his smile was and sometimes I can actually hear his laughter. But most of the time, to be quite honest, it's plain and simply become just another wonderful memory.

While I was standing on the bed, waiting for him to get his breath, I looked out the window and noticed that it had started to rain. How appropriate.

We both acknowledged to one another at the same time, that we could hear the soft pitter patter on the overhang above the window outside.

"Hey," he quipped, "While you're up there, making a fool out of yourself, open the window, would you? I love to listen to the rain. It's one of my favorite things to enjoy."

I looked down at him in amazement as I shared with him that it was one of my most favorite things to listen to also. So I walked across the bed, reached over and cranked open the tiny window that was directly over my dad's head. There is nothing like a Southern California rain!

The wind picked up a little outside, causing a slight breeze to flow through the opening. Looking down at him, I asked if the breeze was too chilly for him. "Hell, no," he said. "Besides, the worst thing that could happen is, I could get pneumonia and die."

We both stared at each other before we began to laugh and as our eyes met, they seemed to hold a sad but true understanding between the two of us.

I leaned down and kissed the top of his head and then took a couple of steps backward and sat down in the middle of his bed, which was, by the way, quite unique, as it was completely round. Another sort of gadget I suppose. I did however ask my dad shortly after I had arrived, why he owned a round bed and he said, "Because it was something else again."

It sure was, I thought, as I sat there wondering where in the heck he bought his sheets.

"OK," I said. "Let's get started."

I asked him if there was anything he wanted to know before we began and he said, "No." It was his life story and he knew where to begin. Of course he did. Perhaps I felt the need to wipe his nose first, or powder his bottom. I turned on the tape and he began.

Appropriately so, he began with when he was born and where, who his parents were, when they divorced, and how he had gone to a private military school during his early years. He then went into how he had opened up a little bicycle fix it shop in his garage to help make ends meet, explaining that in those days, you simply did everything you could just to survive. He told of how he would collect pieces of scrap tin or metal and then turn them into the junkyard for money. And then he began to tell the story of how he was struggling in school around the tenth grade and how making a living was a lot more important to him and his mother. He was seventeen.

He said he had been working so hard after school, that school itself had become a burden. He didn't realize at the time how much of a role a high school education would later play in his life. Unfortunately, all that mattered was paying the bills and surviving. School had simply and sadly become nothing but an obstacle.

So one Saturday afternoon, he and six of his buddies, all of whom were older than he, went down to the Army recruiting office and signed up to go into the United States Army. After long and careful consideration, he felt that this was the only solution. This way he could make good money and send it home to his mother, while being provided with three hots, a cot, shelter, and a paycheck.

Now, I mean to tell you, that while I was sitting there, on that bed, my father went through a sort of metamorphosis before my very own eyes. His eyes lit up, his voice became loud and he was smiling from ear to ear as he recalled those days of his youth. And I was in shock, as I sat staring at the same exact man who I had just had to physically help walk into that bedroom. Or at least I thought it was the same man. To tell you the truth, I wasn't really sure, as I sat in the twilight zone, staring at this person who had all of a sudden taken on the look of someone much younger and so very full of life.

Well, to those of us who are blessed enough to know or to have known a person from that era, it shouldn't really come as much of a shock, now, should it? For this was a time in my father's life that he was extremely proud of; his army days.

As I have already shared with all of you, but I will again, just in case you might have forgotten, my dad believed that every man and woman should fight for this wonderful country of ours. He believed that the draft process should not have been necessary. He believed that every red-blooded American-born citizen should fall to their knees and worship the opportunity to fight for this great land of ours without having to be forced to do so.

Geeze, as I sat there listening to him, I could swear I was about to hear the National Anthem begin to play. Or perhaps, Uncle Sam himself just might come sashaying through the bedroom door. But mostly, I felt very proud of the man sitting before me. As a World War II soldier, he had seen it all. Oh, and just for the record, Uncle Sam didn't come sashaying through the door. However, in my opinion, he damned sure should have.

At that time in history when my dad entered the army, it was just converting from the cavalry of mules and horses to jeeps and tanks. My dad had served as a heavy artilleryman on the front lines, which meant that his platoon was the first to arrive and secure the area. He was most extremely proud of this position that he so bravely completed each time. And again, just for the record, in case there was ever a doubt, so was I.

He told stories of stepping over dead bodies and securing ground, so that the troops could move in. And every once in a while he would motion for me to turn off the tape, as he would have to catch his breath and occasionally wipe the tears from his eyes, explaining to me that those days were very difficult for him because there wasn't a prejudiced bone in his body and it seemed so senseless for *people* to be killing *people*. Nonetheless, it was his duty to protect his country and that's exactly what he did.

Now I have to say—and I'm sure a whole lot of you have either said it yourselves or heard it said from time to time about someone else—but it amazes me how my dad was able to recall details about something that happened fifty some odd years ago better than he could recall what had happened just the day before. This is when it became very clear to me that these were some of the most important years in his life. And as the days went by and his time drew nearer, that little fact would become more apparent than ever. Just you wait and see.

His army days took up more than sixty minutes of that ninety-minute tape and I truly do believe he could have gone on for four more hours if he hadn't grown to be so tired. And that, incidentally, my friends, was also the very reason he ironically gave to me, when I asked why he quit the service. He had simply grown tired. Funny, isn't it? The war made him tired so he quit. And now he was losing patience with another battle, which also, he was growing very tired of and was ready to quit as well. Well, not really funny. That's certainly just another crappy figure of speech.

He then went on to say that after he left the service, he met my mother. It was many years after and he explained that he wanted to settle down and start a family. Lord only knows why he fell in love with my mom, as he put it, because he sure as hell couldn't figure it out nor could he explain it.

He said that he had never really considered himself an intelligent person and that if there was one thing my mom exhibited very well, it was her intelligence. He then went on to say that he was so very impressed with that, as well as her ability to take charge, that nothing else really mattered. He felt that she was a strong woman and would make a great mother because of her abilities. He felt that together, they would compensate for one another's weaknesses, and he made it perfectly clear that at the time, she was very loving. Then, all of a sudden, he motioned for me to turn off the tape recorder.

I obligingly but with a questioning look on my face, reached over and clicked the tiny button. Then he asked, "Is it off?"

I answered, "Yes."

He then said, "Good." Because what he wanted to say shouldn't be for anyone else's ears but mine.

He began with getting that squinty look in his eyes. The very look that always made my heart stand still. Then, he reached down and picked up his pipe from the end table next to the bed, packed it full of tobacco, sat back, and looked at me as he lit it, still squinting every inch of the way. Finally, he pulled it from his lips, and through the smoke I could see him getting ready to share one of his well-known thoughts with me. And just in the nick of time, I might add, for he almost didn't have to wait for the *cancer* to kill him!

He said, "You know, dear, through all the moves from state to state, and through all the yelling and screaming your mother did, and through every birth of all my girls, I just kept thinking it would get better. I could have never imagined in my wildest nightmares what lay ahead for all of us. Maybe if I had stood up to her just once, then perhaps she would have stopped having to always be the one in charge. Then, maybe all my girls would have been OK. I should have known. I should have tried harder!"

I sat there for just a moment, staring into his eyes, aware of the obvious pain he was feeling and I couldn't speak. I swallowed a couple of times and tried to clear my throat but nothing came out. Finally, one more time and a peep came through the tears. Clearing my throat once again, I began to speak. And as I did, his squinting eyes focused on my every word.

"Why, Dad? Why did you stay with her? If you were so miserable and she was so mean, then what in the hell made you stay every time and follow her everywhere she wanted to go?"

Never mind that. Why in the hell had I just asked my dying father that extremely difficult and personal question? Well, I had to, that's why. It had been something that I had always wanted to know. And if you don't mind me saying so, there seemed to be no time like the present, seeing that the present was swiftly trying to become part of the past.

He sat there taking short puffs on his pipe with his eyes focused on mine like he wanted to matter-of-factly tell me to mind my own damned business, and for a split second I truly felt like he might say just that, but he didn't. Thank God! He just simply put his pipe down on the table, sat back against the pillows, folded his arms across his chest, and calmly said, "I guess it was for the family. I just wanted to keep the family together no matter what the cost."

He shook his head from side to side and said, "I know *now* it was wrong, but *then* it was the most important thing in the world to me."

And as his eyes welled up with tears, he then said to me, "I loved you girls and I did love your mother too and all I wanted to do was keep everyone together." And with that, he simply began to sob.

I reached across the center of the bed and took his soft wrinkled little hand in mine and I put it up to my face and I kissed it. And then with tears in my own eyes and my lip quivering right along with every muscle in my shaking body, I said, "Well, I, for one, am so very glad that you did, Dad, and for as long as you did. We sure as hell can't go back now, and we've been through this time and time again. Let's just let it go."

He then cleared his throat, still shaking his head slowly from side to side in disbelief and said to me that if he died tomorrow, he would have to take this pain with him, for he has never found a way to get rid of it.

I still had his warm little hand in mine but that just wasn't good enough for the moment we were sharing. So I leaned forward balancing myself on my knees and I kissed him on his cheek and I told him how very much I loved him and how very much I was going to miss him. And you know, each and every time I said those words to him I realized that I truly felt like they meant something stronger and deeper. Maybe they did. Yes—perhaps they surely did. For with each and every moment that goes by in our lives, we can and do feel differently about certain things now, don't we? Yup, even about the people whom we love. We either love them a lot or just the same and sometimes, we even love them a little less. Funny how we can feel such things in the blink of an eye, isn't it? Well— not really—funny. There's that phrase again.

As I sat on the bed, trying to get hold of myself, I repeated the words again. Trying to create a warm atmosphere instead of a sad one. "Yup," I said, "I sure am going to miss my wise and sentimental dad."

With a cock of his head, he reached for his pipe, put it to his lips, took another puff, and said, "I don't know about wise, but sentimental, I sure are!" We then both sort of made an attempt at a halfhearted laugh and with the patter of the rain still compensating for our uncomfortable silence, he shared another thought with me.

Just out of nowhere, I guess he wanted to discuss *me* missing *him*. And we should all know him well enough by now to understand that he simply said what he had to say *when* he darned well felt the need to say it. So, with the honesty that only he could portray and all the compassion he could muster up, he told me that he felt that missing him was fine, and he felt it was natural. "But," he said, "don't you dwell on my death."

Well, I kind of looked at him like he had just grown a horn in the middle of his forehead and with my own eyes now squinting, along with the rest of my face, I very slowly leaned forward and said, "Dad, I will be devastated when you go. I am losing my buddy, my pal, and my confidant, not to mention my one and only father, for crying out loud. Please don't ask of me things that I can't possibly begin to promise. You're not the one who has to stay behind!"

Well, now he'd gone and done it! It had finally happened. I was right smack-dab in the middle of a full blown crying fit. I had finally had it! I had finally felt like I just couldn't take anymore and to make matters worse, now I had become angry. And I was angry because this wasn't supposed to have happened, damn it. All I had wanted to do was tape his life story, with the rain's pitter-patters gently accompanying us on a gloomy day—and then what? Hell, at that point I had no clue! But I truly never expected either one of us to cry and get upset, for heaven's sake. That little ditty had not been in the gosh darned game plan! Exactly, what in the hell had just happened here? What in tarnation had gone wrong?

Well, well, well. Little Miss Baby Doll had become angry because things hadn't gone exactly as planned once again. How in the heck had I expected to pull off an interview with a dying man about the past, over which he was so emotional about in the first place, without dropping any tears? Well, let's see—huh—beats the hell out of me.

Problem was that there really was no problem, at all. I mean, so what if we were crying? So what if things had gotten a little emotionally out of hand. Who did we hurt? Uh huh, exactly my point. No one. Not even each other.

There are bound to be moments in all our lives when we would rather not make things worse by crying. And I think you all know what I mean. When we want to cry but we hold back those tears with everything we have in us so we may possibly avoid what? Just exactly what harm could possibly take place by crying? So do you think my dad would've gone sooner just because I dropped those tears? Not likely, is it? Or maybe, I was worried about making him feel worse, uh huh, nice try but that was highly unlikely as well. Nope, not a one of those things happened but nonetheless, I felt like I should have been more in control. Well, how de doo! I was missing the point, completely. You see, I was finally feeling and I was doing it out loud. I was finally allowing myself to admit that not even I could save my dad. Things were just the way they were and that would have to be good enough. But most importantly, I had finally realized that saving the world was not my responsibility. Well, for the time being anyway.

After we spent our time crying together, my dad asked me to make another promise to him. Yes, right smack-dab in the middle of our moment he felt the need to ask me right then and there if I would promise him something else. Directly after I had already told him not to ask me to promise things that I couldn't possibly deliver, he went right on ahead and asked me to promise that I would at least try to forgive my mom for all of the mistakes she had made in the past. I tell you, the man never ceased to amaze me right up until the day he died!

Now, please understand, it's not that my mom shouldn't have been forgiven, I mean to tell you that I didn't know if she should have been or not. But either way, I felt that it wasn't up to *me* to forgive her. I was not her judge nor was I her jury. And at that time, my mom had continued to be the same way throughout the years. No matter what I said or did or how much I begged for answers, she refused to take any blame for the loss of our childhood. She simply continued to make excuses for not protecting us when we were children. She said she was always working. She said she hadn't known what was going on because she was never there. And if you don't mind me saying so, that very excuse in itself, was an admission of guilt, for crying out loud!

Nope, my mother absolutely refused to take responsibility for anything at all except having to work to support us—period—end of conversation! And let me tell you, having to explain this to my dad was like pulling teeth without any anesthetic.

So, I finally got the courage up, looked him square in the eye and calmly said, "Dad, when Mom comes to me and asks for my forgiveness, *then* and only *then*, will I be able to make that decision."

Well, he was puzzled, to say the least. He cocked his head to the side just like a dog that has heard a strange noise, squinted his eyes, scrunched up his nose and said to me, "You mean to tell me she hasn't?"

Yes, my friends, my cute, simple-minded, myth-believing, misunderstanding, little dad had just naturally assumed that my mom had already apologized to me and that I was simply holding out on her for punishment. Oh, sure. Why the hell not? And he continued to stare at me in bewilderment, mumbling something to the tune of, "I can't believe it."

Gently and ever so carefully, as not to further break the heart of an already broken man, I told him I wanted nothing more than to hear my mom take responsibility for her part in our abuse, but she never had and I doubted if she ever would. Then, looking into those sad and disbelieving eyes, I shared a comforting thought with him. I told him that I truly believed in my heart that God has a special place in heaven for people like him. So innocent and so caring, people who naturally assume that the human race is honest and giving. It had never even entered his mind that my mom wouldn't have asked for forgiveness. I mean, as far as he was concerned, if you're wrong you're wrong. No big deal! Patch things up and try not to do again whatever it was that you did in the first place and go on with your life. His beliefs had always been to take responsibility for your own actions. And I must say that it broke my heart to have to sit there and witness the hurt in his eyes and his inability to understand what I had just told him. He just sat there shaking his head back and forth, from side to side in disbelief before he finally broke the silence with, "Well, I guess your mother can avoid you and all the other girls and she can even avoid me for that matter, but there is someone she can't avoid and when it comes time for her to come face to face with that being, all hell is going to break loose!" Well put, I thought. Very well put indeed.

So there we sat, staring at each other like we had just arm wrestled and it had ended up a tie. My dad with his arms folded against his chest and me sitting cross-legged on the bed with my hands folded in my lap. And just for the record, I feel it only fair to share with all of you that about a year after my father passed away, my mom did come to me one afternoon with her apologies and sorrows in tow. Oh, and just for the same record, for those of you who might be keeping track, yes, I did forgive her and I asked for God to do the same.

I told my dad that day—that unfortunately, not all people think like him. "No, I guess not," was his reply. "I sure wish they did," I told him. If that were true then there would never be any bad in the world, and all little children would have the wonderful memories that I have from knowing a man like my father. Ah, the wonderful world of fairy tales.

And that, ladies and gents, was the end of our taping session. That was exactly the way my dad saw it. So it is written.

Oh, with the exception of one of my favorite stories, which I had asked for him to tell me just one more time—for the mere sake of getting it on tape.

It was the story of a young man who had joined the volunteer fire department shortly after he had gotten out of the army. And the story goes something like this:

This young man had been called to help fight a fire one day, which actually turned out to take several days before the fire would finally be extinguished. And several days after the fire had indeed been extinguished this young man and a couple of other firefighters were walking through the charred remains of what had once been a beautiful forest, when they suddenly heard a faint whining sound, coming from up in one of the trees. Naturally, they all looked up, searching for this sound, and low and behold, there—about seven feet up in a huge burnt-out tree, clung a baby bear. And he was holding on to that tree for dear life! His fur was charred and he was crying to beat the band. My dad's own words.

Well, one of the rangers sent our young fire fighter back to camp for some wet blankets and Vaseline and when he returned, they climbed up that tree, with soaked blankets in tow and wrapped that charred, little baby bear up tightly. Then, with ropes and *a little help from above,* as my dad put it, they lowered him down safely out of that tree.

They coated his burnt and blistered paws with Vaseline and after they searched everywhere for his mother, to no avail, they took him into the local fire station and that was the last they heard of that little baby bear. Until about a year later when our very same young volunteer fireman saw a poster hanging at the fire station, portraying that same little bear. And it read, "Smokey Says, Only You Can Prevent

Forest Fires." Yes, my friends that young volunteer firefighter was my dad and that must have been about the umpteenth, gazillionth time that I had asked him to tell me that story. Because, even though I certainly knew it by heart, I didn't have it on tape and I all of a sudden realized that day, that once my dad was gone, he wouldn't be able to ever tell it again. Although, I will share with you that this time, he added a very different ending.

Sitting there on the bed, with his arms folded across his chest, staring off into some distant somewhere—with the pitter-patter of the rain beginning to fade, he slowly and quietly whispered that he believed Smokey had died some years ago. Then after another long pause he finished his thought with a statement that to this day, gives my heart great comfort. "Yup," he said, "Smokey went to bear heaven where all little good bears go when they die and soon, I suppose, I'll be seeing that little bear once again."

So, there you have it. Now, is that story true? Well, I never had the heart to ask. But I believe it is, and that's really all that matters.

After I turned off the tape recorder, my dad asked me to hide my eyes so that he could get up and go to the bathroom. And he did it all by himself. Not only that, but I realized that he hadn't gagged even once while he had been smoking his pipe throughout our entire taping session. Here came the hope once again. Or perhaps, it was just good, old-fashioned, plain and simple wishing.

I really *did* think that God *could* heal my dad. I still do believe that it could have happened. I guess it just wasn't in my dad's game plan, that's all—plain and simple. Miracles happen every day! It's just that some are recognized and some aren't. But they *do* happen—and they *are* possible. Just you wait and see!

# Chapter Eleven

## Angels

*In heaven an angel is nobody in particular.*
Man and Superman (1903) "Maxims for Revolutionists: Greatness"

A LOT HAD TAKEN place during the first full week of my stay, but entering into the second week proved to be just as eventful, to say the least.

I had come to be very close to the hospice nurses and I had come to understand a whole lot about death. But most importantly of all, I had come to know my dad in a different way than ever before and he had come to know me in much the same way. I mean, after all, how many times in our lives do we come face to face with such a situation? Well, if we're lucky never. But as we all know, someday, we will all have to face death's door one way or another. And sitting here now, I can tell you that I was once afraid to die. Once—a very long time ago.

My visits with the hospice nurses were long and many. Packed full of question and answer sessions that taught me more about the subjects of life and death than I could have ever imagined I was capable of learning. And most of these questions had honestly been prompted by my strange experiences in my father's home. They were most on my mind—simply because I had a difficult time understanding what was happening. OK, I was scared half out of my wits!

You see, the strange experience I had on my first night there was only the beginning of many to come. I felt sensations of all kinds, all of the time, and by the beginning of my second week there, they weren't only happening at night anymore. Oh, how wonderful, these lessons in life we learn.

It seems to me now, that with every day my dad got weaker, the sensations came more often and stronger. And I must refer to these experiences as sensations, simply because it is the only way I can describe them.

OK, readers, the time has come for me to take the risk of your getting up from wherever you are and tossing this book in the trash while shaking your heads from side to side, wondering just why in the hell you read this far in the first place—as I try to explain things to you just as they happened to me. Bear with me now, this could get a little ugly.

Remember the first night at my dad's house? Well, I truly do believe that it was indeed a hand on my back, a comforting hand that, perhaps, was thanking me for being there. As I explained before, with the help of the hospice nurses and their experiences with the dying, I became aware that it was not unusual for these things to happen. Not unusual for whom, is all I wanted to know.

Now, for those of you who are still with me, I will continue on. For those of you who aren't going any further, don't really throw this book in the trash, please recycle and save a tree.

The hospice nurses explained to me that when it comes time for many of us to go, people, well, no—more like spirits, no—people—might start hanging around, people from another place. Another realm, another plain, spiritual beings.

After I had pleaded with them to listen to me without calling the proper authorities, I told stories that I couldn't believe were coming out of my own mouth. These were stories of feelings and sensations that I had been experiencing at night and now, during the day, as well. Each and every time I entered my dad's room, I felt warm all over and chills or goose bumps usually accompanied it—or as I now like to call them, angel bumps. Just as I began to doze off at night I heard someone clearly whispering my name. I began to see colors faintly surrounding my dad at times, which I had simply shrugged off as me needing new contacts. I saw shadows moving about out of the corner of my eyes. My hair would blow from a slight breeze that would go just as quickly as it came while I was in the house with no windows open. And—I felt—human touch—at times when I was completely alone—or so I thought.

Well, I am pleased to announce that I knew I wasn't crazy, when the nurses simply explained to me that these experiences or *sensations* were all perfectly normal. So in your face, all of you book recyclers! I am perfectly sane! As a matter of fact, I wondered if this was why the witch had decided to stay away most of the time. But then I collected myself and realized that she would not have felt these things. As a matter of fact, she wouldn't even talk to me about them when asked. I don't think angels like witches anyway.

When the hospice nurse asked me if my dad himself had seen anyone yet or if he had been speaking to someone—I all of a sudden got that deer-in-the-headlights look.

I must admit that when that question came at me, it was all I could do not to check out of that place and run like hell to anywhere my scared little legs would take me. Yes, even as much as I have tried to convince all of you, I still had a really hard time believing it myself. What in the hell was actually going on here? Yes, as a matter of stinking fact, my dad had been speaking to someone, and quite a bit, as time grew closer. It seemed that the weaker he got, the more he spoke to someone I couldn't see. And I, quite frankly, did not approve at all. This was twilight zone material, ladies and gentlemen. Definite outer limits stuff that I had no intention of trying to understand.

Well, again, to be quite truthful with all of you, whether I liked it or not, I was right smack-dab in the middle of another situation that I had no control over and could do nothing about. And as much as I tried to tell myself that it wasn't happening, it was real. Very real!

My dad spoke to people who weren't there all right. At least not there that I could see, anyway. But who was I to say? At first I truly thought he was becoming senile. Maybe that is exactly what you all are thinking at this very moment too. If so, it's all right. Don't feel like you have to understand. After all, if I hadn't seen it with my own eyes or heard it with my own ears, or felt it with my own skin, or witnessed it with my own heart, I too would not have believed it. So relax, because I totally understand.

The first week, my dad spoke to these someones only when he thought I wasn't listening. Remember? It was in the wee hours of the mornings when he was throwing up absolutely nothing when we first heard him saying, "Yeah, OK, all right." It wasn't until one day, when the TV kept shutting itself off, that I realized he must have been speaking to and seeing them quite often and the time had come for me to finally confront my dad with the unheard of.

He was sitting in his chair watching one of his shows, with his headphones intact, sort of dozing in and out of sleep, when all of a sudden, the TV turned off. I was sitting next to him on the couch, playing solitaire, minding my own stinking business.

I looked over at him, wondering if he might have accidentally shut the thing off with the remote. Well, it was a nice try, however, the remote was on the coffee table. OK, I thought, probably just a cable surge. You know how the cable will sometime shut itself off? Uh huh, nice try again, Baby Doll, but my dad didn't have cable. OK, I thought, no problem. It must have been a power surge. They happen all the time, however, Little Miss Know It All had unfortunately, overlooked the fact that had that actually been the case, the lights would have surged also. Nitwit!

Well, believe it or not, I didn't really think much about it before I leaned over and with my dad wide awake now and staring at me like I was some sort of fool, I picked up the remote and turned the damned TV back on.

I no sooner sat back down on the couch to finish my hand of solitaire and I'll be darned if it didn't happen again! But this time, my dad opened his eyes real wide and politely asked me to stop it. *Guilty by association, I guess.*

I motioned for him to remove his headphones and as he did I was explaining at one hundred miles per hour that I didn't do anything. He then, very seriously looked me in the eye and said he didn't believe me.

"Look, you little dum-dum," he said, "leave my TV alone."

Well–I–never! I thought as I looked him square in the eye and told him just that. I then proceeded to tell him that I didn't much care for the goings on in his house lately anyway. And that's when it happened. All heaven sort of broke loose, so to speak.

I stood up and began pacing back and forth, ranting and raving about someone touching me at night, and about hearing him talking to someone who isn't there and, "Quite frankly," I said, "I am sick of feeling like I'm losing my mind!"

Now, he sat there for a long couple of minutes looking at me like I had just grown a mustache, before he finally asked me if I had actually seen someone. I was absolutely dumbfounded. *Seen someone? What in the hell sort of question was that?*

"Hell, no," I told him. "If I had, then I might be able to understand just exactly what in the Sam hell was going on here!" Then, in a much calmer tone I asked, "*Who exactly,* am I supposed to have *seen?*" I then made it clear that I demanded an answer by repeating the question. "Who, Dad?"

Needless to say, I stood there for a minute (or ten) with my hot little hands on my impatient bouncing hips like I was some big shot staring at him with probably the most disbelieving look on my face that my dad had ever seen. And all I could think of to say is *who*? Who in the name of God was he talking about?

So, he again told his obviously deaf daughter, that he had no idea who they were, but they had shown up around the same time that I had—and they were there to comfort and help him.

Uh huh, I thought. Let's just hold it the hell right here, you cute little insane dad of mine. Now, not only did I have to deal with the hospice warnings of the unexplainable—but I also had to deal with the fact that my own cute little nitwit minded dad had just obviously gone off the deep end as well! And I was, without a doubt, the only sane human being around! Where in the hell do these people get their nerve?

My dad then reached for his pipe and very nonchalantly packed it and lit it and then sat back in his chair, took in a satisfying puff, and very casually said, "They aren't hurting anyone, dear. They are here to help me when I get sick in the middle of the night. They were sent here from heaven to comfort me. That's all."

Oh—well—heck—that's all?! That's all?! Oh for criminy sakes—I absolutely was losing what little mind I had left!

I walked over very slowly with my eyes never leaving his and I sat down on the couch, as close to the chair as I could get and I placed my hands on my dad's bony little knees and then I leaned as close to him as I could get without falling off the couch and I said, "How do you know where they came from, Dad?" I could not believe I was having this conversation.

He continued enjoying his pipe and he answered me very matter-offactly with, "I know because they told me where they came from." (Duh) "Besides," he continued, "you should be happy—because they like you and me *and* they appreciate you being here."

I carefully chose my words as I offered more information as though I were cracking a cold case wide open. "But you know, Dad, they only come around when you and I are here alone."

"Yah, I know," he said. "She doesn't believe."

Well, of course she didn't believe. Witches don't believe in angels! They only believe in evil stuff, like potions and spells and voodoo and hating, caring daughters.

Now my dad wasn't the type of man to go on and on about something, especially something that he knew nothing about. Well, this is where we differed tremendously because I wanted to drill him until I got an answer that satisfied me. And for those of us who know me, we know that that in itself could've taken all day. Well, all of that is just fine and jim-dandy, but the frustrating truth of the matter was that there were no answers. So I did just exactly what any other normal red-blooded American daughter would have done. Yup, after I had what I know was an absolute nervous breakdown, I turned to the hospice people for help.

Now let's just recap exactly what went on here, shall we? My sick and dying cute little unafraid dad just told me that he has been seeing and talking to people who aren't really there. And that he knows where they came from because they told him. And let's not forget how much they like us. Boy howdy, did that make me feel better! Was I the only one there who wasn't getting this people? I mean, come on! These things don't happen in real life, do they? Well, hell, no, they don't, at least not in my real life. However, my real life had become so confusing by that point that it didn't really matter anymore, anyway. What the hell! Have a party! We'd just invite all of heaven for that silly matter and then at least my dying little socialite of a dad would be happy. Sure, why hadn't I thought of that before? It was a new neighborhood. Go ahead and invite all of your new friends over for pizza! Uh huh, but before that, let's just make a few phone calls, shall we?

Well, both nurses, at separate times (two phone calls) first assured me that there was no reason at all to be afraid. Oh, goody. Wasn't that a sweet relief? I didn't have to be afraid. Why, I might have just danced on the rooftops or no, better yet, maybe I'd just pack my things and join those baldheaded guys down at the airport! Get myself a tambourine and go on the road for a while.

They then proceeded to tell me that it was very rare for someone other than the patient to experience these happenings, however, it was possible that these spirits (if you will), were very appreciative of me. Oh, well, now that was a different story. This was the second time I had been told how much they appreciated me. I felt much better. Halle-flippen-lu-yah! And then, they just as easy as you please, said "It." You know, the words that we hear only in the movies? The words that sound so corny that we automatically think we must have misunderstood? Yup, those words, the words, that haunt my dreams to this very day.

They said that it might be time to have the hospice chaplain come over and talk to my dad. Sure, why not, as my dear old dad would say. Invite everyone was our motto by that time anyway!

Crap! I suddenly felt like I was right smack-dab in the middle of a Marshall Dillon Western. You know? How when some old cowboy is dying and then everyone gets real sad and gathers around him, then the chaplain is called in and the guy chokes a couple of times, maybe says his good-byes to his one and only gal, with Miss Kitty standing idly by for comfort and support and wham! A couple more gasps and he's a goner!

So as I sat listening to these nurses suggesting that it was time to call in a chaplain, it was then and only then that I was sure of the fact that my dad's time to go was really near. I mean after all, when a nurse suggests that it's time to bring in a chaplain, it usually means absolute and near death, right? Oh, sure. But the key word here, folks, is *usually*. And we all know that this is a most "un"usual story to begin with, now, don't we? So don't all of you go getting your bloomers scrunched in an uproar thinking that you have it all figured out, because you don't. Well, not yet anyway.

As the day drew nearer, the strange goings on around my dad's house got more and more intense. The presence of the afterlife had come to hang around quite a bit, as a matter of fact, and my dad and I had come to acknowledge the fact that they must be angels, plain and simple. And I'll be the first one to stand up and say that heavens, yes, it is quite out of the ordinary, but like me, hopefully, as you get closer and closer to the end of this story, you too will feel that they are just as ordinary as you or I. They simply live in another place, that's all.

I believe it was Wednesday of the second week that the hospice chaplain did, in fact, make her debut. And yes, for those of you who think you may have read a misprint, you didn't. I did say "her." She was a very tall, slender woman who spoke softly with a Dutch accent and was angelic herself, as she gracefully swept her way into our hearts and home.

I was scared to death the morning I met her. I guess, somewhere in my strange little mind, I had imagined that because she was a chaplain— that she was physically coming for my dad, or something. Silly, I know, however, it was true. And I was even more afraid to tell my dad that she was coming. I mean, he watched Westerns too, you know. But I am pleased to announce, that just like all the other times, my worry was needless, because, believe it or not, my dad was just absolutely thrilled that a chaplain was coming over. Get that, ladies and gents, absolutely thrilled! Go figure.

It was a definite admission of loss and preparation to me but certainly and obviously not to my dad. And let me not forget to share with all of you that he was also absolutely thrilled that she was a woman! (I have no clue so please don't ask.) Near as I can figure, is I remember him mumbling something about it being "High time that the world began to see women in positions that were once thought to be only a man's job." Yup, as we all already know, that's just the way he was.

On the morning she was to arrive, I was anxiously flittering around trying to keep myself busy so I wouldn't faint or throw up and my dad was sleeping. Get that! Sleeping Beauty had not a care in the world. So how–de–flippin–doo! After this whole thing was over, I'd be going home packing ulcers as well as a nervous breakdown and all he had to do was die! Yes, indeed, this was becoming more and more complicated as the days went on.

The witch had left for work—or wherever it was that she really went during the day and I was in the bathroom, counting all of the newly found wrinkles around my eyes when the chaplain arrived, so the soft knock at the door was a most welcomed intrusion as I rounded the corner of my dad's tiny living room and observed her angelic presence standing at the threshold of my father's tiny palace. And you can laugh if you want to, but I swear she had a sort of purity about her as I glided the door open and invited her in.

Immediately offering her sympathy, as she shook my hand, she led me over to the couch and sat down with me, gracefully turning her lap toward mine, holding both of my hands in hers, as she then quietly requested for me to share my heartaches and experiences with her. She wanted to know everything. And I, my friends, felt like a dreaded weight had just been lifted from my shoulders.

I sat with her that morning, for what must have been the better part of an hour, telling her of my father's declining condition and of the strange goings on that we had come to reluctantly accept. I shared my frustrations and fears as well as my joys and newfound treasures. And perhaps I imagined the relief or maybe there's actually something to be said about confession but I truly did feel like I was safe and like nothing bad could ever come to my dad or me—at least not that day.

Then, it was her turn to speak. And as she did, I felt the strangest, most overwhelming sensation of acceptance and appreciation that I had ever experienced in my entire life, thus far. As if I had just entered into a secret place where no one else had ever gone before. Well, at least not while living here on this earth.

She felt it very odd but also very welcoming for anyone except the patient to experience the happenings that I had indeed been experiencing. Finally, some validation in the midst of this nightmare! Her assumption was that I must be extremely close to my father spiritually and that I had been chosen long ago to lead my dad away from this place. I was a very special person. Yes, very special indeed.

Was this really me, actually sitting on *this* couch in *this* home discussing my father's death with a chaplain? Yup, at least it had been me when I woke up that morning searching for new wrinkles. Was this actually me who was speaking of spirits and strange hoopla that had obviously consumed my every waking moment? Yup, unfortunately, it *was* me and I was becoming emotionally and physically drained before my very own eyes.

A person can only take so much, you know, and then it's retreat time, ladies and gents, plain and simple. Time to take a step back from the front lines and feel for missing limbs, open wounds, check for permanent scarring, making sure at all costs that the damage done isn't so bad. Well, I'm here to tell you that when I took that step back, I realized, much to my own horror, that the damage done was very bad. For I truly believe that on that day back in October of 1992, it was then that I knew beyond a shadow of a doubt that I was not the same person I had been when I got there. No, this war had definitely taken its toll on this soldier. I was tired and dirty and I was beaten beyond recognition. And I'm also here to tell you that no war story I had ever heard could have properly prepared me for the battles past or the battle I was about to experience. I had definitely earned a purple heart. And it was a darned good thing too. For the heart I came with had been broken into a million pieces.

As we sat, continuing getting to know one another, my sleepy-eyed, wandering, little dad emerged from the bedroom, and headed straight for the bathroom. Giving the hospice chaplain a knowing nod, I got up and walked over to the bathroom door and informed him that we had company. And with excitement in his voice, he answered me through the door with "Oh, goody!" Then he assured me that he would be right out.

Oh, goody? Gee whiz, there was a chaplain there. A chaplain who would probably make sure all of his affairs were in order and then give him the ol' kiss off speech as Miss Kitty stood idly by, crying to beat the band—and then would come the few short gasps and bang! He would undoubtedly be history, as we know it—and all this old man had to say was "Oh, goody?" Oh, brother!

I wandered back over and sat down on the futon across from the chaplain and as my dad came out of the bathroom and shuffled his way into the living room, I reached over and turned on the tape recorder.

I made the formal introductions as he was getting nestled into his chair, wrapping himself up in his blanket pausing only long enough to give respect to this woman of the cloth before he continued to finish getting comfortable.

After he became situated, she began with questions regarding his health and well-being and slowly but ever so carefully, she began probing into his spiritual beliefs.

Well, I'll have you all know that my cute, little, angel-befriending dad informed us that he wasn't one bit afraid to die. No, siree. He said that when the good Lord saw it was time—then he would come and get him. And until then, he would simply continue to do just exactly what he had been doing all along, and that, my friends, was that. But I'll also have you know that before their conversation was over, he did mange to say something that absolutely took us both by surprise. And I don't mind telling you, that it also just about brought me to my knees. Imagine that? Not *my* dad.

He looked over at the chaplain, and leaned forward just as far as he could lean and motioned her to come a little closer to him as if he was about to share a secret with her, excluding me from ear shot. (Fat chance) Then, very softly he said to her, "It isn't me I'm worried about." He then pointed directly at me and said, "It's this one here that I'm worried about. Who will be there for her when it's all over?" He then looked down at his folded hands that were sitting studiously in his lap and with tears now staggering down his wrinkled cheeks he said, "There was only one other time in her life that I wasn't there for her and it damn near killed her. And I won't be able to be there for her this time either. I've tried to be there every other time"—his voice trailed off and with a turn of his head, he softly whispered, "But not this time."

Trying to feel my legs and at the same time trying to see through my own tear-filled eyes, I swiftly slithered to my knees from the couch and scooted across the floor to my sobbing, hand-wringing little dad and kneeling before him, I reached up and took his face into my hands and told him that I loved him and that I'd be OK.

And then it hit me! Yup. For one heart-stopping screaming second Little Miss Baby Doll thought she just might be on to something once again. Sheesh, I never cease to amaze my silly self! Was he holding on for me? Naw. Just as quickly as that thought fleeted in, I dismissed it. No way was I going there. No way in heaven or hell was I going there at all. My bravery just simply astounds me.

With a gentle and comforting hand the hospice chaplain assured my dad that they are also trained to support those who are left behind, and she made a solemn promise to him that someone would absolutely be there for me long after he was gone. Oh heck, I felt better already. OK, maybe I didn't, but it was obvious that he sure as heck did and, quite frankly, I guess that was all that really mattered. He was relieved. You could tell by the look on his face. I was exhausted. And I guess I was also just a little bit more afraid because weren't we just a few steps closer now to saying good-bye? Well, perhaps in the large scheme of things, I suppose we were. But truthfully and realistically we were quite a long ways off. Well, heck, you can look at the number of pages there are left to read and know that! However, I am about to share another little secret with you. Ready? OK, here it is. I was learning all along. Yup, learning life's lessons. Lessons that take most of us an entire lifetime to understand. Amazing, isn't it? Yes, indeed, it sometimes truly is.

You see I had learned something most precious. Something that I will cherish for as long as I, myself, live here in this place. I learned about another world, another world where people or angels if you will, actually come to lend a helping hand to those of us who are in need. And you want to know something else? An angel can come into your life and appear as a real person too. Someone who just happens to show up and help you through a difficult situation, like the hospice people, for instance, and it's not always just for the dying as you too are about to learn. And as your mind begins to wander now to a person or a certain happening that you have experienced at one time or another, just do me a favor and think about it. Just consider the possibility. Because once you allow yourself to consider, the most wonderful things begin to happen in your life, because belief is a very important part of our learning experiences here on this earth. From Santa Claus to angels, really, just trust me on this one. Yup, as a matter of fact, sometimes, I think those angels, both the real ones and the sight unseen ones, were there for *me* even more so than they were for my dad. And believe you me, by the time we get to the end of this story, perhaps even some of you nonbelievers will even start to wonder. Yes, if I have done my job as a writer, you too, just might wonder the next time someone special enters into your life, or each and every time you get a chill or think you saw something move out of the corner of your eye, or think you could've sworn you heard someone whisper your name; yes perhaps even *you*, the most stubborn of believers will wonder—could it have been an angel?

# Chapter Twelve

## *Friends*

*Oh I get by with a little help from my friends.*
John Lennon 1940–1980 Paul McCartney 1942

O
N THE VERY same morning that I made the brilliant discovery of angels, I also made the astounding discovery that the hospice chaplain was in fact, not Miss Kitty after all! Nope. And I know because she left that day and my dad was still breathing. Truly remarkable! And after I discovered each of these absolutely miraculous findings she had to be going. Probably had all one could take for a morning whether one is an angel or not. However, before she went riding off into the sunset or the heavens or wherever people like her really *do* go, she had to ask some questions, probably part of her job. Either that or she really was from hell and truly sent here to do nothing but torture me, because one of the questions on her list was THE ONE! You know, the question that seemed to be the most popular amongst the dying? Yup, that one. As she turned to leave after saying her good-byes she turned back around and had the audacity to ask if all of my dad's affairs were in order. Yesiree! Just as I was beginning to *really* like her, there was that absurd question again. Damnit! And right smack-dab in the middle of our moment, for cripe's sake! Why couldn't everyone just stop reminding him of the fact that everything had been done so that he could just go peacefully at any time? Quite frankly, I was getting just a little bit sick and tired of this! Who made up that rule anyway? Once everything is in order you can die? Ha! That's the most ridiculous thing I have ever heard of! And why, might you ask. Because everything *wasn't* done. Everything is never really done completely. Duh! If it were, then people would be able to choose their destiny! Which probably means that the world would really be more than overpopulated. Brilliant deduction on my part! Besides, my dad still had some things left to do. My sisters hadn't been there yet. So it wasn't time to say good-bye just yet. Ha! Ha!

It seems that I could have continued to find all sorts of reasons to keep my dad holding on. And—I'm ashamed to say, that I would have continued to find more and more reasons for the rest of my own life if God had allowed it. Selfish, I know, but oh, so very truthful.

Yes, each and every time I tried, I could always come up with one silly reason or another to make him stay here in this place for just a little while longer. But you know, on this day something began to change. Yes, I do believe it was then, on that very day that I realized I was slowly and ever so slightly beginning to find more and more reasons to let him go. Letting him go was suddenly beginning to outweigh keeping him here. Not like I really had a darned thing to say about it anyway, but I sure as heck thought I did at the time.

So what was the big deal anyway? Affairs in order or not! How come all of a sudden that question finally held a deeper meaning?

Well, I'll tell you why. Because it had finally come to the point that the hospice nurses couldn't believe he was still holding on, that's why. And—let–me–tell–you, it's bad enough when an RN can't figure it out, but when a hospice nurse can't find justification for life, you've just about bought the farm, my friend. Plain and simple.

At that point in our journey, my dad was losing about a pound a day, give or take. He hadn't eaten for almost two weeks excluding an occasional bite of a milkshake or two. He was having difficulty going to the bathroom and was sleeping most of the day and when he wasn't sleeping he wasn't real—shall we say, responsive. Well, not to anyone living anyway. Yes, my friends, he was slowly shutting down. His body was tired and it seemed that the time had finally come for this old man to go rolling home, and one of the most horrible nightmares I had been dreading all of my life was on it's way to becoming very real. So, that's what the big deal was. I just didn't know it at the time. And worst of all was, I didn't really care. I didn't care what his existence was. I just wanted him to stay. You see—the hospice nurses seemed to have just a little more respect for my dad than I did. Well, sort of, perhaps in a different sense. I guess they must have known something that I didn't. DO YA THINK?

I think the most embarrassing of all is that I wanted to know just exactly *how. How* exactly would he die? You see, this damn well mattered to me. Probably a little bit of my background shining through; nonetheless, it was vitally important to me, but not to worry. The hospice people were quite used to these absolutely stupid questions being asked by absolutely scared–half–out–of–their–wits family members. Part of their job, I suppose. Lucky for me.

So, when I asked how and when they thought "IT" might happen, the most common as well as cordial response was that more than likely, they expected my dad to go peacefully to sleep and never wake up again. Well, quite frankly, this just wasn't logical enough (good enough) for me. I needed (wanted) to know exactly *how*. I mean, people don't just go to sleep and shut down, for hell's sake. Something has to happen first, right? Well, doesn't it? I sure as heck thought so. Would his big and caring heart just finally stop beating? Or would he go into a violent cardiac arrest? Or maybe his liver would fail? Might he go into a coma? What would happen, damnit, and how bad would it hurt? That's all I wanted to know! Do you hear me? That's *"all"* I wanted to know! Pitiful, huh? All I wanted to know were the answers that held the very key to the whole entire universe. And those answers just plain and simply and quite frankly would never be told. They just couldn't. Imagine that. I was asking something of those hospice people that they couldn't possibly have given me. Yes, now that I think about it, I most certainly and pitifully was, and do you want to know what else? I didn't really give a rip! Gosh, that was so unlike me not to care about logic. But so many things were not like me at the time. And so many things in my life sure as heck had been far from logical. What in the hell was happening to me? After all, I still *was* my father's daughter. How could I have become this creature who was so very selfish? Well, you see, from my point of view at the time all I was asking (wishing) for were some answers as well as a cure for the horrible disease that had consumed my daddy's body turning him into God only knows what, because I sure as hell couldn't figure it out! That was about it in a nutshell. Not a whole lot to ask, or so I felt at the time. Huh, not a whole lot to ask, yet then it leaves me wondering just exactly *why*, as I am writing and remembering, do I feel like such a fool? Probably another one of those keys to the universe answers that will never be told, I suppose— and so the story goes.

I know my dad enjoyed his little chat with the hospice chaplain, simply because he told me so, himself. He told me that he liked talking about what would happen when it was all over. He said it made him feel like a little mouse in the corner and that it actually comforted him in a way. Uh huh, wonderful, go figure. It made *me* feel like I wanted to puke, void, and crap all at the same time, and not necessarily in that order.

When it came time to end her visit, she promised to return the following week, or sooner if need be and, I gotta tell you, I wanted to grab onto her leg as she was walking out the door begging her to stay every inch of the way. Not to worry though, I contained myself for the mere sake of appearances. But in all honesty, I think I actually believed that because she was a woman of the cloth that perhaps there might be some bargaining power here. You know, maybe she was tighter with the big guy than most. Oh, I know it was silly and I know that you don't really have to be someone of the cloth to be tight with God either, but just like everything else that I had experienced up to that point, I really didn't give a rat's patoot. I would've tried as well as believed anything. Imagine that!

Shortly after she had gone just as gracefully as she had arrived, my dad all of a sudden, wanted to take a walk. A walk? You mean outside, with your legs moving and everything? Like, healthy people do in the evenings after supper? That kind of walk? Holy heck! The hospice chaplain had performed an absolute miracle! My dad had been cured and wanted to take a walk!

Here came that never-ending hope once again. Yes, I thought (prayed) that this could be a sign. Maybe he had to go outside in the fresh air for God to kiss him and he would be better! Yes, that was it! Of course! How had I overlooked one of the most well-known facts in little kid history? God can only see you outside where he has a clear view from heaven! Well, I guess I overlooked that little fact the same exact way I was overlooking the other little well-known fact that I was completely out of my ever-loving mind. Oh well, whatever it takes sometimes, I guess.

So, I did what any other out-of-her-mind daughter would do. I helped him up out of his chair and about killed myself racing to the bedroom to grab a T-shirt for him, yelling back into the living room every step of the way, for him to stay right there. No problem spazoid—like where was he going to go? Frantically searching in every direction—*Ah Ha!*—There was his little T-shirt, hanging over the back of the chair! Grabbing it with such excitement that I about ripped it in two as I ran back into the living room to low and behold find him standing right where I had left him. Whew! Do the true wonders of the world never cease to amaze? I then, very carefully and ever so gently put the little cotton tumor hiding magic cloth on him and then I *tied his sweatpants just a little tighter so he wouldn't lose them on his walk (Hadn't I just done that yesterday too?)*. Oh well, it didn't matter, because my adventureseeking little dad wanted to take a walk to be cured by God and we headed for the door.

"Where do you want to walk to?" I asked. Maybe Siberia? With a little luck—we can probably make it by your eighty-fifth birthday! But my simple-minded little walking dad just wanted to stroll out to his pickup. That was all. He simply wanted to walk out to the tiny driveway that ran alongside of his little trailer and say hello to his good old friend, his 1982 Chevy Pickup. Plain and simple. OK, that was a great start, today to the Chevy, tomorrow, who knows, could be all the way to the neighbor's house—and after that, the possibilities were endless!

So, we strolled out onto the porch and I helped him down the steps, and we began our journey to the side of his mobile home. We are probably talking about ten feet or so, but it took quite a while to get there. And that's when it happened! Reality reared its ugly head once again as my dad had to stop at the bottom of the steps just to catch his breath. He stood there for a minute or two (or six) but who was counting, and with all of the pride he could muster, he then shook my hands free and away from his own and told me he would be fine to walk on his own now. Of course he would. This was a moment between a man, his pickup, and God.

I followed closely behind him anyway but not so close that he could tell what I was doing. Actually, I didn't even know what I was doing. I guess I was just preparing to catch him if he fell.

Oh, how I wish all of you could have seen how he looked when he rounded that corner and saw his Chevy sitting there under the carport awning just waiting for him to crawl in and go. It was like watching the scene of a classic love story. They just don't make 'em like that anymore.

He slowly walked around the front of that beautiful piece of machinery running his hand over the hood and then around to the driver's side of the door. And I stood completely frozen, up against the corner of our little home, as I watched him so fondly reminiscing with an old friend.

He then, all of a sudden startled me by turning toward me and asking if maybe one of the girls might want to wash the old Chevy when they arrive. Regaining my composure from imagining that I was invisible, I assured him that it wouldn't be any trouble at all.

Still standing by the driver's side door, he put his hand on the door handle and attempted to open it. It was locked. Of course it was. He babied that truck like it was a child. He wouldn't have dared to leave it unlocked. He then turned to me once again and asked me to go into the house and get the keys.

The keys?! The keys?! Why, where did he think he was going? For hell's sake he couldn't even walk straight let alone try to drive! And even though I was panic stricken as well as confused, I studiously ran like a mad woman into the trailer to retrieve the tiny pieces of metal that could magically bring his old friend to life. And as I blazed around the corner of the kitchen, there they were, hanging proudly from the bulletin board. I grabbed them and whipped myself back outside and down the steps to where he was, thank God, still standing. I carefully placed them in his hand and he rewarded me with a simple and polite thank you. No problem, I thought, that is unless you actually think that you are going somewhere because if you do then we do have a problem—and a big one.

But no, he sadly knew he couldn't drive. He simply wanted to sit in his pickup and start her up, for old times' sake. And that was all.

He then crawled up inside of her, placed the key inside the secret slot and turned her over. With the purr of a mighty kitten, she came to life, and so did he. And he sat there, with his arms resting on the steering wheel, staring out over the hood, with a wanting look in his eyes that could not be mistaken for anything but pure desire for the better part of about twenty minutes, and I mean to tell you that I felt like I was eavesdropping on the hottest love affair of the century at that very moment. So

I decided to give him some privacy and leave him with, once again, a little much-deserved dignity. So with my head down, I walked around the corner of the house really slowly until I was out of his sight and then I ran like crazy, up the steps and through the door and into the living room. I then perched myself on the couch, which was directly below a window that looked out onto the carport. And there I sat, hiding behind the curtain, watching my dad, through a haze of sheers and tears.

He revved the engine just a couple of times, but mostly, he just simply sat there listening to the hum of life, reminiscing like two old friends about dreams that had so unfairly slipped away.

He must have sat there for the better part of a half hour or more, before he slowly reached for the key, shutting her down for the very last time. And you know, as I sat there watching him through the curtains that day, I couldn't help feeling the absolute finality I witnessed in his good-bye. I knew in my heart just as well as he knew in his heart, that he would never again drive his beautiful Chevy Pickup.

He sat there for just a few more minutes after she had shut down before he attempted to hop down out of his love of the past, as I quickly took that as my cue and hopped off the couch and made a beeline for the door, swiftly setting myself on a lawn chair that proudly sat perched on the front porch, just like I had been sitting there all along, without a care in the world. It took him a good minute to round the corner. As a matter of fact I started to get a bit worried; however, here he came walking ever so slowly and completely out of breath. I wanted so badly to get up and help him, but I didn't—no, I *couldn't*—no, I absolutely *wouldn't!* This had been a special moment for my dad and I, for one, was not going to interfere or even attempt to take that away from him.

He hobbled up the three steps and took a seat next to mine, with his chest heaving and his eyes full of tears. I pretended to pay no attention to his pain, until he invited me into his thoughts. And I knew he would; it just took a little time.

Sure enough, after about five minutes he turned to me and said, "She's a good piece of machinery."

I looked at him and said, "Yup, that she is."

He sat there for about a minute longer in silence, when all of a sudden, still with tears in his eyes he blurted out, "God damnit, this is hell!"

I flinched with the snap of his words as my entire body went rigid, looked down at my feet, as that's where the trail of my own tears were resting, and softly said, "It sure is, Dad."

I couldn't look at him. I just couldn't. For one thing I think to the best of my recollection, it was the first time I had ever heard my dad use the Lord's name in vain like that. But there was another reason I couldn't look him in the eye that day. You see, I was ashamed—for it was the first time during this whole stinking ordeal that I privately asked God to take my dad.

Life for him was over. All of the simple pleasures that had once preoccupied this simple little man were finally over. He couldn't even stay awake long enough to completely finish watching his shows anymore. However, I continued to tell myself that at least he was still making the effort. Sometimes, he would stay awake after the show had ended and I would fool myself into believing that it was a positive sign, knowing that he had slept through the entire show itself. I truly believe that it was a coping technique that I had invented for myself, like a survival tool of hope. No matter how terrible this situation had become, I never once let go of the hope.

In reality, my friends, it was sadly a façade. I couldn't deal with the facts at hand. The hospice people were telling me that it could happen any day. But I just absolutely could not imagine life without my precious dad. Yes, I knew he was dying. My mind was well aware of that fact. It was my heart that couldn't be convinced.

We sat there that day for just a little while longer before my dad got a chill and wanted to go back inside. You got that—a chill in Southern California? But that wasn't the worst part folks. Nope there was plenty more to come.

We got up out of our lawn chairs and choo chood back into the house. And once we were standing inside I looked over my shoulder and asked him where he wanted to go. Well, he said with a little chuckle, we could stand right here and look silly all day.

I reached back like I was trying to hit him and I told him to "Knock it off, old man."

He simply replied with, "I might be old but I am still *your* father and that means you better be nice to me." Again, my silly little dad was displaying his funny side. And you know, he did that quite a bit during his final days with me. I don't know how he kept that sense of humor. That very same sense of humor that had been this trademark throughout his life, but he did. Yup, right to the very end, he sure as heck did. Imagine that. The eighth wonder of the world!

Standing there, we finally decided that it had been a long afternoon and that it was time for him to turn in. So off to the bedroom we scooted.

I got him to the bedroom and settled into bed when he invited me to sit and talk for a while. So I sat down on the floor, next to the bed with my arms resting comfortably under my chin on the side of him, with my hands rubbing his arm. And we chatted about everything and anything that came to mind before he finally drifted off to sleep. And I sat there with his hand in mine, wondering if this is how it would be when he finally did leave me, me sitting there with his hand in mine, looking at him while he appeared to be sleeping. The thought was too painful, so I quickly pushed it out of my mind. But I continued to sit there for quite some time and as I did I began to cry. The loneliness had collided with my spirit and the burden became too much to bear. I suddenly realized that I felt very sorry for me. Here I was sitting on the floor next to my dad's bed while he was sleeping and he would be leaving me soon and there wasn't a damned thing I could do to stop it! So, all that was left to do was cry. To be honest with all of you, I secretly hoped that he might just wake up, putting his soft little arms around me and tell me that everything was going to be all right. But he couldn't, now, could he? Nope, he sure as hell couldn't. But I will tell all of you that what did happen next was the furthest thing from my mind, to say the least!

All of a sudden as I sat there sobbing, minding my own emotions as well as my own damned business, my dad did wake up. Well, sort of.

He opened his eyes sat straight up and stared over in the opposite corner of the room. I quickly wiped my tears off my face so as not to let on that I'd been crying, although it really didn't matter because I don't think he would have noticed if a bomb had dropped on the house.

Still quickly wiping my eyes and staring at him at the same time, I realized that he was in somewhat of a daze. Oh, he responded to me all right. I mean he knew I was sitting there and he acknowledged that, with a simple pat on my hand; however, he was preoccupied with something over in the left-hand corner of the room. Or perhaps I should say *someone*.

He patted my hand once again, but then he ever so slowly lifted his right hand from lying atop mine and with his index finger extended and without making a single sound he pointed up to the corner. And then he did the unthinkable to those of us who consider ourselves sane. As a matter of fact, what he did next sent chills up my very spine. He waved. Just ever so slowly like he wasn't really sure if he should actually be waving or not. So what did I do? Well, to be quite truthful, I really didn't know what to do and I sure as hell didn't begin waving too. But my relationship with my father had grown too strong for me to doubt him in any way, that's for damned sure.

So I leaned closer to him and I whispered, "Who are you waving at, Dad?"

He continued to lie there for just a moment, with his hand still slightly in the air before he said to me, I don't know who they are. I then asked do they know you? He said they seemed to.

Now you should know me well enough by now to know that I felt like running from that room at that very moment, screaming for God to return to me my sanity at once! This was not anything I could have ever imagined in my wildest dreams. Not in my widest imagination for that matter and we all know I truly *do* have one of those. And it wasn't that I believed my dad just because he was my dad either. No, I mean to tell you that I felt something, something very soothing and powerful and something that I just simply could not ignore. I was scared to death. And then I watched in absolute amazement as my dad began to speak.

He shook his head up and down very slowly saying, "Yes, I know, all right." And you know, I have never considered myself a crazy person, even during all of the things I've been through that should have made me crazy, yet I sat there questioning my own sanity for just a second before I realized that I truly believed there was indeed someone there.

I took my dad's hand and slowly lifted myself up from the floor and I carefully sat down next to him on the bed. I then very quietly whispered with tears flowing freely from my eyes, Dad, is it time for you to go? I was scared half out of my wits and, quite frankly, didn't know what in the heck could be happening. Therefore I assumed it was time. What else was I to think? But my simple-minded, angel-beholding dad just simply turned to me and said no, not yet.

Well that's just wonderful, I thought. I mean it wasn't enough that I was sitting there feeling a presence that I couldn't see, as it was. And it wasn't enough that I was just about ready to lose what little mind I had left. But now I had resorted to asking questions of things I knew nothing about regarding people I couldn't even see. And what was worse is the fact that my dad *could* see them but he didn't know them either! Ha, like it mattered to begin with! Yup, this was definitely loony bin material here, folks, not a doubt in my mind.

But you know what I figured out once I stopped long enough to listen to myself? I realized at that very moment that my dad had chosen to share this with me. That is exactly why he had invited me in to his bedroom to talk that very evening. And I realized it because he told me so himself. So put that in your pipes and smoke it!

Now, whoever these people were, told my dad that his time was definitely nearing and they told him I was scared and this just didn't set well with my dad at all. No, siree! He would not have me being afraid. And I have to tell you, I had no clue who this person or people were that told my dad these things and they absolutely and quite frankly pissed me off—but they were absolutely correct, as I have already shared with you. I was scared. Scared to lose him and scared of all of the things I did not understand. My dad felt it very important to address this matter promptly.

So, right in the middle of his gazing session, he turned to me and very matter-of-factly said, "Why are you afraid?"

I sat there for several dumbfounded moments, staring into his eyes before I said, "Afraid? Afraid of what?" Duh! Brilliant response, you lying dum-dum.

Now, I don't know if I was testing him at that point or what the hell I was doing, for that matter. All I know is, I just simply needed to hear what he thought I might be afraid of.

He then said to me, "You know what I'm talking about. Why are you afraid of death and why do you have second thoughts about letting me go when it comes time?"

Well, hallelujah! The cat was out of the bag now! I hadn't told that to *anyone*, not even the damned cat itself! I honestly had not even confronted me, myself with that fact until then. Imagine that! Oh, I could sit there with a straight face and lie my little butt off to anyone who would care to listen about how noble and brave Eddie's daughter was and how she was just waiting for the day to say good-bye to her dear old dad forever. But at that moment, I realized something. A very vital and important part of this whole story, so pay attention. I truly realized I couldn't do it! There—the damned cat really is out of the bag now! Nope, not a snowball's chance in hell! Not one little bit was I going to be able to let him just up and die. Get the picture? And let's not forget the tiny little fact that someone absolutely invisible had just tipped my dad off to that fact. So there I sat, with a dumbfounded look on my face, darned well knowing that what my dad expected was an answer.

I fidgeted a little (quite a lot) before I could finally look him in the eye and when I did, I simply began with, "Look, I told you that when the time comes I will do my best to carry out your wishes, Dad."

Oh, uh huh, that was just great brown eyes! Just Great! Hold on just a minute here, Dad, while I think of an answer that will satisfy you and your dumb little newfound friends. However, at that point it would have taken more than just a minute. It would've taken an eternity. Yup, an eternity would have been real nice right about then. At least that way I wouldn't have had to have made a commitment to the only person in my whole entire life who ever deserved one. Boy, that was great thinking. And do you know what? I mean, of course you don't until I tell you and I'm getting there, believe me. But do you have any idea what he did after that? Well, by now, you could probably just about guess knowing him the way you all do by now. Yes, ladies and gents, my cute little understanding angel-beholding dad, simply reached over and took my hand in his, rubbing it gently as he told me he understood. Good damned thing someone did!

Actually what he understood, was that what he was asking of me, he knew to be very difficult. Especially for me, his cute little baby doll girl, who just about by that time, had lost her cute little baby doll mind.

But nonetheless, again, he felt he needed to remind me that he asked me, and me alone for a reason and if he couldn't trust me, then whom in the hell could he trust? And as I was flipping through the yellow pages of my mind, frantically searching for someone else who could take on this grueling task, anyone other than me, I shared with him that I thought I could do it. I told him that I knew how very important it was to him and that that fact alone would probably motivate me to do the right thing when the time finally did come.

"Don't worry," I told him, "I won't dial 911, I promise." (I sure as hell can't tell you what I will do but I can guarantee you what I won't do.) Chicken! BALK, BALK, BALK, BALK!

"Now," I said, "Let's discuss these friends of yours. How long have you been talking to whoever they are and why did they tell you that I was afraid?" (Tattletales— tattletales!) Oh, for heck's sake! Did I now believe that someone had actually told him something? Huh, guess I truly did indeed.

My dad just simply sat there, kind of rubbing his fingers together, like a child who had just been caught in a lie, before he answered me with,

"They know how very much I want to go naturally when it's time, so they felt it important for me to know that you had some doubts."

Oh, did they now? Well, I'll be go to hell John! How about them apples! Holy Peter, Paul, and Mary!

"OK," I said, "How in the hell do *they*, whoever *they* are, know these things?"

Now, my dad furrowed his brow a bit and I always hated it when he did that because it simply said he was disappointed and as he was furrowing his brow, giving me that dreaded father look, he said, "Well, I think they are from God. You know? They are someone from heaven. Friends. My friends."

Now you have to know that this was a most unusual conversation to begin with, so as my mind was racing, trying to come up with something logical and intelligent to say, I simply and very matter-of-factly said, "How do you know? How do you know that you aren't just imagining these things, Dad?" Oh, God! Had I just called my dad crazy?

"Well," he said, "I know because I've seen them all before and I've seen where they come from. As a matter of fact, I've been there."

Uh huh, OK, now it was definitely time for me to check out of the Bates Motel! Hasta La Vista, Norman! Don't forget to write!

"When?" I blurted out.

He said he didn't know when—or how for that matter. All my cute little miracle-believing dad could tell me, was that he had, in fact, been to a place where there were no limits nor were there any walls or floors there. He said there was a feeling of total and complete peace that came over him each and every time he visited though—and that he didn't have a care in the world.

Staring at him in total disbelief, I asked, "Dad, do you think you have been to heaven?"

He, in return, looked at me with his brow furrowed once again and said he honestly didn't think so, not yet anyway. He felt that the place he had been visiting was more like a waiting area.

A waiting area?! A waiting area?! A waiting area for what? Were you ordering pizza? Or perhaps you went to the big Texaco in the sky while you were traveling in your sleep and decided to stop off and go to the fricking bathroom! A waiting area?! You have got to be kidding me?! Either that or you have a brother named Norman and I won't ever take another shower at your house as long as we both shall live!

Well, my friends, as absurd as it sounded, it was the truth. The whole truth and nothing but the truth—so help him, God! And that was the first conversation I had with my father in reference to the *hereafter*—and I want you all to know that I believed him. Every single solitary word! The conviction and honesty he portrayed could not be mistaken for anything else (including insanity) but the truth. And his sincerity was most honorable. Not to mention the fact that he had obtained exact information regarding *my* feelings that I hadn't told a soul, not even myself at the time. And I'll tell you something else that should just about knock your socks off. When I brought these things up to the hospice nurses demanding an explanation, they both, at separate times told me that they had witnessed these things before. Several times, as a matter of fact, during their visits to the dying. And to make matters worse in an already unbelievable situation, they both recited stories of people waving and talking to someones that *they themselves* could not see. Well, somehow, it didn't make it any easier for me; however, it did solidify the fact that I was not loony and neither was my dad. Whew! What a relief, huh?

No, it didn't really make it any easier—but it was some form of relief nonetheless. So in the weeks to follow, I began to try to accept these happenings as facts and as I continued to do so the strangest thing began to happen. A most miraculous phenomenon. I began to lose my fear of death as well as the unknown. Well, geeze, who in the heck was I to say what he *did* or *didn't* see? I didn't see through *his* eyes nor did I hear through *his* ears. And, well, even if I was wrong—I truly didn't give a rat's patoot at that particular stage of the game and you know—once I took that attitude—another most peculiar thing began to happen. I began to feel tranquility, peace, and some solace. The thought of these people visiting my dad began giving me *great* comfort toward the end of his journey. You see, I knew I wasn't alone anymore and that when the time did come for my dad to cross over, maybe these folks would see it in their hearts to take him quickly and quietly in his sleep. Or so I prayed. And there is a lesson to be learned here, my friends. Praying is just like wishing. Be careful what you pray for—because you just might get it!

After our heartfelt conversation that evening in regard to would I—or would I not—be able to allow the unthinkable to occur, I finally got him settled down enough to go to sleep. But first, I did share with my dad how very special I felt that he had shared his experience with me. For some reason, I knew in my heart it was necessary for me to validate the happenings that had indeed taken place, so I also told him that I believed him, and that I felt extremely blessed in knowing that there were angels (friends) standing readily by to escort him into heaven. They are probably there for all of us, you know? Perhaps it will be someone we knew and loved here in this place who has already gone on or maybe it will be someone we never knew here at all but we will when we see them. I know it in my heart, because in heaven there are no strangers. Only friends. A solemn promise—from the greatest storytelling, monster-fighting, dumbest, overall-sporting, angel-seeking, janitor in the whole–wide– world!

# Chapter Thirteen

## Acceptance

*God works in mysterious ways. Given my love of God
and my belief in God and in Jesus Christ, I have to accept
that I may well be used in this way (as a prophet).*

James Anderton 1932- In radio interview, 18 Jan. 1987
In Daily Telegraph 19 Jan. 1987

RIDAY WAS RIGHT around the corner and it couldn't have come soon enough for me. My sisters would finally be there and I *wanted* as well as *needed* them and their support so very desperately. And in the midst of all of my anticipation I began to realize yet another new feeling. Get that. As if I really needed any more of those, for hell's sake! Well, nonetheless, and I realize that it was a rather bizarre feeling, but here goes; I felt proud of the fact that my dad and I had made it that far. Hang on folks—it gets worse.

I felt a–sort–of–well–protective emotion festering inside of me. I, as absurd as it sounds, found myself wanting to stand proud beside my dad when they arrived, proclaiming, "Yes, he looks like hell, and yes, he is only but a shell of a man—but he's mine and we are bravely fighting this monster together," with the theme from *Rocky* blaring in the background and me wearing my fighting robe and him wearing—well—his boxing sweat shorts—and then, I would proudly take my dad's hand and we would raise them up together in celebration of our proud victory!

Sick huh? Well, perhaps; however, I really felt like I too owned my dad's illness. Like I had been secretly introduced to this intruder, this monster, face to face—and I knew its horrible wrath and power all too well.

191

I guess if we really think about it, sadly, that is *exactly* what had indeed taken place after all, isn't it? Perhaps. But my dad, on the other hand had, entirely different perceptions of the whole damned situation. Imagine that!

All day Friday, for the entire two hours that he was awake, his main concern was only that he thought the girls might be offended by his appearance, asking me several times throughout those couple of hours if I thought they would be shocked.

Honestly, if they weren't shocked, I would have thought there to be something really wrong with them; however, I continued telling him that everything would be fine. I tried to comfort him by telling him that they weren't coming to judge his appearance.

"Oh?" he had replied, "Then why are they coming?"

Now, of course, this was my dad's way of kidding with me but for some unknown reason my sense of humor had slowly been deteriorating right along with his health, so I wasn't really in the mood to joke around with him. As a matter of fact, I got just a little defensive.

In a stern voice, I quipped, "Well, why in the hell do you think they're coming?"

Have you ever said something and even before it was out of your mouth you wished you had kept your flytrap shut? Well, then, you know exactly how I felt at that very moment because he then, cocked his head in a most peculiar way, looking at me with a most disappointing glare on his face which quickly turned to a painful look and said, "Honestly? Do you want me to tell you why I think they are really coming?" And as he sat and fidgeted with his hands in his lap, being careful not to even glance my way, he softly said, "To say good-bye. It is time to say good-bye."

Now, it was me who was sitting there trying to avoid any eye contact as well, when he slowly reached over from his chair and he gently rubbed my hand as he always did when he was feeling sad for me, and he said, "What is it, dear? What is bothering you so much that you can't even bring yourself to look at me when I talk to you?"

I then, knowing damned well I had to face him, cautiously began lifting my eyes to his and when I found myself finally gazing into the eyes that had all of my life been so very understanding, I simply said, "Everything, Dad, everything is bothering me." And with that I began to cry like I have never cried before in my whole entire life. Not up until that point anyway.

He immediately stood up on wobbly legs and, holding on to the arm of the chair, slid his way over to the couch and sat down next to me, making one last attempt to be my dad. He was wearing only a pair of sweat shorts, so as I watched him trying to get comfortable I couldn't help noticing how thin he was becoming with each and every day. He sat back against the back of the couch, allowing his head to fall back, like he was sleepy and took my hand between both of his. I perched myself sideways and propped my arm on the back of the couch, resting my head in my right hand and the other was entwined with his and I sat there also, just staring at him while he rested.

We sat there for just a little while in silence before he tried to open his eyes, rolled his head toward me and very groggily said, "I just can't seem to stay awake, dear."

I took my hand out of his and stroked his hair, which by this time had become much longer than I had ever known it to be. And it was then, that I realized the horror of several tumors growing on the top of his head!

In a state of complete shock, I attempted to try and ask him how long these tiny little intruders had been residing on the top of his head, but I couldn't speak through the tears as well as the lump in my throat. So I simply sat rubbing his head and my hand slowly ran down the side of his face and over the protruding lump on the side of his neck that had now easily grown to be the size of a grapefruit, deforming his appearance horrifically. My hand continued to sooth and comfort as it then made its way down to his right breast where this whole nightmare had begun and I allowed my touch—for the very first time—to wander over the darkened lump which had, in fact, been the reason why we were both sitting there at that very moment. And I have to share with each and every one of you—that I truly felt as though I had just shaken the hand of Satan, himself! And it was then, my friends, that I finally just couldn't take it anymore and gave up. I just couldn't do it any longer. No matter how hard I tried I just couldn't keep hoping. I was all out of hope, just as my dad was all out of chances. My God! This nightmare had gone on long enough and at the expense of my father's quality of life not to mention his disfigurement! So, there I sat—with the bile slithering its way up my esophagus, saying absolutely nothing because there was just nothing left to say.

I continued to cry for a very long time and my dad knew I was crying, but he was simply too weak to even console me. He half opened his eyes and said, "I'm sorry, dear. I just can't stay awake anymore. I'm too tired. I'm sorry. I've tried to hold on as long as I can but it's just not worth it anymore." End of story, folks! He was just too damned tired!

I desperately tried to wipe the tears from my face with my sleeve, but it was no use. They were flowing like a river, so I lay my wet cheek on my dad's shoulder and just let it flow. He reached his hand up and rubbed my hair and it was then that I realized that I had to say something, anything at all to break the silence. So, for whatever reason you all care to give, because I sure as heck can't figure out where it came from, I decided it was time to give him permission to go.

I guess there comes a time in all of our lives when we just have to let go of an unreachable dream—and I believe that on that day and at that particular moment—it was my turn. And it didn't take St. Peter or anyone else to bring it to my attention either. Nope, I just knew that it was time. So, through tears and sporadic sobs, I made myself speak.

"Dad, please don't be sorry, you have nothing to be sorry for. I know you're so tired of fighting and I'm tired of watching you fight so hard. We've finished everything we need to finish, so I want you to know that I understand if you have to go away now. I'll be just fine. I have Uncle here with me and I promise I will take care of everything."

He could barely open his eyes, but he tried so hard to, as he whispered to me, "I love you, Baby Doll. I really do love you so much." Then he paused for just a few moments before I heard him whisper, "My beautiful, beautiful brown eyes."

And that was it. There *was* no symphony orchestra and no violins whining in the distance either. As a matter of fact, I couldn't even hear myself crying. It was nothing like I expected it to be. It—just—was.

I sat holding him that day for a very long time while he slept, actually wondering when he would breathe his last breath in my arms with my tears falling like rain and my heart breaking in two. But he didn't breathe his last breath that day. He simply continued to sleep in my arms until I got him up and soldiered him back to the bedroom, laid him down in his bed and covered him up. And after kissing him good night just one more time with the hope in my heart that I *still*, just *maybe*, had a little bit of Snow White magic in me, I turned to leave him sleeping and made a beeline for the telephone. I then, dialed my home number and as soon as I heard my husband's voice, I cried my tears of acceptance and continued to do so, for a very long time.

At about 7:00 p.m. the witch came home and I tried to share with her all that had happened that day but she wasn't having any of it. At first I thought it might be denial. But then, she snapped at me telling me that she thought that giving permission for someone to go was a crock! She said his body just wasn't ready yet and when it was he would die—plain and simple. And that's when I very calmly asked her why she was so hateful. It came out of mouth just as easy as you please. I was extremely together and peaceful.

She was standing in the kitchen with her back to me and I was in the living room but she whipped her head around in a Linda Blair sort of fashion and she snapped again. "I am not hateful!"

I firmly and very calmly stood my ground. "Then what word would you give it exactly?" I asked. "I have been here for a week and you haven't said one nice thing to me or to my dad, *your* husband," I quipped back.

"What in the world is the matter with you?" I begged. "What could have possibly made you so angry?"

"I'm not angry," she snipped.

"OK, then what would you call it?" I quietly asked. "Are you scared?"

"No, not really," she answered.

"Do you want me to leave," I pushed?

"No, I have to work," she snapped again!

"Is that it? You have to work and you'd rather be taking care of Dad?"

"No," she said. "He would rather have you here. That is more than obvious!"

"Then what?" I demanded. I was growing impatient. And then I added, "And I don't think what you just said is so obvious. For the record, Dad loves you and he never said or did anything to prove otherwise. He loves it when you are with him. No, it is not obvious that he'd rather have me here." Was it?

"And you don't have to work," I pressed, "Because Dad has money put away so that you could take some time off."

"Well, that is all fine and well but your father won't give me the money to help my son!"

I was dumbfounded. She was working to support her thirty-year-old son! She chose this over taking care of my dad! Now I felt rage. Absolute rage!

"No, he won't," I sassed, wishing my words had been flying daggers!

"Have you told Dad all the things you need to say?"

"I suppose," she said. "What is left to say?"

I pressed on. "I don't know. Have you told him how much you love him?"

"Of course," she snapped.

"Have you told him everything? Everything you need to say?"

"Yes," is all she could curtly reply with.

And with that I gave up. There was nothing more I could say. Nothing more I could do. Sometimes, things are just better left unsaid and in this situation, for sure. But I'm not going to lie to anyone. It hurt. I hadn't quite figured out why just yet but it hurt just the same. Perhaps it hurt so bad because I have a soft spot in my heart for broomriding, pointy-hat-wearing, monkey-loving, green-faced witches! Highly doubtful, but maybe.

The next morning was Friday and the hospice nurse arrived bright and early. I was a different person that morning than I had been the day before. For that matter, I was a different person than I had ever been in my whole entire life and would ever be again. Acceptance will do the damnedest things to a person. And not only had I come to accept the fact that my dad was indeed on his way out of this place and probably soon, but I had also realized that, secretly, between the two of us, my dad and I had decided to surrender. I knew it in my heart and I know the hospice nurse knew it just as well the very minute she walked in the door. Must've been the way I looked. And if I had to sum it up in one word, then that word would have to be peaceful.

As my dad and I sat together having coffee in our usual positions that morning, it was very clear that that was the only thing usual about us at all. Certainly, two other very serene and well-behaved people had taken the place of our previous out-of-control, freakish beings. We were at peace. I had not shared with my dad the conversation I'd had with his wife the night before. I let it go.

With him in his recliner and me on the couch, I very calmly and matter-of-factly asked our nurse questions about the tumors I had discovered on my dad's head the day before, while he sat there looking at her with a most peculiar look on his face. Nothing new about that really, he always had a peculiar look on his face, but just as she began to explain about the tumors, my dad smiled, reached over, temporarily interrupting her—touched her hand and said, "No need to worry, it's just the meanness coming out of me. It's my horns!" And with that, she began to laugh and so did I.

I did share with her that morning that my dad and I had come to accept the circumstances at hand (or so we thought at the time anyway) and I shared with her that I had given him permission to leave me. And with all of the understanding, that only she could portray, she simply asked when my sisters were due to arrive. I told her they would be there that evening.

You see, she too knew why my dad was hanging on, or so we all thought at the time anyway. She then looked at my dad and asked him if he was anxious to see the girls.

"Oh, yes!" he said, as his eyes lit up and I watched his soul come to life once again. He shared with her that this would be the first time that all of us had slept together in the same house since 1967! He was so very excited. He then continued on to tell her all about the days when his little girls were still his little girls and he would have to chase us around the house just to get a diaper on one of our butts. Then he went on to say that worst of all was the noise.

"Yakity yakity yak," he said was all anyone could ever hear, when we were all together. And as he sat there shaking his head back and forth, commenting under his breath on how crazy his house would be with all five girls in it at one time, I'm not sure, I mean I can't be positive, but I think I saw just a tad bit of pride, beaming from within my dear old dad. Oh, how I wish I could relive those wonderful conversations. How I so wish I could see that look—that sparkle, in his eyes just one more time. He didn't have enough strength to even walk across the room but by golly, he could go on and on about his five little girls with more energy than a three-year-old! And so the story goes.

Well, folks, hang onto your hats once again because some things never turn out as planned and don't we all just hate that? Well, I know I sure do.

You see it turned out that my middle sister wasn't going to be able to make the trip with the other girls. She was having some sort of personal difficulty and had decided not to come. No big deal, I guess. Well, no big deal unless you're dying, that is. I mean, let's face it, it wasn't like we could say, "Oh that's OK, no big deal, maybe next time." There, quite frankly, wasn't going to be a next time, for hell's sake! And sadly, I knew then—just as well as I know now, that she would regret that decision for the rest of her time here on this earth. Yup—it seems that sometimes, no matter what you tell someone, they just don't get it. And for now, let's just put that little issue to rest because we have more important things to think about. Like who in the hell was going to tell my dad—and worst of all *how*? How was he going to be able to understand this?

Well, the "who" part of that question was pretty darned simple, wasn't it? I mean, I was the only idiot qualified enough to deliver such a message. Lucky me. And the how? Well, I hadn't quite figured that one out yet but I knew I would. I just needed a little time to think about it. Unfortunately, time was not something we had an overabundance of. Gosh, how I hate to be pushed and haven't we already gone over this?

To make a long story even longer, I will share with all of you that I did what most gutless daughters would have done in my situation. Yup— I waited until the very last minute, hoping with everything I had in me that she would change her mind. But as it turned out—sadly—she didn't change her mind, which meant I then, in turn, had to tell my dad.

Before the nurse left that morning, we walked my dad back to his bedroom so that he could lie down for a while and as we did so, she decided to take the opportunity to check his vitals and do a quick once over. She had come to expect a certain ritual by this time as my cute, silly, little, cancer-bestowing Dad would begin making funny noises during the whole exam. He would "Ooh!" and "Aah!" just as soon as she would lay the stethoscope on his chest, or he would yelp out, "Oh, that just makes me feel good all under!" And as always, he would ask if his heart was ticking and she would reply with, "It sounds like it."

"Good," he'd then reply. "Means there's still hope yet."

And as always after these little exams that had absolutely no value what–so–ever–at–all were over with, my dad would then have no trouble in asking us to leave. He would simply say, "OK now, you two get out of here so I can get my beauty sleep." And on cue, we would trot ourselves out of the bedroom and on into the living room where we could then compare notes from the last exam to find out each and every time just exactly what we had suspected all along. My dad was indeed going to die. He had cancer!

Seems kind of senseless, doesn't it? Well, perhaps. However, I don't really think they do those exams for the dying as much as they need to do them for us, the living. And I don't know about you, but I sure as hell felt ten times better. I mean, after all, he *was* still breathing!

As we left him to his much-needed sleep that morning, we walked into the living room to perform our comparison ritual and say our goodbyes when the nurse suddenly stopped and faced me and very softly whispered that she felt he must be hanging on to see the girls. I then told her that my middle sister would not be coming. Funny, came out just as easy as you please telling *her*. Gave me the opportunity to practice for the real thing, I reckon. Uh huh, like any one stinking situation in the world could have done that!

She told me she thought it best to tell my dad right away and like the idiot that I truly was, I promised her I would. She then headed for the door and she turned to me one last time before leaving to ask how long my sisters would be staying. I told her just a couple of nights. She stared at the floor for a long minute before she turned to me and laid her gentle hand on my arm and said, "After the girls leave, it probably won't be long." I looked at her and smiled and told her I knew.

After she left and was clear out of sight, I walked over and sat down on the couch wondering, contemplating, if I should tell my dad about my sister right away, or simply wait until my other sisters showed up without her. Now, that would have been the easiest, however, it didn't seem very fair, not to mention the fact that I already felt guilty for even thinking about lying to my dad.

Well, as it happened, just as I was sitting there trying to decide if I could deceive my dad or not, he yelled from the bedroom for me to please bring him a glass of water. He did this quite often, you see. And I don't mean he yelled for a glass of water quite as often as he always seemed to know when I was up to something. It wasn't at all unusual for him to call for me just as I was contemplating doing something wrong. Must be some sort of universal parental intuition, either that or my dad's special friends tipped him off once again. And I guess I'll never know, because it was one of those things that I didn't pursue. Because some things are just better left un-pursued, if you know what I mean.

I quickly jumped up from the couch, yelling back toward the bedroom that I was coming and headed for the fridge to get him a cold drink of water, still wondering what I should do. And the thoughts of should I or shouldn't I were still going through my mind as I entered his bedroom.

Swinging the door to the wall upon my grand entrance, I found my dad trying to sit up on his own, so I rushed to gently help prop his pillows setting the glass of water on the table next to the bed.

Now, I don't know how he knew, and as I have already shared with you, I never did ask, but the first thing out of his mouth after he got situated was a question. And just as easy as you please, he asked if that *one* particular sister was coming (so much for deceit). I couldn't have lied to him if it would have saved my own life.

I sat down on the bed next to him and looking at the floor I simply said, "No." He sat there for a few minutes before he spoke, which might as well been two hours, before he said, "Well, she has always been the loner, hasn't she? Whatever she is going through, she'll work it out." And that was that—plain and simple.

As I sat there loving my wonderful understanding dad, for being just that, I couldn't help remembering how very many times he had said that exact same phrase referring to anyone at all who had ever had a problem. You see, my dad believed that people had to go through tough times every once in a while in order to appreciate the lives they had. To my dad's way of thinking, this belief would indeed explain why sometimes people would experience more than one mishap or tragedy at a time. He figured that because obviously, the first time didn't get the point across as to how bad things really *weren't*— and how bad things actually *could* become. It's a little deep, I know; however, after sharing most of his philosophies with you thus far, it does make sense, now, doesn't it?

So once again, I had sat around creating ulcers in my already-pitted stomach, for nothing. My dad seemed to understand why my sister wasn't coming, when I, myself, couldn't find one good reason. I was still a little miffed—yet he had moved on. Now, doesn't that just about tick you off? Sure! Maybe I was expecting him to ground her or better yet, maybe I was expecting him to threaten her with never speaking to her again. Yes, I do believe that would have satisfied me to no end, and guess what. Be so very careful what you wish for, especially in anger, because you just might get it. For that is exactly what happened indeed. Sadly, my sister and my father never again had another conversation.

I sat on the bed next to him and gazed lovingly into his tired old chimpanzee eyes, and he obligingly gazed back. We sat there making funny faces at each other, when I leaned forward and kissed him. I told him I felt very lucky to have known him. Sort of a strange thing for one to say to one's parent, now, isn't it? Well, I agree, however, I truly meant it and I felt the surging need to say so right then and there—so I did. I was becoming pretty good at that as a matter of fact. I then shared a secret with him that I hadn't told anyone ever before. Oh, it's not a whopper by any means, but, it was a thought I hadn't shared with him yet or anyone else for that matter.

I told him that I felt it was my early childhood experiences with him that taught me how to be a good mom. I had never forgotten what it had been like to have had a great parent, even if it had only been for a little while. No matter how horrible things became after my dad left home, I always held on to the precious memories I had with him as a child. Sadly, I didn't realize until I was older that I could never have those days back again but I did figure out a way to relive them—and that was through the upbringing of my own children and for that, I was so very thankful to him. I went on to say that because of him, I *did* know that there was another way, therefore I was able to break a cycle that so many unfortunate others aren't able to do. And because of my memories I would be forever grateful that God gave him to me in the beginning of my life.

Well, my hard-thinking, soft-hearted little dad was just a tad bit embarrassed and the look in his eyes told me so. He then, simply took my hand and said he was very proud of me. Then, I was the one who became a bit embarrassed and it was at that moment that my dad asked me to keep yet another very important deathbed promise. And this one, as strange as it was, concerned my husband.

You see, he thought the world of my husband and I think it was mostly and simply because he was a hard-working man who didn't expect something for nothing. He is also a family man whose ideals lie within the family structure. He is the type of person who wouldn't think twice about going on a weekend camping trip without the kids. And let us not forget that my four children are not biologically his and that is what impressed my father the very most.

As I have already shared with you, my dad always referred to my husband as the old man, which is a silly little ditty in itself, because my husband is eight years my junior, which is just another reason why my father thought the world of him. He was a young man with drive and confidence as well as the compassion to make a difference in the lives of my children and to my dad, as we all know, that was everything in a nutshell—plain and simple.

Now, in return, my husband thought the world of my dad as well. Knowing all too well my background, my husband felt that it was indeed my father who prepared a light at the end of the tunnel for me. He also had a mutual respect for my dad, because he worked hard every day of his life and even though he was *just* a janitor, he worked a good, hard, honest living and never expected something for nothing. Heck, I couldn't have had it any better if I had planned it! The two most important men in my life where also very important to one another, kind of a nice little threesome, don't you think? And now that I have explained to you how very important they were to one another, perhaps you will now be able to better understand the request he was about to make.

My dad had a wish that he wanted fulfilled after his death. Oh now, I know what you are all thinking, but relax. It's nothing really dramatic. Well, not yet anyway. He simply asked me to have the chaplain relay a message to my husband at the graveside and *only* at the graveside. Oh, I know it seems a little old-fashioned, but in a sense, that is exactly what made it so very special. And the message? Well it too was very plain and simple. He wanted my husband to know how very much he meant to him and that once my dad was gone, he was leaving the responsibility of looking after my sisters up to him. And to my dad, that was like leaving his whole fortune, quite an honor to say the least!

He was worried about who would look after the girls once he was gone and he felt the only person worthy of that responsibility was my husband. He said that my husband was the closest thing to a son he had ever had, and if he had had a son, he would have wanted him to be just like my husband. My dad was a man of few words as we all know and he never had taken the opportunity to say these things to my husband, and he simply wanted him to know. Oh, of course my dad knew that the girls were all grown-up now and leading their own lives, however, he felt the need to leave someone in charge, and that someone he had chosen very specially.

As always when my dad made me promise something, he repeated over and over again that the moment must be exactly perfect. He absolutely didn't want this secret told to my husband until the graveside service. No ands, ifs or butts! End of conversation.

Now, I will share with all of you that I did indeed keep that promise, and to say that my husband was touched and honored at my father's graveside would be an understatement. He was speechless! Just as my dad probably knew he would be. That's what made it so darned special. A special heart-touching moment—plain and simple.

We sat and chatted some more for the better part of an hour, before my dad drifted off to sleep, leaving me the much-needed time to straighten the house before our guests arrived. I gently lifted myself off the bed in order not to wake him and before I left his bedroom I slowly leaned over and kissed my sleepy, little, sentimental, honor-bestowing dad on the cheek. I couldn't help standing there for just a few minutes watching him sleep as I went over our conversation in my mind.

He wanted to give the honor of overseeing his family to my husband. He didn't want to leave a stone unturned. And as I stood there watching him take small shallow breaths, I realized that the time was drawing nearer and that he, himself, was doing his best to tie up any loose ends. And you know, I still at that point couldn't really fathom the passing of my father. It seemed to always be the closest thing to my mind and yet at the same time the very farthest. No matter how hard I tried to prepare, I just absolutely could not imagine life without my cute, little, sentimental dad. And as I quietly tugged the bedroom door behind me, I glanced back at him one more time and wondered, just how many more times I would be able to close that door behind me before the day would come when he wouldn't be lying there anymore. Sad thought, wasn't it? Yes, it most certainly was and I, for one, can tell you that the very first time I entered that room after his death, I remembered that very same thought and when I went to exit that room for the very last time after his passing, I did not (could not) look back. I simply closed the door behind me and took my last walk down his tiny hallway.

Acceptance is something we all have a tough time with during our lives at one time or another I suppose—especially the kind of acceptance that we have no stinking control over in the first place.

"God, grant me the serenity to accept the things I cannot change, to change the things I can—and the wisdom to know the difference."

# Chapter Fourteen

## Yesterday

*Yesterday, all my troubles seemed so far away. Now it looks as though they're here to stay. Oh, I believe in yesterday.*

John Lennon 1940–1980 and Paul McCartney
1942– Yesterday (1965 song)

I PIDDLED AROUND FOR the rest of the afternoon, trying to keep myself busy until my sisters arrived. How many times do you think someone can clean a home before it just simply falls apart? Well, I'll have you know that I wondered that very thought myself, as I ran a dust cloth over my dad's cherished little stereo. Funny, I thought, how such a simple little gadget could bring so very much enjoyment to a dying man. And I can tell you that I, for one, treated that little musical wonder with the utmost and greatest respect.

I also became extremely overwhelmed that afternoon with sadness and grief. I just could not help thinking what was all of this for? Why? Why are we born to live a certain amount of time and then we are done and we go. Where? Back from whence we came? Why bother? We all end up dying in the end. Some of us live only minutes and some of us live until we are one hundred or longer. Do we pick a number before we arrive? Draw straws? And who is actually the winner anyway? Now, there's a question for us!

I thought I had been facing this situation very well until these bouts of depression would come surging to the surface hitting me like a freight train heading south. How in the world was I to have known that this situation would feel like—well—like hell. I suppose it was like hell anyway. Whatever hell is. Perhaps I had overlooked the fact that dying was sad. No, I think on some intelligent level I had known that when people die it is sad. Other people though. Not my people. Not people I loved so very much. And certainly someone had forgotten to tell me what happens to the human body when it declines. The loss of weight, the fatigue, the loss of appetite, the loss of control over the simple task of going to the bathroom, the loss of laughter, the overabundance of tears, the sickness, the—aw, forget it—this sucked and to top it all off, I had to deal with the witch each and every morning as she readied herself for work at the crack of dawn and didn't return until well into the evening. OK, that part I never really anticipated at all.

Shouldn't this have been a time when the broom-riding mother of Damien and I should be doing some serious bonding? Well, one would have thought so. What in the heck kind of job did she have anyway? Must have been one that was very taxing because once she went to sleep at night she was out like a light and she never heard my dad when he had to go to the bathroom. How could she be lying right next to him and not hear him when I could hear him from the couch in the living room? I was up and down so much during the middle of the night that sometimes I couldn't remember if I was going to get him or if I was taking him back to bed. I reckon, in all fairness, taking care of that castle and supervising those guards and monkeys all day long could be rather tiring. Not to mention the fact that she was probably taking a great deal of time preparing that room with the hourglass especially for me.

Not really caring much about the dust on my dad's stereo that didn't really exist anyway, I walked over to the couch, threw my dust rag onto the coffee table and plopped myself down into the sofa, thinking I would try and watch a little TV to take my mind off things for a bit. Funny how you can actually watch an entire show and not have a clue as to what in the hell is going on.

I must have been sitting there for the better part of about fifteen minutes or so before out of the corner of my eye, I saw my dad walking into the bathroom. Wait a minute! That was impossible, was my first thought, and how in the heck was he able to move so swiftly, was my second thought, and my third thought would have sent chills up my spine had I been as far away as Cleveland because my dad sure as heck wasn't six feet tall!

Scared half out of my bleedy little wits, I jumped to my feet and then just stood there for a second or twenty before I decided to carefully inch my brave little self to the bathroom door, kind of like a child who's trying to run yet they do it in a walking fashion as not to get caught and I must say, with the calmest of nerves, as I then peered into the tiny bathroom to find that there was no one there! No one! I then whirled around and took two steps to the bedroom door and peeked through the crack to find my dad sleeping very peacefully.

This was it! I was absolutely, beyond a shadow of a doubt, losing my flipping mind. Of course I wasn't aware of that fact right then and there because right then and there I was only focused on the fact that I could not have moved a muscle had my ass been on fire. I was petrified! And I must have stood in that hallway for a solid five minutes before I could talk my scared little feet into carrying me back into the living room again.

Walking backward as though whatever it was I saw might just materialize before me again and, surely I didn't want to miss that, I felt my way to the couch and sat down never taking my gaze off the hallway and it was right then and there that I absolutely knew beyond a shadow of a doubt that I was right smack-dab in the middle of an Alfred Hitchcock flick.

I was tired. I wanted to believe that what I had just seen was my complete and total over active imagination. Just as much as I wanted to believe that some miracle would save my dad in the end. And just like that belief, I knew in my heart that I had darned well not imagined what I knew I had just seen. *Whew, what a mouthful!*

I believe that trying to find an explanation for such things is a most difficult task when something like this scares the pee-waddlings out of someone. I must have told myself over and over again at least a million times how very tired I must be. After all, I *was* up and down with my dad all throughout the night, each and every night and I never have been much of a day sleeper so I wasn't sleeping during the day to catch up either. Therefore, to sum it all up in a nutshell, I told myself that I was simply exhausted and that my mind was working a little overtime. Uh huh, the only real problem now was simply convincing my heart. I mean, let's be realistic here. I am well educated and I don't write fiction well at all, so, well—oh, forget it!

I know now, today, that what I saw was definitely someone, although that someone was not in substantial human form, only a human frame, if that makes any sense at all. And I wouldn't blame you one tiny little bit if at this very given moment you got up and this time, really did chuck this book just about as far as it will fly. However, I must say that I am telling you the truth. The way I see it, those of you who have had similar experiences will continue reading, those of you who haven't, might continue reading, if fiction is your thing. Whichever you choose to do, please keep in mind that this is my account of what happened and if you choose not to believe it, I can't blame you one bit. So the choice is yours. But I swear to whatever powers that be, that I saw a very large someone and they were moving, walking, floating?

Assuming I still have somewhat of an audience I will continue on with my story. Thanks for staying yet one more time.

Now, just to add misery to misery, this was not the only time that I would see, what I prefer to call visions. No. I'm afraid to say I saw them quite often as a matter of fact. More times than I care to try and understand anyway and the strange things about these so-called visions were that if I looked directly at them they disappeared.

However, out of the corner of my eye, I could see them very, very clearly. Oh, I know it sounds ridiculous and I don't understand it myself but again, I will say that it is the honest-to-God truth.

Now because of the height of the very first one I saw, I assumed it to be a man but the next one that (who) appeared the following week was much shorter and smaller in frame, so I assumed it to be a woman. And did I tell anyone about these visions? Hell, no! Well, not at first anyway. I wanted to make sure I saw it again before I ran off half-cocked taking the risk of being locked up for the rest of my life. One has to be very careful what one shares in this life. You see, I'm not as crazy as it may appear. Although, the one thing I didn't do, that I really wanted to (really bad), was tell my sisters. Instead, I decided to wait until one of them saw something and told me. That way I could give them a strange look and simply shake my head from side to side in disbelief. Made perfect sense to me. Another lesson in tow— be careful what you plan for—because you just may—aw, forget it.

And speaking of my sisters, they would be arriving before long and not a moment too soon. It was already early into the afternoon and the silence had become deafening. My dad was still sleeping and we already know the house was clean and I was—well, lonely.

I heard a car driving through the park and shot up off the couch only to see— nothing. It had simply passed by. I walked back to my dad's bedroom and he was—still sleeping. So, I walked back into the living room and—paced. This had to be what prison was like. Of that I was sure. Maybe like death row. Sure it was. Waiting for visitors, nothing to do with your time and if you did do something with your time what did it matter? The end result would be the same. I really needed some antidepressants!

The sound of another approaching car! I raced to the sliding glass door and caught just a glimpse of the tail end of a minivan. It was them! My sisters had arrived!

I slid the glass door sideways and stepped out onto the porch. They had passed my dad's house to turn around. I stepped down the front steps and faced the van that was now approaching me. And I must say, they were sure a sight for sore and lonely eyes, but most importantly, they were from home and home is something I had come to miss terribly.

It was nearing the end of October and I had been gone for only two weeks, however, it surely seemed like an eternity. Those two weeks had taken quite a toll on me as well as my emotions. But I hadn't realized how much of a toll until my sisters stepped out of that van.

They were tired from their journey and they looked weathered and beaten and maybe a little apprehensive but to me they were a beautiful sight. The drive had taken them about eight hours and every mile was displayed upon their faces as they were fighting and bickering with each other staggering from the curb, up the stairs, and through the sliding glass door. I couldn't imagine being cooped up in a vehicle with all of them for eight flipping hours, believe–you–me. Nonetheless, I sure as hell would have at the time. Hell, I would have rather been in an arena in Spain, fighting a bull named Ferdinand in the nude—in the rain—well, you get the picture.

As they all filed in, dropping their overnight bags and themselves everywhere— they were griping at each other. However, there wasn't a black eye nor were there any abrasions to be found on any one of them, so I assumed it had been a somewhat passive trip. Oh, they were picking at one another, accusing one another of driving one another crazy, threatening each other that someone was walking home when it came time to leave, but nothing really serious. As a matter of fact, it kind of made me a little jealous. I felt like I had missed out. I wanted to take a road trip with my sisters. I wanted to eat in restaurants and stop for bathroom breaks and then—I remembered all I had been a part of in my father's home and I truly knew at that moment that it was, in fact, *they* who had sadly missed out. Always in the eyes of the beholder, you know.

After they all got settled in and all the hugs had been exchanged, it fell eerily silent. Everyone was looking at me. What?! What in the hell were they all staring at? More silence.

"How's Dad?" my oldest sister finally said, breaking that most uncomfortable stillness.

Oh—he's dying—I wanted to say. He's fine except for the fact that he is not our dad anymore. No, folks—he is a walking, breathing skeleton!

I actually felt an intense urgency to warn them of our dad's appearance, fearing that if I didn't blab it out right away, he might just come walking out of that bedroom at any given moment, drawing embarrassing gasps from everyone. But actually as it turned out, I refrained for just a little while. I motioned with my arm for them all to have a seat. Like Vanna White as she swirled to unveil a new letter.

We all sat down on the living room floor and, once we settled in a circle, I began to speak to them quite matter-of-factly all about my adventure thus far and, as I did, I couldn't keep the tears from spilling down my cheeks. I don't think the gates of hell could have held back the flow.

Damn it! I wasn't going to do this! I was the hero! I was the strong one!

I, in all honesty, was beaten and tired and lonely and that is all I was, plain and simple. My big sister was the first on her knees to lean forward with a most welcome and comforting hug. Of course she was. She was the oldest—she was in charge—she was Glinda the Good Witch and it was her job. And for the most part, I'm not one who likes to be babied—however, I accepted her comfort willingly and submissively hoping that with a wave of her magic wand, she could send me home in a hot air balloon with Toto in my arms—but sadly she didn't—and I had to prepare them for what they were about to see because the man sleeping in that back bedroom no longer resembled our Dad. And so I began.

Gently, I broke her embrace and lingered my touch down her arm until we were both off our knees and in a sitting position once again. Wiping my tears on the sleeve of my shirt, I began by explaining to them that what they were about to see would make them sick, and if it didn't, then I think we could safely assume them not human. They all assured me that they were prepared. It was then that I started to cry again but this time my tears were accompanied by heavy, gut-wrenching sobs. I was so relieved to have them there. I guess I felt a special sort of support now that it wasn't only me there to worry and feel sad. I really don't know. What I *do* know is it simply felt good to have someone comfort and listen to *me* for a change. And if that statement sounds selfish, then so be it.

Well, once it became obvious that I couldn't control my emotions, they all joined in as well. Each of us sitting there sobbing uncontrollably for our own private and personal reasons and one thing I can tell you for sure is this—deep down in the very corner of my heart, without a single doubt in my mind, I know that we all shared not only in the sorrow of our father's absence to be, but also in the sorrow of the absence of our middle sister at that very moment in time. There we were, all together sitting on the floor in a circle, facing something that we as human beings all know will happen someday. We just don't really believe it. We were there to say good-bye to our parent. And although no one actually verbalized it that way during the whole visit, we all knew it was true. And looking back on it now, I actually think we were some of the lucky ones. I mean, I, for one, felt very blessed because some of us only get to say good-bye after our parents are already gone. *We* at least had some warning. And I truly do mourn for those of you who had someone taken away tragically with no time to say good-bye. I pray that I never have to endure that realm of pain.

After we all had a good cry and I was finished preparing them for what they were about to witness, I decided it was time to go in and get my dad. After all, time was a wasting and time wasn't something we had an overabundance of. How many times do you all think I will say that throughout this godforsaken story?

I knew how very embarrassed my dad felt regarding his appearance so I asked the girls to wait in the living room so that he could have time to comb his hair and wake up a little bit. Funny, I thought, my dad had never had hair long enough to comb in his entire life. As a matter of fact, I wondered if we even had a comb in the house!

Remember how in the beginning of this story, I mentioned regrets? Well, here comes one and it's a whopper! One of the regrets I have is that I didn't have someone come in and cut my dad's hair for him during those final days. I tried to talk him into going for a ride over to the barbershop when I first arrived but he really didn't have enough energy to even try. Oh, how he loved those trips to the barbershop. But, he didn't want to shave or cut his hair or do anything really at all except sit and wait to go. Yes, my friends, I do wish that I had been able to get my little dad a haircut. Of course, here again, it didn't bother *him* in the least—it was only *me* it bothered the most.

Angrily swiping at the tears on my face, I stood up and giving them all a glance that was an unspoken warning, I turned and went tiptoeing into the bedroom, gently closing the door behind me to give my dad the privacy we needed to prepare him for his grand entrance. I stood over him for just a minute, watching him sleep as I sometimes did, when I slowly bent forward and gently kissed his wrinkled cheek. He unwillingly opened his eyes and lay there for a second or two trying to get his bearings before he asked me what time it was. I then announced to him that it was time to get up and see his daughters.

His face lit up so brightly with the expression of pure excitement as he hurriedly and awkwardly tried to sit up all by himself asking, "When did they arrive?"

I sat down on the bed beside him, trying to slow him down a bit as I relayed to him that they had only been there a short while. As he was now in a sitting position with his tiny legs crossed over the side of the bed, rubbing his eyes just waking up, he reminded me of a small child trying to hurry and wake up so he could go racing to the Christmas tree to take in the wonder of surprise. But then, out of nowhere, all of a sudden he panicked as he remembered—and he gripped my arm as though he were going to fall from a ten-story building. I was startled but the moment our eyes met I knew. His eyes were begging, pleading and to this day I will never forget the fear and anguish they held, nor will I forget the tenderness between us as I gently placed my hand on his and told him it would be all right. His eyes welled up with moist, silent pain and he said to me, "They will be shocked."

I leaned over and kissed his cheek bringing the palm of my hand up to gently wipe his tears away telling him it would be all right. "You look fine," I said. And as we both sat staring into one another's eyes we both became very aware of the fact that I had just looked my dad in the face and straight out lied to him.

I stood up, trying to avoid his gaze, and then helped him up and into his sweatpants, which once again had to be tightened up another notch. I then asked him if he had to go to the bathroom and he agreed that it might be a good idea. I nodded in agreement and I turned my back to him so he could get a hold of my shoulders when he suddenly paused. I turned my head around to him with a question in my eyes and he simply looked down, away from my gaze now and asked me if I would please put his shirt on for him.

I turned completely around to face him, setting him gently back down on the bed, so I could walk over to his dresser to get him a T-shirt.

"No," he said in a low voice, stopping me dead in my tracks, "Get me a sweatshirt, OK?"

"Sure," I said. "No problem," unless of course you consider your very heart breaking into a million pieces a problem of some sort.

You see, he had developed another tumor on the underside of his right arm, directly above the elbow. And this little dickens was growing more rapidly than the others. No big deal, I suppose, unless of course you consider a tumor the size of a grapefruit on the underside of your father's arm a big deal. What the hell! Come one—come all, I always say. Heck, there was room enough for plenty. Damn it! Damn it all to hell!

The cancer had pretty much taken over his entire body by this time. It was in control for sure. And the only problem I had with this, was just exactly how long would it take to get the flipping job done and what would we have to endure until then? No, let me rephrase that. How much more would *he* have to endure, before it finally claimed its victory?

His right arm was so swollen that it had easily become three times larger than the other arm. And with all due respect, this quite frankly and quite honestly, embarrassed the hell out of my modest, you're-so-vain, caring, little dad. So, I walked over to the closet and retrieved a longsleeved sweatshirt for him.

I carefully stretched the neck and then placed it over his head first, then, one at a time, we slid his arms into the soft sleeves. And as I was standing over him, tugging to bring the neck of the sweatshirt down to rest on his shoulders, I realized I was taking part in yet another role reversal.

I wondered to myself, just how many times had my dad stood over me, pulling a shirt over my head, telling me, "First one arm, then the other." Probably way too many times to count to be perfectly honest— way too many times indeed, and then a fleeting memory flashed just for a moment of how he would tickle my belly, while both of my arms were up in the air. And you know, I sure as hell had no desire to tickle his belly at all. In all honesty, I think I truly wanted to die. Either that or vomit until I choked to death. To be truthful, I really couldn't decide.

With sweatshirt in place, I stood him up once again to begin our choo chooed journey into the living room, making a short pit stop at the potty station. And as

I turned my back to him, placing his hands on my shoulders, I glanced back one more time and what I saw in his eyes could only be described as the look of shame. I reached my hands back to touch his, which were securely attached to my shoulder. Rubbing them back and forth for reassurance, I then whispered to him over my shoulder, "Are you excited?" And he answered me with an enthusiastic, "Uh huh!"

"Good," I said, "You should be." And with that, we headed for the bathroom.

He was still a little groggy, so I entered the tiny bathroom with him, having to repeat our once embarrassing ritual, which, in all honesty, by this time wasn't embarrassing at all anymore. It had simply become a necessity—plain and simply a very *sad* necessity. We didn't even give it a second thought anymore.

He sat down on the toilet to try and relieve himself which had absolutely no significance at all anymore. A couple of tinkles and—he was done. He wasn't really drinking anymore so there wasn't a whole lot to let go of.

I stood with my back to him and then I felt him tugging on my shirt. He was ready to stand up now. I turned and crouched down, placing my hands up underneath his arms and simultaneously, we stood up. I then reached down and pulled his sweatpants up. Only then would I look into his eyes. They were soft and knowing staring back at me as he whispered, "Thank you."

I nodded and gently touched his face. "You're welcome," I whispered.

He then turned toward the mirror as he readied himself for his grand entrance. He leaned over the sink and got closer to the mirror. Then he rubbed his whiskers and shook his head. I knew he was embarrassed. I knew he felt ashamed. So I very quietly and very seriously said, "Hard to believe, you're so damned cute, isn't it?" He turned, looked at me—paused—and then halfheartedly chuckled and said, "Oh, yes, it most certainly is, you knucklehead!" I tilted my head, shrugged my one shoulder, and gave him a half smile as to try and choke back the tears that were ready to spill from my big beautiful brown baby doll eyes. He in return, tilted his head, shrugged his shoulders and looked at me as if to say, *What can we do?*

His gaze then dropped from mine as he took in a deep breath, looked down, and murmured to the floor, "Let's go." And with that, we headed for the living room but, right before we exited the bathroom, he tapped me on the shoulder and waved his hands at me in a let go sort of motion. He wanted to walk on his own, still groping for any dignity he could find. So, I obligingly steadied him and we walked out of the bathroom single file.

As he always did, and he always would right to the very end, my dad somehow found the strength to portray that wonderful smile as he entered the living room with his arms spread wide, exclaiming his wonderful, "Hi there!" And I, for one, was so very relieved that he was too busy hugging and trying to get situated in his chair to see the horror on my sisters' faces. Perhaps he looked away on purpose. Perhaps he knew. Knowing my dad the way I knew him, I'm sure the avoidance was intentional.

Have you ever wondered why we actually take responsibility for things we have absolutely nothing to do with? I know during that time at my dad's, I found myself wondering that very question time and time again. We feel embarrassed if we were molested, or raped, or beat up, or cheated on, or—if we have cancer. Exactly what part of all of that makes one damned bit of sense?

My sisters, like the troopers they were, jumped up and gathered around my dad's chair to hug him and settled in around him, telling him they were so very glad to see him. And as the various conversations began, my mind drifted back to a time when we would all gather around him at my grandma's house, all talking at once, trying to cram two weeks' worth of happenings into a two-hour visit. He would finally start laughing, telling us all to take turns, simply because all the yakking was driving him crazy. And as I tuned back into the present that is exactly what he was saying now, as he chuckled proudly, telling the girls that some things never change.

They all chatted for the better part of an hour when it became apparent that his speech was becoming slurred. I didn't really notice at first until the girls all began looking at each other with horrified questions in their eyes. It was late and he was tired. There would be plenty of time to visit tomorrow. I intervened and asked him if he was tired. His eyes were drooping and it was obvious he was struggling to stay awake. He said he was, as he gathered up the ends of his little blanket and began his attempt to stand. I helped him up and out of his chair and told the girls to say good night. They all said their confused I love yous and hugged him looking bewildered as all hell. I gave them all a reassuring look and turned to my dad and said, "Let's get you to bed." I stayed close behind but he walked on his own until he got behind the privacy of his bedroom door. That's when he stopped and held his hands out in front of him wiggling them in the air giving me my cue to get around to the front of him as he reached for my secret support. I obligingly took him by the hands and walked steadily backward, leading him over to the bed. I then sat him carefully down and kissed the top of his head. He looked up at me and whispered, "Whew," as he wiped his brow. "That's a lot of work," he said. And with tears welling up in my heart, I simply replied with, "I know." And strangely, I did know.

We had become so closely connected that I could actually feel his exhaustion. I could feel his sorrow. But most painfully of all, I could feel his defeat, and his embarrassment.

As I was tucking him in, he asked me if I would be sleeping close to the bedroom that night.

"Would you like me to?" I asked.

He shared with me that he was worried about getting up and down and the girls hearing him vomit. Or—what if he couldn't get his sweatpants on in time and he had to go to the bathroom? The girls might see him naked! I assured him that the girls would all be sleeping and that I would hear the least little noise so I would help him in case he had to get up. I suggested that he wear his shorts to bed, already knowing that he wouldn't. "No," he said, "I just can't handle that." Of course he couldn't. Not only could my dad have been the very first Toys'R Us kid but I swear he must have also been the very first streaker in America as well.

I tucked him into bed and kissed him good night, telling him not to worry, that I'd be right out in the living room if he needed me. He reached forward and grabbed both of my hands, squeezed them twice, and whispered a gruff and humiliated, "Thank you."

"For what?" I whispered.

But silence was all he could muster. His eyes held the peace of my answer.

"You're welcome," I said, "but there's no need to thank me."

Still silent, his soft and wrinkled chimpanzee eyes looked longingly into mine as though there might be some sort of an answer in there if he searched long and hard enough. I sat back down on the bed, our hands still locked together and releasing the grip on one, I reached up and gracefully caressed the side of his face.

"It's almost over," I promised. "Pretty soon we won't have to entertain anymore."

He nodded and swallowed hard.

"I've never wanted to be so alone," he whispered.

"Yeah," I replied softly, "I know, Dad." And then in a Dorothy tone of voice, as though I were trying to tell the Scarecrow how important it was for me to get home to Kansas, I pushed on and said, "But—there are certain people who are going to want to say good-bye to you, Dad, and we shouldn't deprive them of that, unless you really want to because it's OK if you don't want to have anymore company." But it wasn't really OK. Not with me anyway. I honestly wondered how many more friends my dad could have out there who just might want to make an appointment to see him and thinking perhaps we could get him booked solid through the following year as though that just might keep him going.

"No," he said softly. "I don't want to take that away from anyone. Not yet."

I had won again! Another victory! We were still going to entertain!!!!

And just as though he could read my selfish thoughts, he squeezed my hands to get my attention, which it surely did as I looked him in the eye and he said, "I'm tired, dear. I'm tired of pretending that everything is OK while watching the looks of horror on their faces."

Well, he could have left this earth without making *that* particular comment and I wouldn't have minded one gosh darned bit. He'd gone and done it again. Just had to open his big mouth and make me realize once again that this wasn't about me.

We both sat for a few moments in silence, before I cleared my throat to speak.

"Well," I said, "we can do one of two things. We can stop the visits completely—or—we can pick and choose more carefully who comes to visit and for how long—or—we can buy you a pair of sunglasses and tell everyone you have also gone blind and then you can close your eyes when they come in and you won't have to look at anyone at all—or—you can watch them without them knowing it and then when they leave we can make fun of them."

Silence again before he very stoically said, "That was four things."

"Two—four—what in the hell is the difference?" I quipped.

"About two," he said. "Aren't you the one who finished school?" he taunted.

He half chuckled and then I gave him a half chuckle in return and with that, I stood up from the bed, bent down and kissed his soft and wrinkled cheek, told him to get some rest, and turned to leave him to his slumber. But not before he had to give me his opinion.

"I like the sunglasses idea," he murmured.

I turned back toward him with one hand on the doorknob and said, "What?"

"The sunglasses," he slurred as he was fighting to stay awake. "We'll make fun of people when they leave."

"I was kidding," I reminded him.

"Oh," he mumbled, "I'm not."

And with that I informed him of how ghastly of a person he was and that he *was,* after all on his way to heaven and that he had better not say such things until he interrupted me by politely reminding me that it had been my stupid idea in the first place.

"OK," I said. "Since I have more time for redemption than you do, I'll go buy you a pair of sunglasses."

And as I began to exit the room knowing he was on his way to slumber, he whispered, "Be careful—on your way to the store you may just get hit by a bus."

I stopped once again, turned back to look at him and his eyes were closed but he had a half smile resting within the corners of his mouth.

"Mickey Mouse sunglasses," I quipped. "Big ones!" And with that, I finally opened the bedroom door and got the hell out of there.

When I entered the living room, my sisters were all sitting together on the floor again looking like they had all just seen a ghost. About time someone besides me did anyway! Actually, they all looked as if they were mourning, each in her own way. I suppose they really were. And all I could compare it to in my own mind at that moment is that they all looked like I felt when I had first arrived—but that unlike me, they were the lucky ones, for they would, in fact, be able to run all the way back to wherever it is people run to when they are as scared as they all seemed to be. How well I knew.

Just what in the hell do you say at times such as those? Buck up, little buckaroos? How about breaking into song—*The sun will come up—tomorrow—bet your bottom dollar that tomorrow—I'll wish I was— anywhere but here! Tomorrow—tomorrow— there's always tomorrow—oh, what a crock of—Pooh!!!!* Now I'm also a songwriter!

All eyes were on me and I hadn't really broken out in song.

"He's sleeping now," I offered.

All eyes were still searching. OK, now might be a good time to break into that song.

However, I didn't. I simply sat down with them and answered all of their gut-wrenching questions to the best of my ability. And all of a sudden, I realized that I had incredibly become a cancer expert, a hospice caseworker, and a death consultant all in one sitting. Halleflippingluiah!

That afternoon was a long one. My dad slept the rest of the evening and we all found things to talk and laugh about. Laugh and talk—talk and laugh. What I wanted to know was—where were all the tears? This was nothing like I had expected! Of course, I had by that time—come to expect—not to expect. And so the story goes.

Their visit was short but very meaningful and my sisters did, in fact, feel some of the sensations that I had been feeling, but not in the same way. They all complained of not being able to sleep well due to various reasons, none of which I had experienced, or so it seemed. They saw nothing out of the unusual at all, which, quite frankly, made me feel more afraid and alone than special. As I look back now, I feel special, but then, all I felt was alone. Can't see the forest for the—or—don't know what you've got till it's—oh, never mind.

During their two-day stay, they all in their own ways, at separate times, said their peace with my dad. My oldest sister, always the practical one, simply wanted things to be over with. She could see that my dad was withering away to nothing and was willing to let him go simply so that he could be at rest and, although she loved my father very much, she felt it was time for him to be at peace. *Geeze, I now know who got all the unselfishness.*

On the other hand, my next-to-the-youngest sister didn't really know what to feel. Yes, she knew our dad was dying; however, she hadn't really had a relationship with him, so to speak. He was just her dad and that was that, plain and simple. She would miss him and she too loved him. Perhaps the time hadn't yet come in her life for her to get to know the man that she called Dad and I think she sadly had become aware of the fact that time had tragically run out. And on that note I will add that she is actually the only one out of all five of us who acts and looks most like him, and I'm not sure to this day if that is a blessing or a curse. It has to be somewhat of a curse because she walks like him too and she is, after all, a woman!

My middle sister, the one who didn't make it, believe it or not, is perhaps the most satisfied. She has always felt that there was a mutual understanding between her and her father. Somewhat of an unspoken agreement and whatever that agreement is, I might not ever know, but it has given her the peace in her heart and mind to endure. My dad told me that there would come a day when she would want to know everything— and when that day came he asked me to embrace her and tell her that he loved her and that he understood. He made me promise. And I kept that promise when she showed up on my doorstep about three years later—at about 6:00 in the morning and sober as a judge. And as for my youngest sister, the baby, the newlywed, and newly found daughter, well, my friends, this was perhaps the saddest of all, for she simply and desperately, wanted more time. This just absolutely wasn't fair. She was angry and I, for one, can tell you that her anger soon turned to sorrow and to this day, her heart yearns for the relationship that she could have had more of— and at the same time, she is so very thankful for the one treasure already received. The one she went wholeheartedly, head over heals after and as her reward, she will hold just a tiny piece of that treasure in her heart forever. Yes, they all, each in her own way, came to grips with the passing of our dad. I wish I had been so lucky.

During their visit, they did, in fact, witness the vomiting and the sleepless nights and it was all witnessed in absolute and painful silence. After all, what can a person say at times like those? Absolutely nothing, that's what. They were all completely mortified just as I, myself, had been the first time I had to listen to death creeping up from behind my dad to get him. But the only thing anyone can say or do at such times—well—is nothing. It was one of those things better left unspoken.

They also witnessed the absurd behavior of the witch and although this was one subject I really felt *was* better left alone, they would not let me. My oldest sister was the first to say something and for the record, in the end—she would be the last to say something as well. Thank God for big sisters!

What was wrong? Why was she so distant? And never mind that. Where did she go all day? Does she ever help with Dad? Have you even been out of this house? All of these were the questions that came surging forth and then some.

I told my sisters that I felt like she probably felt left out. Best as I could tell, she felt that Dad had chosen me over her and that, quite frankly, made me sick to even say it. There's some kind of thing going on between her, Dad, and the son, I explained, as though I were some private detective who had just cracked a major case. I have tried to talk to her about it but she really harbors some anger toward dad regarding her son.

"Does he live here?" my youngest sister asked.

"No," I answered, "he is in his thirties."

Dead silence. They were all staring at me now like I had just finished the deed and killed our father.

What time does she leave in the morning and what time does she come home and why doesn't she get up with him in the middle of the night and on and on and on.

And all I could say was, "I don't get it either but this must be one of the reasons Dad had me come here."

And just for the record, she *was* a big part of the reason my dad had asked me to come and had I known that day what my dad had up his sleeve for me the following week—I surely would have gone home with my sisters that day and never looked back. Something truly happens to people when they are dying. Some sort of knowing or insight. And I, for one, wouldn't have changed it for the world—but I sure as hell wish that someone would have at least clued me in. I mean after all, those friends of his who had been hanging around could talk about everything else under the sun!

So Saturday went pretty smoothly with plenty of little talk sessions throughout the day. My dad got up a down just a little bit more for brief visits. He tired so easily and his visits didn't last long but they were plenty and for that I was truly thankful, as were my sisters. The witch didn't go to work on Saturday but she disappeared for a while. Probably had to go feed the monkeys or Damien or polish the castle floors. But—when she *was* there, she was very attentive and nice, which, quite frankly, made me a little nervous. Had someone betrayed me and promised her those damned ruby slippers behind my back??? Oh—if only hindsight truly were twenty-twenty.

Sunday morning came quickly and I knew it would soon be time for my sisters to depart. I began to feel the tears building up in my heart early that morning as I got up from the couch and headed to the kitchen for coffee. My dad had had a very busy night of bathroom trips and I had gotten used to not sleeping so coffee had become an addiction of sorts for me. A much-needed addiction to simply function.

Standing at the counter, pouring my much-needed eye opener, I heard all the girls stirring around in the living room and I truly did not want to look at a single one of them for fear I would burst into tears. I didn't want them to leave me. I didn't want to be there anymore. I didn't want to help my dad anymore or fight the witch or any of it. I was tired and I just didn't want to be—period. And now, for another lesson in reality: sometimes in life, we all have to do things we really don't want to do. How's that for poetry in motion?

After my sisters got up and folded their blankets and got their morning drinks and doughnuts (my dad always had doughnuts, thanks to the Indian) we all gathered in the living room as that was the only room in the entire house that would accommodate us all. None of us were really saying much. The witch was in the bathroom, probably trying to decide if she should wear her hair up underneath her pointy hat or down, and my dad was still asleep and all it took was one good solid stare from my big sister from about twelve feet across the room and the dam broke loose, which sent my younger sisters into a frenzy. What's wrong, they were frantically asking as my "Glinda, the Good Witch" came to my rescue. She leaped to the sofa and scooted just about underneath me, cradling me in her arms, and began to rock me and stroke my hair, while telling them I would be just fine and that I was simply tired. She knew what was wrong with me. She had always known when something was wrong and to this very day she still does. The witch came out of the bathroom and Glinda's embrace tightened. She knew that too. She could tell something was amiss there and yet we had not discussed it between ourselves really. I would have but the private opportunity never really presented itself. There was no need anyway because she knew. She could read my heart.

The witch acted generally concerned as she entered the room and cackled the statement: "What's wrong now?" How very empathetic of her.

"Nothing's wrong," Glinda quipped, with daggers in her voice as though she just may have leaped off that sofa at any given moment and thrown that much-needed pail of water.

"Then why is she crying?" the witch asked.

"She's just tired," Glinda answered.

"Well, aren't we all," she stated.

This was it. I really thought there was going to be a showdown— so—I hugged Glinda tighter as to tell her not now. She was fuming and I could feel her shaking with anger.

"Not now," I whispered into her neck. "It will kill Dad."

She let go of me and leaned back at arm's length looking me square in the eye and whispered, "Great, then we can kill two birds with one stone and you can go home with us."

Startled, I stared at her as though she had gone mad before she smiled and then I smiled and then we both began to laugh. I guess in times like those, it is best to laugh rather than fetching a pail of water. Although?

So, the witch went about her business in the kitchen and we sat there on the sofa trying to regain some composure when out from the bedroom walked our sleepy-eyed, stumbling, little dad who wanted to know just exactly what was so damned funny?

"You woke me from my beauty sleep," he said.

"Well, I hate to tell you this but it didn't do much good anyway," I sassed.

"Well, it might have if you had been quiet and let me sleep longer," he guffed as he settled into his recliner, gathering his blanket around himself.

"I seriously doubt that," I said. "It hasn't worked yet."

And with that, he simply gave me a, "Humph!"

But the girls laughed and then began to talk to him and all seemed OK for just a while once again. Well, all except for the witch who had to be well aware by now that Glinda was on to her.

After about an hour the sun came out and we all decided to take our visit out to the front porch where everyone could get some fresh air.

We all got situated out on the front porch with lawn chairs and tucked my dad safely into his blanket and chair with my dad already talking about the old times *(yesterday)* with all of us damned well knowing that it would, in fact, be the last time.

I have this last conversation on tape and I, for one, can tell you, that although I didn't realize it at the time, as I listen to that conversation now, every one of us sounded like we were sick and ready to throw up. All except for my dad, of course, for he was doing what he loved and did best. He was telling stories to all of us, for the last time. Stories of the days when he was with my mother and how he just knew had they stayed together that all of us girls would have gone on to college and so on—and so on—and so on, although, he did share a story that morning that I had never heard before. As a matter of fact, I was shocked, as I'd thought I had heard them all. It was a story about a radio. A radio that he had wanted for a very long time and so he had gone and bought it without my mother's blessing. (*All my troubles seemed so far away.*) Well, it came time for them to need money and what do you think was the first thing on the top of the list to sell? Yup—my dad's treasured, little, voice in a box sort of gadget. It seems that my mother had offered to sell it to my uncle, her brother-in-law, which turned out to be A-OK, in my father's eyes, simply because this particular uncle was my dad's close friend and he had agreed to sell it back to my dad when they were financially better off. But my heart absolutely ached as I watched my dad's eyes trail off into the thick Southern California sky while hearing him painfully describe how he never saw that radio again. Silly, isn't it? For cripe's sake, it was just a silly-ass radio. Perhaps to some, but to those of us who know him, it was a hell of a lot more than that—wasn't it?

Oh—now I realize that my dad allowed those things to happen to him. Just as well as he, himself, realized it, and I will tell you that it didn't hurt as much that he never saw the radio again as much as it hurt to try and understand why. I guess some things just never do make any damned sense at all. Though there is one thing that my dad, my sisters, and I *did* realize that morning. You really and truly can't ever go back. Not realistically anyway. I, for one, could have gone my entire life without hearing that damned story, quite frankly. Kind of made me wonder where he had been keeping that little piece of history for so very long. I mean, just exactly what part of the brain do you suppose harbors such painful memories throughout our entire lives? Well, I myself don't have a clue, and you know what else? I don't give a hoot!!!

Finally, after all of the stories had been told and all the laughs had been laughed, and all the tears had been cried, the dreaded moment had come and it was time for our houseguests to leave. The girls knew it, I knew it and my dad knew it, but nobody wanted to say it. This was it. Their final good-bye with our dad was upon us.

As they were preparing to leave, we were all lingering, dragging our feet, making small talk, literally wasting time. Well, all except for the witch, who obviously had somewhere else to go. She had been antsy all morning. It was Sunday, for hell's sake! Relax, take a load off those ugly green legs, and speaking of green, perhaps she should have had a facial. Maybe do something with that complexion of hers besides hide it under her wide-brimmed hat. She had sat out on the porch and listened to all of the stories. She laughed along with us and she asked questions. Crap—for a moment she almost seemed human. I suppose in all fairness that she was human. She just had a different agenda than the rest of us.

As we all meandered around, I wondered just exactly *what* we were waiting for. Perhaps for my dad to up and die in a hurry so that they wouldn't have to make a second trip? You know as silly as that sounds, I think we all *really* were secretly hoping that he *would* go while we were all together. And I'll tell you something else. I think my dad was hoping too. What better exit than to have your loved ones standing by? Uh huh, well great—it didn't happen. He didn't die before they left. Nope, he sure as hell didn't. As a matter of fact he held on for two more weeks after that. I look back now and wonder just how in the hell he did it and, quite frankly, I don't really know how but he sure as hell did.

As they were all carrying their bags down the front porch steps and out to the van, my cute little automobile-loving Dad, wanted to walk out to the carport and take a look at the eighth wonder of the world; the minivan that my sisters had rented for their journey. My dad actually owned his own minivan as well as his Chevy Pickup and he thought them to be a wonderful form of transportation. He bought his minivan for the witch to get around in. I think the broomstick made it difficult in bad weather. So with my sisters running back and forth from the house to the van, carting luggage and trying to get ready to go home, I walked my dad down the front porch steps, and over to the carport.

With all of my sisters standing around watching my dad admire the van, it seemed like everything was normal. No one seemed to have a care in the world and for just a few brief moments we all seemed to forget the sadness that had been consuming our very lives—and then it was shattered! In the blink of an eye we were all tragically thrown right back into the present as my dad all of a sudden doubled over in pain and began to get sick. It started with a simple cough, and then a gag, and then he began to vomit. So violently, in fact, that he had to hold onto the side of the house for balance, which sent my sisters all scattering back into the house until he was finished, giving him what little privacy and dignity they could, not to mention it was very frightening.

*(Now it looks as though they're here to stay.)* I stood next to him rubbing his back continually telling him it was OK, as he held onto me with one hand and the side of the house with the other. He was truly ashamed, embarrassed and angry and I felt truly the same for him.

When he was able to stand upright and walk back into the house, my sisters made themselves scarce as I paraded him through the living room and straight into the bathroom.

Once inside our locked hollow of privacy, he sat down on the toilet purely exhausted and I wet a washcloth and sat down on the floor directly in front of him wiping the sweat from his face. *(Oh, I believe in yesterday.)*

There was nothing but silence as he sat and stared at the floor just heaving and trying to catch his breath until he regained his composure and then slowly, our eyes met. His were filled with tears— and mine? Well I have no clue what mine looked like but they felt like sandpaper.

"I'm so sorry," he whispered.

"I know, Dad, but there's no need," I said as my words trailed off into some distant daydream of a time when all of this had not yet happened.

"Are the girls still here?" he asked.

"Yes, Dad. They haven't said good-bye yet," I answered, wishing I hadn't said what I had indeed just said. It sure had a different meaning on that day. A much different meaning than ever before.

He was disgusted as he took a deep breath and whispered, "I suppose we should get this over with."

I simply sat there, now on my knees next to him on the toilet and without looking at him, I told the floor, "I suppose so." But neither of us moved.

"I almost wish they hadn't come," he said shamefully. *(Suddenly, I'm not half the man I used to be.)*

"We should have just done this over the phone," he added.

"I know," I whispered. "But that wouldn't have been fair to them, Dad."

'No, I suppose not," he said.

"Or you," I added, as though I were trying to convince a jury.

"No, I suppose not," he answered again.

"Well, what exactly do you suppose?" I quipped with a sick chuckle.

"Hell," he said as he chuckled back, "I really don't know."

"It will all be over with soon, Dad," I sympathetically shared.

He nodded.

"When you feel like you can stand, I will walk back out there with you and you can say your good-byes and then take your nap. You'll feel better when you wake up."

"Oh? And what makes you the know it all?" he quipped.

"I have no clue." I chuckled again. "I'm just a smart gal. I *am* my father's daughter," I added.

"Yes, I suppose you are," he said to the floor. And then added, "My little dumb-dumb."

"Yeah," I mumbled. Your little dumb-dumb, who wished at that very moment that she was anywhere but there. Swimming in shark-infested waters perhaps? Or maybe even sitting in the dentist's chair with the gynecologist at the other end!

"Are you ready?" I asked.

"I suppose I should be," he answered, still looking at the floor with his hands interlocked and resting on his knees. *(There's a shadow hanging over me.)*

"OK," I said, "Just ten more minutes. Can you go out there for ten more minutes?"

"I think so."

"Just don't think about it, Dad. Just pretend you will see them again and go about your day."

"But, I *will* see them again," he said as though I had just tricked him. Maybe not in this place—but in another—I will see you *all* again." *(Oh, yesterday, came suddenly.)*

I felt ashamed. Of course he would.

"I meant here, Dad, sorry."

Silence.

"Do you really believe that?" he asked me. And he wasn't talking to the floor any longer—he was actually looking at and speaking to me.

I sat quietly—thinking—wondering—before I finally said, "Yes, I think I do."

He reached out with the palm of his hand and placed it gently underneath my chin and guided my face upward ever so gently until our eyes met, and he said, "You have to believe that!"

"OK," I said, looking at him with eyes that realistically said, *I'm trying.*

"We *will* see each other again someday," he demanded. "There *is* an afterlife."

"Who do you think these folks are who have been hanging around," he asked, as though we had just celebrated a birthday party.

Uh, quite frankly, at that point I had no clue, but I had been meaning to talk to him about that sooner or later and just about now seemed good.

"I don't know, Dad," was all I could muster.

"Well," he said in a whisper, as though he held the very secret to the universe, "They are from the other side."

"The other side of what?" I asked. Wishing to the very God I prayed to each and every day that I hadn't said what I had just indeed said because the look on his face said, *You are an absolute and undeniable idiot!!!!*

"Heaven!" He blurted out so blatantly in a screamed whisper that it quite frankly scared the living hoopla right out of me and I actually flinched when he said it.

'Oh," was all I could say.

Yup—that's me! Woman of so many wise and wonderful words. Simply just, "Oh."

"You do believe in heaven, don't you?" he begged.

"Of course I do," I said. But I wasn't really sure. I mean, I had never had to really think about it. Streets are paved with gold and all of that stuff. OK, I thought, sure—I suppose I believe.

"Well you'd better," he warned, still screaming in that whisper, which was, quite frankly, getting on my last nerve.

And then he said it. The words I will never forget and yet at the same time I wish I had never heard.

"I've been there!"

OK, this conversation had gone on way too long. I was done and he was understandably in some sort of lunatic state of mind.

Very quietly, I asked, "Been where?"

"Heaven!" he blurted out for the second time but this time I was sure the girls had unmistakably heard him all the way out into the living room.

Staring at him as though he had just metamorphosed into a giant cantaloupe, brow furrowed and head cocked like a dog listening to a high-pitched scream, I scooted on my knees just a tad bit closer to try to get the skinny on this newly exclaimed secret.

"What in the hell do you mean, you've been to heaven?" I whispered with my teeth gritted so tightly I thought I just may snap my own jaw in two, as though he had just perhaps shared with me that he had gambled away the family fortune.

With his hands still folded in his lap, he leaned a little closer, stared right into my eyes and whispered to me that he'd been visiting there in his sleep.

"Heaven," I more stated than asked.

"Yes," he quipped, "heaven!"

With my brow still furrowed and through squinty eyes I stared at him for just a few seconds or years before I very calmly asked again, you have been to heaven—in more of an unbelievable tone like—let me get this straight, you can turn yourself into a toad?

He then leaned back a bit and gave me one good strong nod and replied with a simple "Yup."

Okeydoke, I was done. Everyone out of the pool!!!!

"How do you know?" I whispered. 'I mean, that it's heaven?"

"Because there are people there and they told me so," he answered as though I was an absolute moron and right about then he wasn't really far from being wrong.

"You don't believe me," he said like a kid who had just sworn he had seen Santa Claus.

Still squinting, as if I had entered a Clint Eastwood look-alike contest, I looked him square in the eye and said, "No, Dad, I actually *do* believe you." And I *did*. That is why I sat there looking so damned stupid I suppose because I *did* believe him.

"That's where I go when I'm sleeping," he confessed.

Still squinting, still staring, still being, well, still, I simply sat there allowing this newly found information time to sink in. And then, out of the blue, just like he had been sneaking out late at night and going to the movies, I asked, "Why do you come back?"

And just as matter-of-factly, he quite promptly answered me with, "Don't know. They send me back. Guess I'm not allowed to stay—yet— but I want to," he added.

So, there I simply sat again. Saying nothing because nothing is exactly all that I could think of. We would have to finish this conversation later. My sisters were out in the living room probably thinking he had died and that I was preparing his body for burial, although, it had really only been a few minutes. It only seemed like a lifetime to me, I suppose.

"You can tell me all about heaven when the girls leave," I whispered. And the stupid thing was, I really meant what I had just said.

"But right now, you have your daughters waiting to say good-bye," I added.

"I suppose," he mumbled.

He then outstretched his arms at my signal to help him up. I steadied my hands on his knees and stood up. I then reached down and placed both of my arms under each of his and lifted him from his sitting position. We stood there for just a moment, in that awkward embrace to make sure he could walk on his own when he looked into my eyes and whispered, "Care to dance?"

"Not really," I said lightly tapping his cheek. "You're not my type," I said as I turned my back to him so he could take a hold of my shoulders.

"As a matter of fact," I added, "I don't really even care much for you."

"Oh?" he questioned, "That's not what you said last night!"

"You are a sick man," I quipped. "And too vain for your own good," I added.

"Open the door," he ordered, as though I were really pissing him off.

"Don't tell me what to do," I snapped back at him as I reached for the doorknob to expose our hiding place.

"Just remember," he whispered, "you have to believe. You will need to believe."

And he was right. However, it would take me thirteen more years to get it.

He let go of my shoulders as we walked through the bathroom doorway and out to the living room where he proudly exclaimed to the girls that he was ready to lie down for a while, so it was time now to say good-bye.

They were all getting up slowly from their sitting positions looking as though a rhinoceros had just entered the room.

My dad stood his ground as he held his arms out and pronounced he wanted smooches from everyone so he could get some sleep and they needed to get on their way home. They had a long drive ahead of them. And he—well—he had to die soon so—See Ya!

As they all gathered around him right in the middle of the living room, with each and every daughter, he said his own good-byes, sharing something different with each one of them as they hugged and kissed him for the last time, as the rest of them formed somewhat of a circle around him instead of a line. However I noticed that to each daughter he said, "I'll see you next time, dear." And I couldn't help thinking that there just wasn't going to be a next time. Just as much as I couldn't help thinking that this would be the very last time that my dad would throw his wonderful, loving arms around his little girls and kiss them tenderly. I knew it—and they knew it—and he knew it too. I had, honest to God, entered into a world of absolute insanity!!! But as always, I think my dad felt the need to protect them as well as himself. And then it was time. And with that, he simply and tearfully turned around and headed back to his bedroom, walking a little slowly but perfectly steady, waving his arm over his head in a good-bye fashion. End of scene one thousand. No more takes. End of clip. And that was the end of that—leaving us all standing there, looking and feeling like someone had just stolen our lollypops!!!

That was my dad. Plain and simple Eddie.

After peeking in on him to make sure that he had gotten into bed OK, I then knew it was time for me to say my own good-byes to my sisters. Oh, how desperately I wanted to go home with them. And oh, how I didn't want them to leave me. And as it turned out, this would be the most tearful and most painful experience that my sisters and I had ever experienced amongst ourselves until the death of our mother thirteen years later.

I believe that I cried that day harder than I had ever cried before, thus far. I really and truly thought my heart was actually breaking in two. I couldn't let them leave me. I couldn't let go of my sisters. I couldn't let go of the fact that they were going home and I wasn't. I missed home terribly and I didn't want to stay and face this tragedy any longer, and as I stood there watching them prepare to drive away, I was reminded of a scene from my most favorite movie of all times, as I kissed one sister then another then another, truly realizing that there *is* no place like home. They had all found what they had come for and were now leaving, all with different treasures that they had really already possessed all along. They had simply never been asked to put them to the test. And as for me? Well, no matter how many times I closed my eyes and clicked my heels together, each and every time I opened my eyes they were only filled with tears and I was still standing in a different land, longing with all my heart, to be home again.

It was just as difficult for my sisters to leave as it was for me to watch them leave. They begged me through their own tears, to stop crying, but I absolutely could not. I really wasn't sure at that point if I would ever stop crying again. It hurt so badly that I don't think I can ever forget how it felt, knowing that they were going to the place where my children were and where my husband was. A place that had always been safe with no sadness and no death, a place that had by now, become only a memory.

They circled around the small trailer park block three times, before they were finally gone. And each and every time I felt a little better, just knowing that they didn't want to leave me. Yes folks, I had come to my dad's house for a reason, but at that moment I truly couldn't make one damned bit of sense out of *that* very reason to save my life. I was lost and scared and lonely. And perhaps for the second time in my life, I really wished it *was* me who was dying. It would have been a hell of a lot easier to accept, or so I thought at the time anyway. Funny, isn't it? How we always seem to be able to convince ourselves that when things go terribly wrong, I mean *really, really* wrong, that we'd just like to check out for a while. Aw, come on. We've all done it, and we've all said it—or at least thought it at one time or another in our lives. Maybe we were sick or just sad when we nonchalantly said or thought that stupid phrase, "I could just die." Sure has been easy for some of us to just withdraw and say, so what if I die? Uh huh, real easy indeed unless you're the one sitting in the doctor's office when he comes creeping through the door with your chart in hand and can't quite look you in the eye. Yes, indeedy that sure as hell is a wake-up call now, isn't it? So from now on, let's try—all of us, I mean really try—not to say or think those things anymore when we're down and out, OK? Because the truth of the matter is, is that we really don't mean it. It's simply just an escape, a release of some sort, a figure of speech. And to be quite truthful with all of you, I sometimes wonder just how many times my dad said or thought the same thing during his life. Huh, sure makes you stop and think, now, doesn't it? I wonder how many times he would have taken it back had he known what was down the road for him? Yes, I truly do wonder indeed.

*(Why she had to go I don't know—she wouldn't say. I said something wrong, now I long for yesterday.)*

# Chapter Fifteen

## *Pretending*

AFTER MY SISTERS left that day, I sat out on the front porch for a better part of an hour, crying and trying desperately to make sense out of all that had happened up until that point and you know, I couldn't make a damned bit of sense out of anything at all—and to this day—I still can't. How very doomed I felt when it came time to walk back into that house. I mean, what in the world was there to look forward to? If I stayed, I would have the pleasure of watching my father die a very slow death and when it did finally come time for me to go home I would have just buried him. Sort of makes you want to puke now, doesn't it? Oh, and let us not forget about the witch! She had gone to work that morning and God only knew where work really was. Perhaps some puppy mill or better yet, maybe she really did have a horrible castle somewhere. If she did, I guarantee all of you that not only was *it* horrible—but she did horrible things in *it* too.

Yes, I think that it had finally dawned on me. I was in a lose-lose situation and this truly and very matter-of-factly—was not OK with me. Of course, by this time, nothing was OK with me. Hell, I myself wasn't OK.

So what did I do? Well, after I called home and cried to my husband for about twenty minutes, I did what every other red-blooded American niece would do. I called my uncle the Indian and asked him to come over and console me, which he did very willingly and with all the understanding that only he could portray.

Now I don't know what it is about an Indian and great wisdom, but there has to be some connection between the two and there must somewhere be a darned

229

good reason for it. I mean honestly, have you ever seen an Indian freak out in a time of crisis? Well if you have, then you certainly have one up on me, because I sure as hell haven't, at least not *this* particular Indian. Nope, he is always cool, calm and collected. Always has been and I assume he always will be. And that's exactly why I called him. Because no matter what the situation, no matter what the crisis, I could always count on him to summarize just what in the Sam hell was going on. Kind of a nice relative to have hanging around in times of crisis, don't you think? And I'll tell you something else at the risk of giving every talk show host in the country a screaming heart attack. He is usually right on the money. Yup, my wisdom-sharing, braid-sporting, uncle the Indian is just about as intelligent as any psychiatrist I've ever known. Well, excluding mine, of course. However, when she wasn't available, he sure did do in a pinch.

So it should come as no shock to all of you that on that particular day, while I was crying the blues, and quite simply losing what little mind I had left, and pretty much all at the same time, I figured I might as well go ahead and get *everything* off my chest. Seeing that I had someone who was willing to listen and all. And so I did.

I cried about the pain and I cried about the unfairness and I cried about all of the things that happened twenty years ago, as well as the day before and I did so with my uncle sitting and intently listening to my every word. Oh, but it didn't stop there, my friends. I figured while I was at it I might just as well spill the beans all the way out of the jar and tell my uncle about the witch as well as all those folks who had been hanging around. Yes, indeedy, ladies and gents, while my dad was happily sleeping away back in the snug confines of his bedroom, I confided these insane sightings to my very-believing and by this time probably very–sorry– that–he–knew–the–way–to–my–dad's–house, intent–listening, serious, and consoling uncle, while he sat with his eyes focused on mine the whole entire time, not ever once giving a hint of disbelief before he finally inhaled deeply, exhaled—and then—gave his much-invited opinion.

He had absolutely no clue as to what was happening or what I might have seen. Nice to know that in times of concern, I could depend on him, huh? I mean, honest to Pete, how about a little sympathy here? For hell's sake, the least he could've done was humor me. But in all actuality, I guess he really couldn't, and mostly because there was absolutely no humor in this situation what–so–ever–at–all.

When he did finally choose to share his opinion, *it*—like his brother's—was quite plain and simple. You see, he thought it to be very possible that whoever these people were, they were there to do a job. And with or without my acceptance or cooperation, whether I understood it or not, that job had to be done. He also felt that time was nearing for my dad to depart. Of course you didn't have to be a knowledgeable, braidsporting Indian to figure that one out. However, he felt that the closer the time came, the more I might see these visions, people, whatever, and the more I might find myself going through these crying fits. And as far as the witch went? Well, on that subject my uncle simply listened and squinted and then said to me that he had no words *for* her and he had no words *about* her and when my uncle says that he has no words for or about you—you may as well be dead.

Quite frankly, I was just relieved that he didn't pick up the phone and dial 1-800-Come And Get Her!

In all sincerity and it probably goes without saying, but I'll say it anyway. Without my uncle I probably would have gone insane. *(Even more so than I already had.)* He was always there to pick up the pieces and sweep up the remains when I felt like I just absolutely couldn't handle it anymore. He went out of his way every evening just to come by and visit with my dad and to make sure that I, the lunatic, was hanging in there. He brought me little gifts of encouragement and he always made sure that I had everything I needed. But do you want to know what that wisdom-sharing Indian gave me that meant more to me than anything? His belief and understanding, that's what, and mostly because I was finding it extremely difficult to understand and believe in myself. Yes, my friends, my uncle believed everything I told him to be true and he sympathized with all of my feelings, no matter how absurd they were and no matter how silly they sounded. And let me tell you, some of those feelings were extremely personal and very selfish. And was I surprised? Nope, not at all. I mean, let's assess the situation here. Both my dad and my uncle had been raised by the same wonderful woman. And I think that pretty much sums it all up without even having to utter another word. But you know I will anyway. I felt extremely blessed to have had my uncle around. Actually I didn't feel as blessed then, as I do now. For now, I am able to look back and count the blessings that I was too upset to be grateful for at the time. So this just goes to show you, if you have a relative like this hanging around in times of crisis or sorrow, make a little mental note to yourself to thank them when it's all over. God only knows where we'd be without them.

I sure do wish, however, as I sit here ever so comfortably, reminiscing in the comfort of my own home, that my uncle, the wise and all-knowing Indian hero of my memories could have foreseen the week ahead that had been in store for me because any warning at all would have been greatly appreciated. Of course, there was probably nothing I could have done in this whole world to prepare for it anyway. Well, nothing except for maybe having all of my teeth pulled with absolutely no anesthetic, for the next morning came too quickly as I awoke to a definite as well as disheartening change in the very surrounding of my dad's home.

First of all, I had slept throughout the night. That should have been my first clue that something was amiss. Then, there was this sad and deafening silence around me from the very moment I awoke. I felt *it*—or the absence of *it*. Whatever *it* was or wasn't. And then—there was also that obvious and extreme decline in the very feeling of the house itself and it was unbeknownst to me at the time, but this would become a morning that I would never forget.

It began at seven o'clock when I opened my eyes. It was daylight for starters! I was panicked as I tried to remember if I had heard my dad get up. Had he called for me to come and help him and had I slept through it? I jumped off the couch and ran for the bedroom, which was really just a leap from the couch but for the mere sake of dramatics, it felt like I ran for the bedroom. I slowly pushed the door open and checked to see if my dad was breathing. He was.

Slowly placing my hand on my head with a furrowed brow, I turned and walked back over to the couch, deciding that I should make coffee before I sat down.

I walked into the tiny kitchen with all sorts of thoughts running through my already busy little brain. Had I slept through his early morning smoke? And where in the hell was the witch? I can't believe she would leave without kissing me good-bye!!! Crap—how could she leave without waking me? Was she stupid? He could have died!

Yes, all of this was very serious indeed and yet, there was something else tugging at me. Something about the very feel of that morning that just wasn't quite right.

I had my coffee and took a shower and tidied up the house a bit so that I could sit and chat with my dad about these things when he woke up to watch his morning game show. And it was just about ten minutes after the hour of ten when I knew something was terribly wrong.

He didn't come scooting out of the bedroom to watch his show. He didn't call for me to help him up and how long had he been sleeping anyway? Crap—I couldn't remember. Since yesterday afternoon I thought? Holy—nobody sleeps that long! Unless—

Cautiously, with my heart pounding so loudly I couldn't hear myself think, I lifted myself from the sofa and proceeded to walk back to his bedroom.

Slowly, once again I quietly pushed the door from its ajar position and peeked in with my eyes focused on my dad's midsection the entire time. I then tiptoed to the side of the bed like a predator stalking its prey. It was so cold in there. He didn't stir. Not a muscle, not a sigh, nothing! I felt my heart skip a beat and my knees beginning to give way as I continued to approach the side of the bed watching his chest with every step and it still wasn't moving! Now, standing directly above him I leaned closer to his face like I was half ready to run. Sheer and absolute terror surged throughout my entire being as his chest still hadn't moved. And I became paralyzed, as the first thought that came to mind was that he was gone! He can't be gone! His color was too good. Like I had seen so many dead people before. Like I knew what the hell one should look like. And just as I began to lean over him to touch his face, he all of a sudden took a very deep breath and scared the pee-waddlings right out of me! I was so relieved that I sat down next to him on the bed and all I could do was cry and I continued to do so for a very long time.

I look back on that day now, and I think of how silly it was for me to have been relieved. Because the fact still remains that I *did* eventually lose him and I darned well knew it was going to happen sooner or later, but I will tell each and every one of you right here and now, that each and every time my dad took another breath, I was still holding on to the hope because each and every time just would not have been the right time to let him go. And I'll tell you something else while I'm at it. That third week with my dad taught me a hell of a lot more about living than dying. Yes, that third week, better known as Armageddon in my memory was definitely a crash course in harsh reality—for this was the week that I had to face some facts that most of us only think about when we are alone and scared and at their wits' end. During the third week everything began to snowball, as I was forced to make decisions that I would have never dreamed of. Not even in my wildest nightmares.

As I sat on the bed next to him, now catching my own breath, I reached forward and did actually touch his face anyway. It *was* cold and clammy. Not unusual really. My dad broke out in cold sweats and then hot sweats and then he'd get a chill quite often. It reminded me of someone coming off drugs. It also reminded me of how very strong I was, for each and every time he got these sweats he would begin shaking uncontrollably, which quite sadly made me feel like throwing up. But I didn't. I would simply choke back the tears and bile as I would wrap him up tightly in blankets while rocking him in my arms and then unwrap him and fan away to cool him off, sometimes as many as six times in a period of one hour. Whatever it took is exactly what I did and I will never forget silently asking God, why? Why in his own name hadn't he already done something? Why did my dad have to suffer so and just how many more times would he have to go through all of this before he could finally rest? Sound familiar? Well, if you are someone who has already gone through such an ordeal, it darned well should. Because this is exactly the way we end up, asking God, or whomever to do the very same something that we have been dreading all along. I'm telling you, we as human beings are quite strange, quite strange indeed. And just in case you didn't catch it—that *was*, in fact, me who was actually asking for this to finally be over.

As I was touching his face there was something else that occurred to me right then and there that had never happened before. He didn't respond to my touch! Not one stinking, heart-stopping little bit! He just simply and very deeply continued to sleep.

Well, I simply and very deeply began to cry harder. Was he never going to be awake again? Had he just been waiting to say good-bye to the girls? No! This just couldn't be! I needed to tell him good-bye! He had to realize how much I loved him! I hadn't shown him nor had I expressed it enough! Please, God, not now! Just give me one more chance! One more opportunity! One more second to say good-bye!

Sad wasn't it? Yes it most certainly was. And if my dad had, in fact, gone right then and there, wouldn't he have known how very much I loved him? Hadn't I already done enough to show him? Hadn't I in fact gone to great lengths to tell him? And most importantly of all, hadn't I been the one that he, himself, had chosen to be there? Well, one would think so. Unless of course that someone was me.

You see it wouldn't have mattered when the time came for him to go. I wasn't ready. I still to this day am not ready, because no one ever really is. Isn't there always just one more thing to say, just one more thing to do, just one more pleading minute of a second chance? Of course there is. There's that one more chance in all of us. That's what makes us human. Now, doesn't that just make you want to whoop?

Well, as it turned out, my dad had not in fact slipped into another place that morning. He was merely beginning to sleep a little deeper and a little longer. And with every day that went by he became more exhausted and he continued to sleep deeper and deeper and longer and longer.

This was Monday morning and the beginning of the third week. And as I began to probe my own memory for what this situation of sleep might have been I suddenly remembered what his nurse had said to me three weeks prior to that day. (Three weeks prior. Huh, seemed like such an eternity ago.) Hadn't she said, if I was there that perhaps he might just hold on for four more weeks? Yes, I do believe so. And I also believe that what she said had been the very thing that sent me screaming into a tailspin of urgency and emotion. Yup, I do believe, if I remember correctly, that my conversation with that wonderful nurse person is exactly what sent me crying all the way to Southern California in such a hurry. And since we're on that subject, just what in the hell had been my hurry anyway? Ah, yes, I remember now. I wanted to be there before he got his last boarding call. *Hallelujah!*

Well, my friends, at this point I must share with all of you that I sure do thank God for having the sense to tape when we did and for having the sense to say all I had to say and all I had to do when I said and did it, for my dad would only be awake a total of about one hour a day from that third week forward and that hour was mostly spent with him dozing and me crying hopelessly all by myself.

He did finally open his eyes that morning and slowly, as well as very groggily, turned his head toward me but only to acknowledge my existence. I sat down next to him and asked if he would like to get up and watch his show. He sadly and very weakly told me "No." I rubbed his hair and covered his shoulder with the blanket as he rolled over to get comfortable turning his back to me. And I realized at that moment that for the first time in my entire life, my dad had actually turned his back to me. I began rubbing his shoulders for a time until he fell back to sleep. And then—there was nothing left for me to do. This was it! No more *Price Is Right*, no more *Matlock*. *(Come on down! You're the next contestant on "You're Losing Your Sanity!" Hosted by, yup, you guessed it, that most wonderful little gal, your friend and mine, Daddy's little brown-eyed baby doll girl!)* I was lost. I didn't want him to sleep. I wanted to have another fun-filled conversation and jump on the bed again with him laughing and calling me names. I wanted him to smoke his pipe. I just wanted him to do the things that people do when they are alive and well and have their whole lives ahead of them. Now, would you just listen to that? There just happened to be a slight problem there, wouldn't you say? For he had no real quality of life ahead of him any longer. No—sadly, his whole life had suddenly fallen far behind him, hadn't it? Yes, it certainly had, and instead of *him* clinging to its every precious day—it was *me*.

I really have no clue how I expected all of this to end. When I think back, I truly believe that I thought my dad might just sit up one day and say, "OK, dear, I'm ready to go now, so kiss me good-bye and have a nice life." Or maybe he would wipe his brow with a most relieved look on his face proclaiming how this sure had been a close one, but he feels all better now. I really can't say for sure just what in the hell I expected. And I guess when we really think about it, it doesn't really matter a whole lot now anyway.

I left him sleeping that morning and walked into the living room in a dream state. I don't think I had ever felt so alone in my life. I kept wondering if this was the end. Is this how it's going to be until he stops breathing? And suddenly, I found myself pretending that he was already gone. Silly, wasn't it? Perhaps, but we all do it. At one time or another, especially in situations such as these, we all do it and probably a lot more than we all care to admit. And I'll be the first to tell you that pretending such things only sent me running right back into his bedroom with my heart screaming for another moment. And I did just that. But this time, instead of sleeping, I found my dad with his eyes wide open, and doing something that made time stand completely still. This would, in fact, become the very day that would change my entire life forever. He was talking to someone. Someone whom I, myself, could not see.

I slowly entered the bedroom, half expecting him to stop once he became aware of my presence, but he didn't. As a matter of fact, he looked right at me and then, as if in slow motion, pointed up to the far left corner of the bedroom. Then he turned his head in the same direction and nodded. I slowly and quietly walked over and sat down next to him on the bed and actually heard myself asking who was there. But he didn't say a word. He just continued to gaze into the corner with a most wonderful and peaceful smile on his face. And I wish I could sit here and tell all of you that

I understood what was happening, but I didn't, just as much as I wish I could tell all of you that I wasn't afraid or confused but I can't, because I was. And as I sat there searching my mind for a logical explanation a thought came to me. Hadn't the hospice nurses told me that something like this might happen? Yes, I believed they had but damned if that helped me at all as I was sitting right smack-dab in the middle of this situation. And as I sat staring into a corner looking for something I couldn't possibly have found, something happened to me. Something so unbelievable that it's difficult for me to explain, but I'll try anyway, just for the mere sake of this story. I—all of a sudden, felt at peace. And I wasn't afraid anymore. And laugh, if you must, but I guess if I had to describe what I felt at that very moment besides happiness, it would have to be absolute and complete peace. It was as though time had come to an abrupt but serene halt. Like a blanket of warmth had just been draped upon my shoulders. The entire room no longer existed. We just were.

I wanted so badly to see what he was seeing. I felt them. I knew they were there. I could hear talking but not through my ears. They were thoughts that were not my own. I wanted to ask and then I realized I knew exactly who they were. When they would be taking him would have been my next question but I couldn't speak and that was just fine because I didn't have to. Instead, I simply sat there in silence thankful that I could be a part of whatever was taking place.

After about ten minutes of sitting in complete silence, my dad then turned his head toward me and in a slurred and most tired voice, he tried to speak. Shaking his head from side to side in dismay, he tried it again. Clearing his throat and this time being able to speak a little more clearly, he shared with me that he had been somewhere that morning. Already sitting on the bed, I reached over and took his hand, which to my surprise was very warm. I then touched his face, which I also found to be very warm. He was smiling at me in the most wondrous way and I can't say why but I asked a question that just wasn't something that one would usually ask. However, this was a most unusual situation.

"*Where*, Dad? *Where* have you been?"

He slowly turned his head and gazed at me with those notorious squinting eyes and said, "Somewhere real nice." He then went on to say that this place was beautiful.

I asked with great expectations what this place looked like and he answered me with, "I don't really know."

"Then how do you know it is beautiful?" I asked.

I sat there staring into his eyes with all the understanding and compassion I could possibly muster, when I finally broke the silence by asking him to try and explain it to me. And this is what he said, almost word for word.

"It is a place where there are no limits. There are no floors or ceilings or walls. My body was not limited. I had no hands or anything. I can't tell you what I saw, because there was nothing to see, not with my eyes anyway, but it was beautiful. I felt beautiful. I felt at peace and there were people there. Nice people. But they didn't look like people. I just knew they were people. I didn't feel any pain, nor did I feel any real sensation. Just good. And I will go back."

Now, at the time and to most of us who are among the sane, it honestly sounded like he was losing his mind. I mean, let's go over this, shall we? This place was beautiful, but he didn't see anything. There were people, but they weren't really people. I truly didn't know what in the hell to think. But I will tell you this. I believed him. Oh, yes, I did. With everything I had in me and more—I believed him!

Well, ladies and gents, the hospice people have a term for this kind of experience. Wouldn't you know? They call it "visiting." And my cute little dad being the social butterfly that he was—did a whole lot of it during his final days here on this earth.

Some people who are close to death's door are blessed enough to be able to share these experiences. And some aren't due to extreme weakness, or heavy drugs, or other circumstances but it is the belief of the hospice people and now it is my belief as well, that all people who are dying do, in fact, experience these happenings. It is not really known just exactly *where* this place is, or *what* it is but only that it *does* seem to exist. I myself believe that it is a waiting area before one enters heaven. Simply because when I asked my dad if he thought it might be heaven he said he didn't think so. And he said the reason he didn't think so was because he felt a hesitation to go forward, to go beyond where he was allowed to be. He just wasn't able to go any farther yet.

And now, for the gazillion-dollar question, do you yourselves choose to believe? *Can* you? Remember, it is only my intention to share with you what I, myself, experienced. The rest is up to you. So, in all honestly as well as in all fairness, I must also tell you that I was there and I did, in fact, see and hear all that I have shared with you and I still have a difficult time comprehending all of it. So don't push yourselves too hard. The story isn't over yet. And it wasn't until my dad was gone, that I really focused on what had transpired, which led me to realize that these things *did*, in fact, take place. And in my heart, whether I liked it or not, I knew that what he was telling me was the absolute truth. I'm not saying I liked it. And I'm sure as heck not going to sit here and tell you that at the time I understood it. And I'm sure as heck not going to sit here and tell you that I wasn't afraid either, because I sure as hell was and with every bit of fear I could muster. Yes, I was afraid. I just didn't exactly know what I was afraid of. Perhaps it was the fact that I couldn't see something that I had to believe in for sanity's sake alone. Huh, what a strange thought. For isn't that exactly why those of us who pray do so and to someone we have never really seen? Huh, yes, I do believe we have stumbled onto a very extraordinary thought indeed.

There were a few things that I had to put together for myself during that third week. And let's just say I had to for the sake of just having to. For instance, I chose to believe that if my dad was in a deep sleep, he was visiting. It comforted me. And to be perfectly honest with all of you, not always when he returned, did he share his experiences with me either—only sometimes. Frankly, I feel blessed that he chose to share anything with me at all. And believe it or not, he not only sat there and waved during his brief waking moments but he also spoke and laughed at times—and he cried too. Oh, what I would have given for a crystal ball that morning. Because the experience on that Monday was absolutely nothing compared to what was in store for the both of us that third week. And I am here to tell each and every one of you that even had I been given a magical crystal ball and even had I foreseen the future of the week ahead, it really wouldn't have mattered anyway, for I would have tossed that futuristic little wonder just about as far as it could have flown shattering it into a million pieces along with the many fragments of my broken heart.

# Chapter Sixteen

## *Truth*

*Die Wahrheit hat keine Stunde. Ihre Zeit ist immer und erade dann wenn sie am unzeitgemassesten scheint. Truth has no special time of its own. Its hour is now—always, and indeed then most truly When it seems most unsuitable to actual circumstances.*

Zwischen Wasser und Urwald (*On the edge of the Primeval Forest*, 1922) Chapter 11

s I LOOK back now, it seems to me that during that very same day, the day I refer to as the day of acceptance, so many things took place that had I been twins I couldn't have kept up with it all. For instance, not only did I realize that my dad was going places in his sleep and talking and waving to someones I couldn't see, but I also came to the harsh realization that my absence was taking a terrific toll on my children as well as myself. And how had I come to this brilliant conclusion, you might ask. Uh huh, I thought you just might—so I've prepared a simple and honest answer for you. Quite frankly, at about ten o'clock that very same evening I had a heartbreaking phone call from my eleven-year-old son. Not rocket science at all, just plain and simple human nature.

I had spent most of the day trying to grasp all that had taken place as well as trying to accept the fact that my dad hadn't gotten out of bed all day long with the exception of an occasional trip to the bathroom. So, I spent most of my day perched right by his side watching and listening to the unbelievable until he had finally fallen asleep for the evening. And I must shamefully admit that I felt a certain relief once he had tumbled into solemn slumber as I had become absolutely exhausted! All this hoopla had made me pretty darned tired. Funny how hoopla can do the darnedest things to one's body, isn't it? Well, not funny really, actually it wasn't funny at all. You

239

know, if I myself live a very long time I swear I'm going to wipe that very damned phrase from the English language.

So anyway, I had fallen into a much-needed sleep on the couch, sitting straight up (which was just great for my back) for about an hour before the phone rang, waking me with quite a start. Panicked, I lunged for the phone and on the other end of the line was a very distraught little boy. As a matter of fact, he was *my* little boy and through sporadic sobs, he tried sharing with me that he felt confused. He was losing his grandpa and he couldn't see him and he didn't have his mom there to comfort him and he couldn't see her either. He was having trouble concentrating in school and Halloween was just around the corner. We had never been apart this long and to put it plain and simple, he was completely and entirely fed up! End of explanation! And to be quite truthful with all of you as well as with myself, so was I. And although it is difficult for me to admit, I think I knew then, at that very moment—that I would have to fly home for a few days, but it just wasn't feasible to my conscious mind at the time, so I pushed the thought aside. I mean, after all of the preparation and pain that I had gone through just to complete this task of being with my dad to make it easier for him to leave, the furthest thing from my mind was going home. But after *that* phone call—the phone call to beat all phone calls, the thought began festering in my soul, and soon it became an idea that consumed my mind constantly. Priorities sure do have a way of pushing their way through at the most inconvenient times now, don't they?

To make matters worse, not like I needed anything at all to do that for me at the time but nonetheless, my half sister truly needed a break. And then there was my daughter who was only seven years old also trying to make it without her mom and at the same time she too was trying to deal with losing her grandpa any day now. Yes, my friends, to say that my plate was just a little full, would have been an understatement. My plans were going straight to hell in a handbasket! This wasn't at all what I had planned! What in the hell was I going to do? Who was going to help me get through this mess? Well for criminy sakes, whom do you think? Yup, you have probably already guessed before I can even get it typed. Once again I called upon my uncle, the ever so wise, and truthful Indian, for guidance and the answer I got could've knocked me over with an eagle feather, for he suggested that the time had possibly come for me to go home for a few days.

Now, hold on here just a cotton pickin' minute! Go home? Why, that was absurd! Did John Wayne go home? Did Roy Rogers ever retreat? Would the Lone Ranger himself have ever thought of such a heinous act? What in the hell would Tonto have said about that one? For criminy sakes while we're at it, did Lassie ever once in her courageous adventures back out of a rescue? Why, not just no—but—hell no! Absolutely freaking not with a cherry on top! So how was I to even think about leaving before the job was done? How?

Well, I'll tell you how, ladies and gents—reality. Plain and simple. Well, that and a whole lot of perspective. My dad was dying and *that,* my friends, was obvious. Whether I was there or not—one thing was for sure—he was definitely going to die. But my children were alive and healthy and needing me desperately. Plain and simple. And I needed them in the worst way, as well. I just had to convince the sensible part of my heart of that simple little ditty and we would be on our way. I tell you, the problems I create for myself are never ending!

OK, let's just say for this story's sake that I, Little Miss Chicken Crap, was, in fact, going home for a much-needed break, that only left one problem, one very tiny, minuscule problem actually. *Who* in the heck was going to tell my dad? And never mind that but how? *How* was I going to tell him? How was I supposed to tell the very person who would have given his life for me that I needed to go home to the very little someones who I would give my own life for? Somehow, I think we already know the answer to that question. Yes, of course we do, but remember, at the time I wasn't writing this story and these things didn't seem so clear. As a matter of fact, everything seemed a little muddy. OK, muddy is putting it nicely, but there are small children who may someday read this story and I have to keep it clean.

So now, all that was left to do was to put things in order. And then it hit me! Like a freight train heading south in December—in sub-zero weather—on icy rails!!! The witch person would have to take care of my dad. Oh, crap! Bad idea. Never mind. False alarm!! Everybody back in the pool!!! This just wasn't going to happen. She was up and out of the house at the crack of dawn each and every morning including Sundays and she didn't return until late into the evenings. Come to think of it—she was the hardest working witch I ever did know. And I hate to admit this, but I have indeed known a few in my lifetime.

I had to think long and hard about this. Let's just say for kicks and giggles that the witch was, in fact, able to somehow change into a real person??? OK—probably not feasible. As a matter of fact that wasn't the only problem. No, there was something else. Something that had been subconsciously bothering me for quite some time, however I just hadn't taken the time to sort it out. My dad for some reason just wasn't the same around her. He didn't like her caring for him. Funny, I had never really thought about that before. Or had I? Perhaps we should go back to that when we have more time to ponder. Or, maybe we should just take some cyanide capsules.

So, even if I did go home for just a couple of days and leave his wife with him, God forbid, for better or for worse—in sickness and in health—he might be uncomfortable with that. I couldn't do this. Look him in the eye and tell him I was going home for just a couple of days to be with my kids and SHE would be taking care of him. Nope. Never mind. Seemed like a good idea at the time but not now—not ever! Bad idea, Einstein! Back to the drawing board because even I, Little Miss

Savior, didn't have the ovum to do that! No, siree, Joe! Uh uh—not me! Not Little Miss I Can Do It All! Nope, this was a stupid idea! One of the stupidest since I don't know when! Not me! Well, not me until, of course, my uncle just about slapped me in the face at that very moment hoping to knock some sense back into me.

Knowing my dad as he knew him, my uncle, the ever so intelligent Indian, felt that all I had to do was simply tell him. Plain and simple. Huh, this plain and simple thing seemed to be a family trait until it came to me, which prompted the question that we all ask ourselves at least once in a life time. Could I have been adopted?

My uncle said that if I simply told my dad how I felt and why—that he too would say, your children need you—end of conversation—go home. End of story. And knowing my dad as you all now know him too, I'm sure that most of you are sitting there shaking your heads saying the very same thing. Of course he would understand. My children needed me and if no one else in the whole world could understand that, it was certain that my dad surely would. And to be perfectly honest with each and every one of you, I would like to place all of the reasons right there and nobly say that I went home because my children needed me but I can't. Nope, not and be honest at the same time. Oh, how I hate these moments of truth. Sometimes I truly think that I shouldn't have written this story at all.

I missed my family, yes. My children, my husband, the dogs, the cat, and whatever else I had left behind so long ago and I truly wanted to go home for a visit, yes, I did. I wanted to hold them in my arms and feel them hold me back. But in all honesty—what I really wanted—was to kiss someone whom I loved and whom I knew (hoped) would be around tomorrow. I was fed up with the darkness of dying and I wanted to be amongst the living again.

There. I said it. And let me tell you I'm not very happy about it. Yes—I realize it sounds selfish and that it appears selfish and perhaps it was. But I can tell you with every ounce of honesty I have in me that it was never intended to be or sound that way. I was simply answering my heart's desire. Plain and simple. Or, so I thought at the time anyway. But as you all know, this story has more hidden meanings than a song played backward.

So there I was, about to make what was perhaps to be one of the most difficult decisions of my life. Again. Should I take a chance on not being there when my father died and go home for a few days to be with my children? Or take a chance on him holding on for another two weeks, leaving my little ones to work it out on their own? All of a sudden, I found myself wanting to shut down again and not do a damned thing, except give up. This was just not the way this situation was supposed to have turned out. I was supposed to have come and done the daughter thing as heroic as it could have possibly been, and he was supposed to have died, probably in my arms, leaving me devastated, then I was to go home and resume my life, or what was left of it without my father, to then sooner or later get over his loss, which I might add at this time that we never do, and live accordingly ever after. This situation had not been in the game plan. This was not in the program! This situation shouldn't have even been an option. Yet, again I will remind all of you that things don't always go as planned, and if we don't all know this by now, then we've been sleeping throughout very important parts of this story.

So, there I was, having to once again gain control of a situation that I had no control over in the stinking first place. Talk about getting it by now? *Duh!* The power of love is extremely brutal, isn't it?

Sometimes when I look back, I believe that these feelings of not knowing what to do were a test of some kind. Then again, I believe that everything that happened from then on out, was strategically planned. Did I do the right thing? Well, I have asked myself that very same question time and time again and I always seem to come up with the same answer. So as I share the rest of my story with you, you too will be left to ponder that question. And I will leave the answer up to each and every one of you. I hate to do that to all of you, but then again, let's try and remember that perception is in the eyes of the beholder. I *will* tell you this though, I do feel that the events I am about to share with you, definitely happened for a reason. Huh, don't they always?

The next day was Tuesday, and I woke up with the memory of my son's phone call still haunting me. And as if waking up to that wasn't bad enough, I had something else to deal with, something that I never expected. Of course, how could I have, and I'm sure you will all agree as soon as you read on. But once again, I must warn you to prepare yourselves, for another heartbreaking lesson of love and patience.

My day began at four o'clock in the morning with my dad calling me from the bedroom to help him get up. And I mean to tell you, he wasn't just calling me, he was panicked and more like ordering me to help him get through an emergency! I bolted off the couch in that confused state of mind that happens when we are awakened abruptly from slumber, and I leaped toward his bedroom door. What time was it? Why was it so dark? Why is he yelling? He sounded scared. And where in the hell was that damned witch?

I flipped on the hallway light as I went stumbling into his bedroom. "What's the matter," was coming out of my mouth before I could even focus my eyes.

He was sitting on the edge of his bed bouncing his legs with his arms extended expectantly waiting for me to help him up as though he had to go to the bathroom. The witch had obviously been awakened as I barely felt her sashay by me in the doorway mumbling something I wouldn't really give a crap about until later.

"Hurry up," he demanded. "I need to make a very important phone call."

Yes, you read it right—a phone call! And he was very serious about this call that had to be made, as I almost had to run to catch up with him on his way to the phone. Get that, ladies and gents, I had to run to keep up with a cancer-ridden old man who just the day before couldn't even get out of bed! He was already in the living room, perched in his recliner and reaching for the phone by the time I got my lazy half-asleep keester around the coffee table. I must have looked like one of those circus guys who balance the plates. I had no clue what was going on.

He carefully, with his hands trembling, and very diligently, held the phone tightly in his hands and placed it in his bony lap and dialed a phone number with the determination of a six-year-old.

What in the hell was going on? I was dumbfounded as I heard myself asking, "Who are you calling, Dad?"

"Work," he barked at me!

So I simply and quite cautiously asked him why and when I did, he looked at me like I was an idiot and simply said because he wasn't feeling well and he couldn't go in today. He had to call his boss to let him know. I mean, after all, they depended on him to be there! He was the head custodian! And being a no call/no show was exactly what was wrong with the younger generation of this damned world! You just don't do that!

Now, I reckon I should have been upset or scared is more like it and at first I was. Actually, upset and scared would be putting it pretty mildly. What I really thought was that at any moment, Rod Serling *really* would this time come creeping into the house proclaiming that we had just entered into another flipping episode of *The Twilight Zone!* Yes, folks, I truly thought he had finally lost his cute, little, storytelling mind. Oh, great! Now, who was I going to talk to? Never mind that, what in the hell was the receptionist going to think when their "head custodian," who hadn't been there for three stinking months because he retired due to the sorry-ass fact that he was dying with cancer, called her to ask for his boss, because he wasn't feeling well, and couldn't come in? And you know what? It truly didn't matter because the bottom line was—that he *was* definitely calling his boss and there *wasn't* a damned thing I could do about it. And after I stopped worrying about what an ass he might make of himself, I got to thinking. Yup, I got to thinking about the fact that he had worked for this company for twenty-six long, hard years and if they couldn't handle one strange phone call from him, well that was their problem. However, I did feel sick to my stomach as I sat and listened to him ask for his supervisor. But I'll tell you something else as well, for some strange unknown reason, I also felt very proud.

There was a long pause while whoever answered the phone put him on hold as I was sitting on the futon, elbows on my knees, with my hands over my face trying to grasp what was about to happen. All the while in the back of my mind, I was vaguely aware of the fact that the shower was running. The witch was getting ready to bathe her monkeys no doubt. Either that or drown Toto.

As he sat waiting for his boss to pick up the other end of the line, he glanced my way looking very confident. He was very proud of the fact that he had decided to call in. For many years my dad had worked various shifts for this company but for the last several years he had been going in at five in the morning. This explained his urgency. It was already after four and he hadn't called in yet. He looked over at me and explained with his hand over the mouthpiece that he didn't feel very well. I simply looked at him and said "Well then, it's better if you call in." I mean things could have been worse. He could've gotten up and wanted to go in! Always a silver lining!!!

As my mind tried to imagine what was happening, my thoughts were interrupted by my dad's voice booming the word, "Hi" over the phone. "This is Ed and I won't be able to make it in this morning," he said. "I don't know what's gotten a hold of me, but whatever it is, it's pretty bad." Then I could hear the muffled response of the man on the other side of the line and if I live to be a hundred, I will never forget the relief that came over me when I heard my dad say, "Thank you, sir, I'll try."

His boss had simply told him to take the day off and get better and all I can say to that is loyalty certainly does pay off at times and for that I am truly thankful.

Now, did you all get that conversation? "Something's gotten a hold of me"! Oh, for hell's sake, you don't say! Yeah, something had definitely gotten a hold of him all right! Some damned disease, better known throughout this particular story as the ruthless killer and guess what little Eddie, you are exactly right. It's pretty bad indeed! You—are—dying! Geeze, might we say that I'm just a little angry? Well, perhaps. And so the story goes, once again.

Now, with that little step out of the way, my content and satisfied little dad went shuffling back to bed. End of conversation. End of trauma. And there I sat. Flabbergasted to say the least and not only because of the way this man answered my dad's call, but also because my dad had simply gotten up off the couch and went back to bed all by himself! For hell's sake, yesterday he couldn't make it to the bathroom alone! But you know what? That thought was quickly pushed from my mind as the other thought took over. I just sat there frozen, on that silly futon, feeling nothing but grateful to the man on the other end of the line and for his response. It had given my dad back some of his lost and forgotten self-worth. There are angels among us, folks. Yes, indeed, angels in people's clothing!

I will share with all of you that later on that morning, after I found the strength to pick myself up and off that futon, I too called to speak with the man whom my father had asked for. And when he came on the line, I thanked him for his kindness and his understanding. And it was during this phone call that I learned that this man had been my father's boss for more than ten years and he was very concerned about my dad's condition, for he made it very clear that not only had he been my father's boss, but he had also been his friend. Huh, not so strange, I reckon. I mean, who wasn't Eddie's friend at one time or another? And during that phone call, he asked if he might be able to come by and visit with his old friend before—well—before he left this place. I told him he was more than welcome. And after making arrangements for him to swing by on Wednesday, we both hung up.

Now this wasn't the only visiting arrangements that had taken place between my dad and his coworkers throughout this whole stinking ordeal—nope, not at all. As a matter of fact, during the second week of my visit, two women from my dad's work came by one evening to bring my dad a computer-generated banner sporting many signatures of well wishers from my dad's place of employment. And after a very brief visit with my dad, they both sat out on the front porch with me sharing priceless stories about my silly and crazy dad. One of the women had known my dad for twenty years. As a matter of fact, she had been working in a hardware store that my dad frequented from time to time when they became friends. After knowing her awhile, my dad told her she ought to apply where he worked and she had been there ever since. Those two gals told me stories of beautiful memories. Memories of my dad driving through the front gates of the plant, with his bear buddy right by his side, and as the guard waved him through the gates, the bear would wave a hearty thank you back to him as well as to all who would be lucky enough to see. Everyone knew Eddie and his bear and everyone liked them both. He seemed to have made quite a reputation for himself as all of the office women came to depend on him to walk by the windows in the early mornings, blowing kisses, and making them laugh. He always had a hearty "Top of the morning to you!" ready to start the day and the ever-so-famous "Bye now!" at the end of the day. And no one could ever recall him being any different in twenty-six years.

I do actually have a favorite story of my dad that those gals shared with me. Mostly it's my favorite because it was the one that captured my dad's personality lock, stock, and barrel. And I have told this story over and over again throughout the years so I feel it only appropriate to share it now with all of you. It was the story behind that picture of the man handing my dad a clock for twenty-five years of "keeping it kleen." You know, the one we saw together sitting in his living room on the very first night of my arrival? Yes, that's the one.

Well, it seems that the man in the picture just happened to be the president of the company and on a stage, in front of an auditorium full of employees, when he took that step forward to shake my dad's hand and deliver that clock, my dad was heard to have told this guy that he should mill around and press some flesh. He told him, "After all, the workers of this fine company are who made you what you are today! Without the little guy, you yourself would be no one!" And that, my friends, was that! Now, can you just imagine the look on that guy's face when *that* janitor told him to get out and shake some hands and be thankful for all he had received? Well, I'll tell you what. I sure as hell can—and on some of those sleepless nights that I have told you about, that little thought puts me to sleep with a tickle in my heart and a chuckle in my tummy. My dad— always as honest as the day was long, and then some, and that's all I have to say about that.

After my conversation on the phone with my dad's supervisor, I thought it best to check on my late-sleeping little dad. And as always, my walk back to his bedroom left me full of anticipation and fear. I guess some things never *were* going to change.

As I pushed the door open, hearing a soft whisper as it glided across the carpet, I instantly looked at the blanket that covered my dad's swollen belly. Yup, it was moving up and down, slowly, with about ten second intervals in between, but it was moving. You know, ten seconds doesn't seem like a long time unless you're waiting for someone to breathe. I got really used to watching the second hand on the clock as I waited for my dad to take a breath. This had been a major concern of mine since the beginning of my visit, as I'm sure I don't have to remind all of you, however, I quickly learned from the hospice nurses that ten seconds was nothing really. Oh, and how well I was to soon find out!

As usual, I crept up to the side of the bed, trying to decide if I should wake him or not. And just as usual, the fleeting thought of how I would react if I were to find him gone was darting in and out of my mind at the same time. I leaned over and kissed his cheek awaiting a response.

Nothing. Nope, not even a flicker of an eyelash! Oh, how I wish I had known then just exactly *when* my dad would actually depart, so I could have spared myself all of the agony each and every time he didn't respond to my touch. For each and every time he didn't respond, I just knew beyond a shadow of a doubt that he wasn't coming back.

I gently sat down next to him on the bed, and began stroking his hair with the back of my hand. And as I sat caressing my sleeping little dad, I began to notice changes that had taken form on his face. The wrinkles had become bags of leftover flesh due to weight loss, and were those dark circles forming around his eyes? How had I not noticed that before? The worst shocker was the color of his skin. Not only did it have somewhat of a yellow tint to it but also it had, well, an unhealthy grayish look. Maybe, had I been more experienced at this sort of thing, I would have immediately realized that this was the result of poor oxygen to the body. But you know, I'm kind of glad that I didn't learn these things until after it was too late, for I just might have had a neurotic breakdown otherwise. You know, if I were to count the number of minutes I spent sitting on that bed with my dad, just watching him sleep, I'm sure it would have added up to many hours, maybe even weeks—years! Hell—maybe even decades! I really liked watching him sleep. I studied him. I sat looking at him, wondering about all the wonderful secrets his memory harbored after seventy-two years. I mean, can you imagine all that he had seen? All his body had gone through? All the people he had encountered? And it all came down to this. Lying in a bed so sick he could barely even wake up, with his goofy daughter sitting by his side, studying his face. Pretty sad, huh? Yup, it was painfully sad. And I couldn't help wondering just how many other sons and daughters had done the same exact thing throughout the years. Probably as many as the minutes I spent there at his bedside and more. Now, that thought gave me a considerable amount of comfort. I—*wasn't*—alone! I was certainly not the only poor soul who had ever gone through something like this. Kind of made me want to run into the streets screaming for someone who had survived such a tragedy. Just so I knew that I could and would get through it, despite the pain that was tearing at my insides. Because I can tell you, that no matter how hard I tried to be strong, no matter how hard I tried to be an adult, and no matter how hard I tried to tell myself that other people got through these things, and—that I would too, eventually—I just absolutely could not believe it.

As I was sitting there content in my dream state, my dad began to stir a little. I was quickly reminded of where I was, when he popped his eyes open and asked what in the hell I was doing?

I gathered my words carefully in my mind before I spoke. "I was just sitting here, wishing you would wake up," I said.

"Oh, all right," he answered, looking at me like I was the sick one. Still trying to get his bearings, he asked me to help him up so he could go to the bathroom. "Geeze," I said, "For a guy who doesn't drink a whole lot, you sure have no problem disposing of nothing." His reply was a simple but muffled, "Uh huh."

I stood up and with my eyes focused on the far wall of the bedroom to give him the much-deserved privacy that he needed, I gently pulled the covers back and reached down to get a hold of his hands. I pulled as he pulled creating the leverage needed to bring him to his feet. We then got into our formation and scooted on in to the bathroom. Once inside the small confines of this tiny area, which contained my father's potty, I helped him sit down and quickly took a couple of steps to the side, so that I was now standing right outside the door. I then reached in to close the door behind me, leaving it ajar enough to be ready to retrieve him once he had finished his business. I stood leaning with one leg propped up against the wall of the hallway with my arms folded across my chest, waiting, while I glanced to the left and watched the witch preparing something in the kitchen and obviously getting ready to leave. I thought about saying something like good morning, or how are you, or nice broom—but I didn't. Instead I just stood there watching her and wondering if she worked all of those hours then where was all the money going—when all of a sudden, I heard my dad's gravelly voice from behind the door asking me "Hey, you, what are you doing?"

A faint smile crossed my lips as I replied, "I'm just standing here waiting in case you need something."

"Oh," he said. Then for no silly-ass reason at all he blurted out,

"You're a funny kid, you know that?"

"Yea, I know," I said. Then there was silence. And as I stood waiting for him in the quiet of the hallway, my mind drifted back to a time when it was me sitting on the potty with my short little legs dangling far above the floor and my dad right outside the door asking if I was done yet. And you know, if I could have a penny for each and every memory that pained my heart during those weeks with my dad—well—you know.

Without even thinking, I asked, "Hey, are you done yet?" No answer. "Dad?" Still no answer. With extreme panic rousing my next move, I turned and pushed the tiny door wide open scaring my sleeping Dad almost to death! With a look of embarrassment on my flushed face, I quickly lied, telling him that I had accidentally leaned on the door and it had given way. I didn't want *him* to *know* that *I knew* that he had fallen asleep on the toilet. It was simply my way of saving face for him. And you know, when I think about those kinds of things now, I feel like a real jackass. For you see, my dad probably wouldn't have given a rat's patoot if I *had* acknowledged that he had fallen asleep on the toilet. He was beyond such things at that time. So there I stood, in a complete and utterly ridiculous stance before my father on his sleeping throne. What an idiot! And all I have to say for myself now—is that I wasn't willing to take the risk of embarrassing him, plain and simple, because even if my dad, himself wasn't aware of his dwindling dignity, I sure as hell was—and I wasn't about to do anything to jeopardize it anymore.

It seemed from there on out that the truth was surely mushed up in the pudding, my friends. We were undeniably nearing the end of my father's destiny. Now, I surely don't believe that his destiny was to live long enough to fall asleep on the toilet, just as much as I also didn't believe that his destiny was to live long enough so that he could be the poster elder for cancer-ridden patients. So what then? Why in the world had it gone this far and when would the day come that he had finally paid all of his dues and could go peacefully into eternal rest? Well, the truth of the matter is, is that we ourselves could probably spend the rest of our own lives trying to figure these things out and we would never find the true answers. In the meantime though, we could all probably guess some really great perspectives on the subject and write a book. Huh, and I believe this is where I came in.

# Chapter Seventeen

## *Regrets*

*The follies which a man regrets most, in his life, are those which he didn't commit when he had the opportunity.*

*A Guide to Men* (1922) p. 87

J UST AS SOON as I got him up and running from his nap on the potty, we found ourselves back in the bedroom. The witch was long gone as I had heard the sliding door open and close earlier. And she damned well didn't kiss me good-bye again! Sad thing was, she didn't kiss my dad either. Something was absolutely amiss here.

I fluffed his pillows for him while he sat on the side of the bed waiting for me to finish. And then, he caught me totally by surprise when he asked me to sit him up. He wanted to visit with me for a while.

Visit with me? Why, I was elated! I thought our visiting days were over. Well, at least the ones that I was involved with anyway.

At his very own request I quickly rushed into the living room to fetch his pipe. His pipe! Oh, this was too good to be true. Why, he hadn't smoked his pipe for almost five days. Was he feeling better? Could he actually pull himself out of this? Would his daughter ever stop living in a fantasy world?

Well, my friends, as I look back now, I realize that my dad simply had some unfinished business to tend to that day. There were a few things that he wanted to share with me, and that was all. And I will be the first to tell each and every one of you that although it was painful, I am so very thankful that he did.

After he lit his pipe with me sitting on the end of the bed by his feet like a dog waiting for its next command, he pointed to the closet and asked me to open the door and pull out a box that was hiding on the very top shelf of the closet—and this wasn't just any old box, mind you, this was a specific box; a special box full of memories from long ago. I jumped over the rounded headboard that was sitting in such a way that it made a little corner between the bed and one end of the closet. Once situated, I reached up and retrieved the box from the top of the shelf with the very tips of my fingers. Teetering, I brought it down and over the headboard with a thunk onto the bed. Then I stood waiting for his next request.

"Now," he said, "pull that pillowcase that is hanging in there forward."

I looked to the rear of the closet and sure enough, there was a pillowcase hanging on a wooden hanger. I reached back to pull it forward and, geeze, it was heavy! "What in the hell do you have in this thing?" I asked.

"When you get it out of there, I'll show you, you nitwit."

OK, I thought, but first, the nitwit had to get it the hell out of there. I tugged and pulled and finally lifted the bottom of the heavy pillowcase, so that the top of it would let go of the pole on which it had been hanging for God only knew how long. I then swung it over the headboard, plopping it down on the mattress with a distinct thud.

I really thought my dad would open it up and reach in to reveal its contents but he didn't. Instead, he motioned for me to climb back over the headboard and patted his hand on the mattress inviting me to sit down beside him. And I studiously did so, damn near killing myself in the process.

My silly little secretive dad laughed at me and shook his head from side to side saying, "I don't know about you, you knot head—I just really don't."

Well, I just really didn't know about me either at that point, but that didn't stop me from sitting right down on that bed next to him bursting with curiosity as to just *what* this pillowcase contained. My dad then asked me to untie the knot that had obviously been entwined around the top of the heavy wooden hanger, for what had to have been, forever and a day and reach in to it very slowly. I did. Then he said, "Do you feel something very heavy?"

I did. And not only was it heavy but it was ice cold!

"What is it?" I asked.

"Pull it out and see," he said. "But be careful."

I was, and never in a million years could I have guessed what it was. I pulled slowly and carefully, finally revealing its entire form. It was a beauty and still tucked tightly and securely in its original holster.

As I eyed this newly found treasure, my dad said to me, "When I die, I want you to take that gun home to your old man. Tell him that it will protect him and his family from all the harm that will ever come your way. And tell him something else for me, tell him that it is the very same gun that was tucked into the small of my back one day long ago, when I headed out the door to take care of a long-standing problem. Tell him that I put the bullets into the chamber and after my pop and I had a real good talk, I never did fire that gun. That piece of iron holds one of my most hidden secrets, and I want him to have it from here on out. Do you understand?"

As I sat there totally mesmerized by his every word, I couldn't help but notice how he continually rubbed its ghostly barrel as he spoke. Oh, yes, I understood. Then, looking down at this cold piece of his darkened past, he ended his statement with this:

"Tell him the story behind the gun. Tell him to always remember that even if he were to lose everything tomorrow let this gun be a constant reminder of that story, and tell him that his problems can never be worth someone's life, no matter how they are created or who they are created by."

Then, after thinking about that statement for a few seconds he added, "Although, just between you and me—I will always wonder."

And all I could answer him with were two words, "Me too." I wrapped that beautiful piece of my dad's past very tightly back into its cotton hiding place, and I never looked at it again, until after my dad had passed away and I was sitting in the comfort of my own living room with my husband, trying to recite my dad's wishes to him word for word. And with some reluctance, I'll share something else with all of you: As I sat in the confines of my living room, trying to recite my dad's wishes word for word, I too, rubbed its ghostly barrel. And after all these years, I haven't touched it since.

After we sat in silence for what seemed like an eternity, my dad then reached forward and pulled the box that I had brought forth just before the pillowcase toward himself with its flaps waving as though they just might take off in flight. He reached deep into its shadows, and pulled out what looked like an old picture album. Yup, I was right. That's exactly what it was. But I could have never dreamed what its contents would reveal.

There were pictures upon pictures of my dad's war buddies and of a young Eddie manning his artillery. There was a signed letter from Gracie Allen, dated 1942, thanking all of the servicemen for enduring the loneliness that always accompanies war. And there were meal tickets to the mess hall. There were pictures of really pretty women. Women who my dad would sadly wonder what happened to, out loud, fifty years later.

We sat in silence for most of the afternoon, with the exception of an occasional, "Who is this?" from me, or an inquisitive "Remember this?" from him. He was growing tired now, and I couldn't seem to get myself motivated enough to end our private moments. But the weariness in his eyes told me it was time, but not before he had two more thoughts and wishes to share with me. *Wouldn't you just know?*

First, he wanted me to take that handsome cowboy painting home with me, asking that I hang it someplace in my home with his gun and holster accompanying the corner of that beautiful master piece. No problem! Well, except for the fact that I had absolutely no clue as to where I would hang that painting in my home with that gun and holster proudly accompanying a corner of its magnificence, not to mention the fact that I never really wanted a gun in my house but – this was special and it was from my dad, so I reckoned I would just have to find a place for it. This gift was an honor he had just bestowed upon me, and I became very well aware of that fact as his eyes seeped the moisture of the painting's future departure, and I told him so. My gosh, he must of carried that painting as well as that gun and holster around from place to place with him for most of his life. God only knew how long he had owned both of these treasures because I sure didn't and I didn't ask either. And now he wanted me to do the same, which I have I might add, and the honor of it all still remains with me to this very day.

The second request had to do with the witch and it was a tough one. Squinting his big, brown, chimpanzee eyes and rubbing his chin, he very proudly informed me that he had purchased two tickets a couple of months prior to see Willie Nelson in November of that year. Once again, he proceeded to break my heart as he shared with me that he damned well knew that he wasn't going to be there any longer, so he asked me to surprise his wife with these tickets after he died. He felt the concert would give her something to do, and it would be something to keep her mind off of things once he was gone. He secretly told me that they were hanging on the bulletin board in his little office hidden behind some other papers. Then, he requested the unthinkable! He asked for me to take the other ticket and go with her! *Oh for the very love of God! He just had to be kidding! Go with her? In public? After his death? Not on his life! Not on my life! Not on anyone who was ever someone's life for that matter! Why – we'd have to buy cowboy boots for the monkeys! And she'd have to buy a very wide brimmed black cowboy hat to hide that ugly green face and pointy nose of hers! It would be like the Adam's Family gone country!* Personally, I myself, for some silly ass reason, didn't have one iota of a worry as to her finding things to keep her busy after his death. Hell, hadn't she already done that? She was never there as it was! *Whatever in the world did she do all day anyway?* However, all I could do as I looked into his heartbroken eyes was to promise him I would honor his wishes. *Idiot!! Stupid, stupid, little girl!!*

This reminiscing segment had surely come to an abrupt end. I was done. He wasn't aware but I just couldn't take anymore. Clearly it had become time to put all of our reminiscing to rest along with my dad. I quit!!!! Again.

I began the task of placing all of his memories back into the box, and as I did, I ran across the backside of a small, black, rectangular frame on the very bottom. He hadn't retrieved this frame. He had obviously left it there on purpose. I looked up to catch a glimpse of my dad happily putting his precious treasures in some sort of *Eddie* order, so I felt it safe enough to flip it over, and what I saw shot arrows of sadness straight through my heart.

It was a rectangular picture frame with five (count em my friend) small 3x5 individual school pictures from left to right, of five little girls taped crookedly across the middle underneath the glass. The tape was as old and yellow as its owner proudly holding those priceless treasures securely in place, even after all those years. And as I laid the picture frame face down back into the box, just the way I had found it, I couldn't help imagining a picture of my own, of a man sitting at his kitchen table long ago, holding a roll of scotch tape in his trembling hands, trying to keep his little girls together and with him, the best way he knew how—and the only way he could.

All of the treasures we put back into the box that day are still there. Only now, that box sets a top of a shelf in my own closet. And once in a while, when memories alone just aren't good enough, I carefully reach for that box and relive that wonderful time my dad and I shared. And sometimes, I will bring that leather picture album close to my face and I will close my eyes and take a deep breath through my nose and the smell of its past can bring that memory rushing back to me and I can recall just exactly how wonderful it felt to have my dad sitting next to me, sharing his secrets with me once again.

If I had known that that day was to be the last time we would ever sit together and reminisce, I would have held that box tightly in my hands dumping it out *over* and *over* and *over* again and again. Yes, my friends, it would, in fact, be the very last time that my dad and I would ever be able to talk about the past again. For after that wonderful Tuesday afternoon, the doom of the present began to take over and once it began, there was no stopping its consuming power.

Instead of twice a week, the hospice nurse as well as the caseworker, were visiting every other day now. My dad's visitation with the other side began happening daily. And the situation at home had gotten worse. My children were miserable, my sister was losing her mind, my husband was lonely and I was all of the above. It seemed the time had come for me to make that crucial decision.

Early Wednesday morning, my dad finally fell asleep. I had been up and down with him all night long, fetching drinks of water and helping him to the bathroom, although more times than not, we simply sat up together in the quiet wee hours of the night and well into the beauty of a new morning trying to make him as comfortable as possible. He was experiencing an awful lot of pain through his back, which was undoubtedly due to the tumor that was growing at the base of his spine. So throughout the night, I would sit next to him on the bed, rubbing his back, sometimes with no conversation taking place at all. And you know, I found that situation to suit me just fine. Sometimes, words exchanged between the two of us, were simply not necessary.

By the time the sun came up, my dad was ready for sleep. I was ready for anything that would relieve my tension and heartache.

It was about 6:30 that morning when my dad decided to retire to his recliner from the couch where we had been half dozing, me laying next to him as he slouched trying to sleep. He got situated in his chair when all of a sudden, he very subtly, just like we had been conversing all along, began a conversation with me. My eyes widened as I attempted to sit up and wake up both at the same time. Leaning on one elbow, I turned to face him, asking him to repeat what he had just said. He became a little irritated as it had become difficult for him to speak and breathe at the same time. I apologized for not paying attention the first time, and asked him to repeat again what he had just said.

Slowly, he began, "I said, I had a very strange dream last night."

"Oh," I said, while I quietly reached over and punched the button on my tape recorder. Then I asked him, what made it so strange? He sat quietly for a while, trying to catch his breath, and by the look on his face, I assumed he was also trying to gather his words. He finally broke the silence and began again.

"I dreamed that I was at a meeting with all the world leaders, living and dead, past and present. They were discussing all of the problems of the world. Nobody was upset or anything, they were just talking, you know?" After a short pause, he continued through heavy breathing, to say, "Everyone had coffee or whatever they wanted to drink. It was a big room."

Interrupting I asked, "Where were you, Dad?"

"I was there," he said, "Somewhere in the room. I couldn't really hear all that was being said. I just knew what they were talking about."

I interrupted again asking, "Who was there, did you know anyone?"

"Oh, yes," he said. "Teddy Roosevelt was there and all three Kennedys." Then he shook his head from side to side saying, "It was the strangest damned thing he'd ever experienced in his life." He said, "It was like the peace talks. Everyone was putting in their two cents' worth as to what to do about the world's situation."

Intrigued, I then asked him if he had given any input. "Oh, yes," he said, he had given his opinion on everything he could. Just what the world needed, I suppose, the opinion of a janitor. Now, just maybe we *could* solve all the world's problems!

256

Great, wonderful! No big deal. My dad had just been to a conference with all of the worlds' leaders present and past and I was supposed to pass this off as normal. And to make matters even worse, he truly believed that he had participated. And it wasn't the dream that had me worried as much as it was his description of how it took place. He didn't think he was sitting or standing, you see? He was just there. He couldn't hear anyone but he knew they were speaking. Sound familiar? Yes, I thought it might. So—what do you think? Was he or wasn't he? Could it be possible? Well, who in the hell can stand up and say that it isn't? Sure as heck not me!

Now we had been watching the presidential debates all week, so I thought maybe he was simply carrying what he had seen on TV into his dreams. Not so strange really. As a matter of fact, I didn't even know that my dad had been paying that much attention to the debates. Most of his time in front of the TV had been spent sleeping, or so I thought anyway. However, I learned differently when he gave me his opinion as to how he would vote. And that little tidbit of information came rolling home next.

You see, my dad felt that Mr. Clinton should become president with Mr. Perot as his vice president. In his opinion, they would have made a fine team. Mr. Clinton reminded my dad of President Kennedy and he felt our country needed another young man to get us out of the mess that we were so obviously in. He felt that if Mr. Clinton was too young or inexperienced to handle some of the financial matters at hand, no problem. Mr. Perot was older and a millionaire, so he would be able to pick up the slack. And as for President Bush—well hell, he had already given us four years, he needed a break. After all, he had gotten us through another war for hell's sake and just for that alone, in my dad's opinion, he deserved a vacation. And as I sat listening to the political opinions of a very serious seventy-two year old head custodian, I realized that somehow, in between naps, he had, in fact, been listening to all that had been going on. So I thought I would take this opportunity to ask my dad how he thought the election would go. Hey, you've got to be willing to take risks in life! So I very nonchalantly asked him, "In your dream, did they give any hint as to who would win the election?" And in reply, he turned his head and very matter-of-factly told me no, giving me that look once again, as if to insinuate that I was a dum-dum.

What do I think about his dream? Well, I really didn't give it much thought after that, at least not until I realized that my dad's birthday that year just happened to fall on President's Day—and that's all I have to say about that!

After that early morning conversation, it seems to me that my political opinions would never be the same again. Wouldn't it be nice if it were all that simple though? If we could just put things together like that—one, two, three—simply because they made sense and would work? Uh huh, by the people, for the people. What a concept. Oh, and I will also share with you that I got another little chuckle in my heart that day as my dad was sleeping and I was piddling. If that young Mr. Clinton ever lost sight of what was wrong with *no call/no shows* in this country somewhere along the line, I'm sure Mr. Perot and Mr. Bush would set him straight! And surely looking back now—I can damned well assure all of us that Mr. Clinton wouldn't have been allowed to stray from his wife years later. Mr. Perot and former President Bush would have made sure of that! Boy, was I tired.

The day went by very quickly after that. My dad slept for the rest of the day in his chair with the exception of an occasional trip to the bathroom. And when it came time for him to go back to his bed to continue doing what he'd, in fact, been doing all day long anyway, a very strange conversation took place between the two of us first. Yes, like we had room for another one of those!

He was wide awake, sitting in his chair and looking right at me as I was preparing for our choo choooed journey back to the bedroom. I was standing in front of his chair, folding his blanket, chatting away to him about needing his sleep, minding my own beeswax when all of a sudden he reached up for my arm and had that look on his face. *Oh, Lord!* I immediately sat back down on the couch, stretching my arm between the two of us so that he didn't have to let go. With my eyes focused on his, I leaned forward, taking his hand off my arm and placing it in my own hand instead, rubbing it gently all the while mostly due to my nervousness, I suppose, before I asked, "What is it, Dad?"

Yes, you would think I would have learned by then not to ask, but then again, time wasn't exactly on our side and I couldn't put these things off anymore. After all, I may not have gotten another chance and besides, it turned out that this very conversation that we were about to have would prove to be the conversation that would, in fact, relieve me of any guilt over my father's death during the following week. You might also be interested to know that this conversation would also be the one that would answer that universal question we had all been asking for so long. What in the hell was he holding on for?

My teary-eyed little dad paused just long enough to catch his breath and regain his composure somewhat, before he began. *Why was he crying?* With our hands interlocked together, both leaning toward one another, he looked me in the eye and I looked back into those tired old chimpanzee eyes of his when he told me he was about to ask me a very important question, and he expected me to be truthful with him. Shaking and feeling a little sick to my stomach, I promised him I would, although I had my doubts depending on just exactly *what* question was festering in that busy little mind of his.

He then whispered to me through tears that he was worried about me finding him dead. "What will you do, dear?" And I will never forget the look on his face and the terror in his eyes as he awaited my answer. There, it was out! And to tell you the truth, I didn't have a clue in hell as to what I would do, but I had to give him an answer, and I had to give it to him as convincingly as I could. So, with what was to be perhaps the most crucial performance of a lifetime, I did just exactly what every other red-blooded American daughter would have done. I acted. And I mean to tell you that it was an award-winning moment. Or so I thought at the time anyway.

Still with his hands in mine, I looked him straight in the eye and told him step by step what I would do, just as we rehearsed.

"First," I said, "I will wait about five minutes to make sure you are really gone, just in case the paramedics pick up the call and show up before the coroner. Then I will walk into the living room, assuming you will die in your bed, and I will call the hospice nurse. Then I will call Uncle. Then, I will call the coroner. I will then walk out onto the porch and sit on the step and wait for someone to get here." And by the time I was finished, I too was whispering through tears.

There was nothing but silence for at least three minutes, before he sternly told me in a fatherly tone, "Don't you cry over my body, do you hear? You let me go and then you get the hell out of here, because once I am gone, it's only my body that will remain. I will no longer be in it, so there is no reason for you to stay with me anymore, you hear me? No reason for you to hang around afterward what–so–ever–at–all! You call my brother and he will come and hold you. There are just some things that are not meant to be seen by young women, and a dead body is one of them."

And as he spoke with the sincerity that only he could portray, my mind wandered back to a time when I was riding home in the car with my dad, from my grandma's house and we had come upon an accident in the road. Traffic was backed up for a country mile and there were police cars and ambulances everywhere. After a long, slow, bumper-to-bumper ride, we finally approached the scene of the accident and my dad made me put my head down in my lap until the traffic officer waved us through. When he told me I could sit up again, the accident scene was far behind us and traffic was moving normally. Immediately I asked him, "Why did I have to put my head down?" And little did I know that his reply would be repeated almost thirty years later as he said, "Because, there are just some things that are not meant to be seen by a little girl, and a dead body is one of them." And as I focused back in on the present, I realized that my dad was, in fact, repeating those very same words to me. Only this time, he referred to me as a young woman. And this time, I felt a pain inside my soul that I had never before experienced in my entire life. For this time, we wouldn't just simply pass up a tragedy and then go about our merry way. Nope, this time we were right smack-dab in the middle of our own tragedy, and I would have to go the rest of the way without my dad for the first time ever in my life! And I wasn't real sure at the time, but I had a feeling that after this tragedy, no amount of time spent with my head in my lap was going to be long enough.

Little did I know, that the promises I made to my dad that morning would be challenged that very same night. Yes, my friends, I was about to sadly discover the end result of all of this preparation and hard work.

Now I don't know if what happened that evening was coincidence or a test. Oh, I do have my own opinion; however, I'd just rather keep it to myself. Sometimes, it's just best that way.

Before our conversation ended that morning, my teary-eyed little dad went over his last wishes with me once again. You see, he not only asked me not to look at his expired body but it was also very important that no one else did either. A private man, he was as he lived, and a private man he would be when he died. He shared with me that after the horror he experienced during the war, he felt that a dead body should be laid to rest. It was not to be gawked at. Yeah, I know there was a big difference between the two situations, however, my dad didn't seem to think so. And quite frankly, I'm absolutely sure that my dad's deteriorating body held a close second to those who were found dead on the battlefield. So maybe he was on to something there.

Now, while we were on the subject, my cute little Private First Class Eddie also made another request. Yes, he sure did have a lot of those didn't he? Well, think about it, when you're dying, things just come to mind that you've never really thought about before. That's just the way it goes.

You see, he had decided all by himself, that he should be buried by the United States Army. He felt he had earned the right to receive a full military funeral. Now, I believe that this request meant more to my dad than anything, because as he put it, he might not have been a lot of things throughout his life, and he might not have accomplished a whole hell of a lot, but the one thing he truly felt he did well and the one thing he truly felt he was, was a soldier. A private first class, front lines, artillery soldier who rode a mule named John, to be exact, and it might not seem like a whole hell of a lot to the most of us, but to him, it was everything! And let's face it, ladies and gents, he is the only one that mattered in the end. So therefore, his wishes, all of a sudden, became everything to me too. Funny how priorities change throughout this story, isn't it? Holy crap, there's that damned phrase again. I swear …….

OK, now where were we? Ah yes, last but certainly not least, he wanted to be buried in the nude and let's not go over that again, OK? After a while, that one little stinking request really began to wear on me. And why you might be asking yourselves, well as you read on you'll know why and, quite frankly, fifteen years later, it still gets to me.

Now keep in mind how simple all of these requests were, because later on down the old story road, we will all learn how the simplest of things can be turned into the most complex of problems. Oh, sure they do, for hell's sake—this is life!

Although, it seemed like our little talk went on for hours, upon hours that morning, it actually only lasted about thirty minutes. It ended with both of us pouring our hearts out in one last attempt to make sure we both understood one another. Of course we did. Hadn't we always? Or so I thought at the time anyway.

I gently helped my dad out of his chair once we were through and walked him back to the bedroom. But this time, we were side by side, with our arms around each other's shoulders like two old army buddies coming home from the war. And I guess in a sense, we were.

I tucked him into bed and reminded him that his boss would be by that afternoon to visit. I told him to get some sleep and that I would wake him when his guest arrived and as I turned to leave, he reached out and gently touched my arm and with no words exchanged, we acknowledged how very invaluable we were to one another.

His boss arrived around two o'clock that afternoon, looming through the doorway with a mighty handshake. He must have made three of my dads easily, and he had a smile to match his Paul Bunyan size, ounce for ounce, and after we exchanged introductions, I motioned for him to follow me back out the door so that we might sit on the porch and talk privately. I fell in love with this mountain of a man right away.

Once seated and comfortable, he began with questions regarding my dad's health and I answered his questions as honestly and openly as I could. Then, I ended the conversation with a warning much like you would hear before an adult-geared program.

Be prepared, I told him, for what you are about to witness is of an adult theme only. Some of what you are about to see is graphic in the most inhumane way. Oh, and don't try this at home, folks! Parental discretion is strongly advised. Actually any kind of discretion you can muster would most probably be very helpful.

In all honesty, I told him that the man he had known for years didn't look the same and he probably isn't the same and he never will be the same again. We really never are with each and every day that passes actually, we just don't realize it.

He assured me that he could keep his composure. I then asked him to give me a minute so I could wake him up and get him ready. He obligingly stayed out on the front porch to give me the privacy and preparation time I had requested.

I tiptoed my way back to the bedroom and quietly gave the bedroom door a slight shove across the carpet just as I had done so very many times before. And there he was—right where I had left him. I walked over to the bed and very quietly woke him with the news that someone was there to see him. He sleepily asked who it was.

"It's an old friend," I said. He halfheartedly made an attempt to sit up and in doing so, turned to face me trying to steady himself on one elbow. When his eyes met mine I told him who his visitor was.

He was clearly panic stricken as he then did manage to sit up by himself saying, "Oh, he can't see me like this, he won't believe it!"

I sat down next to him on the bed and calmly told him that if he didn't want to see him, then I would send him away. "It's entirely up to you," I said.

"Yeah," he said, "maybe he should come back another time."

With all of the patience and understanding that I could possibly gather, I softly asked, "When? When do you think will be a better time, Dad?"

He sat there staring down into his lap for just a minute, fidgeting with his fingers before he looked up at me and smiled.

"I guess another time could be too late, huh?"

"Well," I said, "if I could answer that question, I'd have my own talk show." He chuckled and then I chuckled as he motioned for me to retrieve his sweatshirt from the chair.

I pulled the sweatshirt over his head and then I licked my fingers and pretended to brush his hair back. He complimented me with what a goofy kid I was, and I shot him back with a comment of how I simply took after my father and then came that look. The look of ready or not here I am as he shrugged and raised his arms in the air palms side up.

Standing next to the bed, I reached down and gently brushed his face with my hand, one more time.

I asked, "Are you ready?"

And he replied, "As ready as I'll ever be." And with that I walked into the living room to fetch my dad's longtime friend.

When he entered the bedroom his excitement died before he could even get the word "Hi" out of his mouth, and it's only a one syllable word! But, I must say, he covered up his shock pretty well as he walked over to shake my dad's hand. And I'll tell you something else that I will never forget. I can't even begin to express the emotion my heart endured watching my dad prop one leg up with his arm resting over his knee, trying for the very last time to find even an ounce of masculinity left in his tiny withering body, just one last attempt to enjoy some good old wholesome male bonding. I was sick to my stomach once again, and stood motionless in the doorway, as I watched my dad light his pipe and attempt to be one of the guys, just one more time.

After his friend sat down in the chair beside the bed, I left them alone, closing the door behind me, with memories of my dad closing my bedroom door behind him, leaving my first little overnight friend and me to ourselves.

After what seemed to be a short amount of time, my dad's friend emerged from the bedroom and I got a firsthand, up-close and personal peek at what someone looks like when they've just lost their best friend. He stepped into the living room suggesting that my dad might be tired now. I invited him to have a seat, while I went back in to help my dad lie down. And I couldn't help but notice the tears that had welled up in his eyes as he headed for the front porch, shaking his head from side to side. You know, I think there is something that happens to all of us when we witness tears from a man's eyes, especially a man who could have honestly given John Wayne a good run for his money.

When I entered my dad's bedroom everything seemed different in a sense. I mean the air itself felt different. He was still sitting in the very same spot as he had been when I left him, however, that manly arm was now tucked up under the covers and his pipe was lying on the bedside table. And somehow I knew at that very moment, just exactly how it felt to walk through a war zone fresh after battle.

As I leaned over and tenderly helped him to lie back, I asked him, "How was your visit?"

He looked at me through tired eyes and with a worn-out heart he simply said, "It was hell!" Yes, war is hell, isn't it? I mean, haven't we all heard that phrase over and over again at one time or another in our lives? I know I have but somehow it had taken on a whole new meaning at that moment. Bowing my head, I sadly said I was sorry. And he sadly and quietly said, "Me too."

After kissing and telling him good night, I closed the door behind me, once again wondering how many days he would have to endure all of this.

I strolled across the living room and out onto the front porch to thank my dad's friend for coming, and I found him sitting hunched over forward with his head down, hands folded in his lap with his elbows resting on his knees as though he were praying, still trying to hold back the tears. I sat in the chair next to him, and as I gently ran my hand over his arm, I asked him if he was all right. He turned his head toward me and looked at me through swollen, red eyes and said that he was shocked and he couldn't believe it. Me too, I thought. I then told him I was sorry and that I had tried to warn him. He then, very honestly told me that nothing in this world could have prepared him for what he had just seen. He was angry and it was as obvious as the pain that was flowing down his cheeks.

"Why someone like him?" he said. "Out of all the rotten people in the world to choose from, why does someone like your dad have to get cancer?" Yes, I thought, I've heard this somewhere before.

We sat there for the better part of an hour, sharing funny stories about my cute, little, silly dad and the more *he* shared the more I noticed the moisture welling up in his eyes again. This man had truly not *only* been my father's boss for many years as he told stories to me that my dad had told to him about his five little girls. Some I had heard before and some I hadn't. But there was one in particular that I had, in fact, heard my dad himself tell and although I have in fact already shared it with all of you as well, I will share it again as it came from his friend. It had and would always be—my favorite.

He said that when someone would ask my dad if he had any kids, my dad would get that scrunched up look on his face and hold out his hand with fingers extended and he would say, "Five, my friend, count 'em, I got five! And they're all girls!" He said that my dad was always proud to be able to shock people with that fact. He kind of thought he got a kick out of it. And knowing my dad the way we all do, I think we can safely assume that statement to be true. And not only could my dad's friend recall the funny and good things about my dad, but he also remembered a time long ago, when his friend was suffering through a tragic divorce.

Sitting there on the porch with that man was pleasurable and it did my heart good. I always did enjoy a few good stories and especially if they were stories about my dad. I enjoyed it then, just as I enjoy it now and I suppose I always will.

It was painfully obvious that this man was suffering a great deal over losing his long time friend, so I thanked him from deep within my heart for coming. And as he stood to leave I asked if he would mind saying a few words at my dad's funeral. I don't have any idea where in the heck that question came from, but once it was out I was glad I said it, because the expression on his face was priceless, as he graciously accepted my offer with his chest heaving and his eyes still wet with sympathy.

Now I don't know what came over me as this tower of a man turned to leave, but I'm here to tell you that I threw my arms around this gentle giant as if I had known him all my life and I thanked him once again for stopping by. And I reckon if I really had to look for a reason, then it would have to be this: because I felt like it—plain and simple.

I stood on the porch, following his steps as he walked away and I was still standing there long after he was out of sight, and I might have stood there for a couple of more weeks if my dad had not called for me from the bedroom.

Startled out of my moment, I quickly returned to the house and headed in the direction of his room. My first thought was that my dad had been listening to us that entire time, but I ruled it out when I entered the bedroom and realized that he had been sleeping. And it's not that John Wayne and I had said anything bad or that wasn't true, it's just that all of a sudden I felt like I had been secretly planning my dad's future without him. And when you stop and think about it, I guess I was because my dad's future really didn't include him, now, did it? Geeze, that statement in itself sounds awful. Awful? Yes it was, as well as tragic, heart wrenching and a few thousand other things. But you know what? That's just the way it is sometimes and there's not a gosh darned thing we can do about it, now, is there? Perhaps not, but as you follow me through the rest of this story, you just might find yourselves wondering. Yes, indeedy, you just might be asking yourselves that life long universal question. Could it be possible that we are capable of choosing our own destiny?

# Chapter Eighteen

## *Destiny*

*I felt as if I were walking with destiny, and that all my past life had been but a preparation for this hour and this trial. Eleven years in the political wilderness had freed me from ordinary Party antagonisms. My warnings over the last six years had been so numerous, so detailed, and were now so terribly vindicated, that no one could gainsay me. I could not be reproached either for making the war or with want of preparation for it. I thought I knew a good deal about it all, and I was sure I should not fail. Therefore, although impatient for the morning, I slept soundly and had no need for cheering dreams. Facts are better than dreams.*

Sir Winston Churchill 1874–1865 Second
World War (1948) Vol. 1 p. 526

I ENTERED THE bedroom to find my dad sitting on the side of the bed with his hands folded in his lap and his head down.

"What's the matter?" Were the first words out of my mouth. What's the matter? Geeze, besides the fact that he was dying, nothing! Nothing what–so–ever–at–all, you Einstein in dumb daughter's clothing, you!

"My back hurts, dear; will you rub along my kidneys?"

"Of course," I said, as I sat down on the bed next to him just like I had done a million times before and began rubbing his lower back.

Of course his kidneys hurt. I mean, there wasn't anything flowing through them enough to keep them healthy, for God's sake. I hated that job! And not because my arms got tired, Lord—I would have rubbed his back until hell froze over. Nope, it wasn't that at all. It was because he would moan in pain each and every time I did it, and each and every time I did it, the pain seemed to be more intense. And as I was sitting there, doing the daughterly duty that I had obviously become so very fond of, rubbing his back as I watched his face wince in pain, he asked me a question, a question that to this very day stumps the living hoopla right out of me.

"You're homesick, aren't you, Baby Doll?"

Well, to be quite truthful with you, yes, Baby Doll was very homesick, but now wasn't really the right time to talk about it, was it? I mean, not now, while you are sitting here withering in pain with each and every stroke of my hand—no—not now, maybe later on when you're feeling better. Sure, like when your cancer clears up and all those tumors go away and you can eat again and drink again and maybe by then you'll even be able to walk to the gosh darned stinking bathroom alone and perhaps even pee, for hell's sake! Yup, I truly did think that that would have been a much better time indeed. Uh huh, you bet your sweet patooty I did! Problem was—was that it just wasn't very realistic.

Well, I had to tell him sometime. I mean my flight reservations were already made for the weekend and the weekend was getting closer. If I'd put it off any longer, I'd have been on the plane talking to some nice someone sitting next to me, while he was back home yelling for me to come and help him go to the bathroom.

Yes, ladies and gents, you read it correctly, so stop frantically searching for your bifocals. Little Miss Kitty—Cure—All had decided to fly home to see her family and had booked the reservations two days before! Yup, I was being selfish and feeling each and every stinking bit of it. What in the hell kind of a daughter had I become, for heck's sake? Well, I guess a very lonely one and I missed my family so very much. And besides, it was just for the weekend—just for the weekend! Huh, that's funny, it didn't sound bad at the time.

OK, everyone, grab your smelling salts and pick your books up off the floor so we can go forward with the story. Yes, I realize that you are all probably wondering not just how in the hell I could have left him at a time like that—and I ashamedly do not have an answer to that question anyway. But more importantly, you're probably wondering just *who* in the heck was going to take care of "Jack LaLanne." I mean, after all, he *was* just a perfect picture of health!

Oh, for crying out loud! I knew this wasn't going to be easy and I had been dreading this part of the story since it began and simply because I will always wonder if I did the right thing.

But, that's water under a very old bridge now—a very old and rotten bridge. As a matter of fact, it's so decrepit that even the water is rotten, too! OK, enough said and back to the point. I'd had a discussion with Little Miss Green Face earlier on and I had asked her to take a few days off to be with my dad, who also just happened to be her husband, so I could go home for a couple of days to be with my children and although reluctant and that is putting it very mildly, she agreed to do so. I even offered to pay her freaking wages!!!

For reasons I cannot and should not disclose, I think it best to say that I could sadly, no longer justify a relationship with my father's wife after my father's death. It was and still is unfortunate as well as it *was* but still *isn't* painful. So that's it. In a nutshell! However, I will share with all of you, seeing that we've become such close friends and all, that since my father's death, I have realized that these sorts of goings on, happen more often than not, and I could probably write another complete book on this subject alone. And you know, I just might if I take the notion. But for now, I will just have to ask that you trust me on this one and try to understand if you are able, that like my dad, loyalty is of the utmost importance to me and that some things, really are just better left unsaid.

So, keeping in mind that I always told my dad everything and I always felt confident that he would understand no matter what, I will tell you that this time, it wasn't so easy. Ah hell, I felt guilty before I could even open my mouth. I was truly convinced that I was worthless!

So, there I sat, rubbing his back, fidgeting like a three-year-old, trying to answer his question of did I miss my family, when he very slowly turned his head to look at me. And I have to say in all honesty, that for the first time ever in my life, that I could remember anyway, I had a real hard time returning the look.

"What is it, dear?" he asked.

I sat in silence for just a minute before I could swallow enough to be able to speak. And then, just as always, my dad took over. He laid his comforting little hand on my leg and guessed what was bothering me.

"You need to go home for a few days, don't you, dear? You miss the kids and the old man, huh?" he said.

Geeze, this man really had missed his calling in life. Huh, funny thought, a psychic janitor! How did he always know? Ah, the universal parental question of all time!

"Well," I began slowly, still not looking at him, "God knows I can endure a lot, Dad. And it's not me as much as it is the kids." (Cop-out.)

I continued, "Halloween is this weekend and they miss me terribly." (Another cop-out.) And after a short pause, with my head bowed in shame, I sadly admitted that I missed them too.

"Well, hell's bells!" he proclaimed, "Is that all? Why, of course you should go home!"

Well, hell's bells, and just why hadn't I known that *that* was exactly what he was going to say? I mean, after all, this was my dad I was talking to and he thought it was just fine that I go home for a few days. What the hell was keeping me? *Pack your bags, Baby Doll, and get the hell out of here! Hasta La Vista! Have a nice life! Don't forget to write!*

Not knowing how to act or how to react for that matter, I quickly answered his proclamation with the fact that his wife had taken the time off work so she could stay with him, and that I would only be gone for a few days or so, sounding like I was more defending myself than going along with what he had already so wholeheartedly agreed to. And then he made a statement that would be another piece to the puzzle. OK, perhaps we should even go so far as to say it was the missing link! The whole ball of wax! The complete deck of cards! Get the picture?

Very slowly, he turned his gaze to mine and very matter-of-factly said, "Our business together here is done, dear. There is nothing more for you to do here."

*Oh really!* Well, that very matter-of-factly not only pissed me off but it scared the hell right out of me as well! Who in the hell did he think he was talking to anyway? Had I just been dismissed? Yes, as a matter of fact, I felt that's exactly what he had just done. He very politely and very nonchalantly had just told me to go home. How rude! What in the hell was happening here? Hadn't I shared my toys and played nicely with others? Hadn't I done everything right? I didn't even pee in the flipping pool! How could he just up and tell me to go home? Well, how, I ask you? Let's not mention the fact that I had already decided to go. But isn't that just the way it is sometimes? Yup, if I do say so myself, and I do, it most certainly and most sadly is. We think we really want something until we get it and for some silly-ass reason if it comes easily we simply just plainass don't want it anymore. Now, that's sick!

I sat on the bed, still unable to look into his eyes simply because I felt like I was abandoning him, and at the same time I was licking my wounds. I felt like a real dog. No—actually, more like a piece of—OK, enough, you get the picture.

Then—I said it. I had to. And it was out of my mouth before I knew it was coming.

"What's bothering me, Dad, is that I want to be here when you go. I want to be the one by your side just as you have been the one by my side throughout my life." The tears were falling like rain. And I mean to tell you that without even skipping a beat, my dad then said the key phrase that would be my clue as to what in the hell he was hanging on for, although, it wasn't until after his death that I understood its profound significance.

He slowly turned his head toward me again and asked me to look at him. I reluctantly did what he asked and when our eyes met, he then turned his withering body toward mine, grabbed hold of both of my hands, and very sternly, in a fatherly tone began.

"When I die, I will be alone—understand? I will choose the time, the place, and the day, and there's not a damned thing you—or anyone else can do about it. I love you and I want you to go home."

I looked at him as if he had just poked me in the eye—and I just knew I had to come back with something. Anything! Man, he had just kicked me again! So, very angrily I replied with, "Well, that's impossible, Dad, because I have made arrangements for you not to be alone, ever!" *So put that in your pipe and smoke it, Eddie, the ever-so-gallant monster fighting janitor of the whole entire world!* Boy, that was telling him!

Then he looked back at me with a most secretive grin inching across his face and he said, "Mark my words little one," as he patted me on the leg, "I *will* be alone."

Well, I suddenly and very matter-of-factly had the overwhelming urge at that very given moment to slap the crap right out of him. And he deserved it! Relax, folks, I didn't. I refrained. Instead, I just stared at him and this time like *he* was the one who had just grown a horn in the middle of *his* forehead. Then, after I felt I had composed myself enough not to throw up on him or something worse, a sudden and soothing calm came over me. Something so powerful that it actually disarmed my capability to fight. I was ready to surrender.

Yes, my friends, for the first time since I had arrived, I simply wanted to quit. I was done. And what really shocks the living hoopla right out of me, is that I was totally OK with it.

Knowing he was expecting something to come out of my large trap that we have all by now come to know as my mouth, I finally and just simply said, "OK, you're in charge." And with that I got up and sashayed my prissy little bottom around the front of him and ignored his gaze as I began turning his bed down and fluffing his pillows. I didn't want to look at him. I was disgusted with him. He had made me very angry and I was hurt. So now, I would dismiss *him* as I prepared his bed for him, not acknowledging him as a mother would not acknowledge a misbehaved child. And he must have sensed my hurt, as the last thing he tenderly said to me before I put him to bed was this:

"Please try and understand, Baby Doll, I don't think you will be able to handle this, dear. We are too close. And I don't like the thought of you finding me dead."

OK, just when I thought he couldn't shock me anymore, he went and did it again. I *was* stunned at his statement, but I couldn't allow him to see that so I simply looked at him and sputtered, "Well, you're wrong, Dad. And if you'll excuse the expression, you are not just wrong, but you are dead wrong!" *Ha! Take that, Ed! And don't you Baby Doll me, not one more stinking time!*

"I have been preparing myself for this dreadful stinking task since the day I got here and I know I can do it! So stop telling me I can't!"

And to that, my friends, he simply crawled into bed like a little boy, turned over to lay on his back, pulled the covers up over his chest folding his arms accordingly and said, "Uh huh, OK, Baby Doll, we'll see." Just like that! He said, "We'll see." Maybe the old man thought I had just simply asked if we could go get an ice cream after dinner! Hey, he wasn't fooling me one stinking bit! I had said that very same phrase to my own children for years when I just wasn't in the mood to make a decision. Who in the hell did he think he was kidding—with—"We'll see"? What kind of statement was that anyway? Well, quite frankly, even though I, myself, had used that phrase a gazillion times before, I never really *did* know what kind of statement that was. Ah, but little Miss Baby Doll was about to find out, and I mean she was about to find out the hard way. Oh, and just for the record, you can take it from me. "We'll see," simply means that you aren't as tough as you think you are—ever!

# Chapter Nineteen

## Humility

*The churches must learn humility as well as teach it.*
Saint Joan (1942) preface

I T WAS JUST about four o'clock in the afternoon by the time our talk was over and he hadn't slept much at all. So after we were finished with what was to be our last disagreement ever, I gently leaned over and kissed him and told him I loved him, even though he was sometimes, hardheaded. And with a tight squeeze of his hand and a lingering touch, he said he loved me too. Okeydoke—back to square one!

I piddled around that afternoon, pondering our last conversation, over and over again in my head. And to be honest with you, the more I thought about it, the more I walked back to that bedroom to check on my dad. Something was wrong. And something was worrying me! Isn't that a shocker? Something about my dad's attitude. Something that I would not be able to understand until it was right in front of me, bearing down on me like a big foot in a little shoe!

I believe in my heart that during that afternoon's conversation with my dad, my subconscious mind had caught something that my conscious mind wasn't able to comprehend. Another shocker! Whatever it was that was making me feel so uncomfortable that afternoon, I might not ever know for sure. But I do know this; it was extremely overwhelming and it was demanding my undivided attention.

At about eight o'clock that evening, after several trips to the bedroom only to find my dad sleeping, I decided to go in and wake him up. He hadn't even changed positions since four o'clock and, quite frankly, I was more than just a little concerned. He must have needed to go to the bathroom or something, didn't he? Well, sure he did because I was in control and I said so! I also remember wondering when old green face was going to come home—if ever. Perhaps she had stopped off to get her broom tuned up.

I quietly tiptoed into the bedroom and took my usual stance beside the bed. Leaning over to kiss him awake, I suddenly became paralyzed with horror! Extreme panic thrashed throughout my veins! My dad was not breathing!

For a split second or perhaps and more realistically a little longer, I froze. My feet wouldn't move. Neither would the rest of my body. I automatically looked at the second hand on the clock, just as the hospice nurse had taught me. What a good student I had become; Looking at the clock as if I were trying to determine a time of death to report to the coroner. Yes, what a good student indeed! I was flipping petrified!

It was moving slowly—ten seconds. Oh, my God, this wasn't happening!

I wailed out loud, "Not now, please, God," I begged! Twenty seconds, "Please wake up, Dad! Please don't go now," I cried! I'm sorry! I was wrong! I shouldn't have done that! I didn't mean to dismiss you, Please!!!!!"

At just over thirty seconds, just when I was ready to faint or vomit or both, my dad took a deep, agonizing breath. I was relieved, however, my troubles were far from over and I damned well knew it!

His color was bad, real bad. He was gray, for hell's sake and people aren't usually gray—are they? His breaths were at thirty-second intervals and—he wasn't waking up! And when he did finally breathe, his face was contorted with pain and he surely wasn't breathing normally. He was more like, gasping.

THIRTY SECONDS! For crying out loud, what in the hell was going on here? No one waits thirty seconds to breathe! (Unless, of course they're dying.)

OK, enough was enough! I had become desperate! I climbed up over him and sat beside him on the bed. With my heart pounding, I could feel the sweat beading up on my forehead. I took his hand and placed it in mine. He didn't budge. Not even a flicker of an eye! He just absolutely was not responding!

Again, another thirty seconds went by and then a gasp. By this time his skin had turned in color to a permanent and definite blue gray. He was as cool as a cucumber and still no response from my touch. Through tears and sweat, I leaned over and placed my ear against his chest. His heart was definitely working over time. I scooted a little closer to him, clutching his hand tighter inside mine. In a low moan, my tears saturating the tee shirt upon his heaving chest, I begged God not to take him.

"Not now, please! Don't take him from me, please!" I begged.

And then, I did something that was not only forbidden but to this day that I'm horribly ashamed of; I crawled up on top of him, straddled his midsection, and contemplated CPR. Trembling to the extent that I just couldn't get my wits about me, I instead, placed both of my hands, one on each side of his face and I begged with every ounce of strength I had in me for him not to go! Pitiful.

Yes, ladies and gents, there I sat. The brave hospice-trained daughter of a World War II private first classman, who came there for the sole purpose of helping him die with dignity, scared to death and not willing to let go as I begged and pleaded with God to give him back to me! And as I sat and waited for his last breath, holding his face in my trembling hands, bawling like a colicky baby, I whined the word p-l-e-a-s-e over and over again, shaking his shoulders and begging him to wake up.

I couldn't do it! I absolutely could not sit there and do nothing. It wasn't natural. It went against everything I felt in my heart. And it went against everything I'd ever been taught. I couldn't just sit there and let someone die and *least* not—the Greatest Monster-Fighter Who Ever Lived!

So what did the big-shot daughter who could handle anything and everything do? Well, I'll tell you what I did. I jumped off that bed and ran to the phone with the speed of a gazelle, and dialed the hospice number. By God, they would just have to come there and save him! And if they refused, well then by heck, I *would* damned sure call an ambulance! And I meant it!

Standing there, dancing as though I had to go to the bathroom, I heard the receptionist answer on the third ring. In a steady but obviously panicked tone of voice I identified myself and very calmly asked her to send a nurse, *Now!* She asked me to stay on the line as she put me on hold. FOR THE VERY LOVE OF GOD! I WAS ON HOLD IN THE MIDDLE OF A FLIPPING EMERGENCY! *Sort of stupid when you think about it. I mean, how many emergencies does hospice actually deal with? Tad bit redundant, to say the least!*

She quickly came back on the line informing me that *a nurse,* not *our nurse,* but *a nurse* was on her way. She then asked me if I was alone, and I told her yes. She asked me if I could see my dad from where I was standing and I tearfully told her no. She then asked me if I was afraid, and I shamefully told her yes. She told me to go in and sit with my dad until the nurse arrived and whatever I did, *not* to dial 911. I promised I wouldn't—and with the hum of the dial tone—I was all by myself again. I then dialed the number that the witch had given to me in the case of *only* this emergency, and told her that she'd better come home and as I was explaining why, she sounded so perturbed that I simply hung up, dismissing her to smithereens!

I couldn't go in and sit with my dad! I just couldn't. I didn't want to find him dead. I was scared. Scared of the noises his body might make. Scared I might see something or hear something I would never forget. Scared of everything the hospice people had taught me to expect. Hope you got that, folks. I was scared to death and

I didn't want to be anywhere near my father's dead body! So, I simply slumped down onto the couch, dazed and confused, stared at the bedroom door and cried.

I was terrified and if I hadn't been in such a state of shock I might have gotten up off that couch and run right out of there all the way to wherever it is gutless daughters run when their fathers are dying. But I didn't. Nope, I sure as hell didn't and it wasn't because of my fierce bravery either. It was because I simply couldn't have moved had my ass been on fire, plain and simple. All I could do was sit there and cry. My dad could already be gone and I didn't even have the ovum to walk back to that bedroom and be with him. I was ashamed and disgusted with myself and right at that very moment, I, myself, wanted to die, for I truly felt like I had let my father down in the worst way. But most sadly, I had let myself down.

I couldn't just sit there, damn it! What would I tell my uncle and my family? That I just sat there frozen with fear until the hospice nurse arrived? I couldn't do that! They would want details. They would want to know if he had gasped any last words or if he cried or if he suffered or something like that at least! I had to go in there! I just simply had to for the mere sake of all good storytellers if for nothing else!

So, with every bit of courage I had in me, I stood up on wobbly legs and proceeded to drag myself back to the bedroom. Summing up every bit of strength I could find, I proceeded with the long, five-step journey to my dad's bedroom moaning and wringing my hands every step of the way.

Pausing at the bedroom door, with my arm outstretched and stiff as a board, I slowly slid the door open and then I stopped, dead in my tracks, waiting to see if he was still breathing. He was. About every twenty seconds now. And his color wasn't as pale. Feeling sick to my stomach and still on shaky legs, I inched my way over to the bed and climbed up over his body again sitting down cross-legged on the bed next to him. Then, taking his hand in mine I sat with my eyes never leaving his face. I was still crying but now it was for several reasons. Not only did I realize just how much I would miss him but I also realized that he had been right. I wasn't cut out for this. No matter how much I told myself I could do it, my heart wasn't in it. This job was just out of my league. And a small part of me was mourning for the loss of my own bravery, nobility, and dignity.

I laid my head down on his chest with my legs curled up underneath me, just exactly like I had done when I was small and I tried to convince myself that my Dad could never die. After all, he *was* still alive! His heart *was* still beating which meant there *was* still hope!

It was right about then, that I felt his hand on my hair and before I could even look up, as he lay stroking my hair, he said, "It's all right, dear, I'm not going anywhere. Not yet anyway."

Now I don't know how my dad knew what I had been through, but he did. And as I scrambled to get into a sitting position, trying to wipe the tears from my eyes, he asked me not to cry.

"There's no need to be afraid," he said, "I'm all right." And after I regained some composure, I began telling him all that I had been through and for some reason, I reminded myself of Dorothy, frantically trying to explain to her family all she had been through—and Toto too!

Raving at a mach speed of God only knew what, I was babbling on about how scared I had been and that I didn't think I had ever been that scared in my whole entire life! "I didn't know what to do, Dad!" I said, "And I didn't want to let you go!" And looking at me through tired and understanding eyes, still stroking my hair and now my face as well, he simply said, "I know dear, I know."

He did know. He had always known. He knew by the grace of God Almighty that his daughter wasn't cut out for this. Not the end. Not the *very* end. This was the kind of stuff we called upon Superman to do! Not everyday, ordinary daughters. No, siree, at least, not this one!

I lay there beside him with my head on his chest, praying that his seventy-two-year-old heart would continue to beat me to sleep and that when I awoke, this would all have been a bad dream. A really bad dream! Well, it may have worked for Dorothy but sadly, something was telling me, it wasn't going to work for me.

Telling him that the hospice nurse was on her way was the most difficult part of the evening. I was scared to tell him because he hated to be doted over and it was also an admission of my weakness. I had to explain to him that I didn't know what else to do. And as always, he was just as forgiving as only he knew how to be.

"It's all right," he said, "It's no big deal."

Then, he must have felt a little bit of the hanging-on syndrome too or maybe, be was having second thoughts, like perhaps he really didn't wan to die. *Huh, what a concept!* As if either of us really had a say in the matter—well—of course we didn't but just the same, he said something that didn't fit in.

He said, "Goody, maybe she can give me something while she's here, so that I can eat again." He hadn't eaten in days, and we had come to accept the fact that he probably wouldn't ever eat again because he just couldn't. So, when he said that, I felt it odd but simply blew it off for the moment, as I heard a light tapping on the front door. With one last glance of embarrassment I leaped to my feet and ran to let her in.

The nurse they sent radiantly sashayed through the door with her little black bag in tow. Calmly and compassionately placing her hands on my shoulders, she asked if he was gone yet. (I swear they are all angels) "No," I said, "he seems to be doing fine now." And she didn't seem to be a bit surprised as she followed me back to the bedroom.

She entered the bedroom giving my dad a jubilant, "Hi, Eddie! What seems to be the problem?"

"No problem," my dad said, "I guess I just gave my daughter a little scare is all." A little scare? Holy bat crap, if that was a little scare, I just knew beyond a shadow of a doubt that the big scare would surely kill me!

She asked him if he minded her giving him the "old once over," seeing that she was already here.

"No," he said, "go right ahead."

This was the strangest conversation yet! We were all acting like we were just a few friends getting together for the old once over! For crying out loud, a man nearly died here tonight!

She sat him up on the side of the bed and as she was doing her nursely duty and giving him the old once over, listening to his heart, and taking his vitals, my dad shocked the hell right out of me. This was it! This is what this evening had become. I guess hope is catchy. I mean, after all—he *had* cheated death—now, hadn't he? Well, certainly he had because just as sure as I know my own name he was sitting there getting the old once over, by the old hospice angel! So I can tell you right here and now, that yes my friends, he had indeed cheated death and by God— he was ready to fight!

Before I even knew what was happening, the question was out! He asked her if she would place him in the hospital!

I quickly walked from the foot of the bed where I had been happily observing "the old once over," around to where he was sitting and looked at him as if he had just said a filthy word. I was totally confused. He didn't return my look either. His eyes stayed focused on hers and he knew damned well I was looking at him! And then—with tears welling up in his eyes, he asked her again to put him in the hospital.

"Maybe they can get me to take some food," he said, "Then maybe if I can gain some weight, I'll begin to feel a little better again!"

With some confusion in her voice, the nurse asked him if he was sure he wanted to do that. And to be quite truthful with all of you, I can't tell you what his answer was because I was experiencing some audio difficulty.

Maybe seeing me so upset over losing him caused his brain to malfunction and he felt he needed to do something, *anything* to try and hold on for me or maybe, just maybe, he was simply experiencing some good old fashioned hope.

Yes, ladies and gents, for a minute, the hope was back and not only for him but for me as well, as I thought to myself, *hey* maybe if he goes to the hospital, they can hook a tube up to him and feed him! And then, maybe they can hook up another machine that will help him to breathe and another to help him go potty! Geeze—now, wait just a silly little minute here! No, not just wait—but hold it the hell on! What in the name of Jehoshaphat was I thinking? What was *he* thinking? He didn't want to live that way and I truly didn't want to see him that way. So just exactly what in the Sam hell were we doing? What exactly *were* we doing?!

Well, to be quite truthful with all of you, I'm not real sure but I think we were simply being human, because for just a moment, one brief, hopeful, heart-stopping, gosh darned moment, I think that both of us, simultaneously and instinctively grasped for life. Precious and hopeful life. Not so odd really, now, is it? Well, perhaps not—except for the fact that there wasn't any hope left in my dad's case. If we were going to fight, we should have begun months before then. But now, it was too late—way too late. So all we had left to do was give in. Sadly, we had no fight left in us. It was over. Our opponent had long left the ring months ago, screaming its victory, leaving us to lick our wounds and sweep up. The crowd was gone and we were not the heavy weight champions of the world! And I had to tell him before he made a decision that I could not undo.

I quickly rushed over shoving myself between the hospice nurse and him—sat down next to him on the bed, and firmly placing both of my hands, one on each shoulder, I turned him to face me.

"Look at me!" I said.

His shoulders were slumped and he stared at the floor.

"Dad," I said again, "please, you have to hear me!"

Then, in a more subtle tone, I lowered my voice and with all the sympathy that God had the grace to give to me at the time, I calmly began.

"If we put you in the hospital, Dad, yes, they can feed you through tubes and they can help you to breathe with a machine and they can hook IVs up to you from here to hell and back to make everything you have that isn't functioning, functional again—and it just might buy us some more time. And if that's what you want, Dad, if that is truly what you want, I *will* do it! I will do it right now!" And with beckoning tears now flowing a river of pain and confusion onto the sheets that had been coddling his tired, old, cancer-ridden body, I calmly but firmly asked him one last time, "Is that what you want, Dad?" And then again—as I sobbed, cradling his face in my trembling hands, I turned his wrinkled gaze to face me and one last time through my pleading cries I whispered to him, "Is—it—what—you—want?"

Shaking uncontrollably with his hands fidgeting like that of a small child in trouble, he looked into my eyes like he was searching for the answer. Like he just might find it somewhere inside of me if he looked hard enough, before he too began to cry and then, bowing his head in shame or defeat, or both, he whispered, "No, that's not what I want, dear."

And for just a moment—one, brief, heart-stopping moment, I *was* disappointed.

Getting caught up in the moment seems to be a natural part of life, isn't it? Yes—sadly, you bet it is. And for the first time in our relationship together, we had both become weak at the same time. And not being able to draw from one another's strength for just those few moments, damn near turned this situation into more of a nightmare than it had already become, if that was possible. Panic and hope had simultaneously reared their ugly heads once again, and I must share with all of you, how truly ashamed I was of the fact that I was supposed to be the one in charge. Remember, that's exactly why I was there. So there we sat, both of us with our hands in our laps, staring at the floor—both of us waiting for the other to speak and break the silence. Well, neither one of us dared— because neither one of us could.

The nurse had long finished the old once over. As a matter of fact, after seeing what she had just seen, she would probably go home, hang up her smock, and stethoscope and seriously consider another line of work, as I'm sure that skydiving into empty swimming pools seemed a much better profession at the time.

After putting her little once over tools back into her modest black bag, she squatted down in front of my dad, who was still sitting right next to me on the side of the bed, and she asked him how he felt now, "Do you still want to go to the hospital, Eddie?" she asked.

Without looking up, in a low, groveled voice, he told her he felt fine. She started to ask him if there was anything more she could do for him, but he interrupted her by all of a sudden looking up at her from the bed and saying, "No, I don't want to go. Problem is, that I'm just not ready to go *anywhere* just yet." Whatever in the hell that meant, I thought.

"OK," she said, "Well then, I guess my job here is done."

Picking up her bag, she then turned to me and asked if she could talk to me for a minute. Here comes the bad news, I thought, she's going to tell me he's dying. She's probably going to say there is no hope. My God, he probably has terminal cancer!

I turned to my dad, patted his leg and told him to stay put. And you know, that pat on the leg was more of a secret code than it was a pat. As I was saying, we both know, don't we? And of what we both knew, I wasn't quite sure. But the pat seemed to have said it all anyway.

I walked out into the living room with her, and just about the time we reached the front door she turned to me and like a reporter thrusting a microphone at an accident witness, she asked, just exactly what had happened before she arrived.

I thought I had already told her, however, it might do me some good to tell her again, and so I did. I told her everything from the color of his skin to the thirty-second intervals in between breaths—and the fear! I told her all about the fear as well as the conversation that had taken place between my dad and me earlier in the day. Finally, the account of my experience was finished. I was out of breath and she was still standing. *Like the "Rock of Gibraltar," these hospice nurses were.*

Looking at me like I just might not believe what she was about to say, she said, "Well, it sure sounds like he was going." And after a slight pause she then asked if I had given him permission to go? I told her yes, however, that, that very afternoon we had a slight disagreement regarding my inability to handle the situation.

Running her foot along the carpet with her head down, she told me that what she was about to say might not make any sense but for me to try and understand. "OK?" she pleaded. OK, I thought, no problem— shoot!

"This could have been a false alarm. An intentional false alarm," she said.

I was really confused now, as I looked up at her and stared at her with a furrowed brow and a slight squint in my eyes—for just a moment, then saying with disbelief, that I didn't think my dad would ever do such a thing.

She then, suddenly looked up from the carpet directly into my eyes, with all the sincerity and understanding she could muster up and after taking time to clear her throat, she said, "I don't think your dad had anything to do with it"

OK, that sure as hell made my heart skip a beat. As a matter of fact it took me a few seconds to try and understand what she had just said. After all, she had warned me to do so now, hadn't she? Yup, I distinctly remember her asking me to try and understand. Why in the name of God, I had ever agreed to do *that* was beyond me at that very given moment because to try and understand any of this was like trying to figure out the very mind of Alfred Hitchcock—and he was a weird dude!

I mean, I heard what she said, but hearing it clearly and understanding it clearly were two completely different issues.

Ok, this was way too much fun for me and it was clearly time to now - dismiss her! I had to get her out of there because she was quite frankly scaring the living crap right out of me.

I gently reached out and touched the under side of her arm and thanked her for coming and being so nice to my dad, as I escorted her out of the door. Done like a pro, I thought. She had been dismissed, and I was getting pretty darned good at that.

Glancing back over her shoulder, she assured me that if I needed her again, she would be glad to come back.

Uh huh, and that was about as likely to happen as a cure for my dad's cancer! So, you can just go on your merry way, you silly, dumb, little, storytelling nurse, you. I've heard and seen enough for one evening thank you very much. You are dismissed to smithereens!

I stood in the living room for just a few minutes before going back to the bedroom, trying to decide if I wanted to believe her or not. The really awful and frightening matter was that I actually *was* contemplating, believing her. Now, that's sick.

*Was* my dad actually holding on for me? I mean, after all, he really didn't want me to be there when he made his get away, now, did he? No, he didn't and he had already made that very clear. How could this be? Had what happened that afternoon been a test, as she said? Had God decided to see first if I could, in fact, do what I said I could do? Oh this was absurd! This was an outrage! This was absolutely and beyond a shadow of a doubt certainly not acceptable! I had to do something! And I had to do it now!

So, what did I do? Well, I'll tell you. I did exactly what any other red-blooded American daughter of a World War II private first classman janitor would have done—I dashed over to the phone and dialed the hospice number once again, asking the receptionist this time to call *our* Nurse and have her call me back. By God, I was going to get to the bottom of this once and for all! *Our* nurse would have the answers. She was smarter than—well—smarter than any of us, that was for damned sure! Of course, at that time, and especially on that particular evening, so was *Thompson's Colt!*

As I sat waiting for her phone call, I called back to the bedroom asking my dad if he was OK. He answered me with, "Yup, I'm just as happy as I can be." Great, I thought, glad to hear it.

As soon as the phone rang, I about knocked it off the end table scrambling to pick up the receiver. It was her, my lifeline on the other end asking if everything was all right.

No, quite frankly, everything was not all right. As a matter of fact—I had just taken a walk through the flipping twilight zone, *once again,* and I just can't seem to find my way back to reality so, if you don't mind, would you please try pointing me in the right direction because I seem to be more lost than Alice in stinking wonderland!

I quickly went over that day's events and conversations between my dad and me as well as that evening's events, hoping she could give me a logical explanation. I waited—huh, hum, hum—and—well, a couple more hums and—she didn't have the slightest clue. As a matter of fact, I thought she had been captured by the enemy and turned into a drone as she answered my questions with answers that I didn't like at all. She said in her opinion it very well could have been a test and that she was relieved that I had decided to go home for a few days, simply because she had begun wondering about five days prior, if *I was,* in fact, the reason that my dad had been holding on for so very long. She then, speaking to me with all the tenderness she had in her heart, told me not to blame myself. *Oh, sure, easy for her to say.* She said that her ideas were simply speculation and that I might go home and come back and my dad might still be hanging on. But she seriously doubted it. You see, in her opinion, there was just nothing else it could be. After all, she *was* the angel of death, so to speak. She dealt with these situations every day and perhaps that's why I absolutely wanted to puke at that very given moment.

Don't blame yourself, she had said. Ha! Then why even say it? Well, I'll tell you why, because she was right! I couldn't do it! And now it wasn't just the speculation of a cancer-ridden old monster fighter. It was fact. And no matter how much she tried to excuse my afternoon's shenanigans, reality was reality, and I felt humiliated. What a big, bad-ass hospicetrained hero I had turned out to be. Oh crap, I deserved a medal for this! I sure had done my job! And you want to know the very worst part? I still wanted to go home, more than ever! It was almost as if I had secretly known what was in store for me. Easy for me to say now, and isn't that just the way it goes? Well, if your life is anything like mine, then you bet it is. It's always easier to look back and justify. Just ask me. I'm the queen when it comes to justification of any old thing that seems to come along. Hell, I have answers for everything. And if I don't, well then, I'll just make it up. Huh, I wonder where I acquired that talent?

Funny, isn't it, how history and our family heritage just seem to somehow repeat themselves? And I think it goes without saying, but I'll say it anyway, that we seem to realize those wonderful traits we have inherited at the most inopportune times. Hey, we've all said and done it! Oh, don't believe me, huh? Well, I'll prove it to you! How many of you have done or said something and then all of a sudden the next thing out of your mouth was, "Oh, my gosh, I sound just like my mother" (in my case, God forbid), or you'll catch yourselves saying my dad used to do that or, better yet, you're at some family function and some relative will tell you how you act just like your uncle or aunt so and so when they were small. Sick, I know, but I swear to you it's what makes the family world go round. So, it shouldn't surprise any of us that I had completely made up this great scenario just to fit the situation I was in. I had a wonderful and most imaginative teacher. But I'm also going to tell each and every one of you right here and now, that not even *he* could have storied his way out of the events that were yet to come. I don't think Mr. Grimm himself could have come up with a fairy tale wild enough to explain the happenings that were about to take place.

So, I couldn't do it. I wasn't going to be able to sit idly by and allow my dad to die! That had become obvious. So now, here in the present, fifteen years later, I have justified it with knowing what I know now. I've made up a story. One that fits and explains that awful situation years ago. I think my dad's friends on the other side orchestrated that entire evening to prove my dad right and me wrong. And I think they did it so I would have no guilt when I boarded that plane. Oh, yes, being Eddie's daughter has its imaginative advantages in most cases, but even the greatest storytelling, monster-fighting, dumbest janitor in the whole wide world forgot to share with me the story that was about to happen. Not real sure he actually had a psychic side to him—so I really can't blame him for that. But it is another little tidbit I will have to take up with him when I see him again—someday.

# Chapter Twenty

## *Travel*

*I shall be telling this with a sigh Somewhere ages and ages*
*hence: Two roads diverged in a wood, and I– I took the one*
*less traveled by, And that has made all the difference.*
Robert Frost 1874–1963 Mountain Interval (1916) 'Road Not Taken'

W
HEN IT HAD become obvious that our phone conversation had gone on
way too long (*in my opinion*) and it was time to tend to my dad, I told our
nurse that I would see her in the morning. (*Dismissing her.*) She made
promises of arriving early and that she would ask the chaplain to accompany her. I
felt that was a good idea. *(Great, fine, whatever floats your boat, bangs your shutters,
peels your banana, blah, blah, blah.)*

After hanging up the phone, I sat for just a moment, took a deep breath and
then wondered, "Where in the hell was the witch?" Did she work in Albuquerque
for hell sake? Quickly dismissing that thought, as not to lose what little mind I had
left, I then headed back to the bedroom. I was beat. Way too much information for
one evening and I didn't understand all of it even though I pretended to. I didn't like
any of it either, even though I admitted it only to myself. God forbid I admit it to
anyone else. For hadn't I already been made a fool? Yes, I believe that had been me.
The heroic one who was leaving her wounded buddy on the battlefield to fend for
himself, promising that I would return with help as I scrammed the hell out of there
only worrying about saving myself. Ah, what a tangled web we weave.

To say that what I found when I entered the bedroom was unbelievable would
probably be quite an understatement, but by this time in our story, anything you
read from here on out will probably be the same, a big, large, gigantic, humungous
understatement.

I pushed the door slightly and stood completely still. Blinked my eyes a couple of times but it didn't do any good. The scene before me was still there.

My dad was sitting on the edge of the bed, throwing his arms about, barking orders to move artillery that wasn't there. Stunned, I cautiously walked over and sat down next to him on the bed.

He turned his head to look right at me and told me that we had to move these tanks out ASAP! He was more alive than I had seen him be in weeks! What was happening now, for Pete's sake? Had he gone mad? Had he finally lost his cute, little, storytelling mind? Jolting me from my confusion, again he made it very clear to me that we had to move this artillery out now!

With my heart breaking in two, I stood up, faced him, and like the good little soldier he expected me to be, I respectfully assured him that we would. Then, just out of nowhere, like there was no rhyme or reason to his babbling, he pointed to the corner of the room and said, "You see that coin underneath that chair over there? No one has ever found it."

I simply looked to where he was pointing, where there really wasn't a chair, nor was there a coin and said, "I see," as I found myself sitting down next to him again, simply because my legs just wouldn't, couldn't hold me up.

"That sure is an antique by now," he said proudly.

Which one, I thought, the chair or the coin, but it really didn't matter enough to say out loud. My question would have been ignored anyway, as he jumped to another subject immediately.

"There's a Budweiser stand on the corner," he exclaimed with sheer delight. "They sell cool, frosty mugs of Budweiser there," he said with a mile-wide grin.

"Where?" I asked.

"Well, in heaven," he answered me with his dumb-dumb tone. And all I could answer him back with, was that I sure was happy to hear that. And he simply turned to me with a smile on his face and a blank stare in his eyes and just as simply replied, "Uh huh, me too, Baby Doll."

He then shared with me, like he had just walked in the front door from a short jaunt in his 1982 Chevy Pickup, perhaps hanging his keys upon his studious bulletin board during a *hello, I'm home* conversation, that he had met the founder of Anheuser-Busch. "Nice fellow," he nonchalantly said. Oh, I'm sure, I thought, as I sat in total disbelief.

Now before we all simply get up and really this time, once and for all, chuck this book just about as far as it will fly, relax. Everybody just sit down and take it easy, because what was happening was completely and totally normal—well—for someone who is dying anyway. You see, my dad was simply reliving his past as some people do when they are dying. Oh hell, we have all heard it said at least a million times, we simply just never really understood it. "I saw my life flashing before my very eyes!" Sound familiar now? Yes, I thought it might. Well, that is exactly what was happening. My dad was simply reliving his most favorite time of his entire life: His army days.

Heck, after I had gotten used to it, I was actually quite fascinated. I wanted to stay there forever, watching, like a mouse in the corner of his barracks long ago, sharing in the experience of his enthralling past. The sparkle in his eye was priceless and the happiness in his heart was overflowing. And he was just about ready to bellow another order, when he suddenly stopped, put his hand to his ear and said, "Do you hear that, dear?" Lord almighty, now what was happening?

"Hear what?" I asked, as I quickly panned the room for intruders.

"What do you hear, Dad?"

"Beautiful music," he said. And with that, he began to imitate the music he was hearing.

He began to sing the popular music chord, that rises four notes and then drops three? Up, Up, Up, Up—Down, Down, Down. Only he was singing, bum, bum, bum, bum, bum, bum, bum.

"Isn't that just beautiful, dear?" he asked.

"Yes, it is," I told him. "Very beautiful," as I watched his hands follow the music like a talented orchestrator, floating his arms in the air, eyes closed, creating a masterpiece.

I was sure that this was the end. Of course, how many times have I written that statement throughout this story? And as I'm sure I don't have to tell you, but I will just for the sake of saying it, I was just a little baffled, to say the least. Wouldn't any of us have been? Well, perhaps; however, being baffled didn't stop me from spending most of the night this way and I don't mind telling you that there isn't one single doubt in my mind that my dad *really was* seeing and hearing all of the things he was indeed sharing with me that evening. Speaking to invisible someones that I, myself, could not see, humming to music that I, myself, could not hear and every once in a while, he'd grace me with the honor of looking my way and sharing a thought or two with me.

While we're on the subject of I, myself—I'll share with you that had someone been watching me, I, myself, must have been quite a sight that evening. I would imagine I looked as though I were watching a most incredible movie on the big screen. My head darting from side to side watching every move the characters made. This place had become far greater than wonderland! And I believe it was the closest I will ever come to seeing the other side, until I, myself, arrive.

His friends in the corner of the bedroom were back as he nodded to them and spoke in whispers. But this time, all of a sudden, it became very obvious that someone else had arrived. Someone of authority! Military personnel—as my dad began talking to this person, answering questions with respectful and admirable, "yes, sirs" and "no, sirs," when all of a sudden, just out of the blue, his shoulders straightened up, he sat erect and turned his entire torso toward that particular corner of the room and his arm slowly began to form a most perfect half triangle. And with fingers stiff and his thumb tucked neatly into place, he slowly brought his hand up to the brim of his eyebrow, held it there for a few soldier seconds and then lowered his arm back down again to his side in the most perfect salute I think I have ever seen in my entire life. And if I live to be very, very, old myself, I will never forget the seriousness of pride on his face nor will I forget the tears in his eyes as he completed that salute. And after its completion, he turned to me as he proudly explained in the way that only someone like my dad could, that "*That,* my friend, is a soldier's masterpiece!"

I sat totally mesmerized, nodding as I slowly and methodically replied, "Yes, it most certainly is." And I'm here to tell you, it truly and most certainly was.

The witch finally did come home, sometime during all of this hoopla, toting a gallon of milk in her hands! Did you all get that? I called her during '*the*' most final crisis upon all final crises that we will ever have to face in our entire lives, and she stopped to get milk! She never even bothered to ask me if her husband was dead or alive–nor did she ask if I wanted any cookies! She simply walked into the kitchen, put the milk away in the fridge, and went over and sat down on the couch exhaling a heavy sigh. Now, actually, and in all honesty folks, *had* my dad already died, we all know that I would have been laying on the floor in some sort of contorted dead chicken pose. Therefore, I really can truthfully understand her not asking as much as I hate to admit it. Although, just the same–and I know this may come as a shock to all of you as well–but she seemed not to care!!!

Now during all of this time, as she was sitting and exhaling her heavy sighs on the couch, I was standing in the hallway staring at her as though she were an alien. I merely cocked my head to one side, then the other, in a rather slow, head clearing moment as if I had forgotten what exactly I had walked into the hallway for in the first place, before I slowly turned around and went back into my dad's bedroom.

The witch did eventually enter the bedroom sometime after the phenomenon of the coin and the chair that didn't exist and then just shook her head in absolute disgust, rolled her eyes and went out into the living room. I was so sorry that she chose not to share in the happenings of her dying husband. I was even more sorry that for whatever reason she didn't like me being there. Then I became really sorry and a little scared at the fact that I had to leave her with my dad while I went home for a couple of days. I would try and talk to her once again before I left.

It was about two o'clock in the morning before we got to sleep that night, and to be truthful with all of you, I didn't really feel much like sleeping. Something else was happening to me that night. Something I still don't fully understand to this day. But I will tell you this, whatever it was, it gave me serenity and tranquility like I have never experienced before in my whole entire life and probably won't ever again until it's time for me, myself, to say good-bye. I no longer felt the anxiety over my dad's condition. I no longer felt the grief that had been eating away at my heart. And even though I knew he was closer to death's door than he had ever been throughout this whole ordeal, I wasn't afraid anymore. And I find that to be somewhat of a miracle in itself. I don't exactly know what took place that night. I can't explain it. Chances are I never *will* be able to either. But I will tell you this: from that night forward I no longer feared death. Not one stinking, heart-stopping, little bit! Oh, I suppose, just like the rest of us, I truly do enjoy my life and I'd like to stay just as long as time—or God will allow, however I now have a strong belief that when it is time to go, no matter how it happens, there is no fear nor is there pain! There is only solace and comfort. And that is just one of the special gifts I received from my father during his final days with me. Who would have ever dreamed that I would have come out of all of this with *those* feelings? Well, certainly and least of all not me.

That night, just like many years ago, I slept with my daddy for just a little while—and not outside the bedroom door, but right beside him on the floor next to his bed. I don't know what the heck time it was when I finally couldn't take the floor anymore and wandered back out into the living room, plopping myself onto the couch, but it didn't matter. Sleeping had become a pleasure of my past. By that time, I had mastered that technique standing up, sitting down, or any old way I could get it done no matter what time of the day or night it was. At some point I noticed the witch had gone to bed as she was clear over on her side of it when I got up from the bedroom floor. And I remember wondering for just a brief moment—why she even bothered to sleep beside him anymore. But I was so sleepy and I dismissed that thought quickly. Perhaps I was just too tired to deal with it at the time—or—perhaps I really just didn't give a damn anymore.

I know I couldn't have dozed off for very long though, before I woke up to the awful sound of a most ghastly thunk. And then—water rushing and then—my dad cussing at himself and crying out for help!

I bolted up off the couch like someone had lit it on fire and in one leap I cleared the coffee table and raced for the bathroom yelling his name, "Dad!?"

I rushed to the bathroom door, which was standing wide open, my heart pounding to beat the band—and there he stood, with water gushing from the base of the toilet, forming a pool around his feet. He was stationed with his head down and his arms outstretched as if he were trying to stop the stream from flowing with magical powers, helpless, and crying in a pool of toilet water.

He was weeping just as though he were a three-year-old. I stepped into the bathroom, immediately throwing my arms around him, telling him I was there and that everything was all right. And in a motherly tone, while trying to comfort him, wrapping him in the towel that was conveniently hanging from the shower door, I asked what had happened. Well, he didn't really know, but he thought he had fallen asleep on the toilet and when he went to get up he fell backward. My heart was once again in fragments.

I immediately noticed blood on his hand as well as a horrible blue and red bruise beginning to form. I summoned for the witch to turn off the water outside as I told him to hold on to me so I could get him out of the bathroom. "Do you know how to swim?" I joked.

"Sure do," he assured me through his sobs.

"Good," I said, "because I don't and I may need you to save me!"

He answered with the half chuckle I had been hoping for.

We both somehow knew we didn't dare choo choo this time. For this time, what we had both been dreading had finally come. He was very obviously no longer able to stand on his own as he begged for me not to let go of him. My dad, the courageous, monster-fighting, janitor who worked all of his life and who barely stopped long enough to sleep during his seventy-two short years of life, could no longer go to the bathroom by himself. My God, I thought, so this is what it feels like to finally reach that point. And if it is necessary for me to share with some of you what the moment of realization feels like, or perhaps I should say the moment of dreaded arrival, then I must say, it feels like absolute terror! And I don't guess I need to tell any of you what *that* feels like, now, do I?

So once again, in our wounded soldier formation, we both, with our arms flopped over one another's shoulders, limped out of the bathroom leaving yet another battlefield of sorts, I suppose. Yes, I guess that's a good way of putting it and, quite frankly, I was getting just a little bit sick of winning each and every one of those small victories, because if we really think about it, what in the hell were we fighting for anyway? In the end we were going to lose. We damned well knew that. So what in the hell were we still fighting for? Ah, well—great question. We were fighting for one more small victory, of course. Think about that for a little while. You'll get it sooner or later, as my dad used to say.

I limped him into the bedroom and carefully unwound his arm from my neck, turning him at the same time to sit him down on the bed facing me. Then, kneeling down in front of him, I proceeded to dry his feet with his T-shirt that had been neatly laid on the floor the day before.

As I was trying to calm him down he continued to cry in a low whine, rubbing at his sore hand, looking at it and then at me and then at his hand again, through eyes that told a story of wet and tender embarrassment. I sat down on my knees in front of him, and I reached up and took his face in my hands. I asked him to look at me and he did, with his bony shoulders heaving from his sporadic sobs. When he finally focused on me and he was looking directly into my eyes, I asked him not to worry. Then I asked him if he had hurt himself anywhere else. He said no.

"Did I break the toilet?" he asked.

"Oh," I said, "It doesn't matter if you did. The silly toilet can be replaced. But my silly Dad can not," I added.

I then, still holding his face in my hands, wiping his tears with the tips of my thumbs, making sure we still had eye contact, very tenderly asked him not to get up by himself anymore.

"From now on," I said, "call for me and I will get up and help you, OK?" And right after I said it, I was sorry that I had, for the look on his face was absolute shame. Immediately realizing what I had just said, I quickly covered my big mouth tracks by telling him that I knew he could get up on his own, I was simply concerned about him doing so half asleep. (*Good save, Bambino*). And, of course, right away he agreed that he shouldn't have gone to the bathroom while he was so sleepy and he promised to sit on the edge of the bed from now on and wake up first. OK, I thought, we'll leave it at that for now, but I knew in my heart that he could never be left alone again.

I washed his face with a warm washcloth, put socks on his feet and powdered his tummy before we slipped a clean T-shirt on him and proceeded to lay him down for a much-needed rest.

As I was laying him back on his propped up pillows, I once again told him not to worry about a thing. We would call someone to come and fix the toilet.

"How much will it cost?" he asked.

"Oh, not much, I'm sure," I told him. "It's no big deal, Dad. It's probably just the seal." Uh huh, now I had also become a plumber!

Well folks, it wasn't just the seal. Nope, and a plumber I surely was not. Guess I needed a little more training because the whole damned toilet had to be replaced.

It seems that my sleepy-eyed, cancer-ridden, little toilet-seeking dad had lost his bearings as well as his balance and had fallen backward and in doing so had cracked the whole base of the tank. No big deal really. It was an old toilet. The big deal was the way this incident had injured his pride. And even a real plumber couldn't fix that. And I oughta know, because I asked.

It was a busy morning as the plumber and the chaplain and the hospice nurse were all there at the same time. And I think on that very given morning, I realized that I hated crowds. Trauma can teach you so many things about yourself, you know. And if you didn't know, you do now. And to make matters worse, the water had to be turned off so there was no way to make coffee and my nerves were running on empty, while at the same time, my guilt had a full tank.

How could I have allowed this to happen, I wondered? He could have been seriously hurt, for crying out loud. And although he was on his way out anyway, I sure as hell didn't want to lose him to a careless accident. Especially being killed by a broken toilet. How do you think that would read in an obituary?

How had I not heard him get up? What the hell sort of care taker was I anyway? And each and every time I thought I could forgive myself, the horrible bruise on his hand, which had grown to be about six centimeters around and was a brighter red than most apples, was there to remind me that I could not possibly be forgiven for this mistake. For gosh sakes, I should have been flogged!

Now, let's get a grip here. OK, I'm ready now. Of course I realize that it wasn't my fault. Today I do. But then, at that period in time, those angels who were hanging around themselves couldn't have convinced me. And speaking of those feather-backed guardians of all that's good—where in the anthill were *they* when this whole thing went down? Uh huh, gets pretty bad when you start to blame God's own for something you could do nothing about, now, doesn't it? It also makes me wonder when I read an obituary now. So and So died at home. Huh, I think to myself, was it really an illness like my dad's or were they killed by a toilet?

The witch was furious that morning. First of all, she had to go out in the dark and turn off the water. I truly don't know what her problem was. I mean it wasn't in a bucket or pail so there was no chance of it touching her for crap's sake so she couldn't melt—so just exactly what was the deal????? Probably forgot the cookies to go with her milk, which would in turn explain why she hadn't offered them to me earlier! But more so than her anger I realized that morning that they didn't really speak to each other a whole lot. Had it always been this way? Or had I just noticed it that morning when she should have been consoling him instead of complaining about getting to work with no shower. Like taking a shower would have removed the green from her face anyway! And just exactly how did she take a shower without withering away?

Huh, maybe it was a hoax. She probably never really even took a shower. Perhaps that is why she seemed angry all of the time. And not just at me—but at my dad too. Like she had no time for all of this and we definitely bothered the living crap out of her, no doubt. She actually snipped at my dad while getting dressed, that she had told him time and time again that he shouldn't get up by himself. Well, where in the hell was *she,* I thought? And why didn't my dad feel comfortable enough to wake her? Well, I may not have known those answers at the time but I can tell you what I did know. That this dialog between them seemed much too familiar to me and that my father had married my mother's clone. She was still barking at him through pursed lips about getting up alone as she sashayed from the bedroom to the living room.

Well, just for the record, let the truth be known that he just wasn't real steady on his feet anymore, plain and simple. We knew it was bound to happen sooner or later. I have no clue as to why this had become such a stupid mystery all of a sudden. After all, he had been on borrowed time as it was. But come to think of it, aren't we all just on borrowed time? Sure we are. Every day we are here surely isn't ours, so to speak, now, is it? Chew on that for a while—and maybe—after a few days you'll get your appetite back.

As a matter of fact I began to think about what it had been like to watch my dad walk lately and it had quite frankly reminded me of a toddler just learning to take its first steps. He leaned in a sort of forward motion and once he got going he couldn't stop. Yes, it is sad and once again I will remind all of us that if we are fortunate enough to leave this world with some sort of warning (*or unfortunate enough, depending on your druthers*) we do go out much the same way that we come in. I don't know how each of our destinies is chosen. Haven't quite been able to figure that one out yet. Oh, I know this comes as a shock to most of you in that even Eddie's daughter can't peg fate, but I'm working on it.

While the plumber was working tediously in the bathroom, the hospice nurse and I stayed in the bedroom with my dad. He sat hunched over the little wastepaper basket that I had lined with a plastic bag for him so that he didn't always have to run to the bathroom each and every time he felt sick to his stomach. It had become unbearable to get him there each and every time he felt he had to vomit, which was just about every half hour—on the half hour. Not to mention how very heartbreaking it had been to have to stand there and watch him throw up over the sink when he was barely able to stand. Standing by his side, rubbing his back while he threw up mostly nothing had become a most dreaded ordeal for the both of us. Sometimes, as I stood there with him, I would secretly ask God to allow him to vomit up the cancer so that we could go on with our lives. I don't guess that's the way it works though. Too bad. Sure would be nice.

While he was sitting in his hunched over state of sickness, the nurse decided to check his vitals while I sat next to him, holding his hand and rubbing his back. The old once over again! Geeze, wasn't it about time to put that damned ritual to rest? I could tell her what his vitals were; they were really bad. He was dying, for the love of God, so would you please just stop with the old once over! And as my mind was secretly screaming at the unknowing angel of mercy, my cute little announcement-making Dad had a request: he had to go to the bathroom!

I looked at the nurse and she looked at me and we both probably looked pretty stupid. The bathroom! There was no toilet! And God only knew I couldn't have asked him to hold it anymore than I could've asked a three-year-old.

So, what did I do? Well, I did just exactly what anyone else would have done in that sort of predicament. (*I think*)

Without giving his request a second thought, I quickly stood up in front of him, moving the trash bin over with my foot, grabbed the blanket off the bed to use as a curtain and holding it up around him, I told him to go in the bucket.

He looked up at me as his eyes answered me with sheer terror.

"It's OK, Dad," I prodded, "No one's here," as the nurse took my head-waving cue and quickly left the room.

"Are you sure?" he asked.

"I'm sure," I said.

"And you won't peek?"

"No way," I said. "I wouldn't do that."

And with that, he scooted forward and proceeded to relieve his much hurting bladder.

Yes, it breaks my heart to remember his embarrassment and I also remember that the less that was said, the better he seemed to feel about the whole matter. So it became very still and quiet in that bedroom for just a few moments as I allowed my father his much-deserved dignity and at the same time I allowed my mind to wander back to happier times of walks to the ice-cream store.

I waited for him to say "OK," before I dropped the blanket and neatly placed it back over his bed allowing him to sit back down.

I then called for the nurse and she accommodatingly took the bucket out to empty it and replace the plastic bag. Task accomplished. No harm, no foul.

Another moment, another hurdle, I thought, as I was glad to have gotten through yet another uncomfortable situation, until—he asked me to come closer to him. Closer? I was nearly on his lap as it was. I had just placed the blanket back on the bed and I was standing right next to him so I simply turned and sat down right next to him on the bed, put my arm around him and asked, "What is it, Dad?"

"No," he said, pointing to the floor in front of him, "here." I got up and took a step, turned to face him, then squatted down in front of him placing my folded arms across his knees.

"What is it, Dad, "I asked again, only this time, I said it in more of a whisper.

He leaned forward seemingly searching into my eyes with all the compassion that only *he* could portray and said something I had never heard before in my whole entire life!

"I can taste death," he whispered.

I carefully looked back into his eyes with I'm sure what was a most *What the hell did you just say?* kind of look on my face and not because I meant to be rude, but because I truly just didn't understand. I mean, what in the hell kind of statement was that anyway?

I then, very seriously and very quietly asked, "What do you mean?"

He said he didn't know if he could explain it.

"Try," I whispered.

"Well," he began, "it's like a taste in my mouth," he said. "I can smell it through my skin. It seeps out of my pours. Can you smell it, dear?" he asked.

I leaned forward and put my nose to his soft wrinkled face. Taking a deep breath, my mind was thrown into a frenzy as I took in his sweet fatherly scent. The same scent I will always associate with all that is safe and loving and good. It was a mixture of Borkum Riff pipe tobacco, and well—my dad.

"No," I said, once my mind was clear, "I don't smell anything, Dad." He said, "Then lean a little closer and see if you can smell it in my mouth."

I looked at him with just a little hesitation before I realized that the look in his eyes was most pleading.

"Please," he begged.

I leaned forward again and as I did, a memory came to me. It was a most wonderful memory of a Christmas morning long ago.

I was four years old and my dad had tiptoed into my bedroom gently waking me with his finger pressed to his lips telling me to be very quiet. I sat up on the side of

295

the bed rubbing my eyes, with my feet dangling as he put my slippers on. I hopped down off the bed, holding on to his tender hand, as he quietly led me into the living room with my slippers shuffling and scraping across the hardwood floors.

As we entered the living room, there were presents galore and the twinkling of red, green, and blue shimmering ever so illuminating from the tree. But he didn't lead me to the tree. He led me over to the sliding glass door and slid it wide open chilling my little body with a burst of early morning frosty air, instantly bringing tears to my eyes and a cold sting to my cheeks. Then, bending down beside me with one arm around my tiny waist, and the other pointing to the sky, he said, "Do you see them?" Looking up to the dark morning sky I squinted.

"Do you see them?" he asked again. "It's Santa Clause and his eight tiny reindeer," he exclaimed! And as I looked just as hard as I could possibly focus, I believed I did. Yes, I did see them—and to this very day, I still believe I did, because even though I was young, I realized how very important it was to my dad that I saw them. It was more important to *him* than it was to me. But most important of all, was the secret moment we were sharing between the two of us that morning.

So now, sitting there with that memory streaming down my cheeks, I leaned forward and took in a deep breath and exclaimed, "Yes, Dad, I do, I smell it!"

He then, as if very satisfied, leaned back and gave me a look of, see I told you so, nodding his head only once.

"Strange isn't it?" he said.

"Yes," I said, wiping the tears from my face, "It most certainly is." And I'm here to tell you that it most certainly was and probably always will be.

What a gentle man my father was, to take the time to share such a fantasy with a tiny little girl one Christmas morning, so long ago. And who would have ever guessed that that very same tiny little girl would have the chance to relive for her father a moment of much-needed belief again—thirty-three years later. Well, sure as hell not me, folks. Sure–as– *hell*–not–me!

I got up from the floor and sat back down next to him on the bed and there we both sat, in absolute silence, with our heads down, arms resting on our legs, staring at the floor as if perhaps it might just sprout an answer at any given moment.

After about five minutes of that absolute silence, I felt the need to ask a question. I don't know why I had to ask, I just did—and I'm afraid we'll just have to leave it at that.

Interrupting the tranquility, I turned my face toward his and very seriously said, "Dad, do you think it will be soon?"

And without even batting an eye, without even skipping a beat, he knew exactly what I was talking about. He never even asked what did he think would be soon. He never even looked up. He simply continued looking at the floor as he replied, "I really don't know, dear; I wish I did."

Me too, I thought, as we both just sat there and processed—and you know, if I really think about it, what in the hell kind of a question was that, that I had just asked him anyway? Had I lost my mind? How can someone know if they will die soon? And that's not even the worst part. The worst part is how could someone who loved someone else so very much even think of asking that sort of question? Well, sadly, I don't have any answers to those questions either, folks. I truly wish I did, but I don't. And I am ashamed to say that to this very day, even Eddie's daughter still can't figure it out. Hell, she can't even come up with a good story to cover her ignorant tracks. Perhaps I'm losing the magic; God forbid because that would mean that I have grown up and I don't want to grow up—ever! So I'm going to give it some time and I'm going to come up with an answer as to why I asked that question of my father on that very morning, and I'll get back to you on that.

Shortly thereafter, the nurse came back through the door proclaiming that the toilet was now in service! The toilet, I thought. Had that just happened that very morning, because it seemed like it had been days ago. I studiously got up and went into the living room to write a check to the plumber.

When I returned to the bedroom, my dad was concerned about the amount. I simply lied and lessened the amount, praying that he wouldn't ask to see the checkbook. For heaven's sake, the man was dying, what the hell did it matter anyway!

The witch was pleased in that she obviously had somewhere to go so she could now take a shower and fly—or whatever she really did in that bathroom.

Shortly thereafter, the chaplain had joined us in the bedroom for a while, sitting on the end of the bed observing all that was going on. She was a very quiet and reserved woman by nature, so you can just about imagine what it was like for her to spend time with my dad and me. Poor woman.

My dad had finally settled in and laid back on his propped up pillows and was dozing while she and I chatted a bit. Things had finally settled down.

I took this opportunity of quiet time to share with the chaplain what had happened the night before as well as my guilt over my dad's early morning accident. I guess there's just something about a holy person that makes you want to get it all out.

She listened intently for what seemed to be a very long time before she answered some of my, well, I'll call them concerns (*confessions*).

"Sometimes," she began, "we can't always be there. So please don't blame yourself for your dad's accident."

Hallelujah! I was off the hook! The holy person said so!

She then continued on to share with me that sometimes we are allowed to relive our past as well as view a piece of heaven before we actually depart from this world and it was, in her opinion, that this is exactly what had happened to my dad the night before. Well, off and on anyway. Oh, and by the way, just for the record, the chaplain was elated to hear that they serve Budweiser in heaven.

As we sat there engrossed in our conversation, we were all of a sudden interrupted by my dad's stirrings. We both, at the same time, very slowly and quietly turned to face him and as we did we were able to witness a most secretive sight.

My dad was waving and pointing in his sleep. Well, not really in his sleep, his eyes were open, but let's just say for the mere sake of argument that he didn't seem to be aware of his mortal surroundings.

The chaplain was delighted that she was able to witness such wonderful happenings. I myself had quite frankly become sick of it already. Perhaps it was because the more he displayed these surges of the unexplainable, the more I knew in my heart that his time was nearing.

After a while though, my silly, little angel-seeing, heaven-visiting dad fell back to sleep, and he slept for the rest of the day.

Long after my company had gone, including the witch who had once again forgotten to kiss me good-bye—and I had time to enjoy my solace, I began feeling the homesick thing all over again. I had to go and I wanted to go, but I didn't want to go. Now, I don't know about all of you—but this sure as heck confused the crap out of me.

I was very excited about seeing my family again, yet on the other hand—could I really and truly leave my dad? Could I handle it if he did, in fact, pass away while I was gone? Well, how in the hell did I know? I mean we are talking about the same woman who just knew beyond a shadow of a doubt that she could handle letting her father die, without screwing things up, yet wasn't she the one who panicked like the house was on fire when she thought the time had come? Yup, I think that had been me all righty. So, I came to realize that having to make the decision to go home was a gamble, as well as a chance I knew I had to take. I missed my family. Not so much to be ashamed of really. Well, unless you are me—and trust me—I can find blame where others fear to tread. But that wasn't what I was really most ashamed of. I wish it were that simple. You see, what I was most ashamed of, was my desperate need to get the hell out of there. There, I said it. I felt selfish. And I don't mind boasting to all of you that I'm just truly not a selfish person by nature. I'm really not, or I didn't used to think I was anyway, until then.

I simply had to go home where—well, you know, where death wasn't constantly looming. I needed to be someplace happy and alive for just a little while. Not so bad really—well, not until you put it on paper anyway. Gosh, this sucks.

I decided that day, that the irony of the whole situation was that my very devotion to both my dad and my family had been taught to me by none other that the very same guy who was caught in the middle. Well now, wasn't that special. Sure as heck didn't seem to make it any easier though, because the bottom line was this: I knew I was going, but I couldn't get excited because of the guilt. Great way to punish myself, wouldn't you say? Not to mention the fact that I had to leave him in the care of the witch wife person who did nothing but persecute him constantly. Maybe she would be nice once I was gone. After all, they seemed to have lived together for those few years and my dad never said anything that led me to believe that she was mean. But what would he know about mean? He was oblivious to mean.

After I'd had enough of browbeating myself to smithereens, I took another stroll back to the bedroom to peek in on my dad just to make sure that—all was well. Of course, all *was* well, simply meant that he wasn't dead.

I stood hiding behind the crack in the door and as I watched his breathing, waiting for God only knew what, something came to me. A thought. Yes, another one.

I realized that not once during my whole visit, had I given my dad oxygen. And before I got my bowels in an uproar over this thought, I then very pleasantly remembered why. Plain and simply, it was because he wouldn't have it. As a matter of fact, he ordered me to have the oxygen people come and pick up their equipment, so that they could give it to someone who really needed it. And I want all of you to know I did just that, or tried anyway; however, they refused to come and get it for the simple reason that if they took it away and then my dad changed his mind, there might not be one available, so it was better to leave it there, and not use it. Sounded logical to me—sort of, but certainly not to my dad. For cripe's sake, someone could be gasping for air and he had their flipping oxygen tank! Which leads me to another little story within our story.

You see, I never did mention this oxygen dilemma to my dad, simply because I didn't want to upset him. And, as luck would have it, the oxygen guy had to come out to service the tank weekly anyway, whether it was being used or not. Standard operating procedure, you see. So I simply told my dad that they would be there soon to pick the darned thing up.

On the day that the oxygen guy arrived to service the tank, my dad thought that he had come to take the damned thing away to a dying, gasping-for-air, sickly person.

And boy, did he get bent out of shape when the guy refused. So I did what any other red-blooded American daughter of a cancer-ridden old man would have done. I lied to him. Yup, I sure as hell did and only because I had to. Well—just exactly what in the hell would you have done?

When I signed the paper saying that this man had, in fact, serviced the unit, I told my dad I was signing a permission slip for them to haul it away. I then told him that this guy couldn't take it. He had to send someone else to do it, because it simply wasn't his job. Well then, my dad understood completely. And with that, I had the oxygen guy haul the damned thing into the spare bedroom and never gave it a second thought again. And neither did my dad, thank God. Out of sight out of mind.

Now look, it didn't hurt anyone. And I'll tell you what, ladies and gents, it was a heck of a lot easier to lie to my dad, than it was to fight with him. You know, with some sickly person needing that oxygen and all, so I did what I had to do. If I hadn't lied, he just might have slung that two-hundred-pound tank right over his bony little shoulders and hauled it out of there himself, just knowing every step of the way that he was saving someone else's life who needed that damned tank more than he, the brave soldier that he was—and so the story goes.

Walking away from watching him sleep, I wondered if my dad would be ashamed of me for lying to him once he got to the other side and as the thought of that moment began to fade away, right along with the thought of ever having to use that damned old oxygen tank, I began to pack a few things for my journey home.

My dad slept soundly from that afternoon well into the evening. He didn't wake up to watch TV nor did he call out for me to take him to the bathroom. He simply slept. I, on the other hand, had a little chore to tend to as I tied bells from my dad's Christmas box to a string and stretched them across the bedroom door threshold. We weren't going to have another accident! Of that I was positive!

It was pretty quiet for the most part, as the day came to a close and along with the silence, also came an air of sadness—the kind of sadness that rudely rushes in with the wind of change.

I decided to watch a little television to try and occupy my emptiness for a while and as I did, I began to reflect and want for those first days of my visit all over again. Oh, how I wished I would have known that things could've gotten this bad. How badly I wished at that moment that it was the very first night again, when my dad was still spry, obnoxious, and full of conversation. My God, how I knew I would miss him. And as I sat on the couch reminiscing over the last three weeks feeling an emptiness that would only get worse in the week to come, I fell asleep. I never even heard the witch come home.

It was very dark and very quiet when I awoke to his scream followed by a horrible rumble that had to be the very essence of fear itself. In an instant, trying to wake from the deepest of sleep, I leaped up off the couch once again, clearing the coffee table with a single bound. But this time, his cries were coming from right in front of me!

"Help me! Help me, dear! I've fallen down!"

I nearly tripped over him in the dark, as I felt my way to his shaken body that lay on the floor directly in front of the coffee table. Immediately, I dropped to my knees, crawling my way up to his shoulders and propping my arms up underneath his head. And now, I too was shaking, as I felt for his face and panic seized my heart as blood was coming from somewhere within my dad as it was warm and flowing freely down my arm, which was supporting his neck.

"It's OK, Dad, it's OK, I'm here, shhh. It's all right now," was all I could say, as I sat rocking his frail and frightened little body in the dark, trying to calm him down. And as I sat there, holding the very person who had always been my protector, my monster fighter, my hero, I myself began to cry.

Calling (screaming) through throat-clutching sobs for the witch to turn on the light, I didn't think I had the strength to do this anymore. I couldn't breathe.

As the witch came from the bedroom and fingered her way along the wall to the light switch, horror slapped me with the flick of the switch, as his bloody face flashed with the shock of the light.

Cradling his head, searching with my fingers, I tried to find the source of the bleeding, which to my relief, was right under my nose, and his too for that matter, for he had fallen flat on his face.

The carpet was full of blood as my eyes frantically searched the room for something to cover his naked body. Sitting him up, I asked him if he was steady. He said he was, so I made him promise to stay put while I grabbed his blanket from his chair.

I wiggled my way out from underneath him and got to my knees, keeping one hand on him while stretching over at the same time trying to reach his modesty. I quickly snatched it by the very tip of its corner and reeled it closer to me, grabbing the bulk of it and then wrapping his body up tightly. I then, kneeling before him, slightly turned his timid and sobbing face to look at me and asked him to stay right there, I was going to the bathroom to get a washcloth. He looked up at me, sniffling uncontrollably, as he nodded in agreement.

I raced into the bathroom, grabbing a washcloth off the towel rack and then, turning to the sink, I ran the warm water until it became hot, glancing briefly at the image in the mirror that reflected back a fear-stricken stranger with dark circles around her tearful eyes. Quickly dismissing that image, muttering the word *idiot*, as I wrung out the washcloth and headed back into the living room, with my dad's tearful voice echoing throughout the night. "Why do I always have to foul things up? I got blood all over the carpet and my face hurts."

"Hey," I whispered, "I don't want to hear anymore of that," as I stooped down in front of him and began to gently wipe the blood from around his face.

"I can get the blood out of the carpet," I promised. "And you didn't foul anything up," I said, gently wiping the last of the blood from underneath his nose.

"You simply fell down is all. Plain and simple," I said. "Looks to me like the only tragedy we have here is a bloody nose and some bruised pride and that can be fixed, OK?" I asked him, praying that I was right.

And in an almost childlike voice, he whispered, "OK, dear." And after I wiped the blood, sweat, and tears away from his face, I steadied him on his feet and soldiered him back to the bedroom. The bells were streaked across the hallway.

As we neared what had seemed to have become his only safe place, just as I turned him to face me before setting him down on the bed, he reached his foot over and kicked the tiny trash can out of the way, tipping it over and sending it rolling into a round circle on the carpet. He then, with not a moment's hesitation, tapped me on the arm and said, "Hey," pointing to the trash can, "I just kicked the bucket."

Closing my eyes and shaking my head in disbelief, I sat him down on the bed.

"You're a real comedian," I said.

"Yeah, I know," he replied. "That's where you get it from." *Great,* I thought, perhaps after all of this is over, I'll seek my newly found flipping fame and fortune. Now performing, live on stage—the janitor's crackpot daughter! Watch her dance, watch her sing, watch her cry at everything! She's amazing!

As I was getting him situated, I thought to ask him, "Where were you on your way to when you fell down, Dad?"

After a brief pause, as if he really had to think about it, with eyes wide and the childlike sincerity that had recently become a part of his personality, he quipped, "Why—I was going to get me a drink of water!" *Like, Duh!*

"Well," I said, stooped in front of him with my arms resting on his legs, "I'll go get it for you now. I would imagine you need it now, more so that you did when you started out, huh?"

And as I stood up, using his legs to steady myself, he suddenly grabbed my arm, almost pulling me down on top of him, and with his eyes focused intensely on mine, he said, "I'm sorry, Baby Doll, I truly am."

Once again, but this time with my heart-weeping sorrow, I stooped back down in front of him, and holding his precious little face in my hands for what was to be the next to the very last time, I whispered, "I know you are, Dad," and after I paused for just a brief moment, I returned his sincerity and told him he had no reason to be sorry for trying to help himself.

"I didn't want to wake you," he said.

And with all the anxiety I had built up inside, I exhaled my answer of, "I know, Dad, thank you." And the only thing on my mind as I walked out of there and headed for the kitchen to fetch his drink of water was, how in the hell can I leave him now?

I returned faithfully with his drink in one hand and Band-Aids and Neosporin in the other. Already forming above his right eye and a little below his cheek was a rug burn bruise to beat the band. And I decided right then and there that bruising is cancer's way of showing us who's boss. Perhaps like a constant reminder that although we can't see it, it is still there, looming ever so boldly, just waiting to snatch our loved one away.

I set my makeshift first aid kit down on the bedside table and helped him to steady the glass to his lips. "Ah," he said, "That's good stuff. Nothing like a stiff belt after an accident to steady the nerves."

Great, I thought. He's fine and cracking jokes and I'm a basket case walking around in zombie's clothing.

I took a Band-Aid out of its tin container and tried desperately to undo its tiny paper wrapper. My hands were still shaking enough to make this seemingly simple task quite an operation but finally, I pulled the wrapper from both sides, stripping it slowly to reveal the soothing little patch of comfort. As I unscrewed the lid to the tube of Neosporin, my inquisitive little dad wanted to know my intentions.

"I'm going to patch up your face," I said.

"Why, does it look bad?" he asked with some alarm.

"Well," I said, "it doesn't look real good. You've taken a pretty nasty fall and, because you have cancer, you bruise very badly and very quickly," I explained, knowing damned well that my vain and cute little answerseeking dad just might want to see a mirror.

His hand was still bruised from the toilet spill the night before, and, to tell you the truth, I wondered if this is why they called it the "battle" against cancer. Looking at those bruises churned my stomach with grief. And not so much because it looked bad, but simply because of what it represented. The cancer, as well as my failure to hear him get up once again, was staring back at me from his shaken body.

After I bandaged over my guilt, covering it all up so as not to have to look at it, I asked him, "Dad, how in the hell did you get through the bells without waking me?"

"Are *you* the idiot who pulled those across the door?" he perked.

"I am," I snipped almost defensively.

"Geeze," he mused, "Those damned bells could have tripped someone—so, I untied them."

He was awake enough to untie the bells yet he couldn't take ten steps without falling down. For the very love of God—I was surely on another planet!

"I tied them there for your safety, Dad," I snipped.

"Oh," he said with a hint of sorrow in his voice. "What were they supposed to do?"

"Wake me up!" I snipped back at him, tearing up.

"Oh, well, I guess in a sense they did just that in a roundabout way," he said with a snicker.

Smiling, I answered him, "Yes, I suppose they did."

I laid him back down in his bed, and after he had fallen almost immediately asleep, I tiptoed into the living room wondering if I was really going to be able to get that blood out of the carpet as I had promised as well as was I really going to be able to get on that plane in less than eighteen hours.

Because my dad's personality had taken on that of a child's, I felt as though I was leaving him unattended. That "Lone Ranger" attitude was back and this time it was dragging not just Tonto, but a whole posse of guilt behind it. As if I had proven that I could take care of him any better than anyone else. Oh hell, yes, that was a given! I mean all we had to do was just look at him and we could see that he had been taken care of so flipping well! Criminy sakes alive, I should be thankful that the old folks' social services department didn't come in and arrest me! What a screw-up I turned out to be!

OK, now that my heart closely resembled my dad's face; enough was enough. Because, the truth was, was that my dad had a mind of his own (imagine that), and he wasn't about to give in just because I told him to. He really thought he could do these things on his own and no amount of scolding from me was going to change his ways at all. End of conversation! That is who he had always been and that is who he was going to stay, come hell or high water. No one was going to have to wait on him hand and foot! For gosh sakes, he had cleaned up after everyone else for more than the last twenty-six years! It had become who he was. So you see, for him to sit on the edge of the bed and call out for me to get him a drink of water or to come take him to the potty just wasn't going to happen. I realize this now, but then, it was just a tad bit difficult for me to comprehend. And besides, I had grown quite fond of blaming myself for things I had absolutely no control over. Or do I need to remind us of that?

I didn't go back to sleep that night. I just couldn't. Each and every time I'd start to doze off, I just knew I heard him stirring. It was official—I was a nutcase. Hearing him fall down and desperately call for help not just once, but twice, had been devastating. And I, for one, sure as heck didn't want a replay. And I'll share something else with all of you that, quite frankly, lies deep within the confines of my saddened heart—another little secret of sorts, if you will. It took me months after his death to get over that last fall he had taken. Months of closing my eyes at night to go to sleep and hearing nothing but his scream for help. Until the day I finally had to let it go. And with a whole lot of therapy and a truckload of prayer, I was, in fact, finally able to stop carrying the burden of guilt that came along with that fall. However, sometimes on those familiar sleepless nights we have already talked about so very many times throughout this story, I still have to chase that memory from my mind. And chasing memories from my mind is something I've sadly become pretty darned good at throughout the years. And so the story goes once again.

I finally got up off the couch at around five o'clock, giving up on sleep altogether and welcoming a new day. A new day that would have me on my way home on a plane that evening and back to my husband and children and along with that new day came a brilliant idea to my beady little brain. BELLS! That was it! The BELLS! No, I wasn't hearing them, not yet anyway. Why hadn't I thought of this sooner? I didn't need to *string* them! I needed to *tie* them to the doorknob on the outside of the bedroom door and keep the door closed! Then if he got up unannounced, we would hear him for sure because he wouldn't be able to untie them from the inside! Hell's Bells, why hadn't I thought of that before? And I'd find more of them. A whole flipping container of them! Finding those tingly little objects around my dad's house had been a cakewalk in that every gadget owner in the United States of America had bells somewhere in the house—as he sure as heck had. So, problem solved. I'd hook those tiny little jingles to a long thin something or other and then I'd tie them around the doorknob and voila! No more accidents, no more tumbles, no more tears, no more guilt. What a genius!

I smugly began making coffee, prancing around as if I had, in fact, been the very one who actually invented sliced bread and, as I did, I found myself studying my dad's little kitchen. What tiny treasures his cabinets held with their see-through glass doors. My mood was suddenly kicked back into reality.

305

Staring back at me through the glass cabinets, I noticed his work coffee cup and sugar bowl proudly displayed and standing at attention, sitting exactly where he had left them after coming home from his last day of twenty-six years of "keeping it kleen." The cup, sported stains from the years of use, the sugar bowl probably still had sugar in it. I didn't really care to look. What would it matter if it did? He'd not ever be reaching for it again.

There were tiny clips scattered about just waiting for an opened bag of chips, and an array of coffee cups on each shelf, some of which I had given him as gifts throughout the years. And I suddenly realized that this was it. This is how it all ends up, folks; all of our things, our trinkets and treasures, will someday be divided up amongst those who loved us and the rest end up in garage sales to be passed from one household to another, until every trace of our very existence is erased. Scary, isn't it? I mean, why in the hell even go on?

I poured my cup of instant coffee, I guess so that it might somehow instantly wake me up, or slap me—and walked back into the living room, remembering again that this was the day. Tonight, I would be home with my family and I'm not sure but I think I actually felt a twinge of excitement. Hold on a minute. Yes, I do believe it most certainly was excitement I was feeling. Well how about them apples! I was still able to experience normal human feelings of joy! Human feelings. What a concept. After all, I was only depressed, not dead, for crying out loud and at that thought, it dawned on me how my dad had kept his sense of humor all along.

I walked over and sat down on the couch and proceeded to make my morning phone call home, telling the kids to have a good day at school and that I loved them. I was still calling home three times a day on the average—sometimes more, depending on the circumstances, but never less.

I called in the morning before they left for school, then in the afternoon right after they returned home and then at bedtime. By the time my father passed, my phone bill was more than his funeral expenses, no joke!

I didn't tell the kids that I was coming home. I wanted to surprise them and it was becoming more difficult with every call as they would ask each and every time when I was coming home. I was feeling the excitement mounting as I told my youngest son, that it wouldn't be long. Poor little guy, he'd been hearing that line for three weeks now and I think he was beginning to believe that the phrase "it won't be long" meant never. I'm sure he just knew that I would be gone forever. (Forever—only when someone dies.)

My absence didn't seem to affect my daughter in the same way at all. Oh, she missed me (I think); however, she—like her mother—was a daddy's girl and she had her daddy there. Huh, and I had my daddy where I was with me too. We had a lot in common. Yes, indeed, and each and every time I see her take her daddy's face in her hands trying to get his full and undivided attention, as she says something to him that is extremely important to her, I know in my heart, that for the rest of her life she will continue to practice this act as a way to make him understand how very important it is that he listen to her. God forbid, that she will ever have to endure the pain of that very same little gesture during the last three weeks of his life. Come to think of it, *God forbid* seems like an understatement.

After my phone call, I began to piddle around by packing just a little bit at a time. Packing just a little bit here and a little bit there, seemed to be more respectful to the situation. Uh huh, I know how silly it sounds but it's the truth. And I'll tell you something else that's silly but truthful. I think that if I had mistakenly packed all of the guilt I was carrying around with me that morning, I wouldn't have been able to lift that flipping suitcase from the floor. As a matter of fact, it would have given Hercules, himself, a good run for his money.

The witch was up and out the door by seven o'clock. I reminded her just before she left, that I would be leaving that evening and could she try and be home by five. She mumbled something to the effect that she was perfectly aware that I was leaving and she would be there. Good then. Be gone with you! Fly! Fly!

At about nine thirty I walked back to the bedroom to peek in on my dad. He was still sleeping. His breaths were at about twenty-second intervals and he seemed to be in pain as he grimaced with each and every inhale. I stood with my shoulder against the door frame, arms folded across my chest, just lingering, gazing at him. And I might just still be standing there today had I not needed to go to the bathroom sooner or later. I slowly turned from the door, walking back into the living room eyeing my suitcase as if it had just insulted me.

What in the hell was I doing? What in the hell was I about to do? How could I leave him? What in the hell had I been thinking and whom did I think I was kidding? And it was right then and there, that I decided! *No—not to jump off a cliff*—but to open up my little bag of survival techniques, once again, and begin digging for answers. Frantically I searched. Searched for something that would make me feel better. Searching and digging, digging and searching, searching, searching—and finally—there it was! Hiding under my *What's the worst thing that can happen?*

Pulling and tugging it forward, I brought it up close to my heart.

It was my, *You can always change your mind tool.* Gosh I had almost forgotten I owned it. Uh huh, like what was I going to do with it? Like I was going to change my mind. Like what could possibly happen that would make me change my mind? Well, like unless he died that very afternoon or perhaps grabbed my ankles at the door, nothing. And somehow, after that thought, tool or no tool I felt worse than

I had before I started. Quite frankly, I truly believe I should have been an enemy torturer during the war.

The first thing I had to do just for the sake of getting it over with, was take a shower. I had had a rough night and the hospice nurse would be there soon. But I had just one teeny, tiny, little problem. Well now, you had to know that even such a simple task as taking a stinking shower had to be a major production. And it most certainly was in that I was deathly afraid to leave my dad unattended. I was scared that he might get up and wander out of the bedroom and fall again. So what did I do? Well, for starters, I tied the bells to the doorknob, those wonderful little jingly warners of danger. But there was just one more little thing I neglected to overlook. Wouldn't you just know? If they would wake me up when jingling, then how in the heck was I going to string them without waking him? And worse yet was what in the heck was he going to think when he saw the door completely closed? Would he be scared? Would he yell for me? Would I ever stop being neurotic?

Of course, then again, I could have strung them across his doorframe again like someone's over starched laundry? I mean, as much as he liked them being there, that would have gone over about as well as a cat in a mouse closet. Oh, for hell's sake, was there ever any rest for my weary mind? Well, quite frankly—no. Therefore, I opted for leaving the door open and stringing them across the threshold. At least then—I could hear him if he called for me.

I quietly tiptoed to the threshold of his bedroom door and with a thumbtack *(smart thinking, huh)* I stuck one side and then very carefully and very quietly pulled the string and stuck the thumb tack to the other side and voila! Ding Dong the deed was done! Geeze–La–Weeze! Stress much?

Hurrying into the bathroom, I undressed quickly and right before I opened the shower door to turn on the water, I scampered over to the door and looked outside into the hallway. Damn, I couldn't see my dad through the crack in the door because some idiot had failed to leave it enough ajar. Therefore, yours truly, wrapped the towel around her naked body and took two steps into the hallway and lightly gave the bedroom door a shove. There, I thought, so far so good. And with that, I quickly turned scurried into the bathroom and leaped into the shower.

I'd been in there for about three minutes, when a most horrible thought hit me once again. I had to check on him! I mean, what if he heard the shower running and got a little curious and wandered into the hallway to take a look and all of a sudden he fell, tripping over that string of bells, cracking his head on the corner of the wall never to regain consciousness again or something worse. Yes, this could very well happen and I, for one, would be responsible again! Not to mention the fact that the mere thought of such a thing happening was ruining my damned shower. So without turning off the water, I slid open the shower door and hopped out soaking the floor below me tiptoeing over to the door and peeking out. Nope, he was still sleeping away. *Imagine that, you moron!* I scurried back into the shower, rinsed the shampoo out of my hair, quickly lathered up with soap, rinsed off and then turning off the shower I wrapped my already soaked towel around me once again opened the slider door and once more tiptoed to check on my still-sleeping little dad. *Criminy sakes alive!* It was truly time for me to go the hell home!

Now if he got up, I would surely hear the bells because the shower wasn't running anymore. Boy, was he lucky to have such a conscientious daughter, huh? I mean, after all, who else would have gone to such lengths just to make sure he was all right? Well, I'll tell you, no one with half a brain, that was for sure. And please allow me to remind all of you that this is a true story.

I quickly dressed and put on what little face I could, before I walked out of the bathroom and ran smack-dab into my dad!

"Ah!" I yelled, and he returned the yell with, "What in the hell is the matter with you?"

"You scared the crap out of me!" I cried.

"Well, geeze," he said. "I was only waiting for you to get out of the bathroom so I could go potty. I didn't mean to scare you."

"Well, you did!" I said. "And while we are on the subject, how come you got up alone? You promised not to and how did you undo the bells?"

He once again flashed that notorious look of you dumb-dumb, before he answered me with, "Well, I called for you but you didn't answer me, so I figured I'd better get up and go on my own before I wet the damned bed! And I almost killed myself on that string of bells you concocted up in the doorway, so I pulled the thumbtack out of the door frame and headed for the bathroom. That is when I ran into you."

Oh wonderful, Pocahontas. While you were primping in the mirror, your father could have been killed by a string of bells or worse yet—he could have wet the damned bed, you idiot!

Just a tad bit overly dramatic, wouldn't you agree? Well, perhaps. However, I had become an overly dramatic extremely tired mess by that time (like the shower escapade hadn't already convinced us all of that), and that little act of ridiculousness was only a sample of some of the things I did. Jeepers, Wally, no wonder your dad told you to go on home. He was probably afraid for his very life! I mean, after all, his once, very intelligent and extremely calm, clear-thinking daughter had transformed herself into a cross between Stan Laurel and Dr. Jekyll, for Pete's sake! And you know, when I take the time to stop and think about it now, it seems like the more out of control I became, the more in control my dad seemed to become. And—quite frankly—I don't really know what that meant. I might not ever be able to figure it out either. Nonetheless, it's embarrassingly true. Uh huh, and how would you like to have to live with all of that on your conscience? It's not a pretty picture, folks.

Sadly, when I do bring myself to think about it as I am telling this story, to go to the bathroom was the only reason my dad got out of bed that whole day. And I'll share another sad thought with all of you: that little bit of conversation that took place between the two of us in the hallway that morning was the last meaningful conversation we would ever have between the two of us again. And if hindsight were, in fact, twentytwenty, I would have grabbed him and kissed him for all it was worth standing in that hallway that very morning, holding on to him and trying to savor every moment until—well—probably until this very day! But we don't have hindsight on such things, now, do we? No—sadly—we sure as hell don't. And *that,* ladies and gents seems to quite frankly suck more than anything else thus far.

After he went potty and without my clumsy help, I might add, as I walked him back to the bedroom, he, all of a sudden became extremely groggy. What in the hell had just happened to the guy that was standing in the hallway? I laid him back in his bed and tucked him in which would be the very last time for me to do so, and I kissed him on his cheek and told him how very much I loved him. And I remember being very aware of the urgency I felt that day just to love him. But then again, hadn't I become an urgent mess anyway? Each and every time I said "I love you" and each and every time I touched him, I acted as though it could be the last. And for that, I am forever thankful. And let this be just one more reminder to all of you that that's the way it should be. And as we go on with this story if you take nothing else but that little ditty with you as you close this book, please, oh, please remember just how very precious each and every touch and kiss we give or receive is. And I really just can't stress that enough.

Just about the time I got to the bedroom door, pulling it shut behind me, thinking he was fast asleep, he startled me by asking me a question.

"Will you be going home tonight, dear?" he asked.

I turned back around from the bedroom doorway and slowly walked back over to the bed. Standing there with my stomach in knots, I realized he had rolled over so that for the third and final time in my entire life his back was turned to me. I began to shake and fidget from one foot to the other before I answered.

"Yes, Dad, I will probably return in a couple of days though," I replied with the courage of a mountain lion. (*Mouse.*)

And then there was silence once again, but this time to say that it was merely uncomfortable or just casual silence would have been the understatement of the decade.

After a moment or two of just standing there for what seemed like a deafened eternity, with his back still turned to me he finally replied, "You should stay home now, dear; those kids need you more than I do."

And what do you all think I said to that? Well, quite honestly—not a stinking gosh darned thing, that's what. I just simply stood there, looking at his backside before I turned and quietly walked out of the bedroom. And that was the very end of that!

I had obviously been dismissed for the last and final time. And at that very moment I realized that it seemed like forever ago that we had been best friends, buddies, so close and spontaneous to have fun and laugh and reminisce. Yes, forever ago indeed. (Forever—only when someone dies.)

I ask myself today—as I'm sharing my story with all of you—why hadn't I turned around that day, walked back over to the bed and sat down with my dad at that moment as I had done so very many times before and just enjoyed the comfort of his arms around me, or the pleasure of brief conversation, or the mere plain and simple peace we always felt when we were together. Why? And just about the only answer I can come up with—is that it was over, that was why. We had already said and done all there was to say and do, in my dad's opinion. Otherwise, he wouldn't have purposely turned his back to me that day. And whether it is true or not, I choose to believe it. I have to. It's all that saves my sanity.

The day went relatively fast after what was to be our last chance to, well, to—just be, I guess. Last chances are strange in that sometimes just like only chances, or first chances, we don't really know what they are until they're over. Oh, Lord, do you think we'll ever get it?

I glanced back just one more time before I pulled the door behind me, leaving it just a tad bit ajar. And I swear to you that I *still*, yes *still*— thought he would never die!

As the day wore on, I have to ashamedly admit that I did get a little more excited with each and every hour that passed. I was going home!

The hospice nurse came and looked in on my dad that day; however, there was only conversation between the two of *them*, just her and my dad. And that was just fine with me. Isn't it strange how my need to be right smack-dab in the middle of things had diminished? Yes, strange indeed. Then again, perhaps right smack-dab in the middle of things had changed locations. Yes, now that I think about it, that's exactly what had happened. And that's not all that happened either. No, I must say that a lot of things were happening right before my very eyes, yet, I could not see them at the time. Or maybe, *would* not, might be a more honest statement.

My dad had become very groggy, very quickly and he obviously didn't have a whole hell of a lot to say that day. He simply slept, waking up occasionally to go to the bathroom but that was all.

The hospice nurse probably had it figured out long before anyone else, for as she was leaving that day, her visit brief, she took the time to hug me like never before and told me to enjoy my family and to have a safe trip home. Yet, this hug from her, this last and final embrace, seemed to linger just a tad bit more than I had experienced in the past. And as she was showing herself to the door, she turned and made me promise to go. "Don't change your mind," she said. "Your work here is done."

Huh, I thought, what the hell? Had someone taken a poll? And just exactly what had happened in the bedroom between her and my dad? Had he turned his back to her also? Had he not responded to her caring personality and perhaps that was why she had told me to go? Maybe it was her way of getting back at him. Maybe because he hadn't responded to her, she had decided not to like him anymore. Or perhaps she and he had a private conversation regarding getting me out of there so he could die. Or maybe, just maybe, I had become nuttier than a tick on an outhouse rat! Probably so—that seemed more likely.

Had it occurred to me that perhaps it was just time to go? That maybe all had been said and done and just maybe this time, just and only once in my life, it was OK for there not to be a mystery behind something? Well, quite frankly, no. Not on your life, folks! Not then anyway. Only now. And oh, how I was longing for the hindsight once again.

For the rest of the afternoon I prepared, and not to go home, mind you. Oh gosh no. I was already packed, prancing, and chewing at the bit for that trip. You see, I was preparing to say good-bye. What a dope. Like I really knew.

Would I sit down gently on the bed, taking his face in my hands and say to him, "Dad, if you aren't here when I get back, please know how very much I love you and that I'll see you again someday." Or perhaps I would simply give him that look and he would in return give me his and there would once again be an unspoken understanding between the two of us. Or maybe he would cry and say, thank you, dear for making this easier for me, and then I, in return would say through sporadic sobs, no, thank you, Dad, for teaching me how to let go, how to wrap things up, how to love without any expectations in return and how to feel and endure the worst pain imaginable—how to reminisce and how to believe in things I can't see, like God and angels and love.

Is this how it would be? And if so, which scenario? Maybe all of them—or—maybe none of them? None–of–them. Not–a–single–one. We'd have to wait and see. But it didn't matter. I was prepared. Sure I was!

The witch was home by five thirty, and I surely appreciated her promptness when I asked her to be home by five!!!!! I went over some things with her but she just continued to remind me that she already knew. And perhaps she did. Perhaps I had been a little too hard on her throughout this entire ordeal. Maybe she felt left out. Maybe this would make her be nice. Maybe she would sit with my dad and never leave his side and hold his hand and tell him all the things she needed to say. Or maybe—hell would really and truly freeze over and I would finally learn to ice-skate!

I did spend my last couple of hours just standing in the bedroom doorway, gazing at my dad while all he did was sleep. I'd walk to the side of the bed and lean down and kiss him but he never stirred. Then back to the doorway. This is how I spent my final time at his home.

At six thirty, my uncle pulled up in front of the house, bounding from the car and racing inside to remind me that traffic would be heavy and that we'd better get a move on.

A move on? Like now? I felt terror strike as I panicked and whirled around to face the witch, knowing that it was time. It was finally here! Sweet Jesus! My feet wouldn't move, couldn't move! I had to walk into the bedroom and it felt as if I had left my legs somewhere else. Could I do this? Could I actually walk into that bedroom and say good-bye to my dad? My uncle was looking at me in such a way that it made me feel as though I just might puke. And actually, that might not have been such a bad idea at that very given moment. I sure as hell felt like it.

"We really need to go," my uncle prodded. Gosh damn! Wasn't there something else that stupid Indian could be doing right then and there? Go chase a cowboy, Tonto!

Well, I had to do it. I had no choice although I thought about just darting out the door. Sorry, had to go, had a plane to catch! Have a nice death! Don't forget to write! How sick was that? Never mind. I don't really want to know.

I quickly headed for the bedroom and swung the door open with hopeless dread and there he lay, on his back sleeping peacefully, unaware of the panic and terror I harbored within my breaking heart. Or maybe not.

I swiftly but quietly made my way to the bed and bent down to kiss his soft and wrinkled cheek and just as I prepared myself for the moment of all moments he opened his eyes, propped himself up on one elbow and announced that he had to go to the bathroom!

Now? You can't go to the fricking bathroom now, you stupid, old, cancer-ridden, monster fighter, you! This is our moment, you moron! I have a plane to catch and you have to go to the damned bathroom??? Now???? No–No–No!!! This was all wrong! This is not the way it was supposed to be! And just as I felt another silent insult coming on, the witch interrupted my destructive train of thought by reminding me of the time, and as I followed both of them to the bathroom, I still couldn't believe this was happening! She then turned and left me standing alone with him in the bathroom. And there I stood. Oh, this was not at all what I had planned. Not one stinking iota! This was not OK!

With his back to me, leaning with one arm to steady himself on the wall behind the toilet, there he stood and there I stood. I took a couple of steps so that I stood right behind him and placed my right hand on his right shoulder. It was sort of a warning. He didn't move. And he purposely didn't want to look me in the eye. Softly I said, "I gotta go now, Dad." He froze. He didn't utter a word.

I arched my neck around his shoulder and went to kiss him on the cheek, but just as I attempted to do so, he turned his head, making sure to have no eye contact, and kissed my lips and simply said, "Good-bye, dear, I'll see you again." Not "next time," as he had said to me all of my life but, "I'll see you again."

Standing there, with my heart screaming in pain, I gently brushed his face with the underside of my hand and told him I loved him. And the last words my dad ever said to me in person were, "I love you too, Baby Doll." And with that, I turned and walked out of the bathroom, telling him to be careful standing there. Come to think of it, why in the hell (how) had he been standing there? He usually sat. But of course that would have meant he would have had to face me. Geeze, must have taken all the strength he had to stand there like that. All eighty-six pounds of him. He must have not wanted to look me in the eye in the very worst way. And that's all I have to say about that! Actually, it's really all I *can* say about that.

Meeting the witch in the hallway, I gave her a quick hug and a kiss reminding her that he was standing and with that I was gone. And that, my friends, was the last time I would ever see my daddy alive. No dramatics, no symphony orchestra, no serene peaceful setting. Not even one last reminiscing glance as I was racing out the door. Nope. Nothing. Just him standing over the toilet going to the bathroom. Now doesn't all this just damned well fit? Well, it should because it's life. Plain and simple. And if I had just one wish given to me today, it would be to brush the underside of his little face with my hand just one more time and to tell him just one more time how very much I loved him. Toilet and all!

You see, contrary to popular belief, I have finally learned to take it or leave it. I have also learned that only sometimes do things go exactly as planned. Most of the time not. Unfortunately, those sometime things don't include death. That's why I'm telling this story. The last visual memory I have of my dad is of him standing over a toilet, for the *very* love of God! And I wouldn't trade that memory for all the tea in China. Never did care much for tea, anyway so that's probably not a good example. How about—oh never mind—because there is nothing in this world I wouldn't give—except for the lives of my children—just to have one more moment—with my dad. One more glance. One more touch. And that's all I have to say about that.

# Chapter Twenty-One

## *Hindsight*

***Hindsight is always twenty-twenty.***
Billy Wilder (Samuel Wilder) 1906- In J.R. Columbo
Wit and Wisdom of the Moviemakers (1979) ch. 7

O H, HOW WE always seem to wish for the things we cannot have. That's just the way life is, I'm afraid. And probably somewhere along the line for some good reason, I suppose. But it doesn't really matter because we wish and wish anyway. How well I know because I still, to this very day wish that somehow I could have known. Oh, how I wish that some angel would have tapped me on the shoulder that night and told me not to go. One of my very good friends who is also deceased used to say, "You can wish in one hand and sh__ in another." I never really got the true meaning of that little ditty until my dad died. Then it was like the light came on. Finally—duh!!!

I guess I wanted to go home so badly that a whole band of angels could have tackled me, throwing me to the ground, and I still would have gone anyway. Why? Well, I reckon because that's the way God planned it. I have decided that although we wish for hindsight so many times in our lives, the answer is and has always been God's decision. And I'm sure each and every one of you is so thankful that it took reading this story to learn that. Geeze. Oh, and for those of you who don't really believe in God or for those of you who aren't quite sure, just keep on wishing. See how far it gets you.

The very second I stepped out onto the porch that night, I began stuffing my dad's memory to the back of my mind. I would love to be able to say that I did it just for my family. I would love to be able to say that something horrible might have happened if I hadn't gone home. But I can't. Nope, not and be truthful, I can't. I *wanted* to go home, plain and simple. I wanted to go home and cover up my head and pretend none of this was happening. I wanted to go home and feel safe where there wasn't any dying going on. I just wanted to go home, period. And that, my friends, was the hardest thing to deal with the night my dad died. And I'll tell you something else that was a pretty tough nut to crack the night he died: trying to remember just exactly what kind of urgency I had felt that allowed me to leave. It was pretty darned hard to remember that feeling of urgency when it came time to face the fact that he was gone. I went through a lot of, why did I's and why didn't I's, but the bottom line is this: All things happen for a reason and I know in my heart (now) beyond a shadow of a doubt (sort of) that I could not have stood there and allowed my father to go without doing something, anything—other than just standing there and allowing it to happen. Just wasn't me! Perhaps I was a coward. I suppose I was in a sense, or maybe—it's a long shot—but just maybe I was only human. I might not ever know all the answers until I see my dad again someday, but the truth of the matter is this: I obviously had to go home, more than I had to stay. And that is exactly what I did. I can't change it now and I can't go back—and *that* decision, my friends, is something I will ponder for the rest of my life. And so the story goes.

My ride to the airport was riveting as we darted in and out of traffic trying to make my flight on time, with my uncle telling me every step of the way, not to worry.

"Whatever happens—happens," he chided. "And it will do so for a reason. If he goes before you get back it was meant to be. And if he doesn't, then it too was meant to be."

Yeah, yeah, yeah, I thought. Blah, blah, blah. I'm sure he thought that if he didn't drive fast enough and get to the airport quickly enough, I was going to change my mind. And I gotta tell you, if he rode a paint horse anything like he drove a car, it's no damned wonder in this world why everyone thinks that all Indians are drunks!

At the airport, I left my heroic Native American uncle with a big hug and a kiss, making him promise to check on my dad daily. And with that, once again, I found myself walking through the same crowd of nameless faces, wondering if they had any idea what I was going through.

Yes, they all looked like the same faces that I had wanted to address three weeks before. I mean, if you've seen one nameless face you've seen them all. But this time, I wasn't so proud. This time around, I would have to have stood up on top of my soapbox in the middle of the airport yelling, "Hey! Hey everyone! I tried but I just couldn't do it—you see? I gave it three weeks and I just couldn't take anymore!"

And then they would all turn, walking away, shaking and hanging their heads with sighs of disbelief and disgust, and I would board the plane with my head down between my shoulders, with all of them waving their hands at me in a *get the hell out of here* motion. Chicken chit they would all be saying. Coward! Coward! Coward!

My flight home was dark and lonely and I continued searching the darkness of the sky for answers that were nowhere to be found. I tried to read a book, but it just didn't fill the void. And still, as I sat on that airplane searching strange faces in the darkness, I couldn't believe I was going home. Perhaps I would lean over telling the man next to me, that I had just left my dying father standing at the toilet because I was homesick. Uh huh, and wouldn't he simply look at me extending both arms toward me, running one index finger over the other saying shame on you. Yup, he most probably would have, because that's exactly what I felt I deserved.

The plane's landing was little rocky; however, the fear I had once experienced from such an episode had dwindled to nothing. Afraid to fly? Whatever had I been thinking? After what I had just gone through, I found it hard to believe that I had ever been afraid of anything. I leaned forward in my seat and reached underneath to retrieve my purse that had been hiding there throughout the short trip home, desperately wishing that it had been me under there instead. And as I stood to wait my turn to deplane, the gentleman who had been sitting just behind my seat was standing in the aisle behind me motioning for me to go first. Oh, he must not of had a clue as to who I was or what I had just done, obviously, for if he *had* known, wouldn't he then have stuck his foot out into the aisle and tripped me just when I took my first step? Yup, he sure as hell would have and then he might have stepped, placing his large foot directly in the small of my back, bent over while I was laying face down on the floor of that airplane and very quietly whispered in my ear, "Coward," as he then would have proceeded to step with all of his weight on my back to get out of there and as far away from me as he could have possibly gotten.

Yup the guilt was looming stronger than I could have ever imagined it could, but I got a slight reprieve as I stepped out into the looming vast energy of the terminal and saw a friendly face. And I had forgotten just how friendly until he locked his arms around me and whispered in my ear, "I'm so glad you're home," and for just a moment, the previous three weeks seemed to be somewhat of a very sick and twisted nightmare.

As we walked to the area where I was to retrieve my luggage, my husband asked questions about my state of mind, as well as my dad's. Gosh, what do you say to someone about your state of mind in a situation such as that? Quite frankly I had forgotten just exactly what in the hell a state of mind was. Oh, I might have said, I've become somewhat of a sinister lunatic in that all I think about anymore is death and how it will happen to each and every one of us—oh, and my dad? Well, he's dying but just fine. You know, dwindling away to nothing but a shell, and did I mention that besides the fact that he looks like Twiggy's brother he really is doing well even if he does sleep about twenty-three fricking hours a day, which in turn just might account for the Betty Davis bags under my eyes. So, my state of mind? Oh hell, it's simply become nothing but a mere pile of happy horse pooh!

We actually chatted about the sadness of things in between grabbing the luggage and walking around all those nameless strangers before he motioned with a wave of his arm for us to exit the big doors leading to the outside. But before I left the terminal, I glanced back at all of my friends whom I'd never met and I felt sort of sad. Because even though they *were*, in fact, strangers, they were people, and I missed being around people—living, breathing, and probably for the most part—healthy people.

It was the end of October and as I stepped out into the crisp night air, I looked all around in every direction, turning in a complete circle with my arms out to my sides, taking in the beauty of the snow-capped mountains under the light of the beautiful full moon. I was indeed so very glad to be home. And as we drove away from the airport, I caught a glimpse of that full moon once again and I swear it seemed to be following me. We actually did not go home that night. Instead, we headed in the direction of home, however my husband made a slight detour and we ended up on the twentieth floor of a beautiful hotel suite for the night with a picture window the length of the room, so that I could view the mountains in the morning while having my coffee. He thought that I might need some alone time to unwind and gather my thoughts before I went racing back into the swing of things. Good damned thing someone was thinking for me, because I was on autopilot somewhere between Southern California and hell!

We lay on the bed that night, in front of the open sky and talked into the wee hours of the morning before we finally fell asleep. It felt good to have someone to confide in who understood my loneliness and my sorrow over all of the things that had taken place in my life. Someone who wasn't familiar with death, someone who, like me, could not bring himself to believe that it was almost over. And I must confess that as we lay there, sharing stories and enjoying each other's long awaited company, in the back of my mind, I wondered what my dad was doing.

The next morning, I awoke to a beautiful sunrise just beginning to peek over the mountains and I looked at the clock. Four thirty. Geeze, I had a built-in alarm. I sat on the side of the bed gathering my thoughts before I got up and walked over to the coffee pot to turn it on. I was excited at the thought of seeing my children. I was excited at the thought of how very excited *they* would be when I walked through the door unexpectedly. Yes, the guilt seemed to be finally giving in to reality. Hallelujah!

At seven o'clock, I phoned my dad's house. The witch said that he had gotten up only once during the night. Strange, I thought, but that thought was quickly dismissed as I noticed my husband beginning to stir, leading me back to the conversation, making promises to call around lunchtime.

Throughout the next week, these phone calls would take place at least three times a day and always with the same results. He was continually sleeping. Perhaps that is why each and every day seemed to slip by with no sense of urgency to return.

At least once a day, I also phoned the hospice nurse. And with each and every phone call it became very clear that my dad wasn't responding to a whole hell of a lot anymore. He was waking up only to go to the bathroom and then back to bed. When I asked if he had said anything the reply was always "No."

Overnight, he had become only a breathing body. He didn't talk, he didn't share any thoughts, and he didn't—well—he didn't do much of anything, he simply existed.

The reunion with my children was full of excitement and conversations taking place all at the same time. They all seemed to be running in four completely different directions, wanting to show me schoolwork papers and just about anything else they could get their hands on to make me sit there forever. (Forever, only when someone dies.)

At last came the questions I had been dreading. The questions about Grandpa. And, believe it or not, some of those questions not even I could answer. Questions like: "When will he finally go to heaven? Why is he still holding on? Why did someone like Grandpa get cancer?" And all of a sudden I felt a deep compassion and need for my hospice friends. Leave it to a child to stump even Einstein!

It took me really no time at all to feel at home again. Yes, even in a home where it was obvious that they had done perfectly fine without me. The floors were clean, the beds were made, and the laundry had been caught up, probably for the first time in eight years or so it seemed and it wasn't long before I was fitting in again, into a world that harbored no sadness, no sorrow, no pain, and most of all, no death! However, in the back of my heart and mind, hidden away in a dark tiny corner, there was always my dad, a memory that came alive three times a day and then dwindled again. And I'll tell you something else, my friends. Not one day went by that I didn't wonder if I could have handled the emotion involved watching my dad do nothing but sleep. And each and every time that thought crossed my mind, I was indeed, once again, very glad to be home.

That Tuesday, I was scheduled to fly back to Ontario, however, I too had recently been diagnosed with a serious illness (when it rains it pours) that needed a specialist's attention and it just so happened that he was only in on Tuesdays. So I had to postpone my flight to take care of the matters at hand.

On Wednesday, I spoke with the hospice nurse and she shared with me during that conversation that she couldn't see any significant decline in my dad's health. He was simply sleeping the rest of his life away. She said that she wished she could tell me when and how, but she couldn't.

Well, for Pete's sake, of course she couldn't. For crying out loud! How many times was I going to put her through this? But I *wanted* her to tell me. Oh, how I wanted her to be able to give me all of the answers. Our conversation finally ended with her telling me that if there was time they would call and possibly I would be able to make it before he died. Then, with grave sincerity she said, "And then again, there might be no warning at all and you have to decide if you can live with that circumstance if it happens."

I told her that that was something I had to decide within my own heart. She, as always, understood, as well as agreed, and with that, we hung up.

Come Friday, I had made the decision to go back. (Some people never learn, I guess.) I made arrangements to fly out on Monday morning. That would have given me a full week at home and I felt that although it wasn't really fair to the kids, it was fair enough considering the circumstances. We'd had Halloween together and what in the hell did fair mean anymore anyway? God only knows; I, myself, had forgotten long ago.

In my mind, I knew that if my dad went before Monday, then it was meant to be and if he didn't, then that too was meant to be. Some lunatic, car-racing maniac Indian had told me that once so I knew it to be true. Famous last words.

The weekend had already come and gone and by Sunday evening, I had begun packing once again. I had gone to the market that afternoon and bought groceries including the ingredients for a new recipe I had planned to prepare for that evening's dinner. Guilt had prompted me to want to cook one great last surprise meal for the family before I gallivanted off for NutVille again as sick as it was. Damn, I've said it before and I just have to say it again: Guilt, shame, and fear can turn a somewhat ordinary person into an extraordinary weirdo! I hate to cook!

The excitement was building slowly with each and every hour that went by as I realized that the very next day I would be with my dad again. I would once again, stroke his wrinkled face and kiss his withered cheek taking in his scent, while tears of absolute victory would coddle my tired eyes. I would kiss his hands and rub his back until those lopsided cows finally—and this time *really* did—walk back up that hillside. I was going to be able to savor just a few more weeks of his wonderful love. I had won!

I called and spoke to the witch earlier that afternoon and I had asked her to wake him up while I was on the phone and to tell him that I would be there the following day. Hesitant, she asked why, and not hesitant at all, I told her because! With a heavy sigh, she walked into his bedroom and I heard her gently calling his name, once, twice, three times, before he finally gave her a faint and groggy reply. I heard his voice and I was thrown back into wherever it was from where I had come. Hell, I think. Faintly, as if she was holding her hand over the receiver, I heard her through muffled tones telling my dad that I would be there the next day. And through the same muffled tone, I heard him reply, "Oh, goody!" Oh, goody? Yes, he *had* said,

"Oh, goody!" He was glad I was coming! Hold on, Dad, I wanted to scream! We have beaten time as well as death! And he knew it as well as I did! Was there nothing that could stop this dynamic duo? We made it!

I packed a few items such as pictures of the kids, and a few little treasures that they wanted to send to Grandpa and as I was doing so, I got a tickle of excitement. I would be on my way to see my dad the next morning and he was still alive! I was overwhelmed with the feeling of triumph. And as I headed for the kitchen to prepare dinner feeling as if nothing in the world could go wrong, I whispered under my breath, "Hold on, Dad."

It was coming up on five o'clock and I had just taken dinner out of the oven. The kids were outside in the backyard playing and my husband was laying on the couch, enjoying a movie as I called to him that dinner would be ready soon, making jokes about using him for a guinea pig and for a split second, I found myself wishing that my dad could taste what I had just created.

It just all of a sudden crossed my mind of how very much he once enjoyed a Sunday dinner. I mean to tell you, I could actually hear his voice booming with compliments. He was saying, "This is good stuff, dear!" Followed with a very impressed, "MmmMmm!" One of those Oklahoma boy compliments that make you feel good all over. It was five o'clock exactly. And I know it was five o'clock exactly because as I turned from the sink to the stove I felt like one of the kids had snuck up behind me, so I whirled around to say boo, like you do when you want to get the best of someone first when they sneak up behind you, but—there was no one there. No one! A chill—or perhaps I should say, more like a sensation, filled me with despair. I was bewildered and quickly checked with darting eyes to make sure no one had seen me do such a silly thing. As I turned very slowly back to the sink, sort of tilting my head to one side trying to shake the feeling of—well—bewilderment, I just so happened to look at the clock. It was one of those moments in my life that I will never forget, and I would imagine it's due to the chain of events that followed, for at twenty minutes after the hour the phone rang and my life, as I had known it, would never again be the same.

With my hands full of dinner preparation, I picked up the receiver with my thumb and forefinger and placed it on my shoulder. Tilting my head to hold it in place, I said, "Hello?" Nothing. And then again with a little bit of irritation in my voice, "Hello?" I said for the second time, feeling my impatience rising along with the tone in my voice, when very quietly, someone on the other end of the phone said, "Hello," back to me. It was a very soft and muffled "hello." It was not a happy "hello." As a matter of fact, it was the kind of "hello" you never forget. It was the kind of hello that Stephen King writes about, the kind of hello that nightmares are made of. It was the kind of hello that makes the first four letters of its name very proud.

It sort of sounded like my uncle, I thought.

"Is that you?" I asked.

"Yes," he said, in an almost comforting tone, "it's me."

Knowing that he would be picking me up at the airport in the morning, I simply assumed (so badly prayed) that he was calling to confirm a time. That's all, I told myself. Just calling to confirm what time my stinking damned flight was due in and nothing more. Nothing more! But somehow I knew. Something else way back in the corner of my heart was telling me, screaming at me. I felt it. Its sinister presence was there with me, inside of me, lurking, just waiting to pounce.

Cautiously, with my heart pounding so loudly I couldn't hear my own self think, I asked, "What's up?" Trying to sound like me or at least who me had always been and in the very blink of an eye, he spoke the words that would forever be embossed in my memory. The very smallest yet two most powerful words I will never forget because they ripped through my heart with such an impact that the damage could never be restored.

With all of the compassion and love he could muster, he cleared his throat (NO!), and in a soft but monotone voice (Please, God, NO!), he flatly spit it out like one would spit out a piece of pepper that had been lingering on one's tongue, more than glad to be rid of it.

"Buddy's gone."

And just like that, my daddy, my buddy, was indeed gone. The all-knowing, monster-fighting, dumbest, gadget-loving, cancer-beaten janitor and best friend in the whole wide world had finally been swept away. And swept away with him, like the rush of an autumn wind, was surely a piece of me. How very precious each and every breath we take truly is, for it can be our last in an instant. And please, for the love of God, if you walk away from this story with anything at all, please, please, take that with you.

I wish I could be writing some dramatic, or perhaps more compassionate words as I share this most intimate as well as painful part of my story with you, but I can't. Because once someone has passed away, there really is no other way to put it. They are simply gone. And no matter who the storyteller, there just really isn't any other way to share such a tragedy. No words are sufficient enough to illustrate the pain, the agony and the heartache that is felt. I believe that only God, himself, could create the appropriate words because they are just lifeless, as is the subject they portray.

The floor seemed to give way as the room began to spin and I heard a scream come from deep within the bowels of hell only to realize that it was my own as I fell to my knees crawling, whimpering, screaming, moaning the cry of disbelief. "NO"!!!!!

Dropping the phone and somehow dinner all over the floor, the room continued to spin and for an instant I thought this had to be some kind of a sick joke. He couldn't have died. It wasn't time to say good-bye! I had to go there tomorrow. He had said "Oh, goody!" We had more to say, more to do. We had beaten time together, just me and him! It couldn't be time, damn it! It wasn't time! It wasn't time! It just damned well wasn't time!

Still on my knees, in a low moan, I cried, "NO"!!!!! again with my husband now standing over me, his hands up under my arms, trying to somehow lift me from the place I had chosen to fall. Pushing his hands away from me, I crawled to the receiver, picking it up again, but his time like it carried a disease and I slowly put it back up to my ear, crying and sobbing uncontrollably, trying to form the words in my confused brain.

Hearing my uncle on the other end of the line asking if I was there and if I was all right, I ignored his questions asking him when? How? And then dropping the phone again, pounding my fists into the kitchen floor, I screamed, "I can't believe it!" And then wails of "Oh, Dad," echoed throughout my home.

He was gone, my friends! Just like that—my dad had slipped away and I hadn't been there nor had I even expected it. He vanished from my life and I hadn't gotten to say good-bye again. And I wanted to, damn it! I wanted to say good-bye just one–more–time! I so desperately wanted, needed to kiss him just one more time. Take his face in my hands and see him smile that smile that only he could portray. And I wonder just how many *one–more–times* I would have wanted, if he had not in fact died that evening. Just how many one more times do we all truly think God would give to us? Well, I can tell you that there aren't enough one more times in the universe to cover that want, that wish, or that need. And isn't that just the way life is? Because no matter how someone goes, with warning like I had, or without, there is always that need and desperation to say just one more thing, to touch them just one more time. To smell their scent and hold them in our arms just one more heart forsaking minute!

Lord knows I knew it was coming just as well as the good Lord knows we didn't leave a stone unturned. Not in this place anyway. But that's the hell of losing someone we love. The finalization of life and the realization that there just isn't going to be one more time. Our one more times had been given and used up. I hate it with every ounce of despair I have inside me, but the fact still remains and it is true.

Trying to gather what little sense I could, I fumbled to pick the receiver back up off the floor attempting just one more time to talk to my uncle, who was obviously hurting too. I hated the words that waited for me at the other end of the line. I hated my uncle. I hated myself and I hated my dad for leaving!

Crawling around on the floor, looking for something solid to pull myself up on, I realized that my husband was gently and carefully helping me up to a standing position. Then, leading me slowly to a kitchen chair, he sat me down and put the phone to my ear, trying to steady my hands. Slowly and quietly I told my uncle I was there. I'm sorry, was the first thing he said to me. Of course he was sorry, for crying out loud! He had just lost his own brother! My God, he was there in the very place where my dad's body was still laying! But I didn't care. Not one damned bit. I had just lost my dad, and no one could be hurting more than me.

I carefully, with tears screaming throughout my soul, tried to compose myself, but all that came out of my mouth, were silly words, questions that probably could have waited, but for some reason didn't. How did it happen? Did he know he was going? Did he hurt? Did he gasp? And for the very love of God, did he call for me or scream my name? And all over again the tears began to flow as I wailed, "Oh God, I can't believe it!!!!! Why didn't you wait for me?!!!!!"

"He died peacefully in his sleep," my uncle was saying, his voice wavering and cracking as he tried to speak. "One minute he was there, and the next, he was gone, just like that." And then he added, "He left just like he said he would." He was alone.

Yes, just exactly like he said he would indeed.

He was alone, in that wonderful garden of memories he had created for himself, tucked snugly and comfortably in his gadget of a bed. It was perfect. He would simply roll over, pull his blanket up around his swollen little neck and go to sleep, the nap of all naps, without a single worry in the world. His silly little story-believing girl was home and safe with her family. There were no more stories to tell, no more monsters to fight, no more pipes to smoke, no more bathroom trips to make, no more back rubs, no more one last things to do. No more worries. None–what–so– ever–at–all! The ice cream had melted long ago and he was so tired, so sleepy. He just needed to take a little nap until he saw someone he knew and they would take him by the hand leading him finally, beyond the waiting area. He never looked back. He didn't have to. Where he was going he didn't have to endure a lifetime of pain from losing his family to the one and only monster he just didn't have the strength to destroy. He would never again have to endure the heartache of losing his one and only true love to that very same monster and best of all, he would never again have to go to sleep wondering about the safety of those five sweet little brown-eyed baby doll girls. The front lines were ready and secure. The artillery was spit shined and polished. Private First Classman Eddie Littlefield was ready for inspection. Everything was done, finally, once and for all. And I just know beyond a shadow of a doubt that somewhere in heaven, standing next to a Budweiser stand, waiting for him, was an old army mule by the name of John.

# Chapter Twenty-Two

## *Alone*

*I must plough my furrow alone. That is my fate, agreeable*
*or the reverse; but before I get to the end of that furrow*
*it is possible that I may find myself not alone.*

Lord Rosebery 1847–1929 (Archibald Philip
Primrose, 5th Earl of Rosebery)

J UST LIKE UNCOMFORTABLE silence, there are uncomfortable good-byes. How do you hang up with someone who just lost his or her brother? Someone who is holding you up when his or her own heart is breaking? Well, you simply just say good-bye. Something I was becoming very good at. What's worse is the silence that looms inside of you once that connection has been broken.

Sitting alone in my kitchen that night is a feeling I will never forget yet one that I don't care to remember. Being alone is a most horrible thing after someone dies. You can't call them up to tell them that you just don't like it and can't do it so will they please come back just for a little while until you get used to the idea. No, sadly, we can't. It sure would be great if we could but we can't. End of conversation.

But was I really alone? I mean, perhaps I felt lonely but truly and surely I wasn't really alone. I had my family. My husband was busily picking dinner up off the floor making sure to brush me with an occasional touch or grace the top of my head with an occasional kiss. I had my children, who were all out playing somewhere. Somewhere where the news of death hadn't yet touched them. And I had my sisters.

My sisters! My God, I hadn't even thought. I didn't want to think. I didn't know what to say and besides, I didn't want to say anything anyway. All I could do is let go of that river of silent rage that had been building up inside of me. Someone had to call them. Someone had to tell them, someone else besides me. I couldn't say the words. Because if I said those horrible words then all of this would be real. What was I going to do? I was in such a state of disbelief that I wanted to just pick up the phone and call my dad. He'd know what to do for sure! Because he was my knight in shining overalls! My monster fighter! My storytelling, dumbest, hardest-working janitor in the whole wide world of stinking worlds! Damn! Damn! Damn! This just couldn't be happening! I wanted him back! Now! He never told me what to do here in this place after he died. He never shared with me how to call and tell his pride and joys of 1968, five—count 'em, my friend—with all fingers spread apart, arm extended and out in front of him—I got five beautiful brown-eyed baby doll girls! My God, this wasn't happening. Couldn't he make up just one more gosh damned silly-ass story to make it all seem OK? Sure he would and then we'd go get some ice cream and everything would just work itself out. But those days were gone forever and somewhere deep down inside—I damned well knew it.

How do you tell a daughter that her dad has just died? (Buddy's gone.) I simply wanted all of this to go away. Just like the cancer. I didn't want to deal with any of it. I still couldn't believe he was gone. I couldn't fathom it. This all just had to be a bad dream and it was, the nightmare of all nightmares. But thus began those little chores that I spoke of in the beginning of my story. You know, the ones that are most likely responsible for your insanity? Yup, those ones.

In between breaking down and crying at the realization that the time had actually arrived, I, of course, phoned my oldest sister first. My sissy. My Glinda the Good Witch! She'd know what to do. She'd take over and handle this whole gosh damned out-of-control situation once and for all! The all-knowing and all-powerful wizard was gone but alas, Glinda the Good Witch was still there with wand in hand. Thank God.

When she came on the line, I couldn't speak. I got her name out and that's all I needed to do as she assured me that she was on her way, without a moment's hesitation, not even a question. I never spoke a word to her, other than saying her name.

My fingers then found their way to the secret code that would connect me to the baby. My dad's baby, the bride of all brides. And his last experience of justifiable pride on this earth, as she answered the phone with a cheery "Hello," before I proceeded to demolish that cheer with two simple words. "He's gone." And then, just like my father's life, our connection became silent and still. Lifeless, before she finally said something. Minutes don't really matter after someone dies. Time just happens to run amok.

"I'll be right there, after I call the other girls," is all she solemnly said to me, before I was faced once again with the deadly hum of a lonely dial tone. Relieved that I didn't have to call anyone else, I then dropped the receiver back onto the cradle, drew my knees up close to my chest, rocked, cried, and waited.

I am thankful that my children hadn't been in the house when the phone call from hell had come through. Thankful that they had been somewhere else out in a wonderland of happy. It simply gave me some time to form the words. And as I shared with each of them, individually that Grandpa had finally gone to his last and final janitorial job in the sky, I realized that things weren't really as bad as they seemed. Yes, things could have truly been worse. I had never lost a child. And as I cupped my hand over the wetness of each of their cheeks, brushing their tears with the soft touch of my thumb, I silently thanked God for reminding me of this.

We all expect to lose our parents someday. It's practically a given. Losing a child has only happened to me in my worst of the most unimaginable nightmares. Yet, I know that there are some of you who have suffered the unimaginable and lost a precious child. How very thoughtless of me to go on in such a way about just my father. I pray that the very grace of God blesses each and every one of you with strength as well as courage for in spite of the context of this story, *you,* my friends, are the true heroes. I would now like to end this paragraph with just a moment of silence for all of you and I'd also like to share with all of you a sweet reminder. My dad is now in heaven too. Perhaps God has assigned a new keeper of the children.

\*\*\*\*\*\*\*\*\*\*\*\*\*\*\*\*\*\*\*\*\*\*\*\*\*\*\*\*\*\*\*\*\*\*\*\*\*\*\*\*\*\*\*\*\*\*\*\*\*\*\*\*\*\*\*\*\*\*\*\*\*\*\*\*\*\*\*\*\*\*

I have often wondered why I took my father's passing so hard. I mean, other people have lost loved ones and they didn't carry on like the world had ended. Nor did they feel the need to write a book on the subject. Well, I can't explain it myself, because I don't really know why. Maybe it's because I had never lost anyone close to me before my dad. Maybe it's because before his passing, death scared the living hell out of me—or maybe it's because he was so much like a child, that I truly felt I was losing not a father but an actual piece of my childhood. After all, without him, I wouldn't have had a childhood, an imagination, nor would I have known the magic that I have now shared with all of you. So, for now, we'll simply throw this one to the wind.

As I sat waiting for my big sister to arrive, my husband made sure to intermittently remind me of all of the wonderful treasures my dad had shared with me, also making sure to remind me that he had now gone on to a better place. A place he liked visiting. A place where he knew he was going and wanted to be. A place where children made Christmas toys and really could talk to the man in the moon—I had known that place once too. It was heaven right here on earth.

Three of my sisters showed up all at the same time. The middle sister once again, did not come. Talk about throwing reasons to the wind— better yet, read the epilogue.

I can't really remember what took place after that. I guess the same things that take place after someone dies, perhaps a lot of laughter, along with the tears that come from reminiscing. And, of course, questions. Perhaps the same questions that all of you may have. How did he actually go?

Well, just exactly like he said he would. He was alone. And as for the time and the place and the day, well, you can all decide for yourselves.

He died on a Sunday evening at five o'clock, suppertime. And Sunday evening suppertime to an old Oklahoma boy is the best. And he died in the peaceful serenity of his own bed. Coincidence? Perhaps, however, his wife (yes, I said his wife) had somehow described an exact replay of the night I had been there thinking it was his last; "the dry run," as I refer to it now.

She had gone in to wake him, yet he did not respond to her touch nor to the sound of her voice. Thirty second intervals between breaths and his grayish skin tone sent her rushing to the phone. She called hospice and when she returned—he was gone. Just like that. He had waited for her to leave the room. And in spite of the goings on that happened between his wife and me, after my father's death, my heart went out to her. I was thankful then—and I am thankful to this very day that I was not there. I couldn't have and still cannot imagine.

Long after the other two girls went home, my big sis and I sat watching the wedding video into the early morning hours of a rainy day and Monday (always get me down). She sat with me on the couch, arms locked together, comforting me with her words of wisdom, trying desperately to see signs of life in my eyes as we sat in the dark of my family room, playing the tape over and over again and again.

Gosh, my dad was proud. And what a silly man he was as he tapped my new brother-in-law on the shoulder during the bride and groom's first dance and when the groom stepped aside, giving his bride to her father, my dad grabbed *him* instead and began dancing. Portrait of an absolute jackass, my mom would say. But I just simply call them precious memories. My sis commented on how she couldn't believe he had done that. She went on to say that no one should ever interrupt the bride and groom's first dance. Nope, I guess they shouldn't, I thought, but my dad did and that was simply that. He had been somewhat of an embarrassment to each and every one of us at different stages in our lives. Until we got older—and then those silly little bits and pieces of embarrassment that formed his personality became cherished memories. And I can tell you all right–here–and–now, that I would give anything to see him do something embarrassing just one more time.

That first night was the longest and the most difficult, although the night before his funeral could have given it a good run for its money. We must have sat there for hours, playing that tape over and over again, pausing it completely still from time to time to capture a smile or one of his funny faces and I will never forget how it felt to be able to keep him alive at the touch of a button. And when it came time to finally turn it off, the screen fell silent with an eerie stillness. It was over. Just like his life. And I sat there, long after my sis had gone home, alone, in the darkness consumed in the comparison.

I couldn't really sleep that night. My mind was too busy trying to grasp the reality of the tragedy. I would doze off only to be suddenly awakened by a memory or a dream. I finally gave up around five thirty, rising wearily from my sofa and stumbling to the coffee pot. I got as far as the cabinet to grab a mug, when the violent rage of tears began to flow once more. I just couldn't believe it was over. I couldn't seem to grasp the fact that I would never again be able to pick up the phone on a Sunday morning and call my dad. I would never again hear him call me baby doll or nitwit or dumb-dumb. He would never again, take me by my hands swinging me around, singing "You Are My Sunshine." I positively, absolutely knew beyond a shadow of a doubt that I was dying inside. I felt so—alone.

I poured my coffee through my haze of tears and suddenly realized that I didn't want to sit or stand anywhere. I simply just didn't want to be, period. But I had to do something, for my tears were turning to sobs and my sobs soon turned into hysteria and my hysteria turned to sorrow and my sorrow sent me lurching for the counter as I lost the strength in my legs to hold me up. And there I stood (crouched) grasping the counter for strength on the morning after my father had died. This is what loss can do to a person.

There is a certain indescribable aura of hopelessness that hovers after the loss of life. It's as though the air itself is different. Like the whole world will change in one way or another because of the loss of one single person. I believe that with all of my heart—and that's all I have to say about that!

I grabbed my cup of coffee and managed to stumble into the living room, making sure to steer completely clear of the couch where we had sat so many times together and enjoyed the morning sunshine. Instead, I strolled over to the rocking chair, set my coffee on the table in front of me, sat down, put my face in my hands and simply cried. And I cried until I couldn't cry anymore. That first morning after losing someone just has to the very worst. It is the very first day that we wake up in this place, here on earth, without our loved one. We realize that they are gone and there isn't a damned thing we can do about it. And ever so sneakily, time just seems to trudge forward without our permission.

When I felt the comfort of a second wind, I tried to regain some composure. And as I sat there I realized that it was finally happening.

It was me sitting there experiencing the mourning process. Then I felt somewhat of a little chuckle in my heart as I thought about me mourning in the morning and how, if I had said that to my dad, how he would have given me one of those looks of his and then he would have shaken his head from side to side proclaiming that there must be something really wrong with me. I halfheartedly made an attempt to laugh at how he would of then probably mumbled something about my mother and just at that very thought, I missed him terribly all over again and I knew that I had to get on that plane and go to his house and he wouldn't be there— and then—I began to cry, all over again.

I spent most of the morning crying, packing, and preparing to leave. The mood in my house was quiet and solemn. The kids stayed home from school but you would have never known it. It was like a morgue. Now, how in the hell did I know that? I had never even been in a morgue. Not yet anyway. Oh, and what a treat that will be when we get there, folks.

By nine thirty, I was ready to go. I kissed my children one by one, so very thankful for them, remembering what God had so tenderly reminded me of the day before and headed for the airport. But this time, there was no chaos and this time I didn't feel the urgency that I had experienced four weeks prior. No this time there was no reason for any urgency at all now, was there? The atmosphere was calm and organized as well as orderly as we all robotically kissed each other good-bye and prepared our hearts for this separation just one more time. And perhaps it was my imagination, but I could swear I felt a different sort of caring between my family and I that day as I walked out the door to face what we had all come to realize could happen to any one of us. Yes, come to think of it, I am positive that we had all come face to face with the fact that death is so very final, so very looming and so very mean and lonely.

When I arrived at the airport and began my long walk through the terminal once again, I happened upon all of my nameless friends once again, all hustling about, heading for their own appointed destinations, but this time I didn't have the heart to stand in the middle of the airport and exclaim anything. Nope, this time I sadly just dragged myself to the gate and very quietly waited to board. I did, however, feel the incredible urge to thank everyone for their support. It's finally over I would've said, he's gone, I'm devastated and—well, it's just finally over. And then, all of my stranger friends would have hung their heads in disbelief and went their separate ways. Perhaps some of them would have walked by to maybe brush a caring hand across my back or maybe even some of them, probably an elderly person, might have even brushed a caring palm across my cheek. Maybe. For sure though, all of them, each and every single one, would have felt so very sorry for me. I just know it.

I said my good-byes to only my husband this time, as I prepared to board. He and my Glinda would be flying out together later on in the week for the funeral. Huh, the funeral. Weird thought.

There was no lingering at the gate this time. Nor were there any misgivings about who I was or who I might be when I came back. Strange as it seemed, I knew exactly who I was and exactly who I would be when I returned this time, as I hugged and kissed my forever friend and headed down the ramp to board the contraption that would be taking me into the very bowels of hell.

My flight was lonely. As a matter of fact, I can't remember the last time I felt so alone. Well, maybe if I tried hard enough I could have—but those times just like this time was a memory better left un-remembered.

Airborne, staring out the window at the clouds, and feeling like I didn't have a friend in the world, I wondered if my dad just might be out there somewhere. Being up high, closer to heaven made me feel like I could talk to him, call out to him, "I know you're there, Dad," but I didn't. No, I couldn't actually do that and mostly because I was sitting next to one of those nice elderly people who had so tenderly brushed my cheek back at the terminal, and I didn't want her to have a full-blown heart attack a gazillion feet up in the air, and surely not on my account, anyway. I already had one death on my conscience and I truly didn't need another one. Now, why in the heck had I thought that? Why in the name of St. Peter should I have felt guilty about anything? Well, I'm not real sure. But I did. I felt like I damned well should have been there and that's all I have to say about that! Well, for now anyway.

When my flight landed in Ontario and I stood to deplane, I looked around for the guy who had stepped on my back a week before. I was safe! He was nowhere to be seen. Lucky me. My uncle however, was somewhere to be seen as I trotted down the steps from the plane, straight for his arms. And as I buried my face into the softness of his shoulder it occurred to me how very tired he must be of saying good-bye to his loved ones. Perhaps it was the look in that old Indian's eyes that told the very story of those losses, for his brother's death was grimly peering at me through his very soul.

We exchanged few words as we walked to the carousel to retrieve my luggage and then headed for the car. Strange I thought, just exactly what was there to really say? Nothing but maybe, geeze it's so hard to believe it's finally over. Then again, was it really? Should it have been? Shouldn't we have expected this? I mean after all, we did have plenty of time, plenty of warning. Yes indeed we truly did. And I'm sure there are those of you who are still sitting there in some sort of disbelief as well. So why in heaven's name should anyone of us have felt, well—shocked? Well, I'll tell you why: just because we are sitting on a train track and we hear and see the train coming—surely doesn't mean that it will hurt any less when it hits! That's why!

I looked around the airport at all of my nameless friends once again. Were they shocked? No, at least they didn't seem to be as they all hustled about retrieving their luggage and heading for their own destinations. Perhaps they knew the answer to this perplexed question. Perhaps as they were shuffling out of the terminal one of them, probably the spokesperson for all nameless friends, might have just brushed by me, pausing just for a second, tilting their head to one side and quietly whispering into my ear, *Preparation, my dear. You told us yourself at the very beginning of this story that there is never enough time to prepare to say good-bye to someone we love,* they might have said. And then, patting me on the back, wouldn't that spokesperson have then, as they were walking away, waved a warning finger in the air high above their head exclaiming, *You shouldn't have left! You needed more time! It wasn't him, it was you! It was damned sure and absolutely all you!* Perhaps.

The drive to my dad's house was long, lonely and silent as it occurred to me that this wasn't his part of the world anymore. This place no longer held any meaning for me. It had simply become just somewhere else. After this week, I doubted if I would ever have another reason to return. Why in the heck would I? He had gone and left me alone. And just how in the hell does someone feel alone in Southern California? Beats the heck right out of me. I guess the same way someone feels alone in a car with someone else who loved and had just lost the very same someone you just loved and lost and had not one thing at all to say. Doesn't make one damned bit of sense now, does it? Of course it doesn't. Well, unless of course we can think realistically and just simply ask ourselves—just what in the hell did I expect him to say? And I wasn't really alone, now, was I? Well, of course I wasn't. The Indian was there in the car with me and he was driving and yet I felt that surely no one else, including him, could have possibly felt like I was feeling. No, surely not! And truly the rest of the world seemed to go about their business just like nothing at all had happened. I couldn't believe it! My dad had just passed away and the world just didn't seem to care! There had been no special news report interrupting the Sunday evening movie, not one single representative from the White House called to offer condolences and worst of all that damned stinking symphony orchestra never did get their freaking act together. Bob Barker continued to host the flipping *Price is Right* and Andy Griffith continued to portray that stupid, dumb-ass *Matlock* and neither one of them even having a clue to the fact that they had just lost a most loyal and cherished best friend of all best friends! What I really wanted to know quite simply and actually, was how? How in the Sam hell did the world continue to turn when my dad had just died? That was all. And then it hit me. That was it! That was why I felt so alone! Because I was. We all are after losing someone we love because our relationship with them is truly unique and one of a kind no matter who they are. I was alone and lonely and sad and miserable and angry as well as guilty and no amount of anything what–so–ever–at–all was going to change that. And I would unknowingly at the time, continue to feel that way long after those lop sided, silly ass cows finally did come home.

Now, hold on to your aching hearts, ladies and gents, as we prepare to go forward through our journey, closing this chapter with a quote of my own.

"Perhaps it's who we *choose* to be and not who we *really are* that creates the mourning process." M. Tote 1958- "When It's Time to Say Good-Bye" (ch 22)

# Chapter Twenty-Three

## *Journey*

*Whenever I prepare for a journey I prepare as though for death.*
*Should I never return, all is in order. This is what life has taught me.*

Katherine Mansfield (Kathleen Mansfield Beauchamp)
1886–1923 Journal 29 Jan. (1922) pg. 224

A S WE ROUNDED the corner turning into the tidy, little, mobile home park, I panicked as I realized that the very same neighborhood that had once been such a nice place for my dad to have lived had sadly now become a nice place for my dad to have died.

Was there a different feel to this wonderland of his past? Yes, I believe there was. It was final and no longer full of hope as we passed each and every dwelling. I no longer had the capability to change the future—for what I had once so desperately wanted to change had already happened.

We pulled up in front of what used to be my father's home and my heart began to pound as his little paradise seemed to be saying something to me. What was it? Was the canopy above the window actually drooping? Yes, I believe it was. Had the little flowers in the flowerbeds always been so dry and lifeless? And the mailbox—it was—it seemed to be leaning with its tongue hanging open in a frozen cry or scream of disbelief. Yes, my dad's once well-kept and tidy little home had taken on a ghostly image of some kind. This home was speaking to me. It was saying he's gone, daughter of Eddie, and I no longer have a reason to stand proud.

I sat in the car for just a moment as dry leaves blew hastily across the little street, as if scattering the news throughout the community. Now, gazing through the window, not able to take my eyes off the house, I slowly began to emerge, holding on to the door for security. Lingering with some of the remaining leaves, I stood and looked around before I leaned back into the car to retrieve my purse. *My God, how could this be happening?*

When I stood upright, clinging once again to the car door, I summoned the courage to turn and face the front door. I had to go in there. I glanced around once more as if I were waiting for some savior who was very late and in doing so, my eyes finally panned toward the carport and I truly thought my heart was going to stop beating, as my eyes met the hallow and glooming headlights of that old Chevy Pickup.

There it sat, with its lifeless stare, silently still. I slowly and methodically strolled toward the comfort it had to offer, totally mesmerized as my eyes were fixed upon my dad's oldest and dearest friend, with its once purring engine looming of emptiness and silence as it seemed to be mourning its loss in the quiet confines of the carport. And as I stood over the hood, gently brushing my hand along the front of the grill, the memory of a reunion spread across my lips in the form of a smile.

I slowly turned from the truck and faced the steps that led up to the front door. Staring at them as though they had taken on the appearance of snakes, I hesitated, as I knew what I now had to do.

My uncle was patiently waiting, holding my suitcase with the understanding of a saint. When our eyes met, he gave me a longing gaze as if he wished he could bring him back. I in return gave him forgiving looks of "I know you can't" as I began the journey of my green mile.

I put one hand on the railing and one foot on the first step and stood there with a memory pushing its way into the forefront of my mind. It was during the first week of my stay and my dad and I were sitting on the top step having coffee one morning. We sat and chatted about the birds and the air and how the world was going to hell in a handbasket when we both all of a sudden fell silent, enjoying the quiet and the fresh morning air. After about five minutes or so, my dad put his hand on my knee and in a raspy whisper, he said, "A penny for your thoughts." And you know it was a funny conversation after that because I then had to share with him that I had been thinking about how his wrinkly old feet had been carrying him around for seventy-two years and I had found that to be so very amazing. He called me a couple of names, stood up and turned to go back inside shaking his head and mumbling something to the tune of how he didn't understand who I had inherited my ignorance from. And the last thing I heard him say as he closed the screen door behind him was "Must have been your mother." I got a little chuckle in my heart as I began to take those very same steps, one at a time, knowing in my heart that an empty house lay ahead of me and that only my memories were left to keep him alive.

Suddenly, I found myself standing at the very threshold of insanity.

Taking hold of the slender handle, I slid the screen door to the left and stepped into reality pushing the curtains aside as not to take in their smell—his smell. I didn't want to breathe as I slowly looked around his home, my home, the last home we had ever shared together—however— the need for air brutally overcame my resistance. It was no use. *I had to breathe—most people do in order to continue living.* I closed my eyes and took in a deep breath and as I opened my eyes the tiny hallway that led to his bedroom came into view and another memory was cued by a slight ghostly path that *really* had begun to form in the carpet from the sofa to the bedroom door.

The smell of this place overwhelmed my senses with warm and powerful memories—of *him*. Him: my old and tired knight in shining overalls - my brave and now sleeping monster fighter. Him: my all knowing—and all-powerful—dad.

With my arms falling down to my sides in total despair, I slowly walked over to his chair and on the arm of that chair rested his cherished headphones. On the back of that chair lay his blanket. Faintly aware that my uncle was now standing beside me, I picked up that soft bundle of memories and held it close to my face—took in another deep breath and began to cry. I didn't want to exist. I didn't want to be there anymore, and I didn't want to be home either. I simply just didn't want to be—period.

What was I to do? This home was so tiny that there really was nowhere to go to get away. No matter where you stood, you were right smack-dab in the middle of nothing but memories. I wanted to run, but there was nowhere to run to. I wanted to hide, but where? I didn't want to sit down because then my eyes would be forced to look around. So—I did nothing. I simply stood there with my dad's blanket huddled up under my chin and I cried.

My uncle was trying to give me the space I needed when I turned and looked at him and realized that he had the same dilemma. Where could he go? Nowhere really. So he just simply stood there as well. Maybe he was preparing to catch me just in case I fainted dead on the floor, which is exactly what I truly wanted to do. Why was he standing there like that? Why was my father's witch—and now also his widow—sitting motionless on the sofa just staring at the floor? Had she been there when I came in? Why hadn't she at least said something? Anything! And yet she hadn't—had she? And my uncle was just as silent. How about a hug or something? Isn't that what people do when there's been a loss? Sure it is. I saw it all the time on TV. But she didn't make one move to get up off that couch and to be quite and sadly truthful with all of you, I'm glad she didn't. My days of being nice to her and trying to understand her were over—just like my father's life. And I don't think she really wanted me to anyway.

It seemed as though they were waiting for something, like they knew something that I didn't. But what? What more could there possibly be? And then—it hit me.

Like a hurricane of gut ripping, hair-thrashing, heart-stopping emotional winds—it hit me, slugged me, kicked me! The bedroom!

I glanced just a few feet away from where I was standing and for the very first time since I had come to this place, his place, this home, the bedroom door was closed. Shut tight. Just like his life.

Still clutching the blanket close to my nose, with tiny sniffles jerking my shoulders back and forth, I peered up from my foxhole of cotton and tried to hide from the idea of going near there. So many times I had wondered how I would do it. How would I go in there with him gone? And it seemed that that time was now here.

Maybe I didn't have to go. There were no rules that said I had to take that journey. I actually never had to go in there again if I didn't want to. Problem was that I did have to. I had to because I knew if I didn't—if I never passed through that door again, I wouldn't—couldn't—be sure he was truly gone. Oh God, why did I always have to be so damned sure about everything? Hell, if he was still in there then he could just call me up on the phone, once he was feeling better and if I were to never receive that phone call then wouldn't that have been good enough? Uh huh, sure it would have, as nice people in bleached white coats carefully served me my meals three times a day through a tiny window of my dwelling door, making sure not to spill anything on my plush padded surroundings. I had to go in there. Sadly and mostly because I had been raised in a world where nothing is as it seems. I had to be sure. I had to go. I had to get it over with.

Still standing, holding on to his blanket like my very life depended on its security, my eyes met the Indian's. I pleadingly shook my head from side to side with the fear of realization streaming down each cheek.

"I don't want to," I whispered.

"I know," he said, "Whenever you are ready."

OK, how 'bout never? Because at that very moment I truly felt like *never* would do just fine. I glanced at the widow witch and she wouldn't look at me. And I was just about to say something nice to her like: I'm sure you are so very hurting as well or—I'm sorry—or—well, anything nice at all until she just simply and very coldly said to the floor, "Go on in—he's not there." At that very given moment—I truly thought I just might finally, once and for all—just get it over with and slap the crap right out of her. But I didn't. No. Sadly—I simply and very cautiously, as if those snakes had come back, started for the bedroom. *Please be in there. Please can't you make up just one more stinking damned fairy tale and we will be done with all of this nonsense once and for all?* Now standing before the very door that for sure opened into the very bowels of hell, I began wringing the blanket with both hands, shifting my weight from one foot to another. *(I do believe in spooks, I do believe in spooks, I do, I do, I do believe in spooks.)*

I knew what waited for me beyond that door was the very same room where we had spent so many wonderful hours together. Where we had laughed together and cried together and told stories to one another. A place where we had touched each others hearts with all we had to offer and clung—groped—at life for all it was worth. I placed my grip tightly on the knob and slowly turned until it popped.

Pushing with what little strength I had left inside my trembling arms, I opened the door and stepped through its powerful threshold as a rush of Borkum Riff threw me into confusion. His smell! His very existence consumed my senses. I felt dizzy as I stood paralyzed, eyes closed, unable to move until finally, I fearfully opened my eyes—and—he wasn't there!

All that remained of the world's greatest monster-fighting, storytelling, dumbest janitor in the whole entire universe, was his disheveled bed, his belongings and—and—well—his feeling, his past existence—his memory.

Suddenly I found myself at the side of his bed, and now falling onto the very same sheets where he had taken his last deep and tired breath. Taking hold of his pillow, I curled up into a ball, pulled the covers up around my shoulders and laid there rocking—plain and simply crying for my daddy.

Through sobbing and muffled tears I wailed, "I want my dad!" And with that, my uncle quietly walked over, closed the bedroom door and pulled up a chair.

"I want him back," I screamed, as if someone could actually have produced him just to quiet me. "Just for a little minute," I pleaded. "P-l-e-a-s-e," I begged! "Just one more minute," I sobbed. "I–just–want– to–kiss–him–good-bye!" And as I lay there crying, my mind wandered back to a cold winter's morning of long ago.

I had been sleeping until the rumbling of my dad's jeep traveling down our long gravel driveway woke me with a start. Panicked and half asleep, I leaped to my chubby little feet, racing from my bed to the bedroom window, only to see the tail lights of his jeep disappear into the early morning fog. I was devastated and I began to cry. "Wait, wait, Daddy, I forgot to kiss you!" I screamed, banging my tightly closed fists on the closed and fogged up window. But it was too late. He had already gone. I was devastated.

Now, with that memory swarming about my already pounding head, also came a reprieve of comfort when I further recalled his homecoming that evening as he wearily walked through our kitchen door, plopping his old metal lunch pail down on the counter. I could still recall the feel of his overalls as I clung to his legs. I could feel his hands on my tiny back as I desperately held on trying to explain how

I missed kissing him good-bye that morning. And I could still smell his Borkum Riff-scented cheek as he stooped down and began kissing me all over, with my head thrown back in laughter with him promising to never leave me again without kissing me good-bye.

Sadly, as I lay there now, eyes closed, swimming in the warmth of my recollection, I realized he had kept his promises. But how was I to ever know that one day *that* kiss good-bye would be his last? How was I to know that one day, he would not be coming back? *How do any of us ever know?* And the tears began to flow freely once again.

Turning my head from the pillow, I saw my uncle stoically sitting in the chair next to the bed gazing at me with sympathetic eyes. Elbows resting on the arms of the chair, hands folded, fingers interlocked together tucked underneath his chin, like he was praying.

Still cradling the pillow snugly close to my chin, I propped myself up against the headboard, legs drawn up tightly as though someone just might try and take it from me.

"I can smell him," I said. "I can feel him here. I want him back, Uncle. I want my dad back," I tearfully whispered.

He leaned forward resting his elbows on his legs and with the understanding and sympathy that only he could portray he reached for my hands, softly patting them and quietly said, "He's not coming back. He's gone."

He was right. He was gone—and no amount of blubbering was going to change that. I was sitting on his empty bed to prove it. But somehow, that just wasn't good enough. No! His memory just wasn't gonna do anything at all for me at that point! I could still feel him! I swear I could! I swear I could! I swear I could!

Perhaps I really could, perhaps this was one of those precious miracles of life. Or perhaps our minds just allow us to think and feel such things only to pacify our hearts. Perhaps. Or perhaps, just perhaps—his existence was indeed very much there. Who's to say?

Drying my eyes and trying to focus on my surroundings, my gaze found its way to the table next to the bed and I began visually going through my dad's belongings. His change jar, his reading glasses that I rarely saw him use, his ashtray and—his pipe—in that ashtray exactly where he had left it. His pipe. That wonderful retired smoke stack of my father's very being. I reached over, picked it up—closed my eyes and put it to my lips. Emotion began surging as its billowing antique and lingering ghost cascaded throughout my already broken heart and I began to sob once again.

My uncle sat motionless, eyes fixed on me, not speaking. What could he say?

Finally, breaking the silence, with my dad's chimney proudly protruding from between my lips, I quietly muffled, "Where is he, Uncle? Do you think he's here?"

"Do you feel he is?" he replied.

"Yes," I said. "I think I do."

"Then he is," said the Indian with much compassion.

"But I want him to be *here* with *me* now," I said.

And without a moment's hesitation, not even skipping a beat, my uncle replied, "He will always be with you. Each and every time you smile—and—each and every time you give your children an understanding ear, he'll be there. Each and every time you laugh or do something silly, he'll be there. Once in a while," he continued, "You might even catch yourself using one of his phrases or you will admire something that he would have admired and you might all of a sudden say, boy, Dad would have loved that! He will always be with you and his memory will grow to become a part of your personality. That is the true cycle of life."

So there we all have it, straight from the Indian's mouth. And how in the hell he got all of that out so sincerely with me sitting there with that pipe dangling from my lips is beyond me.

I continued to sit there in the comfort of my dad's bed for a very long time, pondering, contemplating (pipe in mouth, rubbing my chin, just like he used to do), and then finally deciding it was time to go. It was time to leave this place now. I had finally faced my biggest and most horrifying hurdle. (Or so I thought at the time anyway.) It was indeed over. And as I carefully placed the pillow back up against the headboard, giving it a final but loving pat, also placing my pipe back in the ashtray, I glanced over beside the end table and there sat Joe, the orangutan, my dad's most loyal companion.

It saddened my heart so, to see Joe sitting there alone, never again to be addressed by my funny and imaginative little dad. And as I stood up from the bed to exit the room, I smiled a most inspiring smile at the simple thought of my dad's memory living on through his lifeless little friends. What a legacy he had left behind, I thought to myself, as I now stopped and turned to take a final and forgiving look at what had once been our haven. With my hand resting on the doorknob I simply just stood and stared before I pulled the door shut behind me like the end of not just a chapter this time, but a complete novel, one of those in which the good guy dies. And as I did so, I couldn't help but wonder if all of the stuffed animals in the world would now come alive forever as their sleeping master would continue to sleep forever. Watch 'em close, folks— while you lay waiting at night to hear your house settling noises—and for the love of God, listen to your children!

I laid on the couch that night wide awake, long after my uncle had gone home and the widow witch had gone to bed in that chamber of horrors that used to be such a place of solace and comfort and memories. But I wasn't listening for house settling noises as I laid there. I was simply recalling memories; memories of our long and tedious journey swarming throughout my tired mind. The hell we had gone through only to lose the battle. The good times we shared in this place even though we were right smack-dab in the middle of a war. One might wonder why, I suppose. Why did we try so hard and fight so long only to succumb to this in the end? Well, my guess would have to be because it's all simply part of the journey. No one really knows how and when his or her journey will end. But it will. It's inevitable. It's all in the plan.

I searched my tiny surroundings for answers until I just couldn't take anymore. Sitting amongst all of my dad's cherished belongings it suddenly dawned on me that they weren't cherished by him anymore— but by me. His turntable sat completely still, his headphones lay across the arm of his chair not crackling anymore, but deathly silent. All of his furry little soldiers sat so still and lifeless. Everything was still and lifeless, lifeless like forever—only when someone dies. At that thought, I reached over, took my dad's blanket off the back of my dad's chair, tucked it up under my chin and as I reminisced my dad's life, I finally fell asleep on what used to be my dad's couch. And I'm not sure, but I could swear that my dad's house made settling noises throughout the rest of the night just as sure as I was that shortly after I had fallen asleep, his stuffed animals came to life.

# Chapter Twenty-Four

## *Perserverance*

*Perseverance, n, continuance, permanence, firmness, stability, constancy, steadiness, tenacity or singleness of purpose, persistence, plodding, patience, industry, pertinacity, gameness, pluck, stamina, backbone, indefatigability, bulldog courage, sand, grit, patience, determination, Colloq., stick-to-itiveness.*

Roget's College Thesaurus in Dictionary Form Encyclopedic Edition Grosset & Dunlap 1975 printing page 262

T HE NEXT MORNING I awoke with a start. I was so tired that I had forgotten why I was there and I somehow thought I had slept through the night without hearing my dad! And then it hit me! I would never hear my dad again. And all of a sudden I became all too well aware of that present and looming cloud of sorrow that followed me to the coffee pot—again.

Accompanying that sorrow was also a flood of tears and I believe I decided on that very morning that I really didn't like waking up that way. It's an awful way to wake up. I mean, no one really likes to feel sad to begin with—but to wake up feeling sad has got to be the worst! And I don't know about all of you, but beginning my day with tears isn't exactly my idea of a good time. But there was something else. Something even more treacherous than sadness was bubbling inside of me. Hard to believe, I know. Yes, ladies and gents, the guilt had arrived! Like a bubbling volcano of emotion—and, oh, how I don't ever want to feel that way again. I just couldn't shake the image of my dad's final seconds.

All I could conjure up in my beedy little mind, was how my dad might have wanted me there during his final moments. And I was actually able to get a visual going of my dad frantically searching the room for me, wondering how I could have left him. Oh, I was doing a fine job of beating the hell out of myself alrighty. I had become a prizefighter overnight.

Through tear hazy eyes, I stumbled my way to the couch, sat down, holding my coffee cup with both hands unsteadily in my lap and glanced down the hallway toward the bedroom door—wondering. Did he wake up at the last second realizing he wasn't going to take another breath? Did he try to call for me? Was I the last thought on his mind? Did I let him down? Was he scared? Would I—could I—ever stop blaming myself? And, quite frankly, I just couldn't take one more thought along those lines; I finally reached for the phone and dialed the hospice number.

The receptionist answered and just upon hearing my voice she immediately expressed her sorrow regarding the loss of my father as she then asked me to stay on the line while she paged our social worker.

Gosh, I thought, as I sat listening to how a summer breeze could make me feel fine (liars), word sure travels fast down there at hospice headquarters. What in the hell must they do, post a death notice on the bulletin board in the break room? Sure, they must! I mean after all—this *was* hospice. Heaven's own travel agency, with plane-less flights departing at all different times of the day and night. Ticket-less travel for sure! No lines, no pushing, no shoving. When your number comes up, you simply go!

My rude and uncalled for emotions were interrupted as the social worker came on the line with her soothing and sympathetic voice.

"Hi, honey," she tenderly quipped. "How are you holding up?"

"Not very well," I said, beginning to sob as I tried to speak. Nope, not very well at all. As a matter of fact, "honey" was on the very brink of a nervous breakdown, because somewhere between last night and this morning, silly little dumb-ass "honey" had gotten the silly little dumb-ass notion that she somehow failed her silly little dumb-ass father!

She was talking now, saying something to the tune of, "It's OK to cry. Just to feel is all you can do and don't fight whatever it is you are feeling." Uh huh, sure enough, sweetheart, I sure as hell won't even begin to try and fight this overwhelming surge of guilt. Nope, not at all. As a matter of fact, I'll keep right on feeling this way until I politely and studiously walk right into the bathroom, grab my dad's razor and carefully put an end to my own sick and pathetic life! Of course, not much could have happened had I done so, due to the stinking fact that my dad never even owned a razor! And I can't recall the last time I ever heard of someone ending their sick and pathetic life with an electric Remington—for the very love of God!

I finally got a hold of myself just long enough to be able to share with her that I was feeling very guilty. She was shocked! She was astounded! She couldn't believe it!

"After all you've gone through with your father, why in the world would you feel guilty?" she asked.

Great question actually. But I didn't have one iota of a clue when it came to the answer. This was genius stumping game show material here. I began with telling her about my vision of my dad's last moments and I shared with her that I didn't think I should have left him.

The other end of the line fell silent. My God, I thought, I've killed her too! But then after taking just a moment to clear her throat, she began to do what she was so very qualified to do. She began to educate, pacify, and nurture.

"Your dad would not have wanted you to feel this way," she began with just a hint of anxiety in her voice. "Your job was done. All business between you and your dad had been exhausted. He knew it—and I think somewhere deep down inside, you knew it too. There was no reason for you to hang around any longer. You leaving is what your dad was waiting for, don't you see? He outwardly admitted to you that he feared for you to be there when he died and then he even tested you. He wanted you to go home to your kids. And believe you me, something tells me that if your dad had wanted you to be there when he died, he would have waited for you. But he didn't, did he? He knew you were coming back but there was just no more to be said between the two of you. So he left. He told you he would choose the time and the place and the day. And he did. You gave him everything he could have possibly wanted from a daughter and he obviously felt satisfied. And I also know that your dad would feel very sad if he knew you were feeling any guilt at all." She continued, "So, you can justify your tears of sorrow, but certainly not tears of guilt. You are going to be just fine," she said. "It hurts to lose someone we love—and God only knows that you and your dad had something very special and unique between the two of you. So mourn him and cry and miss him. This is all very normal—but *you* of all people—should not feel even an ounce of guilt."

Well, I did so hope she was quite finished. And I suppose she had to be, simply because there just didn't seem to be anything else that was left to be said. She had pretty much said it all. And the absolutely horrifying reality of what she had just said—had been true. Now, doesn't that just bang your shutters? Well, I don't mind telling you that it surely banged mine, because I got to thinking about it and she was right. My dad would have, in fact, been so very disappointed in me had he been there to see me feeling and acting this way. I could just imagine him giving me one of those looks and asking me why? Why in the name of God would you be feeling guilty, you dumb-dumb, he would have said. And then he just might of gotten up out of his chair and walked back to his bedroom, shaking his head from side to side in disbelief, mumbling something about my mother once again. Yes, I do believe he just might have done so.

Therefore, I said my good-byes to the social worker, hung up from that conversation, reached deep inside my soul and pulled out all of the guilt that had been festering inside of me—and tossed it over my shoulder. And that was the last I ever felt of it again. Another lesson learned. And I believe for each and every one of us, the lesson is different. Soul searching is an individual task and an exhausting task at that! So, my advice is this: Don't stop until you have searched long enough to find all the answers. It will certainly pay off in the long run. I said so. And I just happen to consider myself an expert on the subject of soul searching. And so the story goes for the umpteenth time.

I spent the rest of my morning trying to decide what to do next. Shouldn't there be something to do after someone dies? I mean besides crying, vomiting and sitting on the couch rocking back and forth? Well, one would think so. And just about the time I was ready to give up vomiting in exchange for diarrhea, the phone rang. It was the nurse. Our nurse. Our angelic little miracle worker, calling to see how I was doing. I'm telling you, they must have some sort of PA system over there. She suggested we go get some coffee and breakfast. "Let's get you the heck out of there for a while," she said. "I'll come pick you up." *(Someone must have tipped her off about the Remington.)*

After hanging up the phone, excited about getting out of there for a while, I walked over to the kitchen sink and rinsed out my coffee cup and while doing so, I heard a faint but audible conversation coming from the bedroom and it startled me just a tad bit in that—well—who was talking in there? Well, it was the widow witch and she was on the phone. She must have been sitting in there waiting for me to get off the phone with the nurse. How could she even go in that room? Never mind that—who was she talking to so privately that she had to call them from the bedroom? Damien!!!! She was probably talking to that no good louse of a son of hers who had taken a swing at my dad one day long ago!!! Oh, great! Now I was thinking like my mother. No person is a no good louse. That wasn't like me to call names or judge anyone. What in the hell had come over me? I mean besides the death of my father? I asked for God's forgiveness as I snuck a tad bit closer to the bedroom as so I could hear—just a little better. Holy crap! The widow witch was laughing—no wait—giggling! I had never heard her laugh out loud. Hell—she sounded almost human! And I couldn't hear through her whispered giggles exactly what was being said but I had a sick feeling in the pit of my stomach that she wasn't talking to her son. Not to mention the fact that she was giggling? I couldn't have even conjured up a half smirk let alone a giggle! Her husband—my father—had just died, for hell's sake! And about that time—just before I truly thought I really could walk into the bathroom and just try and give the old Remington a shot—the nurse came to the door.

Sitting in the coffee shop, trying to eat and function as a normal human being, I just couldn't believe that the time I had been dreading had finally arrived. I couldn't believe that my dad was finally gone. I couldn't believe nor could I understand what had just happened at the house before I left—and most of all—I couldn't believe that I was actually sitting in a restaurant, picking through my breakfast, across from an earth angel, discussing my dad's funeral. Funerals are an odd sort of discussion by far to begin with anyway. I mean, who would ever think that the decisions that have to be made would, in fact, *be* the decisions that have to be made? Confused? Well, so was I, and little did I know it at the time—but I was about to embark on the most challenging of all challenges thus far. In more ways than one!

I gazed out through the big picture window from time to time, admiring the beautiful day and I was amazed at how it didn't seem to matter to others. Every one was hustling about to their appointed destinations without even stopping by to offer their condolences. Instead, all of the nameless strangers simply went about their day, when, in fact, my world had simply stopped turning. Funny isn't it? OK, maybe it's not really so funny. Bad choice of words—again.

When I got back to the house, I bid my hospice friend a farewell, telling her I would see her at the funeral. Lord, that sounded so unfeeling. Hey, I'll see you at the funeral—and maybe afterward we can throw up together, or do something really fun like jump out of an airplane with no parachute!

The phone was ringing as I walked through the door but my attention was diverted as the strong smell of Borkum Riff consumed my senses once again. What— and—how? That pipe hadn't been lit for—I picked up the phone glancing around in confusion as I was saying "Hello?" It was a man. Oh, and not just any man—it was a man who was asking for my father's widow (where was she now?) or myself. A man who never even knew the likes of Eddie—until he had arrived—quiet and still—so unlike my dad at all. It was the representative from the funeral home. And let me share with you, that after this conversation, something tells me that *had* this guy ever met my dad—my dad just may have scared the living hoopla right out of him.

Offering his condolences (*thanks*), he introduced himself and had some questions regarding the preparation of my fathers' body. (*Oh, geeze.*) Sitting down on the couch now simply because my legs had no other choice, I asked what sort of preparation? Well, he continued with graveness that only people like him can portray (no pun intended), he needed to know if they should embalm the body. Oh—my—God!

You have got to be kidding me. Don't you people just do that stuff automatically? I mean, isn't there a Rules and Regs book laying around there somewhere in that godforsaken place? Why in the name of Saint George, or Curious George, or any old George for that matter—would I have to answer that question? OK, look I've got a great idea, don't do anything with the body, how about them apples, huh, Fella? Just leave it alone for–the–very–love–of–God!

I calmly (mostly because these guys quickly rub off on you), yes, very calmly indeed—asked, "Well, what does it entail?"

Dead silence. Oh, my hell—I've killed him too! Stuttering, or perhaps he was actually choking, he replied with an unbelievable, "I beg your pardon?"

OK, so he was a hard-of-hearing funeral parlor guy. No problem—let me rephrase it.

"I simply want (need) to know what embalming entails," I said.

"How and why do you need to do it?" I asked.

He studiously cleared his throat again or perhaps he was throwing up—I'm not real sure as he then informed me that he had never been asked that question before. Well, at least not by a family member of one of their guests. Guests? Well, howdeedoo! Welcome to the Hotel California! Wasn't that cute? My dad had become someone's little overnight guest! Wasn't that special? Well—sweety cakes—hold on to your hat, because you have never had to bury someone like my father before.

"Listen," I said, "please try and understand that this isn't just any old someone we are talking about here. This is," I paused, choking, attempting to clear my throat, "was my dad." And then unwillingly, I began to cry.

Stuttering for just a few seconds he apologized and began to explain that they needed to embalm the body as soon as possible because it preserved the look of the deceased. Now, of course, he continued, if the casket would be closed then there would be no need. Silence again, only this time it was on my end and I hadn't killed myself.

"Uh huh," I finally said, "how is it done?"

Again he nervously cleared his throat and slowly began to speak.

"What do you mean?" he asked. Oh boy, this guy wasn't just hard of hearing—he was downright—well—hard of hearing!

OK, here we go—"How–is–it–done?" I pried.

"Oh," he said, like I had just woken him up, "You mean the procedure?"

Hey, you're catching on—thanks for waking up to answer my questions you dumb-ass funeral guy you!

"Yes," I stammered, blubbering like a baby, "the procedure."

"Well," he said, clearing his throat once more, "Uh let's see—an incision is made under the arm or in the neck and the fluid is then injected into the body."

"Do they have to take my dad's blood away?" I asked, still crying, sounding like a child asking a doctor if it was going to hurt.

"No," he said sympathetically. "There is no need for that." I think he was coming around. I do believe I was hearing just a hint of sorrow in his voice.

"OK," I said simply, still sniffling.

"Please understand," he begged, "It's just that—well—usually people don't ask me these questions."

Poor guy, he had absolutely no clue what he was in for.

OK, I thought, sure I understand. I mean, why would these things be important to someone else? Hey, maybe they weren't. But they sure as hell were important to me. This was my dad we were talking about here! And his body had been his temple for seventy-two years! The cancer had already destroyed what God had so tenderly and perfectly created and so, I simply wanted (needed) to know just exactly what in the hell was going to be done to my dad's body *now*— and *why*—and *how*?

Why was that so difficult to understand? And it wasn't over yet, folks, because then came the million-dollar question. The burning and churning question of the flipping decade.

"And just one more question," he urged. "What do you wish the deceased be buried in?" he politely asked.

"A casket, I suppose," I quipped.

He chuckled a bit or gagged—I really couldn't tell which before he said, "No, I mean clothing."

Here we go—I thought.

"Nothing," I said. "My father's wishes were to be buried in the nude." Put that in your pipe and smoke it, Fella!

He was choking again, I think. Either that or he truly *was* vomiting this time as he stammered that this was not normal. "This was just not done," he murmured, as I could just imagine him pacing back and forth wringing his hands.

"What do you mean it's not done?" I asked just a little defensively.

"Well," he began, "usually the deceased is buried in *something*, anything—but never in the nude!"

Well, welcome to Eddies' World, Fella! Where anything goes! A place where you can talk to stuffed animals and they can talk back, a place where monsters in the closet are done away with once and for all! A wonderland where the Boogeyman always gets a home with some little kid who will actually love him simply because he was misunderstood! A world where children die and go to heaven only to make toys for Santa Claus! A land where all the clothes you will ever need are a pair of jean overalls, a white T-shirt and tennis shoes. Yes, siree, in Eddie's World, the very top of the flipping corporate ladder is no higher than the Head of Maintenance and the highest grade you will ever have to accomplish in school is the flipping tenth grade, so that you could enter the United States Army simply to support your loving mother! So as you can see, in Eddie's World it is perfectly acceptable to be buried in the nude, simply because that's the way he came into the world and by God, that's the way he was damned well going out!

OK, it was time for me to inhale and exhale, inhale and exhale.

You know, I just don't get it. You pay thousands of dollars for a funeral, and let's face it, sometimes the insurance policy doesn't pay for the funeral as it did not in my dad's case, and therefore most of us just don't have this kind of money sitting around in a funeral fund, like a vacation fund. So isn't it usually our savings or vacation fund that we have to dip into for such emergencies?

So it's bad enough that you have to deal with a loss, but on top of that you have to come up with money that you don't *really* have. Then, for the real kicker—some guy who buries people for a living is not only gladly taking your money, but he is also telling you how *not* to spend it.

What should they care how my dad is buried? This matter-of-factly pissed me off to no end. Not like we couldn't already tell. So I very calmly, very politely and very stoically informed this gentleman that my dad would, in fact, be buried buck stinking naked! Like it or not pal, my dad is going out of this world the very same way he came in and simply because that's the very way he damned well wanted it! End of conversation, end of paragraph, end of story!

Thinking that I had just jumped and cleared my only hurdle, I thanked him for his understanding that he actually had not really yet given and then we made an appointment to come in and make arrangements for the service. You know, pick out the casket, write the obituary, snort some arsenic—a regular fun-filled day.

And that's when my next hurdle slapped me in the legs sending me tripping face first into the dirt.

"Before we hang up," he asked, "what sort of service do you have in mind?"

OK, I thought, now I'll get some respect. Now we'll get somewhere, as I proudly announced to him that my America-loving, patriotic little dad was to have a military burial. Huh, didn't know you'd been talking to the daughter of a World War II Vet now, did ya, Fella?

"Oh," he blurted out, "How many years?"

Uh huh, got your attention now—don't I?

With a lump the size of Texas in my throat, I proudly exclaimed, "Six." Not exactly a long time, I realize, however, they were some of the most important years in my dad's life, as we all know. So I felt it only fair to clue him in. I mean, after all, he hadn't yet had the opportunity to read this book.

Silence again. What in the Sam hell was wrong now? Must be choked up. It was understandable. I was really starting to warm up to this guy. I was even thinking that I may end up liking him—and that's when he knocked the wind out of me. Just when you think you like someone and wham, they send you tumbling into Ireallydon'tlikeyouville!

"I'm sorry, Miss," he said, with honest to goodness sympathy, "your father didn't serve long enough in the Armed Forces to receive a burial with military honors."

What in the hell had he just said? I truly thought my hearing had gone out on me.

"What?" I asked in a tone as though he had just told me that Martians had just landed and peed on his leg. Please repeat that because I think the audio portion of our conversation just shorted out. Silly me, I could've sworn you just said that my dad had not served long enough to receive full military honors.

Well, my friends, I didn't misunderstand. I heard him right—and you all read it right. That is exactly what he had just said to me. It was true. My dad had to be a retired serviceman to receive a military burial. Holy caribou poop! What in the hell?

Oh, I think I get it. Let's review this, shall we? It doesn't matter that he fought in World War Two. It doesn't matter that for six long years he put his life on the line for his country, because he just simply didn't do it long enough. Huh, interesting. Well, all I have to say about that is that you can bet your bottom dollar that every serviceman who ever served and died within six years or two months for that matter, just might beg to stinking well differ with that. However, they aren't here anymore to defend that little oversight, let alone defend my dad now, are they? No! They sure as hell are not! Because sadly, you see, they were too damned busy dying for our freedom! This was insane! This was the most ridiculous thing I had ever heard of in my entire life! This was absurd! This was preposterous! And to say the least—*this*—was totally unacceptable to me!

Very calmly, once again, I began to try and talk to my newfound friend whom I really didn't like at all! We hadn't gotten off to a very good start, you know? So,

I slowly yet very insistently informed him that come hell or high water, which ever came first, my dad would, in fact, somehow, somewhere, someway, be buried with full military honors. A twenty-one-gun salute would be performed and taps would be played on a shiny brass bugle on a green flipping hillside, if I had to do it myself! Silence again.

"I'm sorry," I chanted with tears now exclaiming my future plans, "I have to try. You just don't understand because you didn't know him—and if you had," I continued, "You'd probably be crying right along with me right now."

Just what in the hell was going on here? I thought the very worst part was over, but believe it or not, this was just the *very* beginning, after the *very* end. Pretty dumb if I do say so myself—and I most certainly do!

After a very long period of silence, except for an occasional sniffle or two on my end, my friend finally spoke again.

"When would you like to have the service?"

"This Saturday," I said as I explained that my sisters and husband would be coming in by Friday evening.

"Let's get together this afternoon," he said, "And maybe we can come up with something." Like what I thought—What in the hell did we have to come up with? What could be so damned difficult about getting someone buried? What was there to talk about, for crying out loud? He was definitely the gatekeeper, as I had visions of him peering through a small window with tears just streaming throughout his long mustache. *Oh, Dorothy, come on in, we'll find the wizard somehow. We'll get you home to Kansas some way!*

Silence again. Then, very slowly and timidly he spoke, "There *is* just—one—more—thing—that you also aren't going to be pleased with," he cowered.

Oh, for the very love of God, what now? Had they lost the body?

"We can't perform a service on the weekend in a national cemetery."

And when I asked why (simply because I guess I never learn), he simply answered me with, he didn't know why. "It's just the way things are." And my only answer to that was; then I guess we'd better be calling the ice-cream man because this was only Tuesday and my sisters couldn't be there until the weekend. That would mean that my cute little corpse of a dad would have to be on ice for a solid week! Oh, geeze, this just wasn't happening! Why, for the very love of Pete, do people make up these stupid rules? Who? Who makes up these stupid rules and why do they even matter? Who gives a goat's hind end what day of the week someone is buried? Yet, my reply was a simple and defeated "OK," as I was already tired and we had only just begun. As a matter of fact, by the time I hung up the phone, I wasn't just tired, but I was worried and exhausted as well.

Hey great—nice chatting with you! Perhaps later on—your people can call my people and we can do—wait a minute—your people are dead! Therefore, they can't possibly call my people now, can they? Ha! No they flipping well can't! So never freaking mind!

An uneasy feeling began making itself very comfortable in the pit of my stomach. What was I going to do? How could I possibly even think of burying my dad without military honors? And had we even settled the clothing thing or had that gentleman conveniently went quickly on to something else hoping I would forget? Had he dismissed me? And as I sat in what used to be my dad's living room on what used to be my dad's sofa, wringing my hands with worry, a silly little thought came to me. (*Hard to believe, I know.*) I was sitting in the *living* room! I was fretting over my father's *death* in the *living* room, just like I had been *mourning* in the *morning*! OK, it was official; I was cracking up! Or—could it have been that I was getting a little help from—well—you know whom? Perhaps.

At two o'clock that afternoon, the widow witch, the Indian, and me *(sounds like a sitcom)* skipped on over to the morgue for a fun-filled day at the funeral parlor. Come one, come all to the greatest show on earth!

When we arrived, pulling into the neatly groomed grounds with its long circular driveway, I wondered if my dad was happy there like it was a flipping nursing home—knit whit! And then another little bed bug of a thought began racing around inside my beady little brain. Surprising isn't it? Where was he? *Oh—my—God! My dad was at this place! Somewhere inside they were holding him hostage!* Getting hold of myself, I thought I had better put that little idea on ice for a while—just like—where in the hell did that come from? Oh God, he must be freezing! Geeze, would I ever grow up? *Hopefully not.*

Strolling up the Durastone walkway (they pave them that way, as not to allow some demented daughter of her deceased father to lose her footing, slipping in the puddles of her own tears, cracking her head on the pavement killing her instantly so she could join her father inside the funeral home freezer!)—as I was saying, strolling up the beautiful and safe Durastone walkway, my legs began to shake and I found myself searching for my tail, frantically wringing the frayed and fluffy end of it, chanting I do believe in spooks, I do believe in spooks, I do, I do, I do believe in spooks—over and over again in my mind. What might it look like in there?

As we approached the double doors of this fine establishment, my uncle grabbed a hold of the vertical brass handle like he was going to arm wrestle it and swung it open wide, as to allow his guests to go in first. *Chicken!*

Once inside, it was beautiful with its marble floors gleaming our reflections. (*Where was he?*) I looked around the silent hallway (*deathly silent*), and spotted my newfound friend pattering his way toward us.

He looked just exactly how I had pictured him with his hair plastered neatly in place, suit pressed and just as quiet natured as his silenced surroundings. (*Deathly silent.*) Must take a lot of guts to work in a place like that, like running a twenty-four-hour sleepover. Cute thought. My dad had probably already made new friends.

Ushering us toward a small room with a circular table, its chairs silently staged around it, anxiously awaiting their prey, he was obviously eager to get this whole ordeal over with as quickly as possible. (*Can't imagine why.*) And never mind that— but do you think that these guys are all related? Somehow, they all look alike. And if they aren't all related in one way or another, I know for sure that they all go to the same tailor. And they all smile the very same way. Like aw, shucks, isn't this just a sad, sad situation?

Even with his aw shucks of a smile, my friend was extremely pleasant as well as accommodating. Must be tough to have to be accommodating to the bereaved. I mean, what in the hell did I expect, maybe a dancing clown, milk, cookies and a nap? Perhaps.

From the very moment we walked through those looming double doors, I couldn't shake the thought of how this just couldn't possibly be happening. Yet, there I was - in the flesh - standing on the beautiful marble floor of a funeral home waiting to make arrangements to bury my dad. And I was absolutely certain it was, in fact, me because I caught a glimpse of myself in the hallway mirror on my way in.

My new friend seated us in the little room where people have to go to carry out the task of which none of us in our right minds enjoy doing. The round table took up most of the room in that little ten-by-ten space. My God, I thought, I'm going to faint. Woman dies from a claustrophobic seizure in local morgue. Boy, wouldn't that be a hoot! Not only would it have been a hoot, but it may also have raised an eyebrow or two as well.

As I pulled my chair out and sat down I noticed a smaller table situated in the corner where there sat a phone as well as literature probably thanking us for choosing their funeral home for our loved one's final resting needs. Now, isn't that rather silly? I mean, think about it—who cares? It's not like the Holiday Inn. Dead bodies reside there! It's a flipping morgue! They are all nice—and they are all neat—and they are all clean—and they are all dead silent! And after someone dies don't we just pick one with or without a brochure? I mean, what if we don't like any of them? What if none of them, not–a–single–one tickled our fancy for our loved one's final resting needs? What would we do then? Not bury Uncle Marvin ever? I told you it seemed silly. And the phone—why would you need a phone? Oh, I know—probably just in case there happened to be an emergency? OK, now, that's funny. An emergency at the morgue—like what in the hell could happen that would require an emergency situation at the morgue? That is flipping hysterical! Just about as hysterical as I had obviously become at that very given moment.

What in the hell was the matter with me? I was freezing. Shivering down to the very core of my bones. As a matter of fact, I can't ever recall being so cold. And I hate more than anything to be cold!

With my arms folded across my chest, waiting for everyone to get seated around our little conference table in our little room my little mind seemed to be playing tricks on little old me. Where was he? I thought I could hear him. And I swear I could smell him! And—I was scared. So afraid of—what? Something—anything, you name it! And all of a sudden I realized just exactly why the brochure, as well as the phone had been placed there. So that my Uncle could read the address of the brochure while he was dialing the phone, calling the funny farm to come and get me!

I was sad. So sad that all of the ice cream in the universe, the North Pole and Cleveland couldn't have done the trick this time. And worst of all, I was worried. Worried about burying my dad without military honors as well as when? When would we be able to bury him? Would his body have to stay in the flipping freezer until Monday? How long could his body take that cold? Oh, this was dreadful, just dreadful! (*We've got to get Dorothy home!*)

You know, through all of my paranoia and hysteria all it amounted to was this: I missed my dad and I wanted him back. I didn't want to be sitting there. I wanted to go home—to his house and sit on the bed with him and laugh. (*Would I ever laugh again?*) I wanted to kiss him and listen to his silly stories. I wanted all of this to go away. And as I sat there shivering, truly hoping that my Uncle wouldn't look over at me during this chilling moment simply because he just may have mistaken my shivers, that had now become full blown shaking body tremors, for a heart attack, something strange happened. Yes, something very strange indeed, for all of a sudden, without a word spoken from anyone, I began to relax.

Out of nowhere came this incredible feeling of warmth. (*I could feel him.*) And not only did I feel warm, but I felt a peace and serenity come over me (*I could smell him.*), that to this very day I truly can not explain it. It was as if someone had thrown a heated blanket over my shivering heart. (*I could hear him.*) And just as comforting, I wasn't afraid anymore, nor was I sad. (*I could see his smile.*) I suddenly and simply felt—well— that I had a job to do and I needed to get it over with. Even with all the turmoil looming over how and when my dad would be buried, my heart simply knew that everything would be OK. Coincidence? Perhaps.

355

We began with filling out a form as to what the obituary for the newspaper would say. *Now, wasn't this going to be a whale of a good time? Halleflippinglujah!* You live seventy-two years and you get a paragraph or two in the *Daily Tribune* What did I expect? Well, quite frankly, I'll tell you. I think everyone who dies should have a movie of his or her life produced. Because I think everyone's time here is so very precious as well as important. Believe you me—we are all important to someone—somewhere—somehow. Of course, then again, all of the endings would be sad and there probably wouldn't be a whole lot of action in most cases and perhaps Hollywood just might have a problem with this. But it's a nice idea anyway—very nice.

We listed my dad's name, his widow, his daughters ("Five, my friend, count 'em—I've got five beautiful brown-eyed baby doll girls"), his grandchildren, and one great grandchild. And as we then came to the part where you list his life accomplishments, I sat there—dumbfounded. How in the name of God do you do that in two or three lines? Where do you start? I mean, that's where this whole story began and I ended up with a novel. So here you go, Dad—the obituary of all obituaries!

Remembering how my dad would simply shake his head in disbelief and marvel at the thought of having so many daughters and grandchildren delivered a smile to my pursed lips. And it also brought a simple thought to my already overloaded brain. Why hadn't we, my dad and I, written his obituary together? What had I been thinking? Criminy sakes alive, we had certainly thought of everything else! OK, everyone, here's another lesson to be learned. Let's not leave it all up to whoever is left behind. Over the next week or two, everyone sit down and write a paragraph or three about your life accomplishments, and hide it away somewhere in your underwear drawer. If we all write what we want people to most remember about us then we won't leave this world with Aunt Emma's haunting story of how we got drunk, picked our nose, passed gas, and then threw up at somebody's bar mitzvah! Get it done!

When it came time to list my dad's occupation, the widow witch stated he was a janitor and I immediately had to object, leading her as well as my Uncle to stare at me like I had just lost my ever-loving mind.

I refused to allow the word janitor to be typed in black and white. Yes, he had indeed been a janitor when he started out, but he sure as hell wasn't one when he had finished twenty-six years of "keeping it kleen." No, siree! He was the head of maintenance, by golly, and that's exactly what I wanted them to print. There was no way in hell my mother was going to get *that* satisfaction! Positively—absolutely—not!

After all of the paper work had been filled out, we then came to the subject I had been dreading, the service itself. Military honors—that prompted the funeral director to pick up the phone (*there is another reason it was there*), and dial Fort

Ord Army Base, leaving a message for the sergeant in charge to return his call. He obviously must have picked up on the fact that I wasn't going to take no for an answer. While we then all sat waiting with fake smiles on our faces, like this guy was going to call back any minute, we were asked to pick out the announcements. Oh, goody, another fun-filled task down at the county morgue!

Now we had another problem because none of those little folded bearers of bad news even came close to sounding like my dad. He was a unique and one of a kind human being, a simple man. These already printed notices informing my dad's friends and relatives that he had departed were all too formal and elegant to represent my father. What in the heck was I to do now? Why did we need them anyway? Another mystery. I mean, everyone who comes to the funeral already knows who's dead. Why do we have to put it in print? Well, I'll tell you why. Because that's the way it's done. I guess it all has something to do with closure. Although I still think it's kind of silly. We can all sit around at the funeral exclaiming how we didn't know that so and so's birthday was when it was. A little late, don't you think? Another lesson to be learned. Ask now!

Trying not to upset anyone with yet another delay, I explained to the funeral director that my dad had always been extremely proud of my writing ability. He loved for me to read my poetry to him and it delighted him so to hear me sing a song I had written (*definitely must have been love, because I can't carry a tune in a wheelbarrow*), and to a man who could hardly spell, I explained, it was an honor that his daughter had such an ability. Therefore, after consulting briefly with the widow witch and the Indian, we decided to take the ones that were blank inside and I, myself, would write my father's farewell message. I knew in my heart what he wanted me to share, so I promised to return soon with a good-bye speech from my dad. And with that little task out of the way, all that was left to do was pick out a casket. What a delightful experience to look forward to, like a day at Disneyland is what this was turning out to be!

Now, I, myself, never had the pleasure or the experience of performing this task so might I say that I wasn't even a little bit anxious to get started. As a matter of fact, standing up in itself was a chore. While waiting for my Uncle, the widow witch and my new friend to all leave our small chamber I was not being polite as much as I was stalling. Stalling for time to get my courage up. Oh, how I so wanted to vomit.

Walking down the long and silent hallway with our shoes making clicking contact with the marble floors it was more than just a little eerie. What in the world could be behind all of those closed doors? (*Where was he?*) Geeze, what a gloomy place. (There's no place like home!)

With no conversation, our friend silently led us to the room farthest down the hallway and to the right. Studiously, he swung the door open and with an arm extended holding that door he invited us to enter first. (*Like hell!*) Stepping past him and into the—*my God, it was a tomb with no bodies!*—tiny, dimly lit room, there were several final sleeping beds crowded neatly about in various areas of the arena of final peace. Why in the hell wasn't there more light? *It wasn't likely that we would wake anyone for Pete's sake!* And why was there music playing so damned soft and gloomy as though it were coaxing us along. *OK, this was downright morbid!*

Once inside, I expected to hear a heavy creaking door slam shut behind us trapping us forever—never to be seen again! Not alive anyway. Yet it didn't. And there we stood, with an assortment of *Dracula's own* staring back at us. Geeze, why don't they just make one model and leave it at that, for crying out loud! I mean, it's not like it really matters until you have to make a choice—and if we didn't have to choose wouldn't what they had on hand just have to be sufficient enough? Well sure it would. But, oh—no! They have to have as many models as there are makes of cars, so that you have no other choice than to be nothing but confused over the whole stinking ordeal. And then the guilt begins to seep in. Geeze how could I live with myself, knowing that I picked the cheapest model for my father's final resting? It's all a conspiracy I tell you! A commie plot! So, with no other choice presented to me, I began to look around at all they had to offer. What an experience. I mean to tell you that this is something I will definitely want to share with my grandchildren!

There was nothing I wanted. All of these dressed up boxes looked like Cadillacs and my dad had been a pick-up man. And while we're on that subject, why are they all lined with silk? My dad had been a cotton man. Nothing really suited the likes of my dad—so what to do now? *Hey*—nothing here seems to suit me really so I figure we'll just leave things as they are. Maybe pay rent or something so he can just stay where he is—on ice—or in the freezer—or—just where in the hell was he anyway?

Really dreading what I was about to have to say to my newfound friend, I slowly inched my way over to him and just stood there for a moment before I leaned close to his shoulder and whispered, "Is this all you have?" Looking at me like I had to be the most ungrateful daughter on the planet, I quickly, before he had a chance to slap my face, expressed my concerns. Putting his hand to his chin, resting his elbow in the crook of his other arm, he looked as though he was actually trying to come up with something—and he did! All of a sudden, he remembered that they had some other models down the hall. Oh, how I hated to leave this room, as I was the first one to hit the door.

The funeral home had been undergoing some construction changes and he had forgotten all about them. Actually, I had to chuckle a bit, as I think that by this time, this poor guy probably hadn't a doubt in his mind that if he didn't find something that suited me and soon, I might just go into the freezer, pick my dad up, throw him over my shoulder and take him home!

He led us back out into the dark and once again clicking hallway, down through a much narrower hallway, where there must have been a least fifteen more caskets lined up along the wall, all blanketed with heavy brown paper to protect them from the sawdust. (Butcher paper at the morgue? Now, that's a hoot and a half!)

One at a time—the widow witch, who by this time was more than ready to have me happily join my father, the Indian, and I took a hold of the heavy paper and carefully lifted the crinkly wrap off each and every casket together, peering ever so carefully underneath each and every one and I'm sure it was only I who had suspicion that there just might be an inhabitant in one of those human Tupperware containers—and at any given moment, someone was without a doubt going to reach out and grab my arm from underneath exclaiming that we were being too damned loud! *Prozac! That had to be the answer.*

Still not finding anything that seemed appropriate, I was losing faith as we strolled along the wall coming to the end of our selections— and then—there it was! I knew it the minute I laid eyes on it. It was magnificent and I thought I just might pee my pants as we struggled to lift the heavy paper completely off it to reveal its deep pine luster and beautiful brass handles. It was a simple, yet beautiful piece of wood. No, wait a minute—I actually heard my dad say, "Wow, what a beautiful piece of wood. Man, that's nice, dear!"

Could have been my environment, yet I know I heard him just as plain as day. Quickly glancing at the Indian and the widow witch, to see if they might have heard it too, hoping they may have heard it too, praying for the very love of God that they heard it too—but they didn't. Or if they did they didn't let on because they were simply standing there, holding the weighty paper up looking at me and I must have looked like I'd heard a ghost because my uncle asked me if I was all right. *Huh, let me think—uh, no! No I wasn't all right! Of course not, you stupid dumb-ass Indian, because you see, people who hear dead voices talking to them aren't really all there let alone all right, now, are they?* I know I heard my dad and what was worse—was I know I felt him and the worst chill of all horrific chills raced up and down my back and arms like it had a destination. And then came the tears. I have no clue why, but I began to spill tiny droplets of weariness from my tired eyes.

Looking at my uncle, I said, "This is the one, isn't it?" Half asking a question, as he and the widow witch agreed yet reluctantly so, trying to understand my tears. Clearing my throat, I quipped, "I can just hear Dad now. He would think that this is a beautiful piece of wood, it's so simple and so beautiful," I whimpered.

Coming to my aid, my newfound friend rushed to pull the paper completely off the casket. I think this poor guy had either developed compassion over the past twenty minutes or he was just damned glad we had finally made a decision. Whatever the case may have been, his task revealed a once hidden beauty in its entirety.

Now, completely in view, I ran my hand over the top of it and all the way down the length of its Pledge shine. With butterflies swarming about my stomach, I then did something that I, myself, couldn't understand and mostly because, as you all well know, I'm a coward. I reached underneath, feeling for the seal (*how creepy*) and with a soft, yet audible pop, I lifted the top half of the casket upward. It didn't creek like in the movies nor did a ghoulish someone inside sit straight up and grab my hand. Instead, it propped open quite nicely—revealing not a silk lining—but, to my surprise, cotton! An off-white cotton lining with a cotton pillow and on the inside of the top half of the casket that I had just so carefully raised, was the painted image of a leafless tree. A beautiful tree, standing all alone.

A rush of something (realization) suddenly made me dizzy for just a moment as I stood there gazing upon my dad's final napping place knowing that this simple box would soon be cradling him in eternal darkness. And I have to say if you ever need a wake-up call, go casket shopping!

I turned to look at my friend who was hastily wiping his brow with a hanky. "How much?" I asked.

"Twelve hundred dollars," he whispered.

I looked at the Indian, he looked at the widow witch and she in turn looked at me before we all gave simultaneous and agreeing nods. This would, in fact, be the one. It was simple, yet elegant, and it may not have purred like the roar of a now forgotten and silent friend, but it was fitting for the occasion at hand.

As my friend began marking model numbers down on a pad just as fast as his nimble fingers could go, I interrupted his concentration with another question. Still writing yet turning a listening ear toward me as if to say, *Go ahead,* I hesitantly asked him to open the bottom half of the casket. He turned toward me now, looking up from his order pad, with a furrowed brow informing me instantly that I had undoubtedly done it again.

"Let me guess," I said, "People don't usually ask?"

"No," he said, "But no problem, I'll lift it up for you."

Hell, he probably would have spit shined and polished it had I asked him to. Relax, I didn't. Its sheen was just fine. I simply needed to see where the rest of my dad would go. I haven't a clue in snow's hell as to why. I guess just because I needed to at the time.

He slowly unlatched the bottom portion of the top of the casket and lifted the heavy wood to reveal the rest of the inside. It was just the same throughout, billowy and soft and—short? Yes, I did believe this casket appeared to be a little shorter than most. And as that thought began to give me great comfort, I noticed a small cotton bag at the foot of this final resting place, a small cotton bag with a drawstring.

Taking another risk of upsetting the balance of things, pointing to the bag I asked, "What's that for?"

Still writing on the pad without looking up *(just how in the hell long does it take to order a casket anyway?),* my friend proudly announced, "That's where we place the feet of the deceased." Like he had invented the damned thing. And although I didn't understand why, this time I didn't ask. No, this time I simply thought to myself how nice it was that my dad's feet would be kept warm.

Finally finishing his order, my friend tucked the pad away into his coat pocket, gently lowered the lid back down until it rested in place and then half covered it back up with the heavy paper as he then turned with both arms outstretched (*herding*) motioning for us to leave the hallway. He probably wasn't writing an order at all. It had probably been a note that he could conveniently leave behind for one of the construction workers that read HELP ME! CALL THE POLICE!

As we all began our clickety-clacking walk back down the long corridor that would eventually (hopefully) lead us back to the little cramped office with a phone where this guy could actually call for someone to come and pick me up, my friend broke the silence of our journey by proudly announcing that—"Oh," because we had chosen a casket made of wood, there would be a tree planted in a national forest somewhere in my father's name. Now, doesn't that just touch your hearts? Well heck, it did mine! Made me want to do the unthinkable and put my arms around this fella. Don't worry, I didn't. Hell, even I know better than to do something like that. Poor guy would probably have gone into a coma.

As I fell behind to follow the others, I glanced down at the floor and wondered how it might feel under my bare feet as a memory of ice cream and a Sunday afternoon jaunt to the local drugstore surged throughout my broken heart. Where was he, I wondered? Where was my dad? I mean, where did the guests of this fine establishment stay until it was all over? Probably in the basement. I had come to believe that just like in the movies all of the people freezers just had to be in the basement. Problem was, was that I didn't want my dad in someone's basement. No, actually, that wasn't really the problem at all. Oh heck, no. It was much grander than all that. I *needed* to know. I needed to be sure. Had to be sure! Oh– my–heck! I needed–to–see–him! I had to be sure that he *was,* in fact, *dead.*

What if he wasn't? I mean, I hadn't been there when Tonto and Ms Kitty had said their final good-byes. No, I hadn't been! And just what if someone had made a terrible mistake? Oh boy, this wasn't good. No, siree Bob, this wasn't good at all!

Picking up my imaginative pace to catch up with the others, I came up from behind blurting an explosive, "Excuse me?"

Everyone stopped and turned giving me their undivided and much annoyed attention. Eyebrows raised, there they all stood, the Indian, the widow witch and Fella.

"Where is he?" I asked, with desperation seeping from every pore in my body. Now, standing before all three of them, breathing as if I had just run a marathon, searching their eyes for an answer, I asked again,

"Where *is* my dad?"

The Indian was now a pale face, the widow witch was fear stricken and Fella? Well, he simply looked as if someone had just stolen his order pad, but I could swear I saw a trace of a personality coming forward as he smiled, calmly explaining to me that my dad's body was kept in refrigeration until the funeral, slyly slipping the Indian a note begging him to run for help.

Refrigeration? Yuk! If we all just take a little minute to think about this I'm sure we will all come up with somewhat of the same conclusion. This practice of keeping a body on ice seems somewhat—well—morbid, don't you think? I mean, if we were to explain this custom to say, someone from another planet, just think how silly it sounds. We house our dead in a freezer until we dispose of them. Keeps 'em fresh! And then what do we do for the burial? Thaw them out? Oh, for the very love of God! And never mind that just now, but what if the power goes out? I thought this embalming technique was done to preserve the body. Oh, and wait, Mr. and Mrs. Alien, there's more! Then we all pick a day and everyone who ever knew the deceased come to look at them just one more time to say good-bye. We display them in a box of sorts and it's lined with satin or cotton as to add to their comfort because they are DEAD! Then everyone cries—again—as if the very day we lost them wasn't painful enough. We as humans like to drag things out. Double our steps, do things twice—so you see, Mr. and Mrs. Alien, we humans are SICK! And at that very thought—at that very moment, it was then that I decided hands down that I would be cremated. The very thought of laying in waiting with other someones I didn't know, naked in a cold room, covered with a white sheet, while some guy eats a sandwich just doesn't do it for me. I had to stop watching *Matlock*.

Let's see, now where were we? Ah yes—and so the story goes.

Obviously satisfied with his answer of refrigeration, Fella led us back into the tiny room where we had begun this whole ordeal, and what an eye opening ordeal it had been, so that we could all go over what we had just accomplished.

As we all took our designated places around the table, he asked if we would like a flag holder to display Old Glory in the event that Fort Ord actually got their crap together and my dad would indeed have a military burial. Sure, why not? There's another one for you: Take the flag out of the bag, put it on the casket—fold it—hand it to whomever—and then put it in a case on display as a constant reminder. We are sick!

There was a brief discussion over the fact that my dad would, in fact, be buried in the nude—again—and then a promise from Fella that he would continue to try and get a hold of someone to OK my dad's military funeral. The casket would be closed upon my father's request (*and–I–had–to–see–him!*. The feeling was overwhelming. I just couldn't believe he was gone! I had to see for myself! I just had to!

So as we were wrapping things up, I very nonchalantly, very casually dropped the bomb.

"May I see him?" I asked. "May I have a private viewing?"

I'm sure I heard a feather drop. Just as I'm sure it fell straight from the Indian's head as he was on his way to fainting.

"What do you mean?" Fella asked.

"I mean that I need to say good-bye," I shamefully whispered. Sorry, Mr. and Mrs. Alien, that's just the way we are I guess.

My uncle sat very quietly with a look of sympathy as well as understanding upon his once bronze, now slightly pale Indian face. But the widow witch was horrified. And I guess as she well should have been. After all, she had been the one to find him. She had seen him lifeless and still. She couldn't understand what in the hell would compel a person to want to look at such a sight. Well, folks, me neither. I didn't know why I had to, I just did. I needed to see him just one more time. Obviously, everything hadn't been said and done. Perhaps it may have been said—but not done. Yes, I know what my dad had told me. Believe you me. All I could think about was him telling me not to look at him once he was dead. And if I had had any sense at all, I would have heeded his warning, but I felt the need—to be sure—and I had to do—what I had to do for my own reasons, whether they made sense or not. I simply had to make sure, needed to know, that he was really gone.

Fella broke the silence by quickly complying with my request. "We really aren't prepared," he pleaded. "But this won't be a problem," he quickly added. "We'll just cover him with a sheet?" He offered phrasing it as a question. "No," I said quickly, "I'll bring in his sweat-shirt and sweatpants if that's OK."

It's all I had seen him wear during the final weeks of his life and so I had this crazy idea, *thought*, that it would be easier on me if he were wearing the same—not alive.

Fella reluctantly agreed to set up the private viewing for the night before the funeral. And although I couldn't understand why the sudden reluctance, I dismissed it at the time as my over sensitivity.

As we stood to leave, Fella then said something that made me suddenly turn and look at him with what had to be absolute wonderment in my big brown and disbelieving eyes.

"Would you like for us to shave him?" he asked. Maybe give him a little haircut too?

How?—"Yes," I said robotically as if I had been suddenly hypnotized, "That would be very nice." As my mind flashed back to the weeks before, remembering how a shave and a haircut (two bits) had been something my dad had so longed for but had been too weak to accomplish. Oh, how a trip to the barbershop had been such a simple yet unreachable desire. You know, there's just something about a man and his barber that can't be expressed by mere words. It's a male bonding of sorts, I suppose. And did it matter? Perhaps not to some and maybe not even to most—but it did matter to me. And although I was contradicting myself once again to Mr. and Mrs. Alien, I felt good leaving that place knowing my dad would finally receive his shave and a haircut.

What a stressful excursion to say the least. As I pushed the heavy doors out of my way with a vengeance of some sort, I couldn't wait to get to the car. The fresh air was invigorating. It had become very stale inside that awful place although I hadn't seemed to notice until I had exited the building. And, just like Elvis, I'm sure it had been announced once I was gone, which was just fine with me because I was relieved to be gone. And as I was waiting outside for the Indian and the widow witch to emerge from the bowels of hell as well, I began to reflect on the decisions that had just been made. All checked out with no guilt except for one. Hey, one isn't so bad after what we had just been through. And the one I'm referring to was just a little one. And no one else would have even caught it except for maybe the Indian—oh—and maybe all of you.

It was the viewing. I must shamefully admit that we had conveniently arranged for a private viewing to take place the night before the funeral, so that my sis and my husband could accompany me—because—well—I just couldn't do it alone. And if there are those of you who still have to ask why, I guess I also have to share with all of you the reason. I was scared to death! Really scared. But I had to make sure he was gone. And what was I scared of you may all be asking yourselves? Well, duh? Doesn't take much for all of you who know me. And although I had been the one to request a private viewing, I was also the one who *didn't* want to see him. Not like that. I didn't want to look at my dad's body. It frightened me to think of him laying there with no life in him. Not asleep but— dead. And yet, I just had to make sure. Be sure that—well—that he was really gone. To this very day I still cannot figure out for the life of me why it was so very important. All I can tell you is that I truly needed to see him just one last time. I can also tell you that to this very day, for the life of me I wish I hadn't. I should have listened to my dad. And that's all I have to say about that!

The ride home was silent and still just like the rest of the world. The leaves were still falling from the trees; however they seemed to be falling more forcefully now. Could have been the wind that was creating such a fuss or perhaps, just perhaps, they were angry and scared too.

Once we arrived at what used to be my dad's home, I did something that I hadn't done in a very long time. I turned on what used to be my dad's big screen TV, grabbed what used to be my dad's blanket off the back of what used to be my dad's chair and I laid down on what used to be my dad's sofa and I slept. Deeply and peacefully. But right before I dozed off, somewhere on the way to that really good napping sleep, I heard my dad, in a dream or—I heard his deep booming voice singing a song from my childhood. "The old gray mare she aint what she used to be……" And I slept until the wee hours of the morning waking up startled that I hadn't heard him, gagging or calling for me to come and get him—again.

It was two in the morning and once I was fully awake I realized that, sadly, the only one gagging was me.

It was Wednesday. Two more days and it would all be over. I couldn't go back to sleep. Something was tugging on my heart strings. I reached over and turned on the lamp and glanced around the living room just as I had done on my first night's visit. Gosh, that seemed so long ago. Everything was still just as it had been then—except this house was so empty now, so hauntingly quiet. Not even the familiar crackling of the headphones that I had become accustomed to this early in the morning were— the headphones! My eyes instantly widened as I searched the floor—and there they lay, across the room, calm and hushed. What was it he had listened to the very last time he had, in fact, listened to them at all? And when? Had he snuck while I was miles away with my family? Perhaps had he tiptoed out there one morning and maybe gave it one last go around just for Gene Autry's sake or who ever had the pleasure of gracing his presence?

I wondered as I slowly got up from my sofa bed and sneakily shuffled over to the stereo, blanket in tow. Now standing before what used to be my dad's own private concert extravaganza, I reached and softly pushed the glass casing until it welcomed me with an audible click. Pulling my hand back, the tiny door opened on its own as if it knew of my intentions, inviting me to sit a spell and—listen. Making sure the little black dot on the knob was pointed at the word, "Headphones," as not to send the widow witch into a screaming heart attack, I pushed the on button and my dad's old friend came alive with welcoming lights of red, blue and yellow as it lit up like a runway and it occurred to me that my dad had probably delighted in that little display just as much as he did the music as a smile pursed my lips. I sat down on the throw pillow that had cradled my dad on so very many early mornings, reached for the headphones and carefully placed them on my head with the muffs securely over each ear. And as I then reached for the knob that read "Turntable," I wondered if my dad had ever pretended that he was a pilot as he went through this ritual. With the click of ignition, Merle Haggard was just as proud to be an Oakie from Muskokie as I was to have been Eddie's daughter. Of course, I should have known as Merle was twanging away about how they would never burn Old Glory down at the courthouse and how white lightening was still the biggest thrill of all.

Huh, Old Glory. She would hopefully be draped over my dad's casket in a few days. And as Merle continued to sing a medley of his old tunes my mind began to contemplate just how I was going to accomplish that task.

After the Oakie from Muskokie had finished his performance, I noticed that there was another album underneath him on the turntable. Lifting the needle arm, automatically stopping the lazy Susan of my dad's desires, I carefully lifted Merle and placed him aside to make room for—I had no clue. It was dark. Placing the arm back down that in turn began the familiar cycle of the turntable Hank Williams began to crackle out a tune. And as I sat and listened to my dad's old friend serenade me, I began thumbing through the stacked jackets that held his most cherished possessions. My gosh, he had so many friends to keep him company in the wee hours of the mornings. Kitty Wells, Patsy Cline, Porter Wagoner and Dolly Parton, Charlie Pride, and—Freddie Fender—whom he had gone to see in person once while visiting at my home. Oh, how my heart ached as I tearfully recalled my dad coming home from that show and taking my hands high up in the air as he twirled me around booming the melody of how "He'd be there, before the next teardrop fell."

I sat and cried as I whispered the tune along with Freddie until I just couldn't take anymore. With one motion, sweeping the headphones off my head just about taking my ears off with them, I plopped them down beside me with Freddie still faintly singing from the floor. I reached for the power button and as I pushed it to extinguish the display of colored lights, it fell as painfully silent as my world had become. Standing up from the pillow, closing the glass door at the same time, I knew that this would probably be the very last time that my dad's entertainment center would ever perform again—at least for us anyway. And would it survive a new owner someday? Would it even know how to play rock and roll or rap? I truly doubted it. It would probably short out and catch fire first— or so I hoped.

The sun was now peeking through the curtains as a reminder to me of just how long I had been sitting there. It was Wednesday. My family would be arriving tomorrow night all in the preparation to bury my dad on Friday as to accommodate the National Cemetery rules. Another attempt from Fella to accommodate me as to not have to wait until Monday. I really don't think he liked the idea of me hanging around his funeral home any longer than absolutely necessary. Either that or he didn't know the ice-cream man? I had to get going as I had promised Fella that I would be there early to deliver my dad's viewing attire.

Walking to the kitchen to make a pot of coffee I felt as though I were being watched. Like the house as well as everything in it was following my every move. Perhaps it was. I thought as I prepared my wakerupper in the tiny confines of what used to be my dad's early morning preparation station. Soon I thought, this little place as well as all of its inhabitants will be but a memory as I carried my cup of joe into the living room to gather my clothing from my suitcase and then headed for the bathroom trying to be ever so quiet as not to wake the widow witch.

Once showered and dressed I realized while standing in what used to be my dad's bathroom that I loved this little place with all of its memories. And just before I exited the tiny space that had accommodated so much of my dad's last days, I turned and stood next to the toilet, closing my eyes, remembering, reliving the moment I last saw my dad alive. With the door securely locked behind me, feeling safe from being discovered, I puckered my lips and leaned forward and gave a make believe kiss to absolutely nothing, savoring, trying to relive my last moments with my dad. It wasn't the same. But, of course, I don't guess I had to tell you that, now, did I?

I gathered my dad's sweatshirt and sweatpants from the dryer, as well as a pair of socks as I anticipated the Indian's arrival. Folding them up and neatly placing them in a bag I marveled at how very small they were. Had he always been this little of a man? Certainly not, as I remembered him being my monster fighter in what seemed to be another lifetime ago.

Finally, the Indian arrived and just in the nick of time as I just didn't believe I could take not one more stinking memory. I needed something in the present to occupy my time for a while. Of course, the widow witch was now stirring around so I guess for fun we could have held one of her monkeys for ransom. Or maybe hung one up in the living room like a piñata and watched her jump for it. OK—I wouldn't have done such a thing even if she'd had a flying monkey. But I sure did think about it as she had become so damned happy and nice since my father's departure. What was that all about anyway? Like a relief. And all the phone calls? The secret phone calls that took place from the bedroom? Not to mention the fact that she was still coming and going an awful lot. She was very busy. Oh yes, even in the midst of all of my grief, I noticed everything. And then it hit me! Like a blinding snowstorm in mid

June! What if that son of hers, wanted to attend my father's funeral? Oh Dear–Oh Me–Oh My. That was not going to happen. And I would have to tell her so. I didn't want to be cruel but—he just absolutely could not attend. I would speak to my uncle about this immediately. Uh huh—and just as we have all come to know by now—it is never the things we worry most about that ever come to fruition.

My uncle was outside honking as I grabbed my purse and my dad's clothing and headed for the door. The widow witch did emerge from the bedroom asking when I would return. OK—that was new. I told her I wasn't sure, as I'm positive I sounded as though she had just asked me had I seen a ghost. She was acting so out of character. However, I had to dismiss these thoughts at least for the time being as I had to tend to matters at hand. Maybe someone had just informed her that a house fell on her sister. Who knew?

Our drive was quiet as should be expected when driving with a grieving Indian. And—arriving at the funeral home was a tad bit less stressful this time, as I already knew what to expect—well sort of.

We entered the building, but this time Fella was nowhere to be found. Probably quit his job and headed for Albuquerque. So we stood on those beautiful marble floors and simply waited until we heard the familiar clicking of shoes heading our way, as a family of four was following Fella out of that claustrophobic room and as they said their good-byes, Fella turned to give us his attention, greeting us with a half smiled hello. I was really glad to see that he had actually decided to stay as I handed him the bag and explained its contents. He took the bag from my hands and tucked it up under his arm, acknowledging my instructions—until I requested to have all but the socks returned to me. They could leave those on him which gave me comfort, however, I wanted the clothing back as not to allow someone to make the mistake of burying him with them on.

This stopped Fella dead in his tracks, "You want them back?" he asked with eyebrows raised. Oh, Lord, here we go again.

"Yes," I said a little annoyed. What was the problem now, I wondered? Had my dad requested to keep them?

"Is there a problem?" I asked.

"Well," he began, "Quite frankly," he paused then continued, "There might be."

"What is it now?" I asked with my patience wearing a little thin.

Leaning toward me and speaking in a whisper he said, "We'll have to cut them off him."

*Oh–My–God!* "Why?" I asked. Desperately trying to refrain from slapping him across the face just as hard as I could swing my arm.

Still leaning and whispering as not to involve the Indian I suppose, he explained that remmuffled had already set in.

"I'm sorry," I said. "What did you just say? I couldn't understand you."

Steadying himself as if he were preparing to get the hell out of my way just incase I did decide to take a hefty swing, he more clearly repeated what I hadn't heard the first time.

"Riga mortis has already set in," he explained, "And this will make it very difficult to get the clothes on, as well as off, the body."

Well, halleplippinluyah! Riga mortis? Well, why didn't you say so? No problem! Just what I needed to hear—as it was me who was now carefully steadying myself so as not to faint dead on the floor, I suppose.

But I didn't. Nope—I sure as hell didn't. Instead, it was I who was leaning into him as I whispered very carefully as not to take his face and three stooge it into the Indian's.

I had to think—think! Say something to defend my rights. Come on, Baby Doll, let him have it! He certainly has it coming. Go for it, you gutless daughter of the dumbest janitor in the whole wide world. Say something, for the very love of God! 'It's my party and I'll cry if I want to—cry if I want to—cry if I want to—You would cry too if it…'

I began slowly, my voice in a whisper, courage coming up fast from the rear: and it came out of my mouth just as easy as you please.

"If I can dress and undress my daughter's Barbie doll—then you and your qualified staff can damned well find a way to dress and undress my dad, don't cha think?"

He pulled back from me like I had just bit him and I hadn't, I swear, and with a simple nod as well as traces of a smile forming on his face he assured me that they would return the clothes fully intact. Perseverance ensued as I continued in a whisper to explain to Fella that if I didn't get the clothes back, then how would I know that they didn't just get lazy and bury my dad in them anyway. Hey, this stuff happens all the time. I watch *Dateline*! I know how all sorts of morbid things go on behind the closed doors of a funeral home. Sometimes they lose whole bodies! Which, by the way, absolutely shocks the hell out of me, I mean how does one lose a corpse? Never mind that, who in the hell would want one?

I truly thought the Indian was going to faint. Oh, hold your water, Tonto, it's almost over.

"Oh," Fella said, as we were leaving, head down and fingers rubbing his head, like he was trying to portray Columbo, "What about music?" Yeah, I thought, what about it?

"What sort of music would you like played at the service?" he asked.

Hesitating, yet turning and walking slowly back toward him, I explained that I would like to bring one of my dad's most cherished albums in and play a couple of his favorites. I thought that would be very nice, I explained. You know, add a little Eddie charm to this whole godforsaken place. Put a little kick in your step, so to speak.

"We don't have a record player to accommodate that request," he said, ducking from my intended blow to his head.

"OK," I said, "Would you like for me to bring one in?"

"Well," he hesitated, "We don't really have any way to accommodate a record player here."

"You don't have an electrical outlet?" I asked.

"Not one in the chapel that would be accessible," he cowered.

OK, let's start over. What *can* you do, you moronic insensitive feeble little fella, you?

Trying to stay calm, I very carefully chose my words. "Just," and then I paused, "play something nice," I said too tired and too close to tears to fight anymore.

Nodding, he assured me that they had a nice assortment of music to choose from. Yet, I wondered if he even knew who Merle Haggard was?

"Fine," I said. "That will be just great." Then turning and taking the Indian's arm, I very calmly and very quietly walked out of there. And as we walked to the car, somewhere deep inside, I didn't hear Merle Haggard, nor did I hear Hank Williams, but Gloria Gainer, nonetheless belting a determined tune of "I will survive—Hey! Hey!"

During the drive home I began to feel uneasy. Sort of like—well— when you buy a used car and you know beyond a shadow of a doubt that you just got screwed. The Indian was somewhere deep in thought, probably in a place where you didn't have to say good-bye to people you love, but I on the other hand, was off somewhere else, buying used cars and getting screwed. I believe they actually have a clinical term for this classic phenomenon. And, no, it's not looney. They don't use terms like that clinically. It's called "good old fashioned anxiety." And if I could have bottled that stuff and sold it to the powers that be who are in charge of chemical warfare, I would have been a millionaire—or at least a brigadier general.

I simply needed some rest. That was all. It was almost over. This whole terrible ordeal was about to come to a screeching halt. The next night I would view my dad's body (pass the peas) and then would come Friday, when I would have to go through the motions of a task that I had dreaded all of my life. Well, or at least from the very night I had slept by his bedroom door so very long ago. And once I got home to what used to be my dad's house, noticing the mini van was gone again which meant so was the widow witch, I bid my Uncle farewell and sashayed through the sliding glass door, waving my arm behind me through the blowing curtain as a cue for him to pull away, just like nothing at all was wrong in the world, except—I really needed to talk to him about the witch and her odd behavior. Huh. I suppose it could wait. And now it would have to because I had just dismissed him.

I had become very familiar with the consuming scent of my dad's pipe tobacco greeting me upon each arrival, but nonetheless it always sent me to the couch and off my feet to ponder. And there I sat as I glanced over at his stuffed animals all sitting studiously lined up on their perch.

Maybe they were lighting his pipe while I was gone. Or maybe—movies like *Chuckie* made me feel just a little bit uncomfortable as I looked away, trying not to have eye contact with a silly ass-stinking stuffed animal, of all things! I reallio, trulio, very seriously needed to get some sort of psychotic fighting medication or more rest or both.

It was almost over. This whole terrible ordeal was coming to an end. Two more days and then what? I wondered how long it would take for me to return to normal? I wondered if I had *ever* been normal? And at that point, I then wondered just what in the hell normal was?

Just as I rose from the sofa to do—what—anything at all but sit there avoiding eye contact with a stuffed animal, the phone rang, scaring the crap right out of me. It was Fella. He must have missed me.

"Hello," I began like most people do when they answer the phone. Then words— then—absolute disbelief. My dad WOULD NOT be having a military funeral!

My dad, the same exact man who had cried buckets of tears the day John Fitzgerald Kennedy was assassinated; The very boy who lied about his age just to join The United States Army; and that very same boy who became a soldier and who would have proudly given his life for his country at the tender age of seventeen.

The very same man who felt that protesters who burned Old Glory down at the courthouse should be given life in prison, Private First Classman Eddie Littlefield, who in his final days did not relive the births of his daughters (Count 'em, my friend; Five! I've got five beautiful brown-eyed baby doll girls!), nor did he relive the days of his childhood—but my dad did, in fact, relive the six years that he secured ground for the troops to arrive safely as a front lines artillery man—who rode a stinking mule by the name of flipping John! Yes, ladies and gents—*that* very soldier—had not earned a funeral with full military honors—because that young soldier had not served a long enough tour in the United States Army! Well, all I had to say about that was BULLSHIT! And I'll tell you something else. This would have brought tears to that old soldier's eyes as well as shame to his heart, and to tell you the God's honest truth—that's exactly what it did to me.

Now look, I could let the music thing go and I could ignore the fact that my cancer-ridden proud-minded silly little dad wanted his five beautiful brown-eyed baby doll girls to sit with his casket in the back of his Chevy Pickup all the way to the cemetery. Some things just aren't feasible. And even I will admit that I never even gave that request the good old college try. Hell, I didn't even give it a first thought let alone a second or third because even I know that some things are just not possible. But we are not talking about something that is so damned impossible here. This is something as simple as a few shots fired and a bugle played on a hillside. My God, if my dad had had any idea that this might of happened—why—I couldn't even think about it. It was too painful. "I did everything I could," Fella was saying, as I tuned back in to a conversation that was taking place without me once again. I sure hoped that once this was all over I would stop doing that. It was very rude!

I kindly thanked Fella for his bad news—and asked for the number he had called. "Certainly," he said as he read me the numbers with sweat probably dripping from his brow. Then, thanking him again, not really meaning it, I curtly hung up realizing all of a sudden that it really hadn't been Fella's responsibility to get things done. I mean after all, Eddie had been *my* dad, not *his,* and that was obvious because had Eddie, in fact, been anything at all to Fella—he definitely would have smiled more!

Reaching for the phone once again, I picked it up, lifted it over the arm of the sofa and placed it securely in my lap as if to admit to myself that I just might be there a while. Where would I begin? Who would I ask for? And why did I even care as I dialed the number I had obtained from Fella and a woman promptly answered introducing herself as a sergeant.

Silence. She once again said her name obviously losing patience and from somewhere far away I heard myself speak as I slowly began with who I was—and who my father had been—and as soon as I got the whole story out, and I mean the whole entire story just as I have shared it with all of you, from the lying about his age to join—all the way to what the punishment should be in his opinion of the burning of Old Glory—I began to cry. Well, blubber would be a more accurate description actually. And I didn't think they took too kindly to blubbering idiotic daughters in the United States Army, however, she patiently listened and then—silence again—except for my sniffles. She's gonna hang up, I thought, as I tried to gain some sort of composure.

So you see, I continued through sporadic sobs, I simply can not bury Private First Class Eddie Littlefield AKA my dad, in a normal fashion because he just wasn't a normal guy! Did she get that? Did anyone? And then—something miraculous happened. She became another woman.

Not a Sergeant but a woman who also, must have had a father at one time or another in her life. A woman who wasn't afraid nor was she embarrassed to speak her tearful opinion of what the rules were, a woman who wasn't too proud to ask for an exception to the rule, as she asked me to hold, while she began to climb the ladder of the chain of command.

No music. But that was OK, because I made my own as I sat quietly squeaking out a tearful tune of "Be all that you can be—in the A-r-m-y!" I have always been very capable of entertaining myself. That is actually the beauty of being me. No worries about how ridiculous I must have looked, sitting on what used to be my dad's sofa, rocking back and forth singing some damned commercial tune that had actually been intended for Army recruitment. Nope, not a care in the world as my tears fell like rain, sanity intact—well sort of.

I sat on hold for quite sometime and started to wonder if maybe she had forgotten me (ditched me). OK, now that worried me as I began to rock faster and my song became rock and roll, before she finally came back on the line asking if I was still there.

"Yes, I am," I answered with hesitant anticipation.

"Well," she began, "I'm sorry, I had to do a lot of talking."

Silence. I was holding my breath.

She cleared her throat. She was stalling. Oh—my—God! She was trying to catch her breath before she had to break my heart! It was nice of her to take this extra precaution. I suppose. I guess they must teach this tactic in basic training. How to snap a daughter's heart completely in two without even touching her! Impressive to say the least; however, you would think they could have chosen a more suitable subject. I mean, after all, I was hardly a threat to the United States Army. Well, not yet anyway.

I tuned back in once again to a conversation taking place without me. *I really did have to stop doing that!*

She began slowly, "Well, it just so happens (her voice was unsteady) that there is another military service that will be taking place on the very same day as your dad's (no, her voice was cracking) just one half hour before his—right next to his, as a matter of fact (I hadn't shared with her where) and that they would be more than happy to walk over to the next gazebo (she was unmistakably crying) to honor your father with a service—WITH FULL MILITARY HONORS!"

I couldn't believe it! All I could say is Oh–My–God!

"A twenty-one-gun salute?" I asked. (I'm going home.)

"Yes," she proudly replied, a twenty-one-gun salute. (You're going home.)

"A bugler" I asked. (And Toto too?)

"Yes," she proudly exclaimed, a bugler on the hillside behind the gazebo. (And Toto too.)

She continued, "As far as we are concerned, your father was a WWII veteran and he has earned a burial with full military honors, Ma'am.

Ma'am? Wow, she called me Ma'am.

She continued, "We would be more than proud as well as honored to perform his final burial."

I couldn't speak. But neither could she. Silence again.

When I finally caught my breath enough to be able to utter a whispered "Thank you," she returned my thanks with an insistent, "No, thank you, Ma'am—and your father."

Criminy sakes alive, I could swear she was saluting me! And it was at that moment that I realized why my dad had chosen that particular branch of the service we all know as the United States Army.

She then informed me that she would call the funeral home and make all the arrangements. And with that, she thanked me once again, and said that on behalf of the United States Army, they were proud to have had my father serve their branch of the service. And then she hung up.

And there I sat—in silence—with tears streaming in the celebration of perseverance once again!

And as I sat back, basking in the feeling of triumphant ecstasy, clicking my heels together, eyes closed, chanting, "There's no place like home, there's no place like home, there's no place like home," I don't think I could have possibly fathomed at the time what I had just accomplished. However, now, as I sit and reminisce— well, never mind, you'll see when we get there. Let's just say that out of all the tasks I had accomplished thus far, that this particular one - had been the very best of all! However, I do have one regret, as I close this next to the last chapter of my story. One that actually and still to this day can bring a smile to my lips. I would've given almost anything to have been a mouse in the corner when Fella received that call!

# Chapter Twenty-Five

## *Good-Bye*

*I believe that every person on this earth who dies— has touched*
*someone else in a special certain way— and because of that touch, we*
*who remain behind, will in some way be just a little bit different.*

"When It's Time to Say Good-Bye"
Chapter Six, Realization M. Tote (1958-)

A s I SAT, absolutely stunned long after the hum of the dial tone had been silenced, I felt as if I was on top of the world. Yes, I guess you can actually feel triumphant even when it's time to say good-bye. Baby steps, folks, that's what it's all about. One minute turns into thirty then an hour and so on and so on. Pretty soon, before you know it, it's fifteen years later and you're finally sharing your story.

While sitting and basking in the warmth of my victory, I happened to glance down the hallway and sadness overcame me once again. A feeling of gloom began to seep in like a hovering cloud. Would it ever end? Would I ever be myself again I wondered as I glared at the closed bedroom door. Well, quite frankly, no—I wouldn't ever be myself again or at least not the me I had been when I had arrived at this place. No, my friends, for she too had left with my dad. Who remained now looked like me, but I was so much wiser and so much more appreciative of— well—just life in general I suppose. It's funny how a death will do that to a person. Well, not really funny. As a matter of fact, it's not very flipping funny at all.

I was alone. Alone in what used to be such a happy place of years gone by. What happens now, I wondered. Who will love my dad's stuff the way he did? Who will even know the secrets these walls held? Who, for instance, would ever understand what Joe the orangutan had been through? Watching my father's every move, listening to his every breath as he slowly had no more. Poor Joe, I thought as

I cautiously got up from the sofa and headed for the bedroom. What was I doing? I couldn't go in there! He was gone! However, it certainly was me who had my hand on the brass doorknob as I turned it with an audible pop once again as I'm sure that Joe was probably scurrying back into place. I gently shoved as the bottom of the door slid with a swoosh against the carpet. And there I stood. Eyes closed, taking in the smell and waiting for—what? Perhaps I was giving Joe a little extra time? Heart pounding, I slowly opened my eyes. The room seemed to swell or breath or - something. Then again, I felt like I just might faint—again. That smell! The same smell it had always harbored yet, my dad was no longer there. Everything looked the same. Just as if he may come up from behind me at any moment after taking one of his much anticipated trips to the bathroom. But he didn't. Nope—and something was telling me that those days were, in fact, over, forever. Well, of course they were. But it was going to perhaps take an army to convince me—once again—no pun intended.

Joe was studiously sitting in his designated spot right next to the end table by the bed. Eyes open and fixed on me. I almost asked "What?" out loud. Panning the room I realized I was looking for something. A sign. Anything at all that might clue me in on the fact that this all had been just a bad dream. Oh, how I wanted it to be. Oh, how I missed him so very much.

Quietly, as if I didn't want to wake anyone, I slowly walked over to the tiny dresser that held all of the treasures that had once been my dad's. And at that very given moment, I truly wished for two things. One—was that when someone died everything they owned would simply vanish with them and the second wish - was for Joe to please stop staring at me for the very love of God!

So, what in the world do you do with things that don't mean anything at all to anyone else at all—except the deceased? Well, I'm not real sure, however, I will attempt to tell you what I did at the risk of— oh—never mind, we are way past that stage of the game. You simply go through them, that's what—and all of a sudden— you just may find, as I did, that those things suddenly mean more to you than they ever did to the deceased. Yes, magically, they somehow become the possessions of a museum of love that lives on in your heart forever. What a comfort.

Where to begin I wondered. Could I begin? And never mind that, but *why* begin? Well, I reckon, because—I simply felt the need.

Standing before the tiny little built-in dresser I reached for the rounded knobs as if they were the tiny hands of a child and gave them a tug with both hands, instantly displaying its guarded contents inside. Should I be doing this, I wondered? I needed to—what? I needed to touch and feel what was once his—that was all.

Top drawer, now hanging open at a slight downward slant, as if it's bottom lip were puckered, I glanced the contents inside of its guarded walls. There they were.

His trademarks. All neatly folded in a continuous row of cotton. All white and all wondering where Eddie had gone.

I lifted each row and gently laid them on the bed clearing a space inside the treasure trove revealing the bottom of the drawer. I noticed a small box seemingly trying to hide from the unwelcomed light. Reaching for it, I felt like an unwelcomed intruder as well. Gently and ever so carefully, I lifted the tiny white cardboard lid and inside resting on a square patch of white cotton was a watch, a beautiful gold watch that had obviously been given to the "Best damned head of maintenance for twenty-five years of keeping it kleen." And as I stood there holding the proof that my dad had, in fact, succeeded in life, I realized that I had never known him to wear a watch. Funny, I thought, that I hadn't noticed until now. And then, somewhere deep within the channels of my mind I heard my mother chanting that he probably never even learned how to tell time. Closing my eyes to shut her up, I dismissed this irrational thought with a tear. It wasn't important. He sure didn't need to tell time where he was now.

I continued to open and close drawers taking his belongings out and placing them on the bed in the exact same order. Underwear, socks, and two pair of suspenders were among some of the many treasures these drawers held. As I opened the bottom and last drawer, it was deeper than the rest, revealing rows of sweatpants. All studiously lined up next to one another arranged by color. Cute, I thought, as I lifted them up and out to join their fellow partners on the bed. To the right of this drawer, hiding underneath a knitted cap was something blue. As a matter of fact this item was recognizable to me. I reached in and moved the cap to reveal a blue denim, shaving bag with the word "Grandpa" glued in sparkly letters across the front of it. Oh, how my heart whined as I recalled my daughter giving this treasure to my dad one beautiful July day two years before. She had raced through the door from pre-school, me hurrying behind, giggling hysterically just knowing that Grandpa would never guess what she had made for him. The paper she had wrapped it in was folded neatly beneath it. Oh, how my dad had carried on as he whooped and yelled with excitement as he opened his precious gift. And for just a moment, I was able to relive how very wonderful it had felt to surprise my, always grateful, little Dad.

There were buttons strewn about all of the drawers, obviously waiting for the day when he meant to sew them back on to whatever they had fallen off of. And there were small tools lying about as well. They had obviously never been used. Gadgets. That was all they were. Probably saving them for a rainy day.

How would I begin to know what to do with all of these things? I couldn't throw them away and I couldn't give them away either. I mean, who else would ever be worthy of wearing those trademark T-shirts, or his size eight socks, or his two pair of suspenders, one red and one blue? No one that's who! Not one—single—solitary—soul on the face of this earth. So, I slowly opened every drawer in the opposite order from which I had commenced, and began to put everything back into their perspective homes, just as I had found them. Why I had taken them out in the first place was a mystery to me. Guess it was just some neurotic move of a grieving daughter. Pretty silly as I look back on it now.

At the request of the widow witch, I will share with all of you that I did end up taking all of his clothing home with me. And—it will continue to sit in storage until I figure out what to do with all of it, however, I am leaning toward going down to the river and handing it all out to the homeless. I think my dad would have liked that.

I was emotionally and physically drained by the time I finished absolutely nothing. I sat down on the end of what used to be my dad's round bed and glanced up toward the headboard. It was hard for me to believe that just three weeks before—my silly pipe-smoking little dad and I had spent such wonderful hours on that bed, talking and taping and laughing and joking. I leaned up toward the headboard, stretching my arms up to grab his pillow. Half crawling to accommodate my inadequate reach, I swiped the pillow with a single swoop and brought it up to my face, resting it under my chin. I then lowered my face into its softness and I could smell him. I could feel him once again, and with that - the tears began to flow once more.

"I miss you, Dad," I said aloud, "I miss you and I want you back. I don't want to do all of this alone," I croaked, and for some silly reason I peered up from the pillow and glanced toward the headboard once again, remembering the day my dad had shared with me the story of "Smokey the Bear." How he had scrunched up his wrinkly face and held out his hand in a matter-of-fact sort of manner, explaining to me that Smokey had gone to bear heaven where all little good bears go when they die. How he had been so serious as his gaze wandered once he had shared that little tidbit with me. And with that, a smile soon replaced my tears of sadness as I got up off the bed, gently placing the pillow where I had been sitting, saying aloud, "Tell Smokey hi for me, Dad," as I then did the unthinkable. I walked the hell out of there. There would be another time when I could do this. Right then, I was tired. Another time when it just might be less painful. Probably when hell froze over and now that my dad was in heaven that quite possibly and very probably could very well happen. Yes, I do believe that if there ever was someone who could have ever frozen hell over, it sure as heck could've been my dad.

It was dark now as I entered the living room and I had had a very long and trying day. Sitting on the sofa, I reached over and turned on the light—sitting in such a familiar place in such uncomfortable surroundings once again. And I sat there reminiscing long into the wee hours of the morning.

Ended chapters, that's what we all become when we die. One long continuous novel that somewhere along the way becomes a mini series that never ends. And as I sat directing and reminiscing one of the greatest movies of all times; my dad's life, I must have fallen asleep during a commercial.

I'm not sure when the widow witch came home. It must have been around way past my bedtime and hers for that matter but I woke up as she slid the sliding glass door open and half sat up and if you were to ask me why to this day I sure as hell couldn't tell you but I felt the need to have a talk with her. Yup—right then and there on that night I wanted— needed some answers.

When I said hi she whispered hi back to me and told me she didn't mean to wake me and for me to go back to sleep. Well, quite frankly I didn't want to go back to sleep.

Running both of my hands from my forehead back through my hair, now sitting up completely, I answered her with, "Actually, I would like to sit and just talk to you for a few minutes, if you're not too tired."

She walked into the tiny kitchen, stood at the sink facing me over the small breakfast bar counter, sat her purse down and asked me what I wanted to talk about? Oh hell—I had no clue. Like let's start with—just how do you keep your skin so green and beautiful and why do you hide that flawless complexion of yours under that dark brimmed hat?

"Well, for starters—you," I said.

"What about me," she snipped?

Gosh, did she always have to want to make me slap the crap out of her?

"Well," I began again, "*My* dad was also *your* husband and I haven't really seen much of you and I simply wondered how you are doing?"

"Didn't know you cared," she snipped and very quickly, I might add.

Boy, oh, boy was she a witch in widow's clothing for sure.

"Well," I continued, "I do care and that is why I'm asking." Dumb- Ass!

"I'm doing fine I guess," she said, as her voice trailed off into the depths of the house somewhere.

"Would you like to sit with me?" I reluctantly asked. Why, oh, why do I open my mouth?

"I suppose," she answered. Great, I thought.

She very unenthusiastically came around the counter and walked around the front of the coffee table and sat down next to me on the couch. Now what, I thought.

After a few seconds of very uncomfortable silence, which actually felt like an eternity, I decided it was time to lay our cards on the table. It was time to have a good old fashioned step mother–stepdaughter talk, which reminds me, now that I think about it, not to ever do something like that again!

I began with asking if she was angry with me. I asked if there was something I did to make her not like me. She instantly answered me with no.

"No what? No you don't like me?"

"No," she said. "I am not mad at you and, no, you have done nothing to make me not like you. It was your father."

Oh, crap. She didn't just say what she had, in fact, just said.

"What do you mean?" I asked, although I could feel the heat in my cheeks beginning to rise as I asked that question.

"He ignored me," she said. "He was mad at me because of my son. He was angry at me because I loved my son. How fair is that?" she asked.

And at that particular moment I had so many feelings running through me that I had no clue what to say. She was clearly angry with my father and she was hurt but I still couldn't buy the answer she was giving me. So I very carefully and very sympathetically asked if she thought that was the real reason my dad was mad at her, if, in fact, he even was mad, something he'd never shared with me. I had been watching those two for weeks and I felt that *she* had been angry with my father. Quite the opposite of what she was saying now. I was confused, to say the least, and I wanted so desperately to try and understand her.

She went on to say that my dad had no compassion, no sympathy and that he was cruel.

OK—everybody—out of the pool!!!! Was she an idiot? Was she blind? Or could it be that our perceptions of such things are in the eyes of the beholder?

I knew to be careful here. She was obviously angry and hurt. And no amount of sticking up for my father was even necessary at this point. He was gone now—although her words cut through me like a knife. It was like she knew it too, as though she was saying these things about him to hurt me. And all I could think about is how my dad would have wanted me to handle this conversation. Oh, Lord. I did so hope that that little trait wasn't staying.

"OK," I began. "Tell me why my dad wouldn't have wanted you to love your son?"

"Well," she said, "I suppose some of it was because they had gotten into that fight years ago."

Geeze! Did she have to remind me of that now? Well—I suppose she did, seeing that I had asked.

"Oh," I cautiously inched, "I don't think my dad would have held that against *you.*"

She continued, interrupting me, almost talking over me, as she added that my dad had no respect for her son because he couldn't find a job. So she had been supporting him, she explained, because he tried but just couldn't find a job because he was also an addict and everyone wanted a drug test before they would hire him. He couldn't help it that he had an addiction, she explained, as I felt as though I had been dropped off on another planet.

Okeydoke—it was clear to me now. It came down to lack of respect not dislike and my big mouth told her so in so many words.

She instantly reminded me of how perfect my father's daughters were, because we never asked for money. And at that very moment—I truly wished that house would have fallen on her instead of her sister!

Very cautiously again I began by telling her that we never asked for money because we knew dad didn't have any money. Plus the fact that my dad had always told us that you work for a living. Handouts were for those who were not able to work. The less fortunate. This conversation was going nowhere fast. She was really angry with my dad, and I was heartbroken to have to sit there and listen to all of this crap. Her son was in his thirties, for hell's sake. Hell, yes, my dad would have had no respect for him at all. Now it was clear to me as to why my dad would never talk about him. He wasn't worth an honorable mention in my father's vocabulary. Her son was an addict and he was living off his mother!

But I never spoke those words. I wanted to and I really deserved to but I didn't. I simply told her I was sorry because I truly was. At that very moment—I was sorry my dad had ever met her.

"So you see," she continued, "that is why I was mad at your father."

I said nothing.

"Do you understand?" she asked.

"Yeah," I said, "I understand. *You are a codependent idiot with a drug addict son whom you have supported for God knows how long and my dad had probably lost respect for you as well as your son a long time ago.*

Now it was all very clear. And I'm not real sure if I, myself, wasn't just a tad bit angry with my dad at that given moment for not telling me all of this. I had many feelings running through me at that given moment and some of it was fear.

For you see, two weeks before that very day, my dad had called the HR person at his place of employment and had her come out to the house and he changed his beneficiary to me. He told me he wanted me to cut his wife a monthly check for what she was making at the time so she could quit work and still have an income. His life insurance would have only lasted her about two years. Not long, I realize, but this was a gift to her as far as my dad was concerned. Or so I thought at the time. But right then it had become very clear to me that he did this because he was afraid that if they cut her that check all at once—that she would give it all to her son. I promised my dad to carry out his wishes and I was instructed by him not to tell her until he was gone. Now I knew why. I had thought it was for the element of my dad's notorious surprise factor. But it was because she would have blown a gasket. And she was about to because I had to tell her as she was now talking about getting her son his own place as soon as my dad's money came in. My dad had been right. He had known all along. Oh, and don't I wish it all ended there—but oh, no—not in this story. Not on your life!

Why had I even begun this stupid conversation anyway? Well, I suppose it was because I was trying to do the right thing. I didn't want the widow witch and me to end on a bad note. Crap—bad note is putting it lightly. For once this story is over—it will seem more like a bad scrap book.

I did, in fact, explain to her very gingerly that evening what, in fact, my dad had done and why. So that she wouldn't have to work. And for the mere sake of prohibiting me from vomiting—I will skip the details of that conversation. But I can tell each and every one of you that it was a disaster! She blamed me. She blamed my dad and she cursed the very day she had met him. Well, that now made two of us. For before that conversation was over that night—she informed me that she had met someone else. And I'm not real sure, but I think I felt like that notorious house had actually fallen on me as I was now the one who was green in the face. Guess she showed me—didn't she?

I ended the conversation—shortly thereafter—after she had dropped the same bomb my own mother had dropped so many years ago, but not before I had to tell her about the tickets. Oh crap! I had promised! I didn't want to. What I truly wanted to do was march right back in to that little office of my dads and lift the paper they were hidden behind, upon that cute little message board of his and snatch them from their little place of serenity and then burn them to smithereens right along with her stinking broom! But for some Godforsaken, unknown reason, I didn't, so we can all relax. But oh, how I so desperately wanted to! I *had* to tell her. I had promised my dad–and so I did and–she had no reaction. She simply sat there staring off into someplace other than where we were right then and there. I was kind of hoping she just might be contemplating–no–I'm not that vindictive, thank God! I then told her that due to the fact that I was going home and wouldn't be there, (*chicken chit*), perhaps she could take someone else with her. Like maybe her, 'Not so bad daughter' would like to go? Hey, now there was a hell of an idea!

Why–Oh–Why I have never learned to keep my big mouth shut is beyond me folks, because what she said to me next sent me into *the* tailspin of all tailspins!

She wasn't really sure that her daughter would enjoy seeing Willie Nelson, but perhaps her newly found friend would. Her newly found friend!? What in the hell had she just said? I'm sorry, but once again I do so believe that the audio portion of my brain just went on leave, right along with Private First Classman Eddie Littlefield, so please forgive me if I actually and this time, really do reach out and slap your pitiful, ugly, green face you–WITCH!!!

Oh–My–God!!! She had just gone and said the unthinkable! What in the hell did she think I was made of!? Kryptonite? I was so dumbfounded that I couldn't speak! Yes–Me! I was–well–speechless!!

*Go get that pail of water NOW you idiot daughter of Eddie! And just before you throw it on her, make damned sure you tape those tickets to her precious broom because we all know it burned as well! No–on second thought–get the gun! Shoot her–and then her monkeys! No wait–better yet–shoot the monkeys first! Make her watch in absolute horror as you take something that is more than precious to her!!! What the hell–just burn the whole damned castle down!!!! What are you waiting for you COWARD!!???*

What in tar nation had just happened? She had replaced my father not just *once*, but now *twice*? What–in–the? And then–I simply just died inside. I very politely, without even killing one monkey–ended our conversation. I've never really had a murdering bone in my body anyway. What was the use? I was tired and beaten and she sure as hell wasn't worth my breath any longer. I had no words mean enough or ugly enough. I just simply had no words–period. And for the first time in my life, I understood the Indian's very soul. I finally had no words! She had won and I didn't give a damn!

I was so very sad. Isn't it strange how in the middle of one tragedy another one can rear its ugly head? Yes—very strange indeed. And the last thing on my mind that night as she sashayed into the bedroom to turn in—and I was trying to fall asleep—was did he know? My God, how he had loved her—and instead of visions of sugarplums, all I could see was the memory of their wedding day in my backyard and my dad's smiling face.

Thursday morning came very early as I once again stumbled to the coffee pot. Wondering if I would ever sleep normally again, I realized that although I was still stumbling—I wasn't crying on this morning. No, it seemed that time was trying to do its part. Either that or the well had just run dry. Yes, now that I think back, I truly do believe that I had just simply run out of tears for the time being. My eyes were feeling the sensation, but they were dry. And I haven't yet decided which is worse. Crying for so long that your face becomes a permanent wasteland of tears, or feeling like you want to cry but you just can't seem to find the faucet. I guess it doesn't really matter. Both yield the same result, a broken heart that will never mend.

The widow witch—actually—on second thought—she didn't deserve the title of widow after our conversation the night before—so please allow me to rephrase that. The witch—which is a title that was most fitting even more so now—must have left early because when I awoke she was nowhere to be found. Just as well. I wasn't quite sure how I was going to ever look at her again. A couple more days and it would all be over. I would leave that house and never look back. Sad—but true. I went over our conversation in my head again and again. How she had tried to justify her loneliness. How my dad had been—as she put it—emotionally absent. Geeze–La–Weeze! No kidding? The guy was dying. He had cancer and he was dying!! So she went out shopping for a new partner? Holy crap—I needed to get some Valium!

At ten o'clock there came a knock at the door and I was suspicious to say the least. Who in the world would come calling? And perhaps I was a little annoyed as well as I pushed the curtains back and reached for the handle of the sliding glass door.

Oh–my–heck! It was the oxygen guy! He was there to pick up "the hidden" oxygen tank and as I slid the door open to welcome his entrance, another memory pushed its way through right along with him. As we said our hellos I realized he couldn't look at me. Did he know I was ashamed? Or perhaps printed across his clip boarded papers in big red letters was stamped the word DECEASED. Or perhaps it said LYING DAUGHTER!

Uncomfortably, I lead him into the spare bedroom that had secretly harbored "Bertha." With a wave of my hand I presented her to him as our eyes finally met. He had sympathy in his as I had sadness in my own. And there we both stood for just a couple of seconds before I finally broke the silence with an explanation.

"He wanted me to give it back," I said, staring at the floor watching the toes of my right foot slide back and forth across the carpet like a child who had just been caught lying.

"I know, I remember," he said.

"He wanted it to go to someone else who may have needed it more than him, so I had to hide it," I added. "Someone who may have had a chance," I trailed off.

Hoisting it up on to his dolly, and securely wrapping the belt around it, our eyes met again. "I'm sorry for your loss," he said.

"Me too," I replied, "Thank you."

"Well," he continued as he wheeled old "Bertha" into the living room,

"Maybe now it *will* go to someone else who will need it," as he stopped and set "Bertha" upright on her dolly, shoving the clip board toward me, prodding me to sign on the dotted line. It didn't have DECEASED or LYING DAUGHTER stamped across the page in big red letters. Instead it simply had my dad's name typed across the top with his address and phone number and I thought that to be very strange because—Eddie didn't live there anymore.

As I signed the piece of paper that was proof in the pudding that my dad had, in fact, died or was at least gone from this place, he added, "Your dad was a funny man."

Handing the clipboard back to him I replied, "Yes, he was. Sometimes too damned funny for his own good."

"Still," he continued, "it was thoughtful of him to want to give this to someone else."

"Yes," I said, "that's just the way he was," realizing that I had just for the very first time referred to my dad in past tense. We were having a small talk conversation and it was *me* who was telling someone how my dad had once been. And—it made me—proud. Proud that even someone who had only met him once had remembered how funny as well as thoughtful he had been.

Once again, putting the "Bertha" toting dolly into motion, my friend was on his way out. I rushed a little ahead of him, sliding the door open, thanking him as he and "Bertha" made their exit. And as I turned to face my lonely and quiet surroundings once again, I couldn't help but imagine my dad standing somewhere near by, arms folded across his chest, shaking his head back and forth in disbelief with a tisk, tisk sound spewing from his lips that made me feel just a little bit ashamed but only for a minute as I realized that if he had, in fact, been standing there in such a fashion, then he also must have been aware as to why I had lied, end of conversation - as I dismissed that vision with an out loud tisk, tisk of my own. Silly, some of the things we do when we're alone, I thought as I headed for the spare room that had served my dad as his own private little office.

Now standing in the doorway of the office, with my hand upon the knob, another funny thought came to me as I glanced around. With every intention of closing the room up tight just as it had always been, I paused. Why in the heck had my dad even needed an office? Perhaps it made him feel important, I thought, as I eyed the beautiful little roll top oak desk that had served my serious office-needing little dad at one time.

I strolled over and pulled out the matching oak armchair and sat down wondering if my dad ever pretended he was Perry Mason as he sat in this very same chair that looked like an old courtroom seat. Running my hands along the smooth arms on both sides, I leaned forward and almost did a head stand as to peek at the wheels underneath. They seemed old and rusted. Digging my feet deep into the carpet, I rolled the chair a little closer to its tabled partner. Now placing both hands on the desk, perhaps it was I, who was pretending. Pretending that I was *him*. Sitting there, late at night, looking at bills and wondering how he was going to make ends meet on a "Head of Maintenance" salary.

Dust had taken over most of the desk along with its inhabitants that were mostly just strewn about envelopes, paper clips and his silly little half moon shaped reading glasses. I reached over, picked them up and put them on, wondering just how many times he had fretted over not having enough money as we have all done from time to time and I realized that worrying about such things was absolutely useless because in the end it didn't really matter what *did* or *didn't* get paid. He was gone.

I reached down to my right and tugged on the bottom drawer. It didn't budge. What in the heck could have been in there to have made it so damned heavy? I wondered as I tugged with a little more might, finally popping it open and dropping its contents inside. Good Lord—cigar boxes! At least a dozen of them, all stacked neatly one on top of another.

I reached in and brought the top one to me. Placing it on the desk, I slid my fingernail up underneath its lid and laid it back to reveal the contents inside. "What–the–heck," I asked under my breath as I began to rummage—pay stubs! Yes, pay stubs, all proudly stacked inside the cigar box, beginning with his very last one!

I reached down into the drawer and pulled out another box. Setting it down on top of the desk beside its twin I opened it as well. More pay stubs! Now I glanced down into the drawer, staring in bewilderment, reaching in and pulling out each and every box, opening one at a time to reveal yet more pay stubs! My God! He had kept every single pay stub from every single check he had ever earned from twenty-six years of "keeping it kleen"!

Why? Must have meant something to my organized, impeccable, record keeping, Perry-Mason-pretending little dad. But what? Perhaps success? Yes, this was definitely proof of success, I had decided. Perhaps when he was feeling unsuccessful, he would come in here and go through each box proving to him self just how far he had actually come. Or maybe he simply thought that he needed to keep twenty-six years worth of pay stubs to buy a new car or a big screen TV or a silly round bed displayed in the front window of a department store.

Staring down into the drawer in disbelief, I then noticed a big brown manila envelope lying up against the side of the drawer, bulging at the sides. I reached in and it took both hands to retrieve it. Moving the stack of cigar boxes aside, I placed it on the desk in front of me with its mouth gaping open. I reached inside and pulled out a handful of papers. One at a time I glanced at each one, quickly setting them down on the desk as my anger began to grow fierce. Taking the bottom of the envelope and now dumping its entire contents out onto the desk, my hands rummaged through all of it. Every–last–one! Child support checks and money orders! All cashed by my mother, dating all the way back to 1968! She had lied! Surprise, surprise!

Swiping his glasses from my face and placing them on the desk I leaned my elbow next to them and rubbed my forehead with both hands. Why hadn't he shown these to me? He could have proven she lied a long time ago. Instead, he simply dismissed her accusations of nonsupport by saying that's just the way she remembered it. Why? Why hadn't he defended himself?

I began shoving the papers all back into the envelope with just as much anger as I had when I pulled them out and it dawned on me that this envelope had not been tidy like the boxes. And as I angrily continued to shove I realized that perhaps they had been shoved into this envelope after being taken out long before I had arrived. And by looking at them and their appearance, I assumed that thought to be true. That would explain why they had not been tidy and neatly placed into a cigar box. How many times had my dad come in here and done the very same thing I was doing and more than likely with just as much anger I wondered? And I decided that by the looks of the envelope as well as its contents, probably too many times to count.

I began placing the boxes all back into the drawer as well as the mystery-solving envelope and then closed it much harder than I had opened it. I wanted to call all of my sisters and share my newfound information. I wanted to scream at the very top of my lungs from the very highest mountain that our dad had not been a deadbeat! And then—calmness came over me and a simple thought of, why bother. He knew and now I knew as well and what did it matter anymore? We were all grown and these receipts were of a time long ago and it was then that I realized why my dad had done the same. I also realized once again what a noble man he had truly been.

I looked to the left of the desk and discovered that it held a large drawer as well. Oh crap, I thought, as I reached down and tugged its contents wide open. Now, what would I find? Perhaps that we had all been adopted?

This drawer contained a large brown accordion mini-file tied together with an elastic string. I reached in and pulled it up and out and set it on the desk before me.

Untying the string it instantly fanned and gapped open. Steadying myself before I reached inside to reveal who my real parents were, I noticed one single paper protruding from the top. I grabbed that one first. It was—The Divorce Decree— stating in big bold black letters that the end of my father's dreams had, in fact, been finalized. After starring at this document for a very long time, I reached in again to a different accordion slot. Grasping onto and pulling up and then out onto my lap a single piece of paper. And as I attempted to reach for the silly little half moon shaped glasses, as I couldn't believe what I was reading, I opted not to, as I realized they wouldn't help. I was holding a document that I never knew existed. I was shocked. I couldn't believe my eyes! It was a restraining order against my father, signed by a judge dated 1969. A restraining order? *My dad?* Why? And then as I sat mesmerized with bewilderment it came to me. If I had been my mother and living the way we had in fact been living in 1969, I wouldn't have wanted my ex-husband snooping around either. It also occurred to me that 1969 had been the very year that my dad had headed for the front door of his mother's home carrying a trouble stopper in the small of his back. So on second thought, smart move. Mom! Although we all know it surely wasn't this piece of paper that stopped him, now, don't we?

I hadn't known any of these happenings ever went on. I felt as though I were going through someone else's things. A stranger. Someone I hadn't known at all.

I reached up and inside again and pulled out a yellow piece of crumpled paper. Another court order. This one had been signed by a judge also as well as my mother. A request for a decrease in visitation to every other weekend. Attached was a reply letter from an attorney stating conditions that my dad would not get out of his vehicle when picking up his children if he could, in fact, continue his weekend visitations. It had been denied due to his threats to my mother. *Threats? My dad?* And why did he agree not to get out of his vehicle? Could it be that in order for him to see us he gave up the opportunity to be able to even come to the door so that he wouldn't be tempted to beat someone up? My dad? My dad? Well—hell, yes, my dad! My hero! My ever-lasting monster-fighting, knight in shining overalls! It was all there in black, white, and yellow! He had fought to see us! It wasn't a fairy tale! And he had obviously been through hell to do so!

How had he afforded an attorney? Why had he kept all of these reminders of the pain he had suffered in his past? Perhaps he would wake up early on a Saturday morning, pipe in mouth, and coffee by his side, and he would go through all of these things just as I was doing, reminding himself that he was indeed a survivor. If so, good for him, and now it was good for me. I probably will never understand why he didn't defend himself. I mean the proof was all out in front of me. Why hadn't he just put an end to her lies once and for all? And as I wrapped the string back around the archives of our past, I realized that my dad never had been the type of man to have to prove himself. Small man, yes. Small man syndrome—never in a million years!

I laid the file back in its perspective hiding place, deep within the confines of all secrets held and I tenderly slid the drawer closed. Now, I knew too, and for some reason the urge to tell my sisters as well as the urge to scream from a mountaintop had vanished. All I felt was peace, the kind of peace that comes from knowing. We had nothing to prove anymore. My days of defending him were over. And his days of defending himself had obviously been over a long time ago.

There were two more drawers I hadn't yet been through. The smaller top drawers directly above the large bottom drawers. My gosh, what in the world could he have been hiding in those, I wondered! I'll probably find out that the Indian is adopted, I thought as I reached to the right and gave it a tug. And with a scoot sound the drawer gave way and its contents practically jumped out to greet me! Pictures! There must have been hundreds of them or so it seemed. I then turned in my chair, slightly to the left and gave that drawer a tug. More pictures. What a relief. This would be more fun.

Small black and white reminders that we did at one time, all have a happy life together, my mom and Dad, my sister and I. And I'm sure if I had taken the time to do so, I could have placed them in story order. Most of them held wonderful memories of Christmas' gone by, lost and forgotten episodes of a wonderful life. Some sported a young and savvy Eddie standing by a different car in various black and white order. Always smiling, always wearing a silly hat or funky shorts or something that absolutely none of the general population would ever wear. My big sis and I were in a lot of them. Always smiling with our long hair flowing freely or in braids. Funny how in those days you dressed up for pictures, I thought to myself, as I could remember my mom always trying to make sure we looked our best. Most of the time we were wearing matching outfits. YUK! My mom—always wanting our faces washed and our hair combed. I could remember her pleading with my dad to allow her to clean us up first before we went somewhere or had a picture taken. Now there was a memory that had snuck up on me unexpectedly. Huh, and it was a pleasant one—of my mom—being a mom. Never say never, another book—another time—another story.

There were pictures of my grandparents from both my mom's and my dad's side of the family, as well as pictures of my aunts and uncles and cousins. There were plenty of my big sis and I and some of my middle sister and only a few of my two youngest sisters. I guess we get just a little busier with each and every child. And I couldn't help but wonder as I glimpsed my dad from long ago, if he had even a clue as to what the future held at the time those shots were taken. That was long before any judge-signed papers were in sight! Long before a real live monster would move in and destroy his world. Long before the very love of his life would, in fact, stop loving him one day. How do our lives lose these precious gifts so quickly? When do things start to go so wrong? As I look back now, it seems that they simply just happened. But surely with each day there must have been some sort of decline, some sort of warning, or—perhaps—these are things that just lie still and silent in our past and they have no answers, like the photos, black and white and silent. Just like the secrets that they don't portray.

I looked through each and every one before I had finally had enough for one day. Stuffing them all back into their hiding place, just exactly the way I had found them, I closed both drawers tucking away the traces of my dad's very existence.

So there I sat, drumming my fingers on the desk, looking around as though I just might find someone who would be sympathetic to what I had just discovered. And as I scooted my Perry Mason courtroom chair backward as if to make room for a quick getaway, I glanced down at the desk just once more as if it had been some sort of close call and I was simply glad to be alive, when I noticed a small sort of hidden drawer tucked up underneath directly in the center. Oh, Lord, what now? What more could this oak freak show be hiding? That my half sister wasn't my dad's? Oh what a tangled web we weave.

I scooted back just a little bit farther as to accommodate the length of the drawer, reached underneath, and grabbed with my fingertips as there was no handle, and I pulled. Envelopes. Just envelopes. Empty envelopes with—my—Dad's—address—printed neatly in the center and MY RETURN ADDRESS in the top left-hand corner! I reached in calmly and slowly at first and then as I found empty envelope upon empty envelope, I began rifling through them like I had just been overcome with some sort of rabid frothing at the mouth sort of illness. No cards, no letters, just empty envelopes. All from me—and all empty. What in the heck did he do with the cards and letters? Why did he keep all of these envelopes? This had to be the strangest phenomenon I had encountered yet! Why? And just as I began to wipe the foam from the top of the desk that had been dripping from my rabid mouth, still pillaging through the drawer as if I needed to find just one more cigarette, I came across another picture. This one was alone and all by itself on the very bottom of the drawer. Trying to pry it up with the tips of my fingers, I finally had to half bend it to get a hold of it. Grasping it tightly, then, bringing it up close to my face as though I might need to smell it, I could clearly read the date, 1961. It was a picture of a small chubby little girl and her daddy! I was three years old and standing next to him sporting a pair of feet pajamas while he sat on a lounge chair sporting a pair of overalls. It was obvious that I had my hand down the back of his shirt, smiling from ear to ear. He was holding a cigar and doing the same. Shoulders slumped and now taking the picture in both hands, I leaned forward, resting my arms on the desk and just simply stared at it. God, how I loved my dad, then as well as now and no amount of anything that had happened in between had ever changed that. So there I sat. Tears silently screaming the rage of his loss down each side of my face and thanking God that someone had snapped that precious picture. And to this day that very same picture sits proudly on the nightstand beside my bed in a double frame, next to a picture that was taken thirty-one years later at my baby sister's wedding, with him sitting in a chair and me ironically standing next to him on the very same side I had so many years before, hand behind his back and both of us smiling from ear to ear. The only difference between the two photos is that we are both just a little bit older—oh, and I seriously doubt that my hand was down his back or so I don't recall. A lot of years had passed between those two pictures, but not between us, I thought as I allowed my fingers to search through the drawer just one more time in one last lazy attempt to find a letter or card or something—anything that may have come to him in one of those paper news carriers. Nothing. I had absolutely no clue what he might have done with them and I have absolutely no clue as to why he kept only the envelopes. Guess it's just another one of those things I'll have to ask when I see him again. Of course, he'll probably just make up some silly ass story as to the whereabouts of all the cards and letters. Yes, I do believe God allows a good story or two in heaven. And if he didn't before my dad got there, I'm sure he had been forced to do so once my dad had arrived. Everyone loves a good story, folks. Probably even God.

It became very obvious to me for the mere sake of my own sanity if nothing else that it was time to close up shop. I was exhausted and once again felt like I couldn't take not one more stinking memory. Leaving the envelopes in the drawer just as I had found them (OK, maybe a little more strewn about), I slid it closed as it cried with a slight but rebellious moan. Picture in hand, I looked at it and then sort of gave it a sure shake in my tightly closed fingers as though it were a rare and precious coin. The picture was going with me.

This had been a fine place for my dad to have played Perry Mason, I thought, as I stood and pushed the chair back in close to its partner, as my eyes then panned and met the tiny bulletin board hanging by the door which harbored those blasted hidden tickets. I just couldn't bear the thought. I never even looked for them. I just simply walked the hell out of there and that's all I have to say about that! This tiny room with its musty smell and its secrets would only be but another memory in a couple of days. And that, quite frankly, was just fine and jim-dandy with me. I'd simply take all of the memories home with me, packed away tightly somewhere in the corners of my mind and sort them out as we all do—one at a time or several at a time whichever just happened to occur first. It didn't really matter. What was done had already been photographed and stored. Sucks, but that's just the way life goes. Anyway, I had some preparation to do before the Indian would soon be arriving with two very old and much-needed friends of mine. Oh-my-hell! What time was it? Oh, my bejesus! What in the Sam hell had I been thinking? *Had* I been thinking was probably a more appropriate question? Of course I hadn't been thinking because I had been too damned busy playing Perry freaking Mason! Almost in a full gallop I headed straight for the living room stopping short directly where my eyes could focus in on the clock, standing as if I were expecting a show down with the Barker boys. DRAW! It was four o'clock! Oh for the love of Pete! I had to prepare! How? How was I going to prepare for- well- I had to settle down. I was having one of the worst anxiety attacks since—well—since— YESTERDAY! What in the heck was the matter with me? I was cracking up! At eight o'clock this very evening I would be arriving at the funeral home to—what in the hell had I been thinking? He told me not to look at him. He told me not to. This was awful, just awful. Tell me what to do, Scarecrow—Tin Man—Lion—ANYONE!

Breathe, Dorothy—and quit squeezing Toto, he's turning blue. Glinda the good witch would be arriving soon along with the Tin Man and the Indian (not usually in the script) and they might know what to do. No, Glinda would arrive in her shiny sparkling bright sun shiny bubble and she *would* know what to do for sure, now just breathe.

I stumbled backward and stopped once I felt the welcome of my dad's chair on the back of my legs. Now I sat, or more like fell backward into the pillowy softness of what used to be my dad's safe and happy place. It was nice, comforting, as I nestled in and took hold of the blanket which was studiously lying across the arm of this cloud and brought it up close around my neck. His smell was strong now. Stronger than I had ever imagined it could be. I had never sat in my dad's chair. This was odd. Why, it had never occurred to me to do so was beyond me at this point. His smell—his comfort—his presence—was all around me. The clock continued to tick, tick, tick away the minutes however they really didn't matter like they had just moments ago. There was no longer any urgency to prepare. I simply sat back and gazed about the room - and I began to remember. What day was it that he had gotten out of his chair and stood before me and asked for my hands to dance? I couldn't remember. I thought it was the first week of my visit. All the days had grown into one. They were no longer separate. I had been wiping the coffee table with a rag reeking of pledge with an album crackling from the stereo serenading my dusting crusade when I turned and noticed him standing there. Arms outstretched, and smiling from ear to ear. His hands beckoned me in a come here sort of fashion and I dropped the rag and slowly walked toward him, giggling and asking what the heck? When he took my hands as if he were Fred Astaire and I, Ginger Rogers—and he twirled me around as we danced some sort of country swing or waltz combination to what song? I couldn't remember. How could I not have taken notice? Well, perhaps it was because he had done this so many times before. He loved to dance. From the time I was very small in the days when I would stand on his feet to accomplish such a task—and that's what it was when I was very small—a task. Oh, Geeze–La–Weeze, Dad wants to dance again. *Please, God, don't let any of my friends see me dancing with my nutty father,* I would pray as he twirled me around. I could feel the slickness of his cowboy boots beneath my socked feet. Slipping and holding on tight and laughing. I mean a good throw yourself backward, forget about your friends finding out, good oldfashioned down-home rib-tickling laugh. God, how I used to think he was a fruit cake. God, how sitting there now I wished we could dance just once more time. But there were to be no more dances. How was I to have known it would have been our last? How do any of us know? We don't. Please always remember that my friends.

My last dance with my father took place just four weeks before he died, in the privacy of his little living room. And knowing me as you all do, I'm quite sure you are all well aware of the fact that I truly *did* know at the time what a gift of intimacy I had been given on that day long ago–and because of *that* moment, Garth Brooks' song, "The Dance" has always been one of my favorites. I could have missed the pain, but I would have *also*, had to miss–'The Dance!' Profound, isn't it? Oh, and if I can survive the embarrassment of dancing with my nutty father then I'm sure you can survive whatever embarrassment awaits you. As a matter of fact, my advice to you is—relish in it. I will be envious.

Funny how the time just didn't seem to matter anymore as I sat huddled warm and safe and reminiscing. It was so hard for me to believe he was gone. I knew I had to see him. I had to make sure he was gone. I knew I had to but I didn't want to. He warned me. He specifically told me not to do what I was, in fact, planning to do. God I was sorry. And I was ashamed. Sounds like a regular parent child dilemma which just goes to show you that it never ends. I glanced at the clock—I had been day dreaming for almost an hour. Soon the Indian would be arriving from the airport with Glinda and the Tin Man. I think Toto had passed out during the last anxiety attack.

I glanced around the room viewing it one last time from a new perspective. My dad's. From this chair he saw his world. He ended each day from that very chair. Most of the time falling asleep with the TV blaring out of each ear muff. I wondered if he reminisced too. Did he sit and think about the old days in that chair? Perhaps it was a magic chair. Perhaps it held all of the memories of that soldier's life. I was sure it did just as I was sure it was time for me to get up and out of it before I fell under some spell disappearing somewhere beneath the cushions, never to return. I really had to get a life once all of this hullabaloo was over. Funny—I thought as I stood and folded the blanket neatly and placed it back across the arm of the chair, I had now begun my day from my dad's world and ended it the same. Why? Ah—such are the mysteries of life. Or—perhaps—such mysteries simply make a great plot for a good book.

It wasn't long after I had exited the magic chair that I heard a car approaching outside. Then, three almost simultaneous slams of car doors and then—the bubble appeared with its rays of sunshine beaming my sister's smile as she waved her wand and entered my father's home. Glinda and the Tin Man had arrived and not by way of a horse of a different color and carriage but by way of the Indian's automobile. I'm sure the Lone Ranger would have been—well—disgusted.

I threw my arms around the Tin Man and melted within the warmth of his touch. Real hugging back arms! Not just memories but honest to goodness love seeping into my heart from another live human being. I felt energized. And as we stood there for what seemed to be an eternity, neither one of us seeming to want to let go yet, I opened my eyes and gazed at Glinda over the Tin Man's shoulder through tear-soaked eyes and as her eyes met mine there seemed to be somewhat of an old familiar look gazing back at me. It was her good witch look, lips pursed in a soothing, satisfied smile as she stood proud, head tilted to one side, gazing in adoration holding her wand in one hand and lightly tapping it's tip in the other, with little starlets dancing all around her and that beaming ray of "everything's gonna be all right" sunshine. But there was more to her gaze as our eyes locked. Her tear-soaked face was all too familiar to me. For when Glinda the good witch cried it was always for someone else and never for herself. Hers were tears of defeat and sorrow. They were the very same tears that had fallen so many times before—so very long ago. Tears that screamed a silent rage of her inability to rescue me.

My husband was whispering something to me as he hugged and cradled me. It was faint, however, audible as I started back from where my mind had been. "I'm sorry, honey," he was saying. "I know your heart is breaking. I'm sorry your dad is gone."

Me too, I thought but only for a moment before I realized how very sorry he really was. How very real his tears of sorrow were for he had lost his own father at the tender age of eight just when most little boys really need their daddies. At least I had been given the blessing to have really known my father. Of course he knew—and all *too* damned well.

I stretched my puckered lips up just as far as they would go and at the same time brought his cheek down to me as to accommodate my inadequate reach and I kissed his—tear-soaked—face! (Oh, please don't cry, Tin Man, you'll rust.) Thank you, I whispered. And somewhere deep within the make-believe channels of my mind I could hear Glinda in that tooting and melodramatic wavering voice asking, "Are you ready to go home now, Dorothy?"

Yes, as a matter of fact, I was more than ready to go home. I had had it with everyone! The wizard was gone and sometimes I couldn't even remember if he'd ever really been there at all! Aunty Em had probably already given up on me. The weather wasn't clearing and somewhere that nasty old witch was still lurking because I was just too damned scared to go get the broom! And just to top off an already bad day, I couldn't even find the stinking ruby red slippers—God only knew if they ever even existed either—and I had probably just about killed poor Toto during the last anxiety attack. I really did need to get a life if it was the last thing I did!

I left my husband's side with a lingering touch and reached my arms out to hug my big sis. We embraced briefly but ever so forcefully. One of those *you're a good old soldier* sort of hugs. She dismissed the hug with a *good old soldier* pat on the back and then I invited them to sit a spell and listen to a most magnificent story of perseverance as I proceeded to share my triumphant experience with the United States Army.

They were aw struck and teary-eyed as I described my dilemma from the embalming process all the way to the present. Dazed is what they were—or maybe bored—no, dazed—I'm sure of it as they both boasted of how very proud they were of me. I was proud of me too as I glanced over at the Indian who somehow had begun to take on the ghostly appearance of the Scarecrow. Always proud and always silently beaming. He had, after all been my first and longest friend during this entire journey and he probably would have dumped me long ago—if he'd only had a brain.

Sitting on the floor I glanced up at the clock and then at my sis who in turn gave me an understanding glance back. The sort of glance when your eyes meet and then dart away from one another as if we didn't really want each other to know that we had, in fact, had eye contact. It was almost time to go. She knew it—and I knew it. And to say that dread was hovering would have been an understatement. The Indian had to leave on that note—promising to return soon.

We all stood as if to stretch our legs and I noticed my sis staring down the hallway toward the bedroom door. *Don't go in there!* I so wanted to scream. *It's painful and ugly in there!* This was a new role for me as I shocked myself into believing that I could actually spare her the pain. *Stay here and I'll go get Joe—because dad's not in there anymore! Joe can share with you what the bedroom looks like and what his last moments consisted of—just please don't open that door!*

She began to meander toward the hallway and I could swear she was acting as if she may just have had to have gone to the bathroom and I half expected her to turn and give me a raspberry, thumbs twinkling from her ears before she then darted for the bedroom door. But that was all in my mind as she very quietly did, in fact, walk toward the bedroom door and did the unthinkable. She took hold of the knob and turned it until the ever so familiar "pop" welcomed her entry.

I plunked myself down on the couch and watched her walk through the looking glass with my hands over my eyes and simply waited for her to emerge. She wasn't in there for very long before she came back through and I almost hoped she would be laughing hysterically exclaiming that her dumb-ass little sister had been mistaken again and that our dad was in there and just sleeping. But she didn't. No, sadly, she came back out through the black hole and gave me another secret glance which told me he really *was* gone before she then faced the door, turning her back to me, locked her gaze upon the door knob and pulled it toward her ever so carefully closing the bedroom door as if it might just bite her. It was done. My big sis had gone in and checked and our dad wasn't in there. It was real. He was gone. Because the good witch never lied.

I looked up at her through my fingers, which were plastered across my face as if I simply were nursing a severe headache and I noticed that she was definitely avoiding my gaze. She seemed to be in deep thought. Probably saying to herself, hey, for once, the little dumb-dumb got it right, our dad really is gone! Highly doubtful, I suppose—however, possible or perhaps she was just processing. After all, that had been her first time through the looking glass since my dad had left and I do believe the realization of it all had probably just smacked her in the heart. Oh heck, our realization happened chapters upon chapters ago. But she didn't write the book nor had she read it yet. How was she to have known? Either that or Joe had insulted her.

She sat down across from me on the futon and after a moment or two of just sitting there rubbing her hands together, brow furrowed and staring at the floor, she finally turned her gaze toward me and very quietly asked, "Are you sure you need to go tonight?"

Now it was I sitting with furrowed brow staring back at her as if she had tried to spit on me. "I just mean," she continued, "Dad won't be there. Just his body will; do you understand that?"

Oh for the very love of God! I was thirty-four years old! A mother of four! Intelligent, practical, and, quite frankly, no, I don't think I *did* understand that—but I told her I did.

"Of course," I said, with all the confidence in the world or at least in my dad's living room. *Geeze, Glinda, I'm not a dumb little Munchkin!*

"OK," she said, as if she knew me better than I knew myself, "Then we'd better get ready to go and get this over with."

*GO? NOW?* "Why now?" I asked, trying to calm my voice into human tone. Both she and the Tin Man stared at me like—duh—before one of them, and I truly don't know which one, because I could have sworn I had fainted, said, "Traffic's going to be heavy." Oh, traffic. Sure, I was so concerned about getting there on time. I mean, heck, if we were held up by traffic my dad might just get pissed off and leave. So what if we hit traffic, I thought to myself. So what if the rest of my entire life consisted of nothing but the journey to the funeral home. Now that wouldn't be so bad really, would it? Actually, no, not at all because it seemed like the first part of my life up until that very point had been spent dreading this very day anyway. Don't we all? Sure we do if we are at all honest. And no, not every moment of every day, but I'll bet not a one of us can count the times in our lives, actual moments when we glanced at our moms or dads and a quick but fleeting thought of what life would be like without them would scurry across our hearts. We all do it. And it's not because we are strange or weird or in my case even a little, shall we say imaginative? No, it's because we are perfectly normal. Well, most of us anyway. So what the hell did I care about traffic? What was one more decade compared to what faced me that evening? Not realistic I know but it was how I felt at the time. What's new?

I stood up from the couch simply because my sis had said let's get ready and she was the boss. Someone had to be or I might just still be sitting there to this day. However, once standing I felt lost, disoriented and I really didn't know what to do first to *get ready*. Get ready, how? I mean, we were going to see our dad but there was no need to call first, we knew he'd be there. This was really weird. *Do tell Glinda— how does one get ready for the viewing of one's dead body?* Then came the real stumper. What does one wear to view a dead body? I should have been a game show host. I mean, here we go again with traditions that are just a little bit silly. What do you wear to go look at someone who can't look back at you, can't talk to you, can't hug or smell you? What's the use? No wonder my dad wanted to be buried naked. He must have known all along. Or perhaps, he thought that that just may have clenched it and that I wouldn't have dared viewed his body for sure. My God, what was I doing? What had I already done? I shouldn't go. He begged me not to do exactly what I was, in fact, planning to do. And right then and there for some stupid reason—or not—another precious memory came pushing its way through. I didn't need another memory or so I thought. However, this particular memory was of great significance to me. This one had a lesson in store for me. It was pushing its way through to remind me of who I had always been.

I was five years old and we lived on the farm in Ohio. That is where I was born. Ohio. We refer to it as "The Farm," because that's exactly what it was. A most magnificent place where we all once lived happily, as a family with its acres of rolling lawn and apple tree orchards and corn fields that seemed to go on for as far as the eye could see. And it was all ours. A large, white, two story farmhouse with hard wood floors and a big country kitchen and, my God, what I'd give to own that place now.

We had a pasture and a barn with no horse and my dad just couldn't live with that. Just didn't seem right to him. So, one Saturday morning, my silly little pony-seeking dad, woke me and my big sis up early to go fetch us a pony for our pasture. We were going to a pony farm! Another magnificent place where one could go to pick out a pony of any size and color and bring it home. What a day that was! I had never seen nor been to a pony farm but as always, my dad had told us all about it. It was a place where all the ponies in the world lived just waiting to be adopted by none other than us! My heck, they had created these pony farms just for me and my sis to go and adopt us a pony! We had to be the luckiest girls in the whole wide world!

The trip was long but it didn't seem so with my dad chatting away the whole drive about how exciting a place a pony farm really was. And finally, we turned from one country road onto another that was adorned with a white split rail fence that seemed to go for miles and miles with nothing but green pasture as far as the eye could see. My dad kept saying, keep looking you'll see the ponies soon and we kept looking and looking until we did! We did see the ponies! Thousands and thousands of beautiful ponies of all sizes and colors just like my dad had said. I sat in the back seat with my face and hands plastered upon the window staring and trying to contemplate just which pony we would take home for our very own.

When we finally turned again and drove up the long dirt driveway that led to a huge red barn, I noticed a man waiting outside by the fence. This must have been the pony farmer my dad had told us about. We all got out of the car and my dad shook hands with the pony farmer and I just knew that my dad had to be more important than the president of the United States of America! He knew the pony farmer! As a matter of fact, they were both wearing overalls which only further convinced me that my dad and the pony farmer must have gone way back together as my grandma used to say.

While standing and gazing through the fence as I waited for my dad and the pony farmer to finish talking pony talk, I noticed a wire that topped the entire perimeter of the fence. And it seemed just as I was contemplating touching that wire, my dad turned and told me not to. "Don't touch that wire, it's hot," he had said and turned back around to continue his conversation.

Hot? How could a wire be hot, I thought? Didn't make a damned bit of sense to me. So as I waited—I reached down and pulled up a long thick blade of grass. Glancing once to make sure my dad wasn't looking I carefully took that blade of grass and ever so slowly, very lightly, touched the tip of the blade of grass to the wire and—OH MY HECK—IT SHOCKED ME, making me drop the blade of grass and immediately left me inspecting my thumb and forefinger for injury.

As I stood rubbing my hand I looked up and both my dad and the pony farmer were staring at me.

"Did you touch that wire?" my dad asked.

"No," I quipped, dropping my chubby hands to my side yet still rubbing my thumb and finger together.

"Don't touch that wire," he said again. "It's hot," as he turned back around to continue his conversation.

He told me not to touch that wire—it was hot. Clearly I heard him yet I had to see for myself. I had to see what *hot* meant. Just like I now had to see what *dead* meant. I was only five. Now I was thirty-four. But I had always had to make sure. It is who I am. I'm sure my dad knew it then just as well as he must have known it up until the very day he died and nothing I could do would ever change my need to "know." It's who I was and who I had obviously always been.

My sis was staring at me with grave concern (no pun intended) as I came back from this wonderful memory into the present.

"Where were you?" she asked, just a little concerned. I looked into her eyes, still trying to focus on the present, dazed and just a little confused and all I could say was, "Do you remember Spotty our pony?"

"Yeah," she said slowly as she looked as if she might slyly find her way to the door and then dash out through the blowing curtains never to be seen again. "What in the world made you think of Spotty," she asked, more than just a little concerned. The Tin Man looked totally bewildered, as if the entire yellow brick road had just completely vanished before his very eyes.

"Nothing," I said, as I made my way past both of them and headed for the bathroom to get ready. "I just hate electric fences," I mumbled and I closed the bathroom door behind me, leaving both of them standing there, looking at each other as if one of them just knew that the other had, in fact, stolen our only golden path to Oz.

When I emerged from the bathroom, both my sis and my husband seemed to be standing where I had left them. Probably trying to look inconspicuous before they made their getaway.

"Are you ready?" Glinda asked.

"I guess as ready as I'll ever be," I replied, not knowing what in the hell I was talking about.

The Tin Man seemed to still be searching for the right road, however, when our eyes met he held that look. The look of knowing that I was getting in that hot air balloon and there wasn't a damned thing he could do about it.

The Indian arrived right on time whatever that meant. In the Westerns it was the Lone Ranger who always arrived just in the nick of time. However, I don't think there was such a thing as in the nick of time in this situation because had there been, my dad would've still been alive.

We spoke about everything but the obvious on the way to the funeral home. My husband's job, my uncle's job, the flipping weather. I remained very quiet. My dad would've died all over again as I remembered how he used to pay me to be quiet in the car. Hell, I should've collected and cashed in back then, I would've been a millionaire by now.

At last, we arrived at the funeral home. My heart was pounding so loudly that I was afraid once my uncle took the keys out of the ignition, everyone would be able to hear it just as loudly as I was feeling it, which lead me to wonder if anyone had ever had a heart attack at a viewing. I was just a little concerned as one of the worst anxiety attacks in funeral history began to fester inside of me like a tornado trying to gain momentum before it touched down.

I secretly tried to imagine what my dad would look like but they *had* after all, dressed him in his sweats so perhaps he would look as though he were simply sleeping. Yes, I had decided that that is exactly how he would look. What an idiot!

The witch had decided a couple days earlier not to accompany us and I had not yet told anyone the secrets that had, in fact, been revealed the night before. She was still gone when we left the house and I truly didn't feel like going into it. Quite frankly, I was afraid to because this little tidbit of info just may have sent Glinda into a rage like no other thus popping her everlasting bubble of sunshine never to be seen again— proving that the apple doesn't fall far from the witch tree. Good witch or bad witch—we are all very capable of losing it if pushed far enough.

As we walked up that sidewalk to the big front doors, I decided that I didn't like that place anymore. Yes, I believed I wouldn't go there anymore and that was that. From the tear slip proof sidewalk to the clickity clacking hallways I hated that place. My uncle was swinging the big double doors open and now I felt as though I just might want to vomit. *And who in the hell named him the doorman anyway?*

As we entered what had become my worst nightmare (although unbeknownst to me the worse was yet to come) the hospice chaplain was waiting in the entry. Her presence was that of an angel as she stood with arms open wide to great me, her reflection illuminating from the marble floors. I melted in her embrace as she whispered to me, her Dutch accent echoing throughout my heart: "He's here, my dear, I can feel him."

I backed up a couple of steps still holding on to her hands, looked up into those honest eyes of hers and for just a moment, I thought someone *had,* in fact, made a terrible mistake. However, I quickly realized before I embarrassed myself as well as her that she was simply speaking of his presence in a spirit sense. People ought not to say such things to certain people such as myself. For people such as myself just might do something crazy like run throughout the funeral home screaming, "Come out, come out, where ever you are! Ollie, Ollie, Oxen Free!"

I politely introduced my sister and husband to the hospice chaplain and I suddenly realized we were all whispering. Now, there's another one for all of us who just might be keeping track. Why in the name of God do we whisper inside a funeral home? Who in the hell might we be disturbing? And all of a sudden, I could've sworn I heard my mother's voice from somewhere far away, deep from within my past telling me to shut up before I woke the dead. I could've only wished.

The hospice chaplain was saying something as I tuned my mother out and focused back in on the present conversation-taking place without me once again. She was whispering something to my sis. What? What was it they were saying? I lifted my eyebrows at both of them as if to say, *I'm sorry, I didn't catch that*—but neither one of them cared to share anything at all with me. They both just stood there for a brief moment before my sis gave the hospice chaplain an understanding nod, turned to face me, took me by the hand and led me over to the antique sofa in the foyer. Once standing in front of it, she then placed both hands on my shoulders, slightly turned my shoulders toward her and then ever so carefully she sat me down. Stooping down in front of me, both hands on my knees, she whispered, "I'm going to go in and see Dad first, OK?" I stared with no response. They knew something I thought as I sat staring at her. Ah Ha! He *was* still alive! They were going to surprise me!

"Why?" I asked, snickering to myself.

"Well," she stalled, before her Glinda the good witch voice took over and she ever so politely and matter-of-factly explained to me that it was because she needed some time with him first.

Uh huh. OK, whatever you say, I thought.

She was going in to hush everyone before I came in. Probably all of my sisters as well as all of my dad's friends from work were all in there just waiting to yell SURPRISE! When I walked through the door. My dad would be standing there, arms wide open, head slightly tilted to one side as if to say, *No, no, Baby Doll, it's all right, I've been here all along. It's all over now, this has all been just a bad dream.*

I would then melt in his arms and we would go home to his house and eat some ice cream. Oh what a day this was going to be! Wait a minute, if this had, in fact, all been a bad dream, then wouldn't his cancer be gone too? Oh–My–God! His body would be back to normal! He wouldn't gag or throw up absolutely nothing anymore and I would go home with my husband and big sis and prepare for the greatest Thanksgiving ever!

"Are you all right?" she asked.

Blinking at her, coming back from a place where I'm sure only *I* have ever been, I robotically replied, "Yeah, I'm ok. I'm fine."

"You sure," she said. "Do you *not* want me to go in there without you?"

OK, this was turning out to be not so good after all. Why was she asking me that if a surprise was waiting?

"No," I said, "It's OK. I'll wait here." As a matter of fact, take all the time you need because I couldn't stand up had I wanted to at the time so what difference did it make?

She stood and motioned for my husband to come sit next to me on the sofa.

"I'll be right back," she promised.

And with that—she walked around the corner and was gone.

As I sat waiting, I noticed my knees beginning to shake. My husband, sitting on the right side of me, reached over and placed his left hand on both of my trembling knees.

"You OK?" he asked.

I turned my head slightly to face him and as I looked into his eyes I wanted to tell him of my suspicion in the worst way—but I didn't dare. I would have spoiled the surprise.

"I think so," I finally replied.

"It's almost over," he whispered.

I said nothing as I sat confused and scared to death. The hospice chaplain was standing in the tiny windowed room talking quietly to Fella. What could they be talking about I wondered, as I sat waiting? She shouldn't be talking to him, I thought. He's the enemy. He harbors dead people in this tangled web of no return. Keeps 'em in freezers and doesn't let you see them.

Just as I was about to launch into another wild and crazy dream state, my husband asked, "Are you sure you need to do this?"

OK, this wasn't at all the question he might ask had there been a surprise waiting. Because the pleading look in his eyes was that of a man who would have much rather of swooped me up and whisked me out to the car had I just said the word.

Trying not to look at him, I fidgeted in my seat staring down at my hands, which were wringing the hell out of one another and said, "I have to."

And after a long pause of silence, he simply said, "I know."

Where in the hell was Glinda? How in the hell long did it take her to say good-bye anyway? And just as I thought I might bolt from that antique sofa and storm down that corridor to snatch her by the hair of her pretty little head, she floated around the corner, saving herself the unknown embarrassment of becoming bald.

Her face was ashen and her eyes looked as though they held a terrible secret and I knew that look all too well. She spotted Fella and she made a detour to speak with him briefly. Her voice sounded far away and in a whisper, however, I could tell by the rise and fall of both their conspiratorial whispers that she had some sort of a misgiving or concern. Then, Fella seemed to be trying to explain something to her with complete compassion, palms up and animate.

My gaze found hers as she turned now to walk toward me and our eyes seemed to lock together in a silent tug of war as we stared at each other, my gaze following her all the way to the sofa where she then stood directly in front of me, stooping down and taking both of my hands in her own, once again.

Reaching up with the softness of one palm, she caressingly took my chin and turned it so there was no mistake that we were to be eye to eye.

"I need for you to listen to me," she began. "That is not our dad in there. Our dad is gone. What lies in there is simply his shell. It doesn't look a thing like our dad. They waited too long to embalm the body. Do you understand?"

Sure, I understood. Someone had, in fact, made one of the biggest boo-boos in morgue history! Our dad wasn't in there, she had just said so herself, which meant that someone had better be to finding him and fast! Thanksgiving was only two weeks away!

I sat and I simply just stared at her. Brow furrowed and head tilted as though I were a dog who had just heard an eerie sound.

She continued, "His skin is very pale and he is very swollen and I truly wish you would change your mind and just not go in there." (Don't touch that wire—it's hot!) "Are you sure you have to go?" she asked as if we were simply pulling the car over from taking a long drive.

No, I wasn't sure. Now I was scared. This was exactly what I had been afraid of. She wasn't able to face reality, the poor dear. Of course he was swollen and pale. He had cancer!

I swallowed hard, trying to make my mouth come alive with the gift of communication. It was no use, not yet anyway. I had to choose the right words, you know, take it easy on her. Finally, after several attempts, with tears welling up in my already so very tired eyes, I managed to speak.

"I don't want to," I pleaded, "but I have to. Do you understand?"

She sat on her haunches just a second more before she then, leaned on my legs, balancing herself to a standing position and answered me with, "Yes, I understand. I was just hoping," and her thought trailed off in to silence.

I didn't know what she was so worried about. I knew how bad he looked. After all, I *had* been the one who had tended to him. I had spent many a sleepless day and night upon day and night watching him deteriorate. I wasn't afraid of how bad he looked, I knew. What I didn't know or should I say what I didn't, couldn't get through my thick skull was that he was dead! I have no clue what I had been thinking that late November evening. God only knew and I'm sure as always when it came to me, his plate was more than full.

Following her lead I too stood up, cueing my husband to then do the same. This was it. We were going in.

The Indian also took the hint and as Dorothy, the Tin Man, the Scarecrow and Glinda the good witch interlocked arms and began our walk to finally come face to face with the all knowing and all mighty, powerful, Wizard of OZ *(death)*, I realized we were missing someone and had been all along.

We rounded the corner where my sister had mysteriously disappeared just moments before, and with the clickity clacking of our shoes on the marble floors, we began our journey down the long, dark and echoing hallway. About halfway down we came to an open door to the left of us from whence there came faint but unmistakably sad music. "This is it," Glinda said, stretching out her arm as if to say, *After you*.

Hesitantly, I entered through the threshold of the dimly lit room, arms still interlocked, with Glinda and the Tin Man still by my side and the Scarecrow close behind. I stood completely frozen and stared at the far end of the very long room were I spotted that beautiful piece of wood which had a draped curtain encased around the pedestal of which it was obviously sitting atop of. Of course he was on a pedestal. For hadn't I placed him there long ago during an era of monsters and all that could go wrong? Yes, I believed the pedestal was very fitting. I took two more steps closer. I couldn't really see him yet. Two more steps—and then—I could make out the profile of his face just barely protruding over the horizon of the casket and resting underneath that unmistakable propped up leafless tree. I stood completely still as the room began to turn. I became light headed and woozy. Two more steps—which placed me right in the center of the room. I could see his chest now, arms folded neatly and peacefully across it—and—IT WASN'T MOVING!

Without realizing it, I shook my arms loose from my escorts as if to free myself and in a swift and determined walk as if to get to the bottom of this, I made the rest of the journey all the way to the casket. Once before him I stopped and from somewhere far in the distance I heard someone who sounded much like myself moaning "Oh, Dad!"

Now that same someone was crying, uncontrollably. "Get up! Come out of there!" she was begging.

"P-l-e-a-s-e! Please wake up." I reached out to touch him, to gently shake him awake. But before I completed that forbidden task, Glinda was right behind me, arms wrapped around my now flailing body and with both of her arms she strapped both of my arms around my body, hugging me and through tear-wrenching sobs she whispered, "Don't touch him, honey!" He's not warm and soft anymore. He can't come out of there. He's gone."

Turning now to face her, still locked in the embrace of her hug, my eyes were searching, wildly searching hers for an answer. "He's gone," she repeated.

"NOOOOOO!" That someone was now screaming. "I want him back," she was wailing! Wild-eyed and now frantic, I grabbed my sis's shoulders and whispered as though this had become some sort of a conspiracy, "That's not him! He's not in there! There's been a mistake! Don't you see?" Now dropping my hands from her shoulders, I raced to my husband, frantically searching his eyes for some sort of sanity, recognition, "It's not him!" I exclaimed. Now turning and pointing with my entire arm, palm extended upward I tried to reason with him, "That– is–not–my– dad!" The Tin Man tried to hold me, tried to grasp me and console me. "NO!" Where was the Scarecrow? Surely he would see! Surely he would be able to convince these people that someone had indeed made a most horrific mistake! I frantically glanced around the room. The Indian and the hospice chaplain were now coming toward me in almost a full gallop. Thank God! They would know! They would take one look at whoever this man was and surely damned well stinking know that it was NOT MY DAD! The Indian was teary-eyed. HOW? Indians never cry! And the hospice chaplain was fogging up too. Where in the hell was I? This place was strange! No one here could grasp reality! Couldn't they see?! Didn't they know?! For the very love of God—had they all lost their fricking minds?! I turned in circles, searching for someone, anyone who would listen. Where was Fella? He would know. I spotted him at the other end of the room. He was shamefully backing out of the room, head bowed, closing the door behind him. COWARD! Coward, I wanted to scream! You come right back in here and admit that you switched bodies!

Swiftly so as not to lose any time, I half ran back to the casket. "I'm— sooo-s-o-r-r-y," I was now saying to the man who lay there. "I'm sorry for your family and I'm sorry for this mixup." And I wondered if he had had a daughter as loving and devoted as my dad had had in me. And as I tearfully wept before this stranger, remembering not to touch him (this wire was damned hot), a spark of recognition slapped me directly in the face!

Those hands! Those hands, which were folded so neatly across this mans chest, seemed—so—familiar. Unmistakably familiar! Those hands had rubbed mine together when they had been cold. How could this man have had those hands? I knew those hands. They had never touched me in anger. They had wiped many a tear from my eyes. They had slayed many a monster in their day. They had held me in times of trouble and they had patted me on the back when I'd done well. Those hands–were–my–dad's– hands. And that must have meant that—NO!—it couldn't be! It didn't look a thing like him! OH–MY–GOD! What–in–the–hell–had death done to my dad? Hadn't it been enough just to take him away? Why did it have to destroy his body too? GOD–DAMN–THAT–CANCER–TO– HELL!

I was on my knees now. Wrenching tears streaming from my eyes. Glinda and the Tin Man were right beside me, standing me up. The Scarecrow was wiping my face with the softness of his straw hands. (I shouldn't have touched that wire—why hadn't I listened?)

*Don't you all see? He wasn't a coward after all, was he? He had had the courage all along. Always in search of his courage—and he had never really lost it to begin with!*

Glinda took me by the hand, and led me to stand at the head of the casket, peering down at my father's body from behind his head. She whispered in my ear, "That is Dad's hair and those are Dad's hands. See the bruise from the morning he fell? It's still there," she whispered.

I didn't want to see it. That bruise should have died right along with my dad. It pierced my heart with forbidden memories. Memories I had chosen to forget.

"Don't look at his face anymore," she continued, "because it doesn't even resemble our dad."

But I didn't want to say good-bye to this body. I came to say goodbye to my dad. And I think somewhere deep down inside my childlike mind, I had hoped to have just one more heart-felt conversation with him. Perhaps be able to hold him just one last time, kiss him just one last time and tell him I loved him—just one last time.

But—they were. They were my dad's hands and it was indeed his beautiful, full head of now gray hair. This was his crew cut and those were his sweatpants and I could clearly see that he was indeed wearing his cute little blue sweatshirt—however, my dad was warm and caring and this body was cold and lifeless. And as I stood there with tears still seeping from within the cracks of my broken heart, I simply cried.

I cried for all the years missed and I cried for all the time that we *hadn't* shared. I cried because I knew that I would never again feel his touch to mine. And I cried because I knew his journey was over and he wouldn't be coming home again. But mostly, I cried because I just plain and simply wanted my daddy!

The cancer *had* finally won. And there I stood—in the middle of a deserted battlefield—alone. I was the sole survivor of this horrific nightmare, however, as I stood there, searching the smoldering wilderness for any signs of survival, there came somewhat of calmness about me as I realized something that most of us probably do at times such as I have just described to all of you. He was at peace. He would never again feel discomfort. He would never again be tired or hungry or sick. Yes, most of all *sick*. I would never again have to listen to him gag when he tried to eat—or hurt when he had to go potty—I would never have to rub his ailing kidneys again. I would never have to wonder if he would ever eat again or drink again or walk again. I would never have to hear him cough and choke again either! But most importantly of all, I would never have to relive those terrible tears, which fell each and every time he spoke of the divorce. It was all over—once and for all.

Yes, I suppose the cancer *had* indeed won. It had finally chased my dad from his place of occupancy. And it had indeed destroyed that as well. But you know what else? I get a lot of comfort from the fact that the cancer was dead too! Because, you see, cancer is like the sting of a bee. Once it has bitten, it too dies. So, no one really wins. But at least it can't move on to sting someone else. Nope, each particular bout of cancer dies right along with its victim, never to infect anyone else again. And in my dad's own words, "If it had to infect someone, better him than a child."

As I stood there, pondering all of these thoughts, I could hear my dad. Not with my ears but inside my mind. And he wasn't saying everything's going to be all right either. He was saying I'm sorry. I could hear him clearly inside my mind. I could feel his sadness in my heart. And then a feeling of warmth came over me that to this very day I have never experienced again. A heaving flow of warmth and serenity that surged throughout my heart and soul causing me to turn to my sis and very quietly, very calmly and very rationally ask her to close the casket. Our dad just simply wasn't there anymore. Plain and simple—and final. And I have absolutely no recollection of what I'm about to share with you—but rumor has it—that I very peacefully stepped away from the casket, whispered that everything was going to be all right and that he was OK now. "He doesn't want me to cry anymore." I turned and simply walked away.

And that was, in fact, the very last time I ever saw my dad. Wandering to the far end of the room from where I had entered, I found a chair, turned my rump to it and sat down in it and watched as my sis closed the casket and gingerly brushed her hand across the top of it as if she were admiring its shine. For just a moment I panicked—what if he couldn't brea….and then—a deep breath of my own and much like my father's life, the panic passed.

The hospice chaplain graced me with her angelic presence standing next to me placing one hand on my shoulder as if she were my guardian. The Indian stood on the other side of me both probably breathing sighs of relief that the worst was over.

And had they ever spoke of it again to one another, I'm sure the conversation would have sounded like that of a bad storm which we all had lived through not really sure at times if we were all going to make it.

The Indian's eyes were still wet with the pain of realization and as I glanced up at him and then quickly away I was reminded of an Indian chief of long ago who at the end of a TV station's day in the wee hours of the morning, would stand crying over the loss of the beauty of our country as they played the National Anthem. And then—the screen would go blank informing the viewers that, that particular day's programs had ended and that tomorrow was another day. How fitting.

I was exhausted. Watching my sis stand over my dad's casket, all of a sudden seemed redundant. I wanted to scream at her, tell her he was gone, not in there anymore, to face reality! However, I refrained from doing so. I simply sat and waited until she was done. My husband was by her side. They seemed to be having a quiet conversation between themselves. They too were probably discussing the deadly storm, which had just passed.

As they turned and began to walk toward me, I knew it was time to go. Hell, it had been time to go for hours. I stood up from my chair— and without waiting for them, I walked out of that horrible room. I actually had the incredible urge to run from that chamber of horrors but I refrained from doing so as not to draw attention to myself. God only knew I had done enough of that already.

Out in the hallway it still didn't feel far enough away. I turned to the right and kept walking toward the light of the reception area. Once there, it still wasn't far enough away, as a matter of fact I could've walked right out that front door and probably all the way to Missouri (poor little robin) and it still wouldn't have been far enough. However, once in the reception area I managed to stop and function somewhat normally, whatever somewhat normally was.

I could hear footsteps coming up from behind me. My fan club was hot on my heels. Or perhaps they were no longer a fan club at all but an angry mob instead, which caused me to turn around and glance. Nope, I was safe. They weren't carrying torches or clubs nor were they yelling angry obscenities. I wandered over to the window, which was plated as a twin to the door in size and width, and there, I stood—gazing, longing for my freedom.

It seemed as if all I had just gone through was already so far behind me. I felt as though my dad had already been buried and there was nothing more left to do but go home and grieve. In my heart—it was over. My dad had become nothing more than someone I had loved and lost. Someone whom I would miss so dearly for many years to come, I was certainly sure of that. I hated that place and I wanted to go home as soon as I figured out *where* and *what* home meant. I couldn't wait to get out of there. And as I stood staring out the window, waiting for everyone to do whatever else it was that "everyones" *do* after the viewing of a body, I heard the rise and fall of Fella's whispered voice. And then my sis. A whispered conversation that they were trying desperately not to share— so—I listened more intently.

Fella was *very* concerned because he had heard me wailing like a lost calf about how *my dad*, hadn't looked like *my dad*. And actually it was quite comical, as he must've been talking faster than a salesman at a used car convention.

With my back still turned to them, gazing out the window, a smile pursed my lips as he explained to my sister that *had* they embalmed the body right away, *my dad* would have in fact - looked like *my dad*. My sis couldn't get a word in edgewise as he continued to babble on about how it just wasn't their fault. Geeze–La–Weeze, Fella—give it a rest, for the love of Pete! What had I done to this poor guy? As I stood with my back to them, acting as though I were thousands of miles away, it was almost comical as then my husband as well as the hospice chaplain got involved, all whispering at the same time and all trying to explain that it WOULDN'T HAVE MATTERED!!! The room fell silent. I believe it was actually the angelic hospice chaplain that finally broke up the commotion with that shouting statement. I knew she had it in her! *Way to go! God's team one—the opponent—zero!*

Back to whispering, the chaplain seemed to be trying to explain that, "She didn't think it was her dad, period! Don't you see, she actually didn't think it was *him* at all—and long before she saw the body," she whispered. "She cannot grasp the fact that he has passed on," she was now whispering in a low and husked voice. Everyone fell silent once again.

Uh boy, they all thought I was a nutcase. For the very love of God, and I *felt* crazy as I stood listening to them explain to this guy that I couldn't accept the fact that he had died at all! Aw come on, folks, give me some credit—or not—because what they were saying—was— true.

I strolled over to the big double doors and I gave them an arrogant shove as I politely walked the hell out of there. The night air felt good. Crazy people tend to love the night air. My God, I thought, what in the hell had I done to all of these people? Poor Fella. I had had him hopping from the moment we met. And what about my sis and husband? Had they all been tiptoeing around just waiting for me to crack? Well, probably. I then wondered what it felt like *to* crack. Had I already cracked? It sure felt like it. So, I reckoned that that was that. I had probably already cracked and life as I had known it would never again be the same. Wow it sure takes a lot out of a person to be nuts. I was exhausted!

I stood out by the car, waiting for Glinda, the Tin Man and the Scarecrow to emerge with the broom, burnt and frayed beyond recognition but nonetheless, proof that they had, in fact, slayed the wicked witch – well – of death I mean. Not the real wicked witch for heaven's sake! Not even *they* were capable of doing that! Besides, she wasn't even there! Footsteps. Surprised that they weren't running in a full gallop because the nutcase had disappeared, I leaned up against the car, arms folded across my chest and simply stared at them. I wanted to say something clever but all of my cleverness had escaped me. I've heard that happens to crazy people.

All three of them looked like the cats that had eaten the canaries as they rounded the corner and slowed their pace—thus continuing to walk toward me all together and all in cadence.

"Everything all right?" I asked.

"Yeah, sure," they all replied in unison.

"Fella OK?" I nonchalantly inquired.

"Oh, yeah, he'll be fine," the Indian answered, as he unlocked the car door for me.

"He didn't seem fine," I added.

"Oh, he was just a little concerned about you, that's all."

"Me?" I asked in disbelief, "Why in the world would Fella be concerned with me?"

No one said a word. They weren't budging. They were as tight lipped as a submerged submarine. Of course, then again, how in the heck do you tell a crazy person that you think they are crazy? Ah, ha! They had no clue—and—neither did I.

Once inside the car, all was silent. My husband, sitting next to me in the back seat, reached over and lightly touched my knee. "You OK?" he asked.

"Sure," I said, "I'm fine." *But could you please ask the rabbit to put his pocket watch away, the ticking sound is really bothering me.*

I was tired and quite frankly, no, I didn't know if I was OK. I felt numb. Like all that had just happened had been nothing but a bad dream. Had it been real? Maybe I *was* crazy. I couldn't get the image of his body out of my mind. When I closed my eyes it became worse. And now I knew *why*. Why my dad had told me not to do what I had just indeed done. What in the hell could I have possibly been thinking? Boy this wire was hot! Hotter than I could have possibly imagined. Why hadn't I listened? Why?

Well, shucks, we all know why—now—don't we? Unfortunately, I had to do what I had to do—for the very same reasons I had to do what I had to do, years before at the good old pony farm. It's who I was—it's who I am—and I'm sorry to have to say, but it's who I reckon I will always be. I had to be sure. And somewhere deep down inside that silly little brain of mine, I knew I would have to work on that issue in the future as not to have it become the death of me!

At last, we rounded the all too familiar corner into the mobile home park. All was quiet. I supposed that because most of the residents who lived there in that tiny haven were elderly, it surely wasn't a rare scene to see an ambulance or county wagon at someone's residence every now and again. This place was peaceful and it seemed to cradle an understanding of endings.

My next-to-the-youngest sister as well as my baby sister were at my dad's house when we got home, arriving a day early as to accommodate the national cemetery rules and regulations handbook: Section eight; Article32, which clearly must have stated that no burials can take place in a national cemetery on a weekend. Damn, I wish I had read that before all of this hullabaloo had taken place. And for just a second I panicked at the thought of someone being in *that* house without me, the honorary tour guide. My God, had they entered his bedroom without me? The minivan was in the carport, which meant the witch was home—and all of a sudden a weight had been lifted from my shoulders. Let her be the tour guide, I thought. I quit! This was *her* home now—and perhaps it had always been. Perhaps. However, just the same, this home still called to *me*. This home still grieved with and for *me*. And its very existence would always have my blood running through its soul foundation.

As we entered the living room through the sliding glass door, my two little sisters jumped up from the futon sofa to greet Glinda and me. They looked ashen. Tears were abundant as we hugged and comforted each other. I was thankful that the witch had not eaten them.

"How did he look?" They were asking in unison.

"Was he peaceful? Did he look like Dad?" And before I could open my mouth to reply, Glinda was upon them with her words of wisdom, knowledge, and comfort. I was thankful. For I simply stood there with my mouth agape preparing a statement that would never find its way to my lips.

I strolled over to my perch on the love seat and sat down as I listened to my big sis sharing our dad's place in this world now with my dad's two youngest daughters.

It was late and I was so tired I could barely make sense out of anything. Of course, Lord knows I didn't have to be tired not to be able to make sense out of anything. I hadn't been able to make sense out of anything since this whole escapade began.

It was nice having, well, almost all of us together again. The absence of our middle sister needed not to be discussed. This was not a time for judgment and per my dad's wishes as well as his ways, it never would be. Another book, another story, another time.

Despair and anxiety hung heavily in the air, like a thick, cloud of smoke that if not lifted soon was sure to choke all of us to death. The Indian stood solemn and silent as if on guard for the night. Legs spread apart and hands clasped together neatly in front of him, like a stone faced secret service agent. What must have been going through his mind, I wondered, stealing glances as not to let on that I was looking at him. Perhaps he was reminiscing of a time long ago when this scene in my dad's living room would have brought him much joy watching his big brother so happy and proud with all of his girls together again—*minus one*. Then again, I suppose some things are better left unreminisced.

Sleep came fast and deep to me that night. And I dreamed. I dreamed my dad was in a beautiful white casket, flowers carved into the wood so exquisitely that I had to get closer to admire them. It was safe. The casket was closed. And as I neared this beautiful work of art it began to tumble—and it fell off its pedestal! I was horrified as the body began to fall and I awoke with such a start, I found myself sitting straight up on the love seat. I thought my heart might truly stop beating. And perhaps it really did, as it surely felt broken. I frantically searched for and tried to focus on the clock through tear hazy eyes. Five in the morning. The service was at nine. I laid back down plopping my head on the pillow leaving me to stare up at the ceiling in total darkness. It was Friday, November 13th. Today we would bury my dad. And I realized that once again in my life, there I lay, in total darkness, dreading a nightmare that had this time come true. I didn't feel any different than I had when I was only five or six, lying on my bunk bed, shivering after a horrible nightmare. They still had the power to scare the hell out of me. However, sadly, *this* morning I had nowhere to go. Nowhere to run for comfort. I couldn't just shuffle down the old hallway to safety and crawl in bed with my dad. He was finally gone and my worst nightmare had finally come to pass. I was finally a grown-up. I remembered my dad telling me of such things. But it had all been a bunch of hullabaloo then - for surely it had to have been just another silly little story he had made up. And one that I found to be not so entertaining I might add. But it clearly wasn't hullabaloo now. It was pure unprecedented horror! It was sad becoming a grown-up. It hurt and there quite frankly was absolutely no up swing to this new found position. I hated it. I felt so empty inside that no amount of ice cream in the whole universe could ever fill me up. What was happening to me? What would life be like without my silly little storytelling dad? Well, I'd had a week to try and figure this out and I still hadn't come up with anything at all comforting to say the least. Life as I had known it to be, was different now. *Everything* was different now. And as I lay there in the darkness, pondering the knowledge of the universe it came to me. A statement that would for sure go down in the history books and would have to be one of the most famous quotes of the entire United States of America! Being a grown-up sucks! Yup, I was going to be famous.

The sun was now pushing its way through the cracks in the curtains. A sunny day—Huh, who in the hell had ordered *that* I wondered, as I steadied myself to stand and fold my blanket?

The others were stirring now also and as I shuffled my way into the kitchen to make coffee, I thought it very odd that I hadn't curled up next to my husband to sleep the night before. What had I been thinking? *Had* I been thinking was more like it? I couldn't even remember falling asleep. Which then lead me to wonder if the Indian was, in fact, still standing there on guard. And who *had* covered me up? Uh boy, I had to get a hold of myself—and soon. People who do such things usually *are* committed to places where they really *do* see white rabbits running around worrying about what time it is.

My big sis was up now and folding her blanket as well. I wondered if she could remember who covered *her* up? Oh, I was quite sure she could. She could remember stuff that happened before she was even born! Memory like an elephant, that big sis of mine. Wasn't afraid of a damned thing either. She would never crack up over something as Minot as losing a parent either. Oh, hell, no! She was always in control and ready to handle anything. Made me want to walk right over to her as she was undoubtedly coming into the kitchen to make sure I was OK because *she was,* and slap the pee-waddlings right out of her! Yesiree and then I might just slap her for peeing! This wasn't fair! He had been her dad too! How come she wasn't freaking out? How could she remain so calm and knowing? Just like the Indian. I could slap him too. What had they learned that I hadn't? I never skipped a grade but maybe I *had* slept through the course on how to deal with death and the dying. I must have because no one else was acting like me which was a sure fire comfort. *Oh, here she came in her blasted magic bubble.*

"Good morning," she lulled. "Did you sleep well?"

How in the hell did she do that I wondered, as she rubbed my back with her big sister comforting hands?

"Who covered me up last night?" I asked, as though I were on to them.

"I did," she answered, rather puzzled.

"You fell asleep sitting straight up on the love seat."

*Oh, OK, you lying witch of a bubble floater you. Ah Ha! I'm on to you! I didn't really fall asleep now, did I? NO! I didn't! I must have been drugged and then, once asleep, you all—uh—geeze, they all what? Turned me over to aliens for blood work?*

415

What in the hell was the matter with me?

"You had a very stressful evening," she continued. "You obviously needed to sleep. You didn't move a muscle even when we laid you down. I'm worried about you," she mused. "That is a sign of depression."

*Well halleflippenluyah! You don't say? Depression? Geeze, who would have ever thought? We have only just lost our father, you nit-wit, and today we will bury him! Oh, and let's not forget that I only spent the last three weeks watching him succumb to his demise. I've seen things that other people can't see and I've heard things that other people can't hear and I sat idly by while our father did the same. I found out that our father's wife is just like our mother—how fitting and I haven't partaken in a good night's sleep since I arrived at this godforsaken haven and then I had to deal with the ignorant jackasses at the funeral home planning a service that I have since chosen not to believe in! SO WHY—I ask would I have one gosh darned stinking ass reason to be depressed?*

"I guess I could be," I whispered, as I turned to face her before I simply lost my legs, falling to the kitchen floor and began to wail.

"I–CAN'T–DO–THIS," I sobbed!

"I–don't–want–to–go–today! P-l-e-a-s-e," I begged through sporadic sobs. And as I looked up to meet her eyes, face wet and tired, so very tired of channeling tears, I realized that she, as well as my husband, were now down on their knees on the floor next to me. Both had hold of my shoulders and both looked like they had just seen a ghost. Good, it was about time someone else had besides me anyway.

Glinda took hold of me and pulled me to her chest, caressing my hair and cradling my head in her hands. "It's OK," she was whispering, "It's all right. The worst is over now. You don't have to see him today."

This was so embarrassing. These little bouts or tantrums of crying fits, which would come on out of nowhere taking my legs out from underneath me had to stop! My gosh, who in the world ever heard of such a thing? I wasn't *really* Ms. Kitty! Why was this happening to me? I felt so foolish. Like Scarlet O'Hara—so frail and dramatic. Perhaps I might just swing the back of my arm up and gently touch it to my forehead next, then pivot and fall exclaiming, *Oh, woe is me Rhett!* Geeze- La–Weeze. This was really getting old! I was ashamed—and—well—felt stupid and—quite frankly—there didn't seem to be a damned thing I could do about it. I was devastated and sad and I have come to realize that sadness and devastation can and *will* do the damnedest things to a person such as taking your legs out from underneath you and making you do and say things that you never thought possible. Just the same I was "acting a fool" as my dad used to say and I couldn't allow this to happen anymore. He was just my dad! People lose their parents every day! And then, like a load of wet cement, it hit me! He hadn't been *just* my dad. He was a missing piece of my mom as well. He was the brother I never had and the playmate we only dream of as children. He was like Peter Pan and The Waltons, all wrapped into one superb human being. He was— well—my very best friend. And he died with secrets about me that only his ears would ever hear—and feelings I would have never shared had he not been dying. And as much as I tried to let all of that go I just couldn't because—I knew I would never again know or love anyone like him in my entire life.

Taking my chin gently in her hands, Glinda was turning my face upward toward hers to look into my eyes.

"You don't have to see him today," she was quietly repeating.

"His casket will be closed. But someone *does* have to deliver his eulogy and, as I recall," she continued, "I believe he specifically asked *you* to do that."

Oh great. Now, not only did I have to go to that godforsaken place again but I was also expected to stand up at a podium in front of a whole bunch of people I didn't even know and deliver my dad's final words, his farewell speech, which left not a doubt in my mind once again that we do this funeral thing all wrong and backward!

Sitting on the kitchen floor feeling humiliated and dumbfounded once again, I wiped my cheeks with the sleeve of my sweat shirt and glanced up to see both of my younger sisters standing by the counter starring down at me with complete horror in their eyes. Tears of fear, sadness and disbelief were seeping through the very pores of their cheeks and I was sadly reminded of a time when I had seen that look in their eyes before. I glanced back at Glinda and then at the Tin Man and wondered if I clicked my heels together—no—those dreams were long gone and faded. That movie had become old.

I had to get up from the floor somehow and stop this nonsense! I had to somehow keep my legs underneath me. I had to "get a grip" as the saying goes. Grip on *what* is what I wanted to know. What exactly does one grip on to when one has lost it? Well, I wasn't quite sure at that very moment, but I was willing to find out. And I did. When one has lost their grip, one grabs onto the knees of ones big sister and hoists oneself up into a standing position. If one doesn't have a big sister knee, no need to worry—any sturdy object will do. And unlike other warnings, I do suggest you try this at home and practice, practice, practice before you lose someone very close to you.

Now standing at eye level with everyone else in the room, I gazed down at the floor and made an apology. "I'm sorry," I whispered as if I were apologizing to the tile. My husband simply poured his coffee and walked into the living room. My two younger sisters stood completely still and staring at me as though I had just urinated on the kitchen floor—and beside them stood the witch—with a look of pure and identifiable disgust on her face. And Glinda? Well, I think I had finally burst her damned bubble once and for all. No harm done, it had become rather a nuisance anyway.

This day before me held despair and gloom. I could hear my father in some distant silly voice booming that whether we like it or not the sun is going to come up tomorrow. Might as well make the best of it. What a bunch of hullabaloo! Probably just another damned story he'd made up somewhere along the way.

"All a service is, is a chance for the living to say good-bye, you know." Glinda was at it once again.

"What?" I asked as I turned to look at her.

"That's all we do it for," she said. "Dad would have hated to see you go through this," she continued as she chose her drink of the morning to be a can of Pepsi. Then, closing the refrigerator door with a snug thunk, she turned her gaze to meet mine dead on and very matter-of-factly continued her opinion.

"All of Dad's coworkers and friends will be there today and they will surely want to meet us. I mean all he ever did was brag about us." (Five, count 'em, my friend, I've got five beautiful brown-eyed baby doll girls!)

"The hospice chaplain, the nurse and social worker will all be there as well," she continued. "Might as well make the best of it because come hell or high water his service is today," she proudly announced as though she herself had invented the whole damned idea of a funeral ceremony.

Now it was I who was staring at her in disbelief. Where in the hell was all of this coming from I thought. Come hell or high water? Oh brother!

"And if you don't read Dad's farewell poem," she continued, then who will - because I'm sure as hell not getting up there to do it," she quipped!

"You wrote it and it's already been printed. All you have to do is get up there and read it," she matter-of-factly snipped!

*She thinks I'm not going!*

"And after all you went through to get him his military honors, it would be a shame for you to miss that. It's going to be beautiful. Don't you want to be there to see them fold that flag? Don't you want to hear them play taps on the bugle? After all, this is Dad's final hurrah," she proudly exclaimed! "He earned it and you saw it through," she boasted. And as I opened my mouth to reply I realized that finally, Glinda's bursted bubble was leaking from her eyes. My God, she *was* human. She wasn't just a made up rendition of strength and courage. She was hurting and—and—she—was—crying!

Oh what to do—what to do? One just doesn't hold a good witch when she cries. She won't have it. All one can do is wait for her spell to pass.

Still standing there, with my mouth open trying to reply, I realized I couldn't! My God, I was at a loss for words! Speechless! Perhaps for the very first time in my life! And oh, how I wished my dad had lived to see it. I had to do something. Oh, I had really done it now. I had made tears come from the eyes of a good witch. Or perhaps, just perhaps, the heart of a good witch is very fragile also. And I'm only assuming for the mere sake of kicks and giggles, but maybe, *just maybe*—good witches miss their daddies too.

Glinda was now quickly wiping at her eyes as though they were only watering from a severe and very annoying allergy. She then, very proudly stood up a little straighter and pursed her lips as though she might just be thinking about finding a new doctor for those damned allergies.

I walked over to her and very awkwardly made an attempt to console her. This however, was not and had never been my role. I felt like a preteen trying to plan the strategy of a first kiss.

"I'm all right," she quipped. "Let's get ready to go, the drivers will be here at 9:00."

"You're not all right," I snapped, causing her to whirl around and face me directly.

*Oh, Lord, she's gonna cast a spell—she's gonna cast a big-ass spell on me!*

"It's OK not to be all right," I said ashamedly looking down at the floor as though I were addressing the carpet.

Slowly, trying not to move my head too quickly, my eyes then began their journey, starting at her feet and climbing their way up her body until our gaze was unmistakably locked into a stare. I then, turned around and began to walk away but not before I whispered, "Those days of not being aloud to feel are over!"

Yes indeed, those days *were* truly over, however, I have found that certain situations in life which are completely unrelated, can throw you right back into an extreme situation. Strange how that works—and what's even more strange, is how we all tend to take the same role in each and every one. Huh, could very well be the plot of another book.

My two youngest sisters were hastily getting their clothes out of their hanging bags and all of us seemed to be reliving yet another familiar scene as my mind was wandering through the pages of our past, back to a time when we would all get ready for church, my dad's voice booming with hymns as we readied ourselves to go to God's house to worship. My mom was always yelling and my dad was always singing. Can't imagine why I had the issues I had.

When it came time for me to use the one and only bathroom, I got in, closed the door and locked it tightly behind me securing my privacy as well as my safety from all that loomed beyond the other side of that door. And, as always, I found myself standing in front of the sink, staring directly at my own familiar reflection in the mirror beyond. I liked my own face. It was comforting and understanding to my feelings. It had been this way since I was a child in a place where children should never be. I found reassurance in my own eyes. I knew this woman all too well and it felt good to have a friend. Leaning with both hands one on each side of the free standing sink, I focused in a little closer to my reflection. New lines adorned certain parts of my face. Lines that weren't exactly welcome but that told a story. *This story*—and they would always be a reminder of courage, strength and perseverance. Yes, I could have done without them, but since they were already there, I felt it essential to find acceptance for them. Staring back at me was someone I felt truly sorry for. She had lost her father to cancer and today she would bury him. How awful. I wanted to hug her for I knew of her past and I wondered just how much more this little gal could endure. She knew *what* and *how* I felt for her. I could tell by the way she was looking at me. So with one last glance, I turned from her—leaving her to stand alone once again and began to prepare myself to go along with her on her final journey through this devastating nightmare. At least she wouldn't be alone, I thought, as I prepared the shower water to its perfect temperature. And as I stepped into the shower, I hoped that when I died, someone would throw away my shampoo, conditioner and soap—for it seemed disrespectful to use a deceased person's stuff. I wouldn't want someone using my stuff, once I was gone. Oh for the very love of God! What in the hell difference did that make?

The limousines were due to arrive at nine per Glinda's orders. And at exactly nine o'clock arrive they surely did with their stretch in cadence with one another and their drivers appearing as though they had to have been plucked as two mice straight from the home of Cinderella, herself. Funny how everyone involved with this death thing all seemed to look alike. And what was even more strange, was that in some way, they all resembled Fella! Oh God, could this situation get any worse?!

Both gentlemen got out of their cars and stood next to them as though they were retired palace guards. I opened the slider and held one finger up in the air (incidentally, it was my index finger) to let them know we would be along soon.

Turning from the door, I then found my whole family staring at me as though they were waiting for me to perform.

"T-h-e-y-'r-e H-e-r-e," I chimed.

The Indian had arrived just before them dressed in a dark blue suit, which was very *unfitting* to his heritage, in my opinion, but looking dapper just the same. He was handsome and stoic and although he wasn't in war paint it was obvious he was duly prepared for battle just the same.

Giving in to a tradition I had come to despise, I had chosen a dress from my closet before I had left home, that my dad had seen on me just once and absolutely went haywire over. It was a simple black cotton dress with tiny little white flowers all over with a beautiful starch, white, laced, breasted collar. Oh how he had crooned over that dress, twirling me around in elegant circles begging to have another look at me. It embarrassed me at the time—and—I must say—I would have given anything to have that embarrassment back, just one last time—then another—and – another—and …

The witch entered the living room from the bedroom and she was dressed in a beautiful black flowing chiffon dress with—and I am not lying—a black hat with a veil! My hell she looked like first lady Kennedy at John Fitzgerald's service! Her hair had to have been tucked up in that hat somewhere and actually—she was beautiful. I was angry. Oh, my dad would have flipped over how elegant she looked and well— she looked like a widow and I think that is what made me angry. Of course, I had told no one else of the secrets I knew of, therefore, the girls were very sympathetic toward her and very complimentary and doting. I quite frankly wanted to vomit. Who had she met I wondered and how long had it been going on and was he younger than my dad? Did he have money? And–OH–MY–GOD! Would–he–be–there? How would I know? I really should have pulled Glinda, the Tin Man and Tonto aside before this. I should have told them the secret. No—I did the right thing by waiting— for I cannot imagine what sort of nightmare this would have become had they known what I already knew on that day. It was a nightmare already without that information. I would tell them all soon enough. However— the blade of truth that was really stabbing my gut—was—I'm not sure it really *was* a secret. I mean—she had been so matter of fact about it. Like what else was she supposed to have done? She was lonely and my dad didn't want her loving her son and blah—blah—blah! My dad was dying and this other someone was not I suppose. Made me want to glide right on over to the side of her and very nonchalantly put my arm around her waist as I leaned in and lifted that hat and veil just slightly off one ear and whisper to her, "We are all born dying sweetheart." But I didn't. But I wanted to. But I didn't. Mostly because I just knew underneath that hat and veil was a green face and a long pointy nose and she had that hour glass somewhere—I just knew it! She just may have taken me back to my dad's Perry Mason office and locked me in there—flipping that hour glass over—laughing that most hideous laugh with her winged monkey clapping hysterically by her side as she demanded those ruby red slippers or else! I really needed to get home to my therapist!

The girls were dressed in blouses and slacks and they looked very nice. Glinda was in a sweater and slacks also. My husband was in Dockers and a dress shirt. I must not have gotten the memo.

It was finally time to go as we all single filed out the door to our awaiting coaches. And I'm sure we all looked like a bunch of school kids who had been made to perform fifty fire drills in the same day as we dragged our feet, making small talk with one another as to who would go in which car.

"Hey, wait a minute, who in the heck asked for two limos, anyway" I quacked as we came down the front steps? "Do we need two limos?" I asked.

"Does it matter?" Glinda quipped in a whisper.

"Well—no," I stammered trying to cover up my concern about the money while I simultaneously began to configure in my mind just how in the hell much two limos could possibly cost by the hour. And—yes it *did* sort of matter—I mean after all, there wasn't a whole lot of money laying around after the funeral had been paid for and quite frankly, my dad had failed to leave me the magic beans to grow the money tree. Minor details I will take up with him when I see him again. But nonetheless, I myself didn't remember ordering these *two* coaches of luxury. Which then lead me to—Damn that, Fella! Now, what had he done? Although, had I not failed to look at the paperwork before I signed it—thus damning Fella all the way to China, perhaps I would have noticed that the limos were part of the package. Isn't that a hoot? They have funeral packages, like two for one's and free limo rides! Crap, talk about a vacation!

Our drivers were both staring at me now. Where had I been? Geeze, I really had to stop doing that! Both very solemn and standing at attention, I realized they looked as though they were waiting for an answer. Oh hell, someone was asking me a question that I had once again missed because I was somewhere else. Driver number one in the lead car, I think I'll call him Gus, was standing with the back door open and waiting as was his twin in the second car, I think I'll call him Hector, was doing the same. *These guys had to be twins!* Probably a family-owned and run operation. How nice that must have been for them.

What? What in the hell was the big flipping deal? Couldn't we just get in the damned cars before we were late for our own father's funeral, for the very love of God?!

I acknowledged Gus with a half nod and tried to smile but it wasn't happening for me. But that seemed ok, because he wasn't budging either. I don't think they're allowed.

Leaning so close to him I could smell his hair I whispered, "You a good driver?"

Pulling back just far enough to make it obvious that I had either insulted him or he just developed a nervous twitch he very matter-offactly answered me with a curt, "Of course!"

*I'm sure Fella had filled him in on me.*

"All right," I said, "Then, I'll ride with you."

And with that, I climbed into the backseat.

Glinda, the Tin Man, and the Scarecrow followed me, although Glinda climbed over me as to sit by the door. The widow and my two other sisters went with Hector. My Lord—I surely hoped they would be OK. They had no clue who she really was. If she could replace my dad before he died—she probably really could eat someone.

Once settled in our luxurious form of transportation, I realized after about five minutes, that we were not moving. I had heard the driver's door close shortly after ours so I knew he was up there, although there was a smoked privacy glass blocking our view to the front seat of the car. Leaning forward, I knocked on the glass divider, which was probably installed to protect Gus more so than it was to give us privacy. *Fella probably had that done at the last minute.*

"Excuse me, driver?"

The glass slid down with a whispered purr. Without turning around, Gus simply replied, "Ma'am?" *Huh boy.*

"I just wondered why we aren't moving," I inquired carefully as though he just may reach back and slap me.

"We are waiting for the widow's car to lead," he answered and with that, the window went right back up.

*The widow's car? The widow's car?* Crap, I had no clue! They both looked the same to me! The widow's car, huh? So did that mean that by total accident I had picked the right car after all—and no one even had to tell me? Which lead me to wonder if I had, in fact, boarded the daughter's car? Is that what they called it? Or perhaps they called it "the rest of the family car." And then I wondered if my other sister's had been made to walk! Fella was indeed behind all of this—I just knew it! Just as sure as I knew that the *widow's* car didn't have bullet proof privacy glass!

Leaning forward again, I tapped on the window and with the same familiar whisper, it whirred down again.

"Ma'am?" Gus questioned with a slight bit of irritation in his voice.

"Do you guys have radio contact with one another?" I asked.

"Ma'am?" he questioned again. *Geeze, was this guy hard of hearing?*

"I was just wondering if the widow is having some sort of crisis?" I asked.

*Silence.*

"I'm not sure, Ma'am," he answered.

"When they are ready they will pull around us and we can go." And the window went right back up. When they are ready—or—do you mean after she has killed and eaten my two little sisters and the driver?

Uh no. This wasn't OK. How come Gus didn't like me I wondered? Still leaning forward with a look on my face as though I had just learned that Aliens had, in fact, landed and taken over the country, and I know that look was on my face because I could see my own reflection in the glass, I turned around to my right and looked at Glinda and then I turned around to my left and looked at the Tin Man and the Scarecrow and then I turned back around, stared at the great glass wall of China, and tapped on the window again.

With just a moments hesitation the window whirred down once more.

"Ma'am?" he questioned again—and this time there was a definite irritation in his voice.

"Why is this window here?" I asked. Which then prompted the good witch to slug me in the leg.

Hesitation again and then, "It's to give the passenger privacy," he quipped as I noticed him looking at me through the rearview mirror.

"Uh huh," I murmured. "But what if we don't want privacy?" I said.

"What if we want to talk with you? You know, ask a few questions, get to know one another?"

*Another slug in the leg.*

"Ma'am, I can leave the window down if you prefer," he said, still not turning around.

"No," I said, "I'll just knock if I need you."

*Silence.* Hesitation and then, I asked, "Do you know who's funeral were going to, Gus?" "No, Ma'am," he answered with a slight bit of sympathy in his voice. *Liar! I know Fella must have filled him in. I knew by the way he watched me in the rear view mirror.*

"My dad's," I said.

"I'm sorry," he answered.

"Me too," I replied. "He was a great man, you know?"

"Yes, Ma'am, I'm sure he was."

"He was funny too," I added.

"Yes, Ma'am, I can somehow see that. How many of you are there?" he asked as though he were anticipating an ambush.

"Five of us," I answered proudly! (Five, count 'em, my friend, I've got five beautiful brown-eyed baby doll girls!)

"No boys?"

Now why is it people ask that? Did I say there were any boys? Had I ever said there were any boys *ever* in my whole entire life? NO! No stinky, smelly, burping, gas-passing, puppy-dog-tail, nasty freaking boys! Although, I had always wished I had had a brother.

"Nope," I answered, perhaps with a slight hint of sorrow in my voice, not a one.

"We're surprised he lived as long as he did," I joked as if to relieve Gus from obvious discomfort.

He laughed uncomfortably yet compassionately.

Sitting back on my seat, folding my arms across my chest, I caught a glimpse of the widow's car pulling around us slowly, moving to take its place in front of us. It was time to go.

"You can close up for now, if you like," I said.

"Yes, Ma'am," he answered. "If you need anything at all, just knock on the glass."

"Will do," I replied, as the whirr of the window ended our conversation.

Will do? Will do? Now, where in the Sam hell had that come from? I had never said that before in my entire life! Never! It sounded so oldfashioned. So out of character for someone my age. So, my dadish! Oh, my heck—I was doing it already! Doing what we all do sooner or later. Doing what some of us hate and some of us love depending on the circumstance I suppose. I was continuing the cycle of family—the cycle of life.

The ride was smooth and quiet. I guess there isn't really much to say when you're on your way to a funeral. Just a whole lot of thoughts and memories to ponder which, if we really think about it, is where this journey actually began. Another full cycle had run its precious course.

My stomach felt like the Santa Monica Loop had been miraculously constructed around my intestines. My God, I wondered. You don't suppose people do stuff like pass out, vomit or actually loose all bodily functions at a funeral do you? Oh for cripe's sake, here came the anxiety again. Geeze-La-Weeze! Doesn't a person have enough to worry about when it's time to say good–bye? Well, for the very love of God, one would certainly think so!

Tree lined streets of falling leaves were now coming into view. We were almost there. And I was almost ready to vomit. Yup, I could feel the vile rumbling around somewhere between my upper stomach and throat. What a comforting feeling. Especially knowing that other people would be there, lurking, watching, just waiting for me to—Oh, crap!

We were finally pulling into the familiar circular drive of Dracula's castle. Lord almighty, how I truly had come to despise that place. There were cars parked everywhere. Nameless faces of men and women were filing in through the front doors. And either my dad had a whole lot of friends I had never met, or the people from the airport had come to pay their respects.

People were stopping to stare now at the two coaches pulling into the drive. Sorrow and sympathy were worn on their faces as though masks had been handed out before hand in duplicate. Great! I hated those looks. However, I realized that most seemed to be directed toward the widow's car. Oh, my hell! Not the widow's car again! Hey, excuse me! Over here folks! It's me you want to feel sorry for! H-e-l-l-o? Anyone paying attention out there? I'm hurting more than she! She was only his wife. And she has already replaced him! I was his daughter! Known him all of my life. Took care of him through his whole damned stinking illness! Damn it! What was wrong with these people? Didn't they have a clue? Didn't they know?

We exited our luxurious coaches with the assistance of our door opening drivers and I was determined not to lose my footing *or* throw up. No one would have noticed anyway. They were all following the widow. Damn her!

Same old sidewalk, same old doors, same old marble floors waiting for me. God, I couldn't wait to be done with all of this. It was so—well— old, so used—so terribly worn out. So—dead.

My sisters, my husband and I, all entered the funeral home together as though we were connected to one another, standing collectively as one—with the Indian close behind. My father's pallbearers. This was his wish, his desire. His son-in-law, his brother and his daughters, minus one, which led me to wonder if the middle sister had never been meant to have been there all along. For had she been there, someone would have been left to walk behind the casket and perhaps my dad had known all along that this is how it would have turned out. "She'll find her own way," he had said. "She'll get it sooner or later," he had promised. Get what? That there wasn't enough room anyway? No, I seriously doubt that that had been his point. Just the same, there we all were without her and I missed her all of a sudden like she herself had perhaps died without us knowing. And to be perfectly honest with all of you, my faithful friends, she had in a sense done just that. Next book for sure!

So this was it, I thought as we trailed into the funeral home behind the widow of course, whom I simply wanted to trip, sending her sprawling face first into that beautiful marbled floor. Just so I could then bend down beside her and tell her to take a good look at herself in her own reflection. This is the face of a cheater I would have said. Now, take off that ridiculous hat and veil and you walk behind me! My God, what was wrong with me? I suppose this was what the moment of a funeral really felt like. Huh, it struck me sort of funny that I had never really thought about it until then. Well, not to the limits of reality anyway. Besides, we don't know what the limits of reality really are until we're upon them. And quite frankly, I had decided that it sucked.

As we entered that familiar chamber of horrors with its magnificent marble floors looming and ever so inviting for a good old fashioned down home tripping, I froze as there stood the hospice chaplain with her arms spread out wide, her head tilted slightly to one side and that smile! She was wearing a beautiful flowing robe of white over her clothes and, quite frankly, I had to take a second look, as at first glance, well, her purity and calmness flowed so freely that—well—she was just beautiful, that's all. There would be no tripping. There would be no name calling nor would there be any nonsense of ill feelings. The Lord's Lamb herself was standing before me. She would be performing the service today. I found it comforting that a person of the cloth had come to have known my dad so well in such a short time. Although, I guess anyone who had ever met my dad even for a short time had actually come to know him so well. That's just the kind of guy he was. But she was, well, you know, close to God. One of his own—not to mention the fact that she did not correct my dad when he spoke of Budweiser stands on every corner in heaven. No, she didn't. Instead, she asked him to elaborate. And she smiled and squirmed with the excitement of a child as he did so. She was an angel in my eyes and still is to this very day.

I magnetically walked toward her already knowing how those outstretched arms would feel around me. And as I snuggled into the warmth of her hug, I heard a familiar voice. Still taking in the comfort of her smell, I heard it again thus causing me to this time, turn my head just slightly to the side, and out of the corner of my eye—there he loomed.

I turned my head just a little more to get a better look at the giant of a man who could drop tears to match his size over the loss of his friend. The man who had called himself my father's boss.

He was standing Paul Bunyan style, with legs spread and his hands trembling holding some sort of little card. He stood proud and dapper in his blue suit that he had chosen over a plaid Pendleton, suspenders, logger boots, and jeans. However, his shoulders were bent slightly forward and his eyes had been dampened with the apparent loss of his buddy. He looked lost and scared. My gentle giant.

Releasing my hugging grip on the chaplain, I slowly turned toward him and floated right into his looming arms. They swallowed me up at once. His magnificent trembling arms told a secret of how the loss of a friend can bring even the biggest of men to their very knees.

I took just a small step backward and looked way up into his dampened eyes. He stared down at me in return, arms still trembling.

"You OK?" I asked.

He looked up from me and around and then back down at me before he bellowed a whispering thought.

"I keep thinking he's gonna be here, you know, come walking around the corner any minute," he said as he looked past me now and down at the floor as if he were ashamed.

"I know," I said. "Me too."

"What's on the card?" I asked pointing to his trembling fist.

"Oh, it's some notes I've prepared so I don't forget to talk about some things. You know, memories."

My heart was breaking. Oh, yes, I knew all too well what memories were as well as what they meant at times such as these.

"That's nice," I said. "You are a very special person," I added as I reached way up, taking each side of his face in my hands, and then I tugged downward as to bring his cheek to my lips and I kissed it. He blushed but awkwardly returned the kiss just the same.

"I don't really like talking in front of people," he whispered in that deep raspy tone of his. "Makes me nervous."

"You get nervous?" I asked.

"Oh, hell, yes," He answered still whispering.

"Well, I'm a little nervous too," I told him.

His eyes were still glistening the reflection of his pain when he asked if we should go on in to the chapel.

I turned slightly to my left and glanced over my shoulder then turned back and looked all the way up and into his eyes. "I guess that's what we're here for," I smirked.

"I guess so," he smiled back and with that we both turned and faced the chapel.

"I think this is when we put one foot in front of the other," I joked.

"Yah," he stammered. "I know, I just can't seem to get my feet moving."

"Well," I told him, "We seem to be the only ones left standing out here so we'd better figure it out before the service is over and everyone's gone home."

"OK," he said bravely, "Let's go."

And with that we headed for the chapel.

As we entered the peaceful surroundings of the confines of the chapel, I heard that horrible funeral music—organ music, which in any other situation might have been beautiful. Sure as heck wasn't Hank Williams I thought to myself. And once inside the chapel room I felt as though a big door had slammed shut and I was trapped. But there wasn't a door at all. No, I could've just turned around and walked right out of there, of my own free will but something stopped me from doing that. And actually it wasn't a *some* thing as much as it was a *some* sight. Yes, as I walked into the chapel and turned to the left to walk up the main aisle I stopped abruptly—dead in my tracks—no pun intended. I couldn't have taken another step had I wanted to at that moment—for the view before me took my breath away.

I stood mesmerized by the display of my father's casket, on its pedestal at the front of the chapel which was proudly and sweetly cascaded with the American flag. And as this sight *was* breathtaking, it seemed to hold an even deeper meaning than that as I slowly walked closer. Yes, it seemed the colors were whispering a silence that could be heard only by my heart. Yes, it was whispering! *I am honored and proud to accompany this soldier to burial. You're welcome, daughter of Private First Classman Eddie Littlefield - you are so very welcome!*

I respectfully continued to walk up the aisle toward the draped idol and as I got closer, my looming friend tapped me on the under side of my arm as to let me know he was taking a seat in one of the pews to the right. I nodded and continued my journey toward the front of the chapel and it was then that I noticed my youngest sister getting up from the front pew to the left and inching her way to the main aisle as well. By the time I reached my destination, I was standing next to her in front of the beautifully draped casket. She had her hands laid ever so slightly upon the flag and her tears laid ever so slightly upon her cheeks. She bowed her head and then whispered something that I couldn't understand. And as I stood beside her, embracing her with my touch, I watched the pitter-patter of her broken heart fall softly upon Old Glory.

Everyone else had taken their places now as the chapel became a little quieter. And I all of a sudden felt a little dumb. OK, truthfully—a lot dumb as I glanced over my shoulder and realized that people were staring at us.

"We'd better go sit down now," I whispered to her. "I think we may be getting ready to get this over with."

She didn't budge. She was whispering again.

"I didn't know him long enough."

I realized at that moment that it wasn't going to be *me* at all who would be creating a scene. It just may be the youngest. Which would, in fact, make this situation just a tad bit more complicated in that my mind couldn't talk her through it like it could me. Where in the hell was Glinda????

"No, you didn't," I whispered. *Please don't freak out.*

"Actually, none of us did," I whispered. She still wasn't budging. *Yup she's gonna freak out big time—thus creating the most gigantic, catastrophic scene in funeral history!*

"I don't blame Mom," she continued. "I don't really blame anyone actually."

*Great—glad to hear that—now, can we sit down?*

I glanced over my shoulder and locked a stare with Glinda, which didn't take but a second because she, like everyone else was looking right at us. A stare that said, "Get your ass up here now!" *And bring your freaking magic bubble, your wand, the ruby red slippers, the damned broom, the Cavalry, and an ambulance!*

Glinda stood immediately and began her slithering journey to the center aisle, holding on to the banister which slid the length of the front pew probably put there for times like these just in case someone stood and felt the incredible urge to faint! And why they don't make those rows just a little bit wider is beyond me!

The widow witch was sitting in the front pew of course on the end closest to the main aisle, and the next to the youngest sister was sitting to the left of her, then the

Indian then my husband and then Glinda. She had to squeeze past everyone to get to the main aisle, which frustrated the living hoopla right out of me.

*Any day now, Glinda, you giggly, stinking, good-hearted dumb-ass, why didn't you just walk around, good witch big sister of mine?*

Finally, here she came.

She shuffled up to the left side of our baby sister and put her arm ever so gently around her waist. Then, leaning into her and around the front of her she locked a stare with me and whispered, "What are we doing?"

*Hum, let's see, what are we doing? We're milking a freaking cow for the love of God what does it look like we're doing you moronic stupid jackass good witch of the North, South, East or West or whichever part of the damned country your from!*

"I think she's having a moment," I whispered.

"OK," Glinda replied. "She's entitled."

Well, halleflippenluyah! I felt much better now. She was entitled! Entitled, meaning she was allowed, permitted to hold up a whole entire funeral service! Great! And just how long was she entitled to do so? I mean, just how long were we going to be standing up there? Hell, if I had known this, I wouldn't have refrained from vomiting on the marble floors!

So there the three of us stood—before Glinda whispered leaning into her, "Are you ready to go sit down now, honey?"

Yeah, honey, are you ready to go sit down—now—that you have stolen my moment of insanity? Now that you have just accomplished what I, myself, tried so desperately not to do?

"You can spend all the time you need when we get to the cemetery, OK?" Glinda added.

Yeah, hell, we'll even let you jump in the hole with him if you want to—you moment-stealing baby sister of ours!

Tears still dripping, she looked at me and then at Glinda and then back down at Old Glory before she finally surrendered herself to the idea of sitting down.

But before she turned to do so, she asked a question. A question that made me sick to my stomach as well as it probably flipped my dad upside down inside of that box he was laying in, although I didn't hear any ruckus going on.

"Do you think he loved us? Do you think he loved *me*," she sobbed?

OK, now I was sure beyond a shadow of a doubt that my heart was, in fact, breaking as I tried to answer but Glinda beat me to it.

"With every little thing he had in him, I'm sure he loved all of us and he especially loved you."

"I wasn't much of a daughter," she whimpered.

"You were just as much of a daughter as any daughter could have been in our situation," Glinda told her. "Now let's go sit down and get this over with."

And with that, the three of us turned around and walked to the pew to take our perspective seats.

Squishing our way back through everyone's already cramped legs, we all took our seats and just in the nick of time before the side door to the chapel opened and the chaplain stepped through and walked to the podium.

The entire chapel fell completely silent except for the ruffling of a few papers and the swoosh of the chaplain's robe.

She stood looking down at first as though she might be praying and then brought her head up to address the congregation. This was it!

"I want to thank you all for coming," she began. "We are all here to pay our last and final respects to a most wonderful person who touched my life as well as the lives of others, I'm sure. And most who knew Eddie, also knew that he had a way of doing just that; touching if not changing your perspective on life."

She went on to speak of precious gifts and memories. She spoke of stuffed animals coming alive at night and of Santa's elves and how they came to be. She spoke of a man who all of his life beamed as he boasted to anyone who would listen that he had Five—*Count 'em, my friend—I've got five beautiful brown-eyed baby doll girls.* She spoke of how we would all miss him and how he touched our lives with incredible, child like honesty. She spoke of how he loved the simplest things in life and how those simple little things made him so happy. Life *itself* made Eddie happy and when life had become too difficult to bear how he had decided on his own that it was time to say good-bye. She shared how he had planned his own exit with such precision, that she truly believed that he and God had come to some sort of agreement as to how, when - and where he would have his last and final curtain call. And then she spoke of longtime friends, which led her to introduce Paul Bunyan.

The giant of a man stood, shoulders still bent slightly forward as he inched his way to the main aisle and completely dominated the space as he strolled up to the podium, causing her to stand off to the side, bible in hand and head bowed.

Once standing at the podium, both of his enormous hands gripping each side of it, he finally looked up from his notes revealing tear-filled eyes. He stoically cleared his throat once and then again, swallowing hard before he began his valued memories of his most cherished friend.

He began by sharing how long he had known my dad. He told of how anyone who ever knew my dad, was a friend, "And if you weren't welcome as a friend, he let you know right away!"

He told of how his friend would drive through the gates of work each morning, with a teddy bear riding shotgun and if it was a lucky day, that silly bear would give you a wave or two. He spoke of his blatant honesty as well as his natural ability to listen. "Always giving the human race, the benefit of the doubt." He told of an always-cheery fellow who never showed any emotion other than happiness even through his divorce, which the speaker was sure, beyond a shadow of a doubt, had totally destroyed him. He told of memories that brought laughter as well as tears and with his giant shoulders heaving in sorrow, he ended his memoirs with, "I'm going to miss him terribly." And just before he stepped down from the podium, head hung in grief and shoulders slumped forward, he suddenly but slowly turned his tear-filled gaze to the ceiling and said, "I'm sure he's happily sweeping those gold paved streets above—and hopefully with a new broom!"

There were a few giggles and a few tears as the giant then carefully stepped down and began his stroll back to his place on the pew—but not before he glanced over, shoulders still hunched forward and rolled his boyish eyes at me as if to say, *Whew, glad that's over.*

I returned his look with a heartfelt smile and mouthed a silent thank you to him. He nodded as he passed our pew and my attention was then drawn to the front of the chapel once again as the hospice chaplain took her place behind the podium, placing both hands, one on each side of it and looked out at the congregation. She then began her next sentence with, "I have seen a lot of death in my position. And I have also seen a lot of relationships. Most of which end in sadness—and that it is where my job begins; to help teach the loved one's being left behind how to cope and deal with what has happened. But—very seldom, do I have the opportunity to happen upon a situation such as the one I have just encountered in that I was the student and the dying was the teacher. I have been blessed for I have learned so very much about heaven and faith from two people. I have witnessed a relationship that goes far beyond what mere words can express." Then she paused, looking down at the podium again as though she were trying to catch her breath. However, that wasn't it at all as she returned her gaze to the audience before her and her eyes were wet with sorrow. She swallowed and excused herself for just a moment by placing one hand slightly in the air and the other to her lips—and then—she apologized, and continued.

433

"When I met Eddie and his daughter, I was truly amazed that such a bond could exist. He had already prepared himself for his own journey and was teaching his daughter how to say good-bye. He was teaching her how it was perfectly natural to let go." Looking down, she paused again. Then, returning her gaze back to the congregation, hesitantly, she continued.

"We are all born dying, is what Eddie had said—and very matter-offactly I might add—and he shared with his daughter as well as myself, that some of us just make it a little longer than others. He also taught us the true meaning of the word forever. Forever—is only until someone dies—or until someone changes their mind." She smiled.

"How very true that statement is. He simply wanted to make the best of the time he had left remaining here in this place until his forever was finally over. He believed that everyone should live each day just as he had during his last year. You see, oddly enough, Eddie believed he was one of the lucky ones because he had been given the opportunity to say goodbye. Ridden with tumors the size of soft balls, losing at least one to two pounds per day toward the end and not having had a decent meal in six months because he just couldn't seem to keep anything down as his body declined—he felt lucky! Imagine that! Perhaps, he knew a secret." She paused again. "No, I'm sure he knew a secret," she continued, "because when he slept, he went places and then he came back to us and he shared his experiences and he did so in explicit detail—so much detail, in fact, that I will now feel comfortable in telling all of my hospice patients that there is, in fact, cool frosty mugs of Budweiser waiting for them on every corner." (Laughter as well as sniffles in Surround Sound)

"And now," she continued, "I would like to introduce to you, the second oldest of Eddie's five daughters."

I was mesmerized. I had been so caught up in the wonderful person she had just been describing that I had forgotten where I was! I had forgotten who I was! As a matter of fact, I had the urge to turn around and look for Eddie's second oldest daughter. She had to be amazing!

"I can't begin to explain the relationship they shared," she was now saying. "It was exquisite as well as remarkably spiritual. And if ever I had to describe it in just one word—it would have to be unique."

*I liked that word, unique. Made me feel—well—sort—of—unique!*

"Theirs was a relationship that comes along just once in a lifetime," she continued. "A relationship that could—and *has* redefined the word sacrifice."

*Wow, this daughter of Eddie's was absolutely incredible!*

"She has prepared Eddie's final words to all of you," she continued.

"The way he felt and some things he wanted you all to know." And with that, she looked at me and nodded.

Holy crap! Why in the hell was she looking at me? I didn't even know this daughter of Eddie's! I was no way worthy of even being in her presence! And then something horrific occurred to me! It was me! I—was—the—daughter! I had to get up there now and read my father's farewell speech! Oh, hell, I felt sick. As a matter of fact, I thought I just might vomit! Why couldn't that nice daughter of Eddie's read his final words of farewell? She was so brave—and such a heroine! She had already endured so much that surely, one last and final little farewell wouldn't kick her precious little ass! However, as I stood to make my way through the pew and up to the podium, I thought that this little scene just might kick her little keister more so than any other thus far. All of a sudden, and I must say for probably the very first time in my life—I wasn't real sure I wanted to be Eddie's daughter. Not if it meant I had to get up there in front of all those people and share. This had been such a private ordeal up until now. I wasn't sure if it was proper to share my dad's final thoughts. Silly I guess, when you really stop and think about it. I mean, my dad had asked me to. That is why I had written the poem and had it printed on the little brochures that everyone had been handed as they entered the funeral home. Hey—since everyone already had a copy of what I had written, then why did I have to get up there and read it? I mean beside the fact that my dad had asked me to. Boy—I had a good mind to have a few words with him when this was all over!

After making my squished journey through the pew of horrors, I now found myself standing next to the hospice chaplain, facing the congregation but not yet looking at them. I had the brochure in my hands and, quite frankly, I could have wiped my face with the dew it had seeping off it. I made sure not to take my eyes off the pulpit as the chaplain still standing next to me, leaned down and whispered something in my ear. I jerked my head sideways to look at her and as our eyes met we both began to smile.

"He's here" is all she needed to say to give me the courage to share his thoughts. And with that, I looked up from the podium and out at all of the people who for one reason or another were there to say good–bye.

"In the final weeks of my dad's life," I began, "He asked that I share with all of you how he felt about leaving."

I paused, looked down and then up again and continued.

"You know, he should have left us weeks before he actually did." Pausing and then swallowing hard I continued.

"The hospice people and I just couldn't imagine what he had been holding on for."

I paused again but this time it was because I wasn't real sure if I could make the words come out. Up until that point, I had only heard them yet I had never spoken them from my own lips. I continued, my voice beginning to waver.

"We now know, however, that he was simply waiting for me to leave."

There I said it. It was done.

I continued, "He said he would chose the time—the place—and the day—and I guess he did, of course this shouldn't come as a shock to those of us who knew him so well. My dad always seemed to do things his way."

There were a few chuckles and nods from the audience undoubtedly coming from the people who indeed knew him very well. I smiled and continued.

"It was very important to my dad that no one carried on in such a way that it might make others uncomfortable for he felt that death, like birth is a natural thing. He wanted all of you to know that he was OK with leaving and that he would see you all again in another time and another place." And with that, voice already shaky and cracking, I began the poem:


To My Dear Friends and Relatives

While I was asleep, I slipped away, I chose the time, the place, the day. I waited till I was all alone, To begin my peaceful journey home.

Please don't be afraid, I wasn't scared I knew a lot of people there. They were all so very kind to me I'm truly where I want to be.

In my final days still here with you, I did everything I knew to do To stay as long as I could stay I didn't want to leave this way.

But there's a plan for me no doubt I believe that's what it's all about So keep in mind through all your grief That my final rest was true relief.

Oh, I know you'll cry but that's all right Just hug and hold each other tight That's just what I would like to see When you come to say good-bye to me.

In all your hearts is where I'll be If you feel the need to talk to me, Your memories will show the way To bring back all our yesterdays.

I'm so glad you all came here To share the memories, laughs and tears. So until that day when we meet again I'll leave you now, with a thanks My Friends. Bye Now!

Eddie

Perhaps it was because I was bawling through the last stanza, I'm not real sure, but when I finished, there didn't seem to be a dry eye looking back at me when I looked up and out at the congregation.

Sometimes, I think that tears catch on like yawns. I couldn't seem to make anymore words come out as I stared out at all those tear streaked faces. So I didn't for a moment. Instead, I swayed from one foot to another trying to compose myself enough to thank everyone for coming. It was no use. I knew if I tried to say anything else, it would simply sound as though a dying cow were moaning for support while birthing her calf. I was whipped and the realization of what I had just read had made me actually wish that I *had* been giving birth or maybe even having a tooth extracted with no anesthetic once again—anything other than what my heart seemed to be enduring at that very moment. My God, I could have never dreamed that the human heart could withstand such pain. My dad was gone! And I would only have my memories to serve me now when I needed to talk to him or feel him or hug him. I would simply have to turn now—to *only* my memories when I needed advice or just a simple straightening out of sorts. And I believe this is where we all came in to this story now, isn't it? Another full circle.

Where had I been? Hadn't I realized that this is why we were all gathered together? My gosh, *had* I been dreaming?

The chaplain's gentle hand was now around my waist cluing me in to the fact that I was still standing before a whole congregation of people! That was beautiful she was whispering to me. Oh, My God—sit down! It was time for me to step down! But I hadn't thanked everyone for coming! I had so much yet to say! But I couldn't find the words. I couldn't find my voice. I think it must have been somewhere between my stomach and my broken heart. So, I did just exactly what any other red-blooded American daughter of a World War II private first classman would have done. I took my little announcement paper and stepped down from the podium, lip quivering, and my tears cascading to the floor.

And as I tried to focus through the haze as to where I was supposed to go, there stood Glinda, bubble looming with brightness—eyes glistening the reflection of my pain, head tilted sideways, arms extended as always just when I felt I had no where else to turn. And it was times like these when I wanted to—and did—take back every rotten thing I had ever said or done to her. It's a sister thing, I suppose.

Once seated and wishing I could just close my eyes and disappear, the chaplain was speaking again. I believe she thanked me and then announced that in closing she would like to read Eddie's favorite passage from The Good Book—The Ten Commandments. And before she did so, she felt the need to share with everyone why it had been his favorite. You see, she began, Eddie shared with me that during difficult times throughout his life, when he had to make a decision, sometimes as he put it, it became difficult for him to know which was the right way to go (you can go this way—or you can go that way—or you can go both ways). So, she continued, he would pick up the Bible and read The Ten Commandments. This way, perhaps *what* to do still may not be very clear, but what *not* to do was crystal clear. She then chuckled a bit and added, as Eddie would say; "It will sure as hell keep you on the straight and narrow."

*And to think, all this time we've been giving the credit to my grandfather! Thou Shall Not Kill!*

She closed the service with an announcement as to where my dad would be finally laid to rest as well as the fact that he was very proud to have his daughters as his pallbearers—and then she bowed her head cueing the rest of the congregation to do the same and ended the service in prayer.

I truly felt like I was going to faint as I bowed my head with the realization that the first part of the service was now over and I was still breathing. However, like an arrow shot through me, I then also realized that we now had to carry my fathers casket to the hearse. My God, was there no end to this misery? I mean, just exactly how does one carry a casket anyway? I, myself, had never been asked to do such a thing and quite frankly, no one really bothered to give us any sort of schooling on the subject. Therefore, I supposed you just grabbed a handle and gave it the old heave ho! Where in the hell was Fella? Shouldn't this have been his responsibility? And just as I thought I might just track our old friend down and give him a tongue lashing he would never forget, I realized that everyone was standing—except the witch—whom I guess somewhere in the rules and regulations book for funerals had been excused from standing. She was to sit and grieve until someone who liked her—took her by the arm to escort her saddened ass out to her limo: the widow's car. My aching ass! And I didn't wait to see who that someone was either— however, I realized out of the corner of my eye as myself, my sisters, my husband and the Indian were on our way up to fetch our father's casket, that it was, in fact, my father's boss who was helping her to stand. Oh, God—if he had only known what I knew—she would have still been sitting there to this very day. Of that I am sure!

The Indian was now at my side and whispering instructions to me.

Now, I want you all to know, that the carrying of one's casket is considered an honor—well—in our world anyway. What a bunch of hullabaloo! It's morbid! And it's downright un-American if you ask me! Someone should obtain a business license and commence a casket carrying service so that the emotionally unattached can do the honors! Any takers? Probably not. Can't say that I blame you. It's morose, horrific, downright gruesome I say! And it shouldn't come as a surprise to any of us that the Indian seemed to know all about these sorts of things. I swear in my next life, I want to come back as an Indian!

"What do we do?" I whispered, as my sisters were now gathering around us obviously wondering the same.

Three of us line up on one side and three on the other he explained. There are handles to grip on each side. We take hold of the handles—and on the count of three we lift all together. *Break!*

I wish I could remember who went on which side but I can't. All I know is we lined up just the way the Indian had instructed us to do so and on the count of three it's a wonder that casket didn't go flying through the ceiling! The old heave ho was sadly not needed for this casket. It was more like the old pee wee ho, as it's tenant barely weighed eighty pounds when he passed and as we all simultaneously lifted that beautiful piece of wood, I know we were all thinking the same thing as all of our eyes were darting toward one another in recognition of this terrible sadness.

We marched like little soldiers, the six of us and I found myself thinking thoughts to my dad. I hope you're proud. This is what you wanted. But most of all I was still in shock over the feather weight lightness of this final resting box. And for a split second, I wondered if Fella had, in fact, performed the old switcheroo. Sure, you numbskull— and just exactly what would he have gained by doing so? Well, of *that* I wasn't quite sure but I wasn't real fond of Fella and that in itself gave me reason enough to think what I was indeed thinking. And I swore to myself, that come hell or high water after this was all over, I really was going to once and for all—get a life!

As we began our journey in cadence down the main aisle I noticed the back side door was opening allowing the sunshine to cascade upon the carpet a spotlight showing us the way. We came to the end of the aisle and turned in sync to the left, leaving those in the rear to step in place for a moment before we headed for the door.

Once facing the side exit I saw the dreaded hearse. It was in full view of the doorway and I suddenly realized that my dad would be riding in a separate car! I have no clue what else I could have possibly been anticipating. I don't really think I had given it a second thought up until then. Wow, I really needed some serious therapy.

Outside the sun shined so brightly that I wondered if God had, in fact, made a mistake. How could a day so beautiful have been tainted by death?

We marched forward through all of the nameless faces who were whispering to each other; some wiping their eyes with tissue and some just beaming proud smiles back at our solemn faces. I suppose it had been quite a sight to behold. Eddie's daughters carrying his casket. And once that thought crossed my mind then I too was very proud and I'm not real sure but I think my posture may have improved just a tad bit. We marched forward to the hearse and had to turn to the left and then turn again in order to face the rear of this morbid vehicle as its side was facing us.

Once facing the crude and gaping hole that was just waiting to swallow my dad I felt my knees beginning to buckle. Wow, what a lonely consign the back of a hearse appeared to be. And as we scooted the casket up and slid it in, it reminded me of an ambulance. However, that's a car that harbors hope and this was a car that signifies none.

Once scooted in place, we all took a step back and just stood there. I had the incredible urge to ask if I could ride with my dad; however, I managed to refrain from requesting such permission. And as I stood staring into the back of that beast, I noticed the driver standing at attention ready to close the rear door. A small man, in a handsome little suit and tie with absolutely no expression on his face what–so–ever–at– all. Oh, Lord—he was probably related to Fella! They all were!

I obviously wasn't budging as I stood, knees actually touching the bumper of this carriage of death, gazing at the casket which was now in its place and the driver standing next to me—just as obviously waiting for me to move so that he could close the heavy door. My eyes wandered to meet with his and as they did, his still held no expression. The others had walked back to the limos, which were parked behind the hearse, drivers studiously waiting beside open doors.

I just couldn't move. My dad was in that flag-draped box and I couldn't move. And to my surprise it wasn't Glinda or the Indian who came to my rescue: It was the driver, who was saying, Ma'am, as he gently placed his hand under my arm to wake me from my gaze.

"I need to close the door now," he was empathetically saying.

I took just one step back—my gaze still resting upon Old Glory. The driver, then addressing me with Ma'am once more, guided me backward.

"Sorry," I mumbled.

"It's quite all right," he was whispering as he had one arm extended to me and the other on the edge of the door which once shut would entomb my dad. *God, please don't let that door slam shut because it will surely clunk with that horrible sound of finality!*

Leaning close to the driver, I sort of put my arm around his bony little shoulder and reached my lips toward his ear and whispered a request for him to sing a song to my dad on our long drive to the cemetery. He pulled back slightly and it was obvious that I had gotten his attention as he stared at me with brow furrowed and a most bewildered expression on his face. But then, to my surprise, with absolutely no hint of emotion he flatly asked me what I would like for him to sing. Stunned, I removed my arm from around his shoulder and started to walk away, hence turning around walking backward toward the limos I quipped, "How about Happy Trails to You? "You know that one?" I asked.

"Yes, Ma'am, I do," he answered without a moment's hesitation— obviously amused.

"Good," I quipped as I turned to walk toward my waiting limo,

"That one will be just fine," I said over my shoulder as my back was now turned to him—wincing as I heard the heavy door finally slam shut behind me.

When I climbed in to the daughter's car, which was, of course, parked behind the widow's car—Glinda was ready and waiting to give me what for, for picking on the little fellow.

"I didn't pick on him," I exclaimed! "I only tried to cheer him up a bit—put a smile on his face. He looked a little lonely to me," furthering my explanation. "Geeze," I continued, "We only live once. Life is too stinking short to be so damned serious all the time!"

And as we watched the glorious widow's car pulling forward, I realized that what I had just said sounded exactly like something my father would have said and my only regret was that my mother hadn't been there to hear it.

We had at the very least, a forty-minute drive ahead of us as my father chose to be buried in the same cemetery as my grand folks. Of course, anywhere you went in Southern California was a long drive due to the superb traffic situation but we have already gone over all of that—now, haven't we? Yes, I believe we have however, I would like to clarify that as embarrassed as I am to admit it, after complaining as much as I did in the beginning, that I would have given anything at all that day for one of the worst traffic jams in Southern California history! Although, I guess all things actually do happen for a reason and seeing that my dad was no longer on ice, traffic did seem to move quite steadily that day. Thank God for little green apples!

Somewhere around the halfway point, as we all rode in utterly, ghastly silence, I'd had just about enough. I didn't smoke a whole lot, as a matter of fact I never smoked in public or in the car or around my kids. I was what you could call—a closet smoker— but at that very moment, I felt this incredible urge to puff. Therefore, I leaned forward and tapped on the driver's window. It immediately slid down with a whir.

"Yes, Ma'am," Gus questioned with anticipation in his voice.

441

"Hello," I sang with a happy heart.

"Hello, Ma'am," Gus answered back with a hint of a smile in his voice.

"Do you think we could pull this wagon train over so that perhaps we could stretch our legs a bit?" I asked with a slight Southern drawl.

"Ma'am?" He questioned with just a little more concern in his voice.

"Can we pull over?" I asked again with just a little hint of urgency.

"Well, Ma'am," he began, "We *are* in a funeral precession he pleaded and the widow's car is leading.

"Uh, no—it really isn't," I quipped.

"My dad's car is actually leading this circus and I don't think he would mind a bit if we pulled over. As a matter of fact, he was quite the adventurer and I'm real sure he wouldn't mind."

Silence.

More silence.

*Hello, Gus, I do so hope you haven't died up there. For one thing you're driving and for another, we only have one hearse!*

"I have no way to signal the other cars," Gus pleaded.

"Don't you know the way to the cemetery?" I asked.

"Well, yes, Ma'am," he stammered.

"Look," I explained, "This has been a very trying week and my sister needs to have a cigarette before she tears apart your beautiful leather upholstery and since none of us drink, your alcohol back here is doing us no damned good, therefore, might I suggest that we pull this damned caravan over before it appears as if someone let the Samsonite gorilla loose right here in your own backseat? A crippling slug from Glinda walloped my leg. I didn't even look at her.

Gus was now looking at me through the rearview mirror and I was looking right back at him. I think the Tin Man and the Scarecrow had fainted.

"We *are* the third car," Gus answered as though it had taken him all morning to discover this unknown fact. And to my surprise, still smiling, he flashed his lights at the widow's car, which, in turn, must have flashed their lights at the hearse because everyone took the next exit and pulled over. Everyone—including all of the cars behind us!

Well, how about them apples! I had managed to stop an entire funeral precession! Hearse and all! My dad would have gotten a kick out of this one! My mother would have had a coronary!

"What in the hell are you doing?" Glinda whispered with a razor sharp tone in her voice.

"I'm lightening things up a bit," I answered, as though I had only just told a seemingly harmless joke.

"You–know–who isn't going to like this," she chimed in, almost singing the statement speaking of my father's widow.

"Yeah, I know," I said. But the girls are going to think it's a hoot!

The hearse pulled over far enough ahead in the dirt of the off ramp as to give ample room for the widow's car as well as our own. When all the cars had come to a complete stop, the hearse driver was the first to get out of his car. Then, Hector emerged from the widow's car both holding on to their doors and looking back at Gus. This situation looked like a scene from a comedy.

The backdoor of the widow's car slowly opened and our two youngest sisters stepped out at the same time as Glinda, the Tin Man, the Scarecrow and myself. They looked back at our car and slowly walking toward us with questions in their eyes. My dad stayed put.

The Indian was cracking up. He loved to smoke.

Gus waved at the other drivers with a motion of his right hand and yelled, "Just need to stretch their legs!"

Both drivers nodded reluctantly and got back in their vehicles.

Gus remained outside of ours as though he were watching over us.

The two youngest girls were sashaying back to our car, giggling and asking just what in the heck we thought we were doing.

"Stretching our legs!" I answered. "Duh! Didn't you hear Gus?"

"The Indian needed to smoke," I said and giggled as my uncle very obligingly, held up a lit cigarette.

I looked behind us and all of the other cars were pulled over as well. Some of the folks got out and stretched their legs and some stayed in their cars, but all pulled over! This would go down in our family history book as the biggest bonehead stunt of the century! Man, I was proud! It was fun and for just a moment, I felt as though my dad had never left. Hell, even the witch got out, shook her head from side to side and got back into the limo thus signaling to all that we'd probably better do the same. The stunt was over and I was satisfied.

The Indian doused his smoke and with that, we all began climbing back in to our respective coaches. We'd only lost ten minutes. What's ten minutes when you've lost your father? Nothing! And that's all I have to say about that!

Once back in the car, the window still down, Gus turned his head slightly to the right and asked, "Ma'am?"

Leaning forward, I answered, "Yes?"

"You don't have to go to the bathroom or anything, do you?"

Smiling, I softly said, "No, I'm fine."

"Just checking," he smirked and the window whirred the end of our conversation.

I sure had taken a liking to Gus. He was a good sport.

The remainder of our ride was silent as we all unwound from my little escapade. All of us still smiling–but serene and the closer we got to the cemetery the more our smiles faded as reality began to rear its ugly head once again.

The huge iron gates of the cemetery loomed our arrival as we passed under them and took in the breathtaking view of the mountains in the distance. My dad had chosen a most wonderful place to rest. Acres upon green roving acres of beauty surrounded this place. It was like heaven here on earth. This was my dad's heaven—or about as close as I was going to get to see of it anyway—well at least on that particular day.

We drove slowly through the beautiful tree lined drive with the reflection of its magnificence, fluttering back at me through the smoked glass window of our car.

Our precession came to a slow stop as we waited for another service to come to a close. I sat and silently gazed upon the pain of another family, wondering whom they might have lost.

We sat for only moments before our drive continued forward with the crackling of the tires on the peed gravel signaling my stomach to do complete flip flops.

Our car pulled around into a circular turn out and came to a halt in front of a white gazebo off to our left and as the whirr of the window came down I, all of a sudden felt Glinda's fierce and sudden grip on my knee. What? I wondered as I shot her a look of don't do that again, it hurt! I didn't tap on the damned window this time! Gus pushed the button on his own! But she wasn't looking at me. She was staring straight ahead through the now open cubicle which gave her a perfect view through the front windshield. Turning my gaze from her, I too allowed my eyes to wander through the front of the car and what my eyes beheld was breathtaking!

Standing at full attention, gathered around the rear of the hearse, were seven full-dressed United States of America, Army soldiers! Our car door opened with Gus's assistance and as we slid sideways careful not to take our eyes off this sight as though it may disappear if we did, we got out of the car still gazing upon that magnificent display of respect.

My husband took hold of my hand and squeezed it gently as we ventured forward toward the back of the hearse. "Oh–my–God," I whispered as we came upon them.

Three stood to one side of the rear of the hearse and three stood to the other side with one in the rear center, all statues of patriotic bliss, starring out at nowhere, as though we weren't even there. They then, taking whispered orders from their superior officer all seven turned toward our family, clicked their heels together and saluted us. Another Oh–-my–God gushed from my lips.

The rear and center soldier, who was indeed the superior officer, then whispered another husked order and all six of the remaining soldiers then turned and faced each other once again, with the click of their heels. With three on each side of the unopened back door of the hearse, the superior officer then marched up through the center of them and swung wide the big heavy door. With a stomp of his foot and another whispered "Huh!" Three of the soldiers stepped around the door in cadence and were now standing in front of the opening to the rear of the hearse facing their partners once again. The superior officer then pivoted on one foot, did a precise about face and marched to the rear and center once again performing another about face, which turned him in the direction of the rear of the hearse. With another whispered huh! All six soldiers marched in place as they removed my father's casket from its coach and keeping in step the entire time they then turned and marched with the clickity clack of their shiny black shoes on the pavement, carrying that beautiful piece of wood draped with Old Glory into the gazebo. I was mesmerized.

We followed them seemingly awestruck and once inside another bellowed whisper of an order husked through the breezeway of the gazebo and they laid the casket to rest on a pillar worthy of supporting its soldier. Another gut-wrenching, "Huh!" And they all six, turned to face one another, three on each side of the casket, took one step back away from it and saluted my father. A whispered husk of, "At ease," swirled through the air and with that, all six soldiers spread their legs, hips apart and placed their arms behind their backs and stood there.

Another whispered, "Oh–my–God," pursed through my lips, accompanied by tears of pride. It was now time for *us* to enter the confines of the gazebo all the way and take our seats and as I proceeded to do so, another spectacular vision caught my eye.

Halfway up the roving hillside of lawn behind the gazebo stood seven more soldiers in full dress uniforms, standing at attention, bearing arms. And behind them on the very top of the hill stood a lone soldier also standing at attention grasping a solid brass bugle at his side.

I took my seat and silently thanked God for the gift I had just received.

The hospice chaplain stepped up to the podium which was directly next to the casket and began this final ceremony with a prayer as we all bowed our heads.

With the closing of the prayer, the soldiers came to life once again. Standing at attention they received a huffed order from their superior officer and then took two steps toward the casket and in unison they lifted that beautiful cloth of American glory from the casket and with the precise expertise of surgeons, they systematically folded Her Majesty.

The flag was then placed in the awaiting arms of the superior officer and he clicked his heels together, pivoted completely around to face us and presented the emblem of the land we love ever so softly into the lap of my father's widow. Then, taking two steps backward, he stood, clicked his heels together again and standing at attention they all seven then saluted her. If it hadn't been so breathtaking—I would have thrown up. She didn't deserve that flag and I surely had not anticipated that move.

The superior officer then huffed another order and all seven of them turned to face the soldiers on the hillside. A moment of silence and then - Another order and three rounds of synchronized shots were fired from seven rifles. One simultaneous crack—followed by a click, click and then another—and then another. My shoulders jerked and segments of my heart were shattered with each round as though those shots themselves were intended for me.

Another pause of silence and then Taps began to beautifully mourn from the soldiers battle horn and as it did, I reached for my husbands hand, bowed my head and I cried with the whine of the bugle. *There it is, Dad. You have now received a burial with full military honors from the United States Army. You have been graced with the presence of your fellow soldiers.* And just as the soldiers were now at ease, so was my aching heart.

I'm not real sure if I will ever experience pride like that again in my life but I would venture to guess, probably not. Pride like that comes only once in a lifetime and of that I am quite sure.

The chaplain began once again with the reason as to why we were all there however, she then hesitated but continued slowly: "Eddie had a request that he asked for me to share at this time." She then looked at my husband, said his name and went forward with my father's wishes.

"Eddie never had a son," she began, "and therefore, he wanted you to know that he leaves you with the responsibility of looking after his daughters. He knew you would take care of things and watch out for them just as he would have done."

The Tin Man was honored as he bowed his head and with his shoulders wrenching, he allowed his painful loss to flow freely from his closed and stinging eyes.

Another prayer was said. More tears fell like rain. And then, like his life, my father's funeral was over.

The soldiers came back to life as if they had suddenly been recharged. Once again, in complete intonation, they lifted the casket and stepped in place ever so slowly and marched back to the hearse transporting their fellow soldier to burial. We all stood as they left the gazebo and followed them to the hearse. Respectfully they slid the casket back into its haven as they marched in place. Another huffed order gave permission to swing the heavy door closed and with one last and final salute, this soldier had ended his enlistment.

Standing in the warmth of the sun, my sisters and I joined hands and stood in a circle and sang a verse in harmony of "You Are My Sunshine" followed by a verse of "Beautiful, Beautiful, Brown Eyes." We weren't the least bit concerned with who was watching or listening. We believed we had an audience of only one who really mattered.

People were dispersing now, meandering back to their cars and it was about that time when I noticed the hearse driver coming toward me. He shuffled his short little legs over to where I was standing and leaned ever so carefully his lips to my ear.

"I did it," he proudly exclaimed in a whisper.

Pulling my head back and staring at him in complete astonishment, I replied, "Really?"

"Yup," he answered with two quick nods of assurance and his chest stretched out just about as far as it would go; "Two verses!"

I reached around his small frame and gave him a snug little hug and told him thank you.

"I'll bet my dad was dancing in heaven," I said.

"Probably was," he replied, "because his daughters are angels." And with that, he turned, and began walking back to the hearse whistling a very familiar tune.

Shocked at his all of a sudden aggressiveness and bravery, I wanted to ask him if he had ever had the urge to buy a pair of suspenders. However, I refrained. Just a thought.

Walking over to the limo, I looked back and caught a glimpse of the hearse pulling up and over the hill with the sun glistening a sparkle off its shiny chrome bumper. And as I tucked my head to get in to my carriage, I could have sworn I heard a familiar voice from somewhere far away saying; "Man, that's a beautiful piece of machinery!"

I wanted to hug the whole entire United States Army and thank them for what they had just done. I'm sure they had no clue. Oh sure, full military honors but the soldier they had just patriotically put to rest wasn't just any old soldier. As a matter of fact, his war began long after his years in the service had ended. Nonetheless, he was still a true veteran as perhaps we all are when we leave this world.

On the way home, I lowered my power window from the back seat of that stretch limo as we pulled up next to an old pick up truck at a red light. I then leaned out the window just a tad and asked the unshaven gentleman at the wheel if he had any Grey Poupon. He didn't. But as we pulled away from the light and headed for home, I had a flash of my dad, shaking his head from side to side mumbling under his breath how I must have taken after my mother. And I believe it was at that very moment that I knew he would always be such a wonderful part of me and that I would continue to be such a wonderful part of him—and that, my friends, is the very beauty of the precious gift of life.

One at a time, over the next two days, we all left for home. Everyone flew except for Glinda and myself. We had a truck to drive and take home to my father's namesake packed full of memories and keepsakes for all to share.

Leaving my father's home had now become another dreaded task I had to face. Endings are sad and they are final as I should damned well know by now. And if you ever had a doubt—you are about to have that doubt put to rest.

Glinda and I were carrying assigned boxes to the truck. Assigned by my father as to who would get each one with their names scribbled on each one in his notorious chicken scratch.

I still had told no one about the changing of the will or about the witch's secret. I would share it with my sis on our long drive home—or so I thought.

As we both entered my dad's bedroom to get the last of the boxes from his closet, we were greeted with absolute shock and hysteria. The witch was opening my dad's dresser drawers with a vengeance and throwing his T-shirts and sweatpants and all of his possessions all over the bedroom floor! As I watched in complete horror—I was panic stricken! What in the hell was she doing? Jerking in anger with each and every drawer as she yanked it open and continued to throw it's contents to the floor—I slid to my knees across the bedroom floor frantically scooping up his belongings as quickly as I could, holding them to my chest asking— screaming—pleading— begging her to stop!

"What is wrong," I was crying, "why are you doing this?" I was demanding with tears raging from deep within the confines of my broken heart—my eyes begging her to stop—please stop!!!!

She was not crying. She was angry and yelling that she wanted it out!

"All–of–it–out!!!"

With every garment that hit the floor my heart felt its devastating impact as though she were throwing the Bible. And then—the little blue shaving bag with the words Grandpa hit the floor and my tears and pain and confusion were shattered by a bellowing of rage that I hadn't heard in years! A voice of protection that took over the entire room.

It was Glinda the Good Witch and she was in the face of the Bad Witch who she was now backing up to the far wall of the bedroom. She was yelling, "Stop it! What is wrong with you! How dare you!" And then the final threat, "If you touch one more thing of his—I will kill you," she was threatening. "Do you hear me?" she was yelling, still pinning the bad witch up against the wall with her fist planted up underneath the chin of the bad witch. I remembered this scene all too well. I had seen Glinda like this before—but only once—and it wasn't a bad witch she had been fighting—but Satan himself—long ago in a land far away.

I was still sprawled out across the bedroom floor as far as my body would stretch in all directions trying to gather my father's things tears still falling like rain. His things could not be scattered in this way. I was sobbing now.

"What is wrong with you?" Glinda was now demanding.

"Take it all!" the bad witch was yelling! "Get it all out of here! I don't want it!"

"Why?" Glinda was yelling. "What is the matter with you?"

"He would have wanted it all to go home with you anyway," the bad witch was now saying, her voice calming just a tad bit. I don't want any part of him left here anymore.

"But why?" Glinda was now asking, still holding her at bay with one arm, as though she may just have to shoot her.

"Just take it all," the bad witch was saying.

And as I sat on the floor with my father's belongings gathered up in my arms I uttered one single word that answered Glinda's question. The only word I could find to explain all of this mayhem.

"Guilt," I whispered.

"What?" Glinda quipped, as she turned to look down at me with one hand still on the witch's chest."

"Guilt," I said again but this time with more vengeance. "She has been seeing someone else," I whispered. "She was simply waiting for Dad to die."

Glinda looked as though someone had actually shot her. She turned now to the bad witch and then back to me and then—as if she had just chewed a mouth full of dung and swallowed it—she then turned back to the bad witch again, and if there was ever a second time in her life that my big sister could have actually murdered someone, it was at that very moment. But she didn't. She simply let go of the witch and took a couple of steps back, as though she had just touched a leper. Without taking her eyes off the bad witch, she reached down for me grabbing the underside of my arm and she lifted me to my feet as she was saying, "Get up."

I awkwardly but studiously accommodated her command, my arms overflowing with my dad's things, with most still strewn about all over the floor. As I uneasily stood, she ordered me to go get a garbage bag. I stood there for just a moment as my arms were full and I didn't want to let go of my dad's things. Glinda then—very lovingly took my dad's things from my arms and gently placed them on the bed, never taking her eyes of the bad witch. She then very quietly in almost a whisper— very methodically—like a robot with a very controlled temper—repeated herself. "Go get a garbage bag," she said again, as though we had just found a precious dead animal.

Head down, I walked out of the bedroom, which had once been my haven, and into the kitchen and opened the drawer by the sink grabbing a black garbage bag with my mind wandering back to an earlier morning of my dad standing over that very sink vomiting his guts up and, quite frankly, I probably could have done the same had I not had to get back to the bedroom before the monkeys carried Glinda away, although—I seriously doubt on that day, at that particular place in time—that any monkey could have scared Glinda. She would have chewed 'em up and spit em out for sure.

I walked back into the bedroom where I found the bad witch still up against the wall with her head down and Glinda still standing guard over my father's things at the end of the bed. Yet her eyes were still fixated on the bad witch.

"Put Dad's things in the bag," she whispered as though we were robbing a bank.

450

I couldn't feel. I couldn't look at the bad witch. And I couldn't seem to find the strength to place my dad's belongings in a black garbage bag. I hesitated.

"It's OK," Glinda said. "It's only until we can find a box."

I began placing my dad's belongings in the black garbage bag which is a sad realization in itself in that all of his things could actually fit in one big black garbage bag. Of course, how many things does one need anyway, especially when they are dying?

Then the witch broke the silence by spitting the words: "Tell her the rest."

I looked up and directly into her eyes since this whole fiasco had begun just moments before. However, by then it seemed like an eternity. "What?" I said.

Go ahead she continued—tell her how your father changed his will.

Glinda looked at me and raised her eyebrows as she shrugged her shoulders at the same time as if to say, *Is that true?*

I very calmly—although I really wanted to scream—with gritted teeth, said yes, Dad changed his will and left me as his executor so that she wouldn't have to work for two years. He wanted me to issue her a paycheck every month.

"He didn't want my son to get any of his precious money," the bad witch spat!

"No he didn't," I calmly said and enjoyed every savory moment of that sentence.

With a look on her face that said, *You've got to be kidding me*—Glinda said: "That is what this is all about? Money?"

"Well, no," I quipped, "money and the fact that she has been seeing someone else."

"I can't even talk about that right now," Glinda snapped.

"We will gather Dad's things and we will be gone," she said, her eyes never wavering from the eyes of the witch, as if to say, *Don't move or I'll shoot.*

I finished gathering my father's things down to the very last dime in its little case, and I then tied up the bag and heaved it off the bed.

The witch then informed us that she didn't want to be there anymore and she was leaving.

"Good," I said. "Should have done that two years ago. Oh, and pick up some milk while you're out!"

She shot me a look that clearly stated she hated me, maybe even loathed me. And then I said it. I looked at my sister and I said, "Yup, Dad did exactly what he needed to do. He truly recreated his lost dream. He remarried our mother!"

With that, the witch sashayed past us and probably grabbed her broom before she walked out the front door—and without our throwing even one drop of water on her—she was gone. That was the last time I ever saw her. And I was relieved. Although I must admit, I would truly have liked to have been the one to throw that very pail of water on her as she sunk into the earth crooning, *I'm melting—melting— you wicked little girl. What a world—what a world.*

Oh, God, I thought. What must my dad have been feeling as he watched this entire ordeal unfold? The very thought of that was too painful to bear.

I'm sorry, I secretly whispered to him wherever he may have been.

Glinda took the large plastic bag out to the truck. The war was finally over.

Standing at the foot of his bed, I looked around the room one last time as though I were forgetting something. Problem was, I was forgetting nothing. My eyes met the end table that harbored his first aid materials. The box of Band-Aids was still sitting there and a smile pursed my lips as I remembered how innocent he had sounded trying to explain to me as to why he hadn't called out to me before he had gotten up that morning. The chair beside the nightstand was empty. Joe, the orangutan, my dad's buddy and the last one to see him alive, was going home with me. Perhaps someday that damned monkey really would learn how to talk and would need my comfort as he recited what it was like to be the only one in the room when my dad exhaled his final breath.

His pipe and ashtray were going home with me to be lit every Thanksgiving and Christmas in his memory. Thanksgiving. It was only two weeks away. My dad had been right, there weren't going to be anymore Thanksgivings for him.

I walked out into the hallway, turned and took one last look and I want you all to know that two million more looks would not have lessened the pain.

I shuffled the couple of steps it took to get to the bathroom reached out with my arm and swung the door open wide. I could see his smile as I touched his tear soaked cheek and then I glanced at the sink and heard the ghostly sounds of him gagging and ever so carefully, I backed the hell out of that doorway and I pulled the door shut behind me for the very last time.

I walked in to the living room and took one last look around. Those old walls would never again hear the echo of my dad's laughter but they could sure tell one hell of a story someday.

I glanced over at the stereo. The turntable was silent and still. The headphones lay peacefully inside the smoked glass doors, retired, after twenty-six years of keeping him serene.

I heard Glinda outside, yelling for me to hurry up. We had a long drive ahead of us. I walked over and sat down on the couch. Rubbing my hand on the cushion beside me, I leaned back and turned my face into the back of the couch and reminisced. Remembering a day when we sat in that very same place and I wondered what life would be like without him. I just knew at that time, beyond a shadow of a doubt, that I just wouldn't make it without him. That I, myself, just might die. But I didn't.

Glinda was calling for me again. I rose up off the couch, took one last look around the room and the very last thing I saw was that clock. Funny, I thought, somehow it seemed that it should have stopped ticking on the 8th of November in 1992, at exactly five o'clock sharp. But it didn't. And that, my friends, is the very last memory I have of my father's home.

I did, in fact, make it through Thanksgiving. It was the first we had to endure without my dad's lively voice booming throughout our home, but I made it. Made it through Christmas too, although I must admit, I found myself heading for the phone to call him several times throughout the day. Minor details, I suppose.

Every once in a while, I catch myself doing silly things that I have never done before, such as talking back to commercials as I get up to go to the bathroom. Saying things like, uh huh and sure, you bet.

Each and every time I see an old car, I sit up and take notice and usually exclaim how my dad would've loved that one. But for the most part, things have their way of working themselves back to normal. Whatever normal is.

There is one change that I have noticed however, that seems to have followed me home from my dad's. It's somewhat of a new understanding of life. I surely don't take—not even one moment for granted anymore!

No one really knows when it's time to say good-bye. Doesn't really matter when someone leaves us—or how. We are never prepared. There will always be one more thing we wanted to say. One more thing we wanted to do. One more time we wanted to touch. And for each of us, the reasons for all of those one more times are different. They hold special meaning for each and every one of us who has ever been left behind.

The year 1992 was a cruddy year for me. My team lost the World Series, my president lost the election and I lost my dad. Hey, that's life! Or—so they say. However, my blessings that year far succeeded my losses.

On our drive home the old truck broke down on a steep mountain pass and Glinda and I were detained overnight in a ghost town of sorts until a small-town gas station repaired the radiator. And while we were sitting on that lonely mountain road, with the hood of my dad's old friend steaming hot tears and smoke waiting for a highway patrolman, we looked up and saw a cloud formation that very closely, resembled, actually—very clearly looked like, that old painting of the cowboy that resided in my dad's bedroom for so many years. It was as though that painting had been hung in the clouds specifically for our own private viewing. That cowboy, lying on a cloud—head leaning up against his saddle with his hat pulled down over his eyes—asleep. Dreaming of that beautiful woman above him—on a horse formatted of clouds itself. Coincidence? Not this time, my friends. Not this time.

It took me a long time to get over the loss of my dad. And I'm not really sure that we ever really get over a loss as much as we just have to learn to accept it. We simply come to grips with the fact that they are no longer here. That with each and every day that goes by, we simply have to go on without them. We really have no choice in the matter if we want to someday lead a sane and somewhat normal life ever again. Whatever in the hell normal is. Still haven't quite figured that one out yet—and I'm not real sure I ever will. I do still miss him terribly—and not a day goes by that something doesn't remind me of him. And that's OK because you see, my friends—that *is,* in fact, the true cycle of life.

Thank you for allowing me to share my story with all of you. I feel somewhat a sense of sorrow as I close my last and final chapter. Another ending of sorts, I suppose. And, as I'm sure I don't have to remind each of you—but I will anyway—endings just don't happen to assemble with me very well at all; however, it would do my heart pleasure if you walk away from this story with this: Live each and every day with thanks and gratitude. If you are not out casket shopping or attending someone's funeral, you are having a pretty darned good day and the next time you are close to a loved one, reach out and give them a hug or press your lips to their cheek. Take in their smell and cherish it. And above all, don't ever wait to say I love you. Just go ahead and blurt it out! And—if by chance, they turn and give you one of those strange looks or they venture to ask what in the Sam hell has come over you, just simply look them in the eye and tell them a friend of yours passed some information on to you that made you appreciate them as well as life a whole lot more. Trust me just one last time, folks; you'll be so very glad you did!

Happy trails to you, until we meet again.
Happy trails to you, keep smilin' until then.
Who cares about the clouds when we're together?
Just sing a song and bring the sunny weather.
Happy trails to you, 'till we meet again.

**~ Lyrics to "Happy Trails" by Dale Evans Rogers ~**

# Epilogue

WELL, THERE YOU have it, just as I promised. A great story with a not so happy ending. However, as we should all know by now, happy endings are truly in the eyes of the beholder.

The Indian, my precious uncle, whose real name is Calvin, moved to Nevada with me after my father's death and we still remain as close as ever. He still dotes upon me as though I were a child. I am his big brother's second-eldest daughter and he beams with pride each and every time he introduces me to someone as his niece. I, myself, think he truly gets a kick out of watching people's reaction as he is clearly a Native American and I am clearly not. I think my dad planned this relationship. As a matter of fact, I'm sure he ordered it special, as I am positive that Calvin is the brother I never had.

My husband, whose real name is Bob, no kidding, is still my husband and is still employed at the very same company where he worked when my father passed, although he is now the boss. He has been there twenty-one years. My dad would have whooped! We have been married twenty-two years and he helped raise all of my children as his very own. He has eaten, slept and breathed this book with me for fifteen years and has given so very much of himself throughout our entire relationship. How he has endured me after all of these years I may never know but for this—I am so very thankful.

Glinda, my cherished lifeline, my big sister, whose real name is Jodie, lives in Nevada as well. She was actually born Mary JoAnne, however, she did not want to be called Mary as that was my mother's name so she took on a nickname long ago given to her by none other than my father's mother. She is tough and caring and always has been. She got my mother's intellect and my father's heart. To me she is—and always will be my big sister, my protector, my biggest fan—and the very wind beneath my wings.

The two youngest girls, whose real names are actually, Melodie June and Melissa Jan, have endured many hardships since my father's death. Demons left over from the monster, I suppose.

Melodie June, who's nickname is Dee Dee lives here in Nevada as well— and is the only one of us who most characteristically resembles our father in her mannerisms as well as the way she walks and talks. She throws her head back when she gives a hearty laugh and she cries at the drop of a pin. And she waves her arms in the air when she's happy and doesn't give a hoot who's looking at her. Poor thing. She is a girl Eddie.

Melissa Jan whose nickname is Pedie, just recently moved to Wisconsin. She insists upon being called the baby of our family and we accommodate her, mostly because she is the biggest and tallest out of all of us. Where she got her size we have never figured out and she too has many of my father's traits. She loves the togetherness of family. She is the one who always orchestrates us all getting together of course for one more family photo, which she uses as her wall paper on her cell phone. She loves gadgets of any kind—little trinkets of any kind—and the girl absolutely loves and takes impeccable care of her damned cars!

The missing middle sister, whose real name is Margaret Jayne, goes by the nickname of Maggie and lives here in Nevada as well. Her friends call her Magoo as she can not see or hear worth a hill of beans. She did finally find her way just as my dad said she would. Those demons got to her first and she is a survivor. Although, I must admit that I call Maggie my hero as she endured most of the physical abuse after our father left home—and she made it. They all did. Crawling on bare and bleeding knees but they made it. Survivors. I suppose we all are.

My half sister whose real name is Lianne (pronounced Lie-Anne), is also here in Nevada and never really had a nickname, as her father was not an Oklahoma Boy. However, throughout the years we *have* called her Na–Nan from time to time. I have never really thought of her as my half sister. She just came after my dad left home, that's all. She is my little sister—plain and simple. Doesn't matter one iota to me how she got here or who fathered her. As bad luck or fate would have it, those demons found her as well and she is still fighting them but I think for very different reasons. After all, the monster was her father and we cannot change our genetics. She lost her father one year after we lost ours and I was there to pick her up and comfort her. However, I must say that the day he died, the entire Universe felt uncontaminated and I felt free. Lianne touches me in a very special place in my heart and for reasons I cannot even begin to share. Not now anyway. Another book perhaps—at another time and no matter how long it takes—I know she will make it too. She has to. She is a part of all of us and she *will* survive as well. The four youngest have always been and will always be—my baby sisters. Just don't tell Pedie.

After Jodie and I came home, I spoke to my father's widow only one more time and, of course, it was over the money. I received that check about two weeks before Christmas, gave each daughter $1,000, as I felt that is what my dad would have wanted me to do, as it was, after all, Christmas time. I wrote the remainder of that check to the witch and mailed it off to her lock, stock, and barrel. After that, I never heard from her again nor did I try to stay in touch. I threw that relationship to the wind that December of 1992 and perhaps it found its place in the swirl of the changing leaves and the transition of the season. I will probably never know, and that is just fine with me.

My father's wishes were to have his daughters as well as his wife rotate the flag that had draped his casket between all of us each and every year on the anniversary date of his death. Well, sadly, the witch wouldn't give it up so that was the end of that. And you know my friends, speaking of that precious flag, in my own heart of hearts, as much as it embarrasses me to share another self-centered thought with all of you, just one last time–I truly felt that that flag should have been presented to *me* at my father's service. Still being a little selfish? Perhaps. However, *I* was the one who so desperately fought for it and sorrowfully, after my father's death; I was just too darned tired and beaten to fight for it again. So–pitifully, it remained with her. God only knows where it is now. I'm so very sorry dad. I truly am.

And as for me? Well, I came home with knowledge and wisdom and the courage to pursue a gift. Many gifts really. Becoming a writer was one of them. Time is just too darned short. I also became an ordained minister and by profession, a spiritualist and a strong medium. I am a healer of the heart and the mind. I suppose I have had this gift all of my life and was just too darned afraid to admit or pursue it—that is—until I went to my dad's house. I suppose all things really do happen for a reason.

After I came home that horrible November in 1992, I did, in fact, do exactly what my father had asked me to do. I pursued a relationship with my mom and I'm so very glad I did. It was tough going and a long road. OK—in all honesty—it was like pulling the tusks from a bull elephant! But sometimes, because we just can't change the past—I suppose the best thing we can do is just accept folks for who they are and go on. We don't have to forgive the act—just the person. After all—it isn't up to us to judge each other. That just isn't our job. She was my mother and she made many mistakes, and now that my children are grown and have children of their own, I sure hope they don't count mine. We could be here a while.

Fifteen long years have passed and so have others I have loved. We sadly lost our mom in February of 2005 and every one of her daughters was at her bedside. I think my dad would have been proud. She lived thirteen years beyond my dad. The exact same number of years they were married. I would find that to be quite a coincidence—if I believed in coincidences. She died in Jodie's arms and that affair in itself could also be another heartwarming story—someday—maybe—or—maybe not.

My most prevalent hopes are that you have enjoyed partaking in my memories. I was more than glad to share them with all of you. My most cherished desire is that you have learned how to believe. It doesn't matter who or what you believe in—what matters is that you believe in something, anything at all to get you through your own trials so that when the time comes for you, yourselves to have to say good-bye to someone you love—you will remember. Remember this old friend and her story and that if you ever need to go looking for happiness, you need not look any further than your own backyard!

Blessings to each and every one of you as you enjoy the journey and follow that yellow brick road!

# About the Author

MARTI TOTE IS a spiritualist, medium, angelic communicator, and life coach who lives in Reno, Nevada. Her calling is to spiritually heal the heart and the mind. Her passion is her writing. Her peace and solace is the time spent with her horses. However, her most cherished moments are spending time with her husband, children, and grandchildren; for her strongest belief is in God and the very strength of family, as she believes that at the end of each and every day, all we really have is each other!

Made in the USA
Las Vegas, NV
05 January 2024

83951156R00265